Literature of American Music III, 1983–1992

Guy A. Marco

The Scarecrow Press, Inc.
Lanham, Md., and London
1996

SCARECROW PRESS, INC.

Published in the United States of America
by Scarecrow Press, Inc.
4720 Boston Way
Lanham, Maryland 20706

4 Pleydell Gardens, Folkestone
Kent CT20 2DN, England

This is the third volume, covering the years 1983-1992, of a series begun in 1977 by David Horn, called *Literature of American Music in Books and Folk Music Collections: A Fully Annotated Bibliography*.

The second volume, published in 1988 by David Horn, with Richard Jackson, was called *The Literature of American Music in Books and Folk Music Collections: A Fully Annotated Bibliography, Supplement I*.

British Cataloguing-in-Publication Information Available

Library of Congress Cataloging-in-Publication Data

Marco, Guy A.
Literature of American Music III, 1983-1992 / by Guy A. Marco.
p.   cm.
Includes index.
1. Music—United   States—History   and   criticism—Bibliography.
I. Title.
ML120.U5M135   1996   016.78'0973—dc 20   95-26774   CIP

ISBN 0-8108-3132-5 (cloth : alk. paper)

In memory of my parents, who taught me harmony and counterpoint.

Composers! mighty maestros!
And you, sweet singers of old lands, soprani, tenori, bassi!
To you a new bard caroling in the West,
Obeisant sends his love.
—Walt Whitman, "Proud Music of the Storm"

CONTENTS

PREFACE

David Horn, in his two notable volumes of 1977 and 1988 (the second co-authored with Richard Jackson), created a fundamental inventory of significant books dealing with music by Americans and with American musical life. In this third volume of *Literature of American Music* (LOAM) I offer a continuation of the bibliography. While I have observed most of the Horn-Jackson criteria for inclusion, I have thought it advisable to introduce some new considerations. The list is carried forward to cover publications that appeared between 1 January 1983 and 1 January 1993, and were not cited in either of the earlier volumes of LOAM. This is what I have tried to include:

1) monographs in English that appeared in selected source lists, with certain limitations (noted below);
2) monographs in other languages that appeared in the same source lists, if they contain significant reference material (such as discographies) or other important original text.

The selected source lists I have relied on are Illinet, the shared computer catalog of libraries in Illinois; OCLC (accessed through EPIC), the database of the Online Computer Catalog Center; and *American Book Publishing Record* (ABPR). Illinet includes the holdings of the Chicago Public Library, University of Chicago, University of Illinois, Newberry Library, and Northwestern University, and many smaller specialized libraries, such as Columbia College in Chicago. OCLC lists holdings of North American research libraries; the database has about 30 million entries. ABPR is a monthly list, cumulated annually, of monographic publications issued in the United States. Searches of those files, made via subject headings and classification numbers, plus the names of individuals, resulted in an initial list of titles to be examined.

Certain categories of publication were omitted: master's theses and doctoral dissertations, and juvenile books. Other categories have been included selectively: price guides to recordings, music career guides, picture books without substantive text, and books (except discographies) having fewer than 80 pages. For immigrant composers who became U.S.

citizens (Rachmaninoff, Schoenberg, Stravinsky, etc.), a representative group of recent books will have to suffice.

It has also been necessary to limit the coverage of pop/rock performers. OCLC-EPIC lists more than 700 books about Elvis Presley that were published in the 1980s, and there are also hundreds of titles on other major figures. In choosing among those riches I considered several factors. I gave preference for inclusion to issues of established publishers and recognized authors, to books that have received wide attention, and to items that offer useful reference features.

Unaltered reprints, and reprints with minor changes, have been avoided—not always easily, since they often appear without indication of their nature. Lamentably, even respectable publishers are known to list reprint volumes among their new issues, as though they were newborns instead of teenagers. (It is confusing rather than amusing to find reprints reviewed in such media as *Library Journal* without due notice of their advanced years.) Well, the reader of this volume may find some similar misattributions, for which I offer advance regrets.

Volumes that consist entirely or almost entirely of printed music were omitted, unless they contained particularly important prefatory or critical material.

Books that have appeared as units in selected series are occasionally given brief entries; more detail is given in the accounts of the series themselves. One reason for this is that the same description (modified only for the topic or person covered) would usually apply to all the items in the series, and it seems foolish to keep reciting it; but the main reason is that all items in these series were not available for direct examination. For example, the important series of discographies by Charles Garrod seems not to appear intact in any library; but the books are so similar in treatment that it is probably enough to identify the characteristics of the series. Nevertheless, individual series entries have been given full treatment when possible.

The reader will notice a few new features in this volume of LOAM. Each entry has an ISBN and a Library of Congress (LC) classification number. Citations to book reviews appear (to reviews in *American Music* [AM], *American Reference Books Annual* [ARBA], *Choice,* and *Library Journal* [LJ], and there is indication of inclusion in *Books for College Libraries* (3rd ed., 1988), Eugene Sheehy's *Guide to Reference Books* (10th ed., 1986) and the supplement to Sheehy by Robert Balay (1992).

Entry style is based on the second edition of the *Anglo-American Catalog Rules* (AACR2). This style is used by most library card catalogs and computer catalogs, so it will be familiar to the reader. If a book was simultaneously issued by two or more publishers, I have usually identified only one of them.

Probably the most noticeable innovation in this volume is the topical arrangement of entries according to the Library of Congress classification. David Horn's arrangement, into nearly 200 sections and subsections, worked well for him, but brought problems for me. There were many titles that I could not readily place into one of his categories, which made me wonder whether users of the book might have similar uncertainties. So, after consideration and consultation, I switched to the LC classification. The change brought good and bad outcomes. On the favorable side, LC is familiar to American readers, and it is used in other bibliographies (such as *Books for College Libraries*). LC notation acts to organize and separate clusters of titles, eliminating the need for extensive subheadings in the bibliography. LC classification numbers are provided in most new U.S. books, on the verso of the title page. Possibly the main advantage is for the user who wishes to locate books in a research library and who has access to the stacks. Theoretically, the sequence of items in LOAM should correspond to the sequence of books on the shelves.

However, LC brings its share of challenges for the maker of a bibliography. One difficulty is that it may take quite a few years for the classifiers at LC (or those in other libraries who contribute catalog copy to the LC database) to decide exactly how a topic is to be subdivided and notated. For example, ML156 (discography) reveals many twists and turns: it seems to be settling into a pattern that puts label discographies at ML156.2, genre discographies at ML156.4, and performer discographies at ML156.7; but there are innumerable exceptions still to be found on the title page versos of recent books. To address this problem, I have just decided to introduce consistency into the LC assignments of classification numbers, where it seemed necessary to bring like materials together. I know that in doing so I have lost one of the benefits of using LC in the first place: the matches between the classification numbers in LOAM and those in library catalogs. To make up for that, when I have changed a number to achieve consistency, I have included within the entry the original LC number as well as my variant. Another bother about using LC is that the reader will often encounter local library variants that depart from the "official" classification number. So tracking items along the shelves will not always be productive. Most libraries today are dropping the practice of making local variants, so for newer books this is less a concern than for older books.

Another modification that the reader will notice in this volume is in the nature of the annotations. Although I admire and respect Horn's detailed, perceptive accounts, I have thought it best to handle these descriptive notes rather more briskly than he did. I have avoided telling the book's story (for example, in the biographical works I do not say much about the person written about, but summarize the author's approach).

Possibly I have been too crisp—too American?—in this respect. But to atone for that characteristic of the annotations, I have endeavored to give the reader a checklist of reference features in each book, with critical comments on them.

It may be that I am also more inclined than Horn to find faults. I have tried to be clear on what the valuable and less valuable features of these books are, in order to save the reader's time. Not many users of bibliography will care to examine all its titles themselves; it is the bibliographer's task to state plainly what features a book has. I have taken a rather hard line toward one category of writing: the celebrity biography. A high percentage of such books—at least those I have looked at in this project—exhibit qualities that may best be termed "unscholarly." This is not a damning fault, of course. All books do not have to be learned tomes, heavy with footnotes. The audience, the topic, the setting all have a role in determining the scholarly level. For example, I would not have wanted the memoirs of André Previn (S2-961) or Nicholas Slonimsky (S2-971) to be formalized. Still I think the reader of any book that has a factual base—such as a person's life—is entitled to a modicum of credibility. The typical style of the pop-star biography is one that borders on incredibility—a mash of invented episodes and dialogues, often with the feelings of a moment that skipped by decades ago recalled to vivid life. That approach, it seems to me, patronizes and demeans the reader as well as the subject. It has been encouraging to see some objections to this fictionalized biographical approach in recent critiques of such books as the Joe McGinnis treatment of Edward Kennedy and Kitty Kelly's of Frank Sinatra (S2-860). What a person says is a fact: one to be reported exactly if it is known (quoted, with a source note), or offered as "indirect discourse" if it is known only in substance. If what was said has been lost to history (the usual case), let the author and reader share the loss. So I have tried to advise the users of this bibliography about the character of the biographical reportage, leaving the determination of value to the beholder. As a final word on this topic, I should add that the lack of serious treatment of a person's life does not define the quality of that person's contributions; all the master composers have been victims of poor biographers.

Serious treatment is also desirable for the music, both of composers and of performers. In this regard both classical and popular musicians are often mistreated by commentators who offer impressionistic, nonmusical accounts of what they hear. But the classical artists are more likely to have at least a few thoughtful and well-prepared commentators, while unfortunately those in the popular fields may have none. (For example, in the 31 books about Elvis Presley that are included in this volume, there are none that present useful appraisals of his singing, appraisals that would distinguish it from that of his contemporary performers.) In my descriptive notes I have tried to cue the reader regarding the manner in which the author deals with musical events. Alas, quite a number deal not at all with such matters, choosing to recount life stories only.

In trying to present a perspective on each book's reference features, I have been particularly interested in the indexing. An index with subdivisions under main headings ("expansive") is easier to use than one that strings out all page citations under one heading ("nonexpansive"). As a telling example, there is the non-expansive index in the *Guinness Encyclopedia of Popular Music* (S2-76), with its 600 page-references under the heading "Piano." In most cases I have indicated whether the indexing is expansive or not, and I have noted whether the indexing covers only names, or also topics, titles of works, and other categories.

For a time during the writing of this book I was fortunate to have David Prochaska for my student (in the Graduate School of Library and Information Science, Rosary College). As a special study project, he undertook to write annotations for a number of books on jazz. I had thought to use his annotations as the basis for my own critiques of those volumes, but finally I decided simply to print them as they were, identified by his initials, D.P. His knowledgeable comments really need no adjustments; and the reader of them will have some respite from my own more telegraphic idiom. Several other students, named in the Acknowledgments, helped out in various ways.

A final word on the annotations. After considerable effort to locate and examine all titles, I had to give up on some of them. Even the steady cooperation of the interlibrary loan service at Rosary College could not produce all the books I wanted to include. In a number of instances, books that were supposedly owned by a library could not be found there. And some books have no discernible library homes at all. When I did not see a book, there is either no annotation at all, or there is a brief summary gleaned from advertising or reviews.

In preparing the cumulative author index, which covers this volume and its two predecessors, I have tried to make a useful reference tool that could be used apart from the rest of the book. The index gives publisher and date along with author and title. I have named it "Checklist of Books on American Music, 1640–1992" to emphasize that it does have the intention of bringing together—for the first time in print, I believe—the titles of the significant monographic writings on music and musical life of the nation.

ACKNOWLEDGMENTS

Most of the research for this volume was done at the University of Chicago Library (Hans Lenneberg, Bibliographer for Music) and Chicago Public Library (Richard Schwegel, Head of the Music Information Center; Jeannette Casey, Assistant Head). I am grateful to the personnel of those fine collections for their assistance. Many interlibrary loans were arranged for me by the staff at Rosary College Library (Inez Ringland, Director; Kenneth Black, Assistant Director; Corinne Stich, Interlibrary Loan Librarian). Wyn Matthias of the Library of Congress and Michael O'Brien of New York Public Library replied usefully to inquiries.

The contributions of David Prochaska are mentioned in the Preface. Two authors sent me books I was not able to obtain elsewhere: Marion Korda and Bill E. Burk. Rosary College generously provided material support for the enterprise, through the Graduate School of Library and Information Science (GSLIS) (Michael E. D. Koenig, Dean). Searches of OCLC-EPIC, DIALOG, Illinet, and other databases where greatly facilitated by the guidance of MaryFrances Watson, Assistant Dean and Lecturer in GSLIS. Student assistant Penelope Papangelis was a dependable helper in filling information gaps.

INTRODUCTION

"For sheer diversity the music of the United States is not equalled by that of any other country"—so wrote David Horn in the Preface to *The Literature of American Music*. Indeed, that diversity is marked by a steady rise in the international impact of the American musical arts. In 1994 it is reasonable to argue that American composing and music making sets the standards of the world. But how is this grand tapestry documented? Is the literature of American music a worthy partner for the achievements that it chronicles and interprets?

The quantity of literary output is surely impressive. Horn's first two volumes of the present set took note of 3,862 monographs; the present volume brings the total to more than 5,100. There is also a fine variety in the literature. All reference categories are found: bibliographies, discographies, encyclopedias, histories (general, local, specialized by genre), collected and individual biographies, critical studies, resource guides, dissertations, and so on. There are important collections of primary materials also, housed in major libraries. For certain topics, the coverage is solid. But in other areas, we find that development of the literature has been falling behind.

Among the strongest segments in the literature is jazz discography. There are several strong critical histories of jazz as well and of the swing era. Bio-bibliographies of classical composers are another highlight. Surveys of American musical culture in various times and places are excellent.

A number of categories are yet to be developed fully. Local histories are found for many cities and states, but most of the books are old—and whether old or new they tend toward the casual rather than the scholarly approach. Documented histories of organizations—music publishers, record firms, opera companies, orchestras—are just beginning to appear.

Biography is satisfactory for mainstream classical composers, but faint for lesser-known composers and for concert artists. Biography of pop performers after the jazz/swing era is poor; there is scarcely one rock singer who has had the benefit of a thoughtful, studious life-and-works treatment. Similarly, technical musical analysis is a rarity for popular materials of the last quarter century. (Lacking both a firm biographical and an analytic structure, such music remains effectively undefined, except in emotional, political terms.) One or two recent books have addressed thoughtfully the participation of music in contemporary society, but this is a topic that has been allowed to drift, for the most part, into unfruitful byways such as racism or economics.

It should be added that in European countries a similar (usually a much greater) imbalance can be perceived in the coverage of national music panoramas. Frequently, it is an American writer who illuminates aspects of music in another country. Probably the literature of American music is—like the music itself—of unequalled diversity. Those of us who examine that literature, and make it available to others for further examination through bibliographies, may hope that we are displaying its profile in a manner that will bring about needed ameliorations of scope and of a quality that great music deserves.

SAMPLE ENTRY:

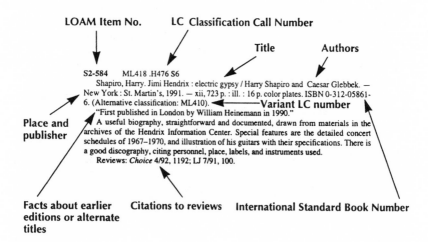

THE BIBLIOGRAPHY

BR–BX : CHURCH MUSIC

S2-1   BR563 .N4 H866
Hurston, Zora Neale. The sanctified church / Zora Neale Hurston. —
Berkeley, Calif. : Turtle Island, 1981. — 107 p. ISBN 0-9136-6644-0.
"Earlier versions of some of these articles first appeared in *New World
Journal* and *Negro: An Anthology.*"
An interesting selection from the work of folklorist Hurston (1901–
1960), dealing with African American lore and legend, with emphasis on
the Southern Black Christian Church. Among the fascinating persons dis-
cussed are Mother Catherine (founder of a voodoo Christian sect) and
Uncle Monday (healer and herb doctor). There are evocative descriptions
of conversions and visions. No sources are cited, and there is no index.

S2-2   BV415 .A1 R64
Rogal, Samuel. Guide to the hymns and tunes of American Method-
ism / Samuel J. Rogal. — New York : Greenwood, 1986. — xxii, 318 p.
(Music reference collection, 7) ISBN 0-313-25123-1.
A valuable "reference guide to the six major hymnals" that "surveys
the specifics of American Methodist hymnody, both texts and tunes,
from 1878 through 1966." Considers which texts may be designated "official" and which tunes are associated with each text; also analyzes
changes that have taken place in the hymnal. Background information is
given on text authors, composers, and arrangers. There is a useful list of
2,005 hymns with citations to their source-hymnals. With a first-line index, composer index, and tune name index.
Review: ARBA 1987, #1250.

S2-3   BX6480 .S8434 T57
Titon, Jeff Todd. Powerhouse for God : speech, chant, and song in an
Appalachian Baptist church / Jeff Todd Titon. — Austin : University of
Texas Press, 1988. — xviii, 523 p. ISBN 0-292-76485-5.
A treatment of Southern Protestant "worship service as the juncture of
language and life," studying the language of the service, the community,

1

individual members of a congregation, pastors, and hymns. The hymns are given in musical notation. With a list of interviews and bibliography of about 250 titles, but without footnotes. There is an expansive index.

Two 12-inch LP discs, with the same title as the book, were issued by the University of North Carolina Press in 1982, with a 24-page booklet by Titon.

Reviews: AM 1991, 102; *Choice* 3/89, 1259.

E : CULTURAL HISTORY; BLACK STUDIES

For black music see ML3556 (beginning with S2-1215).

S2-4   E169.1 .L536
Levine, Lawrence W. Highbrow/lowbrow—the emergence of cultural hierarchy in America / Lawrence W. Levine. — Cambridge : Harvard University Press, 1988. — xii, 306 p. ISBN 0-674-39076-8.

An interesting reflection on cultural categorization, suggesting that we should avoid "frozen categories ripped out of the contexts in which they were created." Some nostalgia is expressed for the nineteenth century, when Americans, "in addition to whatever specific cultures they were part of, shared a public culture less hierarchically organized, less fragmented into rigid adjectival boxes than their descendants were to experience a century later." For example, Italian opera was a pleasure "simultaneously popular and elite"; this is demonstrated in a fine chapter. As the gap between amateur and professional music making widened, the split developed between music in the so-called vernacular and cultivated traditions; but Levine finds the bifurcation neither natural nor necessary. With endnotes and an expansive index.

Review: AM 1990, 233.

S2-5   E185.625 .P373
Pasteur, Alfred B. Roots of soul : the psychology of black expressiveness / Alfred B. Pasteur and Ivory I. Toldson. — Garden City, N.Y. : Anchor, 1982. — x, 324 p. ISBN 0-3851-5880-7.

"Using information about culture, brain geography, and the genetic substance called melanin, this book highlights rhythm as the basis of soul, of black expressiveness, and of popular culture in America and in the Western world." Thus Pasteur offers an approach to the black-versus-white question that does not avoid genetic elements. The thesis is carried further than its evidence allows, however, to the remarkable conclusion that "the pop culture enjoyed by all, music, dance, drama, and so forth, come in large measure from ordinary blacks who are more in tune with the rhythmic pulse of soul." An international review of trends and incidents is presented in support of these ideas. With endnotes and an expansive index.

Review: *Choice* 7/82, 1640.

S2-6   E185.97 .R63 D83

Duberman, Martin Bauml. Paul Robeson / Martin Bauml Duberman. — New York : Knopf, 1988. — xiii, 804 p. : ill. : 112 plates. ISBN 0-394-52780-1.

"Written almost entirely from manuscript sources" at Howard University, and drawing on 135 interviews, this is an outstanding biography of the actor/singer Robeson (1898–1976). Duberman, a professor of history at City University of New York, writes a lively story of the troubled artist, at the same time describing all sources in 197 pages of endnotes. The illustrations are superb. With a partly expansive index.

GR : FOLKSONG

Other folk material is under "National Music," ML3551 (beginning with S2-1206).

S2-7   GR105.37 .C63

Rammel, Hal. Nowhere in America : the Big Rock Candy Mountain and other comic utopias / Hal Rammel. — Urbana : University of Illinois Press, 1990. — xii, 165 p. : ill. ISBN 0-2520-1717-X.

A fabled locale from folklore, Big Rock Candy Mountain, also known as Nowhere, Topsy-Turvey, Ditty Wah Ditty, and so forth, was the subject of a song popularized by Burl Ives and has had other folksong manifestations. Rammel traces them in their American context, relying almost entirely on textual matters, but with some references to music by various performers: Bo Diddley, for one, whose "Diddy Wa Diddy" is explicated (at last) as a variant of Ditty Wah Ditty. Among the other musicians discussed are Jean Ritchie and Spike Jones. With an expansive index.

Review: *Choice* 3/91, 1126.

S2-8   GR110 .N7 B47

Bethke, Robert D. Adirondack voices : woodsmen and wood lore / Robert D. Bethke. — Urbana : University of Illinois Press, 1980. — xii, 148 p. : ill. : music. ISBN 0-2520-0829-4.

A study of folksong among elderly woodsmen in northern New York State, based on fieldwork conducted between 1970–1977. Narratives "are transcribed unaltered" and songs—transcribed by Norman Cazden—are presented as they were performed. Photographs of the lumbermen's living

quarters and work milieu add presence to the volume, which is wonder-
fully evocative of the time and place, the early years of the century. In
fact, the songs included are not more than adjuncts to the main content,
which is made up of individual memoirs and anecdotes. With full documentation and an expansive index.

Reviews: *Choice* 9/81, 74; LJ 1/1/81, 69.

GV : DANCE

S2-9   GV1623 .K5
Kislan, Richard. Hoofing on Broadway : a history of show dancing /
Richard Kislan. — New York : Prentice-Hall, 1987. — xviii, 206 p. :
ill. ISBN 0-13-809484-5.

A casual, undocumented "history of stage dancing from its origins in
Europe through burlesque, vaudeville, and early musical extravaganzas
. . . to the innovative choreography of postwar and contemporary cre-
ations." Along the way, Kislan finds much to admire and very little to
criticize; and he offers many quotes without sources. Some useful technical descriptions of individual dance routines appear, and the photos are
interesting. With a name and title index.

S2-10   GV1781 .S35
Schlundt, Christena L. Dance in the musical theatre : Jerome Robbins
and his peers / Christena L. Schlundt. — New York : Garland, 1989. —
xiv, 247 p. : ill. : 10 p. plates. (Garland reference library of the humanities, 1,213) "A joint publication with the New York Public Library."
ISBN 0-8240-5547-0.

"An alphabetized and numbered list of musical theatre pieces to which
Robbins and/or one of his peers made a contribution during those years
when they were contemporaries: 1932–1965." There are 191 shows,
choreographed by Jerome Robbins, Robert Alton, George Balanchine,
Jack Cole, Agnes De Mille, Doris Humphrey, Hanya Holm, Michael
Kidd, Anna Sokolow, Helen Tamiris, or Charles Weidman. For each
show the theater, number of performances, creative staff, and all performers are given; unfortunately, the performer list does not distinguish
dancers from singers from actors. There are indexes of individuals by
category: choreographers, composers, set designers, directors, and so on.
The "performers" index also fails to identify the dancers, a curious omission in a book about dance.

S2-11   GV1785 .B2
Rose, Phyllis. Jazz Cleopatra : Josephine Baker in her time / Phyllis

Rose. — New York : Doubleday, 1989. — 321 p. : ill. : 16 p. plates. ISBN 0-385-24891-1.

A biography that delineates Baker's Paris triumphs of the mid-1920s, her rise to European stardom in the 1930s, her war work, her activism, and her adopted "Rainbow Tribe" of racially and culturally diverse children. Baker's career as a singer/dancer helped to break the color barrier against black performers; indeed, the book is much concerned with the "racial mythologies that conditioned her success." It is a scholarly treatment, with endnotes, but without direct citations in the text. With a bibliography of 12 items about Baker and an expansive index.

Reviews: *Choice* 3/90, 1160; LJ 8/89, 135.

S2-12   GV1796 .M35 C45

Champe, Flavia Waters. The Matachines dance of the upper Rio Grande : history, music, and choreography / Flavia Waters Champe. — Lincoln : University of Nebraska Press, 1983. — xii, 101 p. : ill. : with one 7-inch 33⅓ rpm disc. ISBN 0-8032-14197.

The Matachines dance is performed on Christmas and on Christian religious holidays. Its history is traced to Spanish America. There is a complete description of the dance, with melodies in score and diagrams of the steps. The accompanying recordings have 13 folk tunes used with the dance. With a bibliography of about 50 items; no index.

Review: *Choice* 1/84, 712.

HD–KF : MUSIC BUSINESS DIRECTORIES

Other directories are at ML12–21 (beginning with S2-26).

S2-13   HD9706.5

Mix annual directory of recording industry facilities and services, 1988. — Emeryville, Calif. : Mix Publications, 1988. — 362 p. : ill. ISBN 0-918371-023.

This is the only annual volume examined. It lists 3,190 recording studios by region, CD pressers, suppliers, trade shows, professional organizations, and record companies, all with contact information and (as appropriate) personnel, equipment, rates, market statistics, and nearby lodgings.

S2-14   KF4291 .A68

Livingston, Robert Allen. Livingston's complete music industry business and law reference book / Robert Allen Livingston. — Cardiff by the Sea, Calif. : La Costa, 1981. — 346 p. ISBN 0-9607-5580-2.

M2-1977 : COLLECTIONS OF PRINTED MUSIC

S2-15   M2 .R233 vols. 11–12

Crawford, Richard. The core repertory of early American psalmody / ed. Richard Crawford. — Madison, Wisc. : A-R Editions, 1984. — 165 p. (Recent researches in American music, 11, 12) ISBN not given.

A well-chosen sample of 101 psalm tunes, representing about 1.5 percent of the entire repertory from the 1550s to the 1790s. The selections are given in score, with extensive critical commentaries. There is also a useful introduction that discusses performance practice and publishing history of the genre. Without index.

S2-16   M3 .B6

Billings, William. The complete works of William Billings / ed. Karl Kroeger; Richard Crawford, editorial consultant. — Boston : Colonial Society of Massachusetts and American Musicological Society; distributed by University Press of Virginia, 1977–1990. — 4 vols. ISBN 0-8139-0917-1; 0-8139-1130-3; 0-8139-0839-6; 1-8785-2801-7.

Billings (1746–1800) was a pioneer American writer of anthems, "fuguing tunes," and other religious music. Kroeger's scholarly presentation of his complete output is graced by valuable introductory histories in each volume, with bibliographic notes and full documentation of all points. Volume 4 includes a 200-item bibliography and a cumulative title index to the whole set. See also S2-159.

Review: AM 1989, 214.

S2-17   M3 .F73

Foster, Stephen Collins. The music of Stephen C. Foster : a critical edition / ed. Steven Saunders and Deane L. Root. — Washington : Smithsonian Institution Press, 1990. — 2 vols. ISBN 0-87474-824-0.

Foster (1826–1864) may be the most popular American composer; many of his 200 songs have become world classics. His output is presented here chronologically, mostly in the form of photocopy of the original publications (a few were newly typeset). Each song is accompanied by a learned commentary covering its history and sources. A useful introduction to the set deals with Foster's style and milieu. Both volumes have indexes of names, titles, first lines, and institutions.

Review: *Choice* 4/91, 1319.

S2-18   M3 .S41

DeVeaux, Scott Knowles. The music of James Scott / Scott Knowles DeVeaux and William Howland Kenney. — Washington : Smithsonian Institution Press, 1992. — 271 p. : ill. ISBN 1-5609-8143-1.

Scott (1885–1938) was "one of the two greatest ragtime composers."

He receives a thorough, scholarly treatment here, with a documented biography, analyses of his compositions, a rollography, discography (in title order; minimal data), and 161 pages of his music in score. With an expansive index to titles and names.

S2-19   M1495 .D36

Jackson, Richard. Democratic souvenirs : a historical anthology of nineteenth-century American music / selected, with introduction and commentary by Richard Jackson; foreword by Virgil Thomson. — New York : published for the New York Public Library by C. F. Peters, 1988. — xvi, 336 p. (The Americana collection music series, 3) ISBN 0-938856-03-0.

A valuable collection of 37 representative songs, piano pieces, choral works, theatrical numbers, chamber music, and two orchestral works, all presented as photocopies of their original publications. Sheet music covers are included. Jackson's perceptive commentaries put the material into historical and aesthetic contexts. Biographical information on the 35 composers is provided. With indexing of composers and titles.

Review: AM 1990, 368.

S2-20   M1629 .D2

Bayard, Samuel Preston. Dance to the fiddle, march to the fife : instrumental folk tunes in Pennsylvania / Samuel Preston Bayard. — University Park : Pennsylvania State University Press, 1982. — 628 p. : ill. ISBN 0-2710-02999.

A fine anthology of 695 tunes, collected in the field by Bayard, presented with extensive commentaries. There is a strong introduction as well, discussing fiddle techniques and other background matters. With a list of performers, list of sources, and index of titles.

S2-21   M1629 .W59

Logsdon, Guy. The whorehouse bells were ringing, and other songs cowboys sing / ed. Guy Logsdon. — Urbana : University of Illinois Press, 1989. — xxii, 389 p. ISBN 0-252-01583.

Voice lines in musical notation (melody only, without chord symbols) for 61 western songs, many of them bawdy, few of them from the familiar cowboy commercial repertoire. A scholarly study of each song includes biographical information (with photos) on the singers, location of manuscripts, secondary references, and recordings. A valuable essay is included on the development of cowboy songs and their distortion in the marketplace. There is a glossary, a bibliography of about 500 published and unpublished items, and a non-expansive index of titles, names, and topics.

Reviews: AM 1991, 316; *Choice* 5/90, 1514.

S2-22   M1629.6 .09 V36
Randolph, Vance. Ozark folksongs / Vance Randolph; ed. and abridged by Norman Cohen. — Urbana : University of Illinois Press, 1982. — xxvi, 590 p. ISBN 0-252-009525.

A one-volume selection from Randolph's four-volume work, published in 1946–1950 (LOAM 499) and reissued with an updated introduction and corrections by University of Missouri Press in 1980, intending to present the tunes that had particularly interesting comments. Citations to recordings; a discography of Ozark folk music; a 23-page bibliography; indexes of song titles, first lines, refrains, contributors, and towns. An indispensable companion to Randolph.

S2-23   9.6 .S7 S68
McNeil, W. K. Southern folk ballads / compiled by W. K. McNeil. — Little Rock, Ark. : August House, 1987–1988. — 2 vols. ISBN 0-87483-038-9; 0-87483-047-8.

Melodies drawn from the states that made up the Confederacy, with substantial commentaries. Arrangement is by topic (war, crime, faithful lovers, cowboys, supernatural, humor, etc.). With a bibliography and discography, and first-line and location indexes.

Reviews: *Choice* 2/88, 918; LJ 10/15/87, 76.

S2-24   M1629.7 .I39 S56
List, George. Singing about it : folk song in southern Indiana / transcribed by George List. — Indianapolis : Indiana Historical Society, 1991. — xxxiv, 428 p. ; with an audiocassette. ISBN 0-87195-086-3.

A scholarly, musical study of 103 songs that sample the regional repertoire from the Civil War to the present. Music and text are discussed, and there are biographies and photos of the singers. Articles from newspapers are reproduced that bear on social aspects of the music. The songs appear in score and on the accompanying cassette. Recordings are cited. With chapter endnotes, a bibliography of 150 items, and a nonexpansive index of titles, places, and names.

Review: *Choice* 5/92, 1486.

S2-25   M1977 .B38 E76
Cray, Ed. The erotic muse : American bawdy songs / Ed Cray. — 2nd ed. — Urbana : University of Illinois Press, 1992. — xlii, 435 p. ISBN 0-252-10781-1.

1st ed., 1969.

A collection of 125 song texts and melodies, from folk sources and modern college and military verses. The explicit lyrics are closely analyzed and traced to origins. Cray provides an informative introduction as well as useful commentaries passim. With citations, a bibliography of about 200 items, and a song index.

Review: *Choice* 7-8/92, 1690.

ML12–18 : DIRECTORIES

Other directories are at HD–KF (beginning with S2-13).

S2-26   ML12 .S26
Sandberg, Larry. The folk music sourcebook / Larry Sandberg and Dick Weissman. — 2nd ed. — New York : Da Capo, 1989. — x, 272 p. : ill. ISBN 0-306-80360-7.

1st ed., 1976 (LOAM Suppl. S-275).

In its revised edition, this useful compilation is not greatly altered; it is "something more than a reprint and less than a completely revised edition." An unusual editorial approach presents new material in a different typeface from the content carried over from the first edition. There are narrative articles on various categories of folk music; and on black, American Indian, Chicano, Canadian, Cajun, Anglo-American, western, and folk-revival music. Reference books, method books, and songbooks are listed with annotations. A resource directory identifies folk music centers, periodicals, films, videos, instrument makers, libraries, festivals, and organizations. With a glossary and a partly expansive index of names and instruments.

Listing: Balay BH133.

S2-27   ML13 .D57
Directory of music faculties in colleges and universities, U.S. and Canada, 1992–1994 / comp. and ed. Craig R. Short. — 14th ed. — Missoula, Mont. : CMS Publications, 1992. — 829 p. Biennial. ISBN not given.

1st ed., *Directory of Music Faculties in American Colleges and Universities, 1967–1970*. The present title was established with the 4th ed.

A list, by state and then by school, of about 1,800 music departments and conservatories, with a faculty roster for each. An index of persons shows where some 30,000 teachers are working. With a useful list of music degrees and the institutions that offer them.

Listing: Sheehy BH157.

S2-28   ML13 .L58
Livingston's complete music business directory. — Cardiff by the Sea, Calif. : La Costa, 1991. — 2 vols. ISBN 0-932303-18-8; 0-923303-19-6.

A miscellany of addresses in such categories as managers, attorneys, publishers, record companies, record producers, studios, and booking agencies. Without a table of contents or explanatory front matter; without index.

S2-29 ML13 .M497
Musical America international directory of the performing arts, 1992 edition. — New York : Musical America Publications, 1992. — 784 p. : ill. ISBN not given.
An annual directory that has appeared since 1968; it has gradually disintegrated into a mere collection of advertisements for artists and managers.

S2-30 ML13 .M505
Music industry directory : formerly the Musician's Guide. — 7th ed. — Chicago : Marquis Professional Publications, 1983. — 678 p. ISBN 0-8379-5602-1.
1st ed., 1954.
An excellent guide to organizations, competitions and awards, music schools, libraries, publishers, orchestras, opera companies, agents, editors and critics, record companies, and festivals in the U.S. and Canada. Well organized, with essential information about each entry, an index by category, and a general index.
Listing: Sheehy BH160.

S2-31 ML13 .W43
Whelan, Keith. Directory of record and CD retailers / Keith Whelan. — Wharton, N.J. : Power Communication Group, 1990. — ix, 368 p. : maps. Biennial. ISBN 0-9627-5920-1.
Descriptions of 1,008 U.S. stores, arranged by state, county, and city, and indexed by recording formats sold (e.g., cylinders, transcriptions) and subject specialties. Access information is given, along with search services offered.
Reviews: ARBA 1992, p. 513; LJ 2/1/91, 75.

S2-32 ML15 .K3 W5.
Wilkinson, Todd R. Kansas City jazz and blues nightlife survival kit / Todd R. Wilkinson. — Kansas City, Mo. : The Ambassadors, distributed by Westport Publishers, 1990. — 72 p. : ill. : map. ISBN 0-9337-0149-7.
A guide to jazz and blues clubs, musical groups and related organizations, individual musicians, and events of the city. Without index.

S2-33 ML15 .W2 H44
Heintze, James R. Scholars' guide to Washington, D.C., for audio re-

sources : sound recordings in the arts, humanities, and social, physical, and life sciences / James R. Heintze; with contributions by Trudi W. Olivetti. — Washington : Smithsonian Institution Press, 1985. — xiv, 395 p. (Scholars' guide to Washington, D.C., 11) ISBN 0-87474-516-0.

An excellent directory of 400 sound-recording collections in the Washington metropolitan area, and also of "organizations that produce sound recordings or provide information, research, or teaching concerning audio resources." Heintze estimates that the collections have some 1.5 million sound recordings. The arrangement is alphabetical by library or institution name, and the information presented includes service hours, use restrictions, name of the director, a description of the sound collection, and a note about listening equipment available. Bibliographic references are given as appropriate. In addition to the familiar governmental and academic libraries, there are entries here for such important but little-known collections as the National Archives for Black Women's History (oral history tapes), the Navy Memorial Museum (many radio receivers), and the Board of Jewish Education of Greater Washington (tapes and discs of Jewish music). With indexes to the subjects of the collections, persons, and institutions.

S2-34   ML17 .F37

Farrell, Susan Caust. Directory of contemporary American musical instrument makers / Susan Caust Farrell. — Columbia : University of Missouri Press, 1981. — xii, 216 p. : ill. ISBN 0-8262-0322-1.

An alphabetical directory of about 2,500 persons, with brief descriptions of their work. List of instruments, with the names of their makers (there are, for example, seven persons who construct balalaikas); lists by state; names of schools where instrument making is taught; societies and groups. With a short bibliography, but without index.

Reviews: ARBA 1982, p. 521; *Choice* 9/81, 47.

S2-35   ML17 .L4

Levine, Michael. The music address book : how to reach anyone who's anyone in music / Michael Levine. — New York : Harper, 1989. — xxii, 231 p. ISBN 0-06-096283-2.

A collection of names and addresses for people and firms in the pop music business, based on no discernible criteria. The arrangement is alphabetic, with only a few persons identified as to occupation. The first pages include ABC, ASCAP (American Society of Composers, Authors, and Publishers), Claudio Abbado, Lee Abrams ("radio programming consultant"), Academy of Country Music, Roy Acuff, the Adventures, Alabama, Peter Allen, and Alvin and the Chipmunks. With no category index.

S2-36   ML18 .A2

Recording industry sourcebook, 1993. — 4th ed. — Los Angeles :
Ascona Communications, 1993. — 562 p. ISBN 0-9624-8822-4. (Alternative classification: ML3790 .R42.)

A useful guide to labels, managers, booking agents, publishers, performing rights societies, attorneys, industry associations, artist organizations, and trade events. Not indexed.

S2-37   ML18 .A21

Blume, August G. The 1987/88 music business directory / August G.
Blume. — San Anselmo, Calif. : Music Industry Resources, 1987. —
vi, 99 p. ISBN 0-932521-02-9.

U.S. record companies listed in alphabetical order, with names of contact persons, addresses, and telephone numbers.

Reviews: ARBA 1989, p. 471; *Choice* 12/87, 603.

S2-38   ML18 .A22

Blume, August G. The 1987/88 music radio directory / August G.
Blume. — San Anselmo, Calif. : Music Industry Resources, 1987. —
vi, 92 p. ISBN 0-93251-03-7.

U.S. radio stations listed by state and city, with names of contact persons, addresses, and telephone numbers.

Reviews: ARBA 1989, p. 341; *Choice* 12/87, 603.

S2-39   ML18 .H1

Handel's national directory for the performing arts. — 5th ed. — New
York: Bowker, 1992. — 2 vols. ISBN 0-8352-3250-6.

4th ed., 1988.

A list of about 7,000 organizations and facilities for music, dance, and
theater, arranged by state. Names of artistic and administrative management are given, with budget and attendance data, hall rental information,
and facts about the buildings. Educational institutions are presented in
the second volume, with data on courses, faculty, degrees, and financial
assistance. This is the most comprehensive of the arts directories.

Listing and review: Balay BG3 (for 4th ed.); LJ 5/1/93, 82.

S2-40   ML18 .P9

Purchaser's guide to the music industries. — Englewood, N.J. : Music Trades, 1897– . Annual. ISBN not given.

The title has varied over the 97-year publication of this directory,
which concentrates on manufacturers of instruments, tuners, technicians,
wholesalers, software producers, schools for the trades, associations, and
publishers. Trademarks of the industry are listed.

S2-41   ML18 .S38

Schreiber, Norman. The ultimate guide to independent record labels and artists : an A-to-Z shop-by-mail source of great music, from rock, jazz, and blues to classical, avant-garde, and new age / Norman Schreiber. — New York : Pharos Books, 1992. — xix, 268 p. ISBN 0-88687-687-7.

A directory of about 500 current, independent U.S. labels, giving the type of music recorded, some principal artists, formats, telephone numbers, addresses, and contact persons. There are also chatty commentaries.

ML27 : ORGANIZATIONS

S2-42   ML27 .U5 A5

Seltzer, George. Music matters : the performer and the American Federation of Musicians / George Seltzer. — Metuchen, N.J. : Scarecrow, 1989. — 369 p. : ill. ISBN 0-8108-2176-1. (Alternative classification: ML3795 .S36.)

A history of the union, with good descriptions of labor legislation. Bibliography and index.

Review: *Choice* 9/89, 142.

S2-43   ML27 .U5 B4

Broadcast Music, Inc. The explosion of American music, 1940–1990 : BMI 50th anniversary. — Nashville : Country Music Foundation, 1990. — 122 p. : ill. ISBN 0-9156-0814-6.

A self-tribute volume for BMI, celebrating how its "open door to all creators of all types of American music and radically new logging and royalty distribution policies" coincided with "a period of unprecedented commercial expansion and stylistic change." BMI was established in 1940 as a performing rights organization in competition with ASCAP, which had restrictive membership. In 50 years BMI acquired license rights for 1.5 million compositions by more than 47,000 writers. This is an undocumented history of BMI, with fine photographs of artists and accounts of hit songs. "Yesterday" by John Lennon and Paul McCartney has been the all-time most performed composition, with 5 million airplays (calculated as 28 years of radio time). Without index.

S2-44   ML27 .U5 N26547

Ringel, Harvey. History of the National Association of Teachers of Singing / Harvey Ringel. — Jacksonville, Fla. : National Association of Teachers of Singing, 1990. — 355 p. : ill. ISBN 0-932761-01-1.

A straightforward chronicle of NATS, established in 1944, with interesting photographs. Although primary sources were apparently consulted, there are no footnotes, and there is no bibliography. Without index.

S2-45 ML27 .U5 S664
Hicks, Val. Heritage of harmony / Val Hicks. — Kenosha, Wisc. : Society for the Preservation and Encouragement of Barbershop Singing in America, 1988. — 230 p. ISBN 0-938627-04-X.
Barbershop quartet singing dates back to minstrel shows of the mid-nineteenth century and was a popular form until the 1920s. The society that published this volume was organized in 1938 to revive and sustain interest in the format. Hicks has written a pleasing history of the society and the revival movement, with charts, facts, and data. With pictures and profiles of the leading groups and strong documentation throughout.
Review: AM 1989, 340.

ML35–38 : FESTIVALS

S2-46 ML35 .R3
Rabin, Carol Price. Music festivals in America : classical, opera, jazz, pops, country, old-time fiddlers, folk, bluegrass, Cajun / Carol Price Rabin. — 4th ed. — Great Barrington, Mass. : Berkshire Traveller Press, 1990. — 271 p. : ill. : maps. ISBN 0-9301-4501-1.
Title varies. 1st ed., 1979 (LOAM Suppl. S-218); 2nd ed., 1983.
A handy descriptive inventory of 160 U.S. and Canadian music festivals, arranged by state under each category: classical, opera, jazz, pop, folk, and country. Dates, types of music featured, director and typical participants, and ticket information are given for each one. Exact locations are pinpointed on regional maps. With an index of festival names.
Review and listing: LJ 7/79, 1456 (for the 1st ed.); Sheehy BH163 (for the 2nd ed.).

S2-47 ML38 .H6 R447
Ravinia : the festival at its half century / Ravinia Festival Association in conjunction with Rand McNally & Company; foreword by Edward Gordon. — [n.p.] : Ravinia Festival Association, 1985. — 160 p. : ill. ISBN 0-528-81066-9.
Ravinia, in Highland Park, Illinois, is the summer home of the Chicago Symphony Orchestra and the site of performances by various other groups. The first season of the CSO was 1936. This is an informal history, notable for numerous photographs of the artists. Without documentation; with a nonexpansive index.

S2-48   ML38 .N69 C6443

Carey, Joseph Kuhn. Big noise from Notre Dame : a history of the collegiate jazz festival / Joseph Kuhn Carey. — Notre Dame, Ind. : University of Notre Dame Press, 1986. — xvii, 207 p. : ill. ISBN 0-268-00677-6.

Carey traces the Notre Dame Collegiate Jazz Festival, a competition among student musicians from various colleges, from its beginnings in 1958 through the 1985 festival. Solo and combo award recipients are mentioned, as are judges. Most information is on public aspects of the event, but Carey describes administration of the 1979 festival, for which he was chairman. One or more photos of performers are included for most years. A discography of nearly 250 collegiate jazz recordings, which were not necessarily connected with the festival, is arranged by state and includes school, album title, record company, leader, and year. Primary and secondary sources are carefully cited, but there is no bibliography. Without index.

Joseph Kuhn Carey has written for *Down Beat, Jazz Times, Rolling Stone,* and the *Boston Globe* [—D. P.].

S2-49   ML38 .W66 M34

Makower, Joel. Woodstock : the oral history / Joel Makower. New York : Doubleday, 1989. — 361 p. : ill. ISBN 0-385-24716-8.

The Woodstock Music and Art Fair of August 1969, with a half million "ebullient children of the sixties descending on a quiet community in upstate New York," was a landmark of festival history, a time of "joy and humanity, and heroics." Makower interviewed numerous survivors of the event to construct this collection of anecdotes and reflections. Without documentation; with a nonexpansive index.

ML49–54 : LYRICS

S2-50   ML49 .H15 K5

Hart, Lorenz. The complete lyrics of Lorenz Hart / ed. Dorothy Hart and Robert Kimball. — New York : Knopf, 1986. — xxvii, 317 p. : ill. ISBN 0-394-54680-6.

A painstaking presentation of 650 song texts, covering 1911–1943, including 300 that were never before published. The chronological arrangement makes it possible to observe the artistic development of Hart, whose early efforts were truly appalling. With a title index.

Reviews: *Choice* 4/87, 1230; LJ 2/1/87, 80.

S2-51   ML54.2 .R3

Stanley, Lawrence A. Rap : the lyrics / Lawrence A. Stanley; introduction by Jefferson Morley. — New York : Penguin, 1992. — xxxi, 397 p. ISBN 0-1401-4788-8.

An uninhibited gathering of 150 rap lyrics by such groups as Ice Cube, Ice-T, 2-Live Crew, and Public Enemy. The author views rap as a "battleground upon which an intolerant and powerful minority—most of whom happen to be white—has attempted to enforce its values against a disenfranchised and largely powerless minority—most of whom happen to be black." He believes that these lyrics express "a mood of renewed black cultural pride."

S2-52   ML54.6 .D66
Sugerman, Daniel. The Doors : the complete illustrated lyrics / Daniel Sugerman. — New York : Hyperion, 1991. — viii, 200 p. : ill. ISBN 1-56282-996-3.

"No modern poet has written better of the alienation and feelings of isolation, dread, and disconnectedness than Jim Morrison" (lead singer of the Doors), opines Sugerman, possibly forgetting T. S. Eliot. He presents his case in the form of song texts, with line-by-line adulatory commentaries. With an index of song titles and many Door photos, showing them in full alienation.

ML55 : LIBRARIES, LIBRARIANS

See also ML111–114 (beginning with S2-89).

S2-53   ML55 .H514
Bradley, Carol June. Richard S. Hill : tributes from friends / ed. Carol June Bradley and James B. Coover. — Detroit : Information Coordinators, 1987. — xv, 397 p. : ill. (Detroit studies in music bibliography, 58) ISBN 0-89990-035-6.

A posthumous festschrift for Hill (1901–1961), musicologist, discographer, librarian (Library of Congress Music Division), and editor of *Notes*. A graceful essay on Hill by Bradley is followed by articles on diverse topics by William Lichtenwanger, Irving Lowens, H. Earle Johnson, Dena Epstein, James Coover, Donald Krummel, and Philip Miller. These are all major scholars, and their contributions are important. There are also five "tribute" pieces about Hill. Without index.

Review: AM 1988, 471.

S2-54   ML55 .S7
Katz, Israel J. Libraries, history, diplomacy, and the performing arts : essays in honor of Carleton Sprague Smith / ed. Israel J. Katz. — Stuyvesant, N.Y. : Pendragon, 1991. — xv, 459 p. (Festschrift series, 9) ISBN 0-945193-13-0.

Smith (1905–) was chief of the Music Division, New York Public Library, from 1931 to 1943, and from 1946 to 1959. One of the essays in this celebratory volume, by Sidney Beck, tells how the collection at NYPL (from 1965 the Library and Museum of the Performing Arts at Lincoln Center) developed under Smith's guidance, leading to the magnificent research resource it is today. Other contributions of importance are David Hall's report of collecting and cataloging challenges at the library, Genevieve Oswald on the dance collection, and Ruth Watanabe's story of the building of the library at the Eastman School of Music. There are also several essays of interest outside the library field.

ML60 : ESSAYS

S2-55　ML60 .F54

Finney, Ross Lee. Thinking about music : the collected writings of Ross Lee Finney / Ross Lee Finney; ed. with a preface by Frederic Goossen. — Tuscaloosa : University of Alabama Press, 1990. — xvi, 203 p. ISBN 0-8173-0521-1.

A thoughtful, well-read composer is represented by essays and lectures that span a half century. His writings are steeped in real music, without fear of technical vocabulary. He avoids the easy chat that characterizes so much composer prose and even quotes Stravinsky on this issue: "But to talk music is risky, and entails responsibility. Therefore some find it preferable to seize on side-issues. It is easy, and enables you to pass as a deep thinker." The most interesting pieces are accounts of Finney's compositional method, with musical examples. Endnotes; but no index. See also S2-473.

Review: *Choice* 11/91, 460.

S2-56　ML60 .L465

Lipman, Samuel. Arguing for music, arguing for culture / Samuel Lipman. — Boston : D. R. Godine, in association with the American Council for the Arts, 1990. — xiii, 448 p. ISBN 0-87923-821-6.

The author, publisher of the *New Criterion,* critic for *Commentary,* and former member of the National Council on the Arts, presents his views on American culture in a collection of previously published essays. His basic perspective is that "as we look around us at the life of high culture in America at present, . . . there is little in blossoming health." He urges government, through the National Endowment for the Arts and other agencies, to stress "not the revolutionary nature of new art but its development out of, and continuity with, the past." The influence of NEA chair Nancy Hanks is well discussed. Other topics include American string quartet writing ("rich indeed"); musical New York ("in a state of crisis"); John Cage's weird nonlecture at Harvard ("as time passed, many members of the audience began to doze, and others started to leave"); the future of classical music (not good: but amateur music lovers will "keep alive the possibility of a small flame of creativity"); and the future of opera (not good either: but could be improved if repertoires of opera companies would move vigorously into twentieth-century works). Lipman has primarily "dismal thoughts on the present and future," negative reactions to such as Zubin Mehta, James Levine, Gian Carlo Menotti, Joan Sutherland, Luciano Pavarotti, Lincoln Center, and Erich Leinsdorf. One reason things are going badly is that Americans have confused democracy with culture, which he believes ought to have an "amicable separation": "It is the task of democracy to govern, it is the task of culture to make the best sense we can, this side of eternity, of life itself." Agreeing or not with these themes and interpretations, the reader will find them fascinating to pursue. With a partly expansive index.

Reviews: AM 1993, 500; LJ 10/15/90, 90.

S2-57   ML60 .P1421
Page, Tim. Music from the road : views and reviews, 1978–1992 / Tim Page. — New York : Oxford, 1992. — xviii, 268 p. ISBN 0-1950-7315-0.

Interesting essays and interviews by a perceptive critic, drawn from *Newsday*. Among the individuals whose work are discussed are George Antheil, Milton Babbitt, Leonard Bernstein, John Cage, Van Cliburn, Philip Glass, Harry Partch, Steve Reich, Leonard Slatkin, Brian Wilson, and Ellen Zwilich. With a nonexpansive index.

Review: LJ 10/1/92, 90.

ML68 : RADIO MUSIC

S2-58   ML68 .J66
Jones, Reginald M., Jr. The mystery of the masked man's music : a search for the music used on "The Lone Ranger" radio program, 1933–1954 / Reginald M. Jones, Jr. — Metuchen, N.J. : Scarecrow, 1987. — xi, 219 p. : ill. ISBN 0-8108-1982-1.

Most people who are old enough to remember *The Lone Ranger* on radio will think of the two familiar musical pieces that were the principal themes: *William Tell Overture* and *Les Préludes*. In fact, there were hundreds of other excerpts heard at one time or another. Jones set out to identify every scrap from every broadcast; and if he has missed any, nobody will ever know it. A large proportion of the mood repertoire consisted of compositions so little played today that a true tune detective was required to name them. Jones has written an intriguing history of the program from the musical point of view, mentioning directors and performers (some of the music was live), citing recordings (some commercial, others made to order). With an expansive index.

S2-59   ML68 .S9
Swartz, Jon D. Handbook of old-time radio : a comprehensive guide to golden age radio listening and collecting / Jon D. Swartz and Robert C. Reinehr. — Metuchen, N.J. : Scarecrow, 1992. — xv, 807 p. ISBN 0-8108-2590-2. (Alternative classification: PN1991.3 U6 S93.)

An excellent survey of about 4,500 radio programs that aired from about 1926 to 1962. It is useful both for radio information and for guidance to collectors of recorded programs. The basic list of shows puts them in category order (music/variety, comedy, adventure, drama, sports, news, etc.) and gives keys to vendors of their recordings. A descriptive section covers about 2,000 programs in title order, giving broadcast dates, credits, duration, story lines, and other facts as appropriate. Performer and program indexes offer quick access to the volume. Many extra features are also provided, such as a directory of collectors and dealers, a useful guide for collectors, a history of the networks, and descriptions of premiums offered on the air. There is a selective, annotated bibliography of some 75 entries.

ML76 : AWARDS

S2-60   ML76 .G7 S3
Schipper, Henry. Broken record : the story of the Grammy awards / Henry Schipper. — New York : Birch Lane, 1992. — x, 271 p. : ill. : 16 p. plates. ISBN 1-55972-104-9.

A breezy, undocumented story of NARAS (National Academy of Recording Arts and Sciences) and its annual (since 1958) awards in about 75 categories of recordings. Schipper emphasizes the conservative bias of the judges and the difficulty of rock musicians in getting recognition. (Other luminaries also missed out on Grammys, for example, Lester Young and Maria Callas.) Numerous quotations appear, without sources, and the factual base is vague throughout. There is a list of winners by category from each year, but not the other nominees (information given in *Variety's Directory,* S2-1288). Label numbers are not given either. Without index.

ML87 : PICTORIAL WORKS

S2-61   ML87 .G185
Gamble, Peter. Focus on jazz / Peter Gamble; photography by Peter

Symes. — New York : St. Martin's, 1988. — 160 p. : ill. ISBN 0-312-02092-9.

A collection of color photos with short biographies; without index or reference features.

S2-62   ML87 .L66

Longstreet, Stephen. Storyville to Harlem : fifty years in the jazz scene / Stephen Longstreet. — New Brunswick, N.J. : Rutgers University Press, 1986. — 211 p. : ill. ISBN 0-8135-1174-7.

This collection of over 150 of Longstreet's black-and-white drawings illustrates locales in New Orleans, Chicago, New York, and Paris. Brief written observations accompany most drawings, but comments and pictures are, in general, only loosely related. Some drawings were made as early as 1925, but most are not dated. The subjects of about a dozen portraits are identified, but most are not. Without a table of contents or an index, the work is most useful as a sample of Longstreet's drawings.

Stephen Longstreet has written novels, biographies, plays (including *High Button Shoes* and *The Jolson Story*), and jazz commentaries. He has exhibited widely as a painter and collagist [—D. P.].

S2-63   ML87 .R4

Reiff, Carole. Nights in Birdland : jazz photographs, 1954–1960 / Carole Reiff; with an essay by Jack Kerouac. — New York : Simon & Schuster, 1987. — 123 p. : ill. ISBN 0-671-63281-7.

In these black-and-white portraits, Reiff shows jazz musicians in performance, posing for her, and in candid moments. The clarity of the images varies, but she often captures strong emotional expressions on the artists' faces. The lack of an index limits its usefulness for reference purposes.

Carole Reiff was a freelance photographer who often worked for record companies; her work has appeared in many magazines [—D. P.].

S2-64   ML87 .T7

Troxler, Niklaus. Jazzplakate / Niklaus Troxler. Waakirchen, Germany : Oreos, 1991. See series note at S2-1111.

ML101–102 : DICTIONARIES AND ENCYCLOPEDIAS

ML101 : General

S2-65   ML101 .U6 N48

New Grove dictionary of American music / ed. H. Wiley Hitchcock and Stanley Sadie. — New York : Grove's Dictionaries of Music, 1986. — 4 vols. : ill. ISBN 0-943818-36-2.

A valuable supplement to the 1980 *New Grove Dictionary of Music and Musicians,* a work whose emphasis was on "European musical and cultural traditions," to the neglect of American topics. Music of Americans and musical life in the United States are dealt with adequately here, with signed articles by specialists. Popular music gets strong attention. The work shares some of the weaknesses of its parent set: lack of an index is the primary defect; the bibliographies are poor (in selection and presentation); many composer worklists, even for prominent persons like John Adams, give minimal data. The whole field of sound recording, which emerged in the United States and was brought to its zenith by U.S. firms, is passed over in silence; there are no articles for the great labels (Columbia, Decca, Victor, etc.), and citations to discographies are few. The exception is in record lists appended to entries for jazz and pop performers, which give label numbers and release years. Despite such problems, "Amerigrove" is the best available conspectus of its topic.

Reviews and listing: AM 1987, 194; Balay BH55; *Choice* 1/87, 724.

ML102 : Topical

Blues

S2-66   ML102 .B6 H39

Herzhaft, Gérard. Encyclopedia of the blues / Gérard Herzhaft; trans. Brigitte Debord. — Fayetteville : University of Arkansas Press, 1992. — 513 p. : ill. ISBN 1-55728-252-8.

Translation of *Nouvelle encyclopédie du blues.*

Biographies, in popular style, of about 300 blues artists, with mention of some important recordings by each. A selection of compact discs, by artist, follows the biographical section. The most interesting part of the book is the list of 300 blues standards, with comments on various renditions of them. There is also a useful list of instruments and their performers. With a nonexpansive name index.

Reviews: *Choice* 5/93, 1442; LJ 9/1/92, 168.

Country

S2-67   ML102 .C7 M2

Marschall, Richard. The encyclopedia of country and western music / Richard Marschall. — New York : Exeter, 1985. — 192 p. : ill. ISBN 0-6710-7606-X.

Color pictures and casual stories of performers, in alphabetical order. Without index or reference features.

Folk Music

S2-68   ML102 .F66 S7
Stambler, Irwin. Encyclopedia of folk, country, and western music /
Irwin Stambler and Grelun Landon. — Rev. ed. — New York : St. Martin's, 1983. — 902 p. : ill. : 56 p. plates. ISBN 0-3122-4818-0.
1st ed., 1969 (LOAM 610).
About 6,000 unsigned articles, mostly biographical, in casual style,
covering mainstream folk, country and western, folk rock, folk blues,
country rock, and bluegrass. Much of the data came from responses to
questionnaires. Important discs are mentioned in the articles, but there
are no discographies. An appendix gives award winners by name (the
most awarded artists being Loretta Lynn, Merle Haggard, Conway
Twitty, Dolly Parton, Tammy Wynette, Roy Clark, Chet Atkins, Waylon Jennings, Charley Pride, Kenny Rogers, and Johnny Cash). There are
also lists of major awards and their winners to 1981. With a bibliography of about 400 items, mostly articles. No index.

Jazz

S2-69   ML102 .J3 C32
Carr, Ian. Jazz : the essential companion / Ian Carr, Digby Fairwea-
ther, and Brian Priestley. — London : Grafton Books, 1987. — 562 p. :
ill. ISBN 0-246-12741-4.
The bulk of the more than 1,600 entries are biographical sketches, but
there are numerous descriptions of terms that often appear in the jazz literature. The entries are more concise than those in the *New Grove Dictionary of Jazz* (S2-73) and less numerous. One or more suggested
recordings are listed for most artists by title, date, and label. Popular biographies are sometimes also listed, but there are no other bibliographical references.
The authors, all jazz musicians, provide an insight that is not always
found in scholarly endeavors. Over 150 photographs are included. Without index [—D.P.].
Review: LJ 9/15/88, 75.

S2-69a   ML102 .J3 C34
Case, Brian. The Harmony illustrated encyclopedia of jazz / Brian
Case and Stan Britt; rev. Chrissie Murray. — 3rd ed. — New York :
Harmony Books, 1987. — 208 p. ISBN 0-517-56442-4.
1st ed., 1978 (LOAM Suppl. S-629) as *The Illustrated Encyclopedia
of Jazz.*
A convenient collection of short biographical sketches, major record-

ings, and color photographs for the principal artists. With a nonexpansive index of names.

S2-70　　ML102 .J3 C6
　Clayton, Peter. Jazz A–Z / Peter Clayton and Peter Gammond. — London : Guinness Superlatives, 1986. — 262 p. : ill. ISBN 0-85112-281-7.
　Cover title: Guinness jazz A–Z.
　A dictionary of jazz terms, topics, places (including landmarks, streets, and sections of cities), instruments, and some groups. There are only a few individual biographies, rather out of place in this handy guide to the nonpersonal aspects of jazz. With a nonexpansive index.

S2-71　　ML102 .J3 E3
　Eckland, K. O. Jazz West 1945–1985 : the A–Z guide to West Coast jazz music / K. O. Eckland; photographs by Ed Lawless. — Carmel-by-the-Sea, Calif. : Cypress, 1986. — 285 p. : ill. ISBN 0-938995-03-0.
　Over 400 bands and 2,400 individuals are included in this directory which encompasses Arizona, British Columbia, California, Hawaii, Nevada, Oregon, and Washington. The longest entries for bands include place and years of most activity, a descriptive paragraph, a list of personnel (with years of association and instrument played), and a brief discography (with label, number, title, and year). However, most entries are much shorter, many no longer than three lines. The longest listings for individuals include instrument played, date of birth (and death), place of birth, vocation (if not full-time musician), affiliations with bands and individuals, and a brief discography. Most entries, however, include only name, instrument, and one band.
　Since the majority of the names do not appear in the *New Grove Dictionary of Jazz* (S2-73), this directory fills a gap; however, idiosyncratic and inconsistent filing arrangements make finding them difficult. A myriad of abbreviations and typefaces makes interpretation slow-going for the occasional user. More than 150 good photographs are a strong contribution; most are placed on the same page as the corresponding entry. With a 12-item bibliography; without index [—D. P.].

S2-72　　ML102 .J3 M455
　McRae, Barry. The jazz handbook / Barry McRae. — Burnt Mill, Harlow, Essex, England : Longman; Boston : G. K. Hall, 1987. — 272 p. : ill. ISBN 0-582-00092-0 (U.K.); 0-8161-9096-8 (U.S.).
　These circa 200 biographical sketches review the musicians' professional careers, focusing on who influenced them and who they influenced. Date and place of birth (and death) are listed along with instrument played and dates of recording career. There is a photograph of each

subject and a few recommended recordings. There are numerous errors
of fact throughout. Entries are arranged by decade and then alphabetically; each decade is discussed in a very brief essay. With a guide to
record labels, a short list of recommended readings, a glossary, a list of
periodicals and festivals, and a nonexpansive index.

Barry McRae has contributed to *Jazz Journal International, Wire Magazine, Jazz News, Event, Jazz Down Under,* and *Down Beat* [—D. P.].

Reviews: ARBA 1991, #1318; *Choice* 11/90, 462; LJ 7/90, 88.

S2-73   ML102 .J3 N48
New Grove dictionary of jazz / ed. Barry Kernfeld. — London : Mac-
millan; New York : Grove's Dictionaries of Music, 1988. — 2 vols. : ill.
ISBN 0-333-393846-7 (U.K.); 0-935859-39-X (U.S.).

Prepared in the general style of other recent Grove efforts, the work is
meticulous in its accuracy. The emphasis of the roughly 4,500 entries is
on biographical articles, which range from a paragraph to several pages,
but there are also many entries for record labels, jazz terminology, styles,
and the like. Most of the signed articles include well-chosen bibliographies; selected recordings are listed for most artists, though the information is terse. There is also a general bibliography of books and
periodicals, with about 2,000 titles. More than 200 photographs are ap-
propriately placed within the text. The biographical and bibliographical
information will be very useful to researchers and to those needing individual bits of information on jazz. One weak area of coverage is ensembles; much information that is given about them in biographical articles
is not indicated by appropriate references. The major weakness is the
lack of an index [—D.P.].

Listing and reviews: AM 1987, 194; ARBA 1990, #1288; Balay BH
119; LJ 1/87, 82.

Music Business

S2-74   ML102 .M85 R3
Rachlin, Harvey. The encyclopedia of the music business / Harvey
Rachlin. — New York : Harper & Row, 1981. — xix, 524 p. : ill. ISBN
0-06-014913-2.

An alphabetical arrangement of 438 entries, unsigned, averaging a
page in length. Coverage includes terminology, associations, copyright
matters, occupations (recording engineer, A & R man, etc.), and media.
Appendix features give acronyms and abbreviations, forms, and winners
of various awards (Tony, Grammy, etc.). No index; some cross-references; no bibliographic references. A numbered list of articles is helpful
for access. The information provided is practical and useful.

Listing: Sheehy BH175.

Popular Music

S2-75   ML102 .P66 F2

Paymer, Marvin E. Facts behind the songs : a handbook of American popular music from the nineties to the '90s / Marvin E. Paymer. — New York : Garland, 1993. — xxii, 565 p. : ill. (Garland reference library of the humanities, 1,300) ISBN 0-8240-5240-4.

A fascinating, unique reference work on popular songs since the 1890s, "where they come from, their subject matter, the characteristics of their lyrics and music, the influences that shaped them, how they were introduced and popularized." The book offers articles in alphabetical sequence on topics relating to songs, such as accompaniment, Africa, anatomy, animals, circus, cities, countermelody, form, humor, octave, questions, rhythm, slang, wishing, and World War II. In each article a number of individual songs are discussed. After the topical entries there is a list of the 4,400 songs cited, with their composers and years, and with references to the articles in which they appear. The tone of the book is light but scholarly. With numerous illustrations of persons, sheet music, and places of interest; and an index to song titles, persons, and subjects.

S2-76   ML102 .P66 G84

Guinness encyclopedia of popular music / ed. Colin Larkin. — London : Guinness, 1992. — 4 vols. ISBN 1-882267-00-1.

A useful but uneven compilation, consisting of about 10,000 entries for persons, groups, associations, and record labels. Most of the authors are British, and only a few are well known in the United States. The language is casual, dates are often vague, and subjective viewpoints frequently take the place of more detached descriptions ("generally accepted opinions" are presented). Discographies for the articles are said to be "exhaustive," but information provided is not consistent with that claim, being limited to albums only, or sometimes "selected albums," and giving no details beyond release dates. Cross-referencing is good, but the nonexpansive index is a trial: There are, for example, about 180 page citations under "Elvis Presley," and about 600 citations under "Piano." The list of entries in alphabetical order is helpful. But the subject bibliography (books only) is completely foolish, listing titles in no order under each topic; omitting certain topics entirely (such as "Rock"); and giving garbled imprint data.

Reviews: *Choice* 3/93, 1112; LJ 1/93, 98; LJ 4/15/93, 60.

S2-77   ML102 .P66 S8

Stambler, Irwin. Encyclopedia of pop, rock & soul / Irwin Stambler. — Rev. ed. — New York : St. Martin's, 1989. — x, 881 p. : ill. : 40 p. plates. ISBN 0-312-02573-4.

1st ed., 1975 (LOAM 1339).

Knowledgeable biographical sketches of about 700 persons and groups, with citations to representative recordings. A useful feature is the identification—with birthdates and birthplaces—of all personnel through the history of major groups. The book is awkward to use because it lacks running heads, and more so because it lacks an index. Appendices give gold and platinum award records from 1958 to 1989, selected Grammy awards from 1958 to 1988, and Academy Award nominations and winners in music from 1958 to 1988. A bibliography of about 600 books and articles—presumably used in writing the entries—appears at the end of the volume.

Listing and reviews: ARBA 1990, #1298; Balay BH134; LJ 2/15/89, 156.

S2-78   ML102 .P66 T9

Tyler, Don. Hit parade : an encyclopedia of the top songs of the jazz, depression, swing, and sing eras / Don Tyler. — New York : Quill, 1985. — 257 p. ISBN 0-688-05079-4.

A yearly chronology of the most successful pop songs from 1920 to 1955, with selections based on Recording Industry Association of America (RIAA) certifications of million sellers (since 1958) and various earlier sources, such as *Billboard* charts. The radio show *Your Hit Parade* was one source, but this book is not about that program. What sets Tyler's approach apart from similar compilations, such as *Popular Music* (S2-102) or *Variety Music Cavalcade* (LOAM 17), are the extensive comments offered about the genesis and later history of the songs. There is a useful biographical section that gives basic data on singers and composers, a title index, and a nonexpansive name index.

Listing and reviews: ARBA 1987, #1266; Balay BH135; LJ 12/85, 92.

Rock Music

S2-79   ML102 .R6 E5

Encyclopedia of rock / ed. Phil Hardy and Dave Laing; additional material by Stephen Barnard and Don Perretta. — [Rev. ed.] — New York : Schirmer, 1988. — 480 p. : ill. ISBN 0-02-919562-4.

1st ed., 1976 (LOAM Suppl. S-1099).

A compilation of brief unsigned entries, mostly for persons (British and American) and labels, with some for topics (e.g., African music, western swing). Information given is inconsistent among entries; birthdates are not always given, for example. Color pictures are useful. Without bibliographies, discographies, or indexing.

Listing: Balay BH126.

S2-79a   ML102 .R6 H37

Clifford, Mike. Harmony encyclopedia of rock /Mike Clifford. — 6th ed. — New York : Harmony Books, 1988. — 208 p. : ill. ISBN 0-517-57164-1.

1st ed., 1983 (LOAM Suppl. SA-651) as *New Illustrated Rock Handbook.*

A useful reference for rock performers of the United States and the United Kingdom, with biographical sketches, lists of hit records with chart positions, and color photos. Without index or documentation.

S2-80   ML102 .R6 H5

Helander, Brock. The rock who's who : a biographical dictionary and critical discography including rhythm-and-blues, soul, rockabilly, folk, country, easy listening, punk, and new wave / Brock Helander. — New York : Schirmer; London : Collier Macmillan, 1982. — xiv, 686 p. ISBN 0-02-871250-1.

All rock and soul acts that have appeared since the early 1950s are included in this useful compilation, with the exception of twist, disco, and white cover artists. Brief biographical notices are given for each person or group, along with a "comprehensive and definitive critical and historical discography." The discography, of U.S. LPs only, mentions labels and release dates (month and year), with notes about platinum and gold albums. Books and articles about each performer are listed, with full bibliographical data; and there are lists of books and articles by each person as well. Index of names; general bibliography. Helander is a country-rock musician.

Listing and reviews: ARBA 1984, p. 453; Balay BH129; LJ 10/1/82, 1866.

Soul Music

S2-81   ML102 .S65 G5

Gregory, Hugh. Soul music A–Z / Hugh Gregory. — London : Blandford, 1991. — vi, 266 p. : ill. ISBN 0-7137-2179-0.

About 600 biographical entries for singers and industry figures, useful for lesser-known persons. Chart songs are identified, and there are selective lists of other records (label name and year of issue).

Reviews: ARBA 1993, p. 546; *Choice* 10/92, 272.

S2-82   ML102 .S65 T43

Tee, Ralph. Soul music : who's who / Ralph Tee. — Rocklin, Calif. : Prima, 1992. — 309 p. ISBN 1-55958-228-6.

"1st published in Great Britain in 1991 by George Weidenfeld and Nicolson Limited."

Casual notices on about 1,800 individuals and groups; vague on facts on dates. Label information is not provided when recordings are mentioned. Without index.

Sound Recording

S2-83   ML102 .S67 E5
Encyclopedia of recorded sound in the United States / ed. Guy A. Marco; contributing ed. Frank Andrews. — New York : Garland, 1993. — xlix, 910 p. ISBN 0-8240-4782-6.

The first extensive reference work to cover a wide range of topics in the area of recorded sound: history, terminology, technology, labels, performers, industry executives, and related subjects. With contributions by 32 specialists. Focused on the United States, but with attention to persons and developments in the United Kingdom, Canada, Australia, New Zealand, and Europe. Includes a list of more than 500 sound-recording periodicals, a list of pseudonyms used by recording artists, and lists of record players produced by Columbia, Gramophone Co., Edison, and Pathé. With a bibliography of about 1,500 entries and an expansive index of names, firms, topics, and categories of performers.

ML105–106 : COLLECTIVE BIOGRAPHIES

S2-84   ML105 .L38
LePage, Jane W. Women composers, conductors, and musicians of the twentieth century, volume 3 / Jane W. LePage. — Metuchen, N.J. : Scarecrow, 1988. — 333 p. : ill. ISBN 0-8108-2082-X. (Alternative classification ML1950 .L38.)

Volumes 1 and 2 in LOAM Suppl., S-22.

The latest volume in this important series profiles 18 composers from various countries. The American-born women are Gloria Coates, Selma Esptein, Priscilla McLean, Mary Mageau, and Joan Tower. For each person there is a biographical sketch, list of works, comments by the composer, and a summary of critical reviews. In the index there is further information under each person's name, including her teachers, institutional affiliations, and orchestras that have played her works.

S2-85   ML105 .V25
Vaughan, Andrew. Who's who in new country music / Andrew Vaughan. — London : Omnibus, 1989. — 128 p. : ill. ISBN 0-7119-1690-X.

Breezy, journalistic entries for performers active in the mid-1980s, without special features and with curious omissions. No index.

Reviews: ARBA 1991, p. 530; LJ 1/90, 103.

S2-86 ML106 .U3 A5

American Society of Composers, Authors, and Publishers. ASCAP biographical dictionary / compiled for the American Society of Composers, Authors, and Publishers by Jacques Cattell Press. — 4th ed. — New York : Bowker, 1980. — ix, 589 p. ISBN 0-8352-1283-1.

1st ed., 1948 (LOAM 1146).

Brief biographies of 8,200 individual members of ASCAP and of 7,000 publisher members, based on a questionnaire conducted in 1980. For each person there is a career summary and list of major works. Without indexes.

Listings: BCL; Sheehy BH184.

S2-87 ML106 .U3 T87

Turner, Patricia. Dictionary of Afro-American performers : 78 rpm and cylinder recordings of opera, choral music, and song, c. 1900–1949 / Patricia Turner. — New York : Garland, 1990. — xxiii, 433 p. : ill. (Garland reference library of the humanities, 590) ISBN 0-8240-8736-4.

A bio-discography of 23 composers, 39 singers, 3 instrumentalists, and 14 vocal groups, all of them performers of classical or religious music. Six operas and musicals are also treated. Books, articles, newspaper notices, and archival collections are cited. Information on recordings is limited to label and number, with approximate release dates, names of performers, and some reissues. Facts about most of the persons included are difficult to locate elsewhere, but there are numerous inaccuracies. Unannotated bibliography of about 250 items. Without index.

Listing and reviews: ARBA 1991, 508; Balay BH87; *Choice* 11/90, 462.

S2-88 ML106 .U3 W2

Warner, Jay. The *Billboard* book of American singing groups : a history, 1940–1990 / Jay Warner. — New York : Billboard Books, 1992. — xvii, 542 p. : ill. ISBN 0-8230-8264-4.

A directory of about 400 American popular vocal ensembles, in alphabetical clusters by decade from the 1940s to the 1980s. A career outline is given for each group, with a selection of hit records (labels and release dates only). No documentation or index.

ML111–114 : LIBRARIES AND PUBLISHING

See also ML55 (beginning with S2-53).

S2-89   ML111 .M9
Music librarianship in America / ed. Michael Ochs. — Cambridge, Mass. : Eda Kuhn Loeb Music Library, Harvard University, 1991. — 144 p. ISBN not given.

A collection of papers read on the occasion of the establishment of the chair in music librarianship at Harvard, the first of its kind in the United States. Michael Ochs, holder of the chair, edited the proceedings, which offer a mixture of scholarship and rambling comments. The more useful contributions are by James Coover (on cooperative approaches to collection development), James Pruett (on service and educational questions), Donald Krummel (on the general failure of libraries to document the music of immigrant groups), and Leo Balk (on the relations between publishers and music librarians). This material had been published earlier, in the *Harvard Library Bulletin,* Spring 1991. Without index.

S2-90   ML112 .K6
Korda, Marion. Louisville music publications of the 19th century / Marion Korda. — Louisville, Ky. : Music Library, University of Louisville, 1991. — xi, 202 p. ISBN not given.

A thorough documentation of the city's place in the early history of music publishing, covering 1832–1882. Following a useful historical introduction, there is a list of 1,450 publications in main-entry order, giving for each its composer, publisher, medium, first line (for songs), bibliographical description with plate numbers, library location, and notes. With a title index and a plate number index.

S2-91   ML112 .K738
Krohn, Ernst C. Music publishing in St. Louis / Ernst C. Krohn; completed and ed. J. Bunker Clark; foreword by Lincoln Bunce Spiess. — Warren, Mich. : Harmonie Park, 1988. — xxiii, 126 p. : ill. ISBN 0-8999-0043-7.

Musicologist Krohn (1888–1975) left this study unfinished; it is ably completed by his colleague Clark. In a scholarly narrative, Clark considers music publishers Nathaniel Philips, Peters & Co., William Foden, Compton & Sons, Bollman Brothers, Kunkel Brothers, Mel Bay, and many lesser figures. With good portraits and illustrations of sheet music, a title index, and a nonexpansive name index.

S2-92   ML113 .I6
Directory of music research libraries / Rita Benton, general editor. — Vol. 1, 2nd ed. — Canada / Marian Kahn and Helmut Kallmann; United States / Charles Lindahl. — Kassel, Germany : Bärenreiter, 1983. — 282 p. (RISM, series C) ISBN 3-76180-6841.

1st ed., 1966–1970.

Public, academic, and private research libraries with significant collections of music materials, arranged by city (states are intermixed). Special collections are identified, and publications about the library are cited. Personnel are not named. With an index of library names and subjects of the special collections.
Listing: Sheehy BH152.

S2-93   ML114 .M4 D59
Directory of music collections in the midwestern United States / comp. Publications Committee, Music Library Association, Midwest Chapter. — Oberlin, Ohio : The Chapter, 1990. iii, 114 p. ISBN not given.
Brief descriptions of library holdings in Iowa, Illinois, Indiana, Kentucky, Michigan, Minnesota, Missouri, Ohio, and Wisconsin, in alphabetical sequence within each state. Personnel are named, facilities and special holdings are identified (including uncataloged material of interest), and access regulations are given. With indexes by subject and staff name.

S2-94   ML114 .N33 D59
Directory of music libraries & collections in New England, 1985 / comp. Publications Committee, Music Library Association, New England Chapter. — 7th ed. — Hanover, N.H. : The Chapter, 1985. — 100 p. ISBN not given.
Basic collection data about the music libraries of the region, in alphabetical sequence by institutional name. Personnel are named, and special collections are identified. There is also a list of libraries by state and a name index.

ML120 : BIBLIOGRAPHY
General

S2-95   ML120 .H6 H4
Heintze, James R. American music before 1865 in print and on records / James R. Heintze. — 2nd ed. — Brooklyn : Institute for Studies in American Music, 1990. — xiii, 248 p. (I.S.A.M. monographs, 30) ISBN 0-9146-7833-7.
1st ed., 1976 (LOAM Suppl. S-1).
This update of a standard source presents new publications and recordings, and fills in information for the period before 1976. Heintze had listed much of the material earlier in two supplements, in *Notes,* to the first edition. There are 1,310 entries in a single alphabetical sequence, with a label index and indexes of composers, compilers, and titles.
Review: *Choice* 4/91, 1290.

S2-96   ML120 .045 D7

Dox, Thurston J. American oratorios and cantatas : a catalog of works written in the United States from colonial times to 1985 / Thurston J. Dox. — Metuchen, N.J. : Scarecrow, 1986. — 2 vols. ISBN 0-8108-1861-2.

An important inventory of 3,450 works by more than 1,000 composers, listed in composer order within genres. Much valuable information is included for each entry: years of composition and publication, publisher, instrumental and vocal forces, timing, length in pages, location of manuscript, premiere data, and citations of reviews. There is an interesting topical index to the compositions, with such headings as baseball, death, flight, Israel, slavery, and weddings. With a name index as well.

Reviews: *Choice* 2/87, 862; LJ 12/86, 94.

S2-97   ML120 .U5 B77

Brookhart, Edward. Music in American higher education : an annotated bibliography / Edward Brookhart. — Warren, Mich. : Harmonie Park, 1988; published for the College Music Society. — ix, 245 p. : ill. (Bibliographies in American music, 10) ISBN 0-89990-042-9.

A list of 1,300 books, articles, dissertations, and master's theses concerned with the history of music in American higher education in the nineteenth and twentieth centuries. Brookhart, a professor of music at University of Texas at Austin and Kansas State University, describes his list as "a limited and selective compilation." Criteria for inclusion are not clear, and there are many strange old items. Not all entries are annotated. An author index and an expansive subject index facilitate access.

Listing and reviews: ARBA 1989, p. 467; Balay BH7; *Choice* 12/88, 622.

S2-98   ML120 .U5 G7

Greene, Richard M. The hit parade, 1920 to 1970 / Richard M. Greene. — 2nd ed. — Riverside, Calif. [12149 Indiana Ave., 92503] : Author, 1991. — viii, 106 p. ISBN 0-1601-0710-0.

1st ed., 1985.

An alphabetical list of some 300 popular songs, presenting for each the publication date; names of composer, lyricist, and singer associated with it; and show in which it appeared (if any). For many of the songs there are also melodic indications in the form of scale letters. Despite the title of the book, it has no connection with the radio program *Your Hit Parade*. No index.

S2-99   ML120 .U5 H46

Heintze, James R. Early American music : a research and information guide / James R. Heintze. — New York : Garland, 1990. — xii, 511 p.

(Music research and information guides, 13; Garland reference library of the humanities, 1,007) ISBN 0-8240-4119-4.

A selective, annotated bibliography of 1,959 books, articles, and dissertations that deal with American music and musicians up to about 1820. Folk music and African-American music are not covered, since they have had good bibliographic attention elsewhere (i.e., Miller [S2-123] and DeLerma [LOAM Suppl. SA-287]). Heintze, music librarian at American University, lists items under customary reference headings (encyclopedias, bibliographies, indexes, etc.) and by historical topics. There are entries under each of 22 ethnic and religious groups; names of collective and individual biographies; titles of critical and facsimile editions of music. Author, title, and subject indexes (not expansive).

Listing and reviews: ARBA 1991, #1253; Balay BH2; *Choice* 10/90, 283; LJ 5/15/90, 70–72.

S2-100   ML120 .U5 J2
Jacobs, Dick. Who wrote that song? / Dick Jacobs. — White Hall, Va. : Betterway, 1988. — 415 p. : ill. : 16 p. plates. ISBN 1-5587-0108-7.

A useful checklist of 12,000 pop songs, identifying for each the publisher, who introduced the song, who sang it on Broadway and in film, and who had the hit records. With a composer index.

S2-101   ML120 .U5 K78
Krummel, Donald. Bibliographical handbook of American music / Donald William Krummel. — Urbana : University of Illinois Press, 1987. — 269 p. ISBN 0-252-01450-2.

A thorough, well-annotated list of 760 major reference works that concern American music; including bibliographies, trade lists, library catalogs, discographies, and guides to the literature. Covers concert music, ethnic music, folk music, sacred music, jazz, and popular music (through rock). Valuable historical surveys and critical comments. Index by author, title, and subject.

Listing and reviews: ARBA 1989, p. 468; Balay BH18; *Choice* 9/88, 82; LJ 1/88, 77.

S2-102   ML120 .U5 S5
Popular music : an annotated index of American popular songs / ed. Nat Shapiro and Bruce Pollock. — Detroit : Gale Research, 1984– .
Vol. 7, 1970–1974. ISBN 0-8103-0845-2.
Vol. 8, 1975–1979. ISBN 0-8103-0846-0.
Vol. 9, 1980–1984. ISBN 0-8703-0848-7.
Vol. 10, 1985. ISBN 0-1-8103-0849-5.
Vol. 11, 1986. ISBN 0-8103-1809-1.
Vol. 12, 1987. ISBN 0-8103-1810-5.
Vol. 13, 1988. ISBN 0-8103-4945-0.

Vol. 14, 1989. ISBN 0-8103-4946-9.

Vol. 15, 1990. ISBN 0-8103-4947-7.

Vol. 16, 1991. ISBN 0-8103-7485-4.

With volume 9 the title was changed to *Popular Music : An Annotated Guide to American Popular Songs*. The first eight volumes were reprinted as *Popular Music, 1920–1979* (1985). Shapiro's books presented songs in chronological arrangement, by copyright year, but the Gale reissue of the first eight volumes rearranged the titles alphabetically; subsequent volumes have been alphabetically arranged. The editors have endeavored to select the most significant songs of each year (about 2,000 in vol. 9). Information on each song includes composer and lyricist, publisher, singer who introduced it, principal recording artists and labels, and awards. With indexes by composer, lyricist, and "important performances"; list of songs and awards by year.

See S2-104 for a companion volume edited by Barbara Cohen-Stratyner, *Popular Music, 1900–1919*.

Listing and reviews: ARBA 1987, #1263; ARBA 1988, #1309; ARBA 1990, #1201; Balay BH132.

S2-103   ML120 .U5 W18

Warner, Thomas E. Periodical literature on American music, 1620–1920 : a classified bibliography with annotations / Thomas E. Warner. — Warren, Mich. : Harmonie Park, 1988. — xli, 644 p. (Bibliographies in American music, 11) ISBN 0-89990-034-8.

A useful gathering of 5,348 numbered entries drawn from about 500 periodicals. The topic is American music from 1620 to 1920, but the periodicals are from all periods—apparently inclusive of those being published up to 1980 or so. There is a mix of music journals and of general journals that contained articles on music. Folk music and American Indian music are not covered, and there are several format exclusions: items of less than a page in length, reviews (of books, recordings, or performances), abstracts of papers, personal reminiscences and anecdotes. The arrangement is by topic according to the author's divisions and subdivisions, not the happiest plan. While there is a subject index to help sort these out, it provides only item numbers under each heading (e.g., one and a half columns of numbers under "Singers"). Some entries have one-line annotations to explicate the titles.

Listing and review: ARBA 1990, #1219; Balay BH25.

S2-104   ML120 .U5549

Cohen-Stratyner, Barbara Naomi. Popular music, 1900–1919 : an annotated guide to American popular songs / Barbara Naomi Cohen-Stratyner. — Detroit : Gale Research, 1988. — xxx, 656 p. ISBN 0-8103-2595-0.

A companion volume to *Popular Music, 1920–1979* (S2-102), listing 2,600 songs.
Listing and review: ARBA 1989, #1229; Balay BH132.

S2-105   ML125 .H4 S76
Stoneburner, Bryan C. Hawaiian music : an annotated bibliography / Bryan C. Stoneburner. — Westport, Conn. : Greenwood, 1986. — x, 100 p. (Music reference collection, 10) ISBN 0-313-25340-4.
An annotated list of 564 books, articles, reviews, dissertations, pamphlets, and miscellaneous items, in author order; nearly all are in English. A useful glossary of Hawaiian music terms, a location list for periodicals, and an excellent expansive index add to the utility of this fine resource.
Reviews: ARBA 1987, #1265; *Choice* 2/87, 867.

S2-106   ML125 .N5
New York Women Composers, Inc. Catalog : compositions of concert music. — North Tarrytown, N.Y. : New York Women Composers, Inc. [114 Kelbourne Ave., 10591], 1991. — 129 p. ISBN not given.
Worklists, by genre, for 50 composers. Information provided for each work varies in detail. While 1,500 compositions are listed, there is no index to bring together those by any one composer.

S2-107   ML125 .P4
Smith, Kile. Catalog of the music of Pennsylvania composers : volume 1, orchestral music / ed. Kile Smith. — Wynnewood, Pa. : Pennsylvania Composers Forum [1210 W. Wynnewood Rd., 19096], 1992. — 60 p. ISBN not given.
Worklists for about 200 composers, with their compositions for orchestra presented in chronological order. Commission, dedication, instrumentation, publisher, and performance information is given.

S2-108   ML125 .P8 T55
Thompson, Donald. Music and dance in Puerto Rico from the age of Columbus to modern times : an annotated bibliography / Donald Thompson and Annie F. Thompson. —Metuchen, N.J. : Scarecrow, 1991. — xv, 339 p. (Studies in Latin American music, 1) ISBN 0-8108-2525-5.
A fine bibliography of 995 annotated entries, including books, parts of books, articles, and dissertations. Critical comments by the knowledgeable authors often point out errors and misconceptions in the writings cited. The arrangement is by topic, covering history, biography, chronicles and travelers' reports, concert music, church music, stage music,

folk and dance music. With a nonexpansive subject index and an author index.

Review: *Choice* 6/92, 1529.

S2-109   ML125 .T2 N4

Neal, James H. Music research in Tennessee : a guide to special collections / James H. Neal. — Murfreesboro : Middle Tennessee State University, Center for Popular Music, 1989. — 75 p. (CPM monograph series, 1) ISBN not given.

Library holdings in music for about 50 institutions are described in this useful directory. While many of the libraries report only basic collections of musical items, others have interesting materials such as scrapbooks, old sheet music, field recordings of folk music, oral histories, and memorabilia of musicians. The Country Music Foundation and Vanderbilt University in Nashville are major repositories for research in the history of Grand Ole Opry and other aspects of country music. With a subject index.

S2-110   ML128 .B23 R46

Renshaw, Jeffrey H. The American Wind Symphony commissioning project : a descriptive catalog of published editions, 1957–1991 / Jeffrey H. Renshaw; foreword by Warren Benson. — New York : Greenwood, 1991. — xix, 383 p. (Music reference collection, 34) ISBN 0-313-28146-7.

A bibliography of 159 works in the American Wind Symphony Editions of the C. F. Peters Corporation. These compositions were commissioned for performance by the American Waterways Wind Orchestra, conducted by Robert Boudreau, an ensemble that has given concerts on a vessel named *Point Counterpoint II* since 1976. The works listed come from many nations and include efforts by well-known composers such as Jean Francaix, Krzysztof Penderecki, David Amram, Robert Russell Bennett, Paul Creston, Alan Hovhaness, Ned Rorem, and Quincy Porter. Information provided for each work is thorough, including composer biography, performing forces, description of style and texture, publication data, and a (usually illegible) page from the score. Appendices list the works by nationality of the composers, by featured solo instrument, by date, by duration, and by type. With a discography and a title index.

S2-111   ML128 .B3 C37

Carner, Gary. Jazz performers : an annotated bibliography of biographical materials / Gary Carner; foreword by John Chilton. — New York : Greenwood, 1990. — xviii, 364 p. (Music reference collection, 26) ISBN 0-313-26250-0.

Consists of 2,927 numbered entries, some with very brief annotations, including books, theses, dissertations, and scholarly articles. Arrangement by person. A useful list, but rendered less valuable for its lack of clear inclusion standards; each title has a "substantive biographical component or aids jazz research," and each book has at least 50 pages. Most of the entries are in English, but a number of European languages are represented. All materials date from 1921 through the 1980s. A topical bibliography, following the person listing, consists of general items; it is of use for the inclusion of European books and dissertations.

Reviews: ARBA 1991, #1316; *Choice* 12/90, 606.

Black Music

S2-112   ML128 .B3 F6

Floyd, Samuel A. Black music biography : an annotated bibliography / Samuel A. Floyd, Jr. and Marsha J. Reisser. — White Plains, N.Y. : Kraus International, 1987. — xxvi, 302 p. ISBN 0-527-30158-2.

An important, extensively annotated list of books about 147 persons, distributed among jazz artists (58 persons), R & B and other popular singers (38), concert and opera artists (22), blues singers (14), and miscellaneous others. Reviews of the books are cited.

Listing: Balay BH89.

S2-112a   ML128 .B45 D445

DeLerma, Dominique-René. Black music and musicians in *the New Grove Dictionary of American Music* and the *New Harvard Dictionary of Music* / Dominique-René de Lerma and Marsha J. Reisser. — Chicago : Center for Black Music Research, Columbia College, 1989. — vi, 56 p. ISBN 0-92991-100-8.

A compilation that is rendered essential by the foolish omission of indexing in *Grove* and *Harvard*. The task has been thoroughly carried out, presenting a basic arrangement by original entry in the source work, plus indexes of authors and their articles.

Listing: Balay BH93.

S2-113   ML128 .B45 G7

Gray, John. Blacks in classical music : a bibliographical guide to composers, performers, and ensembles / John Gray. — New York : Greenwood, 1988. — x, 280 p. (Music reference collection, 15) ISBN 0-313-26056-7.

A useful list of books, dissertations, articles, obituaries, and reviews relating to about 1,200 black musicians who have participated in "art music." The entries are grouped under composers, instrumentalists, vocalists, and opera companies; with sections describing general reference works and major library collections. Indexes of artists and authors.

S2-114   ML128 .B45 H6
Horne, Aaron. Keyboard music of black composers : a bibliography /
Aaron Horne. — Westport, Conn. : Greenwood, 1992. — xx, 331 p.
(Music reference collection, 37) ISBN 0-313-27939-X.
A valuable list of works by five African composers and about 200
African Americans. Arrangement is by person, with genre indexes that
give access to pieces for various instrumental combinations. Facts given
about the compositions are usually minimal. With a discography (basic
information only) and a bibliography of 328 numbered items.

S2-115   ML128 .B45 H7
Horne, Aaron. String music of black composers : a bibliography /
Aaron Horne; foreword by Dominique-René DeLerma. — New York:
Greenwood, 1991. — xx, 327 p. (Music reference collection, 33) ISBN
0-313-27938-1.
An important inventory of 14 African composers, seven Afro-Euro-
pean composers, 10 Afro-Latino composers, and about 150 African-
American composers, with biographical information and worklists. Despite the book's title, compositions of all genres are listed, but there is a
special index of string compositions (various instruments and combinations). With a discography and a bibliography of 138 items. The volume
is enhanced by DeLerma's perceptive introductory essay.
Review: *Choice* 3/92, 1046.

S2-116   ML128 .B45 H8
Horne, Aaron. Woodwind music of black composers / Aaron Horne;
foreword by Samuel A. Floyd, Jr. — New York : Greenwood, 1990. —
xvii, 145 p. (Music reference collection, 24) ISBN 0-313-27265-4. (Alternative classification: ML120 .W5.)
A valuable list of 430 works for (or including) wind instruments, by
90 living composers, most of them African Americans. Biographical
sketches precede each person's worklist. Information about each composition is minimal, sometimes limited to title, date, and scoring. More
data are provided when available. An index gives access to the music for
each instrument and ensemble. There is a 38-item discography and general bibliography of about 60 entries.
Reviews: ARBA 1991, p. 515; *Choice* 12/90, 608.

S2-117   ML128 .B45 S7
Spencer, Jon Michael. As the black school sings : black music collections at black universities and colleges, with a union list of book holdings / Jon Michael Spencer. — New York : Greenwood, 1987. — xvi,
185 p. (Music reference collection, 13) ISBN 0-313-25859-7.
A detailed directory of library holdings at 10 traditionally black uni-

versities, revealing the depths of research material for the study of black music. The universities are Atlanta, Fisk, Hampton, Howard, Jackson State, Lincoln, North Carolina Central, Virginia State, and Tuskegee Institute. With a partly expansive index of the persons and topics in the collections.

Reviews: ARBA 1988, #1274; *Choice* 11/87, 458.

S2-118   ML128 .B45 V3
Vann, Kimberly R. Black music in Ebony : an annotated guide to the articles on music in *Ebony* magazine, 1945–1985 / Kimberly R. Vann. — Chicago : Center for Black Music Research, Columbia College, 1990. — vi, 119 p. ISBN 0-929911-01-6.

A useful index, going beyond the coverage of *Readers' Guide* to include annotations, as well as access by medium and genre. Arrangement is chronological, unfortunately; the least helpful approach. There is a nonexpansive index of names and other indexes of subjects, titles, genres, and "performing mediums."

Genres

S2-119   ML128 .B49 H3
Hart, Mary L. The blues : a bibliographic guide / Mary L. Hart, Brenda M. Eagles, and Lisa N. Howorth; introduction by William Ferris. — New York : Garland, 1989. — xvi, 636 p. (Music research and information guides, 7) ISBN 0-8240-8506-X.

A list of about 7,500 books, articles, and liner notes, mostly biographical items, with several topical groupings (such as "Poetry of the Blues," "Blues and Society," "Blues on Film," and "Blues Research"). Entries are not annotated, but sources of reviews are cited for books. Lack of definite criteria for inclusion is a notable defect: the bibliography "is neither comprehensive nor selective in any systematic way. What we could obtain is included; what we could not obtain is omitted." With an author index and a title index. Hart is a librarian and an editor at the Center for the Study of Southern Culture, University of Mississippi; Eagles and Howorth are colleagues at the Center.

Review: ARBA 1990, #1287.

S2-120   ML128 .C13 M5
Miles, William. Songs, odes, glees and ballads : a bibliography of American presidential campaign songsters / William Miles. — New York : Greenwood, 1990. — lii, 200 p. (Music reference collection, 27) ISBN 0-313-27697-8.

A songster is a "collection of three or more secular poems intended to be sung" having at least four pages, published in book or pamphlet form.

Beginning with the 1840 campaign, 432 such collections appeared; the last noted here dating from 1964. Imprint data is given for each book, with a bibliographic description, but the names of songs in the books are not offered. With a discography, name index, songster title index, and publisher index.

S2-121   ML128 .C2 D4
DeVenney, David P. American masses and requiems : a descriptive guide / David P. DeVenney. — Berkeley, Calif. : Fallen Leaf, 1991. — xvii, 210 p. (Fallen Leaf reference books in music, 15) ISBN 0-914913-14-X.

A useful inventory of 959 sacred works by American composers, providing bibliographic information and (for 28 major works) comments in program-note style with a list of references. A bibliography of 148 writings about the composers and about sacred choral music in the United States has informative annotations. With indexes to the compositions by voice types and groupings, and by title; and an index to the bibliography.

Review: ARBA 1992, #1302.

S2-122   ML128 .C48 D48
DeVenney, David P. Nineteenth-century American choral music : an annotated guide / David P. DeVenney. — Berkeley, Calif. : Fallen Leaf, 1987. — xxi, 182 p. (Fallen Leaf reference books in music, 8) ISBN 0-914913-08-5.

A valuable list of about 1,300 compositions for chorus by 24 composers, including Amy Beach, George Bristow, Dudley Buck, George Chadwick, Arthur Foote, William Fry, William Gilchrist, Charles Tomlinson Griffes, Charles Ives, Charles Loeffler, Edward MacDowell, Lowell Mason, William Mason, John Knowles Paine, Horatio Parker, and Henry Clay Work. The worklists for each composer provide dates, durations, performing forces required, text author, published versions, and manuscript locations, along with brief comments by DeVenney. A useful bibliography of writings about the composers and their choral music follows the catalog. There is indexing by genres, titles, first lines, authors of texts, and translators.

Listing and review: ARBA 1988, #1302; Baley BH116.

S2-123   ML128 .F74 M5
Miller, Terry E. Folk music in America : a reference guide / Terry E. Miller. — New York : Garland, 1986. — xx, 424 p. (Music research and information guides, 5; Garland reference library of the humanities, 496) ISBN 0-8240-8935-9.

A valuable, selective compilation of 1,927 books, scholarly articles, and dissertations, with (for most) one- to four-line annotations. Nine sections: general resources, American Indians and Eskimos, Anglo-American folk songs and ballads, later developments in Anglo-American folk music (bluegrass, country and western, folksong revival), traditional instruments and instrumental music, American psalmody and hymnody, the singing school and shape-note tradition, African-American music (spirituals, gospel, blues), and ethnic music. Author and subject index. Miller directs the Center for the Study of World Music, Kent State University.

Reviews: ARBA 1988, #1311; *Choice* 6/87, 1536; LJ 4/15/87, 36.

S2-124   ML128 .H8 B68

Britton, Allen Perdue. American sacred music imprints, 1698–1810 : a bibliography / Allen Perdue Britton and Irving Lowens; completed by Richard Crawford. — Worcester, Mass. : American Antiquarian Society, 1990. — xvi, 798 p. ISBN 0-912296-95-X.

An important, scholarly work, listing 545 publications of hymn collections and discussing each one fully. Extensive imprint information, variants, provenance, and comments are given. Basic arrangement is by compiler or title, with supplementary lists by date and composer. There are useful geographical lists of printers, publishers, and booksellers. No music is printed. With a general expansive index.

S2-125   ML128 .H8 H86

Ellinwood, Leonard. Bibliography of American hymnals / Leonard Ellinwood and Elizabeth Lockwood. — New York : University Music Editions for the Hymn Society of America, 1983. — 27 microfiche.

An inventory of 7,500 hymnals in 82 libraries, with bibliographic details. The books were published in North and South America between 1640 and 1978. See also S2-126.

S2-126   ML128 .H8 H87

Ellinwood, Leonard. Dictionary of American hymnology : first line index / Leonard Ellinwood. — New York : University Music Editions, 1984. — 179 microfilm reels, 16 mm negative film.

Drawn from material in Ellinwood's bibliography of hymnals (S2-125), this index presents some 1,233,000 entries for individual hymns. Each entry gives the hymn title, author, translator if any, first line, and original-language first line if any. A total of 4,834 hymnals, in all languages using the roman alphabet, were analyzed for the project, which was sponsored by the Hymn Society of America. There is an informative 26-page introduction, in hard copy.

S2-127   ML128 .J3 K45

Kennington, Donald. The literature of jazz : a critical guide / Donald

Kennington and Danny L. Read. — 2nd ed. — Chicago : American Library Association, 1980. — xi, 236 p. ISBN 0-8389-0313-4.
1st ed., 1970 (LOAM 914).
Bibliographic essays with lists of titles after each of them. Covers general works, blues, history of jazz, biography, theory and criticism, jazz education, jazz in literature, and jazz periodicals. One-line annotations; name and title index. One of the most useful guides.
Listing and reviews: ARBA 1982, p. 527; LJ 6/1/81, 1210; Sheehy BH282.

S2-128   ML128 .J3 G7
Gray, John. Fire music : a bibliography of the new jazz, 1959–1990 / John Gray; foreword by Val Wilmer. — New York : Greenwood, 1991. — xviii, 515 p. (Music reference collection, 31) ISBN 0-313-27892-X.
By "fire music" Gray signifies the era of free jazz improvisation in the 1960s associated with Ornette Coleman, John Coltrane, Cecil Taylor, and several other black artists. He lists 7,083 items, most of them brief articles or entries in larger works, under the names of free jazz performers. The bibliography is not annotated. There are also entries under headings, such as countries and regions. Useful appendix features are lists of performers and ensembles by country (even Switzerland had fire music) and by instrument. With a nonexpansive author index.
Reviews: *Choice* 3/92, 1044; LJ 3/1/92, 82.

S2-129   ML128 .J4 H4
Heskes, Irene. Yiddish American popular songs, 1895 to 1950 : a catalog based on the Lawrence Marwick roster of copyright entries / Irene Heskes. — Washington: Library of Congress, 1992. — xliii, 527 p. : ill. ISBN 0-8444-0745-3.
Lawrence Marwick, who headed the Hebraic section of the Library of Congress from 1948 to 1980, compiled a bibliography of 3,427 Yiddish-American songs from U.S. copyright entries of 1895–1951/1952. Heskes has organized Marwick's labors, presenting a valuable resource for study of the genre. The songs are listed by year, with imprint data, descriptions, and comments; the music is not printed. There is a list of publishers, and there are indexes of composers, arrangers, lyricists, and titles.

S2-130   ML128 .M7 L5
Limbacher, James L. Keeping score : film and television music, 1980–1988 : with additional coverage of 1921–1979 / James L. Limbacher and H. Stephen Wright, Jr. — Metuchen, N.J. : Scarecrow, 1991. — xi, 916 p. ISBN 0-8108-2453-1.
"This volume supplements and provides additional coverage for two

previous works by James L. Limbacher—*Film Music: From Violins to Video* (Scarecrow, 1974) and *Keeping Score: Film Music, 1972–1979* (Scarecrow, 1981)."

The 1974 work was noted in LOAM Suppl. SA-594. A list of "films and their composers/adaptors" presents approximately 17,500 titles in date order from 1921 to 1988. The films are then listed under the composers' names. A discography follows, presenting U.S. LP or CD issues of 1980 through 1987; it is in title sequence, with release dates and label names only. There is also a list of collections on disc. With a film title index.

S2-131   ML128 .M78 B6

Bloom, Ken. American song : the complete musical theatre companion, 1990–1984 / Ken Bloom. — New York : Facts on File, 1985. — 2 vols. ISBN 0-87196-961-0 (set).

Volume 1 has a list of 3,283 musicals, giving for each the opening date, number of performances, composer, lyricist, producer, and director. The source of the story is noted, and there are details of production matters. Songs of the show are listed, and cast actors are named. Recordings are not cited. Volume 2 contains an index to the 42,000 song titles and 1,600 personnel. Off-Broadway and off-off-Broadway shows are named, and those that closed before seeing Broadway are listed (including those that did not play in New York at all). Without bibliography, source notes, or discography.

Listing and reviews: Balay BH104; *Choice* 5/85, 1302; LJ 4/15/85, 1302.

S2-132   ML128 .M78 K7

Krasker, Tommy. Catalog of the American musical : musicals of Irving Berlin, George and Ira Gershwin, Cole Porter, Richard Rodgers, and Lorenz Hart / Tommy Krasker and Robert Kimball. — Washington : National Institute for Opera and Musical Theater, 1988. — xv, 442 p. ISBN 0-9618575-0-1.

An unusual song index, with various facts about each number: orchestrator, location of the composer's manuscript, of the sheet music, of the most complete score and lyric, of the original full score, and of the original parts. Comments are appended as appropriate. Songs that were dropped from productions are included. A useful resource.

Reviews: AM 1990, 363; ARBA 1989, p. 470; *Choice* 11/88, 502.

S2-133   ML128 .M78 S34

Salem, James M. A guide to critical reviews, part II : the musical, 1909–1989 / James M. Salem. — Metuchen, N.J. : Scarecrow, 1991. — vi, 828 p. ISBN 0-8108-2387-X. (Alternative classification: Z5781 .S16.)

1st ed., 1967; 2nd ed., 1976.

An important compilation of citations to the reviews of 2,149 Broadway musicals; the reviews appeared in general circulation U.S. and
Canadian periodicals and in the *New York Times*. The shows are listed
by title, with credits, opening dates, number of performances, and then
the references. There are useful indexes to authors, composers, lyricists,
directors, designers, and choreographers.

S2-134   ML128 .M78 S5
Simas, Rick. The musicals no one came to see : a guidebook to four
decades of musical comedy casualties on Broadway, off-Broadway, and
in out-of-town try-outs, 1943–1983 / Rick Simas. — New York : Garland, 1987. — xiii, 639 p. : ill. ISBN 0-8240-8804-2.
Considers about 600 plays identified as "casualties" by rather uncertain
criteria; includes many that had nearly 300 performances. Alphabetical
lists, giving authorship, number of performances, theater, star performers, publication source, and reviews. The same musicals are included,
with more information, in Ken Bloom's *American Song* (S2-131).
Reviews: ARBA 1989, p. 516; *Choice* 6/88, 1567.

S2-135   ML128 .M78 W56
Wildbihler, Hubert. The musical : an international annotated bibliography / Hubert Wildbihler and Sonja Völklein; foreword by Thomas
Siedhoff. — London : K. G. Saur, 1986. — xxiv, 320 p. ISBN 3-598-
10635-1.
A classified list of some 3,600 books, articles, and reviews, dealing
with stage and film musicals. The intent was to give "complete coverage
of the monograph literature" and a "representative documentation" of
periodical writings. About half of the monographic entries are briefly annotated; the periodical entries are not annotated. Most of the entries are
in English, but there are German contributions in sections devoted to
Germany and Austria. The homemade classification of materials is (as
usual with such schemes) an obstacle to access, and within each section
there is further obfuscation in the chronological arrangement of entries
(various editions of the same book in different places). A great deal of
trivia is also in the way: bits from *Senior Scholastic* or *Coronet* will not
hold much interest. Despite all these problems, there are useful items included, more or less findable through the nonexpansive name and subject index.

S2-136   ML128 .M8 S73
Steinzor, Curt Efram. American musicologists, c. 1890–1945 : a bio-
bibliographical sourcebook to the formative period / Curt Efram Steinzor.
— New York : Greenwood, 1989. — xix, 286 p. ISBN 0-313-26197-0.

An interesting overview of the first generation of musicologists in the United States, with brief biographical sketches and lists of writings by and about each one. Of the 35 persons included, 19 were American born, the others European emigrés. By the time that scholarly research was institutionalized with the establishment of the American Musicological Society in 1934, the discipline had good academic roots that would soon flower in the work of natives, such as Otto Albrecht, Warren Allen, Glen Hayden, Otto Kinkeldey, Gustave Reese, and Oliver Strunk. Their work blended with that of such great European scholars as Willi Apel, Manfred Bukofzer, Alfred Einstein, Paul Lang, and Curt Sachs. There is a useful subject index that identifies the special topics associated with each musicologist.

Reviews: ARBA 1990, p. 517; *Choice* 10/89, 294.

S2-137   ML128 .04 E58
Borroff, Edith. American operas : a checklist / Edith Borroff and J. Bunker Clark. — Warren, Mich. : Harmonie Park, 1992. — xxiv, 334 p. : ill. (Detroit studies in music bibliography, 69) ISBN 0-8999-00631.

A useful list of about 4,000 works by 2,000 composers, in composer order. Information given for each opera includes date, publisher, timing, premiere, and other important performances. Without a title index.

S2-138   ML128 .05 K67
Koshgarian, Richard. American orchestral music : a performance catalog / Richard Koshgarian. — Metuchen, N.J. : Scarecrow, 1992. — xiv, 761 p. ISBN 0-8108-2632-1.

A bibliography of published and unpublished concert music by American composers born in the twentieth century, giving the composition date, instrumentation, duration, and publisher. There are lists of the same works by genre and by duration, but none by title. Criteria for inclusion are not stated, but it seems that naturalized U.S. citizens were counted as American. The worklists are reasonably dependable for published material, less so for unpublished items. Omissions of published works, even those currently available on CD, are not infrequent (e.g., for Bernard Herrmann there are three nonfilm symphonic pieces on disc, none of them cited by Koshgarian; for Burrill Phillips there is one work in *Opus* [Winter, 1992/93] not in Koshgarian). Despite such infelicities, which may be inevitable in a compilation of this scope, the book is a valuable resource.

S2-139   ML128 .P3 W3
Walker-Hill, Helen. Piano music by black women composers : a catalog of solo and ensemble works / Helen Walker-Hill. — New York :

Greenwood, 1992. — xi, 143 p. (Music reference collection, 35) ISBN 0-313-28141-6.

A list of nonvocal piano works by about 75 women, arranged by composer. Extensive information is provided about each piece, including many descriptions of the works by their composers. Brief biographies are given as well. With a name and title index.

S2-140   ML128 .P6 T39

Taylor, Paul. Popular music since 1955 : a critical guide to the literature / Paul Taylor. — Boston : G. K. Hall, 1985. — 533 p. ISBN 0-8161-8784-3.

A useful list of 1,600 English-language monographs (including some fiction items) published during 1955–1982. Taylor, a British librarian, has carefully provided full bibliographic detail for each entry and good critical annotations. The books deal with social aspects of music, the music industry, and individual artists. There is a valuable list of 200 periodicals that appeared in the period, with descriptions. The index includes authors, titles, and subjects.

Listing and reviews: ARBA 1986, p. 497; Balay BH139; *Choice* 5/86, 1375.

S2-141   ML128 .P63 I95

Iwaschkin, Roman. Popular music : a reference guide / Roman Iwaschkin. — New York : Garland, 1986. — xiii, 658 p. (Music research and information guides, 4; Garland reference library of the humanities, 642) ISBN 0-8240-8680-5.

A compilation of 5,276 numbered items (nearly all in English), consisting of monographs and names of periodicals (not individual articles) on the several pop genres: country, cajun, ragtime, blues, soul, musicals, and so forth; and on individuals, business aspects, recordings, and literary treatments of pop. Some entries have brief annotations. A good chapter provides the titles of novels with pop music elements in the plots. Criteria for inclusion are not stated: many trifles appear, while substantial works are omitted. Access is awkward, since the author has devised a cumbersome schema of topics and subtopics, and there is no subject index. There is an author and a main-entry index.

Listing and reviews: AM 1989, 346; ARBA 1987, #1262; Balay BH137; *Choice* 12/86, 606; LJ 7/86, 72.

S2-142   ML128 .P63 L57

Lissauer, Robert. Lissauer's encyclopedia of popular music in America, 1888 to the present / Robert Lissauer. — New York : Paragon House, 1991. — xxi, 1,687 p. ISBN 1-55778-015-3.

Not an encyclopedia, but a useful list of 19,000 popular songs,

arranged by title. Information in each entry includes the publication date, composer/lyricist, major recordings, and shows and films in which the song was heard. After the main listing, the songs are grouped by composer, and then by year. Lissauer is identified as a record producer, music publisher, and onetime teacher at New York University.
Reviews: ARBA 1992, p. 529; LJ 6/1/91, 126.

S2-143   ML128 .P63 S9
Suskin, Steven. Berlin, Kern, Rodgers, Hart, and Hammerstein : a complete song catalogue / Steven Suskin; foreword by Theodore S. Chapin. — Jefferson, N.C. : McFarland, 1990. — xxiv, 312 p. ISBN 0-8995-0471-X.
The total song output of the composers mentioned in the title, with the names of shows in which the songs appeared (if any), dates, and publishers. There are 930 by Irving Berlin and 888 by Jerome Kern. With an index of song titles and show titles.
Reviews: ARBA 1991, p. 529; *Choice* 1/91, 764.

S2-144   ML128 .R28 M3
McCoy, Judy. Rap music in the 1980s : a reference guide / Judy McCoy. — Metuchen, N.J. : Scarecrow, 1992. — xiv, 261 p. ISBN 0-8108-2649-6.
"A guide to the literature documenting the rise of rap as a viable pop music genre," including books, periodical articles, news stories, and reviews issued 1980–1990. There are 1,070 annotated entries, followed by a descriptive discography of 76 albums. With a nonexpansive subject index.

S2-145   ML128 .R6 H62
Hoffmann, Frank. The literature of rock, II : including an exhaustive survey of the literature from 1979–1983 and incorporating supplementary material from 1954–1978 not covered in the first volume / Frank Hoffmann and B. Lee Cooper; with the assistance of Lee Ann Hoffmann. — Metuchen, N.J. : Scarecrow, 1986. — 2 vols. ISBN 0-8108-1821-3.
Base volume in LOAM Suppl. SA-647.
An important bibliography of books and articles, in subject arrangement. There is also a discography and a periodical list. With a name index.
Listing and reviews: ARBA 1987, #1269; Balay BH136; *Choice* 11/86, 454; LJ 9/15/86, 78.

S2-146   ML128 .R65 C66
Cooper, B. Lee. Rockabilly : a bibliographic resource guide / B. Lee Cooper and Wayne S. Haney. — Metuchen, N.J. : Scarecrow, 1990. — xix, 352 p. ISBN 0-8108-2386-1.

The authors says there is no clear definition of rockabilly, and the assignment of performers to the category is "somewhat arbitrary." Broadly expressed, the term identifies a stylistic "blending of black blues with white country" in the 1950s. There are 1,945 books, articles, and reviews listed, for about 220 persons, arranged by performer; full imprint data are given. Among the performers in this eclectic inventory are Buddy Holly, Jerry Lee Lewis, Carl Perkins, and Elvis Presley. With a non-expansive author index.

Listing and review: ARBA 1992, #1310; Balay BH125.

S2-147   ML128 .S24 F5

Figueroa, Rafael. Salsa and related genres : a bibliographical guide / Rafael Figueroa. — Westport, Conn. : Greenwood, 1992. — xii, 109 p. (Music reference collection, 38) ISBN 0-313-27883-0.

Salsa seems difficult to define. Figueroa says that it "represents a body of sound that emerged from the Antilles . . . as a result of the meeting of European and African cultures . . . related, of course, to other musical genres of Latin America and the Caribbean . . . based on a unique rhythmic unit (the clave)." The bibliography of 606 items, in subject arrangement, has no clear criteria for inclusion and only a few annotations. Most of the entries are short notices from *Down Beat* and other magazines. With an index of authors and titles, and one of subjects.

S2-148   ML128 .S3 B6

Brooks, Elston. I've heard those songs before : volume II, the weekly top ten hits of the last six decades / Elston Brooks. — 2nd ed. — New York : Morrow, 1991. — vii, 368 p. ISBN 0-9626-2193-5. (Alternative classification: ML156.4 .P6 B6.)

1st ed., 1981.

This edition is titled "volume 2," but it is in fact a revised version of the original publication (Fort Worth, Tex. : Summit Group, 1981). It lists the 10 hit songs of each week from 1930 to 1981, using the titles heard on *Your Hit Parade* (1935–1959) and various sources for the 1960s and 1970s. No information about the songs, or about recordings, is provided. With a title index.

S2-149   ML128 .S3 G2

Gargan, William. Find that tune : an index to rock, folk-rock, disco, & soul in collections / William Gargan and Sue Sharma. — New York : Neal-Schuman, 1984–1988. — 2 vols. ISBN 0-918212-70-7; 1-55570-019-5.

A valuable index by title to 8,000 songs in 400 collections of sheet music. With first-line, composer/lyricist, and performer indexes.

S2-150   ML128 .S3 G8

Goodfellow, William D. Where's that tune? : an index to songs in fakebooks / William D. Goodfellow. — Metuchen, N.J. : Scarecrow, 1990. — vii, 449 p. ISBN 0-8108-2391-8.

Fakebooks are collections of songs that provide for each item the voice line and chord symbols. This useful index locates some 13,500 songs in 64 fakebooks, with the main arrangement by song title. There are indexes to the more than 5,000 composers and the descriptions of the fakebooks that are covered. Many categories of song are included: Broadway, movie, jazz/swing, folk, gospel, rock, and classical.

Review: ARBA 1992, p. 513.

S2-151   ML128 .S3 H4

Popular song index : 3rd supplement / ed. Patricia Pate Havlice. — Metuchen, N.J. : Scarecrow, 1989. — 879 p. ISBN 0-8108-2202-4.

Base volume and two supplements in LOAM Suppl. S-804.

A continuation of the valuable reference series that locates individual songs in anthologies (including fakebooks), covering 181 publications of 1979–1987. Many useful access paths are provided: song title, first line, first line of chorus, composer, and lyricist. Embraced under "popular" are such categories as wedding songs, war songs, folk songs, Christmas songs, Irish songs, Broadway songs, spirituals, Gilbert and Sullivan airs, rock, gospel, jazz, country, cajun, movie songs, and children's songs.

Review: ARBA 1990, p. 540.

S2-152   ML128 .S3 L55

Lewine, Richard. Songs of the theater / Richard Lewine and Alfred Simon. — New York : H. W. Wilson, 1984. — 897 p. ISBN not given.

Supersedes the compilers' *Encyclopedia of Theater Music* (1961) and *Songs of the American Theater* (1973), LOAM 1259.

A useful alphabetical list of about 20,000 songs, with composers, lyricists, musicals they came from, and dates. There is a list of the shows in title order, with opening dates and number of performances, composers, lyricists, songs, and comments. And there are lists of musicals by year, 1891–1983, and films and TV shows made from the original musicals.

Listings and reviews: BCL; *Choice* 5/85, 1306; LJ 4/15/85, 66; Sheehy BH251.

S2-153   ML128 .S4 J3

Jackson, Irene V. Afro-American religious music : a bibliography and a catalogue of gospel music / Irene V. Jackson. — Westport, Conn. : Greenwood, 1979. — xiv, 210 p. : ill. : music. ISBN 0-3132-0560-4.

A subject list of 873 books, dissertations, and articles, not annotated. Criteria for inclusion are not given; "although the bibliography is not nearly complete or exhaustive, it nonetheless constitutes a major effort toward the systematic organization of bibliographic materials." There is also a catalog of "Library of Congress's holdings of Black gospels [songs] copyrighted between 1938 and 1965" in composer order. With an expansive index.

S2-154   ML128 .S75 O2
O'Brien, Robert F. School songs of America's colleges and universities / Robert F. O'Brien. — New York : Greenwood, 1991. — x, 197 p. ISBN 0-313-27890-2.
A list of the alma maters and fight songs of U.S. colleges, grouped by state. For each song the composer and lyricist are given, and sometimes the date, along with the sourcebook where the song appears. With a list of the sourcebooks, a school name index, and a song title index.
Review: LJ 9/1/91, 184.

S2-155   ML128 .V7 D43
DeVenney, David P. Early American choral music : an annotated guide / David P. DeVenney. — Berkeley, Calif. : Fallen Leaf, 1988. — xx, 150 p. (Fallen Leaf reference books in music, 10) ISBN 0-914913-09-3.
A groundbreaking composer catalog of 859 works by 32 persons written from 1670 to 1825, a companion volume to S2-122. Information (as available and appropriate) for each item includes date of composition, text author, biblical citation, duration, publisher, manuscript location, anthology in which it appears, and citations. Various indexes provide access by genre, performing forces, title, and text author. An annotated bibliography of 127 writings on American choral music forms a valuable adjunct to the inventory of works. With lists of published collections and of printers or publishers, and an expansive index to the bibliography.
Listing and review: ARBA 1989, #1218; Balay BH116.

S2-156   ML128 .V7 H67
Hovland, Michael A. Musical settings of American poetry : a bibliography / Michael A. Hovland. — Westport, Conn. : Greenwood, 1986. — xii, 531 p. (Music reference collection, 8) ISBN 0-313-22938-4.
A useful inventory of 5,640 numbered compositions that are based on about 2,400 poems by 99 American authors. Arrangement is by poet, with a composer index. For each entry there are the publication date, editions (for various voices and arrangements), and comments. Anthologies from which songs were taken are identified.

Listing and reviews: ARBA 1987, #1248; Balay BH110; *Choice* 9/ 86, 140.

ML134 : BIO-BIBLIOGRAPHIES OF INDIVIDUALS

S2-157   ML134 .B16 H4

Heintze, James R. Esther Williamson Ballou : a bio-bibliography / James R. Heintze. — New York : Greenwood, 1987. — xii, 125 p. (Bio-bibliographies in music, 5) ISBN 0-313-25068-3.

Ballou (1915–1973) was a little-known composer who lived in Washington, D.C. This inventory describes 116 of her works. Information about each composition includes duration, performances, and publications. With a biographical summary, discography, bibliography of 209 items (including reviews), correspondence, list of interviews, nonexpansive general index, and an index of compositions.

Reviews: ARBA 1988, #1268; *Choice* 7/8/87, 1676.

S2-158   ML134 .B4427 F4

Ferencz, George Joseph. Robert Russell Bennett : a bio-bibliography / George Joseph Ferencz. — New York : Greenwood, 1990. — xiv, 215 p. (Bio-bibliographies in music, 29) ISBN 0-313-26472-4.

A brief biography and worklist for composer Bennett (1894–), listing 175 compositions by genre, with publication and performance information and useful comments. There is a discography of 50 items, including commercial and archival recordings, and a piano roll attributed to Bennett. A bibliography of 531 entries covers writings by and about Bennett, including reviews. The composer is best known for his skillful orchestrations of Broadway and London musicals as well as film scores; a list of theatrical arrangements is included here. With indexes of compositions by title and date, and of all individuals mentioned in the volume.

S2-159   ML134 .B582 K7

Kroeger, Karl. Catalog of the musical works of William Billings / Karl Kroeger. — New York : Greenwood, 1991. — x, 160 p. (Music reference collection, 32) ISBN 0-313-27827-X.

A supplement to the four-volume complete works of the composer, published by the American Musicological Society and the Colonial Society of Massachusetts in 1977–1990 (S2-16). Much of the book is drawn from commentaries and data in the complete works, but there are some additional facts as well, mostly citations to secondary literature. The arrangement is alphabetical in each of two sections: strophic pieces (including the fuguing tunes) and anthems. Incipits are given for all the entries, but in the clumsy method of numbers for scale degrees instead

of in musical notation—a curious defect. With a first-line index, text source index, and incipit index (the number codes again).
Review: ARBA 1992, #1268; *Choice* 2/92, 876.

S2-160   ML134 .B623 K9
Kushner, David Z. Ernest Bloch : a guide to research / David Z. Kushner. — New York : Garland, 1988. — xiii, 345 p. (Garland composer resource manuals, 14; Garland reference library of the humanities, 796) ISBN 0-8240-7789-X.
A briefly annotated list of 579 articles, books, program notes, and reviews; with a worklist and discography. As the longest Bloch bibliography, this compilation has its value. But the uncertain criteria for inclusion (material of "significance," with "representative reviews") and the arrangement (by author or title rather than by subject) render it less satisfactory. The indexing is awkward and incomplete. The discography, clumsily divided by record format, offers inconsistent data and suffers, like the bibliography, from nebulous inclusive criteria.
Reviews: ARBA 1989, p. 481; *Choice* 1/89, 785.

S2-161   ML134 .C69 L5
Lichtenwanger, William. The music of Henry Cowell : a descriptive catalog / William Lichtenwanger. — Brooklyn : Institute for Studies in American Music, 1986. — xxxviii, 365 p. : ill. (I.S.A.M. monographs, 23) ISBN 0-914678-26-4.
A meticulous worklist for Cowell (1897–1965), the prolific experimental composer, "a figure unique in American music." There are 966 numbered entries, the first dating from 1907. For each piece Lichtenwanger provides a description of the draft or manuscript, a musical commentary, performance and publication data, and a wide range of facts relevant to the item. There are no musical incipits, but in many cases these would have been difficult to produce; for example, the beginning (or any segment) of *26 Simultaneous Mosaics* for five players (1963), in which "all players start and stop as they please, and choose the order of movements as they please. . . . There is no score; each is on his own." With a title index and an index of performing forces.
Reviews: ARBA 1988, #127; *Choice* 10/87, 286.

S2-162   ML134 .F47 B5
Bierley, Paul E. The music of Henry Fillmore and Will Huff / Paul E. Bierley. — Columbus, Ohio : Integrity, 1982. — x, 61 p. ISBN 0-9180-930766.
Fillmore (1881–1956) was a bandmaster and composer; 1,030 of his works are listed here, under the eight names he used for publication. One of the pen names happened to coincide with the name of a real person,

William L. Huff (1875–1942), who was also a bandmaster and composer. It is to Bierley's credit that he was able to sort out the situation. The 66 known compositions by Huff are listed here. Both worklists include full information about the compositions and their publication histories. With a name and title index.

S2-163   ML134 .F58 P4
Perone, Karen. Lukas Foss : a bio-bibliography / Karen Perone. — New York : Greenwood, 1988. — viii, 282 p. (Bio-bibliographies in music, 37) ISBN 0-313-26811-8.

Foss, a Berlin-born (1922) naturalized American, composes in many idioms, some of them eccentric (e.g., the "inaudible music performance . . . performer continues to finger or mouth the pitches or words, but no sound is produced"), and has had a career as a conductor as well, notably with the Buffalo Philharmonic Orchestra (1962–1970) and the Milwaukee Symphony Orchestra (1981–1986). This useful resource guide lists his works in genre order, with bibliographies of critical commentaries in the entry. It also presents a discography by genre, has a discography of Foss as conductor, and gives a bibliography of writings about him and his conducting. With an alphabetical index of works and a general index.

Reviews: ARBA 1992, #1271; *Choice* 10/91, 264.

S2-164   ML134 .F6 E4
Elliker, Calvin. Stephen Collins Foster : a guide to research / Calvin Elliker. — New York : Garland, 1988. — xii, 197 p. (Garland composer resource manuals, 10; Garland reference library of the humanities, 782) ISBN 0-8240-6640-5.

A thorough list of materials by and about Foster, including a worklist, iconography, memorials, tributes, and quotations of the songs in works by other composers. The main content is an annotated bibliography of 119 books and articles about Foster. Expansive indexing of authors, arrangers, artists, composers, editors, and subjects. The changing tides of interest in Foster are discussed in a perceptive introduction.

Reviews: ARBA 1989, #1232; *Choice* 9/88, 78.

S2-165   ML134 .G29 R5
Rimler, Walter. A Gershwin companion : a critical inventory & discography, 1916–1984 / Walter Rimler. — Ann Arbor, Mich. : Popular Culture, Ink., 1991. — xiv, 488 p. ISBN 1-560-75019-7.

A useful worklist, presenting all published and unpublished compositions by Gershwin in order of publication date. Information given for each piece includes lyricist, key, time, tempo, commentary, analysis, and pre-CD recordings (some 2,000 in all; label and number only). With a nonexpansive index of names and titles, an index of compositions, and another of recording artists.

Reviews: ARBA 1992, p. 530; *Choice* 2/92, 878.

S2-166   ML134 .H175 S7
Stehman, Dan. Roy Harris : a bio-bibliography / Dan Stehman. — New York : Greenwood, 1991. — xii, 475 p. (Bio-bibliographies in music, 40) ISBN 0-313-25079-0.

Harris (1898–) is a composer who was revered in the 1930s and 1940s, then fell into neglect. A renewed interest in him, and in other conservatives, is under way, and this useful volume will be of value as a documentation for the revival. After a brief biography, there is an annotated worklist—arranged by title—consisting of 178 numbered items, with performance histories. A chronological list of works is presented later. A discography, based on the compilation by William D. Curtis (published in 1981) gives details and comments on 80 recordings. A partly annotated bibliography of articles and parts of books is given, and another list of critical reviews with summaries of them; then there is a compilation of reviews and articles written by Harris. With a partly expansive index.

Reviews: ARBA 1992, #1277; *Choice* 3/92, 1056.

S2-167   ML134 .H46 T9
Tyler, Linda. Edward Burlingame Hill : a bio-bibliography / Linda Tyler. — New York: Greenwood, 1989. — v, 168 p. (Bio-bibliographies in music, 21) ISBN 0-313-25525-3.

A useful study of Hill (1872–1960), a significant composer and educator in the formative period of American composition. His 155 works, mostly unpublished, are listed chronologically, with full information (dates, contents, publications, premieres). There is also a brief biography, a bibliography of Hill's 180 books and articles, and a list of 328 writings about him. Curiously, there are only three recordings to list in the discography (none of them are in print). With a title index and general index.

Review: ARBA 1990, #1255.

S2-168   ML134 .I9 A2
Henderson, Clayton W. The Charles Ives tunebook / Clayton W. Anderson. — Warren, Mich. : Harmonie Park, 1990; published for the College Music Society. — xvi, 293 p. (Bibliographies in American music, 14) ISBN 0-89990-050-X.

A study of songs and other pieces quoted by Ives in his works. In the first section, 224 tunes that Ives used are identified, and the melodies are given in notation; for each, the Ives composition(s)—and movements—

are cited. For example, the song "Nelly Bly" is heard in *Decoration Day*, played by a flute. In another section, the Ives works are listed with all their quoted tunes. A third section presents musical incipits of the tunes. With an index of composers, arrangers, authors, and translators; and an index of the tunes by first lines, refrains, and titles. Exemplary and fascinating research by an Ives authority who has taught at the University of Illinois and served as dean of the music school at Millikin University. Review: *Choice* 4/91, 1290.

S2-169   ML134 .I9 B6
Block, Geoffrey H. Charles Ives : a bio-bibliography / Geoffrey H. Block; foreword by J. Peter Burkholder. — New York : Greenwood, 1988. — xviii, 422 p. (Bio-bibliographies in music, 14) ISBN 0-313-25404-4.
A useful compilation, beginning with a worklist, followed by a thoroughly annotated bibliography of 817 writings about Ives. Criteria for the bibliography are not steady; Block endeavored to cite "all available books and dissertations," leaving "available" undefined, but he also wanted to select "significant writings." Many of the entries are concert reviews. There is a discography, of little value since it is limited to Schwann listings of 1987. Nonexpansive index of names, titles, and topics.
Reviews: ARBA 1989, p. 477; *Choice* 3/89, 1172.

S2-170   ML134 .K79 B7
Bowles, Garrett H. Ernst Krenek : a bio-bibliography / Garrett H. Bowles. — Westport, Conn. : Greenwood, 1989. — xiv, 428 p. (Bio-bibliographies in music, 22) ISBN 0-313-25250-5.
A useful compilation about the twentieth-century Austro-American composer, commencing with a worklist (242 compositions, 105 of them not previously listed). There is a bibliography of 1,530 writings about Krenek, many of them concert reviews, most of them briefly annotated; but criteria for inclusion are unclear. The composer was a prolific author, as demonstrated by the list of 933 writings by him.
Reviews: ARBA 1990, #1240; *Choice* 10/89, 280.

S2-171   ML134 .L79 H3
Hartsock, Ralph. Otto Luening : a bio-bibliography / Ralph Hartsock. — New York : Greenwood, 1991. — xiii, 272 p. (Bio-bibliographies in music, 35) ISBN 0-313-24320-4.
A biography, worklist of 272 compositions, discography of 59 items, bibliography of 34 Luening writings, and bibliography of 586 articles, books, and reviews about Luening and his music. The worklist gives information about premieres and other performances. The discography,

alphabetical by title, gives only label and release date; some noncommercial material is included, but sources for selection of the recordings are not given. With alphabetical and classified lists of the compositions and a nonexpansive index.

Reviews: ARBA 1992, #1265; *Choice* 7/91, 1760.

S2-172   ML134 .M46 P4
Pemberton, Carol A. Lowell Mason : a bio-bibliography / Carol A. Pemberton. — Westport, Conn. : Greenwood, 1988. — xiii, 206 p. : ill. (Bio-bibliographies in music, 11) ISBN 0-313-25881-3.

Composer Mason (1792–1872) is remembered today as a pioneer music educator (who established music in the Boston public school curriculum) and hymnist. His compositions are listed here, 122 of them in date order, with extensive detail on their character and publication history. His writings, and 279 books, articles, and dissertations about him, are elaborately annotated. With an expansive index.

Reviews: AM 1988, 34; ARBA 1989, p. 482; *Choice* 10/88, 327.

S2-173   ML134 .M465 G7
Graber, Kenneth. William Mason (1829–1908) : an annotated bibliography and catalog of works / Kenneth Graber. — Warren, Mich. : Harmonie Park, 1989. — xxx, 349 p. ISBN 0-8999-0046-1.

In his time Mason was one of the leading composers and pianists in the United States, an influential promoter of chamber music, and an innovator in piano pedagogy. Graber provides lists of writings by and about Mason, selected programs of his performances (with extracts from reviews), a worklist by genre (with incipits, comments, and critical notices), a list of library holdings, and an expansive index. A valuable resource on a major figure.

Reviews: ARBA 1990, p. 527; *Choice* 3/90, 1112.

S2-174   ML134 .P264 M3
McGeary, Thomas. The music of Harry Partch : a descriptive catalog / Thomas McGeary. — Brooklyn : Institute for Studies in American Music, Brooklyn College, 1991. — xiv, 186 p. (I.S.A.M. monographs, 31) ISBN 0-914678-34-5.

A thorough worklist, offering great detail on each composition (background, bibliographic description, publication history). Partch (1901–1974) was a composer who made his own instruments, playing unusual microtonal pieces on them. He gained some popularity in the 1950s and 1960s and is represented by reissues on current compact discs. McGeary has included a chronological bibliography of writings about the composer (mostly reviews), an arrangement that is ideal as a document of trends in critical opinion. With a discography, but without index. See also S2-505.

S2-175 ML134 .P48 P3
Patterson, Donald L. Vincent Persichetti : a bio-bibliography / Donald L. Patterson and Janet L. Patterson. — Westport, Conn. : Greenwood, 1988. — xiv, 336 p. (Bio-bibliographies in music, 16) ISBN 0-313-25335-8.
A brief biography of the composer (1915–), and a chronological worklist of 171 compositions. For each work there is detailed information: date, contents, instrumentation, premiere and selected later performances, and publication data. There is a discography of 85 works (some recorded more than once), a list of Persichetti's writings (54 items), and a bibliography of 507 articles, reviews, and parts of books devoted to him and his music. With a title index and general index.
Reviews: ARBA 1989, p. 481; *Choice* 3/89, 1174.

S2-176 ML134 .P667 D4
DeBoer, Kee. Daniel Pinkham : a bio-bibliography / Kee DeBoer and John B. Ahouse. — New York : Greenwood, 1988. — viii, 238 p. (Bio-bibliographies in music, 12) ISBN 0-313-25503-2.
Pinkham (1923–) is a prolific composer, essentially tonal in idiom, with a penchant for choral writing. About 300 works from 1943 to 1987 are listed here by genre, with dates, premieres and other selected performances, publications, and occasional brief comments. A bibliography of articles and reviews includes extracts that present useful descriptions as well as the opinions of the writers. A discography "includes all commercially released records, regardless of current availability." With an alphabetical list of compositions and a nonexpansive index.
Reviews: ARBA 1989, #1201; *Choice* 11/88, 458.

S2-177 ML134 .R12 P3
Palmieri, Robert. Sergei Vasil'evich Rachmaninoff : a guide to research / Robert Palmieri. — New York : Garland, 1985. — xvii, 335 p. : ill. (Garland composer resource manuals, 3; Garland reference library of the humanities, 471) ISBN 0-8240-8996-0.
A valuable guide to the compositions of and writings about Rachmaninoff (1873–1943), pianist and composer, who became an American citizen just before his death, having left his Russian homeland in 1917. Palmieri presents the most complete worklist for Rachmaninoff, arranged by genre, with Russian and English titles, dates of composition and publications, names of movements with their keys, dedications, premieres, and explanatory comments. A list of Rachmaninoff's repertoire

as a pianist and as a conductor reveals the wide range of his mastery. A thorough discography goes back to Edison records of 1919 and Ampico piano rolls of the same year. Full data are given, including matrix and take numbers. The bibliography of articles, reviews, and books about the composer, in various languages, is annotated in depth. With name indexes, a subject index, and an index to names of compositions.

Reviews: ARBA 1986, #1230; *Choice* 10/95, 274.

S2-178   ML134 .R575 D6

Dixon, Joan DeVee. George Rochberg : a bibliographic guide to his life and works / Joan DeVee Dixon. — Stuyvesant, N.Y. : Pendragon, 1992. — xlvi, 684 p. : ill. ISBN 0-945193-12-2.

Composer Rochberg (1918–) was still active in the early 1990s. Having abandoned serialism, he was continuing to "reconnect with the grand traditions of music which were all but lost." His works are listed alphabetically in this useful volume, with full details of composition, performance, publication, recording, and comments by the composer. There are also bibliographies of his published writings, letters, manuscripts housed at the New York Public Library, and critical writings about his works. A chronology of Rochberg's life and compositions takes the place of a regular biography. Without general index.

S2-179   ML134 .R67 M3

McDonald, Arlys L. Ned Rorem : a bio-bibliography / Arlys L. McDonald. — Westport, Conn. : Greenwood, 1989. — 284 p. (Bio-bibliographies in music, 23) ISBN 0-313-25565-2.

Rorem (1933–) is an acclaimed composer of songs, and also a distinguished essayist. His musical works are listed there in chronological order (with a title index), 300 items with performance histories. There is also a discography of 50 recordings and an annotated bibliography of 784 writings and reviews about Rorem's work. His own literary work is also listed and summarized; it covers a wide range of musical and cultural topics, including W. H. Auden, Jean Cocteau, Igor Stravinsky, Paul Bowles, and Cosima Wagner. The most interesting writings are his journals of life in Paris, where he resided for six years. With a nonexpansive index.

Reviews: ARBA 1990, #1248; *Choice* 11/89, 468.

S2-180   ML134 .S398 C4

Carnovale, Norbert. Gunther Schuller : a bio-bibliography / Norbert Carnovale. — New York : Greenwood, 1987. — xii, 338 p. (Bio-bibliographies in music, 6) ISBN 0-313-25084-7.

Schuller (1925–) is a distinguished composer, conductor, hornist, jazz scholar (see S2-1090), and educator. This fine reference source presents a brief biography, an interview, a list of works and performances by genre, a discography of commercial recordings, a descriptive list of 73 writings by Schuller, an annotated bibliography of 469 writings about him (including reviews of concerts and recordings), plus lists of awards and honorary degrees. There are chronological and title indexes to the worklist, and general indexes of names and titles.

Reviews: ARBA 1988, p. 506; *Choice* 10/87, 279.

S2-181 ML134 .S6715 B6
Bierley, Paul E. The works of John Philip Sousa / Paul E. Bierley. — Columbus, Ohio: Integrity, 1984. — xi, 234 p. : ill. ISBN 0-918048-4.

Revision of *John Philip Sousa: A Descriptive Catalog of His Works* (1973; LOAM 1205).

An annotated worklist, in genre and then alphabetical order, with a chronological checklist, 1872–1931. No new titles were added in this edition, but some were deleted. There are 40 new illustrations and (missing in the first edition) a nonexpansive index of titles and names. Much detail is offered on each composition, including historical background, bibliographic description, and publication history. It is interesting that only 136 of the 500 works are marches; Sousa also wrote operettas, songs, instrumental solos, transcriptions, and concert pieces for orchestra. He was the author of many articles too, all listed here. With a bibliography of about 80 items about Sousa, but without discography.

Reviews: AM 1987, 458; ARBA 1986, p. 479.

S2-182 ML134 .T43 M4
Meckna, Michael. Virgil Thomson : a bio-bibliography / Michael Meckna. — New York : Greenwood, 1986. — xiv, 203 p. (Bio-bibliographies in music, 4) ISBN 0-313-25010-3.

A biographical sketch of composer Thomson (1896–1989), and a thorough worklist by genre, consisting of 345 works. Each composition is fully described, with the scoring given, and information about premieres and publications. Reviews are cited with each title. A discography of 78 recordings, a list of 195 articles and books by Thomson, and 288 citations about him offer the most complete research guide on this major artist. An appendix provides descriptions of archival sources. With chronological and alphabetical lists of the works, and a general index.

Reviews: AM 1988, 12; ARBA 1988, #1269; *Choice* 1/87, 746.

S2-183 ML134 .T43 T7
Tommasini, Anthony. Virgil Thomson's musical portraits / Anthony Tommasini. — New York : Pendragon, 1986. — xii, 237 p. (Thematic catalogues, 13) ISBN 0-918728-51-7.

Thomson's fascinating excursion into representing "in an abstract instrumental composition the inner nature of the portrait subject" is fully described and inventoried in this book. The composer "posed" his models as a painter would, making silent musical sketches that he would later fill out into compositions. A thematic catalog offers technical data (incipit, date, instrumentation, discography) along with a photo of each person. Among the individuals thus immortalized were Pablo Picasso, Sylvia Marlowe, Gertrude Stein and Alice B. Toklas, Aaron Copland, Fiorello LaGuardia, and Tommasini himself. Thomson discusses his portraits in an interesting section, explaining his methodology. With a name and title index.

Reviews: AM 1988, 12; *Choice* 11/86, 490.

S2-184   ML134 .W26 K9

Kreitner, Kenneth. Robert Ward : a bio-bibliography / Kenneth Kreitner. — Westport, Conn. : Greenwood, 1988. — 173 p. (Bio-bibliographies in music, 17) ISBN 0-313-25701-9.

A five-page biographical summary for composer Ward (1917–), with a worklist of 86 items in chronological order; the entries give scoring, publications, premieres and other performances, and recordings, along with comments. There is a separate discography of 18 items, a bibliography of 373 writings by and about Ward, and an index of interviews. The works are then listed by genre and title; and there is a general non-expansive index.

S2-185   ML134.5 .D5 L7

Lowenberg, Carlton. Musicians wrestle everywhere : Emily Dickinson and music / Carlton Lowenberg; foreword by Richard B. Sewall. — Berkeley, Calif. : Fallen Leaf, 1992. — xxviii, 210 p. (Fallen Leaf reference books in music, 19) ISBN 0-914913-20-4.

A list of about 1,600 musical settings of the Dickinson poems, representing 276 composers. With a concordance of musical terms used in the poet's writings and indexes to first lines and performance media. Interesting comments throughout.

Review: *Choice* 12/92, 603.

S2-186   ML134.5 .M3

Leiby, Bruce R. Gordon MacRae : a bio-bibliography / Bruce R. Leiby. — New York : Greenwood, 1991. — xii, 230 p. : ill. (Bio-bibliographies in the performing arts, 17) ISBN 0-313-26633-6.

MacRae (1921–1986) is best known for movie musicals of the 1950s, especially *Oklahoma!* and *Carousel*. His earlier career included singing with the Horace Heidt orchestra. This book lists and discusses his stage appearances, radio and television appearances, films, and nightclub and concert performances. There is a discography of 219 items, with minimal information, and a bibliography of 470 entries, including reviews. With a song title index, show and program title index, and a nonexpansive general index.

S2-187　　ML134.5 .M37 R6

Rivadue, Barry. Mary Martin : a bio-bibliography / Barry Rivadue. — Westport, Conn. : Greenwood, 1991. — xii, 234 p. : ill (Bio-bibliographies in the performing arts, 18) ISBN 0-313-27345-6.

Martin (1913–1990) was a Broadway and motion picture singer best known for her roles in *South Pacific, The Sound of Music,* and *Peter Pan.* All her stage appearances are documented here, with full casts, excerpts from reviews, and comments. There is a discography of 105 items, with minimal information; a list of 85 radio and TV appearances; a filmography of 12 movies; and a bibliography of 314 articles, reviews, and miscellany. With a nonexpansive index of names and titles.

Reviews: ARBA 1992, p. 557; *Choice* 3/92, 1038.

S2-188　　ML134.5 .M47 B92

Bryan, George B. Ethel Merman : a bio-bibliography / George B. Bryan. — New York : Greenwood, 1992. — 298 p. (Bio-bibliographies in the performing arts, 27) ISBN 0-313-27975-6.

Merman (1909?–1984) starred in such Broadway musicals as *Girl Crazy, Anything Goes,* and *Annie Get Your Gun,* and had parallel successes in motion pictures. Her voice had "the hard, clarion forthrightness of a jazz trumpet." Bryan has provided a brief biography, chronology, filmography, inventory of stage appearances, radio and television appearances, discography (minimal information, except for album contents), and a partly annotated bibliography of 592 articles and reviews. The infelicitous arrangement of the bibliography, by author, makes it a trial to use. With an index of names and titles.

S2-189　　ML134.5 .R6 P8

Pruett, Barbara J. Marty Robbins : fast cars and country music / Barbara J. Pruett. — Metuchen, N.J. : Scarecrow, 1990. — xvii, 601 p. ISBN 0-8108-2325-X.

A useful gathering of facts about Robbins (1925–1982), country singer and auto racer. The best feature is a thorough discography, with full data (location, dates, personnel, matrix numbers, labels, comments) on all issues. The bibliography, arranged by decade, covers major and minor items, with annotations. With some interviews, a list of Robbins's songs, and a nonexpansive index.

Review: ARBA 1992, #1304.

S2-190　　ML134.5 .S65 P6

Pitts, Michael R. Kate Smith : a bio-bibliography / Michael R.

Pitts. — Westport, Conn. : Greenwood, 1988. — xv, 261 p. (Bio-
bibliographies in the performing arts, 2) ISBN 0-313-25541-5.
  A brief biography (pp. 1–20) with endnotes, then an extensive discography (pp. 21–134), list of stage appearances (pp. 135–138), list of radio
appearances (pp. 139–144), and filmography (pp. 159–167). In the
discography there are session dates, recording locations, matrixes, label
numbers, disc sizes and speeds, and names of accompanists. Unissued
records are noted as well as commercial releases. The discography is indexed by song title, subject, and record label. Smith introduced more
than 1,000 songs and had her picture on the sheet music of 270 songs.
Pitts, a record reviewer and writer about entertainers, has prepared a useful reference volume, including an index of subjects and names (nonexpansive), and an annotated bibliography of 441 titles.

ML156–158 : DISCOGRAPHIES; RECORDINGS

ML156 : Library Collections

S2-190a   ML156.2 .F5 K43
  Keeling, Richard. A guide to early field recordings (1900–1949) at the
Lowie Museum of Anthropology / Richard Keeling. — Berkeley : University of California Press, 1991. — xviii, 487 p. : ill. (University of California
publications, catalogs, and bibliographies, 6) ISBN 0-520-09720-3.
  An inventory of 113 cylinder record collections of North American Indian music. Information for each record includes date, description of
content, duration, and technical specifications. With an index of tribes
and one of collectors, and a bibliography of about 500 items.

S2-191   ML156 .F5 Q56
  Quinn, Jennifer Post. An index to the field recordings in the Flanders
Ballad Collection at Middlebury College, Middlebury, Vermont / Jennifer Post Quinn. — Middlebury, Vt. : Middlebury College, 1983. —
242 p. : ill. ISBN not given.
  A useful inventory of 4,066 songs from the New England region,
arranged by title with a performer index. The Flanders collection was established in 1930.

S2-192   ML156 .I54 S4
  Seeger, Anthony. Early field recordings : a catalogue of cylinder col-
lections at the Indiana University Archives of Traditional Music / An-
thony Seeger and Louise S. Spear. — Bloomington : Indiana University
Press, 1987. — 198 p. ISBN 0-253-31840-8.
  A thoroughly descriptive catalog of an important collection, consist-

ing of cylinders made between 1893 and 1938 by musicologists, anthropologists, linguists, and explorers. Most of the recordings came from Canada and the United States, but there is also extensive material from Colombia, Indonesia, Nigeria, Papua New Guinea, Philippines, and other exotic locales. The material includes all kinds of folksongs (there is a subject list of them), rites, and ceremonies. The editors have written a useful introduction that deals with the mechanics and history of field recordings with the cylinder phonograph.

Review: ARBA 1988, #1273.

S2-193   ML156 .T84

Tulane University, William Ransom Hogan Jazz Archive. Catalog of the William Ransom Hogan Jazz Archive : the collection of seventy-eight RPM phonograph recordings / Howard-Tilton Memorial Library, Tulane University. — Boston : G. K. Hall, 1984. — 2 vols. ISBN 0-8161-0434-4. (Alternative classification: ML156.2 .T84.)

Founded in 1958, the archive consists of oral history tapes (1,500 reels), printed music (16,205 pieces of sheet music), photographs, manuscripts, books, periodicals, and recordings. This useful catalog is in the usual G. K. Hall format, each page made up of 21 photocopied catalog cards, with full bibliographic data.

Listing: Balay BH121.

ML156.1 : General Discographies

S2-194   ML156.15 .B25

Barr, Steven C. The almost complete 78 rpm record dating guide (II) / Steven C. Barr. — Rev. ed. — Huntington Beach, Calif. : Yesterday Once Again, 1992. — 177 p. ISBN not given. (Alternative classification: ML156.2.)

1st ed., 1979 (LOAM Suppl. S-1022).

A useful dictionary of record labels active during 1900–1942, with lists of their series and subsidiaries. For each series there is a guide to the years of issue for clusters of catalog numbers. Dates given are derived from various sources, not all of them agreeing with those of other researchers. Some time series are carried into the 1960s. Facts about the companies are more reliable for U.S. firms than for British entities. A label dating guide describes the appearance of numerous series; it is a valuable section, despite the lack of illustrations. Without index.

S2-195   ML156.15 .G3

Gart, Galen. ARLD : the American record label directory and dating guide, 1940–1959 / Galen Gart. — Milford, N.H. : Big Nickel, 1989. — vii, 259 p. ISBN 0-936433-11-6.

A valuable gathering of information about more than 6,000 U.S. record labels, with descriptions of their material, and names of their A & R men, names of affiliated firms, and addresses. The dating guide gives the record issue numbers that correspond to specific dates; these dates were derived from advertisements, reviews, or other announcements (in some cases, supplied by the author). This book supersedes William F. Daniels, *American 45 and 78 rpm Record Dating Guide* (LOAM Suppl. SA-515) and complements the coverage of earlier labels in Barr (S2-194). With an index of personal names.

ML156.2 : Discographies by Label

S2-196   ML156.2 .A2
Kosht, R. M. A & M records discography : including associated labels and alphanumeric index / R. M. Kosht. — Anaheim, Calif. : A & Mania, 1986. — ca. 300 p. ISBN not given.
A loose-leaf compilation of the A & M issues since 1962, when the label was established by Herb Alpert, whose Tijuana Brass were its first stars. Associated labels are covered, such as I.R.S., Windham Hill, Dark Horse, and Ode. This is a simple number list, with no discographical information, but there is an artist index.

S2-197   ML156.2 .A5 R728
Ruppli, Michel. The Aladdin/Imperial labels : a discography / Michel Ruppli. — New York : Greenwood, 1991. — xv, 727 p. (Discographies, 42) ISBN 0-313-27821-0. (Alternative classification: ML156.2 .R728.)
A list of the output of two important West Coast independent firms. Aladdin, which began with releases under the Philo name, is covered from 1945 to 1961. Lester Young and Billie Holiday were among its artists. Imperial, listed from 1946 to 1969, had a number of subsidiary labels (also covered here): Intro, Jazz West, Bayou, Lamp, Score, Ultra, 7-11, Bonnie, Colony, Knight, Minit, Moppet, Post, Liberty, United Artists, Blue Note, EMI America, and Sunset. Latin and folk material was important on Imperial, but there were stars from other genres as well: Fats Domino, T-Bone Walker, Rick Nelson, Erroll Garner, etc. Ruppli has included singles, 78 albums, EPs and LPs issued in the United States, Europe, and Japan. His discographies are meticulous and detailed, giving locations, dates, matrix numbers, labels and reissues, personnel, and commentaries.
Review: ARBA 1992, p. 530.

S2-198   ML156.2 .B2 K4
Kiner, Larry F. Basic musical library, "P" series, 1–1000 / Larry F. Kiner and Harry Mackenzie; foreword by Richard S. Sears. — New

York : Greenwood, 1990. — xviii, 326 p. (Armed Forces Radio Service discographies, 39) ISBN 0-313-27527-0. (Alternative classification: ML156.4 .P6 K3.)

A detailed label list for the Armed Forces Radio Service popular series (1942–1946). Full discographical data are given for each recording, along with pictures of the discs and comments. Among the artists included are Bing Crosby, Kay Kyser, Dinah Shore, and Charlie Spivak. With a performer index.

Review: ARBA 1992, p. 528.

S2-199   ML156.2 .J3 C87

Cuscuna, Michael. The Blue Note label / Michael Cuscuna and Michel Ruppli. — New York : Greenwood, 1988. — xxxii, 510 p. (Discographies, 29) ISBN 0-313-22018-2. (Alternative classification: ML156.4.)

The definitive label list for Blue Note, in five parts: 1) sessions of 1939–1965, at which time the label was taken over by Liberty; 2) sessions of 1967–1979 (as part of Liberty); 3) Blue Notes issued from EMI sources; 4) reissues; and 5) issues of the revived Blue Note label of 1985. Blue Note was a prime jazz label, featuring such artists as Sidney Bechet, Earl Hines, Thelonious Monk, Art Blakey, Miles Davis, and Dexter Gordon. Full discographical information is provided (matrix, dates and locations, personnel, reissues) for each recording. The basic list is chronological, but there are also numerical listings, of singles, albums, cassettes, and CDs. With an artist index.

Reviews: ARBA 1989, #1235; *Choice* 3/89, 1172.

S2-200   ML156.2 .C15

Bennett, Bill. Capitol record listing, 101 thru 3031 / Bill Bennett. — Zephyrhills, Fla. : Joyce Record Club, 1987. — 52 leaves. ISBN not given.

See note at S2-285.

S2-201   ML156.2 .C4 R7

Ruppli, Michel. The Clef/Verve labels : a discography / Michel Ruppli and Bob Porter. — New York : Greenwood, 1986. — 2 vols. (Discographies, 26) ISBN 0-313-25294-7. (Alternative classification: ML156.2 .R784.)

A valuable list of the Clef and Verve labels with all their subsidiaries, including MGM, from 1944 to 1973. These were the enterprises of Norman Granz, creator of Jazz at the Philharmonic. He consolidated several labels (Clef, Down Home, Norgran) under the name Verve in 1956, then sold it to MGM in 1960. Ruppli presents full discographical detail in chronological lists, then gives numerical and artist indexes.

Review: ARBA 1988, #1282.

S2-202   ML156.2 .C5 B5

Bidwell, Ron. Columbia 78 rpm record listing 37000 thru 41963 : working draft / Ron Bidwell [et al]. — Zephyrhills, Fla. : Joyce Record Club, 1989. — 88 leaves. ISBN not given.

A list of popular releases by label number, without dates (covering 1946–1960). The information given for each record is artist and song title. Quite a few gaps in the sequence remain to be filled in, but this is the most complete list available. No index.

S2-203   ML156.2 .C5 G2

Garrod, Charles. Columbia 78 rpm master listing : Chicago, 501-4999 : January 12, 1933 to February 2, 1949 / Charles Garrod. — Zephyrhills, Fla. : Joyce Record Club, 1990. — 85 leaves. ISBN not given.

S2-204   ML156.2 .C5 L8

Lorenz, Kenneth M. Two-minute brown wax and XP cylinder records of the Columbia Phonograph Company : numerical catalog, August 1896–ca. March 1909 / Kenneth M. Lorenz. — Wilmington, Del. : Kastlemusick, 1981. — 75 p. ISBN not given.

The first published catalog of sound recordings for sale was issued by the North American Phonograph Co. in 1890; it listed wax cylinders produced by Thomas A. Edison. The Columbia Phonograph Co., Edison's major rival in the cylinder business of the 1890s, published its first catalog later in the same year. By the turn of the century Columbia had made thousands of records in the wax cylinder format, records that played for two minutes. Lorenz has used various sources, including company records and miscellaneous lists, to prepare this valuable inventory of about 7,000 titles in matrix number order. Artists' names are given and approximate dates, but no other data are provided. Without index.

S2-205   ML156.2 .D3 G2

Garrod, Charles. Decca New York master numbers / Charles Garrod. — Zephyrhills, Fla. : Joyce Record Club, 1992. — Vols. 1– . ISBN not given.

See note at S2-285.

S2-206   ML156.2 .E33 K8

Koenigsberg, Allen. Edison cylinder records, 1889–1912 : with an illustrated history of the phonograph / Allen Koenigsberg. — 2nd ed. — Brooklyn : APM Press, 1987. — xlii, 172 p. : ill. ISBN not given.

1st ed., 1969 (LOAM Suppl. S-811).

Additional data and corrections serve to update the first edition of this classic work. Two-minute and four-minute cylinders produced by firms associated with Thomas A. Edison are listed by artist and title. The first printed catalog (1890) of the North American Phonograph Co. is reproduced. With a bibliography of about 40 items and a list of U.S. phonograph and record patents awarded to Edison, but without index.

S2-207   ML156.2 .E33 W4
Wile, Raymond R. Edison disc artists and records, 1910–1929 / Raymond R. Wile; ed. Ronald Dethlefson. — 2nd ed. — Brooklyn : APM Press, 1990. — 187 p. : ill. ISBN 0-937612-081.
1st ed., 1985 (by Ronald Dethlefson).
The definitive research on disc recordings produced by Thomas A. Edison, including historical and discographical analyses, lists of artists and of recordings, and numerous essays on related topics. Valuable illustrations of advertising, label variants, performers, equipment, manufacturing buildings, and company logs. The structure of this edition is unfortunately clumsy — as a result of an incorporation of first-edition material — and there is no index.

S2-208   ML156.2 .E4 K8
Korst, Bill. Elite, Hit, and Majestic master listing / Bill Korst [et al.]. — Zephyrhills, Fla. : Joyce Record Club, 1989. — 29, 3 leaves. ISBN not given. (Alternative classification: ML156.4 .P6 K8.)
See note at S2-285.

S2-209   ML156.2 .L4
Raymond, Jack. A numerical list of Liberty Music Shop records / Jack Raymond. — Falls Church, Va. : Author [3709 George Mason Drive, #1011, 22041], 1993. — unpaged.
A useful cumulation, with some revisions, of a serial discography that appeared in issues of *Record Research* from 1981 to 1988. The label issued by the New York record emporium appeared from 1933 to 1942, covering about 214 78rpm discs and 10 LPs. Musicals, jazz, and sophisticated dance or vocal material were featured. Raymond gives all available discographical details, including matrix numbers, recording and release dates.

S2-210   ML156.2 .L536
Lindsay, Joe. Picture discs of the world : price guide / Joe Lindsay. — Scottsdale, Ariz. : Biodisc, 1990. — 205 p. ISBN 0-9617347-1-X.
A list of about 12,000 records on about 50 labels, all of them having surface illustrations of some kind. Arranged by label; with catalog number, artists, and estimated market price. There are good photos of many of the discs.

S2-211 ML156.2 .M3 G2
Garrod, Charles. MGM 78 rpm master numbers listing, 1946 thru 1952 : working draft / Charles Garrod and Ed Novitsky. — Zephyrhills, Fla. : Joyce Record Club, 1990. — 99, 1 leaves. ISBN not given.
A list of master (matrix) numbers, with label numbers, dates, artists, and titles. There are about 5,000 entries in date order, without indexes.

S2-212 ML156.2 .M3 N7
Novitsky, Ed. MGM record listings—30,000, 20,000, 50,000, 55,000, and 60,000 / Ed Novitsky and Charles Garrod. — Zephyrhills, Fla. : Joyce Record Club, 1989. — 18, 2 leaves. ISBN not given.
See previous entry and note at S2-285.

S2-213 ML156.2 .M8 R6
Bartlette, Reginald J. Off the record—Motown by master number, 1959–1989 : volume 1, singles / Reginald J. Bartlette; foreword by Ian Levine. — Ann Arbor, Mich. : Popular Culture, Ink., 1991. — xxxv, 508 p. : ill. ISBN 1-5607-5004-9.
A thorough accounting of issues from 58 labels in the Motown group, with a brief history of each label. Individual disc entries provide matrix numbers, catalog numbers, and dates. There are photos of many discs and indexes by song and record title, artist, and date of issue. A second volume, on albums, was to follow.
Review: *Choice* 4/92, 1203.

S2-214 ML156.2 .M8 B5
Bianco, David. Heat wave : the Motown fact book / David Bianco. — Ann Arbor, Mich. : Pierian, 1988. — xxiii, 524 p. : ill. (Rock & roll reference series, 25) ISBN 0-87650-204-4. (Alternative classification: ML156.4 .S6 B5.)
Motown, established in 1959 by Berry Gordy, quickly became the leading U.S. label in the soul field. Bianco gives a useful miscellany of information about the firm's output, including some 100 biographies and discographies; a chronology covering 1929–1987; 41 short notices about Motown labels and related labels; and label lists for U.S. and U.K. issues. The discographies give release dates and label numbers. The label lists are well indexed, by individual and group names (6,700 of them), song and record titles (8,500), dates, and record numbers. Altogether there are facts about 5,500 commercial discs on 30 American and British labels.
Listing and review: ARBA 1989, #1239; Balay BH123.

S2-215 ML156.2 .O5 M253
Mackenzie, Harry. One Night Stand series, 1-1001 / Harry Mackenzie

and Lothar Polomski. — New York : Greenwood, 1991. — xli, 394 p. (Discographies, 44) ISBN 0-313-27729-X. (Alternative classification: ML156.4 .P6 M253.)

From 1942 to 1946, the U.S. Armed Forces Radio Service played big-band and jazz music transcriptions over military and civilian stations. The broadcasts appeared in several series, among them One Night Stand. This chronological list of 1,000 broadcasts includes programs by all the leading artists of the period, with the greatest number by Les Brown, Jimmy Dorsey, Harry James, Stan Kenton, Freddy Martin, Joe Reichman, and Jan Savitt. The songs played on each date are listed,with vocalists and locations. There is an index of bands, but no title or performer indexes.

S2-216   ML156.2 .P5 R7
Ruppli, Michel. The Prestige label : a discography / Michel Ruppli. — Rev. ed. — Westport, Conn. : Greenwood, 1980. — xiii, 377 p. (Discographies, 3) ISBN 0-313-22019-0. (Alternative classification: ML156.2 .R7842.)

1st ed., 1973 (LOAM 935).

A valuable list of all recordings for the important jazz independent label established in 1949, specializing in the cool jazz artists like Miles Davis, Stan Getz, and the Modern Jazz Quartet. Prestige was sold to Fantasy in 1971, which continued to use the Prestige name until 1979; Ruppli covers the whole period. Sessions are in chronological order, with full details on location, personnel, matrix and release numbers, and comments. With an artist index.

Review: ARBA 1981, p. 456.

S2-217   ML156.2 .S4 P6
Porter, Bob. Signature Record Company master listing / Bob Porter. — Zephyrhills, Fla. : Joyce Record Club, 1989. — 24, 3 p. ISBN not given.

See note at S2-285.

S2-218   ML156.2 .V3 S5
Sherman, Michael W. The collector's guide to Victor records / Michael W. Sherman; in collaboration with William R. Moran and Kurt R. Nauck III. — Dallas : Monarch Record Enterprises, 1992. — 176 p. : ill. ISBN 0-9632903-0-4.

An excellent expansion of Sherman's 1987 book, *Paper Dog: An Illustrated Guide to the 78-rpm Victor Record Labels,* this is an exhaustive guide to all label types used by the Victor Talking Machine Co. There are color photos of the labels, and there is rich historical background, all thoroughly documented. Special categories are fully treated: picture discs, program transcriptions, educational series, children's records, foreign and ethnic items, celebrity records, test pressings, puzzle records, advertising records, and so forth. Coverage includes the early Berliner and Zonophone discs, and the Bluebird series. Useful chronological charts help in the identification and dating of particular labels and label number series. A valuable appendix gives attention to Victor publications. With an annotated bibliography of 32 entries and a non-expansive index.

S2-219   ML156.2 .W8
Garrod, Charles. World transcriptions original series, 1-11268 / Charles Garrod, Ken Crawford, and Dave Kressley. — Zephyrhills, Fla. : Joyce Record Club, 1992. — 84 leaves. ISBN not given.
A listing of issues from the World Broadcasting System, of New York City, which made transcription discs for radio stations from 1933 to 1963.

ML156.4 : Discographies by Genre

Blues

S2-220   ML156.4 .B6 D6
Dixon, Robert M. W. Blues and gospel records, 1902–1943 / Robert M. W. Dixon and John Godrich. — 3rd ed. — London : Storyville, 1982. — 900 p. ISBN 0-9023-9103-8.
1st ed., 1963 (LOAM 806).
A classic compilation, listing "every distinctively black-style American folk music record"—about 40,000 discs. Arrangement is by performer, then chronological. Place, date, matrix, personnel, and release label information are provided for each entry. With an index to the musicians.

S2-221   ML156.4 .B6 L4
Leadbitter, Mike. Blues records, 1943–1970 : a selective discography / Mike Leadbitter and Neil Slaven. — 2nd ed. — London : Record Information Services, 1987. — 798 p. ISBN 0-9078-7207-7.
Supersedes the compilers' *Blues Records: January, 1943 to December, 1966* (1969) (LOAM 808).
This is the first of two projected volumes, covering A-K.
A valuable list that continues the coverage of Dixon (S2-220). Arranged by performer. Information given includes date of recording, place, personnel, matrix and take numbers, issue labels, and comments.

S2-222   ML156.4 .B6 L87
Lornell, Kip. Virginia's blues : country and gospel records, 1902–

1943 : an annotated discography / Kip Lornell. — Lexington : University Press of Kentucky, 1989. — x, 238 p. : ill. ISBN 0-8131-1658-9.

A bio-discography covering "all commercially recorded folk musicians from Virginia and folk musicians closely associated with Virginia up to July 1943." Coverage begins with the Dinwiddie Colored Quartet recordings of 1902. The entries are alphabetical, presenting lists of LP reissues through June 1988, with the exception of Library of Congress records and V-Discs. Dates, locations, labels, matrix numbers, personnel, and comments are given for the records. With pictures of the artists, photos of sheet music, citations to secondary literature, and a performer index.

S2-223   ML156.4 .B6 S26

Scott, Frank. The Down Home guide to the blues / Frank Scott and the staff of Down Home Music. — Chicago : Chicago Review Press, 1991. — 250 p. ISBN 1-55652-130-8.

A discography of about 3,000 LPs, CDs, and cassettes, arranged by performer, with anthologies separately listed. The contents of each album are given, with detailed descriptions and perceptive critiques. The main problem with this inventory is its limitation to material in print at the time of compilation. With the continuing flood of reissues on CD, old material is coming back into print constantly, and it would have been more useful to include items of importance whether currently in print or not. An index would also have been appreciated.

Comedy

S2-224   ML156.4 .C4 C4

Corenthal, Michael G. Cohen on the telephone : a history of Jewish recorded humor and popular music, 1892–1942 / Michael G. Corenthal. — Milwaukee, Wisc. : Yesterday's Memories, 1984. — 108 p. ISBN not given.

The title of this engaging miscellany is that of Joe Hayman's million-selling song, a good representative of the genre covered. Pictures of records and sheet music, and of performers, are the special interest of the book. It also includes some songs in notation, scripts of comic routines, an informal discography (artist and label number only), and much insider commentary. Without index.

Country

S2-225   ML156.4 .C7 G56

Ginell, Cary. The Decca hillbilly discography, 1927–1945 / Cary

Ginell. — New York : Greenwood, 1989. — xxiv, 402 p. : ill. 16 p. plates. (Discographies, 35) ISBN 0-3132-6053-2.

Listings of several Decca series that specialized in country music: the 5000, 17000, Decca Champion 45000, and Montgomery Ward series. Information was drawn from original session books now in Universal City, California, with supplementary facts from interviews with the musicians who took part in the recordings. There are indexes by artist, matrix number, location, composers, and titles, and a guide to release dates. A useful background essay on the Decca Record Co. adds to the value of this excellent research.

S2-226   ML156.4 .C6 H8
Hoffmann, Frank. The *Cash Box* country album charts, 1964–1988 / Frank Hoffmann and George Albert. — Metuchen, N.J. : Scarecrow, 1989. — x, 290 p. ISBN 0-8108-2273-3.

A list of about 2,000 chart albums, following the format of S2-260. There is an album title index, a list of number-one releases by year, a list of 85 albums with the longest chart runs (Willie Nelson's *Stardust* leads all the rest), and a list of artists with the most hits (George Jones at the top).

For the country singles, see LOAM Suppl. SA-667.

Folk, Ethnic

S2-227   ML156.4 .F5 S69
Spottswood, Richard K. Ethnic music on records : a discography of ethnic recordings produced in the United States, 1893 to 1942 / Richard K. Spottswood. — Urbana : University of Illinois Press, 1990. — 7 vols. : ill. ISBN 0-252-01718-8.

A remarkable compilation of about 65,000 recordings, intended to present the entire production of "foreign language records made in the United States and possessions . . . 1893–1942," with the exception of classical and opera material, instruction discs, ethnic humor, and Hawaiian music. Irish and West Indian items are included, although they are in English. Cylinder and disc records are covered. For each one there is full discographical information: date, matrix number, label and catalog number, size, playing time, title transliteration, and performers. The first five volumes are the discography, in geographical arrangement; the sixth volume is an artist and title index; and the seventh is an index by record number and matrix number. An indispensable work.

Listing and review: ARBA 1992, #1305; Balay BH144.

Jazz

S2-228   ML156.4 .J3 B794
Bruyninckx, Walter. Discography : traditional jazz, 1897–1985 /
Walter Bruyninckx. — Mechelen, Belgium : Copy Express, 1985–
1988? — 6 vols. ISBN not given.
Cover title: Traditional jazz. Spine title: Traditional discography.

One of the five major jazz discographers—the others being Jorgen
Jepsen (LOAM 931), Tom Lord (S-241), Erik Raben (S2-240a), and
Brian Rust (S2-242)—Bruyninckx has been prolific and exasperating.
His careful lists of records by performers of many genres have been issued in loose-leaf, in bound cumulations, in poorly identified revisions,
and in a confusing mass of titles and alternate titles. The basic list is S2-
230, the update of LOAM 932. Modern jazz, jazz singers, and swing
bands are treated in separate compilations. The titles cited here are those
in the OCLC database in early 1994, searched through EPIC.

S2-229   ML156.4 .J3 B796
Bruyninckx, Walter. Jazz : the vocalists, 1917–1986 : singers and
crooners / Walter Bruyninckx. — Mechelen, Belgium: Copy Express,
1988. — 4 vols. ISBN not given.
Title from cover. Spine title: Vocalists discography.

An alphabetical list of singers, including big-band vocalists and rock
performers, with inventories of their recordings. Information for each
disc is exhaustive: matrix, location, recording and release dates, labels,
reissues, and personnel. Not every record by each artist is given, for reasons not offered (e.g., Bing Crosby recorded from 1926, but the list here
begins with soundtracks of 1930). With an index of all musicians cited
in the personnel listings.

S2-230   ML156.4 .J3 B797
Bruyninckx, Walter. 60 years of recorded jazz, 1917–1977 / Walter
Bruyninckx. — Mechelen, Belgium : Author, 1980? — 19 vols. ISBN
not given.
Extends the coverage of *50 Years of Recorded Jazz, 1917–1967*
(LOAM 932). Volume 19 is an artist index. A further revision, as *70
Years of Recorded Jazz,* has been announced.

S2-231   ML156.4 .J3 B798
Bruyninckx, Walter. Jazz : swing, 1920–1988 : swing, dance bands &
combos / Walter Bruyninckx. — Mechelen, Belgium : Copy Express,
1988? — 12 vols. ISBN not given.
Title from cover. Spine title: Swing discography.

S2-232   ML156.4 .J3 B799
Bruyninckx, Walter. Modern jazz : modern big band / Walter Bruyninckx. — Mechelen, Belgium : 60 Years of Recorded Jazz Team, 1986. —
2 vols. ISBN not given.
Title from cover. Spine title: Modern big band discography.

S2-233   ML156.4 .J3 B8
Bruyninckx, Walter. Progressive jazz : free—third stream fusion /
Walter Bruyninckx. — Mechelen, Belgium : 60 Years of Recorded Jazz
Team, 1984–1987. — 5 vols. ISBN not given.
Title from cover. Spine title: Progressive discography.

S2-234   ML156.4 .J3 B85
Bruyninckx, Walter. Jazz : modern jazz, be-bop, hard bop, West Coast /
Walter Bruyninckx. — Mechelen, Belgium : 60 Years of Recorded Jazz
Team, 1985. — 6 vols. ISBN not given.
Title from cover. Spine title (vol. 1): Discography. Spine title (vols.
2–6): Modern discography.
Indexed.

S2-235   Not used.

S2-236   ML156.4 .J3 C7
Crawford, Richard. Jazz standards on record, 1900–1942 : a core
repertory / Richard Crawford and Jeffrey Magee. — Chicago : Center
for Black Music Research, Columbia College, 1992. — xxv, 94 p. ISBN
0-9299-1103-2.
An intriguing list of recordings in chronological order for each of 97
songs in the jazz repertoire. For each record there is a place, matrix number, and release label; this information was taken primarily from Brian
Rust's *Jazz Records* (LOAM 930). The book makes possible the examination of a song's recording history and all the facets of interpretation
applied to it during the era of classic jazz. For example, "King Porter
Stomp" is traced from Jelly Roll Morton in 1923 to Bob Crosby in 1942.
An interesting summary of most-recorded songs shows that the winner
is "St. Louis Blues," with 165 versions on disc.

S2-237   ML156.4 .J3 F5
Ferguson, [C.]. Mainstream jazz reference and price guide, 1949–1965 /
[Charles] Ferguson & [Michael] Johnson. — Phoenix, Ariz. : O'Sullivan Woodside, 1984. — xvi, 175 p. ISBN 0-89019-0852.
Author surnames only are given on the title page; Ferguson's first initial is in the copyright statement. Photos of about 60 jazz LP labels, with
descriptions of their output; vague on dates. Alphabetical list of jazz per-

formers, with selective discography (label and release date only). Estimated market prices of the albums, tending toward unrealistic heights (many LPs in the $50–$60 range). Useful for good photos of LP albums, some in color. No indexes.
Review: ARBA 1985, p. 433.

S2-238   ML156.4 .J3 F67
Fordham, John. Jazz on CD : the essential guide / John Fordham. — London : KC, 1991. — 392 p. ISBN 1-85626-014-3.
Casual, rather vague comments about various recordings, arranged in historical chapters, then by performer. Without illustrations. Name index.

S2-239   ML156.4 .J3 H3
Harris, Steve. Jazz on compact disc : a critical guide to the best recordings / Steve Harris. — New York : Harmony Books/Crown, 1987. — 176 p. ISBN 0-517-56688-5.
An artist listing of CD reissues, useful for good comments on the music and for color pictures of the album covers. With a name index.

S2-240   ML156.4 .J3 H33
Harrison, Max. The essential jazz records. Volume 1, Ragtime to swing / Max Harrison, Charles Fox, and Eric Thacker. — Westport, Conn. : Greenwood, 1984. — xii, 595 p. (Discographies, 12) ISBN 0-313-24674-2.
Three British authors have selected 250 "best" jazz records—mostly LP collections of 78 rpm originals, hence mostly recordings made before 1950. Discographical information includes title, label, and number of LP; personnel, places, and dates of original recordings; and song titles. The real purpose of this guide, however, is to discuss the recordings. While some factual information is included about the artists, the compositions, or the recording sessions, the focus is a critique of the recording, particularly of the performances. The work is very opinionated, but the authors write with convincing authority.
Each critique is signed. Secondary sources are carefully cited, and there is a classified bibliography of roughly 150 entries. There are indexes of LP titles and of tune titles, followed by a partly expansive index of musicians.
Max Harrison is a critic of classical music and jazz; he contributed to the *New Grove Dictionary of Music* and has written for many jazz periodicals. Charles Fox is a broadcaster and reviewer, responsible for the radio program *Radio Today*. Erick Thacker has written for *Jazz Monthly, Jazz Express,* and *Composer*. All three contributed to the *New Grove Dictionary of Jazz* [—D. P.].
Listing and review: Balay BH120; *Choice* 3/85, 966.

S2-240a   ML156.4 .J3 J47
Raben, Erik. Jazz records, 1942–80 : a discography / Erik Raben. —
Copenhagen : JazzMedia, 1987– . ISBN 87-88043-06-1.
Four volumes have appeared in this series, which is intended to update
and correct Jepsen (LOAM 931). Arranged alphabetically by artist, it offers full discographical data (date and place, matrix and take numbers,
release labels, performers, and comments) for issues and reissues. Scope
is international, with a substantial representation of European performers. Unfortunately, misspelled names are numerous. With an index of
musicians in each volume.

S2-241   ML156.4 .J3 L8
Lord, Tom. The jazz discography / Tom Lord. — Redwood, N.Y. :
Cadence Jazz Books, 1992– . — Vol. 1, A–Bankhead. ISBN 1-881993-
00-0 (vol. 1).
A work in progress, with 8 volumes available in March 1994, planned
to reach about 25 volumes with a concluding supplementary volume. A
musicians index and song title index are to follow. With "100,000
recording sessions including over half a million musician entries and half
a million tune entries" (publisher's announcement), the compilation will
be the most current and complete of its kind. Arranged by performer, the
entries give full discographical data: date, place, session, matrix, personnel, release labels, and reissues (including CDs). Useful comment are
appended.
Review: ARBA 1993, p. 545.

S2-242   ML156.4 .J3 R9
Rust, Brian. Jazz records, 1897–1942 / Brian Rust. — 5th rev. and enl.
ed. — Chigwell, Essex, England : Storyville, [1982]. — 2 vols. : 1,996
p. ISBN 0-902391-04-6.
1st ed., 1961 (LOAM 930).
The fundamental discography of jazz, giving all known recordings for
each artist, with full details of location, personnel, matrix and take numbers, release labels, rejects, and comments. With artist and title indexes.
Listing: Balay BH143.

Musicals

S2-243   ML156.4 .M6 H3
Harris, Steve. Film, television, and stage music on phonograph records :
a discography / Steve Harris. — Jefferson, N.C. : McFarland, 1988. —
445 p. ISBN 0-89950-251-2.
A thorough inventory of recordings of British and American films
(8,141 items), television programs (1,822 items), and stage productions

(1,797 items). Both original scores and adaptations are included. Titles are in alphabetical order within each section. No information is presented about the recordings other than label and number. Composer index.

Listing and reviews: ARBA 1989, p. 474; Balay BH145; *Choice* 10/88, 292.

S2-244   ML156.4 .M6 L9

Lynch, Richard Chigley. Movie musicals on record : a directory of recordings of motion picture musicals, 1927–1987 / Richard Chigley Lynch. — New York: Greenwood, 1989. — x, 445 p. (Discographies, 32) ISBN 0-313-26540-2.

A list of 666 albums, in alphabetical order by film title. No details are given about the recordings other than label and catalog numbers. For the film itself, information includes composer, lyricist, musical director, cast, and song titles. Index of 6,500 songs and other indexes by per-former, composer, lyricist, and musical director. With a chronology of films. This is a companion volume to the author's *Broadway on Record* (1987; LOAM S-1023).

Listing and reviews: ARBA 1990, p. 523; Balay BH146; *Choice* 12/89, 613; LJ 11/1/89, 84.

S2-245   ML156.4 .M6 L93

Lynch, Richard Chigley. TV and studio cast musicals on record : discography of television musicals and studio recordings of stage and film musicals/ Richard Chigley Lynch. — Westport, Conn. : Green-wood, 1990. — xii, 330 p. ISBN 0-313-27324-3. (Alternative classifica-tion: ML156.4 .O46 L93.)

An alphabetical list of musicals that were made for TV, studio versions of musicals, and some miscellaneous types. Criteria for inclusion are not clear, and information provided is minimal. There are chronological ar-rays for the TV shows and the studio items, and a performer index.

S2-246   ML156.4 .M6 O8

Osborne, Jerry. The official price guide to movie and TV soundtracks and original cast albums / Jerry Osborne; ed. Ruth Maupin. — New York : House of Collectibles, 1991. — vii, 663 p. ISBN 0-876-37846-7.

A title list of material in print in the United States, with price estimates. Reissues and cover versions are included. With performer and composer indexes.

S2-247   ML156.4 .O46 F4

Fellers, Frederick P. The Metropolitan Opera on record : a discography of the commercial recordings / Frederick P. Fellers. — Westport, Conn. : Greenwood, 1984. — xix, 101 p. (Discographies, 6) ISBN 0-313-23952-5.

A list of 477 numbered items, each having the recording date, cast, and release labels. With indexes of artists, operas, and opera arias.

S2-248   ML156.4 .O46 R4
Raymond, Jack. Show music on record : the first 100 years / Jack Raymond. — Rev. ed. — Washington : Smithsonian Institution Press, 1992. — 429 p. ISBN 1-5609-8151-2.
1st ed., 1982 (LOAM Suppl. SA-571).
In this handy compilation the shows of each year are presented, with all their songs; and the recordings of every song are cited. Names and titles are indexed. See also S2-1023.

Popular

S2-249   ML156.4 .P6 A42
Albert, George. *Cash Box* black contemporary singles charts, 1960–1984 / George Albert and Frank Hoffmannn; with Lee Ann Hoffmann. — Metuchen, N.J. : Scarecrow, 1986. — 704 p. ISBN 0-8108-1853-1.
One of the important series of chart books written by Albert and Hoffmann, the others being entered under the latter's name (S2-260 to S2-262). The term "R & B" was used in *Cash Box* magazine, and elsewhere, to identify the popular black idiom during the 1960s and 1970s, with "black contemporary" substituted in the late seventies. Soul music was not given a separate category in *Cash Box,* so that genre falls into "contemporary" along with R & B. About 11,000 singles are listed here, alphabetically under the name of the recording artist, with issue dates, release labels, and chart showings and their duration (the number of weeks is given after the chart positions). A song title index provides convenient access. There are also appendix lists of each month's number-one records, those with the longest chart runs (Patti Austin's "Baby, Come to Me" and Chubby Checker's "The Twist" lead all the rest), and a list of artists with the most chart hits (James Brown is well ahead). For black contemporary albums, see S2-262.
Reviews: ARBA 1987, #1259; LJ 6/1/86, 115.

S2-250   ML156.4 .P6 B35
Banney, Howard F. Return to sender : the first complete discography of Elvis tribute and novelty records, 1956–1986 / Howard F. Banney; photographs by Charles Weitz. — Ann Arbor, Mich. : Pierian, 1987. — xvi, 318 p. : ill. (Rock & roll reference series, 29) ISBN 0-87650-238-9.
A list of records about Elvis Presley, rather than by him: imitations, parodies, cover versions, any songs (686 of them) that mention his name. More than 1,000 songs, on 807 7-inch and 12-inch discs. Label numbers

and release years are the only discographic facts given, but Banney adds interesting comments. Most of the records are from the United States, but 34 countries are represented in this aggregate tribute. Photographs of album covers throughout. Indexes by name, song and album, and record number.

Review: ARBA 1989, #1238.

S2-251 ML156.4 .P6 B4

Birosik, Patti Jean. The new age music guide : profiles and recordings of 500 top new age musicians / Patti Jean Birosik. — New York : Collier Books, 1989. — xxii, 218 p. ISBN 0-02-041640-7. (Alternative classification: ML156.4 .N48 B4.)

New Age music is "a return to roots, to a belief in the primordial power of sound. . . . It offers peace, joy, bliss, and the opportunity to discover within ourselves our own highest nature." Birosik lists New Age musicians in such categories as meditation music, sound health music, and space music. Information on the artists was gathered from a questionnaire that evidently did not ask for biographical information, so the text is mostly devoted to impressions of the various sound products. A few sample recordings are identified, by title only, with no dates or labels. With a list of about 150 record companies that include New Age material among their releases. No documentation or indexing.

S2-252 ML156.4 .P6 B5

Blair, John. The illustrated discography of hot rod music, 1961–1965 / John Blair and Stephen J. McParland. — Ann Arbor, Mich. : Popular Culture, Ink., 1990. — 167 p. : ill. ISBN 1-56075-002-2.

A thorough list of records in the genre that accompanied the other California trend of the 1960s, surf music. Arrangement is by performer; release dates and labels are given, with comments and photographs. There is a label and record number index.

S2-253 ML156.4 .P6 B77

Bronson, Fred. *Billboard*'s hottest hot 100 hits / Fred Bronson. — New York : Billboard Books, 1991. — x, 406 p. ISBN 0-8230-7570-2.

A collection of perspectives on the hit records since 1956: the top 100 of the Beatles, top 50 by Elvis Presley, etc.; top hits by each writer, by producer, and by label; the top 100 debut songs, top male solos, etc. There is also an annual list of top songs from 1956 to 1990, and there are lists by subject (place names, animals, colors, days of the week). A master inventory of the 3,000 great hits of the rock era, and an index to them, rounds off this useful aid, which is further embellished with commentaries and photos.

S2-254 ML156.4 .P6 C66

Cooper, B. Lee. A resource guide to themes in contemporary American song lyrics, 1950–1985 / B. Lee Cooper; foreword by Wayne A. Wiegand. — New York : Greenwood, 1986. — xxiii, 458 p. ISBN 0-313-24516-9.

Lists of songs whose lyrics are concerned with various topics or themes, such as death, education, marriage, race relations, religion, youth culture, urban life, love, sexuality, and poverty; and lyrics that portray personality types (dominant, submissive, independent, rebellious). Thus the book is a kind of emotional history of rock songs, assuming that the words are the bearers of the emotions they write about; nothing is said about the musical elements. An "audio profile of the rock era, 1950–1985" is a discography by style and period, not related to the categories of song lyrics, giving labels and release dates only. Bibliography, not annotated, of about 700 books and articles; criteria not stated. Nonexpansive index of recording artists; index of song titles.

Listing and reviews: ARBA 1987, #1260; Balay BH141; *Choice* 9/86, 138.

S2-255 ML156.4 .P6 C68

Cooper, B. Lee. Response recordings : an answer song discography, 1950–1990 / B. Lee Cooper and Wayne S. Haney. — Metuchen, N.J. : Scarecrow, 1990. — xxiii, 272 p. ISBN 0-8108-2342-X.

A list of recorded songs "marked by a direct lyrical connection to preceding records." The original was usually a hit song, while the "responses" typically failed to make the charts. A total of 674 base records are noted, with 1,252 responses to them issued in 1950–1989. Some of the answer records are humorous parodies, such as Allan Sherman's 1967 "Winchester Hadassah," inspired by "Winchester Cathedral" (New Vaudeville Band, 1966). Others may best be described as cute, such as "Get Off My Tulips" (Caretaker, 1968), drawn from Tiny Tim's hit rendition of 1968, "Tip-toe through the Tulips with Me." With a nonexpansive artist and title index.

Review: ARBA 1991, p. 525.

S2-256 ML156.4 . P6 C683

Coryton, Demitri. Hits of the '60s : the million sellers / Demitri Coryton and Joseph Murrells. — London : Batsford, 1990. — 287 p. : ill. ISBN 0-7134-5851-8.

"Part of this book is based on the 1960s section of *Million Selling Records from the 1900s to the 1980s* by Joseph Murrells, 1984."

While Murrells's 1984 book (LOAM Suppl. S-812) has been criticized for its invented data about sales, from earlier days when reliable figures were not available, this volume—focused on an era of statistic-keeping—is on more solid ground. It lists songs by performer, giving paragraph explanations and sources for each item's million status. There is an artist index and a title index.

S2-257   ML156.4 .P6 D7
Downey, Pat. The golden age of top 40 music (1955–1973) on compact disc / Pat Downey. — Boulder, Colo. : P. Downey Enterprises, 1992. — vii, 453 p. ISBN 0-9633-7181-9.

A useful artist list of chart records, chronological under each performer, that were later released on American commercial CDs. The original label is identified for each song, along with its duration and highest chart position achieved. With the CD label there are interesting comments and technical appraisals. Many songs have numerous CD manifestations (19 for "Great Balls of Fire" by Jerry Lee Lewis; 22 for "I Heard It through the Grapevine" by Marvin Gaye), but they are not all in print. The index of song titles is itself a useful reference, offering quick identification of the artists and dates of the original records.

S2-258   ML156.4 .P6 E8
Erlewine, Michael. All music guide : the best CDs, albums, & tapes : the expert's guide to the best releases from thousands of artists in all types of music / Michael Erlewine, Stephen Thomas Erlewine, and Scott Bultman. — San Francisco : Miller Freeman, 1992. — 1,176 p. ISBN 0-87930-264-X.

About 80 critics and musicians joined to compile appraisals of some 23,000 records, including many varieties of music (rock, gospel, children's, women's music, etc.). With an artist index.

Review: *Choice* 7-8/93, 1748.

S2-259   ML156.4 .P6 G731
Green, Jeff. Green book : songs classified by subject / Jeff Green. — Smyrna, Tenn. : Professional Desk References, 1989. — 326 p. ISBN 0-9397-3503-2.

A subject list—more accurately a keyword list—of popular songs, presenting titles that match with such terms as "farms," "fat," "fear," "fight," "flowers," "food," "fools," and so on. The reason that "keyword" seems preferable to "subject" in these categories is that songs are listed under a term even if the term is used metaphorically. For example, under "fire": "Light My Fire," "Great Balls of Fire," "Play with Fire." Similar terms are treated under main topics, rather than by see also references; under "fire" there also appears "Smoke Gets in Your Eyes." Allowing for this practice, and for the fact that criteria for including songs in the list are not given, the book is a handy reminder of songs that fall into categories. Among the most useful lists are those of songs with women's names in the titles and another for men's names. Without a title index.

S2-260   ML156.4 .P6 H589
Hoffmann, Frank. The *Cash Box* album charts, 1955–1974 / Frank Hoffmann and George Albert; with the assistance of Lee Ann Hoffmann. — Metuchen, N.J. : Scarecrow, 1988. — xv, 512 p. ISBN 0-8108-2005-6.
By "album" the authors mean sets of 78 rpm records and also LP singles or sets. This book complements the coverage of S2-261. The source charts were those that appeared in *Cash Box* magazine. About 6,000 albums are listed, arranged by artist; each with release date (day, month, year) and a list of chart positions, with total appearances. Album title index and chronological list of number-one records for each month of the period. For the singles charts 1950–1981, see LOAM Suppl. SA-676.

S2-261   ML156.4 .P6 H59
Hoffmann, Frank. The *Cash Box* album charts, 1975–1985 / Frank Hoffmann and George Albert; with Lee Ann Hoffmann. — Metuchen, N.J. : Scarecrow, 1987. — x, 546 p. ISBN 0-8108-1939-2.
A list of about 7,000 albums, arranged by artist. Same format as S2-260.
Review: ARBA 1988, #1299.

S2-262   ML156.4 .P6 H77
Hoffmann, Frank. The *Cash Box* black contemporary album charts, 1975–1987 / Frank Hoffmann and George Albert. — Metuchen, N.J. : Scarecrow, 1989. — 249 p. ISBN 0-8108-2212-1.
For scope and format, see S2-249. Covers about 3,000 albums.

S2-263   ML156.4 .P6 J47
Osborne, Jerry. Rockin' records buyers-sellers reference book and price guide, 1991 edition / Jerry Osborne. — Boyne Falls, Mich. : Jellyroll, 1991. — xiii, 524 p. ISBN 0-932117-15-5.
A list of records deemed worthy of attention by collectors, with a price range intended to approximate market value of each. Arrangement is by performer, and release years are given for the records, so there is a quick-reference utility here, whether or not one is concerned about buying and selling.

S2-264   ML156.4 .P6 M2
Mawhinney, Paul C. MusicMaster : the 45 rpm record directory : 1947 to 1982 / Paul C. Mawhinney. — Allison Park, Pa. : Record-Rama, 1983. — 2 vols. ISBN not given.

A monumental compilation of 200,000 listings, arranged by performer. There is indexing by title, label, and year.

S2-265   ML156.4 .P6 M3
Mackenzie, Harry. The Johnny Mercer Chesterfield music shop, with A.F.R.S. additions featuring Johnny Mercer, Jo Stafford, Pied Pipers, Paul Weston and his orchestra / Harry Mackenzie. — Zephyrhills, Fla. : Joyce Record Club, 1986. — 28 leaves. ISBN not given.
At head of title: NBC studios, Hollywood, California, USA, 12 June–8 December 1944.

S2-266   ML156.4 .P6 Q9
Quirin, Jim. Chartmasters' rock 100 : an authoritative ranking of the 100 most popular songs for each year, 1956 through 1986 / Jim Quirin and Barry Cohen. — 4th ed. — Covington, La. : Chartmasters, 1986. — 98 p. : ill. ISBN 0-917190-15-7.
Rock records of the period covered are put in order of popularity, for each year, according to a complex formula. There is an artist index. Annual supplements to this edition have been published.

S2-267   ML156.4 .P6 R62
Rolling Stone album guide : completely new reviews : every essential album, every essential artist / ed. Anthony DeCurtis and James Henke; with Holly George-Warren. — New York : Random House, 1992. — 838 p. ISBN 0-679-73729-4.
1st ed., 1979, as *Rolling Stone Record Guide;* rev. ed., 1983 (LOAM Suppl. S-1120).
Presents critical discographies, for the most part limited to recordings in print as of spring 1992, for rock, soul, country, and other pop performers of past and present. The records are rated with appropriate numbers of stars; while there are plenty of high scorers, a good share of the products are condemned ("pretentious," "a directionless ordeal"). Without index; and not even a table of contents.
Review: *Choice* 7-8/93, 1748.

S2-268   ML156.4 .P6 R63
Rogers, Alice. Dance bands and big bands / Alice Rogers. — Rev. ed. — Tempe, Ariz. : Jelly Roll Productions, 1993. — 400 p. : ill. ISBN not given. (Alternative classification: ML156.4 .B5 R63.)
1st ed., 1987.
A handy list of about 16,000 78rpm records from the 1920s to 1940s, arranged by artist, covering the output of big bands. Titles, vocalists, label numbers, and release dates are given. In addition to discographical

data, which are useful and accurate, Rogers offers indicators of market values for the records.

S2-269   ML156.4 .P6 R88

Rust, Brian. The complete entertainment discography, from 1897 to 1942 / Brian Rust and Allen G. Debus. — 2nd ed. — New York : Da Capo, 1989. — 794 p. ISBN 0-306-76210-2.

1st ed., 1973 (LOAM 1159).

A monument of discography, giving all the recordings for a group of show people, most of whom were not covered in other inventories. Included are such luminaries as the Andrews Sisters, Al Bowlly (a 35-page list), Gracie Fields, Wendell Hall, Danny Kaye, Mary Martin, Will Oakland, Dick Powell, Sophie Tucker, Orson Welles, and Mae West. Excluded are blues and jazz performers, and American big-band artists— two categories Rust has dealt with in other books (S2-242 and LOAM 936). A biographical sketch heads the entry for each person, after which there is a chronological array of the recordings, with dates, locations, matrix numbers, release labels and numbers. Without index.

Listing: Balay BH142.

S2-270   ML156.4 .P6 S66

Shapiro, Bill. Thirty years of rock and roll on compact disc / Bill Shapiro. — New York : Andres & McMeel, 1988. — 188 p. ISBN not given.

A chronological list, by decade then by performer, with lists of CD reissues. Evaluative grades are assigned to the discs, and there are brief biographies of the musicians. With a list of the top 100 CDs, a bibliography, and an index.

S2-271   ML156.4 .P6 T76

The Trouser Press record guide / ed. Ira A. Robbins. — 4th ed. — New York : Collier Books, 1991. — 763 p. ISBN 0-02-036361-3.

Revision of *The New Trouser Press Record Guide,* 3rd ed., 1989. 1st edition, 1983, titled *The Trouser Press Guide to New Wave Records.* British edition, 1987 : *The New Music Record & Tape Guide.*

Trouser Press was a periodical devoted to popular genres outside the mainstream, originally encompassed—in the late 1970s—by the term "new wave." The new edition of "1,600 entries covering 2,500 artists and about 9,500 records" continues to concentrate on "bands and artists who favor experimentation, radicalism, innovation and self-expression," including rap, metal, industrial, goth, and hardcore. For each entry there is a list ("as-complete-as-possible") of albums through early 1991, with release dates and labels. Critical comments on the albums follow, essentially adulatory; but it is impressive that Robbins has listened to them all.

Listing: BCL (for the 3rd ed.).

S2-272   ML156.4 .P6 W43

Whitburn, Joel. The *Billboard* book of top 40 albums / Joel Whitburn. —
Rev. ed. — New York : Billboard Books, 1991. — 347 p. : ill. ISBN 0-
8230-7534-6.

1st ed., 1987.

A list of about 5,000 albums that made the top 40 from 1955 to 1990,
in alphabetical order by artist. For each there is the release date and label, chart position, weeks in the top 40, and comments on the performers. There are separate sections for top soundtracks, Christmas songs,
and other categories. A formula is used to rank the artists. Index of
names.

Review: ARBA 1992, p. 528.

S2-273   ML156.4 .P6 W44

Whitburn, Joel. The *Billboard* book of top 40 hits / Joel Whitburn. —
5th ed. — New York : Billboard Books, 1992. — 674 p. : ill. ISBN 0-
8230-8280-6.

1983 ed., LOAM Suppl. SA-680.

A list of double-sided records, arranged by performer, that reached the
Billboard top 40 charts between 1955 and 1991, with much detail about
chart positions (many positions are adjustments of those given in earlier
editions of the book). Information given for each record includes release
dates, label numbers, and contents. The top records of each decade are
noted, and there is a chronological list of number-one discs from 1955 to
1991.

Review: *Choice* 4/92, 1192.

S2-274   ML156.4 .P6 W445

Whitburn, Joel. *Billboard* top 1000 singles, 1955–1990 / Joel Whitburn. — Milwaukee : Hal Leonard, 1991. — 135 p. ISBN 0-7935-
0247-7.

A revision of *Billboard Top 1000 Singles, 1955–1987* (1988).

A list in rank order, from number one to number 1,000. The title that
heads all the rest is "Don't Be Cruel" / "Hound Dog" by Elvis Presley.
There is also a list of hits by year, a list of top 100 albums, an artist list,
and a song title list.

S2-275   ML156.4 .P6 W457

Whitburn, Joel. *Billboard*'s top 3000, 1955–1987 / Joel Whitburn. —
Menomonee Falls, Wisc. : Record Research, 1988. — 163 p. ISBN 0-
89820-064-4.

1st ed., *Billboard's Top 1000,* 1984; 2nd ed., *Billboard's Top 2000,*
1985.

Whitburn is presenting an ever-growing inventory of singles that have been on the *Billboard* top 10 charts, this edition covering 9 July 1955 through 26 September 1987. The volume includes 3,093 titles. They are listed first by rank (a calculation made by Whitburn, on the basis of positions on the list and number of occurrences), then by artist. With an index of song titles.

Review: *Choice* 4/92, 1192.

S2-276   ML156.4 .P6 W46

Whitburn, Joel. Joel Whitburn presents the *Billboard* hot 100 charts : the eighties / Joel Whitburn. — Menomonee Falls, Wisc. : Record Research, 1991. — Unpaged. ISBN not given.

Photocopies of actual *Billboard*'s weekly "Hot 100" charts, from 1980 to 1989, with a song title index.

S2-277   ML156.4 .P6 W49.

Whitburn, Joel. *Billboard* 1990 music and video yearbook / Joel Whitburn. — Menomonee Falls, Wisc. : Record Research, 1992. — 288 p. ISBN 0-89820-081-4.

Continues a useful reference series of annual chart surveys that commenced with *Music Yearbook 1983*; it became *Music and Video Yearbook* in 1987. Various approaches are taken to the chart hits: There are rankings of all records "that peaked on *Billboard's* Hot 100 chart"; an artist list of singles; artist list of albums; title index to singles; top 20 artists for singles; all number-one hits in chronological order; chronological lists by category; top video rentals and sales; and lists of all number-one videos. These lists vary from volume to volume.

Rock

S2-278   ML156.4 .R6 D9

Duxbury, Janell R. Rockin' the classics and classicizin' the rock : a selectively annotated discography / Janell R. Duxbury. — Westport, Conn. : Greenwood, 1985. — xix, 188 p. (Discographies, 14) ISBN 0-313-24605-X.

An inventory of 862 rock (plus other post-1950s popular genres) recordings that include elements of specific classical compositions. Some of the entries preserve the original name (such as Paul Simon's "Ride of the Valkyries"), while others have new names (such as Louise Tucker's "Midnight Blue," which uses a theme from Beethoven's Piano Sonata, op. 13). Information given for each recording is limited to label number and release date, with useful comments appended to some items. J. S. Bach is the most generous donor to these pop renditions, with strong representation also from Grieg, Mozart, Tchaikovsky, and Wagner. Among the 35 classical recordings said to be indebted to rock material,

only a few works by Philip Glass seem comfortable in the category; most of this group is comprised of "Greatest Hits" records and other anthologies that are classics in original versions. With an index of titles, composers, and performers.
Listing and review: ARBA 1992, #1311; Balay BH156.
First supplement / Janell R. Duxbury. — New York : Greenwood, 1991. — xxii, 168 p. (Discographies, 43) ISBN 0-313-27542-4. (ML156.4 .R6 D90. Suppl.)
Adds 502 recordings to the rock group and 45 to the classical group, and offers corrections and amplifications to material in the base volume. With an index of titles, composers, and performers.

S2-279   ML156.4 .R6 E3
Eddy, Chuck. Stairway to hell : the 500 best heavy metal albums in the universe / Chuck Eddy. — New York : Harmony Books, 1991. — 232 p. ISBN 0-517-57541-8.
Eddy offers rambling, impressionistic accounts of these steely efforts, using picturesque language ("juicy dicehall crotchgrind"). The top rated disc is *Zoso* by Led Zeppelin.

S2-280   ML156.4 .R6 E33
Edwards, John W. Rock 'n' roll through 1969 : discographies of all performers who hit the charts beginning in 1955 / John W. Edwards. — Jefferson, N.C. : McFarland, 1992. — xii, 475 p. : ill. ISBN 0-89950-655-0.
A useful list of recordings by individuals and groups, in date order under their names, with personnel identified and release label given. There is also a chronological list of albums and singles within each year.

S2-281   ML156.4 .R6 H68
Hounsome, Terry. Rock record : a collector's directory of rock albums and musicians / Terry Hounsome. — 3rd ed. — New York : Facts on File, 1987. — xii, 738 p. ISBN 0-8160-1754-9.
1st ed., *New Rock Record,* 1981, 2nd ed., 1983 (LOAM Suppl. SA-677).
A useful gathering of 7,678 entries, representing 45,681 records by some 78,000 musicians from all rock periods and genres. Hounsome "attempts to list every LP record," giving year and label for each.
Review: ARBA 1988, p. 525.

S2-282   ML156.4 .R6 R3
Rees, Tony. Rare rock : a collector's guide / Tony Rees. — Poole, Dorset, England : Blandford, 1985. — 352 p. : ill. ISBN 0-7137-1513-8.
A selection of rock records considered to be collectible, arranged by

performer. There is no estimate of market prices. For the noncollector, the interest in the book will be in its inclusion of unusual materials, such as odd-shaped discs, playable sleeves, promotion records, test pressings, and withdrawn items. Without indexing.

Review: LJ 10/15/85, 80.

S2-282a   ML156.4 .R6 T5438

Tilch, K. D. Rock Musiker / K. D. Tilch. — Hamburg : Taurus Press, 1988. — 4 vols. ISBN 3-922542-30-1.

In German. An alphabetical list of about 80,000 rock performers who have been on LP records. For each person, information given includes: instruments played, album titles and years, and labels. A unique and essential guide.

Steel Band

S2-283   ML156.4 .S8 T5

Thomas, Jeffrey Ross. Forty years of steel : an annotated discography of steel band and pan recordings, 1951–1991 / Jeffrey Ross Thomas. — Westport, Conn. : Greenwood, 1992. — xxxii, 309 p. ISBN 0-313-27952-7.

"The origins of pan and the steel band are relatively recent, dating from roughly the early to mid-1930s," and the first known recordings date from 1951. This is music based in Trinidad, consisting of ingenious performers on zinc pans, tin cans, cement drums, and other "found objects." Musicians have learned to combine these simple materials into percussion instruments with the capability of playing melodies. The tradition has spread to major cities in Britain, Canada, the United States, and parts of Asia. Thomas has compiled 776 LP recordings on labels of various countries, giving dates and label numbers with album contents. Appendix information includes a directory of labels and sources. There are indexes by artist, album title, issue date, and song title.

ML156.5 : Composer Recordings

S2-284   ML156.5 .S9 S88

Stuart, Philip. Igor Stravinsky : the composer in the recording studio : comprehensive discography / Philip Stuart. — New York : Greenwood, 1991. — viii, 96 p. (Discographies, 45) ISBN 0-313-27958-6.

A list of "all Stravinsky's studio performances (except those given primarily for the camera . . .) together with recordings of concerts and broadcasts which have been published on disc or preserved in archive collections." There are 153 issues with the composer as conductor or pianist, plus 29 recordings conducted by Stravinsky's associate, Robert

Craft, and nine miscellaneous items; a total of 191 recordings, given in chronological sequence from 1925 to 1967. Full discographical data are provided: dates, locations, matrix and take numbers, labels and reissues, and names of soloists. There is a supplementary discography of Soulima Stravinsky, son of the composer. With a chronological index of works and a nonexpansive general index.

ML156.7 : Discographies by Performer

S2-285   ML156.7 .A62 G4

Garrod, Charles. Ray Anthony and his orchestra / Charles Garrod and Bill Korst. — Zephyrhills, Fla. : Joyce Record Club, 1988. — 47, 2, 10 leaves. ISBN not given.

Ray Anthony's big band emerged after the prime of the genre, but proved to be enormously durable. This list covers his recordings from 1945 to 1988, with about 200 record sessions and broadcasts described. Full recording information is given: dates and locations, labels, matrix numbers, personnel, and reissues. With a list of albums and an index of song titles. The Joyce Record Club series deals with many other individuals and bands from the jazz/swing era, offering substantially the sort of information described here. The volumes are inexpensively printed, without graphics. References to earlier discographical work on the artists are not made, and sources of data are not given. Other publications of the Joyce Record Club present the output of individual labels; they offer matrix and release label numbers, names of performers, and usually song and artist indexes. For pre-1980 publications of the club, see the bibliography in S2-83.

S2-285a   ML156.7 .A75 J5

Louis Armstrong : the Tsumura collection / J. G. Jepsen; discography by Akira Tsumura. — Tokyo : Author, 1989. — 456 p. : ill. ISBN not given.

A catalog of Tsumura's vast collection of Armstrong recordings, which includes more than 95 percent of first pressings. There are color photos of the labels and album covers, with full discographical details.

S2-286   ML156.7 .B2

Garrod, Charles. Charlie Barnet and his orchestra / Charles Garrod and Bill Korst. — Zephyrhills, Fla. : Joyce Record Club, 1984. — 79 leaves. ISBN not given.

See note at S2-285.

S2-287   ML156.7 .B38 G2

Garrod, Charles. Count Basie and his orchestra, 1936–1945 / Charles

Garrod. — Zephyrhills, Fla. : Joyce Record Club, 1987. — 56, 8 leaves.
ISBN not given.

Count Basie and his orchestra : volume two, 1946–1957 / Charles
Garrod. — Zephyrhills, Fla. : Joyce Record Club, 1988. — 53, 5 leaves.
ISBN not given.

William "Count" Basie (1904–1984) was a prominent pianist and big-
band leader for half a century. Garrod's two-volume discography lists
his studio and radio recordings, presenting full discographical data: locations and dates, matrix numbers, labels and reissues, personnel, and
commentaries. Each volume has a song title index.

S2-288   ML156.7 .B38 S5
Sheridan, Chris. Count Basie : a bio-discography / Chris Sheridan. —
New York : Greenwood, 1986. — xxvi, 1,350 p. : ill. (Discographies,
22) ISBN 0-313-24935-0.

The definitive Basie inventory, superseding Garrod (S2-287), whose
list is not even mentioned by Sheridan. Coverage is 1929 to 1984, in
more than a thousand sessions. Commercial discs, radio transcriptions
(including Armed Forces Radio Service), films, private recordings from
radio, and on-location tapes are all noted in full detail. Information given
for each item: date, location, matrix number, label, reissues on LP and
cassette, personnel, extensive comments, and—an unusual and useful
feature—reference to what Basie was doing at the time. Thus the work
is a Basie chronology as well as a discography. There is a separate list of
all known LPs and one of all engagements from 1936 to 1984. Indexing
offers access by film and video title, radio and TV program title,
arranger, musicians, and song title.

Reviews: AM 1988, 48; ARBA 1987, #1255; *Choice* 1/87, 773.

S2-289   ML156.7 .B433
Garrod, Charles. Ben Bernie and his orchestra / Charles Garrod. —
Zephyrhills, Fla. : Joyce Record Club, 1991. — 19, 4 p. ISBN not given.

Bernie (1891–1943) was a big-band leader whose ensemble was popular in hotel ballrooms and who recorded under various names. This
recording list covers 1922–1941, presenting dates, matrix numbers, personnel, and labels. Among the vocalists were Irving Kaufman, Frank
Luther, Jackie Heller, and Dick Robertson. With a song title index.

S2-290   ML156.7 .B87 C88
DeCraen, Hugo. Marion Brown : discography / Hugo DeCraen and
Eddy Janssens. — Brussels : New Think, 1985. — iv, 44 p. ISBN not
given.

Alto saxophonist Brown (1935–) was a figure in the experimental jazz
movement of the 1960s, achieving international renown on numerous

European tours. The discography covers 1964–1980, offering commercial and noncommercial recordings with full discographical data: locations, dates, matrix numbers, labels and reissues, personnel, and commentaries. With indexes of album titles, compositions by Brown, and musicians on all the records.

S2-291   ML156.7 .C15
Popa, Jay. Cab Calloway and his orchestra, 1925–1958 / Jay Popa. — Rev. ed. —Zephyrhills, Fla. : Joyce Record Club, 1987. — 33, 5 leaves. ISBN not given.
1st edition, 1976.
A detailed discography, with information on all sessions, soundtracks, and transcriptions, including dates and locations, matrix numbers, original labels and reissues, personnel, and explanatory notes. With a song title index.

S2-292   ML156.7 .C52 G24
Garrod, Charles. Bob Chester and his orchestra / Charles Garrod and Bill Korst. — Rev. ed. — Zephyrhills, Fla. : Joyce Record Club, 1987. — 18, 7 leaves. ISBN not given.
1st edition, 1974.
Chester led a big band with a Glenn Miller type of sound. Vocalist Dolores O'Neill brightened the ensemble for two years. This is a thorough discography, covering sessions and broadcast transcriptions from 1936 to 1951, with locations and dates, personnel, matrix numbers, original labels and reissues, and explanatory comments. With a song title index.

S2-293   ML156.7 .C565
Garrod, Charles. Buddy Clark / Charles Garrod and Bob Gottlieb. — Zephyrhills, Fla. : Joyce Record Club, 1991. — 44, 10 p. ISBN not given.
Clark (1911–1949) was a vocalist who sang with Benny Goodman, on his own radio shows, and in motion pictures. His recording sessions are detailed here, from 1934 to 1949. Recordings from radio are included. Among the bands and soloists were Eddy Duchin, Xavier Cugat, Skitch Henderson, Freddy Martin, Percy Faith, Dinah Shore, Jane Powell, Evelyn Knight, and Margaret Whiting. Dates, personnel, matrix numbers, and labels are given. There is a song title index.

S2-294   ML156.7 .C57 W44
Weir, Bob. Buck Clayton discography / Bob Weir. — Chigwell, Essex, England : Storyville, 1989. — x, 258 p. : ill. ISBN 0-902391-119.
Trumpeter Clayton was most prominent in the late 1930s, when he played with Count Basie and recorded with Billie Holiday. This discography covers 1934–1984, giving full data on all sessions, including the

producers' names, dates, locations, durations of the pieces, labels, and reissues. Coverage includes commercial and private discs, tapes, and films. With indexes of musicians, vocalists, band names, songs, and composers.

S2-295   ML156.7 .C65 G24
Garrod, Charles. Larry Clinton and his orchestra / Charles Garrod. — Rev. ed. —Zephyrhills, Fla. : Joyce Record Club, 1990. — 26, 10 leaves. ISBN not given.
1st ed., 1973.
Larry Clinton (1909–1985) was an arranger, composer, and big-band leader, prominent in the 1930s and 1940s. "My Reverie" and "Our Love" were two of his compositions recorded with great success by his vocalist Bea Wain; she also sang on his most acclaimed disc, "Deep Purple." Garrod's list includes commercial discs, transcriptions, films, and tapes that "are today either in the hands of collectors, dealers or libraries." About a hundred sessions are covered, from 1937 to 1961, with all the songs recorded (or broadcast) in each, dates and locations, labels, matrix numbers, personnel, and reissues. With an index of song titles.

S2-296   ML156.7 .C68
Garrod, Charles. Nat King Cole : his voice and piano / Charles Garrod and Bill Korst. — Zephyrhills, Fla. : Joyce Record Club, 1987. — 70 leaves. ISBN not given.
Singer/pianist Cole (1916–1965) had more than 100 chart records over a 23-year span and won two Grammys. See note at S2-285.

S2-297   ML156.7 .C69 H71
Hofmann, Coen. Man of many parts : a discography of Buddy Collette / Coen Hofmann; foreword by Lyle Murphy. — Amsterdam : Micrography, 1985. — Unpaged : ill. ISBN 90-6419-018-6.
Collette is a well-known jazz artist based on the West Coast, who plays flute, clarinet, and saxophone. A 1981 interview gives a background picture of the performer, and the discography lists all his commercial and private recordings and soundtracks from 1945 to 1981. Full information is given for each entry, including locations and dates, personnel, matrix numbers and labels, with commentaries. There is an index of performers.

S2-298   ML156.7 .C7 M67
Morgereth, Timothy A. Bing Crosby : a discography, radio program list, and filmography / Timothy A. Morgereth. — Jefferson, N.C. : McFarland, 1987. — xvii, 554 p. : ill. ISBN 0-89950-210-5.
All known 78rpm recordings (American, British, Canadian, Aus-

tralian, South African) by Crosby are presented in date order with full discographical data (locale, personnel, matrix number, release label, comments). Radio and film appearances are also listed. There are 2,395 entries in all. This valuable compilation includes a nonexpansive index of names and titles.
Review: ARBA 1988, #1298.

S2-299   ML156.7 .C94 G24
Garrod, Charles. Bob Crosby and his orchestra / Charles Garrod and Bill Korst. — Zephyrhills, Fla. : Joyce Record Club, 1987. — 53, 9 leaves. ISBN not given.
Bob Crosby (1913–1993) led a big band that was notable for its up-dated Dixieland style and for outstanding sidemen such as Billy Butterfield, Eddie Miller, Matty Matlock, Muggsy Spanier, Charlie Spivak, and Jess Stacy. A small group, the Bob Cats, was innovative and highly popular. He recorded with great vocalists, such as Connee Boswell, Doris Day, the Andrews Sisters, and his brother Bing. This is an inventory of the orchestra's and Bob Cats' recorded output from 1935 to 1961, including radio broadcasts. Locations, dates, matrix numbers, labels and reissues, personnel, and explanatory comments are given. With a song title index.

S2-300   ML156.7 .D67 R35
Reichardt, Uwe. Like a human voice : the Eric Dolphy discography / Uwe Reichardt. — Schmitten, Germany : Ruecker, 1986. — iv, 80 p. (Jazz index reference series, 2) ISBN 3-923397-03-8.
Consists of "all known recorded sessions" by Dolphy (saxophonist, flutist, clarinetist), excluding unauthorized tapes, 1949–1964. Full discographical data: dates, locations, matrix numbers, labels and issues, personnel, and commentaries. With indexes to album titles, song titles, and musicians.

S2-301   ML156.7 .D69
Garrod, Charles. Sam Donahue and his orchestra / Charles Garrod and Bill Korst. — Zephyrhills, Fla. : Joyce Record Club, 1992. — 21, 7 p. ISBN not given.
Donahue (1918–1974) was a tenor saxophonist who played with Gene Krupa, Harry James, Benny Goodman, Tommy Dorsey, and Stan Kenton; he had his own band at various times and led the Tommy Dorsey Orchestra in the 1960s. This discography is limited to sessions made by Donahue as leader, from 1940 to 1965. Radio broadcasts are included. Dates, personnel, matrix numbers, labels, and comments are given.

S2-302   ML156.7 .D7
Garrod, Charles. Jimmy Dorsey and his orchestra / Charles Garrod. —
Rev. ed. — Zephyrhills, Fla. : Joyce Record Club, 1988. — 65 leaves.
ISBN not given.
Jimmy Dorsey (1904–1957), brother of Tommy Dorsey, was a clar-
inetist in a band that the brothers shared in 1934–1935. Then he formed
his own ensemble, which became one of the premier groups of the late
1930s and 1940s, featuring outstanding vocalists Bob Eberly and Helen
O'Connell. See note at S2-285.

S2-303   ML156.7 .D71 G3
Garrod, Charles. Tommy Dorsey and his orchestra; volume one,
1928–1945; volume two, 1946–1956 [bound together] / Charles Garrod,
Walter Scott, and Frank Green. — Rev. ed. —Zephyrhills, Fla. : Joyce
Record Club, 1988. — Vol. 1, 84, 9 leaves; vol. 2, 72, 7 leaves. ISBN
not given.
1st ed., 1980.
Tommy Dorsey (1905–1956) led one of the greatest big bands, featuring his own dulcet trombone and such star vocalists as Frank Sinatra
and Jo Stafford. This is a fine compilation of Dorsey's recordings (including radio broadcasts) from 1928 to 1956. Discographical information is thorough for each entry: dates, locations, matrix numbers, labels
and reissues, personnel, and comments. With a song title index.

S2-304   ML156.7 .D9
Garrod, Charles. Eddy Duchin and his orchestra / Charles Garrod. —
Zephyrhills, Fla. : Joyce Record Club, 1989. — 28 leaves. ISBN not given.
Pianist and big-band leader Duchin (1910–1951) was one of the most
popular performers of 1934–1940. A motion picture was made of his ca-
reer in 1956. See note at S2-285.

S2-305   ML156.7 .E3 K4
Kiner, Larry F. Nelson Eddy : a bio-discography / Larry F. Kiner;
foreword by Sharon Rich. — Metuchen, N.J. : Scarecrow, 1992. — 709
p. : ill. ISBN 0-8108-2544-9.
The ultimate discography of Eddy (1901–1967), a baritone best remembered for his film musicals made with Jeanette MacDonald (*May-
time, Naughty Marietta, Sweethearts,* etc.). All his performances that
made their way to disc are listed, including radio programs and motion
pictures, from 1929 through 1967. Data for each entry are date and location, matrix numbers and takes, release labels, personnel, and extensive comments. Indexes give Eddy's opera appearances (not many, and
just one at the Metropolitan Opera), his films in sequence, his co-stars
and their films, and song titles. Without a general index.

S2-306   ML156.7 .E3 K5
Kiner, Larry F. The Cliff Edwards discography / Larry F. Kiner. —
New York : Greenwood, 1987. — 260 p. : ill. ISBN 0-313-25719-1.

A thorough record listing for popular singer and ukulele player Edwards (1895–1972), known as "Ukulele Ike" on radio and in motion pictures. His recording sessions and radio transcriptions are carefully described, with matrix numbers, release dates and labels, and personnel. There is also a brief biography, a list of his songs and shows, a filmography, bibliography, and index.

S2-307   ML156.7 .E45 T5
Timner, W. E. Eillingtonia : the recorded music of Duke Ellington and his sidemen / W. E. Timner; foreword by Dan Morgenstern. — 3rd ed. — Metuchen, 'N.J. : Scarecrow, 1988. — xiv, 534 p. (Studies in jazz, 7) ISBN 0-8108-1934-1. (Alternative classification: ML156.5.)

1st ed., 1976; 2nd ed., 1979 (LOAM Suppl. S-648).

The definitive discography of Duke Ellington (1899–1974) and his associates, presented in chronological order from 1923 to 1974. Complete data on each issue are provided, included location, personnel for each number, matrix numbers, and original release labels. An alphabetical list of song titles with their recording dates follows, and there is an ingenious graphic display that shows which musicians performed on given dates. Further lists reveal the recordings made by Ellington's sidemen on their own, or with other groups. This is such a splendid work that Timner will be forgiven for his unhappy inspiration of rendering all personal names and label names throughout in cryptic abbreviations.

Reviews: ARBA 1989, #1237; *Choice* 3/89, 1175.

S2-308   ML156.7 .E6 W37
Wattiau, Georges. Book's book : a discography of Booker Ervin / Georges Wattiau. — Amsterdam : Micrography, 1987. — 29 p. ISBN 90-6419-025-9.

Booker Ervin (1930–1970) was a Texas tenor saxophonist who played with various groups in the 1950s and 1960s. This discography covers his work on 14 labels from 1957 to 1969. Information given is exhaustive: matrix, dates and locations, personnel, timing of each song, reissues, and comments by Wattiau. With an index of musicians and another of song titles.

S2-309   ML156.7 .E9 L31
Larson, Peter H. Turn on the stars : Bill Evans : the complete discography / Peter H. Larsen. — Holte, Denmark : Author, 1984. — 125 p. : ill. ISBN 87-981653-0-5.

A thorough discography of jazz pianist Evans (1954–1980), covering discs and tapes. Dates, locations, matrix numbers, personnel, timings, original labels and reissues, and comments are given for 215 sessions. Eighteen tribute records are also listed. With indexes of musicians, song titles, and album titles.

S2-310   ML156.7 .F46 G24
Garrod, Charles. Shep Fields and his orchestra / Charles Garrod. — Zephyrhills, Fla. : Joyce Record Club, 1987. — 29, 7 leaves. ISBN not given.
The "rippling rhythm" of Shep Fields (1910–1981) was one of the most distinctive sounds of the big band era. He made more than 300 Bluebird records. Garrod lists here about 150 record sessions and broadcasts from 1936 to 1957, and two others from uncertain later dates. The information includes dates and locations, labels, matrix numbers, personnel, and reissues. With an index of song titles.

S2-311   ML156.7 .F58 G24
Garrod, Charles. Ralph Flanagan and his orchestra / Charles Garrod. — Rev. ed. — Zephyrhills, Fla. : Joyce Record Club, 1990. — 41, 5 leaves. ISBN not given.
1st ed., 1985.
Ralph Flanagan was one of the last big band leaders to achieve national prominence. This list covers his commercial discs, broadcast transcriptions, and tapes from 1949 to 1965; there are some 200 sessions in all. Full recording information is given: dates and locations, labels, matrix numbers, personnel, and reissues. With an index of song titles.

S2-312   ML156.7 .F6
Garrod, Charles. Chuck Foster and his orchestra / Charles Garrod. — Zephyrhills, Fla. : Joyce Record Club, 1992. — 31 leaves. ISBN not given.
Foster directed a big band that found a certain popularity on the West Coast and later in the Midwest. See note at S2-285.

S2-313   ML156.7 .G66 C57
Connor, D. Russell. Benny Goodman : listen to his legacy / D. Russell Connor. — Metuchen, N.J. : Scarecrow Press and the Institute of Jazz Studies, 1988. — xvii, 357 p. : ill. (Studies in jazz, 6) ISBN 0-8108-2095-1.
The definitive discography of Goodman, presenting a remarkable richness of detail for all the recordings from 1926 to 1986. All circumstances and personnel of each recording session are given, with elaborate explanatory notes that illuminate the era and Goodman's life, as well as the session itself. Unpublished material, such as rehearsal tapes, is included.

Reissues are identified as well. Indexes of 1,400 performers and some 1,900 song titles.
Reviews: ARBA 1989, p. 489; *Choice* 1/89, 778.

S2-314   ML156.7 .G67 H77
Hoogeveen, Gerard J. Meet Mr. Gordon : a discography of Bob Gordon / Gerard J. Hoogeveen. — Amsterdam : Micrography, 1987. — Unpaged. ISBN 90-6419-024-0.
Gordon (1928–1955) was a tenor and baritone saxophone player who performed with many groups, including those of Jack Montrose, Maynard Ferguson, and Shelley Manne. The discography covers studio recordings from 1949 to 1955, giving full discographical data: dates and locations, matrix numbers, labels and reissues, personnel, and comments. With indexes of album titles, song titles, and musicians.

S2-315   ML156.7 .G78 G24
Garrod, Charles. Glen Gray and the Casa Loma Orchestra / Charles Garrod and Bill Korst. — Zephyrhills, Fla. : Joyce Record Club, 1987. — 38, 7 leaves. ISBN not given.
Named for the hotel in Toronto where it was established in 1928, the Casa Loma Orchestra was one of the outstanding ensembles of the big band era. Gray (1906–1963) was its leader from 1929, though he did not "front" the band until 1937. Garrod's discography covers 1929 to 1961, and includes studio and radio broadcast recordings made under the orchestra's other names (Carolina Club Orchestra, Ariel Dance Orchestra, etc.). Information given is thorough: dates and locations, matrix numbers, labels and reissues, personnel, and commentaries. With a song title index.

S2-316   ML156.7 .H36 G4
Garrod, Charles. Erskine Hawkins and his orchestra / Charles Garrod. — Zephyrhills, Fla. : Joyce Record Club, 1992. — 17, 6 leaves. ISBN not given.
Hawkins (1914–), trumpeter and big-band leader, composed the hit song "Tuxedo Junction." He recorded from 1936 to 1971, with his orchestra or in smaller groups. The discography gives dates, matrix numbers, personnel, labels, and a few comments. With a song title index.

S2-317   ML156.7 .H37 G4
Garrod, Charles. Dick Haymes / Charles Garrod and Denis Brown; with special help from Roger Dooner and the Dick Haymes Society. — Zephyrhills, Fla. : Joyce Record Club, 1990. — 73, 10 leaves. ISBN not given.
Dick Haymes (1916–1980) was a popular vocalist in the 1940s and

early 1950s, often associated with Harry James who gave him an early
break. This chronologically arranged discography includes details of
personnel, place and date of recording, matrix number and song titles,
and label numbers for various releases. Radio and television broadcasts
are also included. There is no explanation about how the discography
was compiled, what releases were included, etc. The index includes only
song titles [—D.P.].

S2-318   ML156.7 .H4 M4
Matesich, Ken. Jimi Hendrix : a discography / Ken Matesich and
Dave Armstrong. — Rev. ed. — Tucson, Ariz. : J. H. Discography,
1982. — 53 p. ISBN not given.
    1st ed., 1981 (LOAM Suppl. SA-802).
    An LP discography, from 1965 to 1970, of the rock guitarist and singer
(1942–1970). Release dates, labels, contents, and personnel are the only
discographical features. Without indexes.

S2-319   ML156.7 .H411
Garrod, Charles. Woody Herman, vol. 1 (1936–1947) / Charles Garrod. — Zephyrhills, Fla. : Joyce Record Club, 1985. — 60 leaves. ISBN
not given.
    Herman (1913–1987) was a major clarinetist and from 1936 leader of
a number of progressive big bands (known as "Herds"). Dave Tough
(drums) and Stan Getz (tenor sax) were among the many star performers who worked with Herman, who remained a prominent figure on the
musical scene into the 1970s. See the two following entries and the note
at S2-285.

S2-320   ML156.7 .H422
Garrod, Charles. Woody Herman, vol. 2 (1948–1957) / Charles Garrod. — Zephyrhills, Fla. : Joyce Record Club, 1986. — 64 leaves. ISBN
not given.
    See S2-319.

S2-321   ML156.7 .H433
Garrod, Charles. Woody Herman, vol. 3 (1958–1987) / Charles Garrod. — Zephyrhills, Fla. : Joyce Record Club, 1988. — 57 leaves. ISBN
not given.
    See S2-319.

S2-322   ML156.7 .H444 M7
Morrill, Dexter. Woody Herman : a guide to the big band recordings,
1936–1987 / Dexter Morrill. — New York: Greenwood, 1990. — xiii,
129 p. ISBN 0-313-27756-7.

After a useful narrative chapter that describes the numerous Herman "Herds" and his various later groups, Morrill provides an inventory of all the recordings (except a few he could not access) from 1936 to 1981, identifying solo instrumentalists, vocalists, and arrangers. Curiously, the original recording information (labels, locations, matrixes) is missing; instead, there is for each number a citation code that brings the user to an LP album list later in the volume. Thus the compilation is more of a checklist (and a useful one) than a discography. With an index of song titles.
　　Reviews: ARBA 1992, p. 531; *Choice* 5/91, 1464.

S2-323　　ML156.7 .J211
Garrod, Charles. Harry James and his orchestra (1937–1945) / Charles Garrod. — Zephyrhills, Fla. : Joyce Record Club, 1985. — 66 leaves. ISBN not given.
Jazz trumpeter James (1916–1983) was a principal soloist with Benny Goodman, then formed his own big band in 1938, achieving great acclaim for 30 years. Among his notable vocalists were Frank Sinatra, Dick Haymes, Kitty Kallen, and Helen Forrest. See the two following entries and the note at S2-285.

S2-324　　ML156.7 .J222
Garrod, Charles. Harry James and his orchestra (1946–1954) / Charles Garrod. — Zephyrhills, Fla. : Joyce Record Club, 1985. — 70 leaves. ISBN not given.
See S2-323.

S2-325　　ML156.7 .J233
Garrod, Charles. Harry James and his orchestra (1955–1982) / Charles Garrod. — Zephyrhills, Fla. : Joyce Record Club, 1985. — 65 leaves. ISBN not given.
See S2-323.

S2-326　　ML156.7 .J62 T84
Trolle, Frank H. James P. Johnson : father of the stride piano / Frank H. Trolle; with contributions by Bill Moss, Kenneth G. Noble, and Michael Montgomery; ed. and annotated by Dick M. Bakker. — Alphen an de Rijn, Netherlands : Micrography, 1981. — 2 vols. : vol. 1, 48 p.; vol. 2, unpaged. ISBN 90-6419-011-9; 90-6419-012-7.
　　A list of 188 recording sessions, from 1917 to 1949, including piano rolls and 78 rpm discs. Locations, dates, matrix numbers, and reissues are noted. With title and label indexes.

S2-327　　ML156.7 .J64 K4
Kiner, Larry F. Al Jolson : a bio-discography / Larry F. Kiner;

foreword by Leonard Maltin. — Metuchen, N.J. : Scarecrow, 1992. — xxii, 808 p. ISBN 0-8108-2633-X.

A splendid discography of Jolson (1886–1950), who was a persistently popular recording artist for 40 years. Kiner's list of records is remarkably detailed, including extended comments on Jolson's life situation at the time of each recording. Radio transcriptions, LP reissues, and cassettes are listed along with originals; information for each entry includes location and date, matrix number, takes, labels, personnel, and comments; sheet music and disc labels are illustrated as well. An appendix list of song sheets with Jolson pictured is of special interest. There is also a list of his compositions, a bibliography of reviews grouped by magazine, a list of his conductors, a list of movie and radio appearances, and a song title index. The only defect in this volume is that it is about twice as bulky as it needed to be, a condition brought about by huge type sizes and empty page spaces.

Reviews: ARBA 1985, p. 433; *Choice* 6/84, 448.

S2-328   ML156.7 .J653 I92

Iwamoto, Shin-ichi. Have you met mister Jones : Hank Jones : a discography / Shin-ichi Iwamoto. — Rev. ed. — Tokyo : Sun Copy Center, 1989. — 420 p. ISBN not given.

A thorough list of recordings, covering 1944–1989, with full discographical detail (location of session, matrix, dates, personnel, reissues). Index of labels, names, and song titles. Jones was a pianist who worked with Benny Goodman, Artie Shaw, and many other groups. User confidence in the facts offered in the book will be disturbed by the extremely poor English and innumerable misspellings (e.g., the song title "Lady in Bed," "dabbing" for "dubbing"); a proofreading by an English speaker would have removed the cloud of carelessness that clings to the volume.

S2-329   ML156.7 .J655

Garrod, Charles. Spike Jones and the City Slickers / Charles Garrod. — Zephyrhills, Fla. : Joyce Record Club, 1989. — 39 leaves. ISBN not given.

Drummer, big-band leader, and satirist, Jones (1911–1965) found sudden fame with his novelty record "Der Fuehrer's Face" in 1942 and was popular through the 1940s for like material. See note at S2-285.

Review: *Choice* 11/86, 489.

S2-330   ML156.7 .J66 M6

Mirtle, Jack. Thank you, music lovers: a bio-discography of Spike Jones and his City Slickers / Jack Mirtle and Ted Hering; foreword by Peter Schickele. — Westport, Conn. : Greenwood, 1986. — xxii, 426 p. : ill. (Discographies, 20) ISBN 0-313-24814-1.

A brief bio-sketch of Jones, followed by a chronology of his recording dates and concert appearances from 1941 to 1965. Discographical information includes dates and locations, matrix numbers, labels and reissues, personnel, and extensive commentaries. Unreleased titles, spin-off records, domestic and foreign LP issues, V-Discs, and Armed Forces Radio Service transcriptions are listed in appendices. With indexes for personnel and song titles.

S2-331 ML156.7 .J67 S6
Sjogren, Thorbjorn. The Duke Jordan discography / Thorbjorn Sjogren. — Rev. ed. — Copenhagen : Author, 1984. — 74 p. ISBN not given.
1st edition, 1982 (LOAM Suppl. SA-377).
Pianist Jordan (1922–) took up residence in Denmark, inspiring this inventory of his recordings from 1945 to 1984, including private tapes and unissued material. Art Blakey, Miles Davis, Charlie Parker, and Sonny Stitt are among the musicians with whom he recorded; there is a list of his partners in the book, but no other indexing.

S2-332 ML156.7 .J9
Garrod, Charles. Dick Jurgens and his orchestra / Charles Garrod. — Zephyrhills, Fla. : Joyce Record Club, 1988. — 35 leaves. ISBN not given.
Band leader Jurgens (1910–) led one of the mellow ensembles of the 1930s and composed several hit songs (e.g., "Careless," "A Million Dreams Ago"). See note at S2-285.

S2-333 ML156.7 .K23 G24
Garrod, Charles. Sammy Kaye and his orchestra / Charles Garrod. — Zephyrhills, Fla. : Joyce Record Club, 1988. — 72, 14 leaves. ISBN not given.
The sweet-style big band of Kaye (1910–1987), with its "singing song title" announcements, was one of the most popular for the longest time; it continued performing into the 1970s. This inventory of his studio and radio recordings spans 1937 to 1971, offering full discographical data: dates and locations, matrix numbers, labels and reissues, personnel, and commentaries. With a song title index.

S2-334 ML156.7 .K28 G4
Garrod, Charles. Hal Kemp and his orchestra : plus Art Jarrett and his orchestra / Charles Garrod. — Zephyrhills, Fla. : Joyce Record Club, 1990. — 30, 6 leaves [for Kemp]; 3, 1 leaves [for Jarrett]. ISBN not given.
Kemp (1905–1940) directed a major big band in the 1920s and 1930s,

featuring vocalist Skinnay Ennis. Recordings are listed here from 1924
to 1940, including early ones that appeared under such names as the Carolina Club Orchestra and the Canadian Club Orchestra. Discographical
information is full: dates and locations, matrix numbers, labels and reissues, personnel, and commentaries. Art Jarrett took over the band when
Kemp was killed in an auto accident in 1940; his records to 1942 are
listed in a brief appendix. There are separate song title indexes for Kemp
and Jarrett records.

S2-335   ML156.7 .K411 G2
Garrod, Charles. Stan Kenton and his orchestra (1940–1951) / Charles
Garrod. — Zephyrhills, Fla. : Joyce Record Club, 1984. — 64 leaves.
ISBN not given.
One of the progressive, sophisticated big band leaders, Kenton (1911–
1979) was prominent for 20 years, performing in Carnegie Hall as well
as on college campuses. Anita O'Day and June Christy were among his
star singers, and such great artists as Lee Konitz (alto sax), Stan Getz
(tenor sax), and Shelly Manne (drums) were in his group at one time or
another. See also S2-336 and the note at S2-285.

S2-336   ML156.7 .K422 G2
Garrod, Charles. Stan Kenton and his orchestra (1952–1959) / Charles
Garrod. — Zephyrhills, Fla. : Joyce Record Club, 1984. — 64 leaves.
ISBN not given.
See S2-335.

S2-337   ML156.7 .K48
Garrod, Charles. John Kirby and his orchestra : Andy Kirk and his orchestra / Charles Garrod. — Zephyrhills, Fla. : Joyce Record Club,
1991. — 16, 2, 14, 3 p. ISBN not given.
Two discographies bound in one volume, covering Kirby (1908–
1952) and Kirk (1898–1992), both big band leaders. Kirby played bass
with Fletcher Henderson and Chick Webb before organizing his popular
Onyx Club Boys in 1937. His recording sessions are detailed from 1938
to 1948; many feature trumpeter Charlie Shavers. Kirk was a bass saxophonist who gained fame directing the Clouds of Joy in Kansas City, featuring his wife, Mary Lou Williams, as pianist and arranger; Pha Terrell
was one of his star vocalists. Kirk's records are listed from 1929 to 1956.
For both discographies, the information given includes dates, matrix
numbers, personnel, labels, and some comments. There are song title indexes for both discographies.

S2-338   ML156.7 .K811
Garrod, Charles. Gene Krupa and his orchestra (1935–1946) / Charles

Garrod and Bill Korst. — Zephyrhills, Fla. : Joyce Record Club, 1984. — 51 leaves. ISBN not given.

The most renowned jazz drummer of the big band era, Krupa (1909–1973) did his most distinguished work with Benny Goodman in the mid-1930s. He then had several bands of his own and toured with Jazz at the Philharmonic. See also S2-339 and the note at S2-285.

S2-339   ML156.7 .K822

Garrod, Charles. Gene Krupa and his orchestra (1947–1973) / Charles Garrod and Bill Korst. — Zephyrhills, Fla. : Joyce Record Club, 1984. — 63 leaves. ISBN not given.

See S2-338.

S2-340   ML156.7 .K92 G4

Garrod, Charles. Kay Kyser and his orchestra / Charles Garrod. — Rev. ed. — Zephyrhills, Fla. : Joyce Record Club, 1990. — 45, 7 leaves. ISBN not given.

1st ed., 1986.

A thorough list of records by one of the most popular of the sweet big bands. Kyser (1906–1985) blended showmanship, humor, innovation, and outstanding vocalists (notably Harry Babbitt, Ginny Simms, and Sully Mason) into a unique entertainment phenomenon. The discography covers 1927–1950, giving dates, locations, matrix numbers, label numbers, personnel, and extensive comments. With a song title index.

S2-341   ML156.7 .M33 G24

Garrod, Charles. Freddy Martin and his orchestra / Charles Garrod. — Zephyrhills, Fla. : Joyce Record Club, 1987. — 68, 12 leaves. ISBN not given.

Martin (1906–1983) directed one of the quintessential dance bands, active in film, radio, and major venues into the 1970s. This discography covers his commercial discs, radio transcriptions, and soundtracks, giving dates, locations, matrix and label numbers, reissues, personnel, and comments. With a song title index.

S2-342   ML156.7 .M35 W7

Worth, Paul W. John McCormack : a comprehensive discography / Paul W. Worth and Jim Cartwright. — Westport, Conn. : Greenwood, 1986. — lii, 184 p. : ill. (Discographies, 21) ISBN 0-313-24728-5.

A definitive chronological inventory of records made by tenor McCormack (1884–1945), who worked for many labels and produced numerous magnificent discs. Worth updates and extends earlier discographies by including LP reissues, unpublished records, alternative takes, film material, and radio transcriptions. Accompanying artists are identified also, locales are given, and playing speeds are specified. With an index of performers and a title index.

Reviews: ARBA 1987, #1258; *Choice* 11/86, 490.

S2-343   ML156.7 .M5

Way, Chris. In the Miller mood : a history and discography of the Glenn Miller service band, 1942–1945 / Chris Way; preface by Herb Miller. — [n.p.] : Author, 1987. — xlix, 613 p. : ill. : 12 p. plates. ISBN not given.

Glenn Miller (1904–1944), a trombonist with several big bands, organized his own group in 1937 and quickly became one of the great names in popular music. His vocalists included Ray Eberle, Marion Hutton, and Tex Beneke. Miller enlisted in the Army Air Force in 1942 and organized the outstanding service band that is chronicled in this book (and also in S2-959 and S2-1139).

S2-344   ML156.7 .M75 B54

Bijl, Leen. Monk on records / Leen Bijl and Fred Canté. — 2nd ed. — Amsterdam : Golden Age Records, 1985. — 99 p. ISBN not given.

1st ed., 1982.

Thelonious Monk (1917–1982) was an innovator in jazz piano, greatly successful in the late 1950s. His studio and radio recordings of 1941–1972 are listed here in great detail, with dates, locations, matrix and label numbers, playing times of individual numbers, LP reissues, personnel, and extended comments that refer to other discographies. About a hundred labels are included. With indexes of performers and song titles.

S2-345   ML156.7 .M85 A87

Astrup, Arne. Gerry Mulligan discography / Arne Astrup. — Soeburg, Denmark : Bidstrup, 1989. — xi, 106 p. ISBN 87-983242-0-9.

The Mulligan studio and radio recordings of 1945–1990 are listed here with dates and locations, matrix and label numbers, reissues, personnel, and comments. With a song title index, musician index, and a list of principal albums.

S2-346   ML156.7 .N4

Garrod, Charles. Ozzie Nelson and his orchestra / Charles Garrod and Bill Korst. — Zephyrhills, Fla. : Joyce Record Club, 1991. — 18 leaves. ISBN not given.

Nelson led one of the smooth big bands, featuring his wife, Harriet Hilliard, as vocalist. The two became famous for their television sitcom *Adventures of Ozzie and Harriet* and for their rock-star son, Ricky Nelson. See note at S2-285.

S2-347   ML156.7 .N6
Garrod, Charles. Ray Noble and his orchestra / Charles Garrod. —
Zephyrhills, Fla. : Joyce Record Club, 1991. — 66 leaves. ISBN not
given.
British-born Ray Noble (1903–1978) led a highly successful sweet-
swing band in the United States during the 1930s and 1940s, with the
great Al Bowlly as one of the vocalists. Among the performers in his
1935 ensemble were Glenn Miller, Charlie Spivak, Bud Freeman, and
Claude Thornhill. See note at S2-285.

S2-348   ML156.7 .O7
Garrod, Charles. Will Osborne and his orchestra / Charles Garrod. —
Zephyrhills, Fla. : Joyce Record Club, 1991. — 22 leaves. ISBN not
given.
Osborne was a vocalist (with Abe Lyman and others) who formed
his first big band in 1935 and had a couple of later groups. See note at
S2-285.

S2-349   ML156.7 .P35 K6
Koch, Lawrence O. Yardbird suite : a compendium of the music and
life of Charlie Parker / Lawrence O. Koch. — Bowling Green, Ohio :
Bowling Green State University Popular Press, 1988. — 336 p. ISBN 0-
87972-259-2.
A useful attempt to document the Charlie Parker records. It is a footnoted, chronological, biographical account, with information and technical comments on recordings as they come along in the narrative. Music examples appear frequently, although they are handwritten and often
difficult to decipher. Koch's unique contribution is to assign catalog
numbers to the records and list them accordingly in an appendix; the result is a kind of Koechel listing of Parker's work from 1940 to 1954, in
which every session has its permanent designator. With an index to song
titles, but no general index.
Review: *Choice* 5/89, 1528.

S2-350   ML156.7 .P96
Osborne, Jerry. The Elvis Presley record price guide / Jerry Osborne. —
3rd ed. — Port Townsend, Wash. : Jellyroll Publications, 1992. — 216
p. : ill. ISBN 0-9321-1717-1.

S2-351   ML156.7 .R613
Boyd, Brian G. Willard Robison and his piano : a discography / Brian
G. Boyd. — Toronto : Author, 1990. — 38 p. : ill. ISBN not given.
A thorough record list for the popular singer/pianist (1894–1968),

active on radio in the 1920s and 1930s. Discs and piano rolls are included, and full discographical information is given.

S2-352   ML156.7 .R73 H69
Hofmann, Coen. Shorty Rogers : a discography / Coen Hofmann and Erik M. Bakker. — Amsterdam : Micrography, 1983. — 2 vols. Unpaged. ISBN 90-6419-014-3; 90-6419-015-1.

Trumpeter Rogers performed with major groups, including those of Woody Herman, Stan Kenton, and Shelly Manne, and also had his own ensemble. These two books list his recordings from 1945 to 1969, giving dates and locations, matrix and label numbers, reissues, personnel, and comments. There are indexes to musicians and song titles.

S2-353   ML156.7 .R95
Hilbert, Robert. Pee Wee speaks : a discography of Pee Wee Russell / Robert Hilbert; with David Niven. — Metuchen, N.J. : Scarecrow, 1992. — 377 p. (Studies in jazz, 13) ISBN 0-8108-2634-8.

A thorough record list for clarinetist Russell (1906–1969), whose sessions began in 1922 and continued to 1968. His notable performances were made with many distinguished artists, including Jack Teagarden, Bix Beiderbecke, Red Nichols, Thelonious Monk, John Coltrane, and Buck Clayton. All known recorded performances are listed, including radio, television, and motion picture work. Dates, locations, personnel, matrix numbers, release labels and numbers, and extensive comments are presented. With a nonexpansive index of musicians.

Review: *Choice* 7-8/93, 1780.

S2-354   ML156.7 .S22
Hall, George. Jan Savitt and his orchestra / George Hall. — Zephyrhills, Fla. : Joyce Record Club, 1985. — 32 leaves. ISBN not given.

Russian-born Savitt (1913–1948) grew up in Philadelphia and formed his first band there, gaining a reputation for attractive swing and dance arrangements. See note at S2-285.

S2-355   ML156.7 .S35
Garrod, Charles. Bobby Sherwood and his orchestra : plus Randy Brooks and his orchestra / Charles Garrod. — Zephyrhills, Fla. : Joyce Record Club, 1987. — 14, 5 leaves; 11, 4 leaves. ISBN not given.

The output of two lesser-known dance bands, covering Sherwood's discs of 1942–1954 and Brooks's of 1945–1948. Information for each record includes location, date, matrix, label, reissues, personnel, and explanatory comment. With song title indexes for each band.

S2-356   ML156.7 .S4
Garrod, Charles. Artie Shaw and his orchestra / Charles Garrod and

Bill Korst. — Zephyrhills, Fla. : Joyce Record Club, 1986. — 64 leaves. ISBN not given.

Shaw (1910–) gained fame as one of the great jazz clarinetists and for his outstanding big bands. Vocalist Helen Forrest made such remarkable recordings as "Begin the Beguine" and "All the Things You Are," and the band's 1940 hit "Frenesi" became a landmark. See note at S2-285.

S2-357   ML156.7 .S56 A25

Ackelson, Richard W. Frank Sinatra : a complete recording history of techniques, songs, composers, lyricists, arrangers, sessions, and first issue albums, 1939–1984 / Richard W. Ackelson. — Jefferson, N.C. : McFarland, 1992. — xiii, 466 p. ISBN 0-89950-554-6.

A useful list of Sinatra's recorded song repertoire, 1,251 titles in alphabetical order. For each entry the information includes arranger, accompanying artists, and citation of the album in which it appeared or the release date for singles. The facts are presented also in several other arrays: a chronological (1939–1984) session list; a chronological album list, with contents and comments; and a singles list. The zealous compiler also offers the songs in order by publication date, by composer, by lyricist, and by arranger. With a nonexpansive index.

S2-358   ML156.7 .S56 G2

Garrod, Charles. Frank Sinatra, 1935–1951 [and] Frank Sinatra, 1952–1981 / Charles Garrod. — Zephyrhills, Fla. : Joyce Record Club, 1989, 1990. — 2 vols. [bound in one] : vol. 1, 92, 8 leaves; vol. 2, 84, 8 leaves. ISBN not given.

A thorough inventory of Sinatra's commercial discs, radio transcriptions, Armed Forces Radio Service material, and film recordings. Information given includes dates and locations, matrix and label numbers, reissues, personnel, and comments. Each volume has a song title index.

S2-359   ML156.7 .S56 S2

Sayers, Scott P. Sinatra, the man and his music : the recording artistry of Francis Albert Sinatra, 1939–1992 / Scott P. Sayers and Ed O'Brien. — 2nd ed. — Austin, Tex. : TSD Press, 1992. — vii, 303 p. : ill. ISBN 0-9343-6724-8.

1st ed., *The Sinatra Sessions, 1939–1980* (Dallas : Sinatra Society of America, 1980).

A list of commercial recordings, giving full discographical data: place and date, arranger, personnel, matrix and take numbers, release label and number, and comments. Reissues, including CDs, are noted. With a song title index. There is a separate filmography and list of soundtracks, a V-Disc list, a list of chart records, CDs, and Grammy nominations and awards. Photos are interspersed. Without index.

S2-360   ML156.7 .S8
Garrod, Charles. Charlie Spivak and his orchestra / Charles Garrod. —
Zephyrhills, Fla. : Joyce Record Club, 1986. — 38 leaves. ISBN not
given.
Russian-born trumpeter Spivak (1905–1982) organized a sweet big
band in 1940, one of the most popular of its type. See S2-285.

S2-361   ML156.7 .T44
Garrod, Charles. Claude Thornhill and his orchestra / Charles Garrod. —
Zephyrhills, Fla. : Joyce Record Club, 1985. — 35 leaves. ISBN not
given.
Pianist Thornhill (1909–1965) played with many of the big bands and
also led his own groups. See S2-285.

S2-362   ML156.7 .V4 B7
Brown, Denis. Sarah Vaughan : a discography / Denis Brown. —
Westport, Conn. : Greenwood, 1991. — x, 166 p. (Discographies, 47)
ISBN 0-313-28005-3.
A detailed array of recordings by Vaughan (1924–1990), one of the
most admired vocalists of the 1940s and 1950s (in one six-month period,
more than 3 million of her records were sold). The basic list is chronological, from 1944 to 1988, with dates and locations, matrix and label
numbers, reissues, personnel, and comments. There is a separate label
listing of LPs, with contents, another label listing of singles and EPs, and
one of reissues and budget LPs. With indexes of song titles, composers,
musicians, and orchestras.

S2-363   ML156.7 .W4
VanEngelen, Piet. "Where's the music" : the discography of Kai
Winding / Piet VanEngelen. — Amsterdam : Micrography, 1985. — 2
vols. ISBN 90-6419-019-4; 90-6419-020-8.
A thorough list of recordings by trombonist Winding (1922–1983),
covering sessions of 1942–1982. Full discographical data; index by performer and title.

S2-364   ML156.7 .Y7 B76
Büchmann-Moller, Frank. You got to be original, man! : the music of
Lester Young / Frank Büchmann-Moller; foreword by Lewis Porter. —
New York : Greenwood, 1990. — xi, 528 p. (Discographies, 33) ISBN
0-313-26514-3.
A remarkable and valuable compilation of all the recorded solos by
Young, published or not; accounting for 251 recording sessions. The pre-
sentation is chronological, from 1936 to 1959. Complete discographical
detail is given, including matrix numbers and takes. An ingenious analy-

sis provides musical examples with symbols to express vibrato, accents, phrasing, and direction of the line. This is the sort of treatment generally lacking in jazz literature; one that is needed and welcome. With source notes, song title index, solo index, and nonexpansive name index. The author is a Danish librarian and saxophone player.

Reviews: AM 1993, 374; ARBA 1991, #1315; *Choice* 7-8/90, 1835.

ML158 : Miscellaneous

S2-365   ML158 .S9

Sutton, Allan. A guide to pseudonyms on American records, 1892–1942 / Allan Sutton. — Westport, Conn. : Greenwood, 1993. — xvii, 148 p. ISBN 0-313-29060-1.

During the 78rpm era, and especially during the three decades after 1910, it was the custom of the record manufacturers to identify many performers on discs with pseudonyms. In certain cases it was the smaller companies that indulged in the practice, companies that "lacking resources to attract exclusive artists, instead created a fanciful array of pseudonyms to lend an air of exclusiveness to the studio free-lance performers on whom they relied." Another reason was that various established artists under exclusive contract with one label "made clandestine visits to competing studios" and of course had to appear in nominal disguise. Then as major labels developed low-cost subsidiary labels, they often masked the names of their performers. To exemplify the extent of the practice, Vernon Dalhart had at least 56 known psuedonyms, and the Peerless Quartet had at least 13. Sutton's valuable research has produced the most extensive list available, some 2,500 *noms du disque* and a cross-list of the real names. Labels that used each name are cited. The user of this excellent work should note that even here not all the pseudonyms appear; in the *Encyclopedia of Recorded Sound in the United States* (S2-83) there is a shorter list (about 700 names), but quite a few pseudonymous instances are found there which Sutton has not included.

ML200–207 : HISTORY OF AMERICAN MUSIC

ML200–200.5 : General

S2-366   ML200 .C44

Crawford, Richard. A celebration of American music : words and music in honor of H. Wiley Hitchcock / ed. Richard Crawford, R. Allen Lott, and Carol J. Oja. — Ann Arbor : University of Michigan Press, 1989. — xi, 519 p. (Michigan American music series) ISBN 0-472-09400-9.

More than any other musicologist, Hitchcock has promoted American music; he is best known for the establishment and successful direction of the Institute for Studies in American Music, authorship of *Music in the United States* (S2-368), and co-editorship of the *New Grove Dictionary of American Music* (S2-65). This volume of interesting essays by friends and colleagues is a well-earned tribute to his decades of service to the cause. Among the scholars who contribute useful studies are Eileen Southern, Dena J. Epstein, Siegmund Levarie, Adrienne Fried Block, Steven Ledbetter, Nicolas Slonimsky, Carol Oja, Charles Hamm, Susan Feder, Wayne Shirley, and Donald Krummel. Richard Crawford presents a biographical sketch of Hitchcock, and someone not named compiled a bibliography of Hitchcock's published writings. With a non-expansive index.

Reviews: AM 1992, 94; *Choice* 12/86, 635.

S2-367   ML200 .C5
Chase, Gilbert. America's music, from the pilgrims to the present / Gilbert Chase; foreword by Richard Crawford; discographical essay by William Brooks. — 3rd ed. — New York : McGraw-Hill, 1987. —xxiv, 712 p. ISBN 0-252-00454-X.

1st ed., 1955; 2nd ed., 1966 (LOAM 25).

A major history, thoroughly revised. While most of the coverage is of classical music, there is new material on ragtime, jazz, and "country to rock—with soul." Chase wrote with graceful enthusiasm and careful scholarship, exploring major movements in a chronological format. One good idea was the restoration of a chapter on Native American music, offered in the first edition as "Indian Tribal Music," but deleted in the second edition. Chapter endnotes; musical examples. Useful bibliography of about 1,200 items, including books, articles, and dissertations. Expansive index of persons, titles, and topics.

Review and listing: AM 1988, 463; BCL.

S2-368   ML200 .H58
Hitchcock, H. Wiley. Music in the United States : a historical introduction / H. Wiley Hitchcock. — 3rd ed. — Englewood Cliffs, N.J. : Prentice-Hall, 1988. — xviii, 365 p. ISBN 0-13-608407-9.

1st ed., 1969; 2nd ed., 1974 (LOAM 30).

A classic history, revised primarily through the addition of a new chapter on developments since the mid-1970s. Hitchcock based his book on primary sources, writing a textbook that is also a footnoted, scholarly document. His own terminology of cultivated and vernacular idioms is used, with heavy emphasis on the cultivated; folk music is treated, and pop, but only a few pages are found on rock and its recent co-genres.

Valuable bibliographic essays conclude each chapter. With an expansive index.

Review: AM 1989, 465.

S2-369 ML200 .K55

Kingman, Daniel. American music : a panorama / Daniel Kingman. — 2nd ed. — New York : Schirmer, 1990. — xix, 684 p. : ill. ISBN 0-02-873370-3.

1st ed., 1979 (LOAM Suppl. S-11).

A fine, balanced account of all forms of American music, with many good illustrations and music examples. For each chapter there are endnotes and bibliographic references, plus lists of recordings and periodicals. Considerable attention goes to pop forms: 60 pages on jazz and 30 on rock. With an expansive index.

S2-370 ML200 .S26

Sanjek, Russell. American popular music and its business : the first four hundred years / Russell Sanjek. — New York : Oxford, 1988. — 3 vols.: vol. 1, The beginning to 1790, xvi, 469 p.; vol. 2, From 1790 to 1909, vi, 482 p.; vol. 3, From 1900 to 1984, 734 p. ISBN 0-19-504028-7; 0-19-504310-3; 0-19-504-311-1.

An interesting historical work by a former vice president of BMI, covering all aspects of the music industry: printing and publishing, concerts, copyright, musical theater, radio, recordings, motion pictures, musicians' unions, television, disc jockeys, legal issues, sales, and marketing. The story begins in sixteenth-century England, and it covers serious as well as popular music. In America musical life began with the earliest colonies, as musicians arrived on the *Mayflower* and in Virginia. Although these books resulted from extensive research, there are no footnotes or citations to sources. Errors of fact are not infrequent; for example, Sir Edward Robert Lewis of the Decca Record Co., Ltd., is renamed "Ted Lewis" and is credited with setting up a firm that never existed, "London Gramophone Corp. of New York." Another organizational name used inappropriately by Sanjek is "Columbia Records Company," which was not the name of any Columbia firm. The American Record Corporation (1929–1938) is confused with the American Record Company (1904–1907). There is no basis for the statement that Columbia introduced a "silent record surface" in 1922. Many similar defects could be listed. Each volume has a bibliography and a nonexpansive index.

Review: *Choice* 1/89, 816.

S2-371 ML200 .S263

Sanjek, Russell. American popular music business in the 20th century /

Russell Sanjek and David Sanjek. — New York : Oxford, 1991. — xxii, 334 p. ISBN 0-19-505828-3.
"An abridgement of the third volume of *American Popular Music and Its Business*" (S2-370).
David Sanjek is the son of the late Russell Sanjek. Covering 1900–1984, the story here deals with music publishing, recording, movies, ASCAP, radio, disc jockeys (and payola), TV, and rock superstars. It is an interesting account, and it was drawn from research sources (1,200 items in the bibliography), yet it does not measure up to scholarly standards: there are no actual citations to the sources, and errors of fact are too numerous to forgive. In the early days of the record industry, for example, we find mistakes of various kinds: the Victrola was introduced in 1906, not in 1896; Thomas Edison did not recognize the superiority of the rival graphophone to his own phonograph and seek to pool patents with Chichester Bell (in fact, the phonograph was winning the market from the graphophone by 1891); Eldridge Johnson's middle name was Reeves, not Reeve, and his discs were of wax, not celluloid; red seal records were first issued in Britain in 1901, not in the United States in 1902; etc. With an expansive index.

S2-372   ML200.4 .T4
Tawa, Nicholas E. The coming of age of American art music : New England's classical romanticists / Nicholas E. Tawa. — New York : Greenwood, 1991. — x, 237 p. (Contributions to the study of music and dance, 22) ISBN 0-313-27797-4.
The composers discussed in detail are John Knowles Paine, George Whitefield Chadwick, Edward MacDowell, Horatio Parker, Arthur Foote, and Amy Beach. Tawa regards this group as "the most important art composers, save for Charles Ives, before the twentieth-century generation"; all were New England born, except MacDowell, who lived for some time in Boston and married a New Englander. There are good background chapters on musical life, audiences, and the struggle of American composers to find their voice and to be heard. The bulk of the book is made up of descriptions of compositions in a program-note style. There are 21 pages of musical examples, curiously unidentified as to their composers. With chapter endnotes, a bibliography of about 120 items, and an expansive index.
Reviews: AM 1993, 114; *Choice* 10/91, 291.

S2-373   ML200.4 .W5
Sablosky, Irving. What they heard : music in America, 1852–1881, from the pages of *Dwight's Journal of Music* / Irving Sablosky. — Baton Rouge : Louisiana State University Press, 1986. — xiv, 317 p. ISBN 0-8071-1258-5.

A fascinating vista of nineteenth-century concert life, taken from the pages of the leading music periodical of the day. Sablosky's graceful comments illuminate the events and their backgrounds. While most of the activity described is on the East Coast, there are also ventures into "the hinterland" of Chicago, St. Louis, and out to San Francisco (where Dwight was surprised "to find much good musical taste and good music in this new country"). Recitals by Jenny Lind, French opera in New Orleans, the Fisk Jubilee Singers, concerts by the Boston Symphony Orchestra — such is the variety of events described with perception and style. Entertaining sidelights abound, none so poignant perhaps than the account of a benefit concert given by the St. Louis Philharmonic Society for its "excellent librarian, Mr. Kuhe," who "devotes his whole time to the interests of the Society, as you can conceive when I state that for the second concert he copied 2,000 pages of music, for the third 1,200, and 700 for the last with a prospect of 1,600 for the next." With a biographical register of artists and an expansive index.
Review: AM 1987, 462.

S2-374   ML200.5 .M413
Mertens, Wim. American minimal music : La Monte Young, Terry Riley, Steven Reich, Philip Glass / Wim Mertens; trans. J. Hautekiet; preface by Michael Nyman. — London : Kahn & Averill; New York : Alexander Broude, 1983. — 128 p. ISBN 0-900707-76-3.
"First published in Belgium in 1980."
It is somewhat painful to get through the "basic concepts of minimal music," founded on a curious dichotomy between "traditional dialectical music," which is "a medium for the expression of subjective feelings" and "repetitive [minimal] music," which "no longer has a mediative function, referring to something outside itself." Mertens has succumbed to the "intentional fallacy," believing that what composers say they are doing is what really happens — that LaMonte Young, for example, has, in his *Dream House,* produced a work "that has no beginning and goes on indefinitely." This whole philosophical discussion is nonsensical, and it finally deconstructs itself: "Yet the freedom this music claims to offer is merely freedom from history as such. It is therefore a negative freedom, paradoxically made possible only by a total addiction to history." Mertens is more surefooted in going through scores and does offer some good technical analyses of various pieces — analyses strictly classical in approach, all about keys, modulations, harmonic structures, and so on. With a miscellaneous two-page bibliography, but no index.
Review: AM 1988, 241.

S2-375   ML200.5 .N55
Nicholls, David. American experimental music, 1890–1940 / David

Nicholls. — New York : Cambridge University Press, 1990. — xiv, 239 p. : 148 music examples. ISBN 0-521-34578-2.

"A much-compressed revision of a Ph.D. thesis submitted to the University of Cambridge in 1985," this perceptive study aims particularly "to try to explain the compositional techniques invented and employed" by a number of twentieth-century Americans. Nicholls documents in technical terms and analyses the rise of a distinctive American (as opposed to Euro-American) music, in which "the main driving force was [Henry] Cowell, and the indispensable chief stoker [Charles] Ives." In addition to Ives and Cowell, persons who receive much attention are Charles Seeger, Carl Ruggles, Ruth Crawford, and John Cage. Techniques explicated include extreme chromaticism, tone clusters, use of unconventional instruments, innovative formal patterns, and chance music. With extensive chapter endnotes, a bibliography of about 125 items, a selective discography, and a partly expansive index.

Review: *Choice* 9/90, 128.

S2-376   ML200.5 .T34

Tawa, Nicholas E. Art music in the American society : the condition of art music in the late twentieth century / Nicholas E. Tawa. — Metuchen, N.J. : Scarecrow, 1987. — viii, 277 p. ISBN 0-8108-1976-7.

As a kind of supplement to *A Most Wondrous Babble* (S2-378), this book deals with "the relationships between the ideals of American democracy, the realities of late-twentieth-century American society, and the condition of art music"—with "art music" meaning "music of artistic intent." Essentially, Tawa is concerned with "forces that shaped American society and the art-music scene after World War II." He is not pleased with what he saw in that period: "the growth of a mass-music entertainment industry, dedicated to creating a vast and uniform market for its goods and unresponsive to the desires of the art-music minority." By abandoning ourselves to the "relentless judgments of the marketplace," Americans were responsible for the "valuation of material improvement over qualitative improvement." In this pessimistic context, Tawa offers interesting observations on public taste, music education, the musical career, music associations, and above all the music business. With chapter source notes, a bibliography of about 300 entries, and a nonexpansive index.

Review: *Choice* 2/88, 918.

S2-377   ML200.5 .T35

Tawa, Nicholas E. Mainstream music of early twentieth-century America : the composers, their times, and their works / Nicholas E. Tawa. — New York : Greenwood, 1992. — ix, 209 p. (Contributions to the study of music and dance, 28) ISBN 0-313-28563-2.

A thoughtful, scholarly account of several American composers: Edgar Stillman Kelley, Frederick Shepherd Converse, Daniel Gregory Mason, Edward Burlingame Hill, Mabel Daniels, Henry Hadley, Deems Taylor, Charles Wakefield Cadman, Henry Gilbert, Arthur Farwell, John Powell, Arthur Shepherd, Scott Joplin, Charles Tomlinson Griffes, Marion Bauer, and John Alden Carpenter. Only a few of those names are found on concert or opera programs today, but as late as the 1930s they were the prime representatives of national composition. Tawa re-examines their music, finding much of it "skillfully crafted and expressively meaningful" with "a wealth of appealing melody." He offers biographical information and program notes on principal works (without music examples), and appends an informal list of recordings. With chapter endnotes, a bibliography of about 200 titles, and a partly expansive index.
Review: *Choice* 3/93, 1164.

S2-378   ML200.5 .T36
Tawa, Nicholas E. A most wondrous babble : American art composers, their music, and the American scene, 1950–1985 / Nicholas E. Tawa. — Westport, Conn. : Greenwood, 1987. — xiii, 284 p. (Contributions to the study of music and dance, 9) ISBN 0-313-25692-6.

Tawa traces the rise of the avant-garde (serial and electronic) composers and the parallel decline of interest in the more traditional school. He sees this development as detrimental to American musical values and to concert life, because audiences who appreciated the traditional writers have not taken the modernists to heart. There is also a sense among listeners that all new music is arid and tuneless, while in fact the composers of the old mainstream wrote (some are still writing) melodic, pungent music of great import. Milton Babbitt, Elliott Carter, and Roger Sessions represent the moderns; Samuel Barber, Walter Piston, Aaron Copland, and Leonard Bernstein are in the losing camp. Tawa's arguments are of interest, although one may doubt whether Copland and Bernstein etc. were really pushed aside by the modernists: they appear to be ubiquitous in concerts and recordings. With endnotes, a bibliography of about 300 items, a discography that offers examples from the various compositional schools, and an expansive index.
Reviews: AM Spring 1993, 114–118; *Choice* 11/87, 487.

S2-379   ML200.5 .T55
Tischler, Barbara L. An American music : the search for an American musical identity / Barbara L. Tischler. — New York : Oxford, 1986. — 235 p. ISBN 0-19-504023-6.

A curious effort, by an academic whose base is history rather than musicology, to deconstruct the idea of American composers as writers of music drawn from the multitudinous American experience. She holds that native composers "have come of age" not as Americans, but as parts of the international search for new music during the twentieth century. The jazz and folk traditions, understood here as peripheral influences, allowed the composer "to be an Americanist if he chose." That major composers such as Harris, Copland, and Bernstein clearly chose that path does not seem to suggest to Tischler any flaws in her viewpoint. There is much confusion of terminology and of music history in this volume, as well as a tendency to wander from the dubious notions it espouses. There are no musical examples and few specific references. Factual and typographical errors are numerous. With endnotes, a bibliography, and an expansive index.

Reviews: AM 1988, 93; *Choice* 12/86, 636; LJ 8/86, 153.

ML200.7–207 : Regional

S2-380   ML200.7 .F6 H7
Housewright, Wiley L. A history of music and dance in Florida, 1565–1865 / Wiley L. Housewright. — Tuscaloosa : University of Alabama Press, 1991. — xvii, 448 p. ISBN 0-8173-0492-4.

A scholarly narrative, told with style, that covers indigenous music (of which none survives) and the music of the colonizers. A section of special interest is "music in the social life" of the nineteenth century: balls, feasts, dances, concerts, opera, military events, etc. "Music of the Negroes" is another fine chapter, one that does not neglect the state's Suwannee River, but concentrates on plantation music and work songs. Folk songs of white people are well described too, and so is Civil War music for voice and band. With endnotes, bibliography of about 600 items, and a partly expansive index of titles, persons, and topics.

Review: *Choice* 6/92, 1555.

S2-381   ML200.7 .H4 N8
Noble, Gurre Ploner. Hula blues : the story of Johnny Noble, Hawaii, its music and musicians / Gurre Ploner Noble. — Honolulu : E. D. Noble, 1984. — 128 p. ISBN not given.

A study of contemporary Hawaiian music and leading musicians. Special attention goes to Johnny Noble (1892–1944), one who had great influence on modern developments.

S2-382   ML200.7 .H4 T15
Tatar, Elizabeth. Nineteenth century Hawaiian chant / Elizabeth Tatar. — Honolulu : Department of Anthropology, Bishop Museum, 1982. — xiv, 176 p. : ill. : with one 8-inch LP disc. (Pacific anthropological records, 33; ISSN 0078-740X.) ISBN not given.

Based on early recordings in the Bishop Museum, this is a scholarly work that examines sources, types (prayer, animal, place-name, love, games, etc.), styles, and social contexts of the songs. Contemporary chant is compared with the historic versions. Spectographic analysis is used to graph minute differences in pitch and vibrato, resulting in a highly refined classification of the material. With a bibliography of about 200 books and articles. No index.

S2-383   ML200.7 .H4 T373

Tatar, Elizabeth. Strains of change : the impact of tourism on Hawaiian music / Elizabeth Tatar. — Honolulu : Bishop Museum Press, 1987. — 29 p. : ill. ISBN 0-9308-9723-4.

"Tourism does modify traditional ways of composing and performing music and dance. In the twentieth century chants, hymn-like songs, and hula songs were reshaped to the taste of the U.S. tourist," and "musicians adapted music to mainland music trends and to rhythms and movements of Tahitian and Samoan music and dance." The modifications are carefully explored by Tatar, who has compressed a great deal of research into a few pages. Sheet music covers serve as interesting illustrations. With footnotes, a bibliography of about 30 items, and a discography of authentic and influenced music.

S2-384   ML200.7 .L8

Allan, Johnnie. Memories : a pictorial history of South Louisiana music, 1920–1980s / Johnnie Allan. — Lafayette, La. : Jadfel Publishing, 1988. — 271 p. ISBN 0-9619335-0-X.

S2-385   ML200.7 .W3

Corenthal, Michael G. The illustrated history of Wisconsin music / Michael G. Corenthal. — Milwaukee : Yesterday's Memories, 1991. — 460 p. ISBN not given.

An interesting gathering of photos and newspaper/magazine stories relating to individuals who took part in Wisconsin musical life. Except for brief introductions to the three periods that Corenthal identifies as "pioneer," "golden age," and "modern era," there is no unifying narrative. Many of the items included have only ancillary connections to Wisconsin. This is a browsing book; it does not follow the implications of its title.

S2-386   ML200.8 .A552 T87

Talley, John B. Secular music in colonial Annapolis : the Tuesday Club, 1745–56 / John B. Talley. — Urbana : University of Illinois Press, 1988. — xvi, 312 p. : ill. ISBN 0-252-01402-2.

A music history of eighteenth-century Annapolis, focused on the Tuesday Club, with a modern edition of music composed by club members and a transcription of minuets from a manuscript by John Ormsby. Extensive minutes and commentaries on the club meetings—which featured musical performances—by one Alexander Hamilton formed the basis for much of Talley's research. Music making was ubiquitous in the Maryland capital: "every gentleman played the violin, and every lady the flute." Other instruments and ensembles were popular as well. The book not only illuminates one city's musical life, but demonstrates the high place held by music among the American upper classes before the Revolution. With musical examples, source notes, and an expansive index.

S2-387   ML200.8 .B5 P56
Pincus, Andrew L. Scenes from Tanglewood / Andrew L. Pincus; foreword by Seiji Ozawa. — Boston : Northeastern University Press, 1992. — xii, 287 p. : ill. ISBN 1-55553-049-4.
Tanglewood, in the Berkshires of western Massachusetts, has been the summer home of the Boston Symphony Orchestra since 1938, as well as a summer school for gifted musicians. About "20 percent of the players in the major American symphony orchestras—and 30 percent of the first-chair players—have gone through Tanglewood." Attendance at concerts reached 328,000 in the 1958 season. This is a straightforward popular history, undocumented, and not without its fictional quotations and conversations. There is an expansive index.
Reviews: *Choice* 11/89, 497; LJ 6/15/89, 60.

S2-388   ML200.8 .B7 B76
Broyles, Michael. "Music of the highest class" : elitism and populism in antebellum Boston / Michael Broyles. — New Haven, Conn. : Yale University Press, 1992. — ix, 392 p. ISBN 0-300-05495-5.
A scholarly discussion of music in Boston during the eighteenth and nineteenth centuries, rendered less effective than it might have been by the author's concern to demolish the "cultivated"-versus-"entertainment" dichotomy and to impose this intent on the historical material. His other thesis is more successfully promoted, but it is also more familiar: that "American musical culture, in spite of its close ties to Europe, developed a distinctive profile as a result of certain cultural forces, intellectual traditions, and political developments whose evolution was unique to America." Topically the book examines the work of Lowell Mason, concert life in Boston, private music making, Samuel Eliot and the Boston Academy of Music, bands, and opera. There are useful appendix listings of instrumentalists. With extensive endnotes, a bibliography of primary and secondary sources, and an expansive index.
Review: *Choice* 4/93, 1322.

S2-389   ML200.8 .B72 S948
Vigeland, Carl A. In concert : onstage and offstage with the Boston Symphony Orchestra / Carl A. Vigeland. — New York : Morrow, 1989. — 270 p. ISBN 0-688-07551-7.

A gossipy account of BSO rehearsals, recording sessions, and personalities, with invented conversations; no notes or index.

S2-390   ML200.8 .N48 B57
Bissonnette, Big Bill [William E.]. The jazz crusade : the inside story of the great New Orleans jazz revival of the 1960s / Big Bill Bissonnette. — Bridgeport, Conn. : Special Request Music Service, 1992. — xviii, 338 p. : ill. : with a compact disc. ISBN 0-9632-2970-2.

A rambling memoir by a trombonist and record producer who was active in New Orleans jazz circles. Bissonnette claims to be a "jazzman; not a musician" and makes no effort to describe the music. So he offers anecdotes and undocumented conversations that cast some dim light on the work of George Lewis, the Easy Riders, Victoria Spivey, Sammy Rimington, Kid Thomas, Punch Miller, and a dozen others. Photos of album covers and an informal discography are included, along with a nonexpansive index.

S2-391   ML200.8 .N48 F8
Friedlander, Lee. The jazz people of New Orleans / Lee Friedlander; afterword by Whitney Balliett. — New York : Pantheon, 1992. — 119 p. ISBN 0-679-41638-2.

A book of photographs, depicting street musicians and jazz players. Without identification of the persons in the pictures, and without commentary or index.

Review: LJ 9/15/92, 41.

S2-392   ML200.8 .N5 A7
Anderson, Gillian B. Music in New York during the American Revolution / Gillian B. Anderson. — Boston : Music Library Association, 1987. — xxix, 135 p. : ill. (MLA index and bibliography series, 24) ISBN 0-914954-33-4.

A fascinating study of the weekly *Rivington's New York Gazette and Universal Advertiser* for the years 1773–1783, seeking out musical notices and advertising. New York is revealed to have a musical life that "resembled that of other predominantly English-speaking provincial towns in the British Empire." A wide range of activity is chronicled: dances, concerts for black residents, announcements of new music published (by about 170 composers), and advertising for music teachers, concert managers, instrument repairmen, and so forth. With a bibliography of about 50 entries; without index.

S2-393   ML200.8 .N5 B37

Bastin, Bruce. Never sell a copyright : Joe Davis and his role in the New York music scene, 1916–1978 / Bruce Bastin. — Chigwell, Essex, England : Storyville, 1990. — x, 346 p. ISBN 0-902391-12-7.

Joseph Morton Davis (1896–1978) was a writer and publisher of pop songs in New York, promoter of early blues and jazz artists, and a pioneer A & R man who developed the race catalog of Ajax records. (Bastin states incorrectly that "Ajax handled only race artists"—their output included jazz and country material.) From Ajax, which folded in 1925, Davis went on to work with Columbia and Okeh, made some records himself, and appeared on several radio stations as a disc jockey. His publishing company, Triangle Music, prospered through the 1920s, and Davis kept going in the 1930s while the entertainment industry floundered. He started a label named Beacon Records in 1942, and in the 1940s worked also as A & R man for Gennett. He went to MGM in 1952, bringing in the Crickets and supporting R & B groups, but only lasted there six months. After that he continued recruiting R & B artists and recording them for Beacon and various other labels. Later he diversified his interests, working with jazz and ballad performers such as Erskine Butterfield and Lee Castle. He continued promoting and supervising recordings into the 1970s. "If anyone in the music business showed himself capable of bending with the wind without breaking, it was Joe Davis." The story is told here in a straightforward manner, with source notes and without invented conversations or anecdotes. With a nonexpansive index.

S2-394   ML200.8 .N5 J63

Johnson, Tom. The voice of new music : New York City, 1972–1982 : a collection of articles originally published in the Village Voice / Tom Johnson. — Eindhoven, Netherlands : Het Apollohuis, 1989. — 543 p. ISBN 90-71638-09-X.

The main topic of these reviews and articles is minimalism, "any music that works with limited or minimal materials; pieces that use only a few notes, pieces that use only a few words of text, or pieces written for very limited instruments, such as antique cymbals, bicycle wheels, or whisky glasses." This kind of definition tends to run loose at the edges and could allow the inclusion of Gregorian Chant or Spike Jones. The author is aware of the scope question, but is undisturbed: "Of course, some pieces are more minimal than others, and some of the music described in the book does not restrict its material much at all." Persons covered most thoroughly by these brief, semitechnical program notes include John Cage, Philip Corner, Philip Glass, Meredith Monk, Phil Niblock, Pauline Oliveros, Steve Reich, Frederic Rzewski, and La-Monte Young. Johnson offers no value judgments on the music he describes, suggesting indeed that it is all just fine. Even a work in which nothing seems to happen, by Harry Budd, gets a straight-faced account: "Budd . . . just lets the music drift . . . he offers no mood changes, no color changes, no tempo changes, no virtuoso licks, no climaxes, no lyrics, and no references to familiar tunes. . . . There is something poignant, even philosophical, about the intentional aimlessness of the music." With a nonexpansive index.

S2-395   ML200.8 .N5 L4
Lawrence, Vera Brodsky. Strong on music : the New York music scene in the days of George Templeton Strong / Vera Brodsky Lawrence. — New York : Oxford, 1987– . — Vol. 1: Resonances, 1836–1850 (1988). — lvi, 608 p. : ill. ISBN 0-19-503199-2.

A splendid research effort, bringing to light the musical culture of New York City. The main source was the diary of Strong, a lawyer and music lover, available only in manuscript in the New York Public Library. Strong's articulate comments on concerts, singers, composers, and all aspects of the cultural milieu are presented in a rich context of explanation and elaboration by Lawrence. Use of the expansive index will lead to great quantities of reference information, such as details on premieres, writings of critics, and addresses of music stores. With a bibliography of about 400 primary and secondary sources.

Reviews: AM 1990, 483; *Choice* 7/88, 1704; LJ 9/15/87, 82.

S2-396   ML200.8 .N52 C338
Schickel, Richard. Carnegie Hall : the first one hundred years / Richard Schickel and Michael Walsh. — New York : Abrams, 1987. — 263 p. : ill. ISBN 0-8109-0773-9.

A good collection of pictures, many in color, in an attractive coffee-table book. There is an undocumented commentary that gives a basic history of the hall from 1891 to 1991, and a useful calendar of seasons from 1891 to 1986/87. With a name index.

S2-397   ML200.8 .N52 P9
Porter, Andrew. Music of three more seasons : 1977–1980 / Andrew Porter. — New York : Knopf, 1981. — 613 p. ISBN 0-3945-1813-6.

In the mode of his earlier collections (LOAM Suppl. S-216, S-217), Porter offers more reviews written for the *New Yorker*. His judgments and style are of high quality. He presents extensive, interesting background material on the works performed. Without index.

S2-398   ML200.8 .W3 K57
Kirk, Elise K. Music at the White House : a history of the American spirit / Elise K. Kirk. — Urbana : University of Illinois Press, 1986. — xviii, 457 p. : ill. : 8 p. plates. ISBN 0-252-102330-X.

A pleasing, scholarly narrative of musical events during the administrations of those who lived in the White House (and in the earlier mansions occupied by George Washington) until the era of Ronald Reagan. The well-documented discussion deals with presidential tastes and musical abilities, instruments, invited performers, and theatrical visits by the first families. The musicians who pass by in this interesting procession represent all manifestations of the art: Marian Anderson, Pearl Bailey, Tony Bennett, Chuck Berry, Eubie Blake, Van Cliburn, Perry Como, the Fisk Jubilee Singers, Martha Graham, Merle Haggard, Vladimir Horowitz, the Hutchinson Family Singers, Al Jolson, Sissieretta Joyner Jones ("Black Patti"), Oscar Levant, Eugene List, the Mormon Tabernacle Choir, Leontyne Price, Thelma Ritter, Ernestine Schumann-Heink, Lawrence Tibbett, Mary Lou Williams, Pinchas Zukerman; plus hundreds of others. With a useful bibliographic essay and an expansive index.

Reviews: AM 1989, 479; LJ 11/1/86, 97.

S2-399   ML207 .P8 D7
Dower, Catherine. Puerto Rican music following the Spanish-American War / Catherine Dower. — Lanham, Md. : University Press of America, 1983. — viii, 203 p. : ill. ISBN 0-8191-3333-7.

A straightforward, documented account of nineteenth-century traditions, the American arrival in 1898, public school music, church music, band concerts, and 15 individual musicians (none of them well known in the United States). With chapter endnotes, a bibliography of about 150 primary and secondary sources, and a nonexpansive index.

ML385–404 : COLLECTIVE BIOGRAPHIES

ML385 : General

S2-400   ML385 .B25
Balliett, Whitney. Barney, Bradley, and Max : sixteen portraits in jazz / Whitney Balliett. — New York : Oxford, 1989. — 213 p. ISBN 0-19-506124-1.

A collection of portraits, all but one of which appeared in the *New Yorker,* between 1971 and 1988 (some revised for the book). Several also appeared in earlier Balliett collections. Subjects include Jean Bach, Max Gordon, Barney Josephson, Bradley Cunningham, Marie Marcus, Claude Thornhill, Jimmy Rowles, Mel Powell, George Shearing, Walter Norris, Harvey Phillips, Benny Goodman, Ruby Braff, Charlie Parker, Buddy De Franco, and Louis Bellson.

Each article is dated. Without bibliographical references or index [−D.P.].

Review: LJ 8/89, 137.

S2-401 ML385 .D29

Davis, Francis. Outcats : jazz composers, instrumentalists, and singers / Francis Davis. — New York : Oxford, 1990. — x, 261 p. ISBN 0-19-505587-X.

A selection of about 40 articles, published in various newspapers and periodicals between 1983 and 1989. Subjects of the longest articles (9–13 pp.) include Duke Ellington's *Queenie Pie,* Mercer Ellington, Gil Evans, Edward Wilkerson, Jr., Billie Holiday, Sheila Jordan, Susannah McCorkle, and the film *Bird.* Shorter articles discuss Sun Ra, Herbie Nichols, Cecil Taylor, Abdullah Ibraham and Sathima Bea Benjamin, Errol Parker, Henry Threadgill, John Zorn, Doc Cheatham, Lester Young, Miles Davis, Frank Morgan, Steve Lacy, Odean Pope, Ran Blake, Borah Bergman, Jane Ira Bloom and Michele Rosewoman, Ella Fitzgerald, Frank Sinatra, Bobby Darin, Bobby Short, Harry Connick, Jr., Mort Sahl, Benny Carter, Charles Mingus, Illinois Jacquet, Steven Coleman, and Wynton Marsalis. Also covered are James Collier's biography of Duke Ellington, George Gershwin's *Rhapsody in Blue,* the Smithsonian releases *American Popular Song* and *The Smithsonian Collection of Classic Jazz,* the American Jazz Orchestra, the films *'Round Midnight* and *Let's Get Lost,* the Ganelin Trio, and the Microscopic Septet.

Recent performances, new recordings, and/or reissues are discussed in most of the articles; label numbers are typically included. Some information comes from interviews with the subjects, but it is often difficult to be sure since sources are poorly cited or are not provided at all. The nonexpansive index covers personal names and groups thoroughly, but includes no titles. Without bibliographical references.

Francis Davis is a jazz critic who writes regularly for the *Atlantic,* the *Philadelphia Inquirer,* and *7 Days* [—D.P.].

Reviews: *Choice* 5/91, 1496; LJ 3/15/90, 92.

S2-402 ML385 .E65

Eremo, Judie. Country musicians / Judie Eremo; foreword by Roy Clark. — New York : Grove, 1987. — vii, 151 p. : ill. ISBN 0-802-10008-2.

Biographical sketches and photographs of about 30 performers, with interview material and selective discographies. No documentation and no index.

S2-403 ML385 .H243

Harris, Craig. The new folk music / Craig Harris. — Crown Point, N.Y. : White Cliffs Media, 1991. — ix, 150 p. : ill. ISBN 0-941677-27-3.

"An overview of trends in contemporary folk music featuring

photographs and interviews with pacesetting musicians," covering many artists not found in the older anthologies. Zydeco, instrumentals, and world music are useful categories. There are sections on musicians from Louisiana, and on British singers in the United States. Basic data of life and career are mixed in with invented quotations and conversations; the photographs are good. Without index.

S2-404   ML385 .K2

Kasha, Al. Notes on Broadway : intimate conversations with Broadway's greatest songwriters / Al Kasha and Joel Hirschhorn. — Chicago : Contemporary Books, 1985. — xvi, 365 p. : ill. ISBN 0-8092-5162-0.

Interviews with Burt Bacharach, Leonard Bernstein, Julie Cahn, Betty Comden and Adolph Green, Sheldon Harnick, Jerry Bock, Alan Jay Lerner, Stephen Schwartz, Julie Styne, and several other composers of musicals. Most of them talk about productions, staging, and one another. There is no documentation. With a nonexpansive index of names and titles.

S2-405   ML385 .N538

Eremo, Judie. New age musicians / Judie Eremo. — Cupertino, Calif. : GPI Publications, 1989. — viii, 111 p. : ill. ISBN 0-88188-909-1.

Material previously published in *Guitar Player, Keyboard,* and *Frets,* consisting of informal presentations on about 22 musicians. The interview format allows the performers to talk freely about this and that. There is some interest in a few compositions given in musical notation. Without documentation or index.

S2-406   ML385 .P4

Pearson, Barry Lee. Virginia Piedmont blues : the lives and art of two Virginia bluesmen / Barry Lee Pearson. — Philadelphia : University of Pennsylvania Press, 1990. — 291 p. : ill. ISBN 0-8122-8209-4.

A discussion of Archie Edwards and John Cephas, giving biographical background, repertoire, and each man's "thoughts on his music." Texts of 83 songs are included, but there is no music in the book and indeed little said about music. Documentation is thorough; there is a bibliography of about 100 items; the index is nonexpansive.

S2-407   ML385 .R53

Riese, Randall. Nashville Babylon : the uncensored truth and private lives of country music's stars / Randall Riese. — New York : Congdon & Weed (Contemporary Books), 1988. — xi, 290 p. ISBN 0-86553-166-8.

A collection of undocumented chat and gossip. Chapter titles indicate the tone: "Con Artists," "Big Balls in Cowtown," "Babylon Bitching,"

"They Fell to Pieces," etc. Casual six-page bibliography; nonexpansive index.

ML390 : Composers

S2-408 ML390 .B76

Borroff, Edith. Three American composers / Edith Borroff. — Lanham, Md. : University Press of America, 1986. — xii, 289 p. : ill. ISBN 0-8191-5371-0.

Borroff examines styles of concert music composed in the United States since World War II. She contrasts a traditional "conservatory" style as represented by Irwin Fischer (1903–1977) with an avant-garde "university" style as represented by George Crumb (1929–). Ross Lee Finney (1906–) is viewed as the fulcrum of the two styles. Short biographies of each composer are followed by detailed musical analyses of several of their works. Borroff interviewed each of the subjects and has included some statements regarding their philosophies and observations on their compositions. Sources are carefully cited. More than 100 musical examples inform the text, and there are worklists for each composer. Without bibliography or index [—D.P.].

Reviews: AM 1988, 235; *Choice* 12/86, 634.

S2-409 ML390 .C59

Claghorn, Charles Eugene. Biographical dictionary of jazz / Charles Eugene Claghorn. — Englewood Cliffs, N.J. : Prentice-Hall, 1982. — 377 p. ISBN 0-13-077966-0.

These terse thumbnail sketches of over 3,000 musicians include birth and death years and places, and a list of collaborators, usually also with dates and places involved. Longer sketches (none exceed one column) often include additional biographical information and comments by critics or peers (most of them carefully cited). A separate alphabetical listing (51 pp.) includes very brief descriptions of over 500 ensembles.

While the entries are much shorter that those in the *New Grove Dictionary of Jazz* (S2-73), this work is still useful. Many persons are included here who do not appear in the larger dictionary (and vice versa). While persons are listed by popular nicknames in the *New Grove Dictionary of Jazz,* here they are usually under full names; since neither work includes an index or much assistance in the way of cross-references, this can help identify musicians whether full or popular name is known. There are numerous discrepancies in dates and places between the two works; this dictionary is somewhat prone to misspelled names.

Charles Claghorn is author of the *Biographical Dictionary of American Music* (1973; LOAM 12) [—D.P.].

Listing and reviews: ARBA 1984, p. 452; BCL; *Choice* 5/83, 1261; LJ 5/15/83, 576.

S2-410   ML390 .E825
Ewen, David. American songwriters / David Ewen. — New York : H. W. Wilson, 1987. — xi, 489 p. : ill. ISBN 0-8242-0744-0.
Replaces *Popular American Composers* (1962; LOAM 1154) and its *First Supplement* (1972). The final publication by Ewen (1907–1985), America's most prolific author of music reference books. Like his other works, this one presents its facts in an interesting way, without scholarly documentation, stressing personal elements and career matters. Musical considerations get little attention. There are no lists of songs. A few bibliographic references are given at the end of each article and each has a portrait. Altogether, 146 composers and lyricists are covered. With an index of song titles.
Listing and reviews: ARBA 1988, #1267; Balay BH109; *Choice* 6/87, 1530.

S2-411   ML390 .F7
Flanagan, Bill. Written in my soul : rock's greatest songwriters talk about creating their music / Bill Flanagan. — Chicago : Contemporary Books, 1986. — xv, 432 p. ISBN 0-8092-5153-1.
Paul Simon is quoted in the book-waxing philosophic: "It's very hard to write about music. What do you say about it? Music is a non-verbal experience. It's easier to address words." His point is amply demonstrated by the laborious interviews that fill the volume; indeed, the respondents also find it hard to say much about their lyrics. The content of their answers amounts to very little beyond sketchy opinions and music business anecdotes. Those involved include Bob Dylan, Chuck Berry, Mick Jagger, Keith Richards, Van Morrison, Sting, Mark Knopfler, Sonny Bono, David Byrne, Elvis Costello, Carl Perkins, Willie Dixon, Joni Mitchell, Neil Young, Lou Reed, and Peter Townshend. With a nonexpansive index of names, titles, and topics.
Reviews: *Choice* 4/92, 1192; LJ 11/15/86.

S2-412   ML390 .G74
Green, Benny. Let's face the music : the golden age of popular song / Benny Green. — London : Pavilion, 1989. — 233 p. : ill. ISBN 1-85145-4896.
Routine anecdotes about the star songwriters George Gershwin, Jerome Kern, Cole Porter, etc. Quotes and incidents are undocumented. With a nonexpansive index.

S2-413   ML390 .P8
Pollack, Howard. Harvard composers : Walter Piston and his students,

from Elliott Carter to Frederic Rzewski / Howard Pollack. — Metuchen, N.J. : Scarecrow, 1992. — xviii, 490 p. ISBN 0-8108-2493-0.

Composer, theorist, and teacher Piston (1894–1976) influenced the course of American music through example, through his conservatory textbooks, and above all through the outstanding composers who studied with him at Harvard. This fascinating book considers 33 of those students, including many of international reputation: Elliott Carter, Leroy Anderson, Arthur Berger, Everett Helm, Norman Cazden, Gail Kubik, Irving Fine, Harold Shapero, Gordon Binkerd, Ellis Kohs, Daniel Pinkham, and Leonard Bernstein. There is technical discussion, with examples, of many works by these men; and often Pollack was able to relate specific compositions to Piston's instruction and comments. Although the individuality of each composer transcends any unifying principle that their music shares, Piston imbued them "with a belief in the continued relevance of the classical tradition . . . this emerged as an appreciation and concern for clear, subtle textures; contrapuntal sophistication; expert knowledge of the instruments; and formal finesse." The expansive index includes lists of the works cited under each composer's name.
Review: *Choice* 4/93, 1324.

S2-414   ML390 .S942
Strickland, Edward. American composers : dialogues on contemporary music / Edward Strickland. — Bloomington : Indiana University Press, 1991. — xi, 220 p. : ill. ISBN 0-253-35498-6.

A collection of taped conversations with 11 composers: Keith Jarrett, Steve Reich, La Monte Young, Anthony Davis, Meredith Monk, Terry Riley, John Zorn, Philip Glass, George Crumb, John Adams, and Ingram Marshall. Strickland's opportunity to extract some musical insights from this group was wasted, as his questions did not probe beneath the surface of personal events, recording dates, and personalities. The tone is that of a "greenroom" interview during a concert intermission. With a nonexpansive index.
Review: *Choice* 2/92, 906.

S2-415   ML390 .S983
Suskin, Steven. Show tunes, 1905–1985 : the songs, shows, and careers of Broadway's major composers / Steven Suskin. — Rev. ed. — New York : Limelight, 1992. — xxviii, 769 p. ISBN 0-8791-0146-6.
1st ed., 1986 (New York: Dodd, Mead).

A composer list of about 6,000 songs from musicals; with a list of the shows in date order, and their songs; and a song title index. There are useful comments throughout.
Reviews: *Choice* 2/87, 893 (for the 1st ed.); LJ 1/86, 73 (for the 1st ed.).

S2-416   ML390 .W274

Reagon, Bernice Johnson. We'll understand it better by and by : pioneering African American gospel composers / ed. Bernice Johnson Reagon. — Washington : Smithsonian Institution Press, 1992. — vii–xii, [3]–384 p. : ill. ISBN 1-5609-8166-0. (Alternative classification: ML394 .W274.)

A valuable collection of essays by 10 specialists, dealing with six major figures: Charles Albert Tindley, Lucie E. Campbell, Thomas A. Dorsey, Roberta Martin, William Herbert Brewster, and Kenneth Morris. Interviews and musical analyses (with 49 works in score) are unified by Reagon into a fascinating picture of the gospel movement. There is an excellent annotated bibliography of gospel music and a discography (labels and numbers only, without dates or other information). With an expansive index.

Reviews: *Choice* 7/93, 1782; LJ 1/93, 120.

ML394–400 : Performers

S2-417   ML394 .C86

Cunningham, Lyn Driggs. Sweet, hot and blue : St. Louis' musical heritage / Lyn Driggs Cunningham and Jimmy Jones. — Jefferson, N.C. : McFarland, 1989. — ix, 245 p. : ill. ISBN 0-89950-302-0.

This work tries, not too successfully, to be both a directory and a collection of profiles of 124 musicians born or raised in the St. Louis metropolitan area. The majority of the musicians are locally known jazz and blues artists, but popular and concert artists are also included. Entries take a variety of forms: some consist almost exclusively of very carefully transcribed interviews with the subjects or their acquaintances; others seem to be based on previously published sources, though none are cited. The alphabetically arranged entries range from one paragraph to eight pages in length. Instruments, places and dates of birth and death, and interviewer are given for each subject.

More than 50 photographs of the artists are placed throughout the text. A six-page glossary defines terms that were used in the interviews. The nonexpansive index includes persons, places, groups, titles, and topics [—D.P.].

Reviews: ARBA 1990, #1286; *Choice* 5/90, 1513.

S2-418   ML394 .E3

Edison, musicians, and the phonograph / ed. and with an introduction by John Harvith and Susan Edwards Harvith. — Westport, Conn. : Greenwood, 1987. — xvii, 461 p. : photos. (Contributions to the study of music and dance, 11) ISBN 0-313-25393-5.

An interesting collection of interviews with 42 musicians, centered on the way performers feel about recording (they usually like it). Among those who offer their views are Lotte Lehmann, Rosa Ponselle, Alexander Kipnis, Jan Peerce, Eugene Ormandy, Aaron Copland, Benny Goodman, Janos Starker, André Previn, Vladimir Ashkenazy, Alicia de Larrocha, and Gunther Schuller. The interviewing is perceptive, and the responses deal directly with musical matters. Some introductory material on Thomas Edison is well presented; it features candid observations by his longtime studio pianist, Ernest Stevens. With a partly expansive index.

S2-419   ML394 .G28
Gaar, Gillian G. She's a rebel : the history of women in rock & roll / Gillian G. Gaar. — Seattle, Wash. : Seal, 1992. — xv, 467 p. : ill. ISBN 1-878067-08-7.

A casual, if impassioned, history of female pop performers since the 1950s. The author is primarily concerned with condemning injustices perpetrated against women by the music industry and takes little time to comment on the music of those talented artists. For such persons and groups as the Shirelles, Ronettes, Carole King, Carly Simon, Tracy Chapman, and Melissa Etheridge, there are anecdotes and undocumented conversations. With informal bibliographies and an expansive index.

Review: LJ 10/15/92, 68.

S2-420   ML394 .H67
Horricks, Raymond. Profiles in jazz : from Sidney Bechet to John Coltrane / Raymond Horricks. — New Brunswick, N.J. : Transaction Publishers, 1991. — vi, 268 p. : ill. ISBN 0-88738-432-3.

A collection of 36 short essays, most of which had been published in *Crescendo International*. In addition to more familiar figures, coverage includes saxophonist and "rehearser" Budd Johnson, saxophonist Arnett Cobb, pianist Al Haig, drummer Roy Haynes, trombonist Britt Woodman, clarinetist/saxophonist Phil Woods, vibraphonist Gary Burton, and bassist Richard Davis. The sketches are informal and pocked with imaginary conversations, but they present an assortment of facts as well. The most interesting item is a long essay, "Classic Ellington," that helpfully condenses the great career, with comments on the major players. With a selective discography of reissues (no commentaries); without an index.

S2-420a   ML394 .J66
Jones, Max. Talking jazz / Max Jones. — New York : Norton, 1988. — xi, 293 p. ISBN 0-393-02494-6.

A collection of interviews and impressions, most of them from the *Melody Maker*. Individuals treated include Barney Bigard, Bud Freeman,

Ben Webster, Red Allen, Ruby Braff, Jonah Jones, Jimmy McPartland, Sy Oliver, Mary Lou Williams, Slam Stewart, Billy Eckstine, and Sarah Vaughn. The conversations (either taped or reconstructed—this is not specified) deal with personal matters, never "talking about jazz." With a nonexpansive index.

S2-421   ML394 .K53
Kiersh, Edward. Where are you now, Bo Diddley? : the stars who made us rock and where they are now / Edward Kiersh. — Garden City, N.Y. : Doubleday, 1986. — 387 p. : ill. ISBN 0-385-19610-5.
Bo Diddley is inactive musically, but planning new ventures that will surprise everyone. Petula Clark is looking for a major comeback, one not connected with her memorable "Downtown." Richie Havens wants to bring an Italian group to the United States for a tour. Such fancies are included in the casual chat produced by 47 old-time rock performers, in response to queries from Kiersh. "The road to gold and the path to obscurity" is clearly plotted for them, marked by the inevitable "struggles with drugs and booze and runaway fame." Without documentation or index.

S2-422   ML394 .K81
Kolar, Walter W. Duquesne University Tamburitzans : the first fifty years remembered / Walter W. Kolar. — Pittsburgh : Tamburitza Press, 1986. — 122 p. : ill. ISBN not given.
In 1936 a peripatetic Balkan string ensemble found a permanent home at Duquesne University in Pittsburgh, eventually taking the name Tamburitzans. Singing and dancing were added to the activities, which represented Slavic folk traditions primarily, but also ethnic music of other groups. This is essentially a scrapbook of the organization with running commentary. The authenticity and the high quality of the Tamburitzan performances have been established through national and international tours. With a list of all performers, 1937–1987. No index.

S2-423   ML394 .L4
Lees, Gene. Meet me at Jim & Andy's : jazz musicians and their world / Gene Lees. — New York : Oxford, 1988. — xviii, 265 p. ISBN 0-19-504611-0.
The title of this essay collection is from a jazz bar that used to exist on West 48th Street in New York City. Lees talks casually about some of the artists who used to congregate there, including Duke Ellington, Artie Shaw, Woody Herman, Frank Rosolino, John Heard, Bill Evans, Billy Taylor, Art Farmer, and Paul Desmond. Invented conversations abound. A few references to actual music appear, but primarily these are personal tales of career problems, race problems, health problems, and miscellaneous escapades. Without notes or index.
Reviews: *Choice* 5/89, 1528; LJ 10/15/88, 92.

S2-424   ML394 .L97

Lyons, Len. Jazz portraits : the lives and music of the jazz masters / Len Lyons and Don Perlo. — New York : Morrow, 1989. — 610 p. : ill. ISBN 0-688-04946-X.

An excellent collection of brief bio-sketches on about 300 jazz artists "whose contributions have proved enduring." "Those who have distinguished themselves over the past decade are represented, but more sparingly: second-guessing history is a risky business." In addition to the usual great names, important individuals of lesser fame are included, such as drummers Airto Guimorva Moreira and Ed Blackwell, vocalists Helen Merrill and Maxine Sullivan, and pianists Ran Blake and Cedar Walton. For each person there is a photograph, life and career summary, and comments on the musical characteristics of the performer. Influences are identified, as are principal recordings (with LP/CD reissue titles). There are no anecdotes or invented conversations. A fine reference list of all the artists under the names of their instruments, in decade order, provides unique perspectives. With a glossary of jazz terms and a nonexpansive index.

S2-425   ML394 .T7

Tosches, Nick. Unsung heroes of rock 'n' roll : the birth of rock in the wild years before Elvis / Nick Tosches. — Rev. ed. — New York : Harmony Books, 1991. — xi, 276 p. : ill. ISBN 0-517-58052-7.

"Revised edition" appears on the cover only.

1st ed., 1984 (LOAM Suppl. SA-760).

An assortment of articles, many published earlier in *Creem,* about 29 musicians. Among those included are Nat King Cole, Louis Jordan, Wynonie Harris, Charles Brown, Ella Mae Morse, Cecil Gant, the Clovers, the Dominoes, and Wanda Jackson. The style is rambling and the language is extremely vulgar. Tosches says, "I wrote it as it came to me, not really caring." Little is said about music. With a chronology, a discography (minimal data), and—what seems to be the only novelty in this revision—a selective CD list. There is a nonexpansive index of personal names.

Reviews: *Choice* 12/84, 568; LJ 6/15/84, 1242.

S2-426   ML395 .B34

Balliett, Whitney. American musicians : fifty-six portraits in jazz / Whitney Balliett. — New York : Oxford, 1986. — x, 415 p. ISBN 0-19-503758-8.

Profiles from the *New Yorker,* 1962–1986, by the magazine's distinguished jazz critic; based for the most part on interviews. Includes essays on Hugues Panassié and Charles Delaunay (two pioneer jazz critics), Red Allen, Jabbo Smith, Doc Cheatham, Art Hodes, Vic Dickenson, Joe Bushkin, Ellis Larkins, Dave McKenna, Bob Wilber, Dick

Wellstood, Jim Hall, Wayne Marsh, Michael Moore, and Gene Bertoncini; plus studies of more familiar artists such as Sidney Bechet and Marian McPartland. Insightful accounts of the music. Without source notes or index.
Reviews: ARBA 1988, #1312; *Choice* 1/87, 771; LJ 1/87, 54.

S2-427   ML395 .D44
Deffaa, Chip. Voices of the jazz age : profiles of eight vintage jazzmen / Chip Deffaa. — Urbana : University of Illinois Press, 1990. — xix, 255 p. : ill. ISBN 0-252-01681-5.
Essays on Sam Wooding, Benny Waters, Bix Beiderbecke, Joe Tarto, Bud Freeman, Jimmy McPartland, Freddie Moore, and Jabbo Smith; shorter versions of seven of them had appeared in *Mississippi Rag*. The author, a jazz critic for the *New York Post*, offers documented (extensive endnotes) views of the men and their work. Except for the chapter on Beiderbecke, the material is based on interviews. For Smith, he gives the "first comprehensive account of his career." All the essays are engagingly written, and most have at least some new information to offer. Bibliography, not annotated, of about 100 general books. Index, not expansive, of names and song titles.
Reviews: *Choice* 1/91, 789; LJ 4/15/90, 95.

S2-428   ML395 .H64
Holmes, Lowell D. Jazz greats : getting better with age / Lowell D. Holmes and John W. Thomson. — New York : Holmes & Meier, 1986. — ix, 150 p. : ill. ISBN 0-8419-0750-1.
A dozen jazz musicians were interviewed to examine the effects of aging on attitude and performance. The transcription of each interview is preceded by a few pages of background information; opening and closing chapters provide context and interpretation. Interviewees: Milt Hinton, Andy Kirk, Mary Lou Williams, Adolphus "Doc" Cheatham, Walter "Foots" Thomas, Eddie Barefield, Johnny Guarnieri, Marshall Royal, Howard Rumsey, Lawrence Brown, Eddie Miller, and Jess Stacy.
A recent photograph of each interviewee is included; there is a brief bibliography, but no index.
Lowell D. Holmes is a professor of anthropology and John W. Thomson is an associate professor of music, both at Wichita State University [—D.P.].
Review: *Choice* 7–8/87, 1704.

S2-429   ML395 .Z56
Zinsser, William. Willie and Dwike : an American profile / William Zinsser. — New York : Harper & Row, 1984. — 170 p. ISBN 0-06-015275-3.

Pianist Dwike Mitchell (1930–) formed the Mitchell-Ruff duo with bass and French horn player Willie Ruff in 1955. They have performed all over the world and have recorded extensively. Ruff is also a professor of music at Yale. Zinsser traveled with Mitchell and Ruff from 1981 to 1983, from Shanghai back to the United States and then to Venice, to collect information for this combination of biography, travelogue, and appreciation. Apparently all of the information came from Mitchell and Ruff, since no sources are cited. Ruff's autobiography, *A Call to Assembly* (S2-666), certainly contains more information about Ruff and probably more about Mitchell as well. The style varies among the chapters, perhaps because parts of the work originally appeared in the *New Yorker* or *Smithsonian*. Without index or bibliographical references.

William Zinsser was an editor, critic, and editorialist for the *New York Herald Tribune* for 13 years. He taught writing at Yale before becoming executive editor of the Book-of-the-Month Club. [—D. P.].

Reviews: *Choice* 11/84, 436; LJ 6/15/84, 1242.

Guitarists

S2-430   ML398 .B53

Obrecht, Jas. Blues guitar : the men who made the music : from the pages of *Guitar Player* magazine / ed. Jas Obrecht. — San Francisco : Miller Freeman, 1990. — vii, 200 p. : ill. ISBN not given.

Interviews and brief biographies of Muddy Waters, John Lee Hooker, B. B. King, Albert King, Willie Dixon, Otis Rush, Freddie King, Albert Collins, and 16 other performers. It is all undocumented and casual, but some facts come through about playing techniques and characteristics of various instruments. With a nonexpansive index.

S2-431   ML398 .G7

Grosz, Marty. The guitarists / Marty Grosz and Lawrence Cohn. — Alexandria, Va. : Time-Life Records, 1980. — 56 p. ISBN not given.

Brief biographies and discographies for Eddie Lang, 1902–1933; Django Reinhardt, 1910–1953; Charlie Christian, 1916–1942; Lonnie Johnson, 1899–1970; Teddy Bunn, 1909–1978; Dick McDonough, 1904–1938; and Carl Kress, 1907–1965. See series note at S2-1114.

Drummers

S2-432   ML399 .H2

Hart, Mickey. Drumming at the edge of magic : a journey into the spirit of percussion / Mickey Hart; with Jay Stevens and Fredric Lieberman. — San Francisco : Harper, 1990. — 263 p. : ill. ISBN 0-0625-0374-X.

An interesting excursion by the percussionist for the Grateful Dead, dealing with the history of drum playing in antiquity and in such locales as Tibet, India, and Africa. Hart includes some discussions with folklorist Joseph Campbell and describes a visit to the Ojibway Indians with Tom Vennum (see S2-998). The author's impressions are provocative and, if not original in a scholarly sense, valuable for the performer's insights they offer. Excellent photographs throughout; without reference features or index.

S2-433 ML399 .K66

Korall, Burt. Drummin' men : the heartbeat of jazz : the swing years / Burt Korall; foreword by Mel Tormé. — New York : Schirmer, 1990. — xvi, 381 p. : ill. ISBN 0-02-872000-8.

These adulatory, sentimental sketches consist primarily of quotations supposedly taken from interviews conducted by Korall or by others with the subjects and their associates. Chick Webb, Gene Krupa, Ray McKinley, Jo Jones, Sid Catlett, Dave Tough, and Buddy Rich are each given 30 to 50 pages of coverage. Much shorter sketches are included for Sonny Greer, George Wettling, Cozy Cole, Jimmy Crawford, O'Neil Spencer, Cliff Leeman, and Ray Baudac. One or more photographs of each drummer are included. Nothing is said about the musical style of individual drummers.

While secondary sources are cited, the interviews conducted by Korall are not documented in any way. A selective discography includes album titles and labels, but not label numbers; many recordings are undated, and no information is included on availability. Personal, group, and club names are included in the nonexpansive index, along with titles of songs, albums, and shows.

Burt Korall is a jazz drummer, jazz critic, and director of special assignments at BMI [— D. P.].

S2-434 ML399 .S8

Spagnardi, Ron. The great jazz drummers / Ron Spagnardi; ed. William F. Miller. — Cedar Grove, N.J. : Modern Drummer Publications, 1992. — 128 p. : ill. ISBN not given.

Singers

S2-435 ML400 .A7

Archer, Robyn. A star is torn / Robyn Archer and Diana Simmonds. — London : Virago, 1986. — 208 p. : ill. ISBN 0-8606-8514-4.

Sentimental, adulatory profiles of women who triumphed over personal problems and prejudice to achieve success, most of them as singers. The book is based on a one-person show of the same name, presented by Archer in 1979–1982. The individuals treated are Marie Lloyd (1870–1922), Bessie Smith, Helen Morgan, Jane Froman, Carmen Miranda, Billie Holiday, Edith Piaf, Judy Holliday, Judy Garland, Dinah Washington, Marilyn Monroe, Patsy Cline, and Janis Joplin. No documentation; with a nonexpansive index.

S2-436   ML400 .B25

Balliett, Whitney. American singers : twenty-seven portraits in song / Whitney Balliett. — Expanded ed. — New York : Oxford, 1988. — x, 244 p. ISBN 0-19-504610-2.
1st ed., 1979.

An expansion of the first edition, from 12 to 25 essays. The artists discussed are Alec Wilder, Alberta Hunter, Cleo Brown, Nellie Lutcher, Joe Turner, Helen Humbers, Ray Charles, Joe Williams, Sylvia Syms, Peggy Lee, Margaret Whiting, Anita Ellis, Teddi King, Mary Mayo, Barbara Lea, Tony Bennett, Mel Tormé, George Shearing, Julius La Rosa, Mabel Mercer, Bobby Short, Hugh Shannon, Julie Wilson, Blossom Dearie, Carol Sloane, Betty Carter, and Dave Frishberg. Except for the Whiting piece, all the essays appeared originally in the *New Yorker*. Balliett is a knowledgeable writer about the music, and he derives most of his biographical material from interviews. Without source notes, index, or bibliography.

Review: LJ 2/1/79, 404 (for the 1st ed.).

S2-437   ML400 .B595

Welding, Pete. Bluesland : portraits of twelve major American blues masters / ed. Peter Welding and Toby Byron. — New York : Dutton, 1991. — 255 p. : ill. ISBN 0-525-93374-1.

Profiles, by various authors, of Blind Lemon Jefferson, Lonnie Johnson, Bessie Smith, Robert Johnson, T-Bone Walker, Big Joe Turner, Muddy Waters, Professor Longhair, B. B. King, Howlin' Wolf, Etta Jones, and Chuck Berry. The style is casual, with undocumented quotations and conversations; the topics are invariably held to a personal level, avoiding discussion of music or of performance. With a nonexpansive index.

S2-438   ML400 .C76

Crowther, Bruce. The jazz singers : from ragtime to the new wave / Bruce Crowther and Mike Pinfold. — Poole, Dorset, England; New York : Blandford, 1986. — 224 p. : ill. ISBN 0-7137-1648-7.

Biographical sketches of some 200 singers are woven together in this historical survey that includes performers associated not only with jazz but also with blues, gospel, ragtime, and their derivatives. Professional and personal facts are accompanied by general descriptions of style;

longer sketches often discuss specific recordings or performances. Connective material places the artists and styles in musical and historical context. The author's evaluations of the singers' talents and significance are carefully written and seem to reflect critical consensus more than personal opinion.

Over two dozen well-chosen photographs are effectively placed throughout the text; most are full-page. There are also about a dozen portraits drawn by Pinfold, which add little. The brief bibliography (ca. 35 entries) is followed by a list of recommended recordings by about 120 of the singers discussed; labels, numbers, and titles are given, but not release or reissue dates. Only personal and group names are included in the detailed, nonexpansive index, which inexplicably ends after "Weiss, Sid."

Bruce Crowther and Mike Pinfold are jazz enthusiasts who have written for jazz magazines and broadcast regularly on jazz radio programs. [—D. P.].

Review: ARBA 1989, p. 490.

S2-439   ML400 .D85
Duncan, Robert. Only the good die young : the rock 'n' roll book of the dead / Robert Duncan. — New York : Harmony Books, 1986. — 192 p. : ill. ISBN 0-5175-5757-6.

"A dark tribute to the excesses personified by Janis Joplin, Jimi Hendrix, Jim Morrison, and other rock heroes who died in pursuit of (or perhaps because of) the rock & roll life style." The sensational aspects of 16 such lives are revealed through vulgar anecdotes, some of them supported by source notes. With a nonexpansive index.

Review: *Choice* 4/92, 1192.

S2-440   ML400 .H43
Hemming, Roy. Discovering great singers of classic pop : a new listener's guide to the sounds and lives of the top performers and their recordings, movies, and videos / Roy Hemming and David Hajdu. — New York : Newmarket Press, 1991. — viii, 296 p. : ill. : 16 p. plates. ISBN 1-55704-072-9.

Short appreciations of 52 blues singers and big band vocalists, movie singers and stage performers, commencing with "crooners and canaries of the 1920s and 1930s" and carrying on to Barbra Streisand and Liza Minnelli. The writing is informal, inclusive of remembered conversations, and undocumented. There is a casual record list for each person, giving minimal data. With a bibliography of about 300 titles and a nonexpansive index.

S2-441   ML400 .H8
Hood, Phil. Artists of American folk music : the legends of traditional

folk, the stars of the sixties, the virtuosi of new acoustic music / Phil Hood. — New York : Morrow, 1986. — 159 p. ISBN 0-688-051916-3.
A collection of interviews and articles that had appeared in *Guitar Player* and *Frets* magazines from 1970 to 1985.
Reviews: ARBA 1987, #1261; LJ 4/1/86, 152.

S2-442   ML400 .M44
Mellers, Wilfrid Howard. Angels of the night : popular female singers of our time / Wilfrid Mellers. — New York : Blackwell, 1986. — x, 227 p. : ill. : 24 p. plates. ISBN 0-6311-4696-2.
Mellers is a British music historian of good repute (see LOAM 27, LOAM A-212, and LOAM Suppl. SA-790), but this foray into American pop raises many questions. In analyzing the work of early blues and jazz vocalists, then of gospel and soul/rock singers, he is tiresomely referential: he plumbs for artistic meaning in racism and in woman's "search for social and creative identity," not making any specific connections between the music of these talented women and any societal elements. For Mellers there is always some external explanation for what happens in art; for example, George Gershwin "revealed through hedonism and nostalgia a profound awareness of what it means to live in big cities." With a glossary, brief discographies (release label and number only), and a nonexpansive index.
Listing: BCL.

S2-443   ML400 .N4
Nelson, Havelock. Bring the noise : a guide to rap music and hip-hop culture / Havelock Nelson and Michael A. Gonzales. — New York : Harmony Books, 1991. — xxii, 298 p. ISBN 0-517-58305-4.
Biographical sketches and discographies for selected rap performers, with a recommended core list of 25 rap records.

S2-444   ML400 .P295
Parish, James Robert. Hollywood songsters / James Robert Parish and Michael R. Pitts. — New York : Garland, 1991. — xiv, 826 p. (Garland reference library of the humanities, 1,164) ISBN 0-8240-3444-9.
Informal biographical sketches of 104 singing film actors, useful for information about singers not much written about (e.g., Bobby Breen, Gloria Jean, Donald O'Connor) and performers who sang only incidentally (e.g., Ann Blyth, Irene Dunne, Lillian Roth, Ann Sothern). Undocumented quotations and conversations are frequent. Discography of LP albums only; filmography, giving studio and release date of each movie. Lists of Broadway and television shows recorded by the artists. Much space is wasted here in accounts of persons well covered elsewhere, such as Fred Astaire, Bing Crosby, Judy Garland, and Elvis Presley. With a nonexpansive index of titles and names.

S2-445   ML400 .S88
Story, Rosalyn M. And so I sing : African-American divas of opera and concert / Rosalyn M. Story. — New York : Warner Books, 1990. — xvii, 236 p. : ill. ISBN 0-446-71016-4.
A collection of appreciations of black singers, from Sissieretta Jones ("Black Patti") to Kathleen Battle, covering many lesser-known artists as well as headliners. The material is undocumented and threaded with "the struggle for racial justice in America." Many direct quotations are included, without sources. There are no reference features other than the nonexpansive index.
Review: AM 1993, 491.

ML404 : Instrument Makers

S2-446   ML404 .W46
Wenberg, Thomas James. The violin makers of the United States / Thomas James Wenberg. — Mt. Hood, Ore. : Mt. Hood Publishing Co., 1986. — x, 399 p. : ill. ISBN 0-938071-05-X.
A 1987 supplement was inserted into the copy seen. About 200 violin makers are listed, with short biographical sketches and photos of their instruments, bows, and labels (some in color). With a bibliography of about 100 entries (incomplete data); without index.
Reviews: ARBA 1988, p. 517; *Choice* 9/87, 142.

S2-447   ML404 .G76
Groce, Nancy. Musical instrument makers of New York : a directory of eighteenth- and nineteenth-century urban craftsmen / Nancy Groce. — Stuyvesant, N.Y. : Pendragon, 1991. — xxi, 200 p. (Annotated reference tools in music, 4) ISBN 0-918728-97-5.
Biographical sketches of about 1,000 craftsmen, with their dates and various street addresses, and the types of instruments they made. The earliest known instrument maker in the city was Geoffrey Stafford, who produced lutes and violins in the 1690s. With a checklist by types of instrument and a bibliography of about 300 books, articles, and manuscripts.

ML410–429 : INDIVIDUAL BIOGRAPHIES

ML410 : Composers

S2-448   ML410 .A235
Adler, Richard. You gotta have heart : an autobiography / Richard Adler; with Lee Davis. — New York : D. I. Fine, 1990. — xiii, 354 p. : ill. : 16 p. plates. ISBN 1-55611-201-7.

Broadway composer Adler (1921–), who collaborated with Jerry Ross in *Pajama Game* and *Damn Yankees,* offers a "moving memoir of deep-felt emotions" and—after his victory over throat cancer—"spiritual awakening." The style is that of imagined conversations. Nothing useful about music is presented. With an expansive index.

S2-449   ML410 .A638
Whitesitt, Linda. The life and music of George Antheil, 1900–1959 / Linda Whitesitt. — Ann Arbor, Mich. : UMI Research Press, 1983. — xxi, 351 p. : ill. (Studies in musicology, 70) ISBN 0-8537-1462-4.
A revision of the author's 1981 Ph.D. dissertation. Antheil was an avant-garde composer who achieved considerable popularity in Europe during the 1920s. In 1936 he moved to Hollywood and took up film scoring, in a more conventional idiom, gradually fading from the concert scene. This is a useful biography, catalog of compositions, discography, and list of writings about Antheil. Indexed.
Review: *Choice* 5/84, 1316.

S2-450   ML410 .B23 .H5
Heyman, Barbara B. Samuel Barber : the composer and his music / Barbara B. Heyman. — New York : Oxford, 1992. — xviii, 586 p. : ill. ISBN 0-19-506650-2.
A study based on the author's dissertation, utilizing interviews, correspondence, and other primary source material. It forms a strong biographical narrative, enriched by Heyman's comments. There are also perceptive observations on many of the compositions, with musical examples from them. With a worklist, bibliography of writings about Barber, endnotes, and index.
Reviews: *Choice* 2/93, 973; LJ 1/92, 130.

S2-451   ML410 .B499 B5
Bergreen, Laurence. As thousands cheer : the life of Irving Berlin / Laurence Bergreen. — New York : Viking, 1990. — xiv, 658 p. : ill. : 16 p. plates. ISBN 0-670-81874-7.
A well-documented and well-told story of Berlin (Israel Balin, 1888–1989), who rose from life in the flophouses of the lower East Side to become America's legendary songwriter. Bergreen concentrates on the composer's life, saying little about the songs as music, but the tale is intriguing enough in itself, and it is related without imagined conversations or episodes. With endnotes, a bibliography of about 100 titles, a list of songs of each five-year period from 1907, and a partly expansive index.
Review: AM 1993, 245.

S2-452   ML410 .B499 W5
Whitcomb, Ian. Irving Berlin and ragtime America / Ian Whitcomb. —

London : Century-Hutchinson, 1987; New York : Limelight, 1988. —
219 p. ISBN 0-87910-115-6 (U.S.).
Originally published London: Century-Hutchinson, 1987.
A casual, anecdotal history of the composer and his times, emphasizing the music business in New York; with undocumented events, conversations, and quotations. A general bibliography of 25 items and a nonexpansive index.
Review: *Choice* 4/89, 1345.

S2-453   ML410 .B566 C5
Chapin, Schuyler. Leonard Bernstein : notes from a friend / Schuyler
Chapin; foreword by Peter Ustinov. — New York : Walker, 1992. —
xii, 178 p. : ill. ISBN 0-8027-1216-9.
Chapin was head of the Masterworks Division at Columbia Records
during the time that Bernstein (1918–1990) made his acclaimed recordings; he was also general manager of the Metropolitan Opera and dean
of the Columbia University School of the Arts. Thus he knew Bernstein
through a number of professional connections, and he was a friend as
well. His affectionate memoir of the musician reveals some episodes not
published earlier, but of little interest. Nothing of substance is said about
the music or the person. Essentially, the story turned out to be just what
the author promised in the Preface it would not be: a book of gossip.
Without documentation; with an expansive index.

S2-454   ML410 .B566 .L56
Ledbetter, Steven. Sennets & tuckets : a Bernstein celebration / ed.
Steven Ledbetter. — Boston : Boston Symphony Orchestra, in association with D. R. Godine, 1988. — ix, 210 p. ISBN 0-87923-775-9.
A tribute volume, made from the 70th-birthday occasion at Tanglewood. Among the contributors are Michael Tilson Thomas, Paul Hume,
and Phyllis Curtin. J. F. Weber's discography gives full information on
all recording sessions and lists reissues as well. A chronological worklist gives minimal data. There is a bibliography of about 120 books and
articles, and an index.
Review: *Choice* 2/90, 960.

S2-455   ML410 .B566 P49
Peyser, Joan. Bernstein : a biography / Joan Peyser. — New York :
Morrow, 1987. — 481 p. : ill. ISBN 0-688-04918-4.
In this story, Bernstein (1918–1990) is portrayed as a Jew, egoist, and
homosexual who also happened to be a musical genius. His compositions are said to exhibit his personal feelings. His sexuality is said to de-
termine his great decisions. "The greater the artist, the more powerful the
sexual drive, whether suppressed or not. . . . The point then is not whether

Bernstein was homosexual or heterosexual and why, but rather how the choices he made affected his life and his art." Such a connection—between the person and the art—is always awkward to demonstrate, and Peyser has the usual problems trying to do it. In the process she does present the major events and relationships of the conductor's life, relying on sources named in the Acknowledgments but not specifically cited. Musical matters are not dealt with, except incidentally as they come up in comments by critics or other composers. With an expansive index.

Reviews: *Choice* 9/87, 148; LJ 6/1/87, 107.

S2-456   ML410 .B6
Gordon, Eric A. Mark the music : the life and work of Marc Blitzstein / Eric A. Gordon. — New York : St. Martin's, 1989. — xviii, 605 p. : ill. : 16 p. plates. ISBN 0-312-02607-2.

A straightforward story of the life and works of Blitzstein (1905–1964), best known for *The Cradle Will Rock* (1937) and other stage works of social significance. The biography is well documented, and there is a complete worklist by genre, offering variable information about the compositions. Recordings are noted for some of them. With a nonexpansive index.

S2-457   ML410 .B97 S5
Simpson, Anne Key. Hard trials: the life and music of Harry T. Burleigh / Anne Key Simpson. — Metuchen, N.J. : Scarecrow, 1990. — xvii, 476 p. : ill. (Composers of North America, 8) ISBN 0-8108-2291-1.

A useful account of Burleigh (1866–1949), the "first black composer to gain recognition both for his art songs and for the elevation of Negro spirituals through his arrangements of them." He had an interesting public life, acting as copyist for Antonin Dvorák (on his American stay)—who got his knowledge of spirituals from Burleigh—and singing at the World's Columbian Exposition in 1893, achieving wide acclaim as a singer. His story is told here in straightforward terms, with chapter endnotes. For many compositions there are musical examples and program notes. There is a worklist, by genre, of 217 items, with dates, publishers, timings, and keys. He himself left no recordings of his singing, but there are many discs of his compositions—listed here with dates and contents. A 300-item bibliography and a nonexpansive index complete the reference apparatus.

Review: *Choice* 6/91, 1650.

S2-458   ML410 .B997 H7
Howell, John. David Byrne / John Howell. — New York : Thunder's Mouth, 1992. — 159 p. : ill. ISBN 1-56025-031-3.

An adulatory, undocumented account of the rock performer and

songwriter whose "inspired work" is "redefining art and entertainment in America." Byrne, former leader of the Talking Heads, was interviewed for the book, and he also offered extracts from his diary. With a discography, bibliography, and filmography, but without index.
Review: LJ 9/1/92, 183.

S2-459   ML410 .C24 F6
Fleming, Richard. John Cage at seventy-five / ed. Richard Fleming and William Duckworth. — Lewisburg, Pa. : Bucknell University; distributed by Associated University Presses, 1989. — 305 p. : ill. 18 p. plates. (Bucknell review 32, no. 2) ISBN 0-8387-5156-3.
A festschrift containing contributions by various scholars. It includes four critical essays; a photo section; an interview with Cage; a conversation between Cage and André Kostelanetz; the text of "Anarchy," an essay/poem by Cage; and some of his correspondence. Without index.
Review: *Choice* 6/90, 1688.

S2-460   ML410 .C24 R5
Revill, David. The roaring silence : John Cage : a life / David Revill. — New York : Arcade Pub./Little, Brown, 1992. — 375 p. : ill. : 16 p. plates. ISBN 1-55970-166-8.
The first full-length biography of the controversial composer (or inventor, as Schoenberg described him), based on interviews with Cage and various associates. Much emphasis goes to Cage's nonmusical activities and interests, for example, his involvement with Eastern philosophies and with futurism. Not much is said about the actual music, and there are no musical examples save six reproductions of pages. A useful worklist covers 1931–1991, giving instrumentation, performance information, recordings, and comments. With source notes (incomplete; many quotations are not accounted for, and exact citations are lacking), a bibliography of about 300 items (also missing important titles), and a nonexpansive index.
Reviews: *Choice* 2/93, 973; LJ 9/15/92, 67.

S2-461   ML410 .C395
Yellin, Victor Fell. Chadwick, Yankee composer / Victor Fell Yellin. — Washington : Smithsonian Institution Press, 1990. — xvi, 238 p. : ill. : 8 p. plates. ISBN 0-87474-988-3.
George W. Chadwick (1854–1931) was an important composer in his day, but his works—in a romantic, Wagnerian idiom—are no longer in the repertoire. Yellin has made a plain, documented biography, with musical examples and program notes. There is an expansive index.
Review: *Choice* 1/91, 791.

S2-462   ML410 .C4

Yoffe, Elkhonon. Tchaikovsky in America : the composer's visit in 1891 / Elkhonon Yoffe; trans. from the Russian by Lidva Yoffe. — New York : Oxford, 1986. — x, 216 p. : ill. : 9 p. plates. ISBN 0-1950-4117-8.

The composer was invited to New York to participate in the opening ceremonies for Carnegie Hall in May 1891. He remained in the United States for 25 days, writing in his diary and providing an interesting outsider view of American cultural life. In addition to the diary (which also recounts in gloomy detail the rigors of ocean travel at the time), Yoffe has drawn on contemporary newspapers to fill out the New York picture; everything shows that Tchaikovksy was greatly admired and appreciated. There are a few chapter endnotes, and other quotes are cited as they appear. With a nonexpansive index. The author is librarian of the Detroit Symphony Orchestra.

Reviews: *Choice* 5/87, 1409; LJ 9/15/86, 89.

S2-463   ML410 .C756 A3

Copland, Aaron. Copland : since 1943 / Aaron Copland and Vivian Perlis. — New York : St. Martin's, 1989. — xii, 463 p. : ill. ISBN 0-312-03313-3.

This volume completes the imaginative biographical treatment begun with *Copland: 1900 through 1942* (1984, LOAM Suppl. SA-118), continuing the combination of interviews with Copland by Perlis, background essays by Perlis, and interviews with Copland's friends and colleagues, also by Perlis. Despite the great difficulties of documenting a life that Copland himself has been reluctant to expose, and musical ideas that he has only vaguely articulated, Perlis has contrived to create an absorbing portrait. Her use of documentation is thorough and scholarly; her choice of graphics is exemplary. With extensive endnotes and a nonexpansive index.

Reviews: AM 1990, 231; LJ 12/89, 126.

S2-464   ML410 .C944 G41

Gillespie, Don. George Crumb : profile of a composer / Don Gillespie; introduction by Gilbert Chase. — New York : C. F. Peters, 1986. — 113 p. : ill. (Composer profiles, 2) ISBN 0-938856-02-2.

A collection of previously published articles and a few original essays, by and about Crumb (1929–), whose compositional process is "not only an involvement in the symbols and sounds of music but a spiritual quest as well. . . . [He] controls all aspects of the aesthetic experience: the visual and auditory, and the intellectual and philosophical" (from an essay by Susan MacLean). The process is ably described in a contribution by Christopher Wilkinson. Perhaps the most interesting elements in the book are ample illustrations of Crumb scores, showing his imaginative variations on the traditional horizontal staff design. A bibliography of more than 400 writings about Crumb is included, with a discography (not detailed), and a list of concert reviews. A worklist features extended commentaries. Without index.

Review: AM 1988, 102.

S2-465   ML410 .D353 B8
Bumgardner, Thomas A. Norman Dello Joio / Thomas A. Bumgardner. — Boston: Twayne, 1986. — xv, 180 p. : ill. (Twayne's music series) ISBN 0-8057-94654.

A scholarly treatment of the composer (born 1913), concentrating on the works. Each chapter takes up a genre, offering genesis and reception studies, along with technical analyses. Interviews and unpublished sources were used; Bumgardner spent four weeks in Dello Joio's home gathering material. The result is a model short biography, interesting and reliable. With a discography, bibliography of primary and secondary sources, worklist, and expansive index.

Reviews: AM 1987, 459; *Choice* 1/87, 772.

S2-466   ML410 .D43 K5
Kimberling, Victoria J. David Diamond : a bio-bibliography / Victoria J. Kimberling; foreword by David Diamond. — Metuchen, N.J. : Scarecrow, 1987. — ix, 178 p. : ill. ISBN 0-8108-2058-7.

A useful biography of composer Diamond (1915–), emphasizing the music rather than the life story. Not that his life was uninteresting; what other composer played in the orchestra for *Your Hit Parade*? He had trouble making ends meet, even when he was most popular; he was widely performed by major orchestras, and he won the Prix de Rome plus three Guggenheim fellowships. Many works are discussed in detail, with musical examples. There is a chronological worklist, 1928–1986, with dates, instrumentations, performances, publishers, and comments. With a bibliography of about 300 items, a discography of 19 recordings, and a nonexpansive general index.

S2-467   ML410 .E44 C6
Collier, James Lincoln. Duke Ellington / James Lincoln Collier. — New York : Oxford, 1987. — viii, 340 p. : ill. ISBN 0-19-305770-7.

In this work Collier focuses on the early life and career of Ellington as he examines the influences on Ellington's musical style. He looks at Ellington not so much as a composer, but more as an improvising jazz musician and bandleader who surrounded himself with good musicians. Collier looks closely at the form, melody, and harmony of many Ellington compositions. His analysis would have been greatly aided by musical examples.

More than two dozen photographs feature Ellington and associates. Primary and secondary sources consulted for this critical effort are carefully cited. A brief discographical note describes various collections that were available at the time of writing. The expansive index includes persons, titles, places, and topics. Without bibliographical references.

James Lincoln Collier is a jazz critic whose books include *The Making of Jazz* (LOAM Suppl. S-693) and *Louis Armstrong: An American Genius* (LOAM Suppl. SA-455) [–D. P.].

Review: LJ 9/1/87, 184.

S2-468   ML410 .E44 D2

Dance, Stanley. Duke Ellington. 1978.

See series note at S2-1114.

S2-468a   ML410 .E44 G2

Gammond, Peter. Duke Ellington / Peter Gammond. — London : Apollo, 1987. — 127 p. : ill. ISBN 0-9488-2000-4.

See series note at S2-1118.

S2-469   ML410 .E44 R3

Rattenbury, Ken. Duke Ellington, jazz composer / Ken Rattenbury. — New Haven, Conn. : Yale University Press, 1991. — xii, 327 p. : ill. ISBN 0-300-04428-3.

A rewarding approach to Ellington that treats him as classical composers are treated. The compositions of 1939–1941 (Ellington's creative prime) are discussed in musical terms. Five of them—"Ko Ko," "Mr. J. B. Blues," "Concerto for Cootie" [later the song "Do Nothin' 'till You Hear from Me"], "Junior Hop," and "Subtle Slough"—are printed in full score notation and analyzed. Rattenbury's scholarly views are counterpointed by comments on the music from Ellington sidemen. With an Ellington chronology, worklist, bibliography, and selective discography. There are endnotes, and there is a nonexpansive index of names and titles.

Reviews: *Choice* 7-8/91, 1791; LJ 11/1/90, 92.

S2-470   ML410 .E44 S9

Stratemann, Klaus. Duke Ellington day by day and film by film / Klaus Stratemann. — Copenhagen : JazzMedia, 1992. — vii, 781 p. : ill. ISBN 87-88043-34-7.

A remarkable gathering of information that lives up to its challenging title. Ellington's life from 1929 to 1974 is charted chronologically, with his performing and personal activities blended; sources are cited for everything. Recordings are noted and discussed as they happened. An appendix offers the names of all musicians who performed in Ellington groups, 1929–1974. There is an extended discussion of the film *A Day at the Races,* in which the Ellington band was thought to have participated; Stratemann says the evidence indicates it was a different band. Other useful compilations are of the Ellington television appearances and of Cotton Club programs and advertisements. There is a bibliography of about 180 books, mostly general in nature. With nonexpansive indexes of cities, persons, song titles, and topics.

S2-471   0 .E44 T8
Tucker, Mark. Ellington : the early years / Mark Tucker. — Urbana : University of Illinois Press, 1991. — xviii, 343 p. : ill. : music. ISBN 0-252-01425-1.

This is both a biographical study, based on interviews and primary documents, and an analysis in technical language—with musical examples—of Duke Ellington's early compositions and recordings. Tucker concentrates on the period before the Duke achieved wide renown with his Cotton Club (New York) appearances in 1927. It is a tale of growing up black in Washington, with no infantile display of musical talent, then of mastering the piano and the jazz/ragtime idioms, with professional performances from age 17. By 1914 he was composing, though his first verified publication dates from 1924, the year of his earliest recording. He led several groups in New York in the 1920s. A valuable appendix in this book lists all the compositions and recordings from 1914 to 1927, with full data and useful commentaries. With extensive endnotes, a bibliographic essay, bibliography of about 150 items, and an expansive index.
Review: *Choice* 7-8/91, 1791.

S2-472   ML410 .F228
Culbertson, Evelyn Davis. He heard America singing : Arthur Farwell, composer and crusading music educator / Evelyn Davis Culbertson. — Metuchen, N.J. : Scarecrow, 1992. — xxix, 852 p. : ill. ISBN 0-8108-12580-5.

A fine biography of Farwell (1872–1952), who made numerous contributions to American music and musical life. He was a critic in New York, director of a settlement music school, and teacher of Roy Harris; he established the legendary Wa-Wan Press (1901) that published the works of 37 American composers—nine of them women. As a composer himself, he was "a fitting figure to be considered as the last of our pioneers." Along with the life story, there is a worklist of 233 compositions arranged by genre, with dates, publishers, performances, musical examples, and comments. A discography lists 26 commercial recordings and 37 private recordings. There are chapter endnotes, and there is a nonexpansive index.
Review: *Choice* 2/93, 972.

S2-473   ML410 .F455 A3
Finney, Ross Lee. Profile of a lifetime : a musical autobiography /
Ross Lee Finney. — New York : C. F. Peters, 1992. — 247 p. : ill. : 16
p. plates. (Composer profiles, 3) ISBN 0-9388-5605-7.
A pleasing story of an interesting, varied life, unfortunately lacking
any substantive information about music. He studied with Alban Berg,
earned a Purple Heart in World War II, established one of the early electronic labs, and wrote in numerous styles. There is a title list of his works
and a nonexpansive index. See also S2-55.

S2-474   ML410 .G1693
Hall, Ruth K. A place of her own : the story of Elizabeth Garrett / Ruth
K. Hall. — Rev. ed. — Santa Fe, N.M. : Sunstone, 1983. — 171 p. : ill.
ISBN 0-913270-68-7.
Garrett (1885?–1947) was a blind musician and composer from New
Mexico, known for "O Fair New Mexico," the state song. She was the
daughter of a popular sheriff, Pat Garrett. The book is an impressionis-
tic treatment, "written in the form of a dialogue," offering no reference
features. Without index.

S2-475   ML410 .G288 D4
DeSantis, Florence Stevenson. Gershwin / Florence Stevenson DeSantis. — New York : Treves, 1987. — 106 p. : ill. ISBN 0-9183-6718-2.
A book of good photos, many of them unusual, a number of them in
color. With an undocumented commentary; without index.

S2-476   ML410 .G288 J2
Jablonski, Edward. Gershwin : a biography / Edward Jablonski. — Garden City, N.Y. : Doubleday, 1987. — xv, 436 p. ISBN 0-035-19431-5.
Edition seen was the reprint by Northeastern University (1990). A
plain, straight-ahead biography, concentrated on the personal life of the
composer (and to some extent that of his brother Ira), and on productions,
performances, encounters with other musicians, etc. With "notes on
sources" for each chapter, but without direct citations. Many of the quotations and conversations remain ethereal. Nothing particular is said
about musical matters. With a selected, annotated discography of reissues and a partly expansive index.
Reviews: *Choice* 3/88, 1106; LJ 9/15/87, 77.

S2-477   ML410 .G288 J22
Jablonski, Edward. Gershwin remembered / Edward Jablonski. —
London : Faber & Faber; Portland, Ore. : Amadeus, 1992. — 222 p. : ill.
ISBN 0-931340-43-8 (U.S.).
An interesting gathering of recollections about Gershwin, from many
contemporaries. Among those who offer observations are Fred Astaire,

Paul Whiteman, Irving Berlin, Oscar Levant, and S. N. Behrman. Comments are set in chronological perspective, accompanying events in the composer's life. There is also a detailed chronology on Gershwin and a nonexpansive index.

S2-478 ML410 .G288 K46
Kendall, Alan. George Gershwin : a biography / Alan Kendall. — New York : Universe, 1987. — 192 p. : ill. : 32 p. plates. ISBN 0-87663-663-6.
A basic biography, using quotes from Gershwin and others without direct citations; but it does not have invented conversations. There is a worklist, giving titles only, from 1913 to 1937, and a partly expansive index.

S2-479 ML410 .G288 R67
Rosenberg, Deena. Fascinating rhythm : the collaboration of George and Ira Gershwin / Deena Rosenberg. — New York : Dutton, 1991. — xxv, 516 p. : ill. ISBN 0-525-93356-5.
A study of songs by the Gershwins, giving the background for each composition. Lyrics and some melody lines (without chord symbols) are provided, along with a sort of analysis that is fixated on the discovery of similar patterns among the tunes. There is documentation in chapter endnotes and a bibliography of about 100 books and articles. Three songs are written out in piano/vocal score. With a checklist of recordings and an expansive index of titles, persons, and topics.
Reviews: AM 1993, 497; *Choice* 5/92, 1402; LJ 10/15/91, 84.

S2-480 ML410 .G398 A3
Glass, Philip. Music by Philip Glass / Philip Glass; introduction by Robert T. Jones. — New York : Harper & Row, 1987. — 222 p. : ill. : 24 p. plates : music. ISBN 0-0601-5823-9.
British edition: *Opera on the Beach* (London : Faber, 1988).
Composer Glass (1937–) is famed as a pioneer minimalist and for several exotic operas, notably *Einstein on the Beach* (1975–1976) and *Akhnaten* (1983). His early study included such diverse figures as Nadia Boulanger and Ravi Shankar; the book offers some "revealing anecdotes" about them and others who helped shape the composer's views and writing. This volume is essentially a genesis account of the operas, indicating a strong concern by Glass with plot and visual elements. Full libretti are given, along with some musical examples in scarcely legible handwriting. With a selective list of works, 1965–1987, and an expansive index.
Reviews: *Choice* 5/88, 1413; LJ 3/1/88, 68.

S2-481 ML410 .G9134
Maisel, Edward. Charles T. Griffes : the life of an American composer /

Edward Maisel. — Rev. ed. — New York : Knopf; distributed by Random House, 1984. — xvii, 399 p. : ill. : 7 p. plates. ISBN 0-394-54081-6. 1st ed., 1943 (LOAM 321). This edition is "updated with a new introduction and notes."

A straightforward life story of Griffes (1884–1920), documented with chapter endnotes. There is a strong analytic chapter on a major work, the piano sonata. With a worklist by genre, giving instrumentation and comments.

S2-482   ML410 .G978 A3

Guthrie, Woody. Pastures of plenty : a self-portrait / Woody Guthrie; ed. Dave Marsh and Harold Leventhal. — New York : Harper & Row, 1990. — xxvi, 259 p. : ill. ISBN 0-06-016342-9.

A selection of writings from the letters and notebooks of folksinger Guthrie (1912–1967), concentrated on the 1930s and 1940s. The editors provide comments and narrative continuity. Song lyrics are interspersed, along with 100 photos and drawings. Interesting, honest material that Guthrie apparently had not thought of publishing. With an appendix that identifies persons and places and relates them to Guthrie, and an index of persons, songs, and subjects.

Reviews: *Choice* 3/91, 1146; LJ 12/90, 132.

S2-483   ML410 .H145 B6

Boeringer, James. Morning star : the life and works of Francis Florentine Hagen (1815–1907), Moravian evangelist and composer / James Boeringer. — Winston-Salem, N.C. : Moravian Music Foundation Press, 1986. — 175 p. : ill. ISBN 0-941642-01-1.

"Morning Star" is a naive Moravian hymn by Hagen, the "last of the classical Moravian composers." Boeringer, former director of the Moravian Music Foundation, has compiled a readable biography from Foundation sources—diaries and family chronicles. There is a survey of settings of "Morning Star," a worklist for Hagen (with title-page facsimiles and bibliographic details), and biographical sketches for persons mentioned in the story.

Review: AM 1989, 219.

S2-484   ML410 .H25

Hamlisch, Marvin. The way I was / Marvin Hamlisch; with Gerald Gardner. — New York : Scribner's, 1992. — xiii, 234 p. : ill. ISBN 0-6841-9327-2.

"A collection of recollections, some good, some not so good," is the author's apt description of this volume. It consists of stories and conversations, some remarkably remembered from age six, and various light comments on people and things along the way. Hamlisch (1944–) is best known for the scores to *The Way We Were* and *A Chorus Line*. With a nonexpansive index.

S2-485   ML410 .H562 S6
Smith, Steven C. A heart at fire's center : the life and music of Bernard Herrmann / Steven C. Smith. — Berkeley : University of California Press, 1991. — x, 415 p. : 27 p. plates. ISBN 0-520-07123-9.
A plain biography, documented with chapter endnotes, free of invented conversations and other fictions. Herrmann (1911–1975) was a leading film composer, winner of an Academy Award for *All That Money Can Buy* (1941), perhaps best known for *Citizen Kane* (1940). He was also a conductor and a writer of concert music. This book has separate worklists for his 61 film scores and his concert works (minimal data given). With a bibliography of about 100 entries and an expansive index.
Review: *Choice* 12/91, 605.

S2-486   ML410 .H685 N5
Neumeyer, David. The music of Paul Hindemith / David Neumeyer. — New Haven, Conn. : Yale University Press, 1986. — viii, 294 p. ISBN 0-300-03287-0.
A highly technical, satisfying analysis of Hindemith's works, set against a study of the composer's methods and principles as outlined in *Craft of Musical Composition*. Neumeyer draws on other published examinations of Hindemith's music, but there had been nothing written to compare with the scope and substance of his approach. He discloses macrostructural designs as well as small-scale patterns, quotations, intervallic practices, and so forth. Luther Noss (see S2-487) prepared a Hindemith worklist for this book, with full details (dates, publications, timings, and notes). With a bibliography of about 150 items and an expansive index.
Reviews: AM 1991, 227; *Choice* 11/86, 490; LJ 10/15/86, 98.

S2-487   ML410 .H685 N7
Noss, Luther. Paul Hindemith in the United States / Luther Noss. — Urbana : University of Illinois Press, 1989. — xiii, 219 p. : ill. : 12 p. plates. ISBN 0-252-01563-0.
A straightforward, documented account of the composer's associations with the United States, commencing with 1920, his emigration in 1940, his teaching at Yale, his creative work and professional activities, honors, and American citizenship in 1946. Hindemith and his wife lived in Europe 1953–1958, then returned to several busy years in America before his death in 1963. Chapter endnotes cite many primary documents, mostly personal letters in the Hindemith Collection at Yale (of which Noss is curator). With a curiously brief (10-item) bibliography, a nonexpansive index of names and topics, and an index of compositions cited.
Review: *Choice* 11/89, 497.

S2-488   ML410 .H86
Soares, Janet Mansfield. Louis Horst : musician in a dancer's world /
Janet Mansfield Soares. — Durham, N.C. : Duke University Press,
1992. — xii, 264 p. : ill. ISBN 0-8223-1226-3.
Horst (1884–1964) was musical director of the Denishawn Dance Co.,
and later for Martha Graham; he was the "first teacher of formal composition for dancers." His career included teaching at the Juilliard School.
His life is told here in an interesting fashion, with a chronology of events,
a bibliography of about 250 items, and a worklist giving dates, instrumentation, and premieres. With a partly expansive index.

S2-489   ML410 .I90 A78
Alexander, Michael J. The evolving keyboard style of Charles Ives /
Michael J. Alexander. — New York : Garland, 1989. — vi, 245 p. (Outstanding dissertations in music from British universities) ISBN 0-8240-
0185-0.
A dissertation presented at the University of Keele, 1984, offering the
first detailed examination of most of the piano works. Half the keyboard
compositions remain unpublished. Alexander considers early influences
on Ives and his youthful experiments; the *Three Page Sonata* (the first
mature solo piano piece); folk implications, especially in *First Piano
Sonata*; the composer's attitudes toward "sound as a natural phenomenon, its spiritual implications and eventual translation into musical effect." Endnotes, general bibliography of about 50 items, list of published
piano music, discography of 12 piano performances (latest record from
1968, with no data). Handwritten musical examples and analyses. Without index.
Review: AM 1992, 98.

S2-490   ML410 .I94 F4
Feder, Stuart. Charles Ives "My father's song" : a psychoanalytic biography / Stuart Feder. — New Haven, Conn. : Yale University Press,
1992. — xvi, 396 p. : ill. ISBN 0-300-05481-5.
A study that "applies principles and formulations derived from clini-
cal psychoanalysis to biographical data," stressing "the critical role of
early childhood experience" with emphasis on "ego psychology." The
relation between Charles Ives and his father is at the center of the analysis, which offers no illumination of the composer's music.

S2-491   ML410 .I94 S7
Starr, Larry. A union of diversities : style in the music of Charles Ives /
Larry Starr. — New York : Schirmer, 1992. — 176 p. ISBN 0-02-
872465-8.
Considering that biographical material on Ives is available in plenty,

Starr concentrates on the music, presenting impressive technical analyses. He intends to "allow the substance of music to inspire and to directly inform the techniques employed to understand that substance." Thus both traditional methods, such as the identification of pitch centers, and fresh techniques, such as tracing of juxtapositions and "journeys," are used. This is insightful and imaginative research, well matched to its complex subject. With indexes of compositions and persons.

Reviews: AM 1993, 488; *Choice* 11/92, 476.

S2-492   ML410 .J67 V6

Von Gunden, Heidi. The music of Ben Johnston / Heidi von Gunden. — Metuchen, N.J. : Scarecrow, 1986. — viii, 204 p. : ill. : music. ISBN 0-8108-1907-4.

The story of avant-garde composer Johnston (1926–), including a biography, chronology, and worklist. For each of the compositions, many of them written in "just intonation," there is information about performances and publications, along with comments. Musical examples are included. Fifteen writings about the composers are listed and 13 recordings. Indexed.

Review: *Choice* 6/87, 1562.

S2-493   ML410 .J77 B2

Balkind, Frankfort Gips. Listen up : the lives of Quincy Jones / Frankfort Gips Balkind, Nelson George, and Courtney Sale Ross. — New York : Warner Books, 1990. — 191 p. : ill. : with a cassette or compact disc. ISBN 0-4463-9233-2 (cassette pkg.); 0-4463-9286-3 (compact disc pkg.).

Jones (1933–) is a trumpeter, pianist, conductor, composer, and arranger, prominent in Hollywood; as of 1991 he had won 25 Grammy awards. In this tribute book, made up mostly of photographs, he gives brief comments on aspects of his work. There is a chronology from 1933 to 1990 by George. With an adulatory essay by Ross and a nonexpansive name index.

S2-494   ML410 .J77 H67

Horricks, Raymond. Quincy Jones / Raymond Horricks; discography by Tony Middleton. — Tunbridge Wells, England : Spellmount, 1985. — 127 p. : ill. : 8 p. plates. (Popular musicians, 2) ISBN 0-87052-214-9.

A straightforward career history, including interviews with Jones and many other quotes (undocumented). There is a selective discography, giving dates and personnel for about 30 albums. No index.

Review: *Choice* 9/86, 138.

S2-495   ML410 .L7986

Lees, Gene. Inventing champagne : the worlds of Lerner and Loewe /

Gene Lees. — New York : St. Martin's, 1990. — xiv, 350 p. : ill. ISBN 0-3120-5136-0.

S2-496   ML410 .M117 H7

Horn, Barbara Lee. The age of Hair : evolution and impact of Broadway's first rock musical / Barbara Lee Horn. — New York : Greenwood, 1991. — xvii, 166 p. (Contributions in drama and theatre studies, 42.) ISBN 0-313-27564-5.

"As a revelation of the hippie lifestyle," *Hair* "shared in the universal appeal of an international movement. Thus, the most compelling reason for looking back at *Hair* is not specific to musical theatre but to its historical and cultural context—the late sixties and the 'Age of Aquairus.'" Whatever its appeal, the musical—by Galt MacDermot, Gerome Ragni, and James Rado—was clearly a great success, running for five years in New York, and to comparable acclaim in other cities. There were 11 cast albums. Horn interviewed many of the principals in constructing an interesting genesis account of the production, emphasizing director Tom O'Horgan's unconventional techniques. She also presents a scene-by-scene description of the opening night performance on Broadway (29 April 1968). Horn's views on the societal impact of the show are not without interest. Nothing is said about the music itself. With cast lists for stage and movie versions, a bibliography of about 150 items (many reviews), and a nonexpansive index.

Reviews: *Choice* 5/92, 1402; LJ 12/91, 148.

S2-497   ML410 .M23 G95

Roman, Zoltan. Gustav Mahler's American years, 1907–1911 : a documentary history / Zoltan Roman. — Stuyvesant, N.Y. : Pendragon, 1989. — xxvii, 544 p. : ill. (Monographs in musicology, 10.) ISBN 0-918728-73-8.

A good choice of documents that presents a chronological view of the composer's time in the United States, when he conducted the Metropolitan Opera and the New York Philharmonic. Contracts, extracts from newspapers and periodicals, letters, concert programs, and miscellaneous items are reprinted, with copious commentaries. There is an expansive index.

Review: *Choice* 11/89, 497.

S2-498   ML410 .M244 A3

Mancini, Henry. Did they mention the music? / Henry Mancini; with Gene Lees. — Chicago : Contemporary Books, 1989. — xix, 252 p. : ill. : 16 p. plates. ISBN 0-8092-4496-9.

A shallow collection of anecdotes and bright conversations, saying nothing about music. Mancini (1924–) won two Academy Awards for Hollywood movie songs and composed much successful light music for

films and television; his work deserves more serious attention. With a nonexpansive index.
Review: LJ 11/15/89, 88.

S2-499   ML410 .M4
Mason, Lowell. A Yankee musician in Europe : the 1837 journals of Lowell Mason / Lowell Mason; ed. Michael Broyles. — Ann Arbor, Mich. : UMI Research Press, 1990. — viii, 243 p. (Studies in music, 110) ISBN 0-8357-2002-0.
Mason (1792–1872) was, in the mid-nineteenth century, the most famous native-born American musician/composer, conductor, organist, and anthologist. His journals, in the Yale University Library, present an acute view of musical life. He spent 14 months in England, Germany, France, and Switzerland, and recorded his critical comments on concert and operatic life there. There is much detail on his hearing of *Messiah* and much interest in church music. He found the quality of vocal performance to be about the same as in the United States, but considered European instrumental playing to be superior. Despite his own musical qualifications, his observations tend to be superficial. With endnotes and an expansive index.
Review: *Choice* 3/91, 1146.

S2-500   ML410 .M452 D5
DiMedio, Annette Maria. Frances McCollin : her life and music / Annette Maria DiMedio; foreword by Sam Dennison. — Metuchen, N.J. : Scarecrow, 1990. — xiii, 168 p. : ill. (Composers of North America, 7) ISBN 0-8108-2289-X.
A sympathetic biography of blind pianist and composer McCollin (1892–), an overlooked artist today who did have considerable renown for a time. Of the 333 compositions in DiMedio's careful worklist— which gives incipits and bibliographical details—93 were published; she had hundreds of performances and received numerous awards. A Philadelphian, McCollin was a musical fixture in her city, frequently performed by such local ensembles as the Philadelphia Orchestra, Curtis String Quartet, and Philadelphia Mendelssohn Club. Her life is admirably summarized in this book, with attention to her religious strengths, influences, and musical thought. DiMedio also considers matters of musical style and development. With chapter endnotes, a general bibliography, musical examples, and a nonexpansive name and title index.
Review: *Choice* 11/91, 114.

S2-501   ML410 .M57 O4
Oja, Carol J. Colin McPhee : composer in two worlds / Carol J. Oja. —

Washington : Smithsonian Institution Press, 1990. — xix, 353 p. ISBN 0-87474-732-5.

The two worlds inhabited by McPhee (1900–1964) were North America (born in Canada; lived in United States; worked in Mexico for a time) and Indonesia. It was his years in Bali that shaped his thought and music, leading to a literary work of importance, *A House in Bali* (1946) and a musicological study, *Music in Bali* (posthumous, 1966). His compositions had exotic qualities drawn from his years in faraway places. He wrote a number of transcriptions of gamelan music (listed here) as well as original concert material (also listed, 1912–1960s). Oja provides musical examples and useful analyses, and documents the biography with endnotes. With an expansive index.

Review: *Choice* 4/91, 1320.

S2-502   ML410 .M7755 S6

Smith, Catherine Parsons. Mary Carr Moore, American composer / Catherine Parsons Smith and Cynthia S. Richardson. — Ann Arbor : University of Michigan Press, 1987. — xi, 286 p. : 6 p. plates. ISBN 0-472-10082-3.

A well-documented and somewhat interesting biography of Moore (1873–1957), with descriptions in program-note style of major compositions. The reception of Moore's work is traced through numerous reviews. A case is made for gender discrimination against her, with the implication that she would have achieved greater prominence had things been otherwise. With extensive endnotes, a bibliography of primary and secondary sources, a worklist, and a nonexpansive index.

Review: AM 1988, 317.

S2-503   ML410 .M948

Head, Heno. America's favorite janitor : the life story of country songwriter Johnny Mullins / Heno Head; foreword by Emmylou Harris. — Independence, Mo. : International University Press, 1986. — 287 p. : ill. : 33 p. plates. ISBN not given.

S2-504   ML410 .P17 K43

Kearns, William K. Horatio Parker, 1863–1919 / William K. Kearns. — Metuchen, N.J. : Scarecrow, 1990. — xvii, 356 p. : ill. (Composers of North America, 6) ISBN 0-8108-2292-X.

Parker was one of the leading composers of his time and a distinguished organist and pedagogue as well. Charles Ives was among his pupils at the Yale School of Music. His opera *Mona* was performed at the Metropolitan in 1912. This is a well-documented biography (chapter endnotes), with program notes and musical extracts, a critical worklist, a bibliography of writings about him, list of libraries with special Parker holdings, a discography of commercial and private recordings, and a nonexpansive index.

Review: *Choice* 10/90, 320.

S2-505   ML410 .P176 A3

Partch, Harry. Bitter music : collected journals, essays, introductions, and librettos / Harry Partch; ed. with introduction by Thomas McGeary. — Champaign : University of Illinois Press, 1991. — xxx, 487 p. (Music in American life) ISBN 0-252-01660-2.

Partch (1901–1974) was an experimental composer who made his own scales (one with 43 tones) and instruments (one with 72 strings), and produced some music that has remained of interest; there are 10 recordings of his complex pieces in the 1993 Schwann *Opus* catalog. He described his ideas and methods in *Genesis of a Music* (LOAM 374). McGeary has listed the composer's output in a descriptive catalog (S2-174). Here he has gathered prose writings, including diaries, essays, and program notes, to round out the picture of a man driven to establish a new basis for music and totally impatient with the world's reluctance to follow his lead.

Review: *Choice* 11/91, 459.

S2-506   ML410 .P7844 G7

Grafton, David. Red, hot, and rich : an oral history of Cole Porter / David Grafton. — New York : Stein & Day, 1987. — 242 p. : ill. 22 p. plates. ISBN 0-8128-3112-8.

An "oral history" in name only, this is a slim, undocumented narrative of Porter's career, interrupted frequently by quotations from reviews or from the composer's associates. The author also introduces "personal impressions of Cole Porter, gained from a number of meetings with Porter himself, and a series of conversational encounters with Monty Woolley." Without index.

S2-507   ML410 .P7844 H8

Howard, Jean. Travels with Cole Porter / Jean Howard; introduction by George Eells. — New York : Abrams, 1991. — 216 p. : ill. ISBN 0-8109-3408-6.

A picture book, offering 300 scenic photos from Porter's two grand tours in 1955 and 1956: He (with his wife and Howard) visited Europe and the Middle East, and evidently a good time was had by all. There are comments to support the pictures, but nothing is said about Porter's songs. With a nonexpansive index of names and places.

S2-508   ML410 .R6315 M7

Mordden, Ethan. Rodgers and Hammerstein / Ethan Mordden. — New York : Abrams, 1992. — 224 p. : ill. ISBN 0-8109-1567-7.

A coffee-table book of photos, showing scenes from the musicals, with program notes. Name and title index.

S2-509   ML410 .R693 A3

Rorem, Ned. The Nantucket diary of Ned Rorem, 1973–1985 / Ned Rorem. — San Francisco : North Point, 1987. — 634 p. : ill. : 16 p. plates. ISBN 0-86547-259-9.

A continuation of the composer's published journals, a series that began with *Paris Diary* (LOAM 343; LOAM Suppl. S-197, SA-137). During this period, 1973–1985, Rorem was widely acclaimed, winning a Pulitzer Prize, teaching at Curtis Institute, and giving frequent performances. He moved with the international set, including Jean Cocteau, Lillian Hellman, Noel Coward, William Inge, Tennessee Williams, and Truman Capote, and presents anecdotes about them. He was also given to much meditation, on nonmusical topics such as sex (which he said he had tired of, but could not help thinking about). With a nonexpansive index.

S2-510   ML410 .R28 S56

Singer, Barry. Black and blue : the life and lyrics of Andy Razaf / Barry Singer. — New York : Schirmer, 1992. — xviii, 444 p. : ill. : 16 p. plates. ISBN 0-02-872395-3.

Razaf was a lyric writer for hundreds of songs, including "Ain't Misbehavin" and "Honeysuckle Rose." This is a plain, undocumented narrative of his rise from Harlem obscurity to a place among the jazz greats of the 1920s and 1930s. With a discography and an index.

Review: LJ 11/15/92, 78.

S2-511   ML410 .S26143 F4

Farber, Donald C. The amazing story of *The Fantasticks* : America's longest-running play / Donald C. Farber and Robert Viagas. — New York : Citadel, 1991. — xi, 241 p. : ill. : 16 p. plates. ISBN 0-8065-1214-8.

With productions in 3,000 U.S. cities and also in 68 foreign countries, *The Fantasticks* by Harvey Schmidt and Tom Jones is surely one of the most successful of musicals. It closed at the Sullivan Street Playhouse in Greenwich Village on 8 June 1986, after 26 consecutive years. A landmark of its kind, the play deserves a better history than this casual gathering of undocumented talk by the actors and writers. Nothing is really said about the musical numbers—except that they were there—and the controversy over some of the show's dubious notions (such as the use of rape in a comical context; the "Rape Ballet" eventually became the "Abduction Ballet") is brushed aside. With an expansive index.

S2-512   ML410 .S283 M55

Milstein, Silvina. Arnold Schoenberg : notes, sets, forms / Silvina Milstein. — New York : Cambridge University Press, 1992. — xix, 210 p. ISBN 0-5213-9049-4.

A valuable contribution to the reconsideration of Schoenberg that has tended toward deconstruction of the 12-tone system he invented. William Thomson (S2-514) has suggested that the composer's theories were faulty; Milstein holds that the music itself "shows tonal considerations to be a primary concern and even an important criterion in the composition of the set itself." In other words, atonal music is in fact tonal, although one must use that term in a certain way to make sense of it. Her argument is not entirely new (George Perle had pointed to the tonal base of Schoenberg's atonality in the 1960s; and Leonard Bernstein made the point in his Harvard lectures), but Milstein is more positive of her purposes and more convincing with her examples. With a bibliography of about 120 entries; without index.

S2-513   ML410 .S283 N4

Newlin, Dika. Schoenberg remembered : diaries and recollections (1938–76) / Dika Newlin. — New York : Pendragon, 1980. — x, 369 p. : ill. : 2 leaves plates. ISBN 0-9187-2814-2.

When Newlin was Schoenberg's student, 1938–1941, she kept detailed diaries that are rich with the composer's presence. She continued the diaries into 1976, with more emphasis on her own ideas, which are of great interest. With a bibliography and an index.

Reviews: *Choice* 1/81, 672; LJ 7/80, 1520.

S2-514   ML410 .S283 T6

Thomson, William. Schoenberg's error / William Thomson. — Philadelphia : University of Pennsylvania Press, 1991. — xi, 217 p. ISBN 0-8122-3088-4.

A critical examination of the theoretical writings of Arnold Schoenberg (1874–1951), father of atonal composition. Thomson believes that the composer "may not have fully comprehended tonality's nature, causes, and history" and that his atonal approach was a "blind alley." Basically his "error is not an uncommon one; it lies in overestimating the influence of our concepts over our percepts": there is something fundamental about the way music is perceived (i.e., with a tonal center and all that such a center implies for consonance, dissonance, macrostructures, etc.), and a composer cannot dispose of this natural tendency by inventing a different theoretical system. Experience supports Thomson's view, since atonal composition has virtually ceased, and it has left scarcely any traces in the concert repertoire. A valuable study that should help to clear the theoretical landscape. With endnotes, a bibliography of about 500 items, and an expansive index. There is good parallel reading in S2-512.

S2-515   ML410 .S33
Schuller, Gunther. Musings : the musical worlds of Gunther Schuller / Gunther Schuller; foreword by Milton Babbitt. — New York : Oxford, 1986. — xii, 303 p. ISBN 0-19-503745-6.
A collection of essays, speeches, liner notes, and miscellaneous writings from 1957 to 1982, by the distinguished composer, scholar (see S2-1090), hornist, and educator. Some of the pieces had been previously published. The material is grouped into three headings: jazz and the third stream, music performance and contemporary music, and music aesthetics and education. All the essays are of high quality and cast in musical language. A stimulating volume, unfortunately without an index. (See also S2-180.)
Reviews: AM 1987, 87; *Choice* 9/86, 140; LJ 2/1/86, 83.

S2-516   ML410 .S36
Gaume, Matilda. Ruth Crawford Seeger : memoirs, memories, music / Matilda Gaume. — Metuchen, N.J. : Scarecrow, 1986. — xvii, 268 p. : ill. (Composers of North America, 3) ISBN 0-8108-1917-1.
The wife of musicologist Charles Seeger (Pete Seeger's father) was a significant composer of great originality. This is a documented account of her life (1901–1953), with a worklist by genre (63 items; with descriptions and manuscript locations). There are also samples of her literary writings—letters and diary notes. A bibliography of 70 articles about Seeger and a checklist of recordings is included, with an expansive index.
Review: AM 1988, 104.

S2-517   ML410 .S473 A3
Olmstead, Andrea. Conversations with Roger Sessions / Andrea Olmstead. — Boston : Northeastern University Press, 1987. — 274 p. : ill. ISBN 1-55553-010-9.
Olmstead, a student of Sessions and author of an earlier biography (*Roger Sessions and His Music,* 1985; LOAM Suppl. SA-138) here compiles into subject chapters the results of interviews she had with him between 1974 and 1980. She strikes a balance in her questions between the composer's personal life and his musical thoughts. Sessions presents interesting observations on other twentieth-century composers and a number of useful technical explications of his own writing. There is also a Sessions worklist, with brief information about each piece, and a discography with minimal data. About 200 items are listed in a bibliography of publications by and about him. With an expansive index.
Reviews: AM 1988, 237; *Choice* 12/87, 623; LJ 5/1/87, 71.

S2-518   ML410 .S473 A4

Olmstead, Andrea. The correspondence of Roger Sessions / Andrea Olmstead. — Boston : Northeastern University Press, 1992. — xxviii, 539 p. : ill. ISBN 1-55553-122-9.

More than 200 letters by Sessions, and 60 letters to him, from 1909 to 1985, are reproduced with extensive commentaries by Olmstead. Among the correspondents (nearly all of them musicians) are Aaron Copland, Luigi Dallapiccola, Ernest Bloch, and Ernst Krenek. Many of the ideas found in the Sessions-Olmstead interviews (S2-517) are aired in the letters; they exhibit a thoughtful, cultured scholar with impressive musical insights. There is a partly expansive index of letter writers, titles of works discussed, and topics.

Reviews: *Choice* 12/92, 628; LJ 6/1/92, 128.

S2-519   ML410 .S6872 G7

Gordon, Joanne Lesley. Art isn't easy : the theater of Stephen Sondheim / Joanne Lesley Gordon. — Updated ed. — New York : Da Capo, 1992. — ix, 363 p. : ill. ISBN 0-306-80468-9.

"An unabridged republication of the edition published in Carbondale, Illinois in 1990, with the addition of a new chapter."

The new chapter deals with the 1990 production, *Assassins*. Like the rest of the book, it is a worshipful account of Sondheim's musicals, through which he "tackles real and complex subjects . . . with intricate music, biting wit, and profound themes." Gordon finds the shows "serious and poignant" and "emphasizes the disturbing content" in them. She does not deal with the music, so her method is essentially one of plot summary with commentary on the lyrics. With chapter endnotes and an expansive index.

S2-520   ML410 .S6872 Z2

Zadan, Craig. Sondheim & Co. / Craig Zadan. — 2nd ed. — New York : Harper, 1986. — viii, 408 p. : ill. ISBN 0-06-0154649-X.

1st ed., 1974 (LOAM 1302).

An undocumented oral history of the Sondheim Broadway productions, revealing the thoughts and dreams of various individuals involved in each show, as set down in taped interviews. Arthur Laurents, David Merrick, and Leonard Bernstein are among those who offer interesting observations on the musical and dramatic elements, but most of the people quoted are talking about themselves or one another. With a useful inventory of the productions and casts, a list of albums, many good photos, and a partly expansive index.

Reviews: *Choice* 3/87, 1081; LJ 12/86, 130.

S2-521   ML410 .S688 B5

Bierley, Paul E. John Philip Sousa, American phenomenon / Paul E.

Bierley; foreword by Arthur Fiedler. — 2nd ed. — Columbus, Ohio : Integrity, 1986. — xxiii, 270 p. : ill. ISBN 0-9180-132103.
1st ed., 1973 (LOAM 1204).

The only full-length biography of Sousa, in a slightly revised edition. An adulatory tone pervades the study, which covers the Sousa family (he was the son of a Portuguese immigrant) and its residences, his military career, and primarily his work with the United States Marine Band and later with his own famous band. The bandmaster was also a frequent contributor to periodicals, as demonstrated by the list of 138 articles; and he wrote seven books. There is a worklist, with no details about the compositions or their publication history (but see Bierley's exhaustive *Works of John Philip Sousa* [S2-181]). With footnotes and sources, and a non-expansive index.

Review: *Choice* 11/73, 1397 (for the 1st ed.).

S2-522   ML410 .S81227
Starer, Robert. Continuo : a life in music / Robert Starer. — New York : Random House, 1987. — xii, 206 p. : ill. ISBN 0-394-55515-5.

Composer Starer (1924–), who emigrated from Austria after World War II, became known in the United States as a Broadway, television, and Hollywood specialist. He taught at Juilliard and at City University of New York. His memoir is of interest for the glimpses it gives of a composer's mentality. For example, there is a confessional chapter on Starer's imperfect memory, leading to reflections on musical memory in general—a topic usually fudged by performers. The whole book is a modest self-appraisal, with generous appreciation to the work of other musicians. Without notes or index.

Reviews: *Choice* 9/87, 142; LJ 3/1/87, 72.

S2-523   ML410 .S855
Still, Judith Anne. William Grant Still : a voice high-sounding / Judith Anne Still. — Flagstaff, Ariz. : Master-Player Library, 1990. — xiv, 309 leaves : ill. ISBN 1-877873-02-0.

"A series of published and unpublished essays" by the composer's daughter, in typescript format. Adulation predominates, but there are useful facts to be found (with difficulty, as there is no index). For example, Still was the first black to conduct a major orchestra and the first black to have a symphony performed by a major orchestra. Still's life (1895–1978) was filled with musical contrasts—he played violin in an Army band, was oboist in the pit orchestra of *Shuffle Along,* studied with avant-garde composer Edgar Varèse—and it produced at least a dozen works that remain in the repertoire.

S2-524   ML410 .S932 B9
Boucourechliev, Andre. Stravinsky / Andre Boucourechliev; trans.

from the French by Martin Cooper. — New York : Holmes & Meier, 1987. — 327 p. ISBN 0-8419-1058-8.

A strong, musical approach (originally published by Fayard in France, 1982), to Stravinsky's works, with many musical examples. The studies of the music are related to the life and events of the composer at the time of composition. With chapter endnotes, a worklist by genre (minimal information), and a nonexpansive index.

Review: *Choice* 3/88, 1106.

S2-525   ML410 .S932 C75

Confronting Stravinsky : man, musician, and modernist / ed. Jann Pasler. — Berkeley : University of California Press, 1986. — xix, 380 p. : ill. : 8 p. plates. ISBN 0-520-05403-2.

An interesting collection of 21 essays drawn from the first International Stravinsky Symposium (San Diego, 1982), presenting scholarly views of the composer's background, collaborations, musical devices and practices, contemporary influences, and California years. Among the well-known contributors are Milton Babbitt, Robert Craft, Allen Forte, Richard Taruskin, and Charles Wuorinen. Footnotes, but no bibliography; expansive index.

S2-526   ML410 .S932 C85

Craft, Robert. Stravinsky : glimpses of a life / Robert Craft. — New York : St. Martin's, 1992. — xv, 416 p. : ill. : 8 p. plates. ISBN 0-312-08896-5.

Another fine book by Stravinsky's close associate and chronicler, this one "half biography and half musical commentary"; it is made up of 15 previously published essays and 10 new ones. Craft writes from a privileged position, as the only witness to the history of "Stravinsky's life vis-à-vis his two families during the years 1950–1971." The composer's love affair with Vera Sudeinka, whom he met in 1921 (both married, he the father of four children) is honestly recounted, although its 14-year unfolding does not put Stravinsky in a good light. On the musical side there is a valuable genesis study of *Oedipus Rex* and perceptive analyses of *Histoire du soldat, Rite of Spring,* and *Symphonies of Wind Instruments.* With an expansive index.

S2-527   ML410 .S932 G7

Griffiths, Paul. Stravinsky / Paul Griffiths. — London : Dent, 1992. — xiii, 253 p. ISBN 0-460-86063-1.

A straightforward biography, with program notes on the compositions, of "the dominant, emblematic musician of the twentieth century," who is described as a "splintered man—peasant and sophisticate, classicist and iconoclast, believer and mercenarian, modalist and serialist."

Griffiths does not have the time or space to deal with so many splinters, and his attempt may cancel out some of the virtues of this introductory book.

S2-528   ML410 .S932 O4
Oja, Carol J. Stravinsky in "Modern music," 1924–1946 / ed. Carol J. Oja; foreword by Aaron Copland. — New York : Da Capo, 1982. — xix, 176 p. : ill. ISBN 0-306-76108-4.
"Unabridged republication of articles printed in the journal Modern music . . . 1924–1946."
An interesting collection of 39 articles that comment on many aspects of the composer's work and on individual compositions. Among the authors are Walter Piston, Marc Blitzstein, Aaron Copland, Virgil Thomson, Elliott Carter, Ingolf Dahl, Manfred Bukofzer, and Lincoln Kirstein. Copland's foreword notes that "an astonishing variety of critical attitudes is revealed. Yet within that range one of them persists: the repeated sharp, unexpected turns in Stravinsky's musical style." With an expansive index.

S2-529   ML410 .S932 W2
Walsh, Stephen. The music of Stravinsky / Stephen Walsh. — London : Routledge, 1987. — 317 p. ISBN 0-4150-0198-6.
A perceptive, analytic approach to the Stravinsky works, with references to other studies. With a bibliography of about 200 items and an expansive index.

Note: For a Tchaikovsky item, see S2-462.

S2-530   ML410 .T517
Tobias, Henry. Music in my heart and borscht in my blood : an autobiography / Henry Tobias. — New York : Hippocrene Books, 1987. — xiii, 192 p. : ill. : 16 p. plates. ISBN 0-87052-457-7.
Tobias, a songwriter, pianist, and social director in Catskill and Miami resort hotels, offers a casual memoir, seeking out "memorable and embarrassing moments." With a nonexpansive index.

S2-531   ML410 .T54
Jezic, Diane Peacock. The musical migration and Ernst Toch / Diane Peacock Jezic; with worklist and discography by Alyson McLamore. — Ames : Iowa State University Press, 1989. — xi, 220 p. : ill. : music. ISBN 0-8138-0322-5.
The first biography of Toch, one of the European composer refugees (69 of them, the book tells us) who came to America with the rise of Hitler. It is a graceful, scholarly look at his life, with musical comments on many of the works. Family interviews and unpublished materials

were among the sources used. Of particular interest is the light shed on other musicians who settled in various parts of the United States, doing whatever work was available (much of it for Hollywood), sponsored and partly supported by individuals, institutions such as the New School in New York, and government agencies. Toch's own composing was fairly well received during his lifetime; he had numerous performances and recordings, and wrote the scores for 16 films. Eight or nine of his pieces are available on CD. The book has a good worklist, of published and unpublished compositions, and a discography of 46 recordings (LP commercials only). There is a useful table of emigrant composers and what they did in this country. With bibliographies of 27 writings by Toch and some 50 articles and reviews about his music, and an expansive index.

Review: *Choice* 7-8/90, 1836.

S2-532 ML410 .W2958 B7

Bortin, Virginia. Elinor Remick Warren : her life and her music / Virginia Bortin; foreword by Howard Swan. — Metuchen, N.J. : Scarecrow, 1987. — xii, 269 p. : ill. (Composers of North America, 5) ISBN 0-8108-2084-6.

"One of the most performed women orchestral composers" in the 1970s, Warren (1900–) "during much of her career stood virtually alone as a woman achieving renown in the world of American composition." This is a straightforward life story, undocumented, with program notes on many of Warren's pieces. There are 63 musical examples, and there is a detailed worklist (giving full descriptions and performance information). A discography includes Warren playing the piano and other artists performing her compositions. With first-line and author indexes to song texts, a bibliography of about 300 articles and reviews, and a nonexpansive index.

Reviews: AM 1989, 209; *Choice* 7/88, 1703.

S2-533 ML410 .W395 J37

Jarman, Douglas. Kurt Weill : an illustrated biography / Douglas Jarman. — Bloomington : Indiana University Press, 1982. — 160 p. : ill. : 24 p. plates. ISBN 0-253-14650-X.

A useful biography of the German-American composer (1900–1950) who worked in classical and Broadway modes. In Germany he wrote his most famous composition, *Die Dreigrosschenoper (Threepenny Opera* in the United States); in America he created such successful theatricals as *Lady in the Dark, One Touch of Venus,* and *Street Scene.* Jarman deals with Weill's life, but is most valuable in offering musical commentaries on the compositions. With a chronological worklist and a bibliography of about 80 books and articles; endnotes and a nonexpansive index. Without discography.

S2-534   ML410 .W395 T4
Taylor, Ronald. Kurt Weill : a composer in a divided world / Ronald
Taylor. — Boston : Northeastern University Press, 1992. — xiv, 358 p. :
ill. ISBN 1-5555-3147-4.
"First published in England in 1991."
A straightforward biography, documented with chapter source notes,
of the German-American composer (see annotation for S2-533). This
book lacks a worklist and has only a selective bibliography (partly annotated) of 100 items. With a nonexpansive index.

ML416 : Organists

S2-535   ML416 .B53 O9
Owen, Barbara. E. Power Biggs, concert organist / Barbara Owen;
discography by Andrew Kazdin. — Bloomington : Indiana University
Press, 1987. — x, 241 p. : ill. ISBN 0-253-31801-7.
The radio performances and recordings of Biggs (1906–1977) did
much to establish the organ as a solo instrument outside the church environment and to bring baroque music into the common repertoire.
Owen presents a straightforward biography, undocumented (she did
have access to his personal papers and had help from his widow) but serious in tone and without invented conversations. The arrangement is
chronological, dealing with events and with comments on them by
Biggs. The artist's observations on his European tours are of considerable interest, as he comments on many of the great instruments on which
he recorded. An appendix gives the specifications of three organs most
associated with Biggs. His organ editions and his recordings are listed
also. There is a bibliography of some 200 items and an expansive index.
Review: AM 1988, 467.

ML417 : Pianists

S2-536   ML417 .A825
Asher, Don. Notes from a battered grand : a memoir / Don Asher. —
New York : Harcourt Brace Jovanovich, 1992. — xii, 305 p. ISBN 0-
1516-7281-4.
The author, pianist for several dance bands from the 1940s to the
1960s, was well known at the Hungry i in San Francisco. His memoir is
a gathering of anecdotes and conversations with no particular point and
with no musical reference. No index.
Review: LJ 4/1/92, 120.

S2-537   ML417 .B3 N8
Nolden, Rainer. Count Basie. 1990.
See series note at S2-1111.

S2-538 ML417 .C285
Catrambone, Gene. The golden touch : Frankie Carle / Gene Catrambone. — Roslyn Heights, N.Y. : Libra, 1981. — xviii, 262 p. : ill. ISBN 0-87212-124-0.
A casual life story of the popular pianist and big band leader, made of anecdotes and fictional dialogues. Music is not a subject of treatment. No documentation; but there is a chronological discography (minimal data) and a nonexpansive index.

Note: For Duke Ellington material, see S2-467–S2-471.

S2-539 ML417 .E8
Petrik, Hanns E. Bill Evans. 1989.
See series note at S2-1111.

S2-540 ML417 .E93
Collinson, John. The jazz legacy of Don Ewell / John Collinson and Eugene Kramer; with seventeen piano transcriptions by Ray Smith; and additional contributions by William Russell [et al.] — Chigwell, Essex, England : Storyville, 1991. — xii, 248 p. : ill. ISBN 0-90239113-5.

S2-541 ML417 .F28 A4
Fay, Amy. More letters of Amy Fay : the American years, 1879–1916 / Amy Fay; ed. Margaret William McCarthy. — Detroit : Information Coordinators, 1986. — xx, 168 p. : ill. ISBN 0-89990-028-3.
An earlier collection of letters by Fay (1844–1928), written while she was studying in Europe, was published in 1888 (*Music Study in Germany*). In this set of perceptive epistles, most of them to her sister Zina, Fay comments on musical life in Chicago and New York, where she was active as a pianist, educator, and club woman. She presents sensitive and entertaining appraisals of the conductors, pianists, and violinists of the day, and of the critics as well. With a nonexpansive index.
Reviews: AM 1988, 465; *Choice* 11/86, 488.

S2-542 ML417 .G7
Graffman, Gary. I really should be practicing / Gary Graffman. — Garden City, N.Y. : Doubleday, 1981. — x, 350 p. : ill. : 4 p. plates. ISBN 0-385-15559-X.
A happy, casual memoir by the pianist (1928–), featuring "impishly witty anecdotes" from his world travels. With a nonexpansive index.
Review: LJ 2/15/81, 455.

S2-543 ML417 .H247
Cazort, Jean E. Born to play : the life and career of Hazel Harrison / Jean E. Cazort and Constance Tibbs Hobson. — Westport, Conn. :

Greenwood, 1983. — xviii, 171 p. : ill. (Contributions to the study of music and dance, 3) ISBN 0-313-23643-7.

Harrison (1883–1969), pupil of Busoni and Egon Petri, was the first black concert pianist to achieve international recognition; in 1904 she was a soloist with the Berlin Philharmonic Orchestra. Later she taught at Howard University and Alabama State College. This story is partly based on interviews and is supported by chapter endnotes; nevertheless, undocumented dialogues and anecdotes appear frequently. Press notices and concert reviews are reproduced. With an expansive index.

S2-544   ML417 .H5 D2.
Dance, Stanley. Earl Hines. 1980.
See series note at S2-1114.

S2-545   ML417 .H72 A3
Hodes, Art. Hot man : the life of Art Hodes / Art Hodes; with Chadwick Hansen; discography by Howard Rye. — Urbana : University of Illinois Press, 1992. — xii, 160 p. : ill. ISBN 0-252-01753-6.

Pianist Hodes (1904–), "one of the last survivors of the generation of white jazz musicians who learned their trade in Chicago in the twenties," played with Louis Armstrong, Bix Beiderbecke, Sidney Bechet, Barney Bigard, Jack Teagarden, and dozens of other great artists. He remains active in Chicago and on tour. This is his memoir, heavily edited by Hansen, but remaining informal (with quotes and conversations); there is no documentation. The discography covers all sessions and broadcasts—original issues only—from 1928 to 1988. For each item the date and location are given, with matrix number, label and number, personnel, and comments. With a nonexpansive name index to the text, but no text to the discography.
Reviews: *Choice* 12/92, 627; LJ 12/91, 147.

S2-546   Number not used.

S2-547   ML417 .H79 A3
Vaché, Warren W., Sr. Crazy fingers : Claude Hopkins' life in jazz / Warren W. Vaché, Sr.; foreword by Martin Williams. — Washington : Smithsonian Institution Press, 1992. — x, 134 p. ISBN 1-56098-144-X.

Hopkins (1903–1984) was a pianist and bandleader, most prominent in the 1930s when he recorded for major labels and performed in principal New York venues. He was still active into the 1970s and produced an acclaimed album in 1973, *Crazy Fingers*. Hopkins kept a diary that served as the basis for Vaché's biography, a good deal of which had appeared earlier in jazz magazines. While much of the story is the generic anecdotal road show of the jazz player, there is some interest in the

European tours (Hopkins was bandleader for Josephine Baker). While the diary is presumably the source for most of the material, it is not cited directly in support of episodes and conversations, and there are no other source citations. With a filmography and a good discography (1922–1974), giving full information about locations, dates, matrix numbers, labels, and personnel. There is a nonexpansive index.

Review: LJ 5/15/92, 95.

S2-548   ML417 .H8 D82
Dubal, David. Evenings with Horowitz : a personal portrait / David Dubal. — New York : Birch Lane, 1991. — xxi, 321 p. : ill. : 8 p. plates. ISBN 1-55972-094-8.

Dubal, himself a pianist (teacher at the Juilliard School), was a friend of Vladimir Horowitz (1903–1989) and interviewed him extensively over a three-year period. The conversations were essentially musical, presenting the master's opinions and methods in a detail not otherwise available in print. As the author observes, Horowitz was "far from the unknowledgeable and silly buffoon that he himself had often portrayed." There is also a CD discography, with useful commentary. No documentation is provided; there is an expansive index.

S2-549   ML417 .H8 P6
Plaskin, Glenn. Horowitz : a biography of Vladimir Horowitz / Glenn Plaskin; discography by Robert McAlear. — New York : Morrow, 1983. — 607 p. : ill. ISBN 0-688-01616-2.

A straightforward biography based on 650 interviews with friends and associates of Horowitz, plus 50 interviews with the pianist himself. Extensive source notes. Discography of commercial releases and reissues in the United States and the United Kingdom, arranged by composer, with recording dates, matrixes, and labels—but without release dates. The artist's concert repertoire is listed. With a nonexpansive index.

Reviews: *Choice* 7/83, 1608; LJ 2/15/83, 399.

S2-550   ML417 .H8 S3
Schonberg, Harold C. Horowitz : his life and his music / Harold C. Schonberg. — New York : Simon & Schuster, 1992. — 427 p. : ill. : 16 p. plates. ISBN 0-671-72568-8.

A casual, journalistic treatment of the pianist; without documentation, although it includes long, indented quotes. A discussion of the Horowitz recordings is of interest. The discography itself, arranged by composer (with a chronological index), gives release labels and dates, but no matrix or release label numbers. With an expansive index.

Review: LJ 11/1/92, 89.

S2-551   ML417 .J37 A553

Andresen, Uwe. Keith Jarrett : sein Leben, seine Musik, seine Schall-platten / Uwe Andresen. — Gauting-Buchendorf, Germany : Oreos, 1985. — 187 p. : ill. (Collection jazz) ISBN 3-923657-09-9.

In German. A bio-discography, useful to those who do not read German for its numerous photographs (including the album covers) and the chronological inventory of recordings, with personnel and reissue information. The commentaries for the albums are not of great interest, being of the program-note variety. Andresen's biographical section is undocumented and popular in style. With an index to the photos only and a sketchy bibliography of 12 items.

S2-552   ML417 .J37 C2

Carr, Ian. Keith Jarrett : the man and his music / Ian Carr. — London : Grafton, 1991. — 237 p. : ill. ISBN 0-306-80478-5.

A documented review of Jarrett's career and a thorough discography (matrix numbers, personnel, release labels) of more than 100 albums. With chapter endnotes and an expansive index of names and titles.

S2-553   ML417 .J6 B76

Brown, Scott E. James P. Johnson : a case of mistaken identity / Scott E. Brown; discography by Robert Hilbert; foreword by Dan Morgenstern. — Metuchen, N.J. : Scarecrow Press and the Institute of Jazz Studies, 1986. — viii, 500 p. : ill. (Studies in jazz, 4) ISBN 0-8108-1887-6.

The publication facts above are taken from the book itself; the title has been cited variously. Johnson was a premier artist of the ragtime and jazz eras, known as the "father of stride piano." He also composed successful songs and Broadway shows. He had considerable influence on such jazz figures as Fats Waller and Art Tatum. As a biography, this book demonstrates the benefits of combining serious scholarship with a fascinating life story. Events, quotations, and conversations are documented through endnotes. There are reference lists of stage productions to which Johnson contributed; of his symphonic and other "classical" compositions; of his (about 300) songs; and of 183 recordings (recording and release dates, personnel, reissues; with name and title indexes). Bibliography, primary and secondary sources, of about 250 items. With nonexpansive name and subject index.

Review: *Choice* 1/87, 772.

S2-554   ML417 .J6 K2

Kappler, Frank. James P. Johnson. 1981.
See series note at S2-1114.

S2-555　　ML417 .K27 W5

Page, Tim. William Kapell : a documentary life history of the American pianist / Tim Page. — College Park : International Piano Archives at Maryland, University of Maryland Press, 1992. — 200 p. ISBN 0-89579-298-2.

An interesting book of photos, clippings, programs, and letters—with explanations—that outlines the career of Kapell (1922–1953), a career cut short by an airplane crash. Page used materials in the Kapell Archive at the International Piano Archives. The discography by Allan Evans is unfortunately arranged by composer, but it includes published and unpublished recordings, giving matrix numbers, takes, and release data. With an expansive index.

S2-556　　ML417 .K3

Kartsonakis, Dino. Dino : beyond the glitz and glamour : an autobiography / Dino Kartsonakis; with Cecil Murphey. — Nashville : T. Nelson, 1990. — 187 p. : ill. : 8 p. plates. ISBN 0-8407-7158-4.

The story of "one of the world's best known concert pianists," in which he reveals "how you'll be amazed at God's provisions for his musical education . . . and feel the pain and joy of his search for a wife." Conversations, amazing memories, and uplifting messages are the principal content. With no documentation or indexing.

S2-557　　ML417 .K66 A3

Kirkpatrick, Ralph. Early years / Ralph Kirkpatrick; epilogue by Frederick Hammond. — New York : Peter Lang, 1985. — 128 p. : ill. : 12 p. plates. ISBN 0-8204-0282-6.

A straightforward autobiography by harpsichordist Kirkpatrick (1911–1984), almost entirely devoted to personal events. He had some interesting stories to tell about his Harvard years and about his sojourn in Europe (1931–1933), when he studied with Nadia Boulanger and Wanda Landowska, and toured the Continent researching baroque performance practice, but the tale would have been more valuable had it taken account of his musical growth. Without index or reference features.

S2-558　　ML417 .L646

Lalo, Thierry. John Lewis / Thierry Lalo and Jacques Lubin. — Montelimar, France : Limon, 1991. — 286 p. : ill. (Mood indigo) ISBN not given.

In French. A discography of jazz pianist Lewis (covering 1946–1990) and of the Modern Jazz Quartet (covering 1951–1988). Information given includes date, personnel, matrix, and release label. Reissues are not included. Not documented; with an index of names.

S2-559   ML417 .L67 A3
Liberace. The wonderful private world of Liberace / Liberace. — New York : Harper, 1986. — 222 p. : ill. ISBN 0-06-015481-0.

Walter Liberace (1919–1987) was a flamboyant pianist who transformed his performances of popular songs and light classics into grand entertainment. His lavish lifestyle (including 21 dogs, a glitter wardrobe, and eccentric collectibles) and his bubbling personality were the centers of public interest, and they are the topics of this volume. "Enthusiasm and optimism" pervade the tale, which is notable for its total lack of attention to his music and to his controversial personal relationships (see S2-560 and S2-561). Without index or reference features; but the photographs are gems.

S2-560   ML417 .L67 T5
Thomas, Bob. Liberace : the untold story / Bob Thomas. — New York : St. Martin's, 1988. — xvii, 284 p. : ill. : 16 p. plates. ISBN 0-312-01469-4.

Paperback edition: *Liberace : The True Story* (New York: St. Martin's, 1989; ISBN 0-312-91352-4).

An undocumented assortment of anecdotes and conversations relating to the popular pianist (1919–1987). The untold story is of his death from AIDS. With a partly expansive index.

S2-561   ML417 .L67 T53
Thorson, Scott. Behind the candelabra : my life with Liberace / Scott Thorson; with Alex Thorleifson. — New York : Dutton, 1988. — 242 p. : ill. : 16 p. plates. ISBN 0-525-24653-3.

A maudlin story that offers "details of the fundamentally tender love affair between Liberace and Thorson," including the less than tender conclusion in legal wrangles. Dialogues and anecdotes are provided, in a fictional idiom. Musical matters are not considered. Without notes or index.

S2-562   ML417 .M846 A3
Monk, Thelonious. Thelonious Monk. 1987.
A memoir by the pianist (1917–1982). See series note at S2-1118.

S2-563   ML417 .M846 F4
Fitterling, Thomas. Thelonious Monk : sein Leben, seine Musik, seine Schallplatten / Thomas Fitterling. — Waakirchen, Germany : Oreos, 1987. — 175 p. : ill. : music. (Collection jazz) ISBN 3-923657-14-5.
See series note at S2-1111.

S2-564   ML417 .M85
Albertson, Chris. Jelly Roll Morton. 1979.
See series note at S2-1114.

S2-565   ML417 .P46 L4
Lees, Gene. Oscar Peterson : the will to swing / Gene Lees. — Rocklin, Calif. : Prima Publishing & Communications, 1990. — vi, 293 p. : ill. ISBN 1-55958-037-2.
Originally published Toronto: Lester & Orpen Dennys, 1988.
A casual biography comprised of anecdotes and undocumented conversations, with nothing said about music. Peterson (1925–) is a Canadian jazz pianist most renowned for his ensemble work in the Oscar Peterson Trio. With a list of about 80 sources (no pagination for periodical articles) and a nonexpansive index.
Review: LJ 6/1/90, 130.

S2-566   ML417 . P47 P34
Palmer, Richard. Oscar Peterson / Richard Palmer. — Tunbridge Wells, England : Spellmount; New York : Hippocrene Books, 1984. — 93 p. : ill. ISBN 0-946771-45-6 (U.K.); 0-87052-013 (U.S.).
A documented biography of Canadian jazz pianist Peterson (1925–), best known for his outstanding ensemble, the Oscar Peterson Trio. In addition to biographical matters, which are dealt with factually, there is good discussion of musical elements. The discography is selective, offering about 75 sessions from 1947 to 1982. Without index.

S2-567   ML417 .P77 A3
Price, Sammy. What do they want? : a jazz autobiography / Sammy Price; ed. Caroline Richmond. — Urbana : University of Illinois Press, 1990. — 157 p. : ill. : 24 p. plates. ISBN 0-252-01702-2.
Price (1908–) offers a casual, undocumented memoir of more than 60 years as a jazz pianist. He was a staff pianist for Decca, and he recorded with major artists such as Sidney Bechet and Lester Young. His account is comprised of anecdotes and conversations, offering little of substance about his music or the people who made it with him. A discography of original issues only, 1929–1988, give dates, matrix numbers, release labels, locations, and personnel. With an expansive index of names, places, and song titles.
Review: *Choice* 7-8/90, 1837.

S2-568   ML417 .P8
Groves, Alan. The glass enclosure : the life of Bud Powell / Alan Groves and Alyn Shipton. — Oxford, England : Bayou, 1993. — 144 p. : ill. ISBN 1-8714-7826-X.
A straightforward life story of pianist Powell (1924–1966), undocumented, but without invented conversations. There is a 2-page bibliography, a fully detailed 21-page discography (by Shipton), and an index of names and song titles. The earlier book by Groves (S2-569) is not

mentioned in the front matter and not cited in the bibliography; since the first work could not be inspected, a question remains about how similar the two treatments—with the same number of pages—might be.

S2-569   ML417 .P81
Groves, Alan. Bud Powell / Alan Groves. — New York : Universe, 1987. — 144 p. : ill. (Jazz life & times) ISBN 0-8166-6369-5.
A brief account of the pianist; see comment at S2-568.

S2-570   ML417 .S425
Guerry, Jack. Silvio Scionti : remembering a master pianist and teacher / Jack Guerry. — Denton : University of North Texas Press, 1991. — xii, 220 p. : ill. ISBN 0-929398-27-0.
A fond and laudatory account of Scionti (1882–1973), pianist, teacher, and conductor. He taught at the American Conservatory of Music (Chicago) and the University of North Texas. With endnotes, a bibliography, and a nonexpansive index.
Review: LJ 2/1/92, 90.

S2-571   ML417 .S824 K4
Keller, Keith. Oh, Jess! : a jazz life : the Jess Stacy story / Keith Keller. — New York : Mayan Music Corp., 1989. — 225 p. : ill. ISBN 87-88043-08-8.
A friend of Stacy (1904–) offers casual, affectionate recollections and the results of interviews with him. Stacy, who played with Benny Goodman and Bob Crosby, won the *Down Beat* polls as most popular jazz pianist in four consecutive years (1940–1943). There are 48 photographs. With a filmography, discography (dates, labels, personnel), and a nonexpansive index.

S2-572   ML417 .T39 B83
Buholzer, Meinrad. Auf der Suche nach Cecil Taylor / Meinrad Buholzer, Abi S. Rosenthal, and Valerie Wilmer. — Hofheim, Germany : Wolke Verlag, 1990. — 166 p. : ill. ISBN 3-923997-388.
In German. An impressionistic appreciation of Taylor's life and views, often descending into philosophical babble, with many undocumented conversations and quotations. Useful for the chronological discography, offering location and personnel for 60 LPs and CDs. Without indexes.

S2-573   ML417 .T8
Billard, François. Lennie Tristano / François Billard. — Montpellier, France : Limon, 1988. — 203 p. : ill. (Mood indigo) ISBN not given.
A straightforward, footnoted biography of pianist Tristano (1919–

1978), discussing his stylistic periods, with useful technical comments on his performances. There is a discography of LP issues, covering his sessions from 1945 to 1966, with label, date, location, timing, and personnel data. No index.

S2-574   ML417 .W15 S5
Shipton, Alyn. Fats Waller : his life & times / Alyn Shipton. — New York : Universe Books, 1988. — 134 p. : ill. (Jazz life & times) ISBN 0-87663-687-3.
A brief account of pianist Waller (1904–1943). See series note at S2-1117.

S2-575   ML417 .W15 T5
Thomson, David. Fats Waller, 1980.
See series note at S2-1114.

S2-576   ML417 .W4 G3
Gelles, George. Teddy Wilson. 1981.
See series note at S2-1114.

ML418 : String Players (Violin, Guitar, etc.)

S2-577   ML418 .B17 A3
Barker, Danny. A life in jazz / Danny Barker; ed. Alyn Shipton. — New York : Oxford; London : Macmillan, 1986. — 223 p. : ill. ISBN 0-19-520511-1 (U.S.); 0-333-39909-9 (U.K.).
Shipton, a jazz player and reviewer, has compiled some useful facts about Barker (d. 1994), a jazz guitarist, and (in separate chapters) Jelly Roll Morton, Cab Calloway, and Louis Armstrong. The biographical material is anecdotal and includes quoted conversations. Although the treatment is disorganized and casual, some interesting perspectives emerge, such as one of Harlem club life and another of Barker's performances among old-fashioned Mississippi racists in the 1920s. Without source notes. Nonexpansive index. Chronological Barker discography of 1931–1975, with information on each record including matrix, recording location, performers, and label.
Reviews: AM 1988, 457; *Choice* 1/87, 771.

S2-578   ML418 .D33 A3
Danzi, Michael. American musician in Germany, 1924–1939 : memoirs of the jazz, entertainment, and movie world in Berlin during the Weimar republic and the Nazi era—and in the United States / Michael Danzi; as told to Rainer E. Lotz. — Schmitten, Germany : Norbert

Ruecker, 1986; distributed by Legacy Books, Hatboro, Pa. — ix, 292 p. ISBN 3-923397-02-X.

Danzi (1898–) performed in Harlem clubs, then moved to Germany in 1924. He played guitar or banjo in a 16-year European career of appearances, studio work, and recordings (more than 17,000 titles on disc). Among the labels that carry his work are Electrola, Lindström, Grammophon, Kristall, Homocord, and Telefunken. He was often a sideman with Alex Hyde's orchestra. Danzi was seen in 55 films (listed here). The discography, by Lotz, covers sessions from 1924 through 1939, in date order; it gives personnel, matrix and release numbers, and long commentaries. There are interesting photos of advertising materials and of Danzi performing on location. With a partly expansive index.

Review: AM 1988, 99.

S2-579　　ML418 .H44 W47

Weschler-Vered, Artur. Jascha Heifetz / Artur Weschler-Vered and Julian Futter. — New York : Schirmer; London : Hale, 1986. — 240 p. : ill. : 16 p. plates. ISBN 0-0293-44808 (U.S.); 0-7090-2542-4 (U.K.).

An adulatory account of the violinist (1901–1987), only slightly documented, of some interest for the story of his early life and training. With bibliography, index, and discography of commercial recordings (minimal data).

Reviews: *Choice* 12/86, 636; LJ 11/1/86, 97.

S2-580　　ML418 .H476 M3

McDermott, John. Hendrix : setting the record straight / John McDermott, Mark Lewisohn, and Eddie Kramer. — New York : Warner Books, 1992. — xix, 364 p. : ill. : 16 p. plates. ISBN 0-4463-9431-9. (Alternative classification: ML410.)

S2-581　　ML418 .H476 M5

Mitchell, Mitch. Jimi Hendrix : inside the Experience / Mitch Mitchell; with John Platt. — New York : Harmony Books, 1990. — 176 p. : ill. ISBN 0-517-57716-X. (Alternative classification: ML410.)

Original British edition published under title: *The Hendrix Experience.*

Mitchell was drummer in the Hendrix group; he tells the story of tours in the late 1960s, giving an itinerary. The content is mostly made up of color pictures, with undocumented conversations. No index.

S2-582　　ML418 .H476 M9

Murray, Charles Shaar. Crosstown traffic : Jimi Hendrix and the postwar rock 'n' roll revolution / Charles Shaar Murray. — New York : St.

Martin's, 1989. — viii, 247 p. : ill. : 8 p. plates. ISBN 0-312-04288-4. (Alternative classification: ML410.)

Originally published as *Crosstown Traffic: Jimi Hendrix and Post-war Pop* (London: Faber & Faber, 1989).

Rock singer and guitarist Hendrix (1942–1970) was especially known in the 1960s for his flamboyant instrumental technique and engineering effects, as well as the custom of destroying his guitar on stage at the end of a performance. The chapter of Murray's book that deals with the Fender guitars is of considerable interest. The rest of the book is about the personal problems faced by Hendrix, with much attention to racism and drugs. Sources are given for incidents and conversations. Music itself is not taken up, except for some critical comments in the selective discography. There is a bibliography of about 200 general books on rock. With a nonexpansive index.

Review: LJ 9/15/90, 80.

S2-583   ML418 .H476 R4

Redding, Noel. Are you experienced? : the inside story of Jimi Hendrix / Noel Redding and Carol Appleby. — London : Fourth Estate, 1990. — 231 p. : ill. : 16 p. plates. ISBN 1-8721-8036-1. (Alternative classification: ML410.)

The bassist with the Hendrix group offers undocumented anecdotes about them and their tours. He also relates his own "efforts to win just financial reward for the band itself" after the leader's death in 1970. Concert schedules are interspersed, but they are less complete and reliable than those of Shapiro (S2-584). With a nonexpansive index.

S2-584   ML418 .H476 S6

Shapiro, Harry. Jimi Hendrix : electric gypsy / Harry Shapiro and Caesar Glebbeek. — New York : St. Martin's, 1991. — xii, 723 p. : ill. : 16 p. color plates. ISBN 0-312-05861-6. (Alternative classification: ML410.)

"First published in London by William Heinemann in 1990."

A useful biography, straightforward and documented, drawn from materials in the archives of the Hendrix Information Center. Special features are the detailed concert schedules of 1967–1970 and illustrations of his guitars with their specifications. There is a good discography, citing personnel, place, labels, and instruments used.

Reviews: *Choice* 4/92, 1192; LJ 7/91, 100.

S2-585   ML418 .H5 A3

Hinton, Milt. Bass line : the stories and photographs of Milt Hinton / Milt Hinton and David G. Berger; foreword by Dan Morgenstern. — Philadelphia : Temple University Press, 1988. — xv, 328 p. : ill. ISBN 0-8772-2518-4.

Bass player Hinton (1910–) tells of vivid childhood experiences in Mississippi, where at age seven or eight he witnessed a lynching. Moving to Chicago's South Side at age nine, he took violin lessons at Hull House and played professionally as a teen, and went on to perform with leading jazz artists. After that his story becomes a series of anecdotes about colleagues. There is a selective discography covering 1930–1987, giving dates, labels, and personnel for about 250 items. There are 175 photographs, taken by Hinton. With a partly expansive index.

Review: LJ 12/88, 114.

S2-586   ML418 .J73 A3

Jordan, Steve. Rhythm man : fifty years in jazz / Steve Jordan; with Tom Scanlan. —Ann Arbor : University of Michigan Press, 1991. — 176 p. : ill. (Michigan American music series) ISBN 0-472-10256-7.

Originally published as *Rhythm Is My Business: Fifty Years in Jazz* (Boston: Quinlan, 1988).

"One of the best rhythm guitar players in jazz history," Jordan (1919–) has performed with Benny Goodman, Artie Shaw, Stan Kenton, and other major artists. In a first-person narrative, Jordan describes growing up in New York, his early entry into the jazz world, gigs, and travels. Anecdotes and conversations are the basis for the narrative, which is not documented. There is a selective discography covering 1940 to 1990, limited to LP reissues. With a nonexpansive index.

Review: *Choice* 7-8/92, 1691.

S2-587   ML418 .M4

Viva, Luigi. Pat Metheny. 1990.

A brief study of the guitarist. See series note at S2-1111.

S2-588   ML418 .M45 C6

Coleman, Janet. Mingus/Mingus : two memoirs / Janet Coleman and Al Young. — Berkeley, Calif. : Creative Arts, 1989. — 164 p. : ill. ISBN 0-88739-067-6.

Bassist and bandleader Charles Mingus met the authors in the late 1950s, while Coleman and Young were students at the University of Michigan. They affectionately describe their relationships with Mingus, in a light, reflective style. Roughly two dozen photographs show Mingus, mostly in his later years; their quality is very uneven. Without bibliographical references or index.

Janet Coleman writes frequently for the *Village Voice, Mademoiselle,* and other magazines. Al Young writes fiction, poetry, nonfiction, and screenplays [—D. P.].

Review: *Choice* 1/90, 810.

S2-589   ML418 .M59 A34 B76
Milstein, Nathan. From Russia to the West : the musical memoirs and
reminiscences of Nathan Milstein / Nathan Milstein and Solomon Vol-
kov; trans. from Russian by Antonina W. Bovis. — New York : Holt,
1990. — 282 p. : ill. : 16 p. plates. ISBN 0-8050-0974-4.
A pleasing autobiography, rendered interesting for the cast of characters: Milstein's associates and friends included Vladimir Horowitz,
Sergei Rachmaninoff, Gregor Piatigorsky, George Balanchine, and
Fritz Kreisler. Milstein (1904–) was a violin prodigy from Russia who
studied with Leopold Auer and established a world career that peaked in
the 1980s with a base in the United States (he became a citizen in 1942).
His comments on David Oistrakh and other fellow violinists are candid
and informative. However, the book is without source notes and is
marred by invented conversations. With an expansive index.
Review: LJ 6/15/90, 114.

S2-590   ML418 .P79 S5
Shaffer, Karen A. Maud Powell : pioneer American violinist / Karen
A. Shaffer and Neva Garner Greenwood; foreword by Yehudi Menuhin. —
Arlington, Va. : Maud Powell Foundation, distributed by Iowa State
University Press, 1988. — xx, 530 p. : ill. ISBN 0-8138-0989-4.
Powell (1868–1920) was the first prominent American female violinist,
a student of Charles Dancla at the Paris Conservatory and of Joseph
Joachim in Berlin. She had successful tours in the United States,
1894–1898, was a sensation in Europe during 1898–1900, and performed
in South Africa. The life of the touring concert artist of her day is well portrayed in the book, and contemporary critical comments are given. One of
the earliest violinists to record, Powell was a Victor artist from 1904 to
1917. Shaffer and Greenwood have written a graceful, mostly documented
(and rather adulatory) account of the Powell career, with endnotes, a
chronological discography (with matrix numbers, takes, release dates;
covering published and unpublished items), and an expansive index.
Reviews: AM 1991, 311; *Choice* 9/88, 140.

S2-591   ML418 .S62
Smith, Stuff. Pure at heart / Stuff Smith; ed. Anthony Barnett and Eva
Logager. — Lewes, England : Allardyce, Barnett, 1991. — 61 p. : ill.
ISBN 0-9079-5415-4.
Smith (1909–1967) was a jazz violinist. This is the report of an inter-
view with him conducted in 1965, in which nothing tangible was con-
veyed about his life or his music. An autobiographical fragment of equal
utility is included in the book. With a name index.

S2-592   ML418 .S64 A3
Smith, W. O. (William Oscar). Sideman : the long gig of W. O. Smith :

a memoir / W. O. Smith; introduction ["Fanfare"] by Dizzy Gillespie. — Nashville : Rutledge Hill, 1991. — 319 p. : ill. ISBN 1-55853-132-7.

Smith (1917–1991) was a jazz bassist who performed with Coleman Hawkins, Dizzy Gillespie, Charlie Parker, Miles Davis, and other notables; he also played the classical repertoire, as a member of the Nashville Symphony. Smith studied at New York University and later became a teacher of music at Tennessee State University. His story is casual and undocumented, featuring remembered conversations. Music as such is not discussed. In contrast to most memoirs of black jazz artists, Smith's does not seem focused on racism; indeed, he is able to "rejoice in the victory of black Americans over racism and bigotry. It is not yet a complete victory, but it is substantial and continuing." With a nonexpansive index.

S2-593   ML418 .V23

Hedges, Dan. Eddie VanHalen / Dan Hedges. — New York : Vintage, 1985. — 139 p. : ill. : 12 p. plates. ISBN 0-394-74130-7.

The story of rock guitarist VanHalen is told here in vulgar language with invented conversations. There is a list of recordings, 1978–1986, giving minimal data. Without index or reference features.

S2-594   ML418 .W27 D3

Dance, Helen Oakley. Stormy Monday : the T-Bone Walker story / Helen Oakley Dance; foreword by B. B. King. — Baton Rouge : Louisiana State University Press, 1987. — xiii, 285 p. : ill. ISBN 0-8071-1355-7.

The first biography of Aaron "T-Bone" Walker, blues and jazz guitarist, precursor of rhythm and blues and of urban blues. The writing is casual, with undocumented conversations and quotations throughout, and a narrative emphasis on Walker's gambling and drinking. His actual music making is largely passed over. A good discography presents the recording sessions from 1929 to 1973, with matrix numbers, release dates and labels, reissues, and personnel. A selected bibliography is made up of general material. The piano-vocal score to the book's title song, "Call It Stormy Monday," is included. With a partly expansive index of names and some topics.

Reviews: AM 1989, 91; *Choice* 11/87, 486.

ML419 : Wind, Brass, and Percussion Players

S2-595   ML419 .A3 A3

Adler, Larry. It ain't necessarily so / Larry Adler. — New York : Grove, 1984. — xi, 222 p. : ill. ISBN 0-394-55757-3.

A refreshing memoir, prefaced by a wonderful account of the treachery of memory: Adler (1914–) recounts several incidents as he remembers them, as others remember them, and as they were recorded in contemporary diaries—all different. So he presents his recollections tentatively, as "not necessarily so." They are entertaining in any case. As the first concert harmonicist, Adler got to perform with distinguished orchestras and conductors, and mingled with such persons as Al Capone, Groucho Marx, Eddie Cantor, Fred Astaire, Sid Grauman, Ingrid Bergman (who wanted to go away with him—if that is necessarily so), Humphrey Bogart, Darius Milhaud, and Dwight Eisenhower. He started as a pianist, in Baltimore, switched to harmonica, and heard at many auditions that "he stinks." Remarkably, a thoroughly botched performance of *Bolero* in Los Angeles produced rave reviews and led to a great career. Anecdotes and conversations abound here, but in the stated context they are not distressing. With a nonexpansive index.

S2-596   ML419 .A66
Sudhalter, Richard M. Henry "Red" Allen. 1981.

S2-597   ML419 .A75 A6
Albertson, Chris. Louis Armstrong. 1978.
See series note at S2-1114.

S2-598   ML419 .A75 G5
Giddins, Gary. Satchmo / Gary Giddins. — New York : Doubleday, 1988. — 239 p. : ill. ISBN 0-385-24428-2.
Giddins based much of this biography on several previously unpublished manuscripts by Armstrong, who was a prolific prose writer. Many of the photographs (some in color) are published for the first time. In fact, the book is fairly equally divided between text and photographs. The author attempts to examine what impact these unpublished documents have on earlier Armstrong scholarship.
The discography (5 pp.), primarily of recent releases, is arranged loosely by recording date; it gives label names and numbers. With a four-page bibliography, but without index.
Gary Giddins is a jazz critic and historian. He founded the American Jazz Orchestra in 1985 [—D. P.].
Review: AM 1989, 473.

S2-599   ML419 .A75 P55
Pinfold, Mike. Louis Armstrong, his life & times / Mike Pinfold. — New York : Universe, 1987. — 143 p. : ill. (Jazz life & times) ISBN 0-87663-667-9.
British title: *The Life and Times of Louis Armstrong* (Tunbridge Wells: Spellmount, 1987).
A casual, fast-moving biography, concentrating on Armstrong's life (1900–1971), rather than on his music. It is not documented, although

most of the quotations appear to be real and were probably based on some unnamed sources. The illustrations are well chosen, and there is a useful discographical essay. With a bibliography of about 80 titles and a nonexpansive index.

S2-600   ML419 .B12 M7

Morton, David C. DeFord Bailey : a black star in early country music / David C. Morton; with Charles K. Wolfe. — Knoxville : University of Tennessee Press, 1991. — xix, 199 p. ISBN 0-87049-698-0.

Bailey (1899–1982) was a harmonicist, guitarist, banjoist, and blues singer, as well as a founding member of Grand Ole Opry and a regular performer there from 1925 to 1941. His friend David Morton taped interviews with him and secured letters and other personal documentation for use in this sturdy biography. Source notes are given, including a list of the taped interviews. Only four recording sessions were made by Bailey (one for Columbia, one for Victor, and two for Brunswick), all of them well described in Wolfe's discography, with matrix numbers, labels, and reissues. Bailey's song repertoire is listed, and there is an expansive index of persons, titles, and topics.

Reviews: *Choice* 5/92, 1406; LJ 11/15/91, 84.

S2-601   ML419 .B164

Weber, Bruce. Let's get lost : starring Chet Baker : a film journal / Bruce Weber. — New York : MCA, 1988. — Unpaged. ISBN 0-9621-6580-8.

An album of black-and-white photos about trumpeter/vocalist Baker, with running commentary. He worked with Stan Getz and Gerry Mulligan, among others; the pictures include some good scenes of performers in action. Without index or reference features.

S2-602   ML419 .B23 C5

Chilton, John. Sidney Bechet : the wizard of jazz / John Chilton. — New York : Oxford, 1987. — xiii, 331 p. : ill. ISBN 0-19-520623-1.

Bechet (1897–1959) was a clarinetist and soprano saxophonist who worked in New Orleans, New York, and across Europe. His popularity rose and fell with changing musical tastes, but as early as the late 1930s critics began to recognize the extent of his contribution to early jazz. He spent the last 10 years of his life in Europe, where he was honored as a great jazz musician.

Chilton relies on a wide variety of sources for this detailed biography, including correspondence and conversations with Bechet's associates, recorded interviews, and published materials. He attempts to assess the veracity of Bechet's autobiography *Treat It Gentle* (1960) and to fill gaps in that work.

About 50 photographs are included; none are dated earlier than 1922.

All quotations are meticulously cited, and there is a bibliography of about 100 entries. Includes a partly expansive index of names, titles, and places.

John Chilton is a trumpeter, bandleader, and writer, whose works include *Who's Who of Jazz* (1970, rev. ed. 1985) [—D. P.].

Reviews: AM 1991, 320; *Choice* 9/88, 137.

S2-603   ML419 .B23 K2
Kappler, Frank K. Sidney Bechet. 1980.
See series note at S2-1114.

S2-604   ML419 .B23 Z2
Zammarchi, Fabrice. Sidney Bechet. 1989.
A brief account of Bechet's life, with a discography. See series note at S2-1111.

S2-605   ML419 .B24
Prendergast, Curtis. Bix Beiderbecke. 1979.
See series note at S2-1114.

S2-606   ML419 .B25 C3
Chilton, John. Bunny Berigan. 1982.
See series note at S2-1114.

S2-607   ML419 .B25 D8
DuPuis, Robert. Bunny Berigan : elusive legend of jazz / Robert DuPuis. — Baton Rouge : Louisiana State University Press, 1991. — xiv, 368 p. : ill. ISBN 0-8071-1648-3.
A straightforward, documented biography of trumpeter Berigan (1908–1942), who starred with the Tommy Dorsey and Benny Goodman ensembles. There is a good bibliography that includes unpublished materials and a selective discography that gives matrix and release numbers along with perceptive comments. There is an expansive index.

S2-608   ML419 .B298 A3
Bernhardt, Clyde E. B. I remember : eighty years of black entertainment, big bands and the blues : an autobiography by jazz trombonist and blues singer Clyde E. B. Bernhardt / Clyde E. B. Bernhardt; with Sheldon Harris; foreword by John F. Szwed. — Philadelphia : University of Pennsylvania Press, 1986. — xix, 271 p. : ill. ISBN 0-8122-80180.
The author's long career included associations with King Oliver, Jay McShann, and other leading groups. His reminiscences are anecdotal and casual, relating to his daily activities and including undocumented conversations; nothing specific is said about music. A good discography,

covering 1934–1979, includes matrix numbers, locations and dates, personnel, and rejected takes. With a partly expansive index. Harris is the author of the *Blues Who's Who* (1979).
Reviews: *Choice* 1/87, 771; LJ 6/15/86, 69.

S2-609   ML419 .B5
Bigard, Barney. With Louis and the Duke : the autobiography of a jazz clarinetist / Barney Bigard; with Barry Martin; introduction by Earl Hines. — London : Macmillan, 1985. — x, 152 p. : ill. : 16 p. plates. ISBN 0-3333-9908-0.
New Orleans clarinetist Bigard (1906–1980) had a difficult childhood and initiation into musical life, playing in brothels or wherever he could; then he joined King Oliver in Chicago and went on to a 15-year association with Duke Ellington. Later he was with the Louis Armstrong All-Stars. His memoir is made of invented conversations and anecdotes, revealing nothing about his music. With an expansive index, but without other reference features.
Reviews: AM 1987, 453; *Choice* 6/87, 1561.

S2-610   ML419 .B57 G5
Giese, Hannes. Art Blakey : sein Leben, seine Musik, seine Schallplatten / Hannes Giese. — Schaftlach, Germany : Oreos, 1990. — 217 p. : ill. (Collection jazz, 13) ISBN 3-923657-13-7.
In German. A biography and discography for drummer Blakey (1919–1990). See series note at S2-1111.

S2-611   ML419 .B635 A3
Bogue, Merwyn. Ish Kabibble : the autobiography of Merwyn Bogue / Merwyn Bogue; with Gladys Bogue Reilly. — Baton Rouge : Louisiana State University Press, 1989. — 209 p. : ill. ISBN 0-8071-1498-7.
A spirited, casual memoir by a musician who "had fun almost every day." Cornetist and sometime manager for Kay Kyser's big band, he was best known as a novelty singer; he took his stage name from a song title. His pranks and anecdotes are entertaining, albeit marked with invented conversations. There is no whining about personal problems, but nothing about music either. With an expansive index.

S2-612   ML419 .B735
Lock, Graham. Forces in motion : the music and thoughts of Anthony Braxton / Graham Lock; photographs by Nick White; foreword by Anthony Braxton. — London : Quartet, 1988. — xvi, 412 p. : ill. : 16 p. plates. ISBN 0-7043-2620-5.
Braxton (1945–) is an avant-garde classical composer active also in

popular music. In this book, which seems to be drawn from interviews (no specific sources are given), he makes known his views on many topics, for example, Duke Ellington, John Coltrane, Charlie Parker, chess, astrology, feminism, Egypt, acid rain, racism, and poverty. With an informal discography (minimal data), worklist, bibliography, and expansive index.

Review: *Choice* 10/89, 326.

S2-613   ML419 .B76

Brown, Marion. Recollections : essays, drawings, miscellanea / Marion Brown. — Frankfurt am Main, Germany : J. A. Schmitt, 1984. — 285 p. : ill. ISBN 3-9233-9603-1.

Brown (1935–) is an alto sax player who has performed with many jazz groups, as well as an author and artist. Presented here are five of his essays and 14 drawings, plus five compositions in score. These are backed up by interview material made in Germany during 1983. Full documentation, but no index.

S2-614   ML419 .B89 A31

Bushell, Garvin. Jazz from the beginning / Garvin Bushell as told to Mark Tucker; introduction by Lawrence Gushee. — Ann Arbor : University of Michigan Press, 1988. — xiv, 198 p. : ill. : 16 p. plates. ISBN 0-4721-0098-X.

Written memoirs of clarinetist and alto saxophonist Bushell (1902–) and interviews with Tucker formed the basis for this biographical account. Bushell traveled widely and contributes anecdotal material— much of it relating to encounters with the law—from Europe and South America, as well as tales about Cab Calloway, Chick Webb, Rex Stewart, and others who reached greater stardom than he. Music is not really discussed. Undocumented quotations and conversations abound, although Tucker does provide some chapter endnotes. A discography spans 1920 to 1964, with dates, locations, labels, and personnel. There is a list of musicians with brief biographical data and a nonexpansive index of names, titles, and topics.

Reviews: AM 1993, 493; *Choice* 3/89, 172.

S2-615   ML419 .C11

Berger, Morroe. Benny Carter. 1980.

See series note at S2-1114.

S2-616   ML419 .C594

Hennessey, Mike. Klook : the Kenny Clarke story / Mike Hennessey; foreword by Dizzy Gillespie. — London : Quartet, 1990. — xii, 364 p. : ill. : 16 p. plates. ISBN 0-7043-2529-2.

A casual life story of drummer Clarke (1914–), taking him from early days in Pittsburgh, to house drummer at the Apollo and Minton's in New York, an association with Dizzy Gillespie from 1946, Paris, the Modern Jazz Quartet, and international acclaim. There are long direct quotations without sources and many undocumented episodes. Music itself gets little attention, except for a selective discography (1937–1984) that gives personnel and album contents. There is a general bibliography and a nonexpansive index.

S2-617   ML419 .C6 A3

Clayton, Buck. Buck Clayton's jazz world/ Buck Clayton; assisted by Nancy Miller Elliott; discography compiled by Bob Weir. — London : Macmillan, 1986; New York : Oxford, 1987. 255 p. : ill. ISBN 0-333-41733-X (U.K.); 0-19-520535-9 (U.S.).

Clayton (1911–) is a trumpeter, arranger, and composer. He focuses on his professional career, recounting his relationships with Billie Holiday, Count Basie, Coleman Hawkins, Lester Young, Jimmy Rushing, and other musicians. He also talks about touring in Asia, Europe, and Australia. There are about 30 well-chosen photographs, a detailed discography (25 pp.), and an expansive index [—D. P.].

Reviews: AM 1987, 454; *Choice* 7-8/87, 1703.

S2-618   ML419 .C62 A3

Coleman, Bill. Trumpet story / Bill Coleman. — London : Macmillan, 1988. — 224 p. : ill. ISBN 1-333-45784-6.

First published in French, 1981.

Bill Coleman (1904–1981), swing trumpeter, relates personal and professional aspects of growing up in Cincinnati, becoming successful in New York, and living in Paris after 1948. Highlighted are his relations with Louis Armstrong, Benny Carter, Edgar "Spider" Courance, Roy Eldridge, Duke Ellington, Coleman Hawkins, Fletcher Henderson, Clarence Paige, Luis Russell, Lloyd Scott, Dicky Wells, and Teddy Wilson. He chronicles tours all over the world and describes some of his recording sessions. One recurrent theme is the racial prejudice Coleman encountered throughout the United States, particularly after he married a white woman. The style is straightforward; Coleman includes many details of dates, places, and persons. The 23 photographs, many of various ensembles, are interesting but very poorly reproduced. The discography, compiled by Evert (Ted) Kaleveld and Lily Coleman, documents nearly 100 recording sessions. Dates, places, personnel, matrix numbers, song titles, and original labels and numbers are included, along with some information on reissues. This is followed by a list of Coleman's film appearances. The partly expansive index includes personal names, places, and song titles [—D. P.].

Reviews: *Choice* 9/91, 114; LJ 2/15/91, 195.

S2-619   ML419 .C63 L6

Litweiler, John. Ornette Coleman : the harmolodic life / John Litweiler. — London : Quartet, 1992. — vii, 245 p. : ill. : 8 p. plates. ISBN 0-688-07212-7.

Alto sax player Coleman (1930 or 1931–) was identified with the rise of fusion jazz, as well as the "bop to hard bop succession." He also wrote and performed concert pieces. In this adulatory account, he is placed on a level with Louis Armstrong and Charlie Parker as a jazz innovator. The biography is straightforward, partly documented with endnotes. There are comments of a musical nature, although they run to smoke and mirrors; for instance, no clear meaning appears for "harmolodic." One Coleman solo, "Free," is transcribed. A discography covering 1949–1991 gives location, personnel, titles, and release labels. With an expansive index.

Review: LJ 3/15/93, 80.

S2-620   ML419 .C63 M37

McRae, Barry. Ornette Coleman / Barry McRae; selected discography by Tony Middleton. — London : Apollo, 1988. — 96 p. : ill. (Jazz masters) ISBN 0-948820-08-X.

This brief work, the first monograph on Coleman in English, mixes personal and professional biographical information with criticism, in an effort to identify what makes Coleman's music unique.

A dozen recent photographs show Coleman in performance. The 15-item bibliography, which gives only title, author, and publisher, is followed by a description of Coleman's film and TV appearances. The selected discography provides personnel, locations, dates, titles, labels, and numbers for 36 releases. Without index.

Barry McRae has contributed to *Jazz Journal International, Wire Magazine, Jazz News, Event, Jazz Down Under,* and *Down Beat* [—D. P.].

S2-621   ML419 .C63 W54

Wilson, Peter Niklas. Ornette Coleman : sein Leben, seine Musik, seine Schallplatten / Peter Niklas Wilson. — Schaftlach, Germany : Oreos, 1989. — 186 p. : ill. (Collection jazz, 12) ISBN 3-923657-24-2.

In German. An appreciation of Coleman, with brief consideration of his life story, comments on his performances, and a discography. Source notes are given. A bibliography of about 50 items is useful for inclusion of German writings. The discography (1955–1988) shows album covers, gives personnel, and presents extended commentaries, but omits discographical details. A number of good photos enhance the reference value of the book. Indexes of composers and albums, but no general index.

S2-622   ML419 .C645

Filtgen, Gerd. John Coltrane : sein Leben, seine Musik, seine Schallplatten / Gerd Filtgen and Michael Ausserbauer. — Gauting-Buchendorf, Germany : Oreos, 1983. — 220 p. : ill. (Collection jazz) ISBN 3-923657-02-1.

A useful discography is the highlight of this study, which also presents a plain biography of saxophonist Coltrane (1926–1967); record sessions are listed from 1949 to 1967, giving full data of location, personnel, titles, album cover photos, and extensive comments.

S2-623   ML419 .C645 .P9
Priestley, Brian. John Coltrane / Brian Priestley. — London : Apollo, 1987. — 96 p. : ill. (Jazz masters) ISBN 0-9488-2002-0.

A brief biography of Coltrane (1926–1967), premier saxophonist of the avant-garde in the 1960s. "Virtually everything issued" is listed in the discography, covering 1949–1967, giving matrix numbers, personnel, titles, and brief comments. A more comprehensive list than the one in Filtgen (S2-622), but without the lengthy discussions.

S2-624   ML419 .D35 A3
Darensbourg, Joe. Telling it like it is / Joe Darensbourg; ed. Peter Vacher; supplementary material compiled by Peter Vacher. — Basingstoke, England : Macmillan, 1987. — vi, 231 p. : ill. ISBN 0-333-41735-6.

Reprinted as *Jazz Odyssey: The Autobiography of Joe Darensbourg* (Baton Rouge: Louisiana State University Press, 1988; ISBN 0-8071-1442-1).

Joe Darensbourg (1906–1985) was a clarinetist and alto saxophonist, known as a New Orleans stylist. He describes his early years in Louisiana; later stays in Los Angeles, Seattle, and San Francisco; and long associations with Kid Ory and Louis Armstrong. In a casual tone, Darensbourg combines recollections of his personal life and his professional career, which included such figures as Barney Bigard, Papa Mutt Carey, and Ed Garland. His descriptions of the lifestyle of the 1920s itinerant musician are noteworthy. More than 40 well-chosen photographs from Darensbourg's private and public lives are nicely captioned and reproduced. The discography documents over 100 recording sessions with dates, places, personnel, matrix numbers, song titles, and issuing labels and numbers. Short lists of compositions and film appearances are followed by a chronology (7 pp.) and a bibliography of around 25 titles about Darensbourg. The partly expansive index includes personal names, places, clubs, ensembles, and song titles.

Peter Vacher is a critic and writer on jazz who has contributed to *Coda, Jazz Monthly, Jazz Journal International,* and *Jazz Express* [—D. P.].

Review: *Choice* 9/88, 137.

S2-625   ML419 .D39 A3
Davis, Miles. Miles : the autobiography / Miles Davis, with Quincy

Troupe. — New York : Simon & Schuster, 1989. — 431 p. : ill. : 32 p. plates. ISBN 0-671-63504-2.

Miles Davis (1926–1991), trumpeter and bandleader, has already been the subject of several biographies. Here he casually chronicles personal and professional aspects of his life. He discusses working with John Coltrane, Gil Evans, Dizzy Gillespie, Herbie Hancock, Thelonious Monk, Charlie Parker, and Max Roach. Davis has captioned the over 100 photographs with many personal observations. They range from publicity stills of early idols to fellow musicians in performance. A few pictures from his personal life are included. The detailed, expansive index covers names, titles, and concepts [—D. P.].

Reviews: AM 1992, 89; *Choice* 12/90, 639; LJ 10/1/89, 97.

S2-626   ML419 .D39 C5

Chambers, John Richard. Milestones 1 : the music and times of Miles Davis to 1960 / John Richard Chambers. — Toronto : University of Toronto Press, 1983; New York : Beech Tree Books, 1985. — xii, 345 p. : ill. ISBN 0-688-02635-4 (U.S.).

Considers the life of jazz trumpeter Davis (1926–1991) to 1959, taking him from his early work in East St. Louis, Illinois, to New York City, where he studied briefly at the Juilliard School, and then joined Charlie Parker. He achieved renown in the bebop movement of the 1940s and as a creator of the subsequent cool jazz style. He is characterized by Chambers as a "bebop prodigy, hipster, fashion plate, autocrat, activist, rock star." Unfortunately, much of his life was affected by heroin addiction, and the resulting problems take up a good segment of the book; but there are also some musical discussions. Conversations and anecdotes are plentiful. Documentation is minimal, with no source notes, a bibliography of about 200 items (including liner notes), and a nonexpansive index. See also the following entry.

Review: AM 1987, 329.

S2-627   ML419 .D39 C51

Chambers, John Richard. Milestones 2 : the music and times of Miles Davis since 1960 / John Richard Chambers. — New York : Beech Tree Books, 1985. — 416 p. : ill. ISBN 0-688-04646-0.

Continues item S2-626, taking Davis from 1960 to the late 1980s. His second quintet, fusion, modal experiments, and his emerging preference for loud rock sounds are dealt with. Chambers presents a more scholarly approach in this volume than in his first one, giving chapter endnotes and minimizing conversations and quotes; there is also some useful musical discussion, but without musical examples. A bibliography of about 300 items is included, lacking pagination for articles. With a nonexpansive index.

Review: AM 1987, 329.

S2-628   ML419 .D39 M3

McRae, Barry. Miles Davis / Barry McRae. — London : Apollo, 1988. — 96 p. : ill. (Jazz masters, 14) ISBN 0-9488-20055.

A plain, undocumented life story of Davis, with a selective discography of 1948–1986 material "generally available"; full data are given for the record sessions covered: date, place, personnel, matrix and label number. Without index.

S2-629   ML419 .D39 R49

Reyman, Randall G. An analysis of melodic improvisational practices of Miles Davis / Randall G. Reyman. — Decatur, Ill. : Millikin University, 1986. — 183 leaves. ("Summer Fellowship Grant Project.") ISBN not given.

An intriguing technical study of melodic features employed by Davis performing in four genres: "bop, modal, post-bop modernism, and fusion." Four solos are transcribed and analyzed, and certain melodic patterns are found to predominate. The musical examples are written in a careless hand. With a general bibliography of 82 items; without index.

S2-630   ML419 .D39 W5

Wiessmüller, Peter. Miles Davis : sein Leben, sein Musik, seine Schallplatten / Peter Wiessmüller. — 2nd ed. —Schaftlach, Germany : Oreos, 1988. — 220 p. : ill. (Collection, jazz) ISBN 3-9236-57048.

1st ed., 1984 (LOAM Suppl. SA-473).

In German. Wiessmüller has left the early biographical information unchanged in this edition, but has extended his evaluation of Davis's career in the 1980s. The critiques of early recordings have not been revised, but information about available reissues has been updated. The short article on rare and bootleg recordings of Davis has been dropped. The index has been expanded to include titles of individual pieces discussed in the discography, but personal names are still not included, and the biographical portion of the volume is not indexed. Three biographies have been added to the bibliography [—D. P.].

S2-631   ML419 .D4

Armstrong, Doug. Wild Bill Davison : a celebration : an illustrated tribute / Doug Armstrong. — Ottawa : Leith Music, 1991. — 207 p. : ill. ISBN not given.

A photo album on trumpeter Davison (1906–1989), including advertisements, reviews, programs, and miscellaneous graphics. Pictures taken on international tours are of interest. A discography covering 1924–1989 gives minimal data. Without notes or index.

S2-632   ML419 .D64 H67

Horricks, Raymond. The importance of being Eric Dolphy / Raymond

Horricks; discography by Tony Middleton. — Tunbridge Wells, England : D. J. Costello, 1989. — 95 p. : ill. ISBN 0-7104-3048-5.

A general appreciation of saxophonist-clarinetist-flutist Dolphy (1928–1964), including attention to "Influences," "Development," and "Directions." Undocumented quotations are pervasive. Certain musical matters are addressed, and three solos are transcribed. The discography of commercial recordings made in the United States, the United Kingdom, France, Germany, and Italy (1949–1964) lists personnel for each recording, plus the date and location, but gives no further details. With a bibliography of 10 items; without index.

S2-633   ML419 .E8 A3
Erwin, Pee Wee. This horn for hire / Pee Wee Erwin; as told to Warren W. Vaché, Sr.; foreword by William M. Weinberg. — Metuchen, N.J. : Scarecrow Press and the Institute of Jazz Studies, 1987. — x, 441 p. : ill. (Studies in jazz, 5) ISBN 0-8108-1945-7.

Erwin is a trumpet player who was heard with various big bands (including Benny Goodman and Tommy Dorsey) and in many other contexts from the 1920s into the 1970s. Most of this book consists of an engaging first-person narrative by Erwin, recalling his childhood, then offering a remarkably detailed account of his playing days on the road with one group or another. His memory seems incredible at times; but he does mostly eschew quoted conversations. The story is that of hundreds of itinerant musicians, not superstars, who formed the structural skeleton of the famous bands. A good discography is appended, with descriptions of recording sessions of many bands, giving contents, personnel, and historical details. With a nonexpansive name index.

Review: *Choice* 3/88, 1106.

S2-634   ML419 .F7 A3
Freeman, Bud. Crazeology : the autobiography of a Chicago jazzman / Bud Freeman; as told to Robert Wolf; foreword by Studs Terkel. — Urbana : University of Illinois Press, 1989. — xii, 103 p. : ill. ISBN 0-2520-1634-3.

Tenor sax player Freeman (1906–1991) was one of the Austin High Gang who developed the Chicago jazz style. He was also, according to Studs Terkel, "a natural-born story teller" of "twinkly elegance"—but this gift is not much in evidence here. The book is a gathering of minor anecdotes and invented conversations, undocumented, albeit spiced by the presence of great artists who shared the stage with Freeman at one time or another: Ray Noble, Benny Goodman, Tommy Dorsey, Paul Whiteman, etc. Nothing is said about the music they played. There is some interest in the selective discography, where Freeman drops in some critical comments. The title of the book comes from a song that Freeman recorded for Okeh in 1928. With a nonexpansive name index. Review: *Choice* 2/90, 960.

S2-635   ML419 .G4 P2
Palmer, Richard. Stan Getz / Richard Palmer. — London : Apollo, 1988. — 96 p. : ill. (Jazz masters, 15) ISBN 0-948820-06-3. (Alternative classification: ML156.7.)
A casual but documented biography, concentrating on the personal life (1927–1991) and problems of the saxophonist. There is a brief section that discusses his musical style. With endnotes and a selective (criteria not given) discography. No index.

S2-636   ML419 .G4 T3
Tercinet, Alain. Stan Getz / Alain Tercinet. — Montpellier, France : Limon, 1989. — 222 p. : ill. (Mood indigo) ISBN not given.
In French. A brief biography, followed by a useful discography (pp. 117–212), giving dates, personnel, matrix numbers, and release labels.

S2-637   ML419 .G54 M4
McRae, Barry. Dizzy Gillespie, his life and times / Barry McRae. — New York : Universe Books, 1988. — 136 p. : ill. (Jazz life & times) ISBN 0-87663-746-2.
An adulatory life story (1917–1993) of the trumpeter and bop innovator, with undocumented anecdotes and quotations; nothing is said about music. With a useful discographical essay, covering 1937–1987, that gives extended comments on principal recordings. There is a nonexpansive index.

S2-638   ML419 .G54 W84
Wölfer, Jürgen. Dizzy Gillespie : sein Leben, seine Musik, seine Schallplatten / Jürgen Wölfer. — Waakirchen, Germany : Oreos, 1987. — 195 p. : ill. (Collection jazz) ISBN 3-923657-16-1.
In German. A straightforward undocumented biography of 69 pages, followed by a discography (1941–1984) that is most useful for its long analysis of each song. Release label and selective reissues are given, with personnel. Album covers are illustrated. With a list of Gillespie's compositions, a list of his arrangers, an index of song titles, and one of album names.
Review: *Choice* 9/89, 140.

Note: For Benny Goodman material, see S2-952–S2-956.

S2-639   ML419 .G665 B76
Britt, Stan. Dexter Gordon : a musical biography / Stan Britt;

discography by Don Tarrant. — New York : Da Capo, 1989. — xx, 215
p. : ill. : 16 p. plates. ISBN 0-3068-0361-5.

Original British edition has title *Long Tall Dexter* (London: Quartet,
1989).

Saxophonist Gordon (1923–1955) played with several big bands, including Horace Heidt. His records are listed here from 1941 to 1987,
with all data given on each: location, date, personnel, matrix number, and
release label. Sound tracks and Armed Forces Radio Service transcriptions are included. The biogrpahical section of the book is also useful,
though its extended quotes from other publications are given without citations. There is an expansive index.

S2-640   ML419 .H26
Hampton, Lionel. Hamp : an autobiography / Lionel Hampton; with
James Haskins. — New York : Warner Books, 1989. — ix, 286 p. : ill. :
16 p. plates. ISBN 0-446-71005-9.

A first-person narration by the great jazz vibraphonist, drummer,
singer, and big-band leader (1913–), consisting mostly of dubious recollections (from childhood onward), conversations, and episodes. Nothing is said about Hampton's unique role in jazz—he was the first to play
the vibraphone as a jazz instrument, with Benny Goodman's Quartet of
1936 to 1940—nor about the music of major artists with whom he performed. The book is one of the poorest specimens of musician memoir,
without even a complete discography (there is a selective list). The nonexpansive index is weak.

Reviews: AM 1993, 486; *Choice* 7-8/90, 1836; LJ 10/1/89, 98.

S2-641   ML419 .H35 C5
Chilton, John. The son of the hawk : the life and recordings of Coleman Hawkins / John Chilton. — New York : Quartet; Ann Arbor : University of Michigan Press, 1990. — viii, 429 p. : ill. ISBN 0-7043-27376
(N.Y.); 0-472-10212-5 (Ann Arbor).

Coleman Hawkins (1904–1969), tenor saxophonist, was noted for his
harmonically sophisiticated, improvisational solos. He recorded as
bandleader, sideman, and unaccompanied soloist. In this biography,
Chilton combines a wealth of biographical information with analyses of
many of Hawkins's recordings, emphasizing professional aspects of his
life over personal ones and using primary and secondary sources. The
style is scholarly and engaging. While quotations are carefully cited,
most endnotes lack page numbers. The bibliography of over 50 books is
followed by a list of periodicals consulted. The roughly 30 photographs
do not contribute much to the work. The nonexpansive index consists almost exclusively of personal names. A discography would have made a
useful companion to Chilton's insightful analyses.

John Chilton is a trumpeter, bandleader, and writer, whose works include *Who's Who of Jazz* (1970; rev. ed. 1985) [—D. P.].
Reviews: AM 1991, 320; *Choice* 7/91, 1790.

S2-642   ML419 .H35 J3
James, Burnett. Coleman Hawkins / Burnett James; discography by Tony Middleton. — Tunbridge Wells, England : Spellmount; New York : Hippocrene Books, 1984. — 93 p. : ill. ISBN 0-8705-2009-1 (U.S.).
A brief biographical sketch, undocumented, and a selective discography of material "generally available"; it covers 1929–1966, giving matrix numbers, personnel, and labels. Without index.

S2-643   ML419 .H35 M4
McDonough, John. Coleman Hawkins. 1979.
See series note at S2-1114.

S2-644   ML419 .H45 A3
Herman, Woody. The woodchoppers ball : the autobiography of Woody Herman. — New York : Dutton, 1990. — x, 162 p. : ill. : 16 p. plates. ISBN 0-5252-4853-6.
Herman's life story (1913–1987) was a troubled one, marked by depression and eventual poverty: he was ejected from the house on Hollywood Boulevard that he had bought (in his wealthy prime) from Humphrey Bogart. The tale is told in the first person by Herman, via undocumented reminiscences and anecdotes. Nothing is said about the actual music that brought him fame—his clarinet and his big band's progressive jazz sound. With no reference features, other than a nonexpansive index.
Review: LJ 2/15/90, 187.

S2-645   ML419 .H45 V6
Voce, Steve. Woody Herman / Steve Voce; discography by Tony Shoppee. — London : Apollo, 1986. — 112 p. : ill. (Jazz masters, 11) ISBN 0-948820-03-9.
The colorful, innovative clarinetist and bandleader Herman (1913–1987) is hardly visible in this brief collection of undocumented anecdotes and conversations; nothing is said of the great progressive style developed in his various "Herds." There is a selective discography, but no index.

S2-646   ML419 .H5 D2
Dance, Stanley. Johnny Hodges. 1981.
See series note at S2-1114.

S2-647   ML419 .H67
Horn, Paul. Inside Paul Horn : the spiritual odyssey of a universal traveler / Paul Horn; with Lee Underwood. — New York : HarperSan Francisco, 1990. — xv, 284 p. : ill. : 12 p. plates. ISBN 0-06-250388-X.
Horn (1930–), jazz performer on the flute, clarinet, and saxophone, describes his wide travels (India, China, Egypt, Russia) in terms of musical experiences and spiritual pursuits. He studied Zen meditation and became an advocate of reincarnation and karma. His musical life has included work with many notables, such as Duke Ellington, Miles Davis, Bill Evans, and Charles Mingus. The tale is told informally, with invented conversations and much philosophical baggage. Nonetheless, there are interesting anecdotes, including Horn's effort to exploit so-called pyramid power by playing the flute in the king's chamber of the Great Pyramid at Cheops. With a discography covering 1957–1985 (personnel and album contents given); without index.

S2-648   ML419 .H87 A3
Hutchinson, Sean. Crying out loud / Sean Hutchinson. — Santa Barbara, Calif. : J. Daniel, 1988. — 197 p. : ill. ISBN 0-936784-42-3.
Hutchinson (1948–), a rock guitarist, founded the 1960s group Far Cry. The group performed at Woodstock, but faded after a couple of years. The book is anecdotal and undocumented, but with relatively few invented conversations; fun with groupies is a central theme. Hutchinson went on to become a member of a Balkan folk dance group. Without index, notes, or discography.

S2-649   ML419 .J6
Hillman, Christopher. Bunk Johnson : his life & times / Christopher Hillman. — New York : Universe, 1988. — 128 p. : ill. (Jazz life & times) ISBN 0-87663-685-7.
A plain biography of jazz pianist Johnson (1889–1949), without source notes but free of imaginary conversations. Some useful musical observations appear, along with interesting city maps showing locations of musical points of interest. With a bibliography of some 100 articles and a nonexpansive index.

S2-650   ML419 .J72 C5
Chilton, John. Let the good times roll : the story of Louis Jordan and his music / John Chilton. — London : Quartet, 1992. — 286 p. : ill. : 16 p. plates. ISBN 0-7043-7025-5.
Jordan (1908–1975) was a saxophonist, known for his group the Tympany Five; he has been acclaimed as the father of rhythm and blues. He starred at the Apollo Theater in Harlem and went on to record with Bing Crosby, Ella Fitzgerald, Louis Armstrong, and other stars. This is a

straightforward life story, with endnotes. There is a selective discography, giving minimal information, and a nonexpansive index.

S2-651   ML419 .K58 A3

Kirk, Andy. Twenty years on wheels / Andy Kirk; as told to Amy Lee; discography by Howard Rye. — Ann Arbor : University of Michigan Press, 1989. — 147 p. : ill. : 24 p. plates. ISBN 0-4721-0134-X.

Kirk (1898–1992) was a big band leader and bass saxophonist, director of the Clouds of Joy for 20 years, and performer with many artists and groups. This first-person story was edited from interview transcripts by Lee. It is an informal, anecdotal tale, replete with undocumented conversations and quotes, following the typical format of itinerant musician recollections. Nothing is said about music. Rye's discography includes "all traced recordings on which Andy Kirk played or which were made by his bands, and . . . small groups drawn from the bands" from 1920 to 1956. Unissued material, films, and broadcasts are included, in original issues only. Information given includes dates and locations, matrix numbers and labels, personnel, and comments. The book has a name and title index, but the discography is unindexed.

Review: AM 1993, 493.

S2-652   NL419 .K78 C8

Crowther, Bruce. Gene Krupa : his life and times / Bruce Crowther. — New York : Universe, 1987. — 144 p. : ill. (Jazz life & times) ISBN 0-8766-3670-9.

Krupa (1909–1973) was widely recognized as the premier jazz drummer of his time, performing with Benny Goodman and later as leader of his own band. Crowther aims to illuminate the "social background" and the "environment in which his . . . music was formed." He gives a good account of these elements, beginning with Krupa's childhood in Chicago's South Side, and including a useful review of the false arrest for drug possession in 1943. Musical content is limited to a discussion of the record sessions, which are thoroughly listed.

S2-653   ML419 .K78 K6

Klauber, Bruce H. World of Gene Krupa : that legendary drummin' man / Bruce H. Klauber; with an introduction by Mel Tormé. — Ventura, Calif. : Pathfinder, 1990. — 214 p. : ill. ISBN 0-9347-9329-8.

A biography compiled primarily from previously published Krupa interviews, with added material from colleagues and friends. His experiences and comments combine to make an absorbing volume. With a life chronology, personnel lists of his groups, an informal selective discography, and a nonexpansive name index. Bruce Klauber is a drummer and writer of articles for jazz magazines.

Note: Glenn Miller item at S2-959.

S2-654   ML419 .M79 H7
Horricks, Raymond. Gerry Mulligan's ark / Raymond Horricks; discography by Tony Middletown. — London : Apollo, 1986. — 96 p. : ill. (Jazz masters) ISBN 0-948820-01-2.
A career survey of baritone sax player Mulligan (1927–1996), emphasizing musical considerations. Without documentation, but sparing in its use of quotes and conversations. The selected discography offers only items in print at the time of compilation; it gives dates and locales, personnel, matrix numbers, and labels.

S2-655   ML419 .M79 K6
Klinkowitz, Jerome. Listen : Gerry Mulligan : an aural narrative in jazz / Jerome Klinkowitz. — New York : Schirmer, 1991. — xxii, 306 p. : ill. : 16 p. plates. ISBN 0-02-871265-X.
A chronological inventory of the Mulligan recordings, connected with the performer's life story—an interesting approach that illuminates both the art and the person. The period covered is 1945 to 1989; information on each disc includes locations, dates, personnel, labels, and useful technical comments by Klinkowitz. Incidents from Mulligan's life are recounted informally, without documentation, but without fictionalized conversations. There is a bibliography of about 30 items and a nonexpansive index of names and titles.

S2-656   ML419 .N8
DeMichael, Don. Red Norvo. 1980.
See series note at S2-1114.

S2-657   ML419 .P24 G4
Giddins, Gary. Celebrating Bird : the triumph of Charlie Parker / Gary Giddins. — New York : Beech Tree Books, 1987. — 128 p. : ill. ISBN 0-688-05959-3.
An album of black-and-white photos with some interesting shots of saxophonist Parker (1920–1955) in action. The running commentary provides a basic biographical sketch, pocked with sociocultural explanations of the music, undocumented and brightened with conversations. With a checklist of LPs; without notes or index.
Review: AM 1988, 96.

S2-658   ML419 .P24 W74
Wilson, Peter Niklas. Charlie Parker : sein Leben, seine Musik, seine Schallplatten / Peter Niklas Wilson and Ulfert Goeman. — Schaftlach, Germany : Oreos, 1988. — 188 p. : ill. (Collection jazz) ISBN 3-923657-12-9.
In German. A bio-discography, with a discussion of Parker's back-

ground, early work in Kansas City and with the big bands, his move to bebop, his accomplishments and influence, and his personality. The very selective discography (covering 1940–1954) gives information on 62 sessions, including locations, labels and reissues, personnel, and extended critical comments. Photos of albums are interspersed. CD collections are described in detail. Wilson has chosen the most important Parker recordings for elaborate analysis, not attempting to duplicate the four-volume inventory of Piet Koster and Dick Bakker (*Charlie Parker Discography*, Amsterdam: Micrography, 1974–1976). With many photographs, an index of album titles, and one of song titles.

S2-659   ML419 .P67 A3
Porter, Roy. There and back : the Roy Porter story / Roy Porter; with David Keller. — Baton Rouge : Louisiana State University Press, 1991. — xiii, 196 p. : ill. ISBN 0-8071-1689-0.

Bebop drummer Porter worked with Charlie Parker, Dexter Gordon, Eric Dolphy, and other major figures. In this autobiography he "chronicles his life, warts and all . . . not afraid to discuss that considerable portion of his life of all-night performances and the attendant hustling and con for the drug score which kept him going." It is a crude tale, narrated in vulgar language, replete with invented conversations. Porter's arrests and incarcerations are duly ascribed to police racism. Nothing substantial emerges about the innovative music making of the era. There is a discography covering sessions of 1945 to 1978, with matrix numbers, personnel, and labels; a bibliography of 21 items; and a nonexpansive index.

Review: *Choice* 11/91, 459.

S2-660   ML419 .P72
Boulard, Garry. Just a gigolo : the life and times of Louis Prima / Garry Boulard. — Lafayette : Center for Louisiana Studies, University of Southwestern Louisiana, 1989. — viii, 182 p. : ill. : 16 p. plates. ISBN 0-984940-49-0.

A trumpeter and big-band leader, Louis Prima (1910–1978) was also a "wild man" and an "enigma" whose music was "sometimes highly autobiographical." He was successful from the mid-1930s, but was criticized for his flamboyant behavior on stage, prompting one writer to say that he had "sacrificed his musical abilities to become a buffoon." Boulard's adulatory account is undocumented and unindexed, heavy with escapades and conversations, saying nothing substantial about the music involved.

S2-661   ML419 .P76 P7
Preston, Katherine K. Music for hire : a study of professional musicians in Washington (1877–1900) / Katherine K. Preston. —

Stuyvesant, N.Y. : Pendragon, 1992. — xxv, 325 p. : ill. (Sociology of music, 6) ISBN 0-918728-66-6.

Based on the journal of John Francis Prosperi (1840–1923), bandsman and orchestral player who worked in the nation's capital, this is the story of white musicians in sundry occupations. Prosperi was the son of an Italian immigrant who played in the United States Marine Band. The journal deals with parades, theater, dances, riverboats, resorts, parties, sports events, fairs, picnics, and other venues that required music. A valuable slice of Americana emerges from Preston's careful, documented research. There is a useful appendix of places where Prosperi played, a bibliography of about 200 primary and secondary sources, and an expansive index.

S2-662   ML419 .R48
Restum, Willie. They all came to see me / Willie Restum; as told to Paul Willistein. — Allentown, Pa. : Author, 1986. — 132 p. : ill. ISBN not given.

Restum, a saxophonist, was most active in the 1950s; he had a 10-year run at the Dream Lounge in Miami Beach, performing and mingling with a vast array of celebrities—many of whom are photographed with him in this book. The text of his story consists strictly of anecdotes and conversations, with scarcely a fact or date. Without index (except for a list of the personalities in the photos).

S2-663   ML419 .R52 T2
Tormé, Mel. Traps, the drum wonder : the life of Buddy Rich / Mel Tormé. — New York : Oxford, 1991. — xiii, 233 p. : ill. : 16 p. plates. ISBN 0-19-507038-0.

An "honest, loving portrait" of the great jazz drummer (1917–1987), by a lifelong friend. Some aspects of the Rich character emerge, with difficulty, from the cloud of anecdotes and remembered conversations that comprise the book. Tormé might have allowed his own musicianship to come forward on occasion and give the story an artistic dimension, but he chose not to do so. Without notes; with an expansive index.

Reviews: AM 1993, 386 ; *Choice* 1/92, 757.

S2-664   ML419 .R64 A3
Rollins, Sonny. Sonny Rollins. 1988.
See series note at S2-1118.

S2-665   ML419 .R64 W3
Wilson, Peter Niklas. Sonny Rollins : sein Leben, seine Musik, seine Schallplatten / Peter Niklas Wilson. — Schaftlach, Germany : Oreos, 1991. — 216 p. : ill. (Collection jazz, 17)
See series note at S2-1111.

S2-666   ML419 .R84 A3

Ruff, Willie. A call to assembly : the autobiography of a musical storyteller / Willie Ruff. — New York : Viking, 1991. — xvi, 432 p. : ill. ISBN 0-670-83800-4.

Ruff (1931–) played string bass, and French horn, mostly with jazz pianist Dwike Mitchell; had a class with Paul Hindemith; and became a professor of music at Yale. The Mitchell-Ruff duo brought jazz to China (see Zinsser's tour account, S2-429). Ruff's life story is casually told, with invented conversations and anecdotes. He grew up poor in Alabama, became "empowered" as a 14-year-old in the Army, learned to play the horn well enough to get an offer from the Israel Philharmonic (he turned it down), and the drums well enough to appear around the world. His account of the Russian tour with Mitchell is of interest. Without documentation; with an expansive index.

Reviews: *Choice* 12/91, 605; LJ 5/15/91, 84.

S2-667   ML419 .R9

McDonough, John. Pee Wee Russell. 1981.

See series note at S2-1114.

S2-668   ML419 .S61

Laplace, Michel. Jabbo Smith : the misunderstood and the "modernistic" / Michel Laplace; trans. Denis Egan. — Menden, Germany : Jazzfreund, 1988. — 48 p. : ill. ISBN not given.

Trumpeter Smith (1908–) was of that generation of jazzmen that followed Louis Armstrong; others in the second group were Red Allen and Bill Coleman. This book gives a biographical account, with perceptive musical discussions, and an inventory of Smith recordings from 1927 to 1976. Full data are given for each session, including locations, personnel, matrix numbers, labels and release numbers. Eight of Smith's solos are transcribed, and there are some good photos of him in action. Without index.

S2-669   ML419 .S767 A3

Stewart, Rex. Boy meets horn / Rex Stewart; ed. Claire P. Gordon. — Ann Arbor : University of Michigan Press, 1991. — x, 236 p. : ill. ISBN 0-472-10213-3.

Stewart (1907–1967) played his cornet with Duke Ellington's band from 1934 to 1945 and made his best records with the group (one was "Boy Meets Horn" in 1938). This book—edited from Stewart's scattered notes ("only about 500 words were not written by Rex")—covers his early years in Washington, D.C., his work with Fletcher Henderson and others in New York during the 1920s and 1930s, and his time with the Duke, going up to only 1948. It consists mainly of anecdotes and rememberd conversations, with nothing said about the music everyone was playing. Without source notes; with a nonexpansive index of names and titles.

Review: *Choice* 9/91, 115.

S2-670   ML419 .T3
Guttridge, Leonard F. Jack Teagarden. 1979.
See series note at S2-1114.

S2-671   ML419 .W44 A3
Wells, Dicky. The night people : the jazz life of Dicky Wells / Dicky
Wells and Stanley Dance; foreword by Count Basie; introduction by
Martin Williams. — 2nd ed. — Washington : Smithsonian Institution
Press, 1991. — x, 229 p. : ill. : 16 p. plates. ISBN 1-5609-8067-2.
1st ed., 1971 (LOAM 1144).
A trombonist in the big-band era, Wells (1909?–1985) performed with
many ensembles, among them the bands of Fletcher Henderson and
Count Basie. His memoir consists of invented conversations, described
by Dance as "examples of conversation on band buses, in dressing
rooms, and at rehearsal . . . condensations intended to illumine . . . 'big-
band folklore'"; accounts of events that are "not, unfortunately, entirely
clear"; and "obscurantist memories." It is not important how factual the
story is, since it has no relation to music, being fixed on drinking, wom-
anizing, and personal disputes. There is one valuable section in the book,
an essay on Wells by André Hodeir (first published in 1954); it offers in-
telligent, musical comments on the Wells style of playing. A discography by Chris Sheridan covers 1927 to 1981, giving full data on the sessions: dates, personnel, matrix and label numbers, and comments. With
a nonexpansive index of names and song titles.
Review: LJ 1/92, 132.

S2-672   ML419 .W45
Chandler, Edna White. The night the camel sang / Edna White Chandler. — St. Johnsbury, Vt. : New Amberola Graphic [37 Caledonia St.,
05819], 1990. Unpaged. ISBN not given.
The first female trumpet virtuoso to achieve wide acclaim, Edna White
(1891–) was a prodigy who graduated from the Institute of Musical Arts
(later the Juilliard School) at age 15. She toured widely and was popular
on radio. This informal autobiography tells of her "nine riotous years in
vaudeville" and other adventures.

S2-673   ML419 .W48 A3
White, Howard. Every highway out of Nashville / Howard White;
with Ruth White; "Prelude" by Jean Shepard. — [n.p.] : JM Productions, 1990. — viii, 148 p. : ill. ISBN 0-9392-9888-0.

S2-674   ML419 .W54 A3
Wilber, Bob. Music was not enough / Bob Wilber; assisted by Derek
Webster. — Basingstoke, England : Macmillan, 1987; New York : Ox-

ford, 1988. — 216 p. : ill. : 16 p. plates. ISBN 0-3334-4418-3 (U.K.); 0-1952-0629-0 (U.S.).

Not many autobiographies begin with a confession of failure, as this one does; indeed Wilber (1928–), a clarinetist who had been Sidney Bechet's protégé), did not reach the heights in jazz. But he fronted the successful Bob Wilber Wildcats and then his own jazz band, and he recorded with Jack Teagarden, Benny Goodman, Bud Freeman, and other greats. In any case, he is a keen listener and observer, with insightful comments about the players of his day. Invented conversations are relatively few, and musical thoughts are numerous; the writing style is clear and attractive. A white man from an affluent home, Wilber seemed to decide he was an outsider in the jazz world, but he presents an interesting picture of the insider dimension. With a discography covering 1947–1984, giving full data (matrix and label numbers, locations, personnel), and a nonexpansive index.

Review: *Choice* 7/88, 1705.

S2-675   ML419 .Y35 I6
Insana, Tino. The authorized Al / Tino Insana and Al Yankovic. — Chicago : Contemporary Books, 1985. — 127 p. : ill. ISBN 0-8092-5133-7.

Al Yankovic (1959–) is an accordionist and rock performer. This little "concocted chronicle" has a number of unusual and amusing items in it, such as a youthful bowling scorecard, pages from his junior high school yearbook (with marginalia), and plenty of bizarre photos that explicate his nickname, "Weird Al." The text is equally weird, giving a "behind the scenes look at the volatile and superfluous life" that includes "his painful introspective period." With a set of song lyrics by Yankovic. While perhaps not "the most important book ever written in the history of mankind," it is a refreshing spoof of the rock-hero novelette.

S2-676   ML419 .Y7 B75
Büchmann-Moller, Frank. You just fight for your life : the story of Lester Young / Frank Büchmann-Moller; foreword by Lewis Porter. — New York : Praeger, 1990. — xvi, 282 p. ISBN 0-275-93265-6.

A fine biography of the tenor saxophonist and bop pioneer (1909–1959), largely based on interviews and primary sources, with full documentation. Quotations from many individuals present a kaleidoscopic effect of impressions about Young and his troubled life. There is special interest in the court martial transcript that marked the end of his miserable military experience. Appendices present a list of Young's jobs and engagements (1919–1959) and names of the members of his groups (1941–1955). With chapter source notes and a nonexpansive index of names. The author is a Danish librarian and saxophone performer.

Reviews: AM 1993, 374; *Choice* 7-8/90, 1835; LJ 2/15/90, 187.

S2-677   ML419 .Y7 G4
Gelly, Dave. Lester Young / Dave Gelly; discography by Tony Middleton. — Tunbridge Wells, England : Spellmount; New York : Hippocrene Books, 1984. — 94 p. : ill. (Jazz masters) ISBN 0-8705-2010-5 (U.S.).
An undocumented biography, including invented conversations, and a selective list of "generally available" recordings made during 1936–1947. Without index or reference features.

S2-678   ML419 .Y7 L47
Porter, Lewis. A Lester Young reader / Lewis Porter. — Washington : Smithsonian Institution Press, 1991. — xiii, 323 p. ISBN 1-56098-064-8.
A collection of 36 articles, most of them previously published, gathered by one of Young's biographers (see LOAM Suppl. SA-504). Interviews with his brother and with pianist Jimmy Rowles, published for the first time, add some bits to the story of Young's career; and interviews with Young himself give some information on musical matters. Among the 31 contributors are John Hammond, Nat Hentoff, Dan Morgenstern, Whitney Balliett, and Frank Büchmann-Moller. Index, but no bibliography or discography.
Reviews: AM 1993, 374; *Choice* 5/92, 1405; LJ 11/15/91, 84.

ML420 : Singers

S2-679   ML420 .A25 A3
Adams, Edie. Sing a pretty song : the offbeat life of Edie Adams, including the Ernie Kovacs years / Edie Adams and Robert Windeler. — New York : Morrow, 1990. — 366 p. ISBN 0-688-07341-7.
Popular singer Adams (1931–), wife of comedian Ernie Kovacs, was well known on television and Broadway. She recounts her rise to stardom and her life with Kovacs in a series of dialogues and anecdotes. With an expansive index.

S2-680   ML420 .A59
Anderson, Bill. Whisperin' Bill : an autobiography : a life of music, love, tragedy & triumph / Bill Anderson. — Atlanta : Longstreet, 1989. — 464 p. : ill. ISBN 0-9292-6424-X.
Country performer Anderson offers a casual memoir of anecdotes and recalled conversations, without documentation or index. Most of the tale is about the injury to his wife in an auto accident and the subsequent hardships they endured.

S2-681 ML420 .B114 A3
Baez, Joan. And a voice to sing with : a memoir / Joan Baez. — New
York : Summit Books, 1987. — 378 p. : ill. ISBN 0-671-40062.
Also in paperback (New York: New American Library, 1988).
A totally boring anecdotal autobiography by the singer (1941–), with
remembered conversations. Nothing about music. Without index or reference features, except for 32 pages of photos.
Review: LJ 7/87, 71.

S2-682 ML420 .B22 A3
Bailey, Pearl. Between you and me : a heartfelt memoir on learning,
loving, and living / Pearl Bailey. — New York : Doubleday, 1989. —
xiv, 270 p. : ill. : 16 p. plates. ISBN 0-385-26202-7.
Singer/actress Bailey (1918–1990) has turned to biographical and inspirational writing, this being her sixth book of the type. Here she speaks
"from the depth of my soul of joy, pain, loneliness, a word no one but
God understands." She hopes to give others good reasons for carrying
on, specifically in this book to complete college degrees (she finished
hers at age 67) and to counter the decline in American family life through
the wisdom that can be gained from the African experience. The style is
anecdotal, with invented conversations—including one wildly improbable exchange with a psychiatrist, who is said to have cured her depression by advising her not to sing a certain song with gloomy lyrics. Nothing else is said about her singing, or about music. Without index.

S2-683 ML420 .B365 A3
Berry, Chuck. Chuck Berry : the autobiography / Chuck Berry; foreword by Bruce Springsteen. — New York : Harmony Books, 1987. —
xxii, 346 p. : ill. ISBN 0-517-56666-4.
An anecdotal, casual memoir of the rock pioneer (1926–), with quoted
conversations, detailing Berry's numerous adventures with women, the
music industry, the tax collector, and (of greater interest) the segregated
world in which he grew up. He does not elaborate on his music making,
except to offer some background information on individual song lyrics.
Useful reference features include a chronology of 48 recording sessions
(1955–1979), a discography (labels and release dates only), and a filmography. Nonexpansive index of persons and titles, with some topics.
Reviews and listing: AM 1989, 335; BCL; *Choice* 4/92, 1192; LJ
11/1/87, 1281.

S2-684 ML420 .B6 A3
Bono, Sonny. And the beat goes on / Sonny Bono. — New York :
Pocket Books, 1991. — 274 p. : ill. : 16 p. plates. ISBN 0-671-69366-2.

"A man who lived the American dream, got knocked down more than once, yet rose again to new triumphs," Salvatore Phillip Bono (1935–) is best known as one of the Sonny and Cher duo that was prominent in the 1960s and 1970s; they were one of the few husband-wife teams in the world of rock music. The marriage was dissolved after 11 years, having been either happy or not, depending on which participant is reporting (cf. S2-701); Bono quotes her as naming him "a great husband." He was surprised to learn she was miserable and wanted to leave him for a guitar player. Bono recovered and went on to other successes, including election to mayor of Palm Springs. The whole story is in episodic, fictionalized format, with no documentation or index.

S2-685   ML420 .B7 A3
Boone, Pat. A new song / Pat Boone. — Rev. ed. — Altamonte Springs, Fla. : Creation House, 1988. — 1v, 207 p. ISBN 0-88419-211-3.
1st ed., 1970 (LOAM Suppl. S-1071).
Singer/evangelist Boone (1934–) presents an inspirational, born-again message of faith, recounting his rebound from family and financial crises. His mode is anecdotal, with uplifting dialogues. Music is not a topic of discussion. Without index or reference features.

S2-686   ML420 .B777 A3
Bricktop. Bricktop / Bricktop; with James Haskins. — New York : Atheneum, 1983. — xviii, 300 p. : ill. : 16 p. plates. ISBN 0-689-11349-8.
"A scrappy redhead 'colored girl' [real name Ada Smith Ducongé] from West Virginia" became an international celebrity as a singer and nightclub owner in Paris during the 1920s and 1930s. Her story is filled with the activities of the beautiful people of her era: F. Scott Fitzgerald, Cole Porter, Maurice Chevalier, Sophie Tucker, the Duke and Duchess of Windsor, and above all her friend Josephine Baker. She introduced the Charleston to Europe and taught it to the Aga Khan. Her anecdotes suggest something of the wild years when Paris was the center of the elite world. Without documentaion; with a partly expansive index.

S2-687   ML420 .B8
McCall, Michael. Garth Brooks : a biography / Michael McCall. — New York : Bantam, 1991. — 186 p. : ill. ISBN 0-5532-9823-2.
The story of country singer Brooks (1962–), with a discography.

S2-688   ML420 .B818 A31
Brown, James. James Brown : the godfather of soul / James Brown; with Bruce Tucker; epilogue by Dave Marsh. — New York : Macmillan, 1986. — xii, 336 p. : ill. ISBN 0-02-517430-4.

Reprinted with new introduction by Tucker (New York: Thunder's Mouth, 1990; ISBN 0-938-41097-0).

A casual, "loud, proud and soulful" memoir of soul singer Brown (1933–), telling of his rise from poverty to riches, with episodes about income tax troubles, a paternity suit, and other nonmusical problems. Recalled conversations abound, along with anecdotes about such celebrities as Elvis Presley, Tina Turner, Otis Redding, and Michael Jackson. With a chronological list of singles and albums (no contents or discographical data) and an expansive index.

Review: LJ 2/1/87, 80.

S2-689   ML420 .B818 R8

Rose, Cynthia. Living in America : the soul saga of James Brown / Cynthia Rose. — London : Serpent's Tail; distributed by Consortium Book Sales and Distribution, 1990. — 182 p. ISBN 0-85242-209-2.

The godfather of soul, and also "the man who kick-started funk music," is here crowned with undocumented, adulatory quotations and anecdotes. Rose is more concerned with cultural context than with music, about which she says little. With a nonexpansive index.

Review: *Choice* 9/91, 115.

S2-690   ML420 .C18 A85

Ardoin, John. The Callas legacy / John Ardoin; foreword by Terrence McNally. — Rev. "compact disc edition." — New York : Scribner's, 1991. — xviii, 236 p. : ill. ISBN 0-684-19306-X.

Revision of the 2nd ed., 1981, with a new foreword.

1st ed., 1977.

The revision consists of corrections and new listings of compact discs by soprano Maria Callas (1923–1977) from 1982. All of her commercial recorded output is now available on CD. Material in this excellent guide is in chronological order, with perceptive discussions of each record. There is also a list of Callas's recorded interviews, and one of her film performances. With a selective bibliography of about 100 entries and a nonexpansive index by name and place.

S2-691   ML420 .C18 C32

Callas, Jackie. Sisters : a revealing portrait of the world's most famous diva / Jackie Callas. — London : Macmillan, 1989. — 247 p. : ill. : 8 p. plates. ISBN 0-312-03934-4.

A family memoir by a sister of Maria Callas, made up of conversations and anecdotes. Among the prominent topics are the soprano's obsessive eating, her troubled relationship with her mother, the mother's "neurotic possessiveness," and everybody's heavy concern about money. With no documentation or index.

S2-692   ML420 .C18 L37

LaRochelle, Réal. Callas : la diva et le vinyl / Réal LaRochelle. — Montreal : Éditions Triptyque, 1987. — 392 p. ISBN 2-89031-069-8.

In French. Despite the impression given by its title, the book is not primarily a discography although there is a discography at the end. LaRochelle has concentrated on the recording career of Callas, her dealings with EMI and Cetra-Soria, and the making of her discs. There are chapter endnotes. The recording list gives locations, dates, labels and reissues, and personnel for releases of 1949 to 1972. No index.

S2-693   ML420 .C18 C35

Lowe, David A. Callas as they saw her / David A. Lowe; discography by Dominique Ravier. — New York : Ungar, 1986. — xv, 264 p. : ill. : 40 p. plates. ISBN 0-8044-5636-4.

A fine collection of research material on Maria Callas, including an inventory of her performances from 1938 to 1974, with reprinted (in English translation if necessary) reviews. Her 1957 memoir, reprinted from *Oggi* magazine, is of interest. There are two interviews as well, and a number of appreciative essays by fellow artists (Placido Domingo and Joan Sutherland among them). Ravier's discography, billed as the most complete available, is useful for its presentation of locales and casts; however, it lacks any discographical information. The critiques of selected great recordings, by Lowe, are substantial. Without index.

Review: LJ 8/86, 152.

S2-694   ML420 .C18 S35

Scott, Michael. Maria Meneghini Callas / Michael Scott. — Boston : Northeastern University Press, 1992. — v, 312 p. : ill. : 16 p. plates. ISBN 1-55553-146-6.

A well-documented biography, although casual in style. The major interest is in Scott's perceptive comments on the recordings. With a chronology of performances and record sessions (1938–1974), a bibliography of about 90 items, and a partly expansive index of names.

Reviews: *Choice* 1/93, 806; LJ 8/92, 104.

S2-695   ML420 .C18 S413

Segalini, Sergio. Callas : portrait of a diva / Sergio Segalini; trans. Sonia Sabel. — London : Hutchinson, 1980. — 171 p. : ill. ISBN 0-09-143740-7.

A book of black-and-white photographs, with accompanying commentary. There is also a chronology of stage appearances, 1938–1974. Not indexed.

S2-696   ML420 .C18 S68
Stancioff, Nadia. Maria : Callas remembered / Nadia Stancioff. —
New York : Dutton, 1987. — 258 p. : ill. ISBN 0-525-24565-0.
An informal collection of anecdotes written by a friend of Callas, of-
fering no new material. Much of the text is devoted to imaginary con-
versations. Without index, notes, or reference features.
Review: LJ 9/1/87, 184.

Note: See S2-1267 for another Callas item.

S2-697   ML420 .C27 A3
Hart, Kitty Carlisle. Kitty : an autobiography / Kitty Carlisle Hart. —
New York : Doubleday, 1988. — 262 p. : ill. ISBN 0-385-24425-8. (Alternative classification PN2287.)
Carlisle (1915–) sang in Bing Crosby films, refused a marriage pro-
posal from George Gershwin, married Moss Hart, and worked with
artists such as Danny Kaye, Rex Harrison, and Woody Allen. Her memoir is therefore not without interest, but it is casual and undocumented,
with invented conversations. There is a nonexpansive index.

S2-698   ML420 .C258 W5
Wiggins, Gene. Fiddlin' Georgia crazy : fiddlin' John Carson, his real
world, and the world of his songs / Gene Wiggins and Norm Cohen. —
Urbana : University of Illinois Press, 1987. — xxi, 302 p. : ill. : 18 p.
plates. ISBN 0-252-01246-1.
Carson (1868–1949) was a pioneer country musician, who "made the
first discs [in 1923] that made the industry aware of the vast untapped
potential market for southern Anglo-American folk music." His early
days are reconstructed insofar as possible by Wiggins in a scholarly fashion, and his songs are presented in text and musical notation. Good documentation is given in chapter endnotes. There is a discography covering 1923–1934, with full data on each session: date, contents, matrix
numbers, labels, personnel, and comments. With an expansive index of
titles, names, and topics.
Review: *Choice* 5/87, 1409.

S2-699   ML420 .C265 A3
Cash, June Carter. From the heart / June Carter Cash. — Englewood
Cliffs, N.J. : Prentice-Hall, 1987. — 219 p. : ill. ISBN 0-13-530767-8.
The author, wife of country singer Johnny Cash, offers a sentimental
memoir comprised primarily of conversations and family anecdotes.
Without notes, index, or reference features.
Review: LJ 5/15/87, 80.

S2-700   ML420 .C44

Bego, Mark. Cher! / Mark Bego. — New York : Pocket Books, 1986. — 219 p. : ill. ISBN 0-6716-28453.

Cherilyn Sarkisian (1946–), better known as Cher, gained fame as a singer and actress, and for her marriages and romances. Her name was legally changed to the single word Cher in 1979. Bego's undocumented story brings out her "unconventional, flamboyant, and always surprising" nature. Dialogues and episodes are provided to support this portrayal. Without index; with a list of recordings (minimal data).

S2-701   ML420 .C44 T2

Taraborrelli, J. Randy. Cher / J. Randy Taraborrelli. — London : Pan, 1990. — xix, 316 p. : ill. ISBN 0-3303-1483-1.

Gossip and invented conversations are offered to portray "one of the bravest, most exciting women of our times." The main theme is Cher's emergence from poverty as a 16-year-old go-go girl to fame under the "Svengali-like" power of Sonny Bono; after her unhappy marriage to Bono, she developed her career as an actress. Without index or reference features.

Review: LJ 12/86, 104.

S2-702   ML421 .C44 Q85

Quirk, Lawrence J. Totally uninhibited : the life and wild times of Cher / Lawrence J. Quirk. — New York : Morrow, 1991. — 303 p. : ill. : 24 p. plates. ISBN 0-688-09822-3.

A casual, undocumented tale that presents anecdotes, conversations, and Cher's states of mind at various times. With a selective discography (minimal data) and a filmography (casts only). There is a partly expansive index.

S2-703   ML420 .C63 G7

Gourse, Leslie. Unforgettable : the life and mystique of Nat King Cole / Leslie Gourse. — New York : St. Martin's, 1991. — xiii, 309 p. : ill. : 16 p. plates. ISBN 0-312-05982-5.

A plain life story of Cole (1916–1965), jazz pianist and vocalist whose records were on the charts for 23 years. Conversations, quotes, and "thoughts" abound in the telling, which is undocumented and without discussion of musical elements. Sources are said to be interviews, "newspapers and magazines, occasionally liner notes on record albums, and a few books." The book title comes from a Cole song, cleverly overdubbed into a 1992 Grammy-winning duet by his daughter Natalie. With a selective discography that gives minimal information and a nonexpansive index.

S2-704   ML420 .C65 A3

Collins, Judy. Trust your heart : an autobiography / Judy Collins. — Boston : Houghton Mifflin, 1987. — 275 p. : ill. ISBN 0-395-41285-4.

An informal memoir, made up of undocumented events and conversations; hardly anything is said about music. Of some interest for 16 pages of photographs. The discography is just an album list with titles of songs and release dates. Without index.

S2-705   ML420 .C72 A3

Joseph, Pleasant. Cousin Joe : blues from New Orleans / Pleasant ("Cousin Joe") Joseph and Harriet J. Ottenheimer. — Chicago : University of Chicago Press, 1987. — xi, 227 p. : ill. ISBN 0-226-41198-2.

Pleasant Joseph made numerous recordings as a blues vocalist between 1945 and 1954. He also played piano, guitar, and ukulele with blues and jazz musicians. This autobiography is based on narratives recorded in the 1960s, supplemented by additional narratives recorded in the 1980s. The style is loose, as Joseph recounts personal and professional aspects of his life. There is little in the way of factual detail, but Joseph is candid in his descriptions of events throughout his life. The 24 photographs, which date mostly from the 1970s and early 1980s, capture Joseph nicely. The chronologically arranged discography documents over 20 recording sessions by date and place, personnel, titles and composers (mostly P. Joseph), matrix numbers, and labels and numbers of various releases; there are separate lists of song titles, albums and singles released (by label), and personnel (by instrument). The bibliography includes roughly 40 articles and monographs. Without index.

Harriet J. Ottenheimer is a professor in the Department of Sociology, Anthropology, and Social Work at Kansas State University. [—D. P.].

Reviews: *Choice* 4/88, 1254; LJ 9/15/87, 77.

S2-706   ML420 .C935 A3

Crosby, David. Long time gone : the autobiography of David Crosby / David Crosby; with Carl Gottlieb. — New York : Doubleday, 1988. — xvii, 489 p. : ill. ISBN 0-385-24530-0.

This is the Crosby (1941–) of Crosby, Stills, and Nash. He has made a rambling memoir, offering undocumented events and conversations. Much of the story is about his imprisonment and drug addiction; none of it is about music. With 16 pages of photographs; no index.

Review: LJ 11/15/88, 69.

S2-707   ML420 .C94 H4

Haskins, Jim. Scatman : an authorized biography of Scatman Crothers / Jim Haskins; with Helen Crothers. — New York : Morrow, 1991. — 224 p. : ill. ISBN 0-688-08521-0.

Crothers (1910–1986) was best known for TV and movie acting appearances, but he maintained a career as guitarist and scat singer (hence his nickname). He grew up in poverty—dancing for pennies on the streets and shining shoes in Terre Haute, Indiana—and traveled with bands during the 1930s. He suffered all the indignities of the Jim Crow period with a philosophical optimism that was justified with Hollywood success. Interesting incidents are few in the story, however, and it is formed mainly of invented quotes and conversations. Nothing is said about the music played by Crothers. With no documentation, but with an expansive index.

S2-708   ML420 .D54 G8
Grossman, Alan. Diamond : a biography / Alan Grossman, Bill Truman, and Roy Oki Yamanaka. — Chicago : Contemporary Books, 1987. — 235 p. : ill. 12 p. plates. ISBN 0-8092-4825-5.
A collection of anecdotes and conversations, emphasizing the gloom of Neil Diamond's life (1941–): divorce, cancer, and exhaustion. He is also a singer/songwriter. There is a casual "American discography" and a song list, but no documentation or index.
Review: LJ 5/1/87, 142.

S2-709   ML420 .D54 W6
Wiseman, Rich. Neil Diamond : solitary star / Rich Wiseman. — New York : Dodd, Mead, 1987. — xii, 324 p. : ill. : 16 p. plates. ISBN 0-396-08619-5.
Diamond is portrayed here as a "brooding, driven loner" who "packaged himself into a king of pop." The book is not very revealing, however, being a chain of invented conversations and mind-reading exploits by Wiseman. Without sources; with an expansive index.
Review: LJ 5/15/87, 87.

S2-710   ML420 .D56 A3
DiMucci, Dion. The wanderer : Dion's story / Dion DiMucci; with Davin Seay. — New York : Beech Tree Books, 1988. — 221 p. : ill. ISBN 0-688-07841-9.
DiMucci's memoir is the generic tale of growing up in an Italian family in the Bronx, followed by episodes with drugs, marriage, the record business, and so forth; the whole marked by undocumented conversations and quotations. Nothing is said about music. No index or reference features.

S2-711   ML420 .D98 D97
Thomson, Elizabeth. The Dylan companion / ed. Elizabeth Thomson and David Gutman. — New York : Delta Books, 1991. — xxxi, 335 p. ISBN 0-385-30225-8.

A collection of 49 essays about the singer/composer (1941–) by various authors, including Pauline Kael, Greil Marcus, Joan Baez, Wilfred Mellers, and Bruce Springsteen. Most of the entries are documented. With a strong bibliography of about 600 books and articles, a selective discography (minimal data), and a nonexpansive index.

S2-712   ML420 .D98 H49
Heylin, Clinton. Bob Dylan : behind the shades : a biography / Clinton Heylin. — New York : Summit Books, 1991. — 498 p. : ill. : 16 p. plates. ISBN 0-671-73894-1.
A documented narrative of Dylan's life and work, cleverly structured so that quotes from Dylan and others are interwoven with the story. Many interviews are cited, and other sources are identified in endnotes. A list of persons associated with Dylan is given, along with an account of 43 recording sessions (1961–1990) that provides song titles, locations, and notes. There is a partly expansive index.

S2-713   ML420 .D98 H8
Humphries, Patrick. Absolutely Dylan : illustrated with more than 200 photographs / Patrick Humphries and John Bauldie. — New York : Viking, 1991. — 240 p. : ill. ISBN 0-14-016823-0.
A plain, undocumented biographical section is followed by a useful chronology of events, songs and records, press notices, and commentaries. Many of the 200 photographs are published for the first time. Without index.

S2-714   ML420 .D98 R4
Riley, Tim. Hard rain : a Dylan commentary / Tim Riley. — New York : Knopf, 1992. — 356 p. ISBN 0-3945-7889-9.
The commentary is mostly about the lyrics to Dylan songs, taken one LP record at a time. Nothing is said about the musical element. With a casual discography (minimal information) and a nonexpansive index of names and titles.

S2-715   ML420 .D98 S5
Shelton, Robert. No direction home : the life and music of Bob Dylan / Robert Shelton. — New York : Morrow, 1986. — 573 p. ISBN 0-688-05045-X.
An examination of the "myths and distortions surrounding this restless, questing enigma." Some sources are cited in chapter endnotes, but many conversations and episodes go undocumented. There is a list of Dylan songs, with interesting comments. The discography is not too useful, being selective and offering minimal data. With a bibliography of about 100 items and a nonexpansive index.
Reviews: AM 1988, 345; *Choice* 1/87, 772; LJ 9/1/86, 203.

S2-716   ML420 .D98 S6

Spitz, Bob. Dylan : a biography / Bob Spitz. — New York : McGraw-Hill, 1988. — xv, 639 p. : ill. ISBN 0-07-060330-8.

A useful account, based largely on interviews, with source notes. Most of the quoted conversations seem to be traceable to the sources. With a good discography, presenting full information on recording sessions from 1960 to 1973, and a partly expansive index.

Reviews: *Choice* 4/89, 1345; LJ 11/15/88, 70.

S2-717   ML420 .D98 W3

Bauldie, John. Wanted man : in search of Bob Dylan / ed. John Bauldie. — New York : Citadel, 1990. — 224 p. : ill. ISBN 0-8065-1266-0.

An interesting collection of essays and interviews dating from 1959 to 1990, offering the perspectives of many musicians and others who knew Dylan. These pieces are well documented, with all quotations accompanied by exact citations in endnotes. Among the persons involved are Johnny Cash, Paul McCartney, Bruce Springsteen, Allen Ginsberg, and Roy Orbison. With a name and title index.

S2-718   ML420 .D98 W56

Williams, Paul. Performing artist : the music of Bob Dylan : volume 1; 1960–1973 / Paul Williams. — Novato, Calif. : Underwood-Miller, 1990. — 310 p. ISBN 0-88733-101-7.

A discussion of Dylan's public performances in chronological order from 1960 to 1973, providing a useful reference base. The discussions themselves will not be to everyone's taste, as they stem from the naive position that a songwriter means what the lyrics say. For example, in "Talking New York," Williams accuses Dylan of hypocrisy, since the song is about being mistreated in New York, while "from what we know [of Dylan] the opposite is the case." Exclusive concern with the lyrics in their literal sense removes considerations of the texts as poetry and of the musical settings. There is an annotated discography of 35 in-print albums and of seven-inch American singles, covering 1962–1989, with contents and release dates. Films and major television shows are listed. With a bibliography of about 100 entries and a nonexpansive index.

Review: *Choice* 12/90, 642.

S2-719   ML420 .D98 W6

Williams, Richard. Dylan : a man called alias / Richard Williams. — New York : Holt, 1992. — 192 p. : ill. ISBN 0-8050-2255-4.

A chronological photo book about Bob Dylan, with a running commentary. There is a nonexpansive index.

S2-720   ML420 .F52 C64
Colin, Sid. Ella : the life and times of Ella Fitzgerald / Sid Colin. —
London : Elm Tree Books, 1986. — viii, 151 p. : ill. ISBN 0-241-
11754-2.
The first book-length biography in English of singer Ella Fitzgerald
(1918–). Colin relies on secondary sources (poorly or not cited) to create a romantic picture of her career. The selective discography of 25 albums includes album and song titles, pesonnel, label and number, and
release year. About 20 photographs are well reproduced. The partly expansive index includes persons, places, titles, and topics [—D. P.].

S2-721   ML420 .F52 H37
Haskins, Jim. Ella Fitzgerald : a life through jazz / Jim Haskins. —
London : New English Library, 1991. — 280 p. : ill. ISBN 0-450-
48796-2.
A straightforward life story, free of fictional elements, with documentation in endnotes. There is a good discography, covering 1935–1966,
giving full data for each record: date, location, personnel, matrix number, and release labels. With a nonexpansive index.

S2-722   ML420 .F52 N8
Nolden, Rainer. Ella Fitzgerald. 1986.
A biography and discography; see series note at S2-1111.

S2-723   ML420 .F778 B4
Bego, Mark. Aretha Franklin, the queen of soul / Mark Bego. — New
York : St. Martin's, 1989. — x, 340 p. : ill. ISBN 0-3120-28636.
A casual, undocumented narration about soul and gospel singer
Franklin (1942–), with quoted conversations. It is all about her personal
life, with nothing said about her music. There is a discography of album
titles (release dates and contents only). With an expansive index.
Review: LJ 9/1/89, 191.

S2-724   ML420 .G253 C64
Coleman, Emily R. Complete Judy Garland : the ultimate guide to her
career in films, records, concerts, radio, and television, 1935–1969 /
Emily R. Coleman. — New York : Harper & Row, 1990. — viii, 440 p. :
ill. ISBN 0-06-016333-X.
A fact book about the singer/actress (1922–1969), but hardly the ultimate one: considerable information is offered on the topics cited in the
title, but most often with minimal data. The discography, for example,
has no dates for the records and gives only the release label and album
contents. Probably the most useful section is the Garland song repertoire,

a list of 700 songs. There is a bibliography of about 300 items about the singer and a nonexpansive index.

S2-725   ML420 .G305 D37
Davis, Sharon. I heard it through the grapevine : Marvin Gaye : a biography / Sharon Davis. — Edinburgh, Scotland : Mainstream, 1991. — 304 p. : ill. ISBN 1-85158-317-3.
An adulatory, undocumented account of Gaye's life (1939–1984), saying nothing about his music, with fictional conversations. The rock performer, born in a Washington, D.C., ghetto, had a troubled existence with a gruesome termination as his father shot him. A discography covers 1955–1990, giving album contents and release dates only. With a nonexpansive index of names and song titles. The book's title is that of a chart recording by Gaye.

S2-726   ML420 .G39 A4
Gibson, Debbie. Between the lines / Debbie Gibson; with Mark Bego. — Austin, Tex. : Diamond Books, 1989. — 128 p. : ill. ISBN 0-89015-735-9.
A semifictional memoir of the singer/songwriter (1970–), of some interest for the casual comments on individual songs. Without documentation or index.

S2-727   ML420 .G5 R4
Reisfeld, Randi. Debbie Gibson : electric star / Randi Reisfeld. — New York : Bantam, 1990. — x, 98 p. : ill. : 16 p. plates. ISBN 0-5532-8379-0.

S2-728   ML420 .H1165
Haley, John W. Sound and glory : the incredible story of Bill Haley, the father of rock 'n' roll and the music that shook the world / John W. Haley and John von Hoelle. — Wilmington, Del. : Dyne-American, 1990. — 249 p. : ill. ISBN 1-8789-7000-3.
An interesting biography of Haley (1925–1981), the putative father of rock and roll, written by his son. There are many good photos and many unsourced quotations. Newspaper pages recall the strange old days, such as the 1953 event that saw "6,000 teen-agers shake, rattle 'n roll to blatant, blaring music of the Comets." The discography covers 1946 to 1989, presenting "most of the known recordings," with label numbers and contents of albums. Over a hundred musicians who performed with Haley are identified. With a song list and a nonexpansive index.

S2-729   ML420 .H28 W5
Willens, Doris. Lonesome traveler : the life of Lee Hays / Doris

Willens. — New York : Norton, 1988. — xxi, 281 p. : ill. ISBN 0-393-02564-0.

A plain biography, based on interviews, of the folksinger who worked with the Almanac Singers and the Weavers. Hays was an activist, blacklisted after interrogation by the House Un-American Activities Committee; but political matters are muted in this story, which concentrates on personal issues. Indexed.

Reviews: AM 1991, 225; *Choice* 1/89, 817.

S2-730   ML420 .H58 D3
DeVeaux, Alexis. Don't explain : a song of Billie Holiday / Alexis DeVeaux. — New York : Harper & Row, 1980. — vii, 151 p. : ill. ISBN 0-06-021629-8.

The "song" is a poetic account of Holiday's life highlights, without reference features.

S2-731   ML420 .H58 K65
Kliment, Bud. Billie Holiday / Bud Kliment. — New York : Chelsea House, 1990. — 111 p. : ill. ISBN 1-5554-6592-7.

A casual, undocumented account of Holiday's personal life (1915–1959) with invented conversations. The story is basically that of a drug addict and her troubles with the law; nothing is said about her music. With a nonexpansive index.

S2-732   ML420 .H58 M2
Maddocks, Melvin. Billie Holiday. 1979.
See series note at S2-1114.

S2-733   ML420 .H58 O4
O'Meally, Robert G. Lady day : the many faces of Billie Holiday / Robert G. O'Meally. — New York : Arcade, 1991. — 207 p. : ill. ISBN 1-5597-0147-1.

A depiction of the "greatest jazz singer in history," intending to "focus on her achievement . . . and on the ways in which she developed her artistic skills." Indeed the book does concentrate on musical matters, with discussions of Holiday's range, timbre, vibrato, careful improvisation, and so forth. Some of her thoughts are also revealed, along with conversations and anecdotes that intrude on the purpose of the study. Without notes or index.

S2-734   ML420 .H58 W4
White, John. Billie Holiday : her life and times. 1987.
See series note at S2-1117.

S2-735   ML420 .H595

Goldrosen, John. Remembering Buddy : the definitive biography of Buddy Holly / John Goldrosen and John Beecher. — 2nd ed. — New York : Viking/Penguin; London : Pavilion, 1987. — 204 p. : ill. ISBN 0-14-010363-5 (U.S.).

"Based in part on a revised edition of *Buddy Holly: His Life and Music,* first published in 1975."

New in this edition are some useful reference features: tour dates, 1956–1959; a chart file; an alphabetical discography; and a recording session file, 1949–1968. There are many good illustrations, including reprints of reviews and advertising. The text is a casual life story of the rock singer (1938–1959), with invented quotations and conversations. Without source notes; with a nonexpansive index.

Review: LJ 10/15/87, 77.

S2-736   ML420 .H62 H6

Buckley, Gail Lumet. The Hornes : an American family / Gail Lumet Buckley. — New York : Knopf, 1986. — xii, 262 p. : ill. ISBN 0-3945-13061.

The story of singer Lena Horne, told by her daughter, set in the context of the family's life in Brooklyn. Lena Horne (1917–), starting out at age 16 in the Cotton Club chorus, went on to sing with the Noble Sissle band, then become the first acclaimed black chanteuse (see LOAM Suppl. S-1001 and S-1002) of the U.S. nightclub circuit. This is not a fictionalized story, but it does include undocumented quotations from publications. Without index or reference features.

Reviews: *Choice* 11/86, 488; LJ 7/86, 76.

S2-737   ML:420 .H68 A3

Howard, Jan. Sunshine and shadow / Jan Howard. — New York : Richardson & Steirman, 1987. — 490 p. ISBN 0-931933-48-X.

A collection of anecdotes and invented conversations about Grand Ole Opry country singer Howard, concentrating on her personal problems, her "story of love, sadness and devastating personal loss." She was an abused wife who divorced and remarried, only to be deserted by her second husband. The book says nothing about her singing. No illustrations and no index.

Review: LJ 8/87, 127.

S2-738   ML420 .H88

Bego, Mark. Whitney! / Mark Bego. — Toronto : PaperJacks, 1986. — 117 p. : ill. : 8 p. plates. ISBN 0-7701-0543-2.

The "Cinderella story" of Houston (1963–), who became at 23 years of age "the most popular female singer in the world." It is a breezy, undocumented story, based partly on interviews (not with Houston). There is a list of her Grammys and of her records (release dates, personnel, durations of songs). There is a Houston chronology, but no index.

S2-739   ML420 .H948 T4
Taylor, Frank C. Alberta Hunter : a celebration in blues / Frank C. Taylor; with Gerald Cook. — New York : McGraw-Hill, 1987. — ix, 311 p. : ill. ISBN 0-07-063171-9.

A casual compilation of anecdotes and quoted conversations, without source notes, about the blues singer (1895–1984). The focus is on Hunter's personal life, with little said about her music. Useful for many good photographs and for a detailed discography (1921–1983) that gives matrix numbers and personnel for all sessions. With a partly expansive index of names and topics.

Reviews: *Choice* 6/87, 1562; LJ 3/15/87, 80.

S2-740   ML420 .J16 A3
Jackson, LaToya. LaToya : growing up in the Jackson family / Latoya Jackson; with Patricia Romanowski. — New York : Dutton, 1991. — vii, 261 p. : ill. : 32 p. plates. ISBN 0-525-93343-3.

Michael Jackson's sister (1956–), herself a noted pop singer, sets out "to tell the truth—no matter how painful," offering "the dark side of *Moonwalk*" (see S2-742). It seems the family was given to rivalries and jealousies, and there was child abuse as well. The text is a fair script for a soap opera, spun of melodramatic episodes and invented conversations. Without sources or index.

S2-741   ML420 .J17 S41
Schwerin, Jules. Got to tell it : Mahalia Jackson, queen of gospel / Jules Schwerin. — New York : Oxford, 1992. — 204 p. : ill. : 16 p. plates. ISBN 0-19-507144-1.

The author produced Jackson's Grammy recording (1976) and a film about her; he interviewed her as part of the research for his book. The gospel and soul singer (1911–1972) received two other Grammy awards and was internationally acclaimed. Her career is sketched here, but obscured by undocumented conversations and trivial anecdotes. There is a plain record list, alphabetical by label, with no discographical data. Without source notes or index.

Reviews: *Choice* 1/93, 806; LJ 9/1/92, 178.

S2-742   ML420 .J175 A3
Jackson, Michael. Moonwalk / Michael Jackson. — New York : Doubleday, 1988. — 283 p. : ill. ISBN 0-385-24712-5.

The rock star (1958–) meditates about the "crushing isolation of his fame" and gives "personal feelings about some of his most public friends": Diana Ross, Fred Astaire, Marlon Brando, and Katharine Hepburn. He discusses his love affairs with Ross, Tatum O'Neal, and Brooke Shields, and either remembers or invents appropriate conversations. Without index or reference features.

S2-743   ML410 .J175 B3
Bego, Mark. Michael! / Mark Bego. — New York : Pinnacle Books, 1984. — 180 p. : ill. ISBN 0-5234-3223-2.
See note at following entry.

S2-744   ML420 .J175 B31
Bego, Mark. On the road with Michael : the Michael Jackson story, part 2 / Mark Bego. — London : Zomba, 1984. — 128 p. : ill. ISBN 0-9463-9161-0.
This volume and the preceding entry offer a chatty biography of the singer, a discography, and a photo account of the 1984 "victory tour" with commentary.

S2-745   ML420 .J175 M15
Machlin, Milt. The Michael Jackson catalog : a comprehensive guide to records, videos, clothing, posters, toys and millions of collectible souvenirs / Milt Machlin. — New York : Arbor House, 1984. — 128 p. : ill. ISBN 0-8779-5664-2.
A guide to the market values of records, videos, and other "authorized merchandise," such as bubblegum cards, buttons, T-shirts, posters, dolls, and calendars. Sources for purchase of the items are given. The term "millions" in the title evidently refers to the total quantity of all the objects produced.
Review: ARBA 1985, p. 441.

S2-746   ML420 .J175 M2
Marsh, Dave. Trapped : Michael Jackson and the crossover dream / Dave Marsh. — New York : Bantam, 1985. — 259 p. : ill. 16 p. plates. ISBN 0-553-34241-X.
The "first serious biography" of Jackson, "peering deeply into the making of a legend"—a high purpose, not likely to be achieved through undocumented gossip, quotations, and anecdotes. There are some technical observations on the singing. Without index.

S2-747   ML420 .J175 T3
Taraborrelli, J. Randy. Michael Jackson : the magic and the madness / J. Randy Taraborrelli. — Secaucus, N.J. : Carol, 1991. — ix, 625 p. : ill. : 16 p. plates. ISBN 1-55972-064-6.

A fantasy biography, more fiction than fact, featuring remembered conversations, episodes and anecdotes, and vignettes in which the clothing and gestures of the characters are fully described. Some of the sources used are cited in chapter endnotes, but there are no direct citations. The bibliography lists about 500 articles. With a partly expansive index.

S2-748   ML420 .J175 T5
Terry, Carol D. Sequins & shades : the Michael Jackson reference guide / Carol D. Terry. — Ann Arbor, Mich. : Pierian, 1987. — xxxiv, 507 p. : ill. (Rock & roll reference series, 22) ISBN 0-87650-205-2.
A handy compilation of data about the rock star, including a bibliography of 999 articles and 149 reviews; a chronology; a discography, by label, with release dates and comments; and a song list. Indexing is by author, title, subject, date, publication title, and record number. There are good photos of record labels.
Review: ARBA 1988, #1322.

S2-749   ML420 .J36 D4
Denisoff, R. Serge. Waylon : a biography / R. Serge Denisoff; discography by John L. Smith. — Knoxville : University of Tennessee Press, 1983. — xiv, 375 p. ISBN 0-87049-387-6.
A balanced biography of country singer Waylon Jennings (1937–), based partly on interviews, marred by undocumented quoted conversations. "Selected Bibliography" of about 300 articles. Discography, covering 1959–1981, gives matrixes, recording dates, and labels. There are separate lists of singles and albums.
Review: LJ 9/1/83, 1707.

S2-750   ML420 .J735 G8
Guralnick, Peter. Searching for Robert Johnson / Peter Guralnick. — New York : Dutton, 1989. — 83 p. ISBN 0-525-24801-3.
A plain biography of Johnson (1911–1938), "probably the most influential of all blues singers," previously published in *Living Blues* (1982). Guralnick discredits the tale of a "presumed pact with the devil" as the cause for Johnson's early death. Without sources, index, or reference features. In view of Alan Greenberg's full-length biography (1983; LOAM Suppl. SA-320), it is hard to see why Dutton chose to make a hardcover issue of this minor essay.

S2-751   ML420 .J74 G6
Goldman, Herbert G. Jolson : the legend comes to life / Herbert G. Goldman. — New York : Oxford, 1988. — xii, 411 p. : ill. ISBN 0-19-505505-5.

A straight biography of Al Jolson (1886–1950) for the most part, but there are intrusions of conversations and anecdotes not accounted for in the chapter endnotes. The value of the book rests with documentation of Jolson's stage appearances, films, and radio shows, plus a discography of commercial releases covering 1911–1950 (matrix and release numbers, performers). With a nonexpansive index.

Reviews: *Choice* 2/89, 948; LJ 9/15/88, 76.

S2-752   ML420 .J75 A3
Jones, Bessie. For the ancestors : autobiographical memories / Bessie Jones; collected and ed. by John Stewart. — Urbana : University of Illinois Press, 1983. — xxv, 203 p. : ill. ISBN 0-252-009592.

Jones is a folklorist and folksinger (1902–); Stewart is a professor of anthropology at the University of Illinois. The book is an informal effort, with undocumented, quoted conversations. Nothing is said about music until page 135. Photos and a "bio-chronology" are of some reference interest. Without index.

Listing and reviews: BCL; *Choice* 10/83, 321; LJ 6/1/83, 1151.

S2-753   ML420 .J77 A6
Amburn, Ellis. Pearl : the obsessions and passions of Janis Joplin : a biography / Ellis Amburn. — New York : Warner Books, 1992. — xii, 340 p. : ill. ISBN 0-446-51640-6.

The life of blues-rock singer Joplin (1943–1970), assembled mostly through interviews, emerges as a series of escapades based on sex and drugs. There is no documentation for the quotes and conversations, which are cast in vulgar language. Nothing tangible is said about Joplin's unique singing style. The discography is only a list of albums and their contents. With a general bibliography of books and a nonexpansive index.

S2-754   ML420 .J77 D2
Dalton, David. Piece of my heart : the life, times, and legend of Janis Joplin / David Dalton. — New York : St. Martin's, 1985. — 284 p. : ill. ISBN 0-3126-1055-6.

A superficial account based on interviews conducted in 1970; without musical allusions. There are 60 good photographs. No index.

Review: LJ 3/1/86, 97.

S2-755   ML420 .J77 J6
Joplin, Laura. Love, Janis / Laura Joplin. — New York : Villard, 1992. — viii, 342 p. : ill. : 32 p. plates. ISBN 0-679-41605-6.

The younger sister of the singer tells some stories and recalls some very old conversations. There is some interest in a number of previously unpublished letters, although they are of a personal nature and do not illuminate musical matters. Without documentation; with a nonexpansive index.

S2-756   ML420 .K4

Kirsten, Dorothy. A time to sing / Dorothy Kirsten; with Lanfranco Rasponi; foreword by Robert Jacobson; discography by Stanley A. Bowker. — Garden City, N.Y. : Doubleday, 1982. — xiv, 247 p. : ill. : 8 p. plates. ISBN 0-3851-4744-9.

Lyric soprano Kirsten (1915–), recognized for her Puccini roles at the Metropolitan Opera, reduces her career to a series of bright anecdotes and fictional conversations. The discography is of little value, consisting of titles and labels only, without dates or data. With a partly expansive index.

Review: LJ 5/1/82, 891.

S2-757   ML420 .K5

Kitt, Eartha. Confessions of a sex kitten / Eartha Kitt. — New York : Barricade Books, 1991. — viii, 280 p. ISBN 0-9426-3733-X.

Originally published as *I'm Still Here* (London: Sidgwick & Jackson, 1989).

Anecdotes and imaginary conversations about the pop singer (1938–), who rose to sudden fame in the Broadway revue *New Faces of 1952*. With an expansive index.

S2-758   ML420 .L2

Mannering, Derek. Mario Lanza : a biography / Derek Mannering; foreword by José Carreras. — London : Hale, 1991. — 176 p. : ill. : 12 p. plates. ISBN 0-7451-1664-7.

Tenor Mario Lanza (1921–1959), often compared to Enrico Caruso and regarded as his natural successor, never achieved success in opera (he made only two operatic stage appearances and recorded no complete operas). His fame rested on tours, movies—especially *The Great Caruso* (1951)—and recordings. Complications in his personal life interfered with the development of his career. Mannering's approach is casual, without documentation and with invented conversations. His discography of studio recordings, 1949–1959, presents 398 items, but without any reference information except place, performers, and contents (not even the label number). Without index.

S2-759   ML420 .L18

Stoller, Lee. One day at a time / Lee Stoller; with Pete Chaney. — Madison, Tenn. : LS Records, 1983. — 289 p. : ill. : 22 p. plates. ISBN 0-9614-3700-6.

The story of country singer Christy Lane (1940–). The mode is fictional (it begins with an account of a dream that Lane had at age nine), consisting almost entirely of conversations and soap-opera episodes. It includes a Lane poem and some of her recipes. Without index or reference features.

S2-760   ML420 .L249 K35
Kamin, Philip. Cyndi Lauper / Philip Kamin and Peter Goddard. — New York : McGraw-Hill, 1986. — 96 p. : ill. ISBN 0-0703-3499-4.
A picture book about the pop singer (1953–), embellished by adulatory comments, quotations, and conversations. With no documentation or reference features.

S2-761   ML420 .L277 W6
Wolfe, Charles. The life and legend of Leadbelly / Charles Wolfe and Kip Lornell. — New York : HarperCollins, 1992. — xv, 334 p. : ill. : 8 p. plates. ISBN 0-06-016862-5.
Huddie Ledbetter (1885–1949), known as Leadbelly, was a blues and folksinger, discovered in a Louisiana penetentiary by Alan Lomax, who recorded him for the Library of Congress. Leadbelly went on to great success in performance and on commercial recordings. Documentation preserved by Alan Lomax and his father, John Lomax, provided a basis for this volume, which attempts to "sort out the myths from the truths." It is a scholarly, readable book, with chapter endnotes. The accounts of Leadbelly's incarcerations take up a good deal of the story, but they are worth the space: disturbing and understated. After those ordeals, the life of the famous musician must have been a challenge, but he was equal to it, "a powerful creature in front of that mike. He was sure of himself musically. So sure of who he was. . . . No asking for pity because he was poor, black, and discriminated against. . . . He was always this positive creature." There is a definitive discography, covering 1933–1949, with locations, matrix and label numbers, personnel, and comments. With a nonexpansive index of names, topics, and titles.

S2-762   ML420 .L290
Lee, Johnny. Lookin' for love / Johnny Lee; with Randy Wyles. — Austin, Tex. : Diamond Books, 1989. — iv, 183 p. : ill. : 4 p. plates. ISBN 0-89015-731-6.
One of the worst specimens of the pop musician memoir, comprised of undocumented anecdotes and conversations told in a vulgar idiom. The content is totally nonmusical, dealing with marriage, divorce, troubles in the Navy, etc. Without index.

S2-763   ML420 .L294 A3
Lee, Peggy. Miss Peggy Lee : an autobiography / Peggy Lee. — New

York : Donald I. Fine, 1989. — 280 p. : ill. : 32 p. plates. ISBN 1-55611-112-6.

A sentimental, anecdotal account of the singer's personal life (1920–) and career, fact-free and with nothing said about music. Memories of thoughts and conversations long past are ubiquitous. A discography by label gives minimal information. With a nonexpansive index.

S2-764   ML420 .L533
Draper, Robert. Huey Lewis and the News / Robert Draper. — New York : Ballantine, 1986. — 143 p. : ill. : 16 p. plates. ISBN 0-345-33028-5.

A gathering of episodes and conversations illustrating the lives and thoughts of rock singer Lewis (1951–) and his News group. There is also a set of his "wit and wisdom" quotations. The discography is an album list with contents, 1977–1983, giving no details. Without index.

S2-765   ML420 .L534 E8
Escott, Colin. The killer / Colin Escott; discography by Richard Weize. — Bremen, Germany : Bear Family Records, 1986. — 3 vols. : ill. ISBN 3924-7870-26/42/50.

Three pamphlets about the career of rock singer Jerry Lee Lewis (1935–) from 1963 to 1977. There are photocopies of newspaper material and programs (some in German), along with a connecting narrative. The discography gives matrix numbers and release labels, plus extensive comments.

S2-766   ML420 .L534 G9
Guterman, Jimmy. Rockin' my life away : listening to Jerry Lee Lewis / Jimmy Guterman. — Nashville : Rutledge Hill, 1991. — 223 p. : ill. ISBN 1-5585-3081-9.

Rock singer Lewis, "the most profane pop performer and the purest purveyor of sacred music," had many ups and downs, personally and professionally. They are the mileposts of this casual, undocumented tale. The book jacket observes that he has had to endure "books about him full of transparently made-up quotations" and "a flop film based on his life." Yet this volume also features disembodied quotes. There is a brief survey of his recordings, but no discography. With a nonexpansive index of names and titles.

S2-767   ML420 .M1387 A3
Madonna. Sex / Madonna; ed. Glenn O'Brien. — New York : Warner Books, 1992. — Unpaged : ill. ISBN 0-446-51732-1.

A sexual autobiography of Madonna Louise Ciccone (1959–), made up primarily of nude and lurid photographs. There is an appropriate text, in the form of the singer's thoughts and letters. Music is not mentioned. Without index.

S2-768   ML420 .M1387 A5
Andersen, Christopher P. Madonna, unauthorized / Christopher P. Andersen. — New York : Simon & Schuster, 1991. — 350 p. : ill. : 32 p. plates. ISBN 0-6717-3532-2.
An informal life story of the singer, made up of anecdotes and dialogues that are loosely connected to sources named for each chapter. With a nonexpansive index.

S2-769   ML420 .M1387 B4
Bego, Mark. Madonna : blonde ambition / Mark Bego. — New York : Harmony Books, 1992. — xi, 308 p. : ill. : 16 p. plates. ISBN 0-5175-8242-2.
A presentable life story of the singer, depicted as "a pushy bitch" who "slept her way to the top." There is good documentation in endnotes and an index of names, titles, and places.

S2-770   ML420 .M1387 C3
Cahill, Marie. Madonna / Marie Cahill. — New York : Smithmark, 1991. — 95 p. : ill. ISBN 0-8317-5705-1.
A book of good photos, mostly in color, with an accompanying commentary and index.

S2-771   ML420 .M1387 K5
King, Norman. Madonna : the book / Norman King. — New York : Morrow, 1991. — 256 p. : ill. ISBN 0-68810-3898.
An anecdotal tale of the "towering heights and shattering lows of a brilliant career," in which the singer offers a "sassy outspoken commentary on her life and music." In fact, neither she nor King has anything substantial to say about music. Without documentation; with a nonexpansive index.
Review: LJ 12/91, 148.

S2-772   ML420 .M1387 L27
Lagerfeld, Karl. Madonna, superstar / Karl Lagerfeld. New York : Norton, 1988. — 93 p. : ill. ISBN 0-393-307662.
A book of photos, without reference features.

S2-773   ML420 .M1387 M6
McKenzie, Michael. Madonna : lucky star / Michael McKenzie. — Chicago : Contemporary Books, 1985. — 95 p. : ill. ISBN 0-8092-5233-3.

An illustrated biography, comprised mostly of undocumented quotations and stories, with adulatory asides. No index or reference features.

S2-774   ML420 .M1387 R36
Randall, Lee. Madonna scrapbook / Lee Randall. — New York : Citadel, 1992. — 224 p. : ill. ISBN 0-8065-1297-0.
A picture book accompanied by a chronological narrative. Without reference features or index.

S2-775   ML420 .M1387 R54
Riley, Tim. Madonna illustrated / Tim Riley. — New York : Hyperion, 1992. — xvi, 112 p. : ill. ISBN 1-56282-983-1.
A book of 111 photographs, accompanied by an appreciative commentary that includes invented quotations; no documentation or reference features.

S2-776   ML420 .M1387 T4
Thompson, Douglas. Madonna revealed : the unauthorized biography / Douglas Thompson. — Secaucus, N.J. : Carol, 1991. — vii, 180 p. : ill. : 16 p. plates. ISBN 1-55972-099-9.
British title: *Like a Virgin: Madonna Revealed* (London: Smith Gryphon, 1991; ISBN 1-8568-50099).
Gossip, anecdotes, and talk about the singer, concentrating on titillating episodes. Her first kiss, it is revealed, occurred in a convent school. She worried about sex a lot when young. Without index or reference features.

S2-777   ML420 .M219 A3
Mandrell, Barbara. Get to the heart : my story / Barbara Mandrell; with George Vecsey. — New York : Bantam, 1991. — viii, 446 p. : ill. : 32 p. plates. ISBN 0-5532-9243-9.
Country singer Mandrell (1948–) is portrayed here as a "triumphant survivor," having resumed her career after an auto accident and gone on to entertain 48,266 fans in the Astrodome. The story is in fictional style — with many quotes and thoughts — without musical content or reference features. Mandrell's sentimental anecdote about the time she sang "Danny Boy" on request to a dying soldier in a Vietnam hospital will leave "not a dry eye in the house."

S2-778   ML420 .M219 C8
Conn, Charles Paul. The Barbara Mandrell story / Charles Paul Conn. — New York : Putnam, 1988. — 221 p. : ill. : 8 p. plates. ISBN 0-399-13317-8.
Country star Mandrell has a "special dilemma," drawing the line

between "personal privacy and a loyal following who insist on having an inside track to the performer and her family." Conn does all that he can to follow the inside track, offering a book of domestic scenarios and anecdotes, enlivened by unattributed quotes from Mandrell and various invented conversations. Much attention goes to the singer's auto accident and recovery. Nothing emerges about her singing as such. With a chronological recording list (minimal data); no index or other reference features.

Review: LJ 9/1/91, 192.

S2-779   ML420 .M3 A3
Manilow, Barry. Sweet life : adventures on the way to paradise / Barry Manilow. — New York : McGraw-Hill, 1987. — 274 p. : ill. ISBN 0-0703-9904-2.

The adventures of Manilow (1946–) included growing up poor in Brooklyn and subsequently "battling the terrifying risk of a musical career." His book is a medley of "enchanting anecdotes," invented conversations, and inspirational chants (the volume ends with the imprecation to the reader: "Don't give up your dreams"). A discography of albums by release date, 1973–1985, gives contents only. There are 32 pages of photos. Without index.

Review: LJ 1/88, 88.

S2-780   ML420 .M33 T8
Tosches, Nick. Dino : living high in the dirty business of dreams / Nick Tosches. — New York : Doubleday, 1992. — xii, 572 p. : ill. : 16 p. plates. ISBN 0-3852-6216-7.

The story of Dino Crocetti of Steubenville, Ohio (1917–1995), who rose to fame as Dean Martin, popular singer and movie actor of the 1950s and 1960s. It is a colorful tale with a cast of celebrities; Martin was a partner in a comedy team with Jerry Lewis, then a member of the Frank Sinatra "rat pack." Many friends and associates were interviewed for the book. There are extensive source lists, but no actual footnotes to connect the text to them, leaving many episodes and conversations unsubstantiated. A remarkable bibliography was compiled, consisting of some 1,500 entries (articles and reviews). With an expansive index of names and titles.

Review: LJ 6/1/92, 130.

S2-781   ML420 .M3415 C9
Cusic, Don. Reba : country music's queen / Don Cusic. — New York : St. Martin's, 1991. — xii, 234 p. and unpaged index : ill. ISBN 0-3120-6450-0.

A plain, undocumented narrative about country singer Reba McEntire (1954–), with quotes and anecdotes. A rancher's daughter, she sang with rodeos, then went on to become a Grammy winner and to sing in Carnegie Hall. The discography is also casual, giving album titles and contents only. Nothing emerges about her music. With a partly expansive index of names and titles.

S2-782   ML420 .M3415 L4
Leggett, Carol. Reba McEntire : the queen of country / Carol Leggett. — New York : Fireside, 1992. — 208 p. : ill. ISBN 0-6717-5141-7.
A juvenile-style life story of McEntire, "unquestionably the most beloved performer in country music today." The framework is anecdotes and quotations, all undocumented. Much is made of the tragedies in the singer's life, her divorce and the death of her band members in an air crash. Music as such is not brought up. The discography is a chronological list of albums with contents, with no information other than the label names. With a nonexpansive index of names and titles.

S2-783   ML420 .M357 H8
Holmes, Tim. John Cougar Mellencamp / Tim Holmes. — New York : Ballantine, 1985. — 143 p. : ill. : 16 p. plates. ISBN 0-3453-2891-4.
Mellencamp (1951–) is credited with reviving rock in the early 1980s, by presenting "basic, no-frills, authentic" material and his personal "aw shucks" sincerity. This is a rambling account of the singer's career, including many undocumented quotations from him. There is an informal discography (minimal data) and a similar videography. Without index.

S2-784   ML420 .M357 T8
Torgoff, Martin. American fool : the roots and improbable rise of John Cougar Mellencamp / Martin Torgoff. — New York : St. Martin's, 1986. — 222 p. : ill. : 8 p. color plates. ISBN 0-312-02319-7.
The book's title is that of the first hit album (1982) by Mellencamp, whose "improbable rise" included several years of false starts with various labels before he struck the charts. Vulgar language and undocumented sensational episodes form the basis for Torgoff's story. Without index or reference features.

S2-785   ML420 .M376 G4
Garon, Paul. Woman with guitar : Memphis Minnie's blues / Paul Garon and Beth Garon. — New York : Da Capo, 1992. — xi, 332 p. : ill. : music. ISBN 0-3068-0460-3.
Memphis Minnie (1897–1973) was an influential early blues singer, noted for her skillful guitar work as much as for her singing. Garon's biography is documented (chapter endnotes) and imaginative—drawing on "folklore, psychoanalysis, critical theory, women's studies, and surrealism" to "illuminate the poetics of popular culture." In any

case, a readable life story emerges, undiluted by fictional episodes. A useful discography presents the sessions from 1929 to 1959 with locations, personnel, matrix numbers, and labels. With an expansive index.

S2-786   ML420 .M388 H4
Haskins, James. Mabel Mercer : a life / James Haskins. — New York : Atheneum, 1987. — xvii, 217 p. : ill. ISBN 0-689-11595-4.

In this, the first full-length study of singer Mabel Mercer, Hawkins explores her personal life along with her career, tracing her popularity in Britain, France, and eventually the United States. In general, the work seems carefully researched, based on primary and secondary sources. Only published material is cited; much of the information that came from interviews with Mercer's friends and associates is not. Nearly 30 photographs, mostly posed, depict Mercer at different times in her adult life. There is a partial list of songs sung by Mercer and a discography of 14 albums, which gives only album title and label number. The partly expansive index includes persons, places, and titles.

James Haskins has written over 60 nonfiction books for adults and young adults, including *Bricktop, The Cotton Club, Lena Horne,* and *Black Theater in America* [—D. P.].

Reviews: *Choice* 7/88, 1704; LJ 2/15/88, 169.

S2-787   ML420 .M43 B4
Bego, Mark. Bette Midler, outrageously divine : an unauthorized biography / Mark Bego. — New York : New American Library, 1987. — 190 p. : ill. ISBN 0-451-14814-2.

Midler (1945–) is a seven-time Grammy winner, a singer whose "love life, awesome talent, irrepressible energies . . . [and] wrenching heartbreaks" are recounted here in casual style. The book is mostly talk, with undocumented quotes from Midler and others. Music is not discussed. There is a discography (1972–1985), giving minimal data, and a filmography of six movies. No index.

S2-788   ML420 .M43 C6
Collins, Ace. Bette Midler / Ace Collins. — New York : St. Martin's, 1989. — 164 p. : ill. ISBN 0-312-02869-5.

An anecdotal appreciation, resembling a children's book. Without reference features or index.

S2-789   ML420 .M514
Milsap, Ronnie. Almost like a song / Ronnie Milsap. — New York : McGraw-Hill, 1990. — x, 259 p. : ill. : 32 p. plates. ISBN 0-07-042374-1.

A "classic rags to riches tale" of the blind musician (1944–), winner of six Grammys. It is made up of undocumented conversations and anecdotes, without index or reference features.

S2-790   ML420 .M62 A3

Morrison, Jim. Wilderness : the lost writings of Jim Morrison / Jim Morrison. — New York : Villard, 1988. — 214 p. : ill. ISBN 0-3945-6434-0.

See S2-791.

S2-791   ML420 .M62 A31

Morrison, Jim. American night / Jim Morrison. — New York : Villard, 1990. — 212 p. : ill. ISBN 0-3945-8722-7.

"A continuation of the author's *Wilderness*."

These two volumes are of prose by Morrison (1943–1971), who gained fame as leader of the Doors. There are essays and reflections, and many poems in the beat style. With brief editorial notes and first-line indexes.

S2-791a   ML420 .M62 D2

Dalton, David. "Mr. Mojo risin" : Jim Morrison, the last holy fool / David Dalton. — New York : St. Martin's, 1991. — 157 p. : ill. ISBN 0-3120-5900-0.

An adulatory report on Morrison's "mythological dimension," with many photographs. Praise is lavished on the performer's abilities as a poet and filmmaker. Without documentation.

Review: LJ 5/1/91, 77.

S2-792   ML420 .M62 H8

Hopkins, Jerry. The lizard king : the essential Jim Morrison / Jerry Hopkins. — New York : Scribner's, 1992. — 272 p. : ill. ISBN 0-6841-9524-0.

An informal, undocumented report of "startling new information on Jim's life and loves," presented through anecdotes and dialogues. There is some interest in transcripts of seven interviews with Morrison, although the questions are routine. With 70 photographs; without index.

Review: LJ 10/1/92, 90.

S2-793   ML420 .M62 H9

Huddleston, Judy. This is the end : my only friend : living and dying with Jim Morrison / Judy Huddleston. — New York : Shapolsky, 1991. — 212 p. : ill. : 16 p. plates. ISBN 1-5617-1038-5.

A first-person romance, relating the sexual adventures of a groupie and a rock star. Since Morrison is dead, memory and imagination cannot be separated in Huddleston's story.

Review: *Choice* 11/91, 458.

S2-794   ML420 .M62 J7
Jones, Dylan. Jim Morrison, dark star / Dylan Jones. — New York : Viking, 1992. — 191 p. : ill. ISBN 0-1401-6833-8.
A book of 130 photos, many large-size, many in color, with an adulatory commentary. No notes, index, or reference features.
Reviews: *Choice* 4/92, 1192; LJ 3/1/91, 90.

S2-795   ML420 .M62 K4
Kennealy, Patricia. Strange days : my life with and without Jim Morrison / Patricia Kennealy. — New York : Dutton, 1992. — vii, 429 p. : ill. ISBN 0-5259-3419-7.
Morrison (1943–1971), celebrated with the Doors in the 1960s, took Kennealy as his wife in a "pagan Celtic wedding rite," culminating a relationship that included passion and fame as well as "terrible consequences." While this account shares the fictionalized character of most celebrity revelations, Kennealy has some unusual turns. She is a self-declared witch and "astral mourner," one who writes letters to Morrison and speaks to him daily in the great beyond. She expresses venom with vigour, toward Pamela Courson (Morrison's key woman) especially, but in general to all who failed to do justice to his "warmth and generosity . . . and tenderness." But *au fond* this is no more than an undocumented fantasy romance. No index.
Review: LJ 3/15/92, 89.

S2-796   ML420 .M62 L4
Lisciandro, Frank. Morrison : a feast of friends / ed. Frank Lisciandro. — New York : Warner Books, 1991. — 176 p. : ill. ISBN 0-446-39276-6.
A collection of appreciative essays about Jim Morrison (1943–1971), written by various friends and colleagues. The content is anecdotal and bears no relation to music. Without notes or index.

S2-797   ML420 .M62 R6
Riordan, James. Break on through : the life and death of Jim Morrison / James Riordan and Jerry Prochnicky. — New York : Morrow, 1991. — 544 p. : ill. : 32 p. plates. ISBN 0-688-08829-5.
A straightforward, documented biography, avoiding the sensational scenarios that are usually emphasized in the Morrison literature. The performer's philosophical and poetic aspirations are dealt with soberly. With a useful bibliography, discography (minimal data), and a difficult index.
Review: *Choice* 11/91, 458.

S2-798 ML420 .N375 A3

Near, Holly. Fire in the rain . . . singer in the storm : an autobiography / Holly Near; with Derk Richardson. — New York : Morrow, 1990. — 290 p. : ill. ISBN 0-688-08733-7.

Near tells of her "journey from football princess to political and social activist, from movie and television actress to the chanteuse who fills Carnegie Hall." She was a member of the Weavers in their prime. The book title comes from a 1981 album, *Fire in the Rain*. Anecdotes and conversations are the stuff of the story, which has no documentation or reference features except for a nonexpansive index.

S2-799 ML420 .N381

Reisfeld, Randi. Nelson : double play / Randi Reisfeld. — New York : Bantam, 1991. — 115 p. : ill. : 16 p. plates. ISBN 0-553-29285-4.

A breezy, adulatory tale of Ricky Nelson's twin sons, Matthew and Gunnar (1967–), who are rock performers "destined for superstardom." The story is fictionalized and without sources for its numerous quotations from the twins. No index or reference features.

S2-800 ML420 .N3826 B4

Bashe, Philip. Teenage idol, travelin' man : the complete biography of Rick Nelson / Philip Bashe. — New York : Hyperion, 1992. — xxiii, 312 p. : ill. : 16 p. plates. ISBN 1-56282-969-6.

Rock singer Nelson (1940–1985) rose to fame as an adorable child (Ricky) on his parents' television show of the 1950s, *Ozzie and Harriet;* he first sang on the program in 1957 and had a million-selling record in the same year. Nelson became a rebellious teen, married, had an affair with a heroin addict, had an illegitimate son, and died in a plane crash amid allegations of drug abuse. These events are related in a fictionalized style, with dialogues and feelings presented. There is a casual discography (minimal data) and a nonexpansive index.

S2-801 ML420 .N3826 S4

Selvin, Joel. Ricky Nelson : idol for a generation / Joel Selvin. — Chicago : Contemporary Books, 1990. — xiii, 331 p. : ill. : 32 p. plates. ISBN 0-8092-4187-0.

An undocumented tale of Nelson's chaotic life, featuring conversations and dramatized episodes. A bibliography of articles about the singer is of some use. With a discography that offers minimal information and an expansive index.

S2-802 ML420 .N4 A3

Nelson, Willie. Willie : an autobiography / Willie Nelson; with Bud

Shrake. — New York : Simon & Schuster, 1988. — 334 p. : ill. : 32 p. plates. ISBN 0-671-64265-0.

The same book was also issued with the title *I Didn't Come Here and I Ain't Leaving: the Autobiography of Willie Nelson.*

A vulgar memoir of drugs and drink by the country singer (1933–), with undocumented episodes and conversations; there is nothing about music in it. With a nonexpansive index of names and titles.

S2-803   ML420 .N4 N4
Nelson, Susie. Heart worn memories : a daughter's personal biography of Willie Nelson / Susie Nelson. — Austin, Tex. : Eakin Publications, 1987. — 288 p. : ill. : 32 p. plates. ISBN 0-89015-608-5.

The "thorns as well as the roses" are described in this domestic, sentimental memoir. Father and daughter smoked pot together; she was witness to many of his lurid episodes. Dialogues are provided to enliven the events. Music and singing are not discussed. With a nonexpansive index of names and titles.

Review: LJ 10/15/87, 77

S2-804   ML420 .N48 A3
Newton, Wayne. Once before I go / Wayne Newton; with Dick Maurice. — New York : Morrow, 1989. — 269 p. : ill. ISBN 0-688-07973-3.

Singer Newton (1942–), "an integral part of the Las Vegas scene" since the late 1950s, reveals all about his "youthful marriage, his sadness over the bitter divorce, his famous feuds, and his love affairs." Nothing is revealed about his music. Conversations and anecdotes form the core of the narrative. Without documentation or index.

S2-805   ML420 .O29 E4
Eliot, Marc. Death of a rebel : a biography of Phil Ochs / Marc Eliot. — Rev. ed. — New York : Watts, 1989. — xv, 335 p. : ill. : 32 p. plates. ISBN 0-531-15111-5.

"Originally published 1979 in paperback by Anchor Books" (LOAM Suppl. S-1220).

A completely fictionalized story of Ochs (1940–1976), a "sixties rebel/social commentator/student activist/street socialist/poet/pop star and disturbed child of an America gone war-crazy." His life was mostly downhill, from concert stage to jail and a mental hospital. This edition presents "new facts and documents" that "prove Ochs was a target of Hoover's FBI," new pictures, and an updated discography. With a nonexpansive index.

S2-806   ML420 .O3 A3
O'Day, Anita. High times, hard times / Anita O'Day; with George

Eells; discography by Robert A. Sixsmith and Alan Eichler. — New York : Limelight, 1988. — 376 p. : ill. : 16 p. plates. ISBN 0-87910-118-0.

Jazz and scat vocalist O'Day (1919–) was acclaimed in the 1940s when she sang with Gene Krupa and Stan Kenton. Her memoir has little to say about her musical life, however, being mired in the endless personal difficulties she experienced: a teenage marriage, drugs, alcohol, jail, and so on. The format is anecdotal, with undocumented conversations. There is a useful discography, covering 1941–1979, with dates, matrix numbers, locations, labels, and reissues. An album list is given, with contents, but there is no general index.

Review: LJ 8/81, 1546.

S2-807   ML420 .O78 A81

Amburn, Ellis. Dark star : the Roy Orbison story / Ellis Amburn. — New York : Knightsbridge, 1991. — viii, 283 p. : ill. : 16 p. plates. ISBN 0-8184-0518-X.

"Rock's most unlikely and enigmatic star" is traced here "from depths of tragedy and obscurity" to the heights of fame. The death of his wife and children was a turning point in his life, which ended at age 52 with a heart attack in 1988. He enjoyed "motorcycles, smoke and speed." Amburn's account is based partly on interviews, which are cited among other sources used in chapter endnotes. There is a discography of titles and labels only. With a bibliography of about 150 entries, and an expansive index of persons and titles.

Review: LJ 5/1/90, 89.

S2-808   ML420 .O78 C6

Clayson, Alan. Only the lonely : Roy Orbison's life and legacy / Alan Clayson. — New York : St. Martin's, 1989. — 257 p. : ill. : 16 p. plates. ISBN 0-3120-3961-1.

An informal biography of rock performer Orbison (1936–1988), focused on his personal life and problems. Mind reading and invented conversations are everywhere. Footnotes appear at times, but they lead to vague references, such as "Evening News 3 June 1972," or "Veronica Television (Dutch)." With a discography covering 1956–1988, giving only album titles and U.S./U.K. release labels, and a partly expansive index.

S2-809   ML420 .P275 F6

Fong-Torres, Ben. Hickory wind : the life and times of Gram Parsons / Ben Fong-Torres. — New York : Pocket Books, 1991. — xvi, 236 p. : ill. : 8 p. plates. ISBN 0-671-70513-X.

Parsons, who died at age 27 in 1973, was a country-rock fusion singer,

member of the Byrds and the Flying Burrito Brothers, and "intense friend" of Emmylou Harris. He created a cult following and had about 20 songs written about him. In this adulatory biography, not much emerges about his brief life or career except for anecdotes and conversations. The author asserts that interviews and other sources were used, but there are no citations. With a selective record list, giving minimal data, and a nonexpansive index of names and titles.
Review: LJ 7/91, 98.

S2-810 ML420 .P3
Fleischer, Leonore. Dolly : here I come again / Leonore Fleischer. — Toronto : PaperJacks, 1987. — 238 p. : ill. : 8 p. plates. ISBN 0-7701-0751-6.
Grammy winner as best female country vocalist (1978), Parton (1946–) is presented as a "unique composite of country shrewdness, innocence, full-figured sensuality, and backwoods gospel-singing fervor." The story is casual and undocumented, with plenty of quotes from Parton. No index or reference features.

S2-811 ML420 .P321 C9
Cusic, Don. Sandi Patti : the voice of gospel / Don Cusic. — New York : Doubleday, 1988. — x, 226 p. : ill. ISBN 0-385-24353-7.
An adulatory biography of the "voice of gospel music," informal in style, with undocumented conversations interspersed. Patti's Dove and Grammy awards are listed. A discography of just eight records purports to give her "major solo releases," with labels, issue dates, and contents. No index.
Review: LJ 4/1/88, 91.

S2-812 ML420 .P322 C16
Calt, Stephen. King of the Delta blues : the life and music of Charlie Patton / Stephen Calt and Gayle Wardlow. — Newton, N.J. : Rock Chapel, 1988. — 341 p. : ill. : 24 p. plates. ISBN 0-9618610-02.
An inventive blues dance guitarist who accompanied his own singing, Patton (1891–1934) was the first important blues artist from Mississippi. He recorded extensively for Paramount, while living a disordered life that included many wives and periods in jail. This biography is based on numerous interviews, and a few endnotes are given; however, most conversations and quotations are unaccounted for. Musical analyses of Patton recordings are valuable. The music of 16 songs is included. With a discography of reissues only, a chronology, a glossary of song expressions, and a partly expansive index.
Review: *Choice* 10/89, 324.

S2-813　ML420 .P49

Phillips, John. Papa John : an autobiography / John Phillips; with Jim Jerome. — Garden City, N.Y. : Doubleday, 1986. — 444 p. : ill. : 32 p. plates. ISBN 0-385-23120-2.

An "intimate, gritty, all-too-true" account of the rock singer's life, during which he "spent $1 million on drugs" and "ended busted, broke, and burned out." He also founded the Mamas and the Papas, a group popular in the mid-1960s. The book is shaped from anecdotes and invented dialogues, saying nothing about the music of Phillips or his colleagues. Without reference features, but with an expansive index.

S2-814　ML420 .P8 A7

Ponselle, Rosa. Ponselle, a singer's life / Rosa Ponselle; with James A. Drake; foreword by Luciano Pavarotti; discography by Bill Park. — Garden City, N.Y. : Doubleday, 1982. — xxv, 328 p. : ill. : 20 p. plates. ISBN 0-3851-5641-3.

A casual life story as told by American soprano Ponselle (1897–1981), rendered more secure by Drake's documented commentary. The fictional conversations remain unaccounted for. Ponselle started in the theater as a teen in a duo with her sister Carmela ("The Italian Girls"), singing pop tunes of the day. Then she was "discovered" by Enrico Caruso and appeared on the Metropolitan Opera stage at age 21, remaining with the company until 1937. The discography is unfortunately by title, rather than chronological, but it does give full data: locations, dates, matrix numbers, release labels, and comments. Private recordings and air shots are included. With an index to the discography and a general expansive index.

Review: LJ 12/15/82, 2341.

S2-815　ML420 .P96 A4

Adler, David. Elvis, my dad : the unauthorized biography of Lisa Marie Presley / David Adler and Ernest Andrews. — New York : St. Martin's, 1990. — 179 p. : ill. : 8 p. plates. ISBN 0-312-92197-7.

Presley's only child, born in 1968, here reveals—after "a closely guarded life of privacy"—the "good and bad years at Graceland . . . Lisa Marie's battle with drugs . . . scientology and her marriage to musician Danny Keough . . . the sensational birth of Danielle, Elvis' first grandchild." The revelations appear to have been constructed by Adler and Andrews, from interviews with unnamed persons and from other books about Presley; it is not stated that Lisa Marie assisted them. Nevertheless, the authors are ready to describe Lisa Marie's feelings and statements, from the time she was nine years old to the day her baby was born (evidently the birth was "sensational" because the parents practiced Lamaze methods). Without index or reference features.

S2-816   ML420 .P96 B2

Barth, Jack. Roadside Elvis : the complete state-by-state travel guide for Elvis Presley fans / Jack Barth. — Chicago : Contemporary Books, 1991. — viii, 184 p. : ill. ISBN 0-8092-3981-7.

A sensible handbook for Presley fans who visit Tupelo, Memphis, Graceland, Nashville, Hollywood, and Las Vegas, offering advice and what to see and what to avoid. Aside from the main centers, there are Presley memorabilia to be found worldwide; Barth includes a citation to the Lido cabaret in Paris, where soldier Elvis leaped on the stage in 1959 to render a song; and the barbershop in Friedberg, Germany, which treasures a "clump" of hair and a comb that touched the kingly head. With a nonexpansive index of names and titles.

S2-817   ML420 .P96 B80

Brewer-Giorgio, Gail. The Elvis files : was his death faked? / Gail Brewer-Giorgio; foreword by Raymond A. Moody, Jr. and Monte W. Nicholson. — New York : Shapolsky; Toronto : McGraw-Hill Ryerson; Lancaster, England : Impala Books, 1990. — x, 275 p. : ill. ISBN 1-5617-1000-8 (U.S.).

S2-818   ML420 .P96 C6

Cotten, Lee. The Elvis catalog : memorabilia, icons, and collectibles celebrating the king of rock 'n' roll / Lee Cotton. — Garden City, N.Y. : Doubleday, 1987. — 255 p. : ill. ISBN 0-385-23705-7.

S2-819   ML420 .P96 C7

Cranor, Rosalind. Elvis collectibles / Rosalind Cranor. — 2nd ed. — Johnson City, Tenn. : Overmountain, 1987. — 400 p. : ill. ISBN 0-923807-22-4.

1st ed., 1983 (Paducah, Ky.: Collection Books; LOAM Suppl. SA-818).

Illustrations and estimated dollar values of postcards, sheet music, photographs, concert programs, publications, and movie items (lobby cards, posters, etc.) related to Presley. The prices are on the high side, like $35–40 for an Elvis balloon. Without indexing. There is a shorter version of the book available: S2-843.

S2-820   ML420 .P96 D4

DeBarbin, Lucy. Are you lonesome tonight? : the untold story of Elvis Presley's one true love and the child he never knew / Lucy DeBarbin and Dary Matera. — New York : Villard, 1987. — xxv, 324 p. : ill. : 16 p. plates. ISBN 0-394-55842-1.

In this story, cast in the mode of a romance paperback, Presley has a love affair with a teenaged French girl, unhappily married, and sires a daughter he was destined never to see. Lucy DeBarbin remains his lover for many years, keeping the secret of Desirée from him. She "reveals his deepest thoughts" and tells "why he was so lonely, unhappy and empty." Her love is his comfort "in the fog of his final years." A photocopy of the baby's birth certificate does give her surname as Presley; but there is no further evidence offered for the reality of the tale.

S2-821   ML420 .P96 F8

Fortas, Alan. Elvis, from Memphis to Hollywood : memories from my twelve years with Elvis Presley / Alan Fortas. — Ann Arbor, Mich. : Popular Culture, Ink., 1992. — xi, 322 p. : ill. ISBN 1-56075-026-X.

The author was one of the entourage that clustered around Presley; he identifies himself as "traveling companion, bodyguard, chauffeur, gofer, sometimes caretaker, and full-time friend." He offers undocumented anecdotes and conversations, perhaps more interesting than most Elvis storybooks in their vivid descriptions of the singer's sexual entertainments. With a nonexpansive index.

S2-822   ML420 .P96 F9

Frew, Timothy. Elvis / Timothy Frew. — New York : Mallard, 1992. — 176 p. : ill. ISBN 0-3129-2197-7.

Essentially a picture book, with an undocumented life story as counterpoint, offering no new material. The filmography gives dates and credits, plus color illustrations. There is a directory of about 100 fan clubs, worldwide, and an expansive index.

S2-823   ML420 .P96 G4

Geller, Larry. If I can dream : Elvis' own story / Larry Geller and Joel Spector; with Patricia Romanowski. — New York : Simon & Schuster, 1989. — 331 p. : ill. : 16 p. plates. ISBN 0-6716-5922-7.

A bizarre fictionalized tale, told by Presley's hairdresser and "close friend, confidant, and spiritual advisor." Geller's undocumented conversations and activities with the singer are reported, mostly involving searches for truth and the like. Without index.

S2-824   ML420 .P96 G5

Gibson, Robert. Elvis, a king forever / Robert Gibson; with Sid Shaw. — Poole, Dorset, England : Blandford, 1985. — 176 p. : ill. ISBN 0-07-056518.

A book of color photos and adulatory comments, in which the subject emerges as "a colossus," "a living legend," and a "king holding court." Quotations and anecdotes are produced to support these estimates. Without index or reference features.

S2-825   ML420 .P96 G66

Goldman, Albert. Elvis / Albert Goldman. — New York : McGraw-Hill, 1981. — x, 598 p. : ill. ISBN 0-070-236577.

An informal biography, without source notes or bibliography, yet said to be based on "three years of research and over 600 interviews." Of interest is the conclusion that the singer died of an accidental drug overdose (cf. S2-826). Undocumented, quoted conversations abound. With a nonexpansive index.

Listing: BCL.

S2-826   ML420 .P96 G68

Goldman, Albert. Elvis : the last 24 hours / Albert Goldman. — New York : St. Martin's, 1991. — viii, 192 p. : ill. ISBN 0-3129-2541-7.

A journalistic, undocumented story that purports to solve the mystery of the singer's death, reversing the conclusion offered in Goldman's earlier book (S2-825). Here it is said that Presley committed suicide by drug overdose, deliberately taking an excess of central nervous system depressants. The author believes that Presley was anguished over the impending publication of a tell-all book by his dismissed bodyguards (*Elvis: What Happened?*; LOAM Suppl. S-1235). In that volume Presley's dissolute life ("drug addict, sex freak, gun fetishist") was exposed in detail. Goldman views the American icon with contempt: "He made no sacrifices, fought no battles, suffered no martyrdom, never raised a finger to struggle on behalf of what he believed or claimed to believe. Even gospel, the music he cherished above all, he travestied and commercialized and soft-soaped to the point where it became nauseating." He was "a consummate plagiarist, ripping off everybody in sight." His talent "was not for art but for artifice, for the tricks of the crowd pleaser." It is curious to find a biographer who can sum up his subject as "a phoney . . . a failure as an artist [and] as a man." Without index. (For another analysis of the cause of death, see S2-844.)

S2-827   ML420 .P96 G72

Greenwood, Earl. Elvis—top secret : the untold story of Elvis Presley's secret FBI files / Earl Greenwood and Kathleen Tracy. — New York : Signet, 1991. — 340 p. : ill. ISBN 0-4511-7311-2.

The Freedom of Information Act has permitted researchers to see the FBI files on Presley, dating from 1956. There was nothing insidious about the FBI interest in the singer; the agency routinely kept an eye on celebrities. Thus there are no astonishing revelations in these documents (reproduced in small, fuzzy print, scarcely legible): some death threats, phone calls between Presley and Howard Hughes, miscellaneous rumors. Without index.

S2-828   ML420 .P96 G73
Greenwood, Earl. The boy who would be king / Earl Greenwood and
Kathleen Tracy. — New York : Dutton, 1990. — 310 p. : ill. : 32 p.
plates. ISBN 0-525-24902-8.
A Presley history by his cousin and later press agent, presenting "rare
personal insights," including "vivid and colorful portraits of Presley's
parents." Of Presley's later life there has been so much written that the
chance of fresh revelations is dim, though a plethora of undocumented
anecdotes and conversations are applied to the effort. Supposed sexual
fantasies of the King are recounted, along with an actual orgy. Without
index or reference features.
Reviews: *Choice* 4/92, 1192; LJ 8/90, 112.

S2-829   ML420 .P96 H35
Hammontree, Patsy Guy. Elvis Presley : a bio-bibliography / Patsy
Guy Hammontree. — Westport, Conn. : Greenwood, 1985. — xii, 301
p. : ill. ISBN 0-313-22867-1.
A well-documented biography, followed by a balanced "evaluation"
and a useful bibliographical essay in which much of the shabby writing
about Presley is aptly criticized. With a bibliography of about 300 books
and articles, a list of interviews held by the author, a Presley chronology,
filmography, discography of commercial releases (1954–1979, giving
little information), and an expansive index.
Reviews: AM 1987, 337; ARBA 1986, p. 503; *Choice* 7/86, 1686.

S2-830   ML420 .P96 H8
Hodge, Charlie. Me 'n' Elvis / Charlie Hodge; with Charles Goodman. — Memphis : Castle Books, 1984. — 194 p. : ill. ISBN 0-9166-
9300-7.
Hodge was a guitar player and evidently a sort of jester in Presley's
court. He recounts the 17-year association here in fictionalized style, providing dramatic episodes and nonstop conversations. No reference features.

S2-831   ML420 .P96 J8
Jones, Ira. Soldier boy Elvis / Ira Jones; as told to Bill E. Burk. —
Memphis : Propwash [P.O.B. 16792, TN 38186], 1992. — 256 p. : ill.
ISBN 1-8792-0723-0.
An entertaining account of Presley's military service (1958–1959), as
recalled by the master sergeant of his platoon in Germany. The singer is
portrayed (mostly through unsourced conversations) as "very much the
all-American soldier boy," one who took his assignment seriously and
never took advantage of his fame. He and Jones became buddies and
shared typical soldier escapades. The photos are the highlights of the

book, showing Presley engaged in mundane Army tasks. Without index or reference features.

S2-832 ML420 .P96 L37

Latham, Caroline. E is for Elvis : an A–Z illustrated guide to the king of rock and roll / Caroline Latham and Jeannie Sakol. — New York : Penguin, 1990. — 301 p. : ill. ISBN 0-453-00732-5.

A dictionary that gives—in alphabetical sequence—brief, undocumented entries on persons and topics. A sampling: Travis Smith (his uncle); snakes (he was afraid of them); sneering (he forgot how to do it); Snoopy and Brutus (two of his dogs). Without index.

S2-833 ML420 .P96 M32

Marcus, Greil. Dead Elvis : a chronicle of a cultural obsession / Greil Marcus. — New York : Doubleday, 1991. — 233 p. : ill. ISBN 0-385-41718-7.

A collection of writings that appeared after Presley's death, showing "how he remains alive in the cultural image of our place and time." Marcus provides a commentary on the diverse essays included, generally upholding an adulatory position in the face of the few authors with doubts. The language is notably vulgar. With a nonexpansive index of titles, persons, and topics.

S2-834 ML420 .P96 P3

Peters, Richard. Elvis : the music lives on : the recording sessions, 1954–1976 / Richard Peters. — London : Pop Universal/Souvenir Press, 1992. — 144 p. : ill. ISBN 0-2856-3099-7.

S2-835 ML420 .P96 P68

Presley, Priscilla Beaulieu. Elvis and me / Priscilla Beaulieu Presley; with Sandra Harmon. — New York : Putnam, 1985. — 320 p. : ill. : 32 p. plates. ISBN 0-399-12984-7.

Anecdotes and conversations that purport to cast light on the domestic life of Presley, seen through the eyes of his wife. Without reference features.

S2-836 ML420 .P96 Q5

Quain, Kevin. The Elvis reader : texts and sources on the king of rock 'n' roll / Kevin Quain. — New York : St. Martin's, 1992. — xxiii, 344 p. ISBN 0-312-06966-9.

A gathering of reprinted material that deals with various aspects of Presley's life and career. None of it is of special interest. A casual "reference section" presents lists of recordings and films with minimal data. The book has the shortest index known, just two pages (with closer typesetting it would have fit onto one).

S2-837   ML420 .P96 R4
Ridge, Millie. The Elvis album / Millie Ridge. — New York : Gallery Books, 1991. — 304 p. : ill. ISBN 0-8317-2749-7.
A book of pictures, many in color, with some commentary and a name index.

S2-838   ML420 .P96 R5
Rijff, Ger J. Long lonely highway : a 1950's Elvis scrapbook / Ger Rijff. — Reprinted with additions. — Ann Arbor, Mich. : Pierian, 1988. — xv, 200 p. : ill. (Rock & roll remembrances series, 8) ISBN 0-87650-237-0.
Originally published as: *Elvis Presley: Long Lonely Highway* (Amsterdam: Tutti Frutti Productions, 1985).
This is a reprint of the Amsterdam book, with a new introductory essay by Lee Cotten and a name-place index. It presents a chronological view of Presley's activities from 1950 to 1958, via photocopied programs and press notices.

S2-839   ML420 .P96 R7
Roy, Samuel. Elvis : prophet of power / Samuel Roy. — Brookline, Mass. : Branden, 1985. — 195 p. : ill. : 2 leaves plates. ISBN 0-8283-1898-0.
An amateurish appreciation of the singer, marked by much hostility toward the infidels who found fault with him, especially Albert Goldman (S2-825). The message is obscured by the raspy tone and by quite a few misspelled words. Roy does answer the troubling question "What caused and still causes the fanaticism that Elvis enjoys?" The secret was his "ability to achieve the best again and again." With no reference features; with a half index (last names of persons only).

S2-840   ML420 .P96 S7
Stanley, Billy. Elvis, my brother / Billy Stanley; with George Erikson. — New York : St. Martin's, 1989. — xvi, 296 p. : ill. : 16 p. plates. ISBN 0-312-03329-X.
Backstage talk and bus conversations are provided here to enrich the legend, by a brother and "personal aide" of the singer. His loyalty was given the ultimate test by Presley's affair with his wife, which "caused deep pain for Billy and abiding guilt for Elvis." Without notes; with an expansive index.

S2-841   ML420 .P96 S72
Stanley, Rick. Caught in a trap : Elvis Presley's tragic lifelong search for love : as told by his brother / Rick Stanley; with Paul Harold. — Dallas : Word Pub., 1992. — 232 p. : ill. ISBN 0-8499-0979-1.
A very sentimental tale of the singer, including "psychological

analysis" of his problems. It seems there were "forces beyond Elvis's control [that] held him captive." Brother Rick was a "personal assistant" who toured with Presley, hewed wood, and carried water. He prepared an interesting list of the 100 most asked questions about his sibling, including such queries as "Could any woman live up to the standards that Elvis wanted?" ("No, not really.") Without index or reference features.

S2-842   ML420 .P96 S74
Stern, Jane. Elvis world / Jane Stern and Michael Stern. — New York : Knopf, 1987. — 196 p. : ill. ISBN 0-394-55619-4.

A book of interesting photos and illustrations (newspaper stories, memorabilia) that illuminate the "Elvis world"—at the heart of which are "the true believers who consider the 42 years, seven months, and eight days he spent on earth close to sacred." An unusual group of studio portraits is included, some of which show the subject without his trademark sneer. Lyrics to many of his songs are provided, and there is a movie list. With a critical bibliography of books about Presley; without index.

Review: LJ 10/1/87, 95.

S2-843   ML420 .P96 T4
Templeton, Steve. The best of Elvis collectibles / Steve Templeton and Rosalind Cranor; contributing editors John Diesso and Ted Young. — Johnson City, Tenn. : Overmountain, 1992. — xi, 115 p. : ill. ISBN 0-9328-07771.

A short version of Cranor's *Elvis Collectibles* (S2-819).

Well illustrated in color, with estimated values of such items as sheet music, posters, movie posters, and odd things like pocket calendars ($60) and *TV Guide* covers (up to $125).

S2-844   ML420 .P96 T5
Thompson, Charles C., II. The death of Elvis : what really happened / Charles C. Thompson II and James P. Cole. — New York : Delacorte, 1991. — viii, 407 p. : ill. : 22 p. plates. ISBN 0-385-30228-2.

After 10 years of research, including interviews and study of autopsy records, the authors state their well-informed opinion on the cause of Presley's death. It was not suicide and not a simple drug overdose. Rather, it was the result of an accidental overdose of medical drugs, as Presley took codeine pills (to which he was allergic) thinking they were Dilaudid. The codeine reacted with numerous other prescription substances he was taking and killed him. Because of the excessive prescriptions given to Presley, a medical "cover-up" followed, finally penetrated by television investigators and a court trial. This account would have been more definitive if it had been carefully documented and presented without fictional conversations. However, the solution — dramatically held back until the final page — seems to match the facts. (For other interpretations, see S2-825 and S2-826.)

S2-845   ML420 .P96 W3
Westmoreland, Kathy. Elvis and Kathy / Kathy Westmoreland and William G. Quinn. — Glendale, Calif. : Glendale House, 1987. — 312 p. : ill. : 9 p. plates. ISBN 0-9618-6220-3.
A sentimental, fictionalized story told by a singer who performed in 1,000 concerts with Presley and was also his "lover and friend." The two were preoccupied with trying to "discover certain truths about religion and life." Westmoreland offers an idealized portrait of Presley, denying the reports of his sexual excesses. Although the book's blurb refers to the account as "highly documented," there is no documentation to be found. Without index.

S2-846   ML420 .P96 W73
Worth, Fred L. Elvis : his life from A to Z / Fred L. Worth and Steve D. Tamerius. — Chicago : Contemporary Books, 1988. — xvii, 618 p. : ill. ISBN 0-8092-4528-0.
A miscellany of facts and trivia, with a filmography (including story synopses), lists of television and radio shows, and lists of concerts. All the songs he performed are listed also, and there is a discography that covers bootlegs and commercial releases. Without index.
Review: ARBA 1990, #1299.

S2-847   ML420 .P974 F4
Feldman, Jim. Prince / Jim Feldman. — New York : Ballantine, 1984. — 146 p. : ill. : 16 p. plates. ISBN 0-3453-2325-4.
Rock singer Prince (1958–), whose given name was Prince Rogers Nelson, changed his name in 1993 to a symbol that represents man and woman. He made six remarkable multichannel albums between 1979 and 1985, of which the most popular were *1999* and *Purple Rain*. The latter was also a movie soundtrack, selling more than 11 million copies. The life of this talented performer (who plays all the instruments of the pop ensemble) is told here in plain fashion, with no documentation but with minimal fictionalization. Prince's erotic displays ("one minute he teased with his zipper, the next he got it on with his guitar") are contrasted with his "shyness" and his deeply earnest thoughts about sex "as a religion." Nothing is said about the music, although there is an informal recording list. No index.

S2-848   ML420 .P974 H6
Hill, Dave. Prince : a pop life / Dave Hill. — New York : Harmony Books, 1989. — xiii, 242 p. : ill. : 8 p. plates. ISBN 0-5175-7282-6.

An episodic account, spiced with undocumented quotes and conversations, of the singer's life. This is a discography of U.S. and U.K. releases that covers 1978–1988; it shows chart positions, but otherwise gives minimal data. Adulatory comments are offered on the recordings. With a nonexpansive index.

S2-849   ML420 .P974 R3
Rowland, Mark. Prince : his story in words and pictures : an unauthorized biography / Mark Rowland and Margy Rochlin. — New York : Lorevan, 1985. — xiii, 174 p. : ill. ISBN 0-9317-7327-X.

A tale said to be compiled in part from interviews, but with no identified sources. It is a chatty account of the star's life and loves, with undocumented dialogues and revealed feelings. There is a selection of "quotable quotes" (one is "I was lonely as a kid") and a trivia quiz. Some of Prince's albums are discussed and praised. Without index.

S2-850   ML420 .R74 A3
Robinson, Smokey. Smokey : inside my life / Smokey Robinson; with David Ritz. — New York : McGraw-Hill, 1988. — xi, 289 p. : ill. : 32 p. plates. ISBN 0-07-053209-5.

Soul singer Robinson (1940–) tells his tale in soap-opera idiom, through dramatic episodes and sentimental observations. His life deserves a stronger presentation; he and the Miracles gave Motown its initial drive in the late 1950s, and he was still a chart performer through the 1980s. With a discography of titles only and a nonexpansive index.

S2-851   ML420 .R8734
Hume, Martha. Kenny Rogers : gambler, dreamer, lover / Martha Hume. — New York : New American Library, 1980. — 159 p. : ill. ISBN 0-4522-5254-7.

Pop/rock/country singer Rogers (1939–) sang with several groups before going on to a successful solo career in 1975 (with 22 chart albums in 10 years, and a Grammy in 1977). He is portrayed here mainly through photographs (many in color), with a running commentary that includes reflections and anecdotes of his own. There is no documentation and no index, but there is a list of recordings with minimal data.

S2-852   ML420 .R875 B45
Bego, Mark. Linda Ronstadt : it's so easy! / Mark Bego. — Austin, Tex. : Eakin, 1990. — 212 p. : ill. ISBN 0-89015-775-8.

"Is she a rocker? a Mexican folk singer? a country and western cowgirl? a 1940s chanteuse? an operatic diva? or a pop and rock singer turned actress? Actually, she is all of the above." Ronstadt (1946–) has certainly had a varied career, sketched in this book in plain fashion, with

numerous quotations from her (not documented). Her personal life is not a topic. With a list of recordings (minimal data); without index.
Review: LJ 9/1/90, 222.

S2-853   ML420 .R879 T38
Taraborrelli, J. Randy. Call her Miss Ross : the unauthorized biography of Diana Ross / J. Randy Taraborrelli. — New York : Birch Lane, 1989. — 585 p. : ill. : 32 p. plates. ISBN 1-55972-006-9.
An informal, adulatory life story of soul singer Ross (1944–), featuring undocumented anecdotes and conversations. Her life with the Supremes is presented as an unsavory association. The discography offers dates, labels, and album titles only, covering 1959–1989. With a nonexpansive index of names and titles.
Review: LJ 1/90, 112.

S2-854   ML420 .S21 D14
D'Alessio, Gregory. Old troubadour : Carl Sandburg with his guitar friends / Gregory D'Alessio. — New York : Walker, 1987. — 196 p. : ill. ISBN 0-8027-0966-4.
The great poet and biographer (1878–1967) was also a folk artist, who "would sing and play all night if you let him." He carried his guitar with him, describing it as "a small friend weighing less than a newborn infant, ever responsive to all sincere efforts aimed at mutual respect, depth of affection, or love gone off the deep end." D'Alessio, an associate editor of *Guitar Review,* was a friend of Sandburg and his host for a period in the 1950s, the time of most events in the book. Musicians and celebrities are encountered (Ethel Smith, Andres Segovia—who tried to give Sandburg lessons—Tallulah Bankhead, Edward Steichen, and Marilyn Monroe) and credited with imaginary quotations. The anecdotes are of little interest, but are flavored with poems and inscriptions by Sandburg. With a nonexpansive index.
Review: LJ 9/1/87, 182.

S2-855   ML420 .S562 A3
Sills, Beverly. Beverly : an autobiography / Beverly Sills and Lawrence Linderman. — New York : Bantam, 1987. — xii, 356 p. : ill. : 30 p. ISBN 0-553-05173-3.
A continuation of the memoir that began with *Bubbles* (1976). After soprano Sills (1929–) sang for the last time at the New York City Opera in 1980, she became general director of the company. Her bright anecdotes do not really reveal her "on artistic, political and personal issues," but they provide some amusing stories. One memorable appearance at La Scala, in *Lucia,* was marked by the consecutive portrayals of hero

Edgardo by four tenors, each in turn run off the stage by the audience. With no reference features except for a nonexpansive index.
Review: LJ 6/1/87, 108.

S2-856   ML420 .S563 M7
Morella, Joe. Simon and Garfunkel : old friends / Joe Morella and Patricia Barey. — New York : Birch Lane, 1991. — 261 p. : ill. : 8 p. plates. ISBN 1-55972-089-1.
Domestic biographies of the singing/guitar duo, Paul Simon (1941–) and Art Garfunkel (1941–), greatly successful in the late 1960s; they split up, rejoined, pursued solo paths. In this tale the emphasis is on "marriages, divorces, children, disappointments and tragedies," with an effort to show "how creative tension fueled their careers." The writing is generally free of fictional conversations, but it is all undocumented and impressionistic. There is a record list, 1964–1989, giving minimal information. Without index.

S2-857   ML420 .S58 H85
Humphries, Patrick. Paul Simon, still crazy after all these years / Patrick Humphries. — New York : Doubleday, 1989. — 164 p. ISBN 0-385-24908-X.
British title: *The Boy in the Bubble.*
A straightforward life story of the singer (1941–), undocumented and featuring contrived conversations. With an uninformative discography of albums and song titles only. No index.
Review: LJ 2/15/89, 160.

S2-858   ML420 .S5635 A3
Simone, Nina. I put a spell on you : the autobiography of Nina Simone / Nina Simone; with Stephen Cleary. — New York : Pantheon, 1992. — x, 181 p. : ill. : 16 p. plates. ISBN 0-679-41068-6.
Originally published London: Ebury Press, 1991.
Simone (1933–) is a jazz singer and pianist. She offers an undocumented life story, with emphasis on the personal over the musical. It does come out that she is Louis Farrakhan's favorite singer and that her "Consummation" is his favorite song. With a discography (titles and label names only) and a nonexpansive index.

S2-859   ML420 .S6 D6
Doctor, Gary L. The Sinatra scrapbook / Gary L. Doctor. — New York : Citadel, 1991. — 255 p. : ill. ISBN 0-8065-1250-4.
A fine accumulation of memorabilia on Frank Sinatra (1915–), including pictures of records, magazine covers, album covers, comic books, lobby cards, sheet music, photos on the set or in the studio, and

so forth. American and foreign materials are shown, the latter frequently entertaining. This is a collector's guide, but one without price estimates for the artifacts. No index.

S2-860   ML420 .S6 K4
Kelly, Kitty. His way : the unauthorized biography of Frank Sinatra / Kitty Kelly. — Toronto : Bantam, 1986. — xvi, 575 p. : ill. : 32 p. plates. ISBN 0-553-05137-7.

A controversial book, given that status for two reasons: Sinatra's unsuccessful attempt to have publication suppressed, and the vile image of the singer's personality that emerges from its pages. Kelly has nothing good to say about her subject, denigrating even admirable qualities that she has to acknowledge: "Frank's spontaneous acts of kindness laid the foundation for his reputation as a generous, giving man and provided his press agents with what they needed at other times to cover his atrocious behavior." The reader who is interested in the truth about Sinatra's psyche will be dubious about Kelly as a source for it, since her account— obviously loaded with venomous bias—is fraught with imaginary conversations and scenarios that obscure whatever factual base may be there. The extensive list of sources and chapter endnotes present an impression of scholarly research, but there are no direct footnotes to connect her episodes with the individuals "who cooperated" in "875 interviews" or with the many published and unpublished resources she consulted. Nothing is said about Sinatra's singing or acting as such. With a nonexpansive index.

S2-861   ML420 .S6 S6
Sinatra, Nancy. Frank Sinatra, my father / Nancy Sinatra. — Garden City, N.Y. : Doubleday, 1985. — 334 p. : ill. ISBN 0-385-18294-5.

Nancy Sinatra grew up in the Beverly Hills area, with Loretta Young and Walt Disney among her neighbors, and a famous father who was not at home much. Such is the background for her recollections, which reveal not only conversations but many of her childhood thoughts. Some of the family anecdotes are of interest, and there are a number of unusual photographs. Without index.

Review: LJ 12/85, 124.

S2-862   ML420 .S72
Spector, Ronnie. Be my baby : how I survived mascara, miniskirts, and madness : or my life as a fabulous Ronette / Ronnie Spector; foreword by Cher. — New York : Harmony Books, 1990. — xv, 318 p. : ill. : 16 p. plates. ISBN 0-517-57499-3.

Ronnie Bennett was one of the Ronettes, a successful pop group of the 1960s; all went well until she married her producer, Phil Spector: then "her life became a nightmare and her career crashed to a halt." The domestic ordeal that followed is retold here in fictionalized specificity, with details "so bizarre they're almost funny." Among the characters are the Beatles and Rolling Stones, Cher, Bruce Springsteen, and Billy Joel. "The important thing is that she survived and she's still around to tell the tale," as Cher says. With an expansive index.

S2-863   ML420 .S77 C8
Cross, Charles R. Backstreets : Springsteen : the man and his music / Charles R. Cross [et al.] — New York : Harmony Books, 1989. — 223 p. : ill. ISBN 0-5175-7399-7.
The book's title comes from *Backstreets* magazine, whence most of the contents of the volume was derived. There are interviews with Bruce Springsteen (1949–) and others; an inventory of recording sessions, including the unreleased material; a list of all the singer's concerts; and information for collectors of memorabilia. With 150 photos; without index.

S2-864   ML420 .S77 E4
Eliot, Marc. Down thunder road : the making of Bruce Springsteen / Marc Eliot; with Mike Appel. — New York : Simon & Schuster, 1992. — 382 p. : ill. ISBN 0-6717-8933-3.
"The book Bruce Springsteen hoped would never be written," a "no-holds barred" revelation that "lifts the veil of secrecy." It shows the singer as "raw, out of control, self destructive." Actually, the focus of the tale is narrow, concentrating on the legal disputes between Springsteen and his discoverer/manager Mike Appel (co-author of the volume). There is an abundance of photocopied contracts, letters, account books, and the like, which are offered in support of Appel's position. There are also extensive endnotes and a nonexpansive index.
Review: LJ 8/92, 103.

S2-865   ML420 .S77 H4
Hilburn, Robert. Bruce Springsteen : born in the U.S.A. / Robert Hilburn. — London : Sidgwick & Jackson, 1985. — 256 p. : ill. ISBN 0-684-18456-7.
U.S. title: *Springsteen* (New York: Scribner's, 1985).
A picture book, presenting about 200 photos and a running commentary. Without index.

S2-866   ML420 .S77 H8
Humphries, Patrick. Bruce Springsteen : blinded by the light / Patrick Humphries and Chris Hunt. — New York : Holt, 1986. — 176 p. : ill. ISBN 0-03-008532-2.
Primarily a picture book of photos and album covers, with remem-

bered quotes and anecdotes. A useful chronology of life and work covers 1965–1985. There is a song list, with comments, and a discography (including bootlegs), also with comments, from 1973. Without documentation or indexing.

S2-867   ML420 .S77 M2
MacInnis, Craig. Bruce Springsteen here & now / Craig MacInnis. — New York : Barron's, 1988. — 94 p. : ill. ISBN 0-8120-4095-3.
A photo book with adulatory comments and invented quotations interspersed. Without index.

S2-868   ML420 .S77 M35
Marsh, Dave. Glory days : Bruce Springsteen in the 1980s / Dave Marsh. — New York : Pantheon, 1987. — 478 p. : ill. ISBN 0-394-54668-7.
An anecdotal, undocumented account of Springsteen's career, without special features. With a bibliography of articles and reviews, and a partly expansive index of songs and names.

S2-869   ML420 .S915 K3
Kimbrell, James. Barbra : an actress who sings / James Kimbrell. — Boston : Branden, 1989, 1992. — 2 vols. : ill. ISBN 0-8283-1293-5 ; 0-8283-1946-4.
An affectionate life story of Barbra Streisand, the reluctant star ("I don't like to perform. That's true. I don't even like to be watched"). Kimbrell brings out diverse facets of her complex personality, using many anecdotes and quotations, some of them documented. Nothing emerges about her singing. There is an inadequate, amateurish index in the second volume, made up of one-word entries, such as "Bogdonovich's," "Boop," "Booth."

S2-870   ML420 .S915 S93
Swenson, Karen. Barbra, the second decade / Karen Swenson. — Secaucus, N.J. : Citadel, 1986. — 255 p. : ill. ISBN 0-8065-0981-3.
Barbra Streisand's second decade of fame, as described here, ran from 1974 to 1986. (For the first decade, see LOAM Suppl. S-1092.) Swenson gives a straight narrative of those years, with long discussions of each recording and film. There are about 300 photographs, but no sources or index.

S2-871   ML420 .T52 L4
Farkas, Andrew. Lawrence Tibbett, singing actor / Andrew Farkas; introduction and discography by William R. Moran. — Portland, Ore. : Amadeus, 1989. — 160 p. ISBN 0-931340-17-9.

A collection of essays by and about Tibbett (1896–1960), one of the leading baritones at the Metropolitan Opera from 1923 to 1950. A brief biography by Thomas R. Bullard opens the book. Other contributors are John Hyde Preston, P. K. Thomajan, Juliette Laine, and W. S. Meadows. There is the report of an interview with Tibbett, a reprint of his memoir, "Glory Road," and four other articles by him. A definitive discography, a revision of the one contributed by Moran to Tibbett's 1977 autobiography, presents 103 entries in title order, with full recording data. Other reference features of the volume include a list of Metropolitan broadcasts in which Tibbett appeared, his Covent Garden broadcasts, his movies, and his radio recordings. This excellent handbook concludes with a strong expansive index.

Review: *Choice* 10/89, 325.

S2-872   ML420 .T632 O78
O'Connell, Sheldon J. Dick Todd : king of the jukebox / Sheldon J. O'Connell. — Providence, R.I. : Old Jazz, 1987. — iv, 155 p. : ill. ISBN 0-9693-0230-4.

Popular baritone Todd (1914–) was born in Montreal and sang on Canadian radio before coming to the United States; he sang with Larry Clinton, and then successfully on his own from around 1938 to 1945. "Deep Purple" and "Blue Orchids" were among his hit records. This story is a casual, anecdotal one, heavy with imaginary dialogues; it has little to offer beyond a discography (in song title order, with label and date for each). Without index or references.

S2-873   ML420 .T66
Tomlin, Pinky. The object of my affection : an autobiography / Pinky Tomlin; with Lynette Wert. — Norman : University of Oklahoma Press, 1981. — 212 p. : ill. ISBN 0-8061-1719-2.

Tomlin was a popular composer/singer/bandleader in the mid-1930s. His hit song was "The Object of My Affection" (1934); it led to a number of movie roles.

Review: LJ 8/81, 1546.

S2-874   ML420 .T69 A3
Tormé, Mel. It wasn't all velvet : an autobiography / Mel Tormé. — New York : Viking, 1988. — xii, 384 p. : ill. : 16 p. plates. ISBN 0-670-82289-2.

The distinguished jazzy popular singer Tormé (1925–) is not well served by this memoir, which is built of casual chat and undocumented conversations. One incident of interest is his dispute with Richard Rodgers over the phrasing of "Blue Moon"—but such tales are scarce. Tormé's brilliant appearances with George Shearing get little attention.

The discography (1944–1982) gives labels and numbers only. With an expansive index.

S2-875 ML420 .T7 E18
Eatherly, Pat Travis. In search of my father / Pat Travis Eatherly. — Nashville : Broadman, 1987. — 191 p. : ill. ISBN 0-8054-5727-5.

"The discovery of a daughter to the fact of a father who became indifferent to her . . . [and] the secret of mending a broken relationship." Country star Merle Travis (1917–1983) is the parent who went wrong, then right. Written like a children's book, the story has nothing of interest to say about country music or Travis. Without documentation or index.

S2-876 ML420 .T76
Cusic, Don. Randy Travis : king of the new country traditionalists / Don Cusic. — New York : St. Martin's, 1990. — xi, 210 p. : ill. ISBN 0-3120-4412-7.

A breezy, undocumented account of the Grammy-winning singer—the youngest male to sing at the Grand Ole Opry, whose 1986 "Storms of Life" has sold more than any other country song. There is a bibliography and a discography (minimal data), and a nonexpansive index.

S2-877 ML420 .T88 D8
Drake, James A. Richard Tucker : a biography / James A. Drake; foreword by Luciano Pavarotti; discography by Patricia Ann Kiser. — New York : Dutton, 1984. — xvi, 304 p. : ill. : 32 p. plates. ISBN 0-5252-41949.

Tucker (1913–1975) was a tenor who specialized in the Italian repertoire. This account of his life is of some interest as a record of his rise from coat lining salesman in New York to cantor to Metropolitan Opera star of 30 years. It is undocumented and marred by invented conversations and anecdotes. The discography is just a checklist of releases from 1954 to 1967, giving minimal data. With an expansive index.

Reviews: *Choice* 9/84, 112; LJ 2/15/84, 376.

S2-878 ML420 .T95 A3
Turner, Tina. I, Tina : my life story / Tina Turner; with Kurt Loder. — New York : Morrow, 1986. — 236 p. : ill. ISBN 0-688-05949-X.

"One of the most sensational life stories in show business" is attributed to popular singer Turner (1939–), who rose from poverty in East St. Louis to international stardom. She teamed with Ike Turner for many of her hits, married and divorced him, and went on to success as a solo artist, sweeping the Grammys in 1985. The memoir is made of invented conversations and anecdotes, preserving little of the real-life drama that occurred. There is a "cast of characters" that identifies persons of

consequence in the tale, and there are comments on some recordings.
Without index.

S2-879   ML420 .T95 W4
Welch, Chris. Take you higher : the Tina Turner experience / Chris
Welch. — London : W. H. Allen, 1986. — 192 p. : ill. ISBN 0-4910-
3951-4.
An undocumented tale of Turner's rise to stardom, with many anecdotes
and dialogues. A casual discography offers little data. Without index.

S2-880   ML420 .T955 C7
Cross, Wilbur. The Conway Twitty story : an authorized biography /
Wilbur Cross and Michael Kosser. — Garden City, N.Y. : Doubleday,
1986. — xi, 193 p. : ill. : 41 p. plates. ISBN 0-3852-3189-9.
A "quintessentially American rags to riches success story" about
country singer Twitty (1933–1993), made up primarily of "fascinating
anecdotes." Musical matters are not taken up. There is also a discography, 1956–1985, giving minimal data. Without index.
Review: LJ 8/86, 152.

S2-881   ML420 .V2
Mendheim, Beverly. Ritchie Valens, the first Latino rocker / Beverly
Mendheim. — Tempe : Arizona State University Press/Bilingual Press,
1987. — 153 p. : ill. ISBN 0-916950-79-4.
An amateurish biography of Valens (1941–1959), early fusion performer and first successful Chicano in the rock field, famous for his
songs "La Bamba" and "Donna." He died in the same accident that took
the life of Buddy Holly. The book reads like a rough draft; for example,
the discography has uncertain dates and no information about the recordings except the label names. Quotations and anecdotes abound, and the
style is fixedly adulatory. Without notes or index.

S2-881a   ML420 .V25
Bego, Mark. Ice, ice, ice : the extraordinary Vanilla Ice story / Mark
Bego. — New York : Dell, 1991. — viii, 104 p. : ill. ISBN 0-4402-10135.
Vanilla Ice is white, but also a successful rap singer; it is interesting to
find his life marked by racism. The book title comes from his hit record
"Ice Ice Baby." Bego's account is casual and undocumented, with in-
vented conversations. The discography has titles only. No index.

S2-882   ML420 .W12 E5
Eng, Steve. A satisfied mind : the country music life of Porter Wag-
oner / Steve Eng. — Nashville : Rutledge Hill, 1992. — 464 p. : ill.
ISBN 1-55853-133-5.

Wagoner (1930–) is known as a country singer, songwriter, and record producer, and for his successful association with Dolly Parton (he wrote many of her songs and made 22 chart records with her). As producer of Parton's hit discs, he found himself in financial entanglements. This book "cuts through the tabloid gossip to show a complex, adventurous, and enormously methodical man behind the image." Although 160 interviews were conducted by Eng, he does not document numerous conversations and quotations. However, there are chapter endnotes, and there is a partly expansive index.

S2-883   ML420 .W274 A6
Warfield, William. My music and my life / William Warfield; with Alton Miller. — Champaign, Ill. : Sagamore, 1991. — 229 p. ISBN 0-915611-40-6.
Warfield (1920–) is a baritone, best known for his portrayal of Porgy in *Porgy and Bess*. This is casual first-person narrative, presenting anecdotes about his growing years, reconstructed conversations, and meditations on various topics. Without index or reference features.

S2-884   ML420 .W28 H37
Haskins, James. Queen of the blues : a biography of Dinah Washington / James Haskins. — New York : Morrow, 1987. — 239 p. : ill. ISBN 0-688-04846-3.
A casual biography, without source notes or bibliography; quoted conversations abound. The story is of Washington's personal life (1924–1963), with little said about her music. A useful discography is appended, chronological by recording session (1943–1963); it gives matrix numbers, personnel, label numbers, and reissues. With a nonexpansive index of titles, names, and topics.
Review: *Choice* 9/87, 140.

S2-885   ML420 .W4
Whiting, Margaret. It might as well be spring : a musical autobiography / Margaret Whiting and Will Holt. — New York : Morrow, 1987. — 384 p. : ill. ISBN 0-688-06406-X.
Vocalist Whiting (1924–) grew up in a musical atmosphere as the daughter of songwriter Richard Whiting and started her career with a hit record of his "My Ideal." She went on to become one of the leading ballad singers of the 1940s, while marrying three times and dealing with the problems that resulted. Her memoir is mostly people talking, however, and says nothing about music. With a discography by label (minimal data) and a nonexpansive index.
Reviews: AM 1988, 455; LJ 1/87, 90.

S2-886   ML420 .W55 W5

Williams, Jett. Ain't nothing' as sweet as my baby : the story of Hank Williams' lost daughter / Jett Williams; with Pamela Thomas. — New York : Harcourt Brace Jovanovich, 1990. — xviii, 338 p. : ill. : 16 p. plates. ISBN 0-15-104050-8.

Antha Belle Jett was born five days after the death of Hank Williams (1923–1953), her mother being "his sometime mistress, Bobbie Jett, who turned the baby over to Hank's mother and fled to California." The child was in time adopted by another family, who kept her true father's identity secret. Through the efforts of an attorney whom she later married, she established the paternity of Williams and became Jett Williams; later she toured as a singer with her father's Drifting Cowboys. This soap-opera scenario lends itself well to the fictionalized treatment it receives here, comprising long dialogues and dramatic scenes. Without index or documentation.

S2-887   ML420 .W55 W55

Williams, Roger M. Sing a sad song : the life of Hank Williams / Roger M. Williams. — 2nd ed. — Urbana : University of Illinois Press, 1980. — ix, 318 p. ISBN 0-252-00844-8.

1st ed., 1970 (Garden City, N.Y. : Doubleday; LOAM 645).

This is a reprint of the first edition, enhanced with a six-page "Afterword" by the author that reports on the singer's continuing popularity, a thorough discography that notes all reissues, and a nonexpansive index.

Review: *Choice* 11/81, 388.

S2-888   ML420 .W55 W6

Williams, Lycrecia. Still in love with you : the story of Hank and Audrey Williams / Lycrecia Williams and Dale Vinicur. — Nashville : Rutledge Hill Press, 1989. — xiv, 199 p. : ill. : 32 p. plates. ISBN 1-55853-048-7.

Audrey Williams (1923–1975) was the wife of Hank Williams; "when his alcoholism ended their marriage in early 1952, his life quickly descended into extended bouts of drunkenness and sickness." He died at age 29 of alcoholism and medications. This unhappy tale is recounted by their daughter, who carries the story to the success of Hank Williams, Jr. Her memory of domestic events and conversations—from age five—forms the basis of the undocumented, sentimental tale. There are many long quotations, apparently drawn from interviews. Music per se is not discussed. Without index.

S2-889   ML420 .W5525

Wilson, Brian. Wouldn't it be nice : my own story / Brian Wilson;

with Todd Gold. — New York : HarperCollins, 1991. — xiii, 398 p. : ill. ISBN 0-06-018313-6.

The founder of the Beach Boys rock group here tells the "whole amazing story" of his "20-year nightmare of drug addiction, alcoholism, obesity and mental illness." Musical points are not included; the style is anecdotal and conversational. Without reference features, except for an expansive index.

S2-890   ML420 .W68
Wilson, Mary. Dreamgirl : my life as a Supreme / Mary Wilson; with Patricia Romanowski and Ahrgus Juilliard. — New York : St. Martin's, 1986. — xii, 292 p. : ill. ISBN 0-3122-1959-8.

Wilson was one of the original Supremes, a female vocal trio established in 1964 that was centered on Diana Ross. In Wilson's gossipy, undocumented history of the group, Ross appears as treacherous and domineering; Wilson emerges as whiny and malcontent. With a casual discography and an index.

Review: LJ 12/86, 104.

S2-891   ML420 .W836 P5
Peisch, Jeffrey. Stevie Wonder / Jeffrey Peisch. — New York : Ballantine, 1984. — 147 p. : ill. : 16 p. plates. ISBN 0-3453-2309-2.

Blind musical phenomenon Stevie Wonder (1950–), who composes his own songs and plays most of the instruments on his records, has won 14 Grammys. In this informal biography he is often quoted, as though from interviews, but no such source is cited, and Wonder is not among the persons who are thanked in the acknowledgments. With a casual list of recordings; without index.

S2-892   ML420 .W836 S9
Swenson, John. Stevie Wonder / John Swenson. — New York : Harper, 1986. — 159 p. : ill. ISBN 0-06-097067-7.

A rambling tale of Wonder's career, comprised mostly of undocumented quotations and conversations. A chronological discography gives U.S. and U.K. release labels for issues of 1962–1985, with some chart histories and comments. No index.

S2-893   ML420 .Z2 C4
Chevalier, Dominique. Viva! Zappa / Dominique Chevalier. — New York : St. Martin's, 1986. — 127 p. : ill. ISBN 0-3120-0201-7.

A picture book with breezy commentary about Zappa (1940–1993), "jazz pioneer, outspoken satirist, virtuoso guitarist, smutty exhibitionist, serious modern composer." He was founder of the Mothers of Invention group. A discography offers titles only. There are informal lists of Zappa's publications and appearances, fanzines, and souvenir products. Without index.

S2-894   ML420 .Z285 A3
Zappa, Frank. The real Frank Zappa / Frank Zappa; with Peter Occhiorosso. — New York : Poseidon, 1989. — 352 p. : ill. ISBN 0-6716-3870-X.
Zappa presents "inimitable views" on art, beer, symphony orchestras, groupies, and many other topics. Along the way he tries to reveal how he became the "state of the art in weirdness." Without index or reference features.

S2-895   ML420 .Z37 C4
Colbeck, Julian. Zappa : a biography / Julian Colbeck. — London : W. H. Allen, 1987. — 190 p. : ill. ISBN 0-8636-9156-0.

S2-896   ML420 .Z37 G5
Gray, Michael. Zappa / Michael Gray and Mike Teasdale. — London : Proteus Books, 1985. — 159 p. : ill. : 16 p. plates. ISBN 0-8627-6147-6.
Cover title: Mother! is the story of Frank Zappa.
A breezy tale of Zappa and the Mothers of Invention, with many quotes and without documentation. There is a lengthy account of his trial in the United Kingdom (for singing vulgar lyrics) that even gives some transcript material. There are some useful technical descriptions of instruments and combinations, with musical observations. A one-page discography gives minimal data. No index.

ML421 : Musical Groups

S2-897   ML421 .B38 G2
Gaines, Steven. Heroes and villains : the true story of the Beach Boys / Steven Gaines. — New York : New American Library, 1986. — 374 p. : ill. : 32 p. plates. ISBN 0-4530-0519-5.
The Beach Boys, a rock group formed in 1961, were popular for 20 years. Their story is a "gothic tale of drugs, sex, music, greed, booze, and genius," based on interviews with the performers, their family, and their friends. The "multidimensional saga" is comprised of vulgar conversations (undocumented) and crude episodes. Nothing is said about music; there are no reference features except for an expansive index.

S2-898   ML421 .B38 G4
Golden, Bruce. The Beach Boys : southern California pastoral /

Bruce Golden; updated by Paul David Seldis. — 2nd ed. — San Bernardino, Calif. : Borgo, 1991. — 104 p. ISBN 0-8937-0459-1.
1st ed., 1976 (LOAM Suppl. S-1185).

S2-899   ML421 .B38 M5
Milword, John. Beach Boys : silver anniversary / John Milword. — Garden City, N.Y. : Doubleday, 1985. — 240 p. : ill. ISBN 0-385-19650-4.
A picture book with accompanying commentary. No index or reference features.

S2-900   ML421 .B42
Delbanco, Nicholas. The Beaux Arts Trio / Nicholas Delbanco. — New York : Morrow, 1985. — 254 p. : ill. ISBN 0-6880-4001-2.
The distinguished chamber trio, consisting of violinist Daniel Guilet, cellist Bernard Greenhouse, and pianist Menahem Pressler, is displayed here from many perspectives, all of them musical. The author interviewed them, heard their concerts, and attended recording sessions. The discussion is technical, and the more revealing for that; the reader who can follow the vocabulary will gain great insight into the way a chamber ensemble thinks and masters its repertoire. Without documentation (supposedly many of the conversations are so-called reconstructions), without index, and with only a casual discography (minimal data).
Reviews: *Choice* 5/85, 1342; LJ 12/84, 2282.

S2-901   ML421 .B69
Jan, Ramona. Bon Jovi / Ramona Jan. — Toronto : PaperJacks, 1988. — 177 p. : ill. : 8 p. plates. ISBN 0-7701-0807-5.

S2-902   ML421 .C3 G8
Goldstein, Toby. Frozen fire : the story of the Cars / Toby Goldstein; photography by Ebet Roberts. — Chicago : Contemporary Books, 1985. — ix, 118 p. : ill. : 16 p. plates. ISBN 0-8092-5257-0.
The Cars "may seem icy as chrome, but a fire burns within." Goldstein's account fails to demonstrate this proposition, being a collection of gossip and anecdotes with no documentation. The only reference feature is a recording list (album titles with contents only). No index.

S2-903   ML421 .D61
Bego, Mark. Doobie Brothers / Mark Bego. — New York : Fawcett, 1980. — 190 p. : ill. ISBN 0-4450-4595-7.
A story of the middle-of-the-road rock group that was popular in the 1970s.

S2-904   ML421 .D66 D46
Densmore, John. Riders on the storm : my life with Jim Morrison and the Doors / John Densmore. — New York : Delacorte, 1990. — 319 p. : ill. : 32 p. plates. ISBN 0-385-30033-6. (Alternative classification: ML419.)

Densmore was drummer with the Doors from 1965 to 1971; as a companion of Morrison for six years, he offers a recollection that "may not be the whole truth, but it is the way I saw it." Morrison is described as "a guy with a natural instinct for melody but no knowledge of chords to hang it on," unable to read music, and not really musical. He was given to "pranks," such as spraying a recording studio and instruments with a fire extinguisher; and of course he was sex driven. Densmore's own life story is somewhat interwoven, but this is much less his autobiography than an eyewitness account of Morrison's maniacal days. Unfortunately, the useful content of his product is minimal, as it is largely limited to vulgar conversations and episodes. Without index or reference features.

Reviews: *Choice* 4/92, 1192; LJ 8/90, 112.

S2-905   ML421 .D66 D8
Doe, Andrew. The Doors in their own words / Andrew Doe and John Tobler. — London : Omnibus, 1988. — 94 p. : ill. ISBN 0-8627-6869-0.

Originally published as *The Doors* (London: Proteus, 1984).

The "thoughts and philosophy" of Jim Morrison and the three other band members, as "drawn from rare interviews, reviews, and critiques." None of the thoughts are about music. Without documentation or index.

S2-906   ML421 .E93 D8
Dodge, Consuelo. The Everly Brothers : ladies love outlaws / Consuelo Dodge. — Starke, Fla. : CIN-DAV, Inc., 1991. — xii, 344 p. : ill. ISBN 1-879347-09-1.

An adulatory account of the Everlys, told in a casual style with a crude vocabulary. Undocumented, with quoted conversations. A chronology of major events has some information value, and the list of Everly compositions in title order may be useful. With an informal bibliography of 60 items, a list of albums and their songs, and a nonexpansive index of names and titles.

Review: LJ 9/1/91, 192.

S2-907   ML421 .E93 K2
Karpp, Phyllis. Ike's boys : the story of the Everly Brothers / Phyllis Karpp. — Ann Arbor, Mich. : Pierian, 1988. — xiii, 266 p. : ill. (Rock and roll remembrances, 9) ISBN 0-8765-0245-1.

The lives of singers/guitarists Don and Phil Everly are narrated in fictional style, with conversations and anecdotes. The drama of their farewell concert in 1973 gets ample attention, along with their return to the stage 10 years later. There are discographies of singles (1956–1973) and albums (1958–1986), giving titles and label names only. A life-and-career chronology covers 1908–1987. Without notes; with indexes of persons, places, topics, and dates.

S2-908 ML421 .G72 B7
Brandelius, Jerilyn Lee. Grateful Dead family album / Jerilyn Lee Brandelius. — New York : Warner Books, 1989. — 256 p. : ill. ISBN 0-446-51521-3.

"An intimate, elaborate scrapbook . . . assembled from the private memorabilia of the Grateful Dead's extended family, band members, relatives, working associates, and friends . . . filled with histories, anecdotes, testimonials, fragments, artifacts, poems, souvenirs, and . . . hundreds of never-before-published photographs." Without index or reference features.

S2-909 ML421 .G72 G2
Gans, David. Conversations with the Dead : the Grateful Dead interview book / David Gans. — New York : Citadel Underground, 1991. — x, 342 p. : ill. ISBN 0-8065-1223-7.

An endeavor to extract deep thoughts from the members of the group, about music and various philosophical topics. Results are vague at best, with such observations as this one being typical: "It's not always what you're playing that makes it—it's what everybody else is playing too. The holes are just in the right places, or whatever." No index or reference features.

S2-910 ML421 .G72 G74
Greene, Herb. Sunshine daydreams : a Grateful Dead journal / Herb Greene. — San Francisco : Chronicle Books, 1991. — Unpaged : ill. ISBN 0-87701-813-8.

Pictures of the members, and journal pages showing what the group was doing each day of the month in various years. Without index.

S2-911 ML421 .G72 J2
Jackson, Blair. Goin' down the road : a Grateful Dead traveling companion / Blair Jackson. — New York : Harmony Books, 1992. — xi, 322 p. : ill. ISBN 0-5175-8337-2.

The material in this book was previously published in the magazine *Golden Road*. It offers sensible interviews with the group members, including many technical points about their music and their instruments. Background information on the songs emerges as well. A performance chronology covers 1966–1991, with good descriptions of the events. Without index.

S2-912   ML421 .G72 J3
Jensen, Jamie. Grateful Dead : built to last : 25th anniversary album, 1965–1990 / Jamie Jensen. — New York : Plume, 1990. — 96 p. : ill. ISBN 0-4522-6478-2.
A casual history, with some interviews; notable for 120 color photos. Without index or reference features.

S2-913   ML421 .G72 R9
Ruhlmann, William. The history of the Grateful Dead / William Ruhlmann. — New York : Smithmark, 1990. — 96 p. : ill. ISBN 0-8317-3976-2.
With discography and index.
Review: *Choice* 4/92, 1192.

S2-914   ML421 .G72 S3
Scott, John W. DeadBase IV : the complete guide to Grateful Dead song lists / John W. Scott, Mike Dogulshkin, and Stu Nixon. — Hanover, N.H. : DeadBase, 1990. — ix, 502 p. : ill. ISBN not given.

S2-915   ML421 .G72 T8
Troy, Sandy. One more Saturday night : reflections with the Grateful Dead family and Dead Heads / Sandy Troy. — New York : St. Martin's, 1992. — xi, 275 p. : ill. ISBN 0-3120-7759-9.
A book of interviews with the players and various associates, enhanced by color photos published for the first time. The stories concentrate on the notorious public behavior of the group (such as their placement of a flag on the great pyramid in Gizeh) and on numerous drug-related episodes. There are scattered comments of substance about audio equipment and some insider views of the group's concert history. No index or reference features.

S2-916   ML421 .G86 S9
Sugerman, Daniel. Appetite for destruction : the days of Guns 'n' Roses / Daniel Sugerman. — New York : St. Martin's, 1991. — xi, 246 p. : ill. ISBN 0-312-05814-4.
"One part punk-rock attitude, one part rhythmic heavy metal" are the elements that enabled the group to "rescue rock 'n' roll from an early grave" in the mid-1980s. The tale, focused on their lives of "violence, love and energy," is told through vulgar quotations and anecdotes, not documented. The author endeavors to find a rationale for their activities in myth and in poetry. With a partly expansive index.

S2-917   ML421 .G86 W2

Wall, Mick. Guns 'n' Roses : the most dangerous band in the world / Mick Wall. — London : Sidgwick & Jackson, 1991. — ix, 147 p. : ill. : 8 p. plates. ISBN 0-2830-6086-7.

A compilation of "outrageous and candid pronouncements" and "unguarded quotes" about such topics as money, sex, and drugs. The authors are the band members and their manager; the idiom is entirely vulgar; the documentation is absent. Without index.

S2-918   ML421 .H27

Gooch, Brad. Hall and Oates / Brad Gooch. — New York : Ballantine, 1985. — 147 p. : ill. : 16 p. plates. ISBN 0-3453-2271-1.

Daryl Hall and John Oates, cited by *Billboard* as "the most successful duo in the history of the recording industry," offer a "distinctive mix of rock and soul," or—as Gooch says elsewhere—"a blend of funk with Motown and Philly r & b." While much of this plain narrative is about the success story of the pair, there are some accounts of the way they write their songs, albeit vaguely reported ("letting the words steam up out of the music"), and quite a bit is said about work in the studio. A number of invented conversations intrude. With a recording list (minimal data); without index.

S2-919   ML421 .H88 A3

Hutchinson Family. Excelsior : journals of the Hutchinson Family Singers, 1842–1846 / ed. Dale Cockrell. — Stuyvesant, N.Y. : Pendragon, 1989. — xxxiii, 467 p. (Sociology of music, 5) ISBN 0-918727-65-7.

The Hutchinsons "were a most important part of American popular music's nascency," presenting some 12,000 concerts of folk and traditional music from the 1840s to the end of the century. In their own journals—capably edited and annotated here—the family presents a rich view of American cultural life. Aside from musical matters, the journals are a fascinating repository of detail on social conditions in many cities. One appendix gives the concert itineraries of the group; another presents the titles in their song repertoire. With extensive chapter endnotes and a partly expansive index.

Review: AM 1993, 377.

S2-920   ML421 .J82 A3

Judd, Naomi. Love can build a bridge / Naomi Judd and Wynonna Judd; with Bud Schaetzle. — New York : Villard, 1992. — x, 940 p. : ill. ISBN 0-6794-1247-6.

A sentimental account of the life and troubles of the Judds, made up mostly of fictionalized scenes and dialogues. Nothing is said about music. Without index or reference features.

S2-921   ML421 .J82 M5
Millard, Bob. The Judds : a biography / Bob Millard. — New York : Doubleday, 1988. — vi, 206 p. : ill. ISBN 0-385-24441-X.

Naomi and Wynonna Judd are a mother-daughter country singing duo, whose "acoustic approach harkens back to the traditional country roots that they claim." This casual tale concentrates on the country roots, saying nothing tangible about the Grammy-winning music that emerged from it. There is no documentation for the conversations and anecdotes. Their hit records are listed, with personal commentaries. Without index.

S2-921a   ML421 .K33
Blake, Benjamin. The Kingston Trio on record / Benjamin Blake, Jack Rubeck, and Allan Shaw. — Naperville, Ill. : Kingston Korner, 1986. — 272 p. : ill. ISBN not given.

A combination picture book and discography, with a thorough discussion of every recorded song. All the album covers are illustrated. With an index of titles and persons.

S2-922   ML421 .L6 W5
Whitwell, David. The Longy Club : a professional wind ensemble in Boston (1900–1917) / David Whitwell. — Northridge, Calif. : WINDS, 1988. — 199 p. ISBN not given.

Georges Longy, oboist with the Boston Symphony Orchestra, founded the Longy Club in 1900. The chamber group gave concerts for 17 years, evidenced by all the illustrations of programs in this book. All the artists are identified as well, and reviews are quoted.
Review: AM 1989, 220.

S2-923   ML421 .M35
Phillips, Michelle. California dreamin' : the true story of the Mamas and the Papas / Michelle Phillips. — New York : Warner Books, 1986. — 178 p. : ill. : 16 p. plates. ISBN 0-446-51308-3.

The author was wife to the group's leader, John Phillips. She recounts the "wildly decadent lifestyle that embraced LSD and free love," all the way to "burnout, arguments, and the final bitterness and breakup" (in 1968) of the ensemble. Conversations and episodes are provided; reference features are not. The book's title is that of the group's first hit single in 1966.

S2-924   ML421 .M65 B2
Baker, Glenn A. Monkeemania : the true story of the Monkees / Glenn

A. Baker. — New York : St. Martin's 1986. — 144 p. ISBN 0-312-0003-0.

A story of the rock group that was briefly prominent in the late 1960s, with fine photographs of them, and of record labels, advertising, etc. The narrative portion is made up of conversations and quotations. With a discography of album titles (no contents or details); without notes or index.

S2-925   ML421 .M65 L4
Lefcowitz, Eric. The Monkees tale / Eric Lefcowitz. — Rev. ed. — Berkeley, Calif. : Last Gasp, 1985. — 119 p. : ill. ISBN 0-86719-338-7.

A casual history of the group, with a biography of each performer. There is a filmography of 58 items and a record list (album titles and contents only). No other reference features and no index.

S2-926   ML421 .M65 R4
Reilly, Edward. The Monkees : a manufactured image : the ultimate reference guide to Monkee memories & memorabilia / Edward Reilly, Maggie McManus, and William Chadwick. — Ann Arbor, Mich. : Pierian, 1987. — xvi, 307 p. : ill. (Rock & roll reference series, 28) ISBN 0-87650-236-2.

Living up to its subtitle, this is a book that documents the group via a day-to-day chronology (1965–1986), tour schedules, heavily annotated lists of their television and film work, and a thorough discography of U.S. and foreign releases. There are good photographs of album covers and of memorabilia. The general index is nonexpansive and crudely contrived, but the song and album title index is serviceable.

Review: ARBA 1988, #1320.

S2-927   ML421 .M7 D9
Dwight, Billy. Motley Crue / Billy Dwight. — New York : Ballantine, 1986. — 126 p. : ill. : 16 p. plates. ISBN 0-3453-3237-7.

The story of the borderline–heavy metal group that made its debut record in 1981.

S2-928   ML421 .N35 R4
Reisfeld, Randi. Nelson : double play / Randi Reisfeld. — New York : Bantam, 1991. — 115 p. : ill. : 16 p. plates. ISBN 0-5532-9285-4.

The story of twins Matthew Nelson and Gunnar Nelson (1967–), sons of rock star Ricky Nelson, and rock performers themselves. In this adulatory account, made up largely of undocumented conversations, there is some interest in the Nelson domestic setting. Nothing is said about music. Without index.

S2-929   ML421 .N48
George, Nelson. Cool it now : the authorized biography of New

Edition / Nelson George. — Chicago : Contemporary Books, 1986. — 128 p. : ill. ISBN 0-8092-5004-7.

S2-930   ML421 .N5 N35

Nance, Scott. New Kids on the Block / Scott Nance. — Las Vegas : Pioneer Books, 1990. — 94 p. : ill. ISBN not given.

A picture book about the rock group that consists of "the five hardest working kids in show business." A clean image is projected, not only in the photos but in the undocumented remarks by the performers. Without index.

S2-931   ML421 .O2 W5

Widner, Ellis. The Oak Ridge Boys : our story / Ellis Widner and Walter Carter. — Chicago : Contemporary Books, 1987. — xi, 212 p. : ill. ISBN 0-8092-4842-5.

A collection of interviews with the 39 persons who have sung with the Oak Ridge Boys since the group was formed in the mid-1940s. The conversations trace the evolution of the ensemble from gospel roots to country. With a discography and an index.

Review: LJ 7/87, 80.

S2-932   ML421 .P741 C37

Carter, William. Preservation Hall : music from the heart / William Carter. — New York : Norton, 1991. — vii, 315 p. ISBN 0-393-02915-8.

Preservation Hall, which opened in 1961 in New Orleans, has remained a bastion of traditional jazz performance. This is an account of the persons who have been closely associated with the Hall. There were 200–300 performers per year in the early years, but now closer to 75 per year. The initial acclaim given to the Hall and its artists became muted in the 1980s, as "overall quality of the music slipped," but there has been a resurgence with the influx of younger musicians who respect traditional style. Carter's story is partly documented (there are "notes on sources" for each chapter, without direct citations) but overly attached to anecdotes and conversations. With good photographs and a nonexpansive index.

Review: LJ 5/15/91, 84.

S2-933   ML421 .R22 F6

Fletcher, Tony. Remarks : the story of R.E.M. / Tony Fletcher. — New York : Bantam, 1990. — 128 p. : ill. ISBN 0-5533-4920-1.

Originally published London: Omnibus, 1989.

"From humble origins in an abandoned church in collegiate Athens, Georgia" to "worldwide headlines"—such is the saga of the R.E.M. group, told here in plain fashion, without documentation, and with numerous quotes and dialogues. There is a discography (minimal data), but no index.

S2-934 ML421 .R22 G6

Greer, Jim. R.E.M. : behind the mask / Jim Greer; photographs by Laura Levine. — Boston : Little, Brown, 1992. — 139 p. : ill. ISBN 0-3163-2730-1.

A book that reveals how the group has remained famous "without selling out" or "toning down their political views." It is useful for good color photos and for a chronology of tour appearances. The discography gives titles only. Without index.

S2-935 ML421 .R35

DesCordobes, Dominique. Ratt / Dominique DesCordobes. — New York : Ballantine, 1986. — 127 p. : ill. : 16 p. plates. ISBN 0-345-33238-5.

Ratt is the name taken by a heavy metal group from San Diego, prominent in the mid-1980s. This book recounts their 1984 tour and offers little stories about individual performers. The discography and videography give titles only, without dates or data. No index or sources.

S2-936 ML421 .R9

Adler, B. Tougher than leather : the authorized biography of Run-DMC / B. Adler. — New York : New American Library, 1987. — 191 p. : ill. : 16 p. plates. ISBN 0-4511-5121-6.

An informal story of the "most notorious and popular rap group in the world," in which the members "lay it all on the line about their lives, their music, their message, and their projects." The book's title is that of a movie they made. Without index or reference features.

S2-937 ML421 .S86 R9

Ruuth, Marianne. Triumph & tragedy : the true story of the Supremes : a biography / Marianne Ruuth. — Los Angeles : Holloway House, 1986. — 220 p. : ill. ISBN 0-87067-725-X.

Diana Ross established the popular female vocal trio in 1964; the Supremes achieved great success in the new soul style for Motown records (18 chart albums by 1976). This "no-holds-barred" story, in fictionalized style, concentrates on the thoughts and problems of the performers, saying nothing about their music. There is a discography (minimal data), but no index or other reference features.

S2-938 ML421 .S86 T9

Turner, Tony. All that glittered : my life with the Supremes / Tony Turner; with Barbara Aria. — New York : Dutton, 1990. — 308 p. : ill. ISBN 0-525-24910-9.

A gossipy narrative of the soul group, by one of their managers. It concentrates on their childhood situations, disputes, and extramusical activities, offering undocumented quotations and conversations. With a partly expansive index of names.

Review: LJ 10/1/90, 90.

S2-939   ML421 .T27 F6

Davis, Jerome. Talking Heads / Jerome Davis. — New York : Vintage, 1986. — xiii, 146 p. : ill. ISBN 0-394-74131-5.

A plain account of the rock group formed in the late 1970s, known for innovations and variety in their output. Undocumented episodes and conversations are the format. There is a record list, 1977–1985, giving personnel and comments. No index.

S2-940   ML421 .T42

Turner, Tony. Deliver us from temptation / Tony Turner; with Barbara Aria. — New York : Thunder's Mouth; distributed by Publishers Group West, Emeryville, Calif. — xi, 254 p. : ill. : 16 p. plates. ISBN 1-560-25-034-8.

A superficial narrative comprised of gossip, imaginary conversations, and anecdotes, centered on the nonmusical experiences of the Temptations. Much attention is paid to clothing, makeup, and use of drugs. Turner was one of the managers of the group. Without reference features.

Review: LJ 10/15/92, 70.

S2-941   ML421 .T43 W4

Williams, Otis. Temptations / Otis Williams; with Patricia Romanowski. — New York : Putnam, 1988. — 240 p. : ill. : 32 p. plates. ISBN 0-3991-3313-5.

The Temptations were a popular R & B group organized in 1960; Williams was one of the members. They had 46 chart songs in the next 15 years and won three Grammys. Unfortunately, Williams's story captures little of the excitement they generated. It is a casual memoir, undocumented, and heavy with talk and gossip. A discography gives record dates, but no other information. Without index.

S2-942   ML421 .T55

Greenspoon, Jimmy. One is the loneliest number : on the road and behind the scenes with the legendary rock band, Three Dog Night / Jimmy Greenspoon; with Mark Bego. — New York : Pharos Books, 1991. — xiii, 321 p. : ill. ISBN 0-8868-7647-8.

Three Dog Night was one of the most popular groups of the late 1960s and early 1970s. Greenspoon, a keyboardist in the original ensemble, here reveals unsavory details of his life in "sex, drugs, and rock & roll." In time he "lost it" through heroin addiction, then "kicked it" and got back to work. The idiom of the undocumented story is consistently vulgar. There is a record list, giving minimal data. No index.

S2-943   ML421 .T78 B7
Breland, Roger. In search of a lovely moment / Roger Breland. — Nashville : T. Nelson, 1990. — 171 p. : ill. : 8 p. plates. ISBN 0-8407-3014-4.
An account of the gospel group Truth.

S2-944   ML421 .V2
Considine, J. D. VanHalen! / J. D. Considine. — New York : Quill, 1985. — 159 p. : ill. ISBN 0-6880-4299-6.
Anecdotes and undocumented interviews bring forth the "wit and wisdom" of David Lee Roth and the other members of the rock group. A discography gives album contents only. Without index.

S2-945   ML421 .V36 K3
Kamin, Philip. VanHalen / Philip Kamin and Peter Goddard. — New York : Beaufort, 1984. — 128 p. : ill. ISBN 0-8253-0242-0.

S2-946   ML421 .Z98 D7
Draper, Robert. ZZ Top / Robert Draper. — New York : Ballantine, 1984. — 146 p. : ill. : 16 p. plates. ISBN 0-345-3223-04.
The "undisputed kings of American concert halls" are none other than the three-piece band from Texas known as ZZ Top. This book is made up of undocumented stories and talk, shedding no light on their music. With an informal discography (minimal data); without index.

S2-947   ML421 .Z98 F8
Frost, Deborah. ZZ Top : bad and worldwide / Deborah Frost and Bob Alford. — New York : Collier Books, 1985. — 120 p. : ill. : 8 p. plates. ISBN 0-0200-2950-0.
A picture book with commentary about the "sizzling hot Texas superrockers," popular from the mid-1970s. Their album *Eliminator* (1983) sold more than 8 million copies. Anecdotes and quotations appear, but there is nothing said about the music. No documentation or index.

S2-948   ML421 .Z98 N35
Nance, Scott. Recycling the blues : ZZ Top / Scott Nance. — Las Vegas : Pioneer Books, 1991. — 96 p. : ill. ISBN not given.
A personal view of "MTV's glamorboy outlaws," ZZ Top—"one of the most innovative, organic and hottest bands in the world," offering an "intimate exploration of the life and music of each band member,

revealing their motivations, influences, and plans." Interviews are the format here, bringing out anecdotes, pseudo-conversations, modest self-appraisals of the group's top albums, and reflections "on the environment and censorship." Without index or reference features.

ML422 : Conductors

S2-949   ML422 .A24
Durham, Lowell. Abravanel! / Lowell Durham. — Salt Lake City : University of Utah Press, 1989. — ix, 215 p. : ill. ISBN 0-87480-333-0.
A well-illustrated, but undocumented, account of a major international conductor who chose a career with the Utah Symphony Orchestra. In a 32-year reign, Maurice Abravanel (1903–) made an important ensemble out of what had been an ordinary community orchestra. When he retired in 1979, he was asked what he was going to do next, to which he replied he would be "studying music." With a discography of Utah Symphony recordings, 1952–1979 (minimal data), and various tables of works most performed, soloists, and so on. There is an expansive index.
Review: *Choice* 4/90, 1332.

S2-950   ML422 .B8 L5
Lindquist, Emory Kempton. Hagbard Brase : beloved music master / Emory Lindquist. — Lindsborg, Kans. : Bethany College Press, 1984. — xii, 154 p. : ill. ISBN 0-916030-06-7.
Brase (1877–1953) was organist and choral conductor at Bethany College in Kansas for more than a half century; he retired in 1946. His life story is presented in straightforward fashion, with extensive documentation and endnotes, emphasizing primary sources. There is an expansive index.

Note: Duke Ellington material is at S2-467–471.

S2-951   ML422 .E9
Horricks, Raymond. Svengali : an orchestra called Gill [*sic*] Evans. 1984.
A brief account of big-band arranger Gil Evans. See series note at S2-1118.

S2-952   ML422 .G65 C6
Collier, James Lincoln. Benny Goodman and the swing era / James Lincoln Collier. — New York : Oxford, 1989. — xii, 404 p. : ill. ISBN 0-19-505278-1.
An admirable, straightforward account of Goodman's life and career, well documented and free of make-believe. Musical comments are not numerous, but effective when they appear, offering viewpoints between

technical analysis and liner-note style; unfortunately, there are no musical examples to support these discussions. There is no discography or bibliography, but there are extensive endnotes and an expansive index. Reviews: *Choice* 2/90, 959; LJ 9/15/89.

S2-953   ML422 .G65 C7
Crowther, Bruce. Benny Goodman / Bruce Crowther. — London : Apollo, 1988. — 128 p. : ill. : 8 p. plates. (Jazz masters, 13) ISBN 0-9488-2004-7.
A straightforward, undocumented life story, with a selective discography covering "representative listening" from all periods of Goodman's career. Without index.

S2-954   ML422 .G65 F4
Firestone, Ross. Swing, swing, swing : the life & times of Benny Goodman / Ross Firestone. — New York : Norton, 1992. — 522 p. : ill. : with one compact disc. ISBN 0-3930-3371-6.
A straightforward, detailed life story of Goodman, based on extensive sources (which are listed, but not directly cited). It is entirely a personal tale, with no musical considerations. Dialogues of uncertain authenticity appear, but not too often. With an expansive index, but without other reference features. Firestone appears to have been unaware of Collier's biography, which covers the same ground more thoroughly (see S2-952).
Reviews: *Choice* 6/93, 1635; LJ 1/93, 116.

S2-955   ML422 .G65 K2
Kappler, Frank K. Benny Goodman. 1979.
See series note at S2-1114.

S2-956   ML422 .G65 K5
Klussmeier, Gerhard. Benny Goodman und Deutschland / Gerhard Klussmeier. — Frankfurt am Main : H. A. Eisenbletter & B. S. M. Naumann, 1989. — 166 p. : ill. ISBN 3-9273-5503-8.
In German. Of interest for its extensive photocopies of newspaper advertising and concert programs, as well as photographs of the Goodman band in Germany. Without index.

S2-957   ML422 .K35 A69
Arganian, Lillian. Stan Kenton : the man and his music / Lillian Arganian. — East Lansing, Mich. : Artistry, 1989. — xii, 207 p. : ill. ISBN 0-9621116-0-0.
Consists of 20 interviews by Arganian, with friends and associates of the distinguished bandleader/pianist/arranger (1911–1979). Among the persons who recall and admire him are Pete Rugolo, June Christy, Shelly

Manne, and Shorty Rogers. Their memories are primarily on the personal level, with few direct comments on Kenton's music (e.g., Q: "What do you feel was his biggest contribution to music?" A: "You know you're asking for an awful lot there. I can't wrap up anything like that"). Without index or reference features.

S2-958   ML422 .M49
Meyer, Raymond. Backwoods jazz in the twenties / Raymond F. "Peg" Meyer; ed. with an introduction by Frank Nickell. — Cape Girardeau, Mo. : Center for Regional History and Cultural Heritage, Southeast Missouri State University, 1989. — xi, 158 p. : ill. ISBN 0-9344-2619-8. (Alternative classification: ML48.)

Meyer (1903–) was a school bandmaster and musical instrument salesman in southern Illinois and southeast Missouri, with a career somewhat similar to that of the Broadway "music man." He played on riverboats, and he teamed with Jess Stacy. He also led early jazz groups, such as the Melody Kings and the Agony Four. His story is made up of undocumented tales and conversations, but they are unusual; for example, his dance bands had to avoid playing "slow blues or drag" that might "encourage grinds and vulgar exhibitions," and stop watches would be used to check the tempo of the music to insure that the fox-trot would not vary from 70 beats per minute. Without index.

S2-959   ML422 .M5 B9
Butcher, Geoffrey. Next to a letter from home : Glenn Miller's wartime band / Geoffrey Butcher. — Edinburgh, Scotland : Mainstream, 1986. — xvi, 360 p. : ill. : 8 p. plates. ISBN 1-8515-8025-5.

The tale of Miller's Army Air Force Band, with a complete discography and chronology of appearances. There is no documentation. With a nonexpansive index. The study is superseded by Polic (S2-1139).

S2-960   ML422 .P27 A3
Paschedag, Theodore. The music came first : the memoirs of Theodore Paschedag; as told to Thomas J. Hatton. — Carbondale : Southern Illinois University Press, 1988. — ix, 98 p. : ill. : 16 p. plates. ISBN 0-8093-1471-1.

The autobiography of a music instrument salesman and school band director who "came to town [West Frankfort, Illinois] to sell a children's band for a month and stayed on for over fifty years." Paschedag (1905–) was a "Music Man" in real life; he acquired an appreciative following, including Hatton, who interviewed him and edited these folksy memoirs. There are some interesting anecdotes, indicative of the style of life in the American countryside of the time. Without index or any other documentation.

S2-961   ML422 .P91 A3
Previn, André. No minor chords : my days in Hollywood / André Previn. — New York : Doubleday, 1991. — x, 148 p. : ill. ISBN 0-385-41341-6.

A delightful account of a precocious musician working as a film composer, arranger, and conductor from 1948 to 1964. Previn (1929–) is best known today as a symphony conductor, but he has had a brilliant career in pop music and jazz as well. His tour of duty in the film studies is recounted here with humor and irony (and undocumented quotes and conversations, it must be said), and with entertaining profiles of the beautiful people who surrounded him: Louis B. Mayer, Jascha Heifetz (who is portrayed as a cruel, eccentric tightwad), Vincente Minnelli, Alan Jay Lerner, Billy Wilder, and Ava Gardner (who made him an offer he could not understand). Previn won four Oscars and might have stayed on in Hollywood indefinitely, but he was called to a new phase of "worry and self doubt," of being "frightened by the glory of the music I have to work with, and plagued by personal inadequacies"—in contrast to an easy decade in California, "entertaining and educational and highly paid." It is good that he captured some of the entertainment of it in this happy volume. Without index.

S2-962   ML422 .S76 S6
Smith, William Ander. The mystery of Leopold Stokowski / William Ander Smith; foreword by Donald R. Vroon. — Rutherford, N.J. : Fairleigh Dickinson University Press, 1990. — 289 p. : ill. ISBN 0-8386-3362-5.

The Polish-American conductor Stokowski (1882–1977) was renowned for his development of the Philadelphia Orchestra and for his flamboyant public persona. It is the "enigmas and paradoxes of the man and the musician" that are the focus of Smith's book, "hence the word mystery used in the title." The mystery is often explained mysteriously, as in the author's conviction that Stokowski's "paranormal powers" enabled him to produce the wondrous orchestral sounds of Philadelphia and in other ensembles. (Were such powers, one may wonder, also the secret weapons of George Szell in Cleveland and Georg Solti in Chicago?) There is further psychic reflection in the study of Stokowski's personal life, where the author finds a "father-figure role model within the imagined reality of the family romance." Along with these speculations, there are interesting comments on the maestro as a musician, drawn from many of his associates. The whole work is thoroughly documented with endnotes. A detailed discography covering 1917–1977 gives attention to reissues and includes useful commentaries. There is a bibliography of about 250 items and an expansive index.

S2-963   ML422 .T46 S3
Schabas, Ezra. Theodore Thomas : America's conductor and builder
of orchestras, 1835–1905 / Ezra Schabas; foreword by Valerie Solti. —
Urbana : University of Illinois Press, 1989. — xvi, 308 p. : ill. : 11 p.
plates. ISBN 0-252-01610-6.

Thomas was "the most celebrated conductor of the 1880s and 90s"; he
conducted the New York Philharmonic for 13 years, then organized and
directed the Chicago Symphony Orchestra. Less than a month before his
death, he saw the dedication of Orchestra Hall, concluding a successful
drive he had headed. This is a well-crafted, documented biography of a
seminal figure. With a bibliography of about 300 entries and a partly expansive index.
Reviews: AM 1990, 487; *Choice* 11/89, 498.

S2-964   ML422 .T67 H65
Horowitz, Joseph. Understanding Toscanini : how he became an
American culture-god and helped create a new audience for old music /
Joseph Horowitz. — New York : Knopf, 1987. — x, 492 p. : ill. : 24 p.
plates. ISBN 0-394-52918-9.

The premise of this study is that the great Arturo Toscanini was in
some respects a construct of the music industry—a star created by radio
and recording executives, notably David Sarnoff of NBC. A Toscanini
"cult" was said to result from all this attention, though presumably the
conductor's enormous talents had a bearing on his success and popularity. It is argued that Toscanini's version of the standard repertoire was
promoted with such vigor by NBC and RCA Victor that it became the
accepted pattern in the United States: a repertoire based on eighteenth-
and nineteenth-century European classics. Another way of looking at the
matter is that American (and indeed European) notions of the symphonic
repertoire spread out slowly through the early twentieth century, until the
arrival of the LP record accelerated the process. However that may be,
Horowitz has given food for thought and placed it in a scholarly context.
He offers a kaleidoscope of views about the maestro, a fine account of
concert life in the previous and present centuries, and an assessment of
the societal impact of radio and the ever-improving record players. With
endnotes and an expansive index.
Reviews: AM 1990, 366; *Choice* 6/87, 1562; LJ 12/86, 102.

S2-965   ML422 .Z56 C8
Cummins, Paul F. Dachau song / Paul F. Cummins. — New York : P.
Lang, 1992. — xiii, 308 p. : ill. ISBN 0-8204-1729-7.

Conductor Herbert Zipper (1904–), an Austrian Jew who was incar-
cerated by the Nazis at Dachau and Buchenwald, experienced terror and
the ugliness of humankind at its worst. He had just begun a conducting

career, directing the Dusseldorf orchestra, when the Nazis invaded (1938) and imprisoned him for 10 months. His family managed to secure his freedom, and he gained the appointment as director of the Manila Symphony. There he encountered the Pacific War and was for a time imprisoned by the Japanese; afterward he lived through the battles in the Philippines. When peace came he moved to the United States, conducting and teaching, and did further work in the Far East. The story is told here in a sober style, with endnotes, bibliography, and a nonexpansive index.

ML423 : Writers, Critics

S2-966   ML423 .F26 A3
Feather, Leonard. The jazz years : earwitness to an era / Leonard Feather. — New York : Quartet, 1986. — 310 p. : ill. : 16 p. plates. ISBN 0-7043-25799.
Feather has been writing about jazz since 1934, producing many acclaimed volumes and innumerable articles and reviews. This book is a memoir in the form of an essay collection. It brings out several themes that have energized Feather, such as the ugliness of racism and sexism. The actual events of his own interesting life, as a pianist, composer, and songwriter, are muted.
Reviews: AM 1989, 86; *Choice* 6/87, 1562.

S2-967   ML423 .G69 K6
Kodish, Debora. Good friends and bad enemies : Robert Winslow Gordon and the study of American folksong / Debora Kodish. — Urbana : University of Illinois Press, 1986. — xiii, 263 p. : ill. : 16 p. plates. ISBN 0-252-01251-8.
Gordon (1888–1961) was the first director (1928–1932) of the Archive of Folk Song at the Library of Congress, an ethnologist who made some 900 field recordings, one who did much to bring an interest in folk song to the general public. He left the Library of Congress under unhappy circumstances and had a disappointing career thereafter. He was "rehabilitated" by the Library via a commemorative recording in 1978. This biography is a straightforward documented narration, interspersed with interesting correspondence (there are 3,785 numbered letters in the Gordon collection at LC). With a bibliography of about 400 primary and secondary sources and an expansive index.
Reviews: AM 1988, 333; *Choice* 5/87, 1409.

S2-968   ML423 .L3 S5
Shapiro, Doris. We danced all night : my life behind the scenes with Alan Jay Lerner / Doris Shapiro. — New York : Morrow, 1990. — 245 p. : ill. ISBN 0-688-08937-2.

"Both a fascinating behind-the-scenes account of show business history and an intensely moving personal story of obsession and redemption" told by a woman who was Lerner's assistant for 14 years. Her story is a chain of remembered conversations, soap-opera incidents in hospitals, and melodramatic interpretations of Lerner's love life. With no documentation; with an expansive index.

S2-969   ML423 .M2
Browning, Norma Lee. Joe Maddy of Interlochen : profile of a legend / Norma Lee Browning. — Chicago : Contemporary Books, 1992. — xx, 217 p. ISBN 0-8092-3907-8.
Maddy (1891–1966) played in the Minneapolis Symphony Orchestra, then went into public school music supervision. He and T. P. Giddings established the National Music Camp at Interlochen, Michigan.

S2-970   ML423 .S498 P5
Pescatello, Ann M. Charles Seeger : a life in American music / Ann M. Pescatello. — Pittsburgh : University of Pittsburgh Press, 1992. — xii, 346 p. : ill. ISBN 0-8229-3713-1.
Henry Cowell, one of his students, said that Seeger (1886–1979) was the "greatest musical explorer in intellectual fields which America has produced." The musicologist (and "quintessential nineteenth-century New England gentleman") was rightly acclaimed for "the collectivity of all his contributions to the American musical scene and to American society." Among his achievements was the offering of the first U.S. university course in musicology, at Berkeley in 1913–1914. He was assistant director of the Federal Music Project and music director for the Pan-American Union. He was husband of composer Ruth Crawford and father of Pete Seeger. This fine book is nearly an autobiography, drawing on numerous lengthy quotes from Seeger (all documented in endnotes); Pescatello knew him well as a student and friend. With a bibliography of about 150 of Seeger's writings and compositions, and 250 writings about him; with a nonexpansive index.
Reviews: *Choice* 3/93, 1162; LJ 10/15/92, 69.

S2-971   ML423 .S57 A3
Slonimsky, Nicolas. Perfect pitch : a life story / Nicolas Slonimsky. — New York : Oxford, 1988. — 263 p. : ill. : 16 p. plates. ISBN 0-19-315155-3.
A wonderful memoir by one of music's international treasures. Russian-born Slonimsky (1894–1995) mastered English and has become best known today as an author of reference books (most notably *Music since 1900* [LOAM A-84] and recent editions of *Baker's Biographical Dictionary*). But his prodigious musical gifts led him through an earlier var-

ied career of conducting, composing, and playing the piano. Although he never achieved the recognition that was bestowed on persons he knew and worked with, such as Serge Koussevitzky or Henry Cowell, he was universally respected by the musical community. The reader of this book will delight in the Slonimsky wit, his anecdotal flair, his caustic appraisals of certain colleagues (Koussevitzky above all), and the blend of humility and joy in his own accomplishments. With a partly expansive index.

Reviews: AM 1989, 101; *Choice* 10/88, 327; LJ 3/15/88, 53.

ML424 : Instrument Makers

S2-972   ML424 .D29 S3

Schmidt, Paul William. Acquired of the angels : the lives and works of master guitar makers John D'Angelico and James L. D'Aquisto / Paul William Schmidt. — Metuchen, N.J. : Scarecrow, 1991. — vi, 103 p. : ill. ISBN 0-8108-22399.

The story of two Italian-American instrument makers, John D'Angelico (1905–1964) and his successor James D'Aquisto (1935–). D'Angelico set up shop in New York City, making string instruments, and in the 1930s achieved renown for his guitars. Fine photographs of instruments by both men are the highlights of the volume, which also gives some biographical details and comments (not documented) by the craftsmen and by users of their guitars. Actual specifications of the instruments are not given. With pages from the firm's ledger books and an expansive index.

S2-973   ML424 .S54 H6

Holden, Dorothy J. Life and work of Ernest M. Skinner / Dorothy J. Holden. — Richmond, Va. : Organ Historical Society, 1985. — 300 p. : ill. : 18 p. plates. ISBN 0-913499-005.

Skinner (1866–1960) was certainly a unique prodigy, one whose creativity took the form of building organs in childhood (his first attempt at age 12). His father was an opera impresario, but he himself was drawn to the mechanical aspects of music. In time he became recognized as a master, with instruments in such venues as Symphony Hall in Boston and the National Cathedral in Washington. His firm merged with Aeolian to form the Aeolian Skinner Co. Holden's account is scholarly, with extensive notes and a bibliography of some 500 items. An appendix gives the specifications of 24 instruments. With a nonexpansive index.

S2-974   ML424 .S76 R4

Ratcliffe, Ronald V. Steinway / Ronald V. Ratcliffe; foreword by Henry Z. Steinway. — San Francisco : Chronicle Books, 1989. — 204 p. : ill. ISBN 0-87701-592-9.

A valuable, attractive volume that chronicles the Steinway family and firm (1853–), and illustrates their products with about 200 superb photographs (a third of them in color). The historical chapters are thorough and well documented. A technical section on piano manufacture is greatly detailed and benefits from outstanding photographs by Margaret Bourke-White. A useful discussion compares the American and German pianos. Steinway artists are listed and shown at the keyboard. Many of the unique "art case" instruments, such as that in the White House, are described and depicted. A list of Steinway patents appears in an appendix. With an expansive index.

Review: AM 1992, 100.

ML429 : Music Industry Figures: Publishers, Executives, Disc Jockeys, etc.

S2-975   ML429 .D47 A3

DesBarres, Pamela. Take another little piece of my heart : a groupie grows up / Pamela DesBarres. — New York : Morrow, 1992. — 304 p. : ill. ISBN 0-688-091-149-0.

This is a sequel to S2-976, which is blurbed here as "an underground classic." DesBarres goes on to a "postmodern marriage and motherhood"—involving work as an actress and cosmetic saleswoman, and recourse to "spiritual healing." The tale is cast in fictionalized format, with conversations and so forth, and has no classic characteristics, underground or above. With an expansive index.

S2-976   ML429 .D86 A3

DesBarres, Pamela. I'm with the band : confessions of a groupie / Pamela DesBarres. — New York : Morrow, 1987. — 304 p. : ill. : 32 p. plates. ISBN 0-688-06602-X.

An "uncannily sweet and innocent" former singer with the GTOs ("the Frank Zappa masterminded girl group") and dedicated camp follower, DesBarres proudly details her one-night stands with a multitude of rock stars. Among the luminaries she vividly remembers are Waylon Jennings, Jim Morrison, and Mick Jagger. Anecdotes and quoted conversations are plentiful. Without index or reference features. See also S2-975.

S2-977   ML429 .E72 W3

Wade, Dorothy. Music man : Ahmet Ertegun, Atlantic Records, and the triumph of rock 'n' roll / Dorothy Wade and Justine Picardie. — New York : Norton, 1990. — 303 p. : ill. : 10 p. plates. ISBN 0-393-02635-3.

Ertegun was one of the founders in 1947 of Atlantic, a major independent label that featured such stars as Ray Charles, John Coltrane,

Aretha Franklin, and the Rolling Stones. Since the Atlantic saga has been dealt with by earlier writers, the only relatively fresh information here is about the payola scandals and the influx of organized crime into the music business. Unfortunately the book is undocumented, and the style is casual (anecdotes and quoted conversations). With a nonexpansive index.

Reviews: *Choice* 9/90, 129; LJ 3/15/90, 92.

S2-978   ML429 .F75 J3

Jackson, John A. Big beat heat : Alan Freed and the early years of rock & roll / John A. Jackson. — New York : Schirmer, 1991. — xiv, 400 p. : ill. : 32 p. plates. ISBN 0-02-871155-6.

A casual but intriguing narration of the rise and fall of disc jockey/rock promoter Freed, with mostly documented stories and conversations. The payola chapter is most informative (Freed was convicted of accepting bribes, and though he received a suspended sentence his career came to an end). "Rock 'n' roll" was the name he gave to his New York radio show (in around 1954), rather than to the music he played, which was "blues and rhythm." An excellent bibliography includes about 400 books and articles, with interviews by Jackson, plus court documents and publications of Congress. With a filmography and an expansive index.

Review: *Choice* 1/92, 756.

S2-978a   ML429 .G69 A3

Graham, Bill. Bill Graham presents : my life inside rock and out / Bill Graham and Robert Greenfield. — New York : Doubleday, 1992. — 568 p. : ill. : 24 p. plates. ISBN 0-385-24077-5.

Berlin-born Graham, originally Wolfgang Grajonca (1931–1991), had a remarkable life: he was a Holocaust refugee to America, a Korean War hero, and eventually a rock impresario based in San Francisco. He launched the careers of Janis Joplin, Otis Redding, Jefferson Airplane, and the Grateful Dead, and "created the business of rock as it exists today." About 100 persons contributed observations about him in this book, offering interesting perspectives. With a partly expansive index.

S2-979   ML429 .M8 A3

Morrow, Cousin Bruce. Cousin Brucie! : my life in rock 'n' roll radio / Cousin Bruce Morrow and Laura Baudo; introduction by Neil Sedaka. — New York : Beech Tree Books, 1987. — 255 p. : ill. : 32 p. plates. ISBN 0-6880-6615-1.

Bruce Morrow joined WABC in New York in 1961, and over the next 13 years with the station he became "granddaddy of rock radio" and WABC became the highest rated station in American history. His memoir is a casual, name-dropping tale without documentation. Long fictional dialogues abound, separated by anecdotes. Without index.

S2-980   ML429 .P33 V4
Vellenga, Dirk. Elvis and the colonel / Dirk Vellenga; with Mick Farren. — New York : Delacorte, 1988. — x, 278 p. : ill. : 16 p. plates. ISBN 0-385-29521-9.
"The man behind Elvis" was his agent Tom Parker (1909–), who called himself "Colonel." In this book he stands revealed as Andreas van Kuijik, an illegal alien from the Netherlands, and is accused of making poor career decisions that may indeed have "stifled and underutilized" Presley's talents. For example, Presley "never performed outside the U.S. because of Parker's fear of having his [own] citizenless status discovered." It is a good story, although it lacks documentation to support Vellenga's investigative research. There is an out-of-place discography of Presley records and a nonexpansive index.
Review: LJ 10/1/88, 89.

S2-981   ML429 .P92 H66
Hirsch, Foster. Harold Prince and the American musical theatre / Foster Hirsch; forewords by Harold Prince and Stephen Sondheim. — Cambridge, England : Cambridge University Press, 1989. — xvii, 187 p. : ill. ISBN 0-521-33314-8.
Stage director Prince (1928–) is best known for his collaborations with Stephen Sondheim, but he has many other Broadway credits, from *Pajama Game* (1954) to *Phantom of the Opera* (1986). He has also directed at the Vienna State Opera, the Chicago Lyric Opera, and the Metropolitan Opera, among others. This book presents a well-documented (chapter endnotes) account of his career, in almost act-by-act studies of his productions. Many apt illustrations and comments from persons who worked with him supplement the interesting text. With an expansive index. See also S2-1294.

S2-982   ML429 .R4 A31
Reig, Teddy. Reminiscing in tempo : the life and times of a jazz hustler / Teddy Reig; with Edward M. Berger. — Metuchen, N.J. : Scarecrow, 1990. — xv, 204 p. : ill. (Studies in jazz, 10) ISBN 0-8108-2326-8.
Reign (1918–1984) was a record producer for the Savoy label and others, waxing important sides by Erroll Garner, Don Byas, Miles Davis, Milt Jackson, Charlie Parker, and other jazz artists. Along with his casual memoir, there is a discography of his work and a number of informal reflections about him by various associates.
Review: *Choice* 3/91, 1146.

S2-983   ML429 .R6
Gart, Galen. Duke/Peacock Records : an illustrated history with discography / Galen Gart and Roy C. Ames. — Milford, N.H. : Big Nickel, 1990. — iv, 234 p. : ill. ISBN 0-936433-12-4.
A biography of Don D. Robey (1903–1975), "the first successful black

entrepreneur to emerge in the music business after World War II." Working in Houston, primarily with his Duke and Peacock labels and a booking agency, he helped to establish the careers of Bobby Bland, B. B. King, and other exponents of blues, gospel, and soul. This account is straightforward, undocumented, and sparked by the inclusion of photographs that depict record labels and performers. Label lists for Duke, Peacock, Back Beat, Song Bird, Sure Shot, ABC-Peacock, and Giggles are given; and there are data from logbooks and session dates. With a nonexpansive index.

S2-984   ML429 .S64 R5
Ribowsky, Mark. He's a rebel : the truth about Phil Spector, rock and roll's legendary madman / Mark Ribowsky. — New York : Dutton, 1989. — viii, 339 p. ISBN 0-525-24727-0.

Spector (1940–), rock guitarist, songwriter, and ultimately record producer, is portrayed here as an "extraordinary eccentric, a brilliant musical talent, a wizard with a song." His life, which found him living in a huge California estate behind high walls by the time he was 30, was one of "drugs, dreams-come-true and destruction." He emerged from seclusion in time to produce the sensational three-LP *Concert for Bangladesh* in 1971. Ribowsky's biography is shaped of anecdotes and conversations, without identified sources. There is a discography, with dates, labels, and indicators of chart status; and a nonexpansive index.

S2-985   ML429 .Z44 Z4
Zelzer, Sarah Schectman. Impresario : the Zelzer era, 1930–1990 / Sarah Schectman Zelzer; with Phyllis Dreazen; introduction by Daniel Barenboim. — Chicago : Academy Chicago Publishers, 1990. — 300 p. : ill. ISBN 0-89733-351-9.

For six decades the "czar of Chicago's performing arts world," Harry Zelzer (1897–1979) established and operated the Allied Arts Corporation—the city's major booking agency for classical and popular performers. His wife's memoir brings forward hundreds of artists and subjects them to her definite opinions: occasionally negative (Grace Moore, a snob; Judy Garland, her own worst enemy) but mostly adulatory. There is a useful list of all the performers presented by Allied Arts from 1937 to 1977, by category, with dates. With a nonexpansive index.

ML461–1311 : MUSICAL INSTRUMENTS AND ENSEMBLES

ML461–476 : Folk Instruments; Other American Instruments

S2-986   ML461 .S64
Smith, L. Allen. A catalogue of pre-revival Appalachian dulcimers /

L. Allen Smith; foreword by Jean Ritchie. — Columbia : University of Missouri Press, 1983. — 128 p. ISBN 0-8262-0376-0.

A fine, illustrated inventory of instruments made before 1940. Specifications are given, along with detailed descriptions and commentaries. With a list of dulcimer makers, a bibliography of about 150 items, and a partly expansive index.

S2-987   ML476 .I79

Irwin, John Rice. Musical instruments of the southern Appalachian mountains / John Rice Irwin. — 2nd ed. — Exton, Pa. : Schiffer, 1983. — 104 p. : ill. ISBN 0-9168-3888-2.

1st ed., 1979.

An illustrated handbook of instruments, with stories of their makers and players. Dulcimers, fiddles, banjos, and mouth bows are shown in many varieties (such as the cigar box fiddle from the depression years, said to have a "remarkably good tone in relation to its appearance" and several hubcap banjos, made from scrap materials). There also are sweet potatoes, cowbells, fifes, mandolins, and so forth. With an interesting introductory section on "the people and their music," and an index of names.

S2-988   ML476 .L5

Libin, Laurence. American musical instruments in the Metropolitan Museum of Art / Laurence Libin; foreword by Philippe de Montebello; preface by Henry Steinway. — New York : Metropolitan Museum and W. W. Norton, 1985. — 224 p. : ill. : 18 p. color plates. ISBN 0-3930-2277-3.

A picture book of instruments, arranged by category (winds, strings, etc.), giving specifications and descriptive comments. With a bibliography of about 125 entries and an expansive index of names, instruments, and topics.

Reviews: *Choice* 5/86, 1400; LJ 3/1/86, 97.

ML557–561 : Organ

See also S2-992

S2-989   ML557 .L16

Landon, John W. Behold the mighty Wurlitzer : the history of the theatre pipe organ / John W. Landon; preface by Reginald Foort. — Westport, Conn. : Greenwood, 1983. — xv, 231 p. : ill. ISBN 0-313-23827-8.

Theater organs were used to accompany silent films from around 1905 to the emergence of talkies in the late 1920s. The instruments used varied greatly, but were based on the electric action pipe organ invented by Robert Hope-Jones, demonstrated in 1886. Acquiring the Hope-Jones patents, the Rudolph Wurlitzer Company of North Tonawanda, New York, became dominant in the theater organ field. After two decades of neglect, the theater organ was the subject of revived interest in the 1950s, with many old instruments salvaged and rebuilt for use in concerts and silent film revivals. Landon's scholarly narrative expands on these historical facts and discusses elements of manufacture. He takes up the place of the theater organ on radio and recording. Biographical notes are given for about 100 organists, including the popular Don Baker, Jesse Crawford and Helen Crawford, Al Melgard (of the Chicago Stadium), Rosa Rio, and Lew White. A valuable world inventory of instruments, arranged by country and state, gives installation data and specifications, with the names of organists; however, the list is curiously lacking entries for American states other than Alaska and Hawaii. With a discussion of sources, a bibliography of about 150 items, and a partly expansive index.

Reviews: AM 1987, 225; *Choice* 5/84, 1316.

S2-989a   ML561 .C34
Callahan, Charles. The American classic organ : a history in letters / Charles Callahan. — Richmond, Va. : Organ Historical Society, 1990. — xxv, 532 p. : ill. ISBN 0-913499-05-6.

An annotated, indexed gathering of 312 letters by and to organ builders and organists, such as Ernest Skinner, Henry Willis, Carl Weinrich, E. Power Biggs, Alexander Schreiner, and G. Donald Harrison (president of Aeolian-Skinner). In addition there is a valuable collection of specifications for important organs in the United Kingdom and United States, including the instruments at the Anglican Cathedral, Liverpool; St. Paul's, London; Princeton University Chapel; Trinity College Chapel, Hartford, Conn.; St. John's Chapel, Groton, Mass.; Washington Cathedral; Symphony Hall, Boston; and Kresge Auditorium, Cambridge, Mass.

S2-990   ML561 .J86
Junchen, David L. Encyclopedia of the American theatre organ / David L. Junchen; foreword by Q. David Bowers. — Pasadena, Calif. : Showcase Publications, 1985. — 2 vols. : ill. ISBN 0-917800-02-8.

An enthusiastic, monumental tribute to the instrument that was pervasive in theaters and stadiums in the 1920s, with about 1,800 illustrations. The work is organized by firm, presenting photos, blueprints, advertisements, and other documents from 90 organ building enterprises. For each builder there is an "opus list," showing locations and specifications for each organ produced. Major organists are identified. The whole is well unified through an index in volume 2, covering persons, firms, topics, products, and theaters. There is also a useful glossary.

Reviews: AM 1987, 321; ARBA 1987, #1243.

S2-990a   ML561 .095 M7

Owen, Barbara. The Mormon Tabernacle organ: an American classic / Barbara Owen. — Salt Lake City, Utah : Church of Latter Day Saints, 1990. — xii, 116 p. : ill. ISBN 1-55517-054-4.

A history of all the organs in the Tabernacle, emphasizing the present Aeolian-Skinner instrument, installed in 1948. Useful reference features include a list of the organists, a list of the stops on the present organ, and a selective discography. There are illustrations of the pipes, and of stages in construction. With a bibliography of 13 items and an expansive index.

ML651 : Harpsichord

S2-991   ML651 .P3

Palmer, Larry. Harpsichord in America : a twentieth-century revival / Larry Palmer. — Bloomington : Indiana University Press, 1989. — xiv, 202 p. : ill. ISBN 0-253-32710-5.

This is an intriguing "quixotic tale of the return to prominence of an instrument discarded by time, forgotten by the general public"—a revival accomplished by "an intrepid band of dreamers . . . some frankly quite mad." Among the intrepids was Arnold Dolmetsch, nineteenth-century pioneer in authentic performance practice of early music and maker of period keyboard instruments. Another was the first modern virtuoso of the harpsichord, Wanda Landowska. John Challis became the "Dolmetsch of the Middle-West"): the principal American harpsichord builder. Other stellar names include performers Sylvia Marlowe, Ralph Kirkpatrick, and Fernando Valenti; and builders/restorers Frank Hubbard and William Dowd. Palmer tells their story in a pleasing way, letting it flow from their own (documented) quotations and conversations. With a bibliography of about 200 titles and a partly expansive index.

Reviews: AM 1991, 422; *Choice* 9/89, 141; LJ 4/15/89, 77.

ML661–747 : Piano

S2-991a   ML661 .R64

Roell, Craig H. The piano in America, 1890–1940 / Craig H. Roell. — Chapel Hill : University of North Carolina Press, 1989. — xix, 396 p. : ill. ISBN 0-8078-1802-X.

A history of the piano industry, with ancillary discussion of the place of the instrument in American culture. Baldwin and Steinway get the most attention. Production and sales figures are given, and other data of interest, such as the number of musicians and music teachers in the United States from 1900–1940. With many quaint illustrations, extensive endnotes, and an expansive index.

Reviews: *Choice* 7-8/89, 1850; AM 1992, 100.

S2-992   ML711 .C6
Clark, J. Bunker. The dawning of American keyboard music / J. Bunker Clark. — Westport, Conn. : Greenwood, 1988. — xxii, 411 p. (Contributions to the study of music and dance, 12) ISBN 0-313-25581-4.
A scholarly account of piano and organ publications by Americans, beginning with the first such piece to appear, in 1787. Bibliographical and musical details are given for each item, including library locations and comparisons of editions. For many there are musical extracts as well. Method books are listed. Most of the composers are little known today (among the most prolific were Anthony Heinrich and Charles Thibault), but Benjamin Carr and James Hewitt are two of some prominence. Alexander Reinagle is another more familiar composer; his *Philadelphia Sonatas* (1786–1794) are outstanding for their period. Practically all the music seems to be derivative and lacking virtuosic elements; much of it consists of arrangements and medleys of popular songs. With footnotes, a bibliography of about 150 titles (covering modern editions and reprints), a title index, name index, and nonexpansive subject index.
Reviews: AM 1990, 116; *Choice* 4/89, 1342.

S2-992a   ML747 .S54
Silvester, Peter J. A left hand like God : a history of boogie-woogie piano / Peter J. Silvester; with a special contribution from Denis Harbinson. — London : Quartet Books, 1988; reprint, New York : Da Capo, 1989. — 324 p. : ill. : 16 p. plates. ISBN 0-306-80359-3 (U.S.).
The title of this book refers to William Turk, as described by Eubie Blake; Turk was one of the pioneers of the boogie-woogie piano style. Boogie was highly popular in the 1920s, its vogue lasting through the 1940s. Silvester traces its humble roots to barrelhouse pianists in the deep South and carries the story to New York nightclubs. Principal artists such as Albert Ammons, Meade Lux Lewis, Pinetop Smith, and Pete Johnson get justified attention, and lesser-known men such as Charles "Cow Cow" Davenport, Clarence Lofton, Eurreal Montgomery, Joe Turner, Jimmy Yancey, and Bob Zurke are amply treated. The approach is straightforward, with chapter endnotes. There is a selective discography and an expansive index.

ML800–1015 : Violin; Other Stringed Instruments

S2-993   ML800 .T5
Thomson, Ryan J. The fiddler's almanac / Ryan J. Thomson. — Newmarket, N.H. : Captain Fiddle Publications, 1985. — vi, 138 p. : ill. ISBN 0-931877-00-8.
A useful, eclectic volume of material about the fiddle and its players, in the modern folk music context. The fiddle is in fact a violin, and the

fiddler a violinist, so what makes the difference is the music and the manner of performing it. Thomson gives advice on buying and learning, and information about contests and organizations; lists early recordings by American fiddlers; and presents a directory of sources that includes schools, camps, and suppliers. With a glossary and an index of personal names and groups.

Reviews: AM 1988, 326; *Choice* 10/85, 307; LJ 7/85, 60.

S2-994   ML1015 .A9 B6

Blackley, Becky. The autoharp book / Becky Blackley. — Brisbane, Calif. : i.a.d. Publications, 1983. — 256 p. : ill. ISBN 0-912827-01-7.

This history of autoharp design and manufacture also traces the development of its tablature. Autoharp production and marketing by C. F. Zimmermann, the Phonoharp Company, and Oscar-Schmidt-International are chronicled. There is a short chapter on well-known performers and a look at related instruments. The text is well illustrated throughout. Primary sources are heavily used and well cited. The bibliography includes over 100 articles, periodicals, and monographs. There is a separate list of roughly 100 instruction books and songbooks. A discography lists over 200 albums and cassettes featuring the autoharp. There are also short listings of festivals, schools, museums, etc. The nonexpansive subject index is followed by an index to discussions of autoharps by make and model.

Becky Blackley is the editor of the *Autoharpoholic* magazine and has contributed to *Frets* and *Bluegrass Breakdown* [—D. P.].

S2-995   ML1015 .B3 L5

Linn, Karen. That half-barbaric twang : the banjo in American popular culture / Karen Linn. — Urbana : University of Illinois Press, 1991. — xii, 185 p. : ill. ISBN 0-252-01780-3.

An absorbing history of the banjo in its "changing and conflicting images," from pre–Civil War times (the "southern black banjo") through modernization in the 1920s and the "southern white banjo" that followed. A scholarly presentation, with chapter notes, a 300-item bibliography, and an expansive index.

Review: *Choice* 2/92, 905.

S2-996   ML1015 .G9 W5

Wheeler, Tom. American guitars : an illustrated history / Tom Wheeler; foreword by Les Paul. — Rev. ed. — New York : HarperCollins, 1992. — xiv, 370 p. : ill. ISBN 0-06-273154-8.

1st ed., 1982 (LOAM Suppl. A-62).

A dictionary of guitar-making firms and of performers, especially useful for details about the instruments. With an expansive index of personal and guitar names.

S2-997 ML1015 .R3

Ring the banjar : the banjo in American folklore to factory. — Cambridge : Massachusetts Institute of Technology Museum, 1984. — 112 p. : ill. ISBN not given.

An exhibition catalog for a 1984 event at the M.I.T. museum, with 37 color plates and extensive notes. There are also two essays, one on the banjo in history, the other on Boston's banjo makers.

ML1035 : Drum

S2-998 035 .V6

Vennum, Thomas, Jr. The Ojibwa dance drum : its history and construction / Thomas Vennum, Jr.; foreword by J. Richard Haefer. — Washington : Smithsonian Institution Press, 1982. — 320 p. : ill. : with film, The drummaker. (Smithsonian folklife studies, 2) ISBN 0-8747-4941-7.

The Ojibwa—usually identified as the Chippewa—are dispersed over the western Great Lakes area. When the fur trade that sustained them began to vanish in the mid-nineteenth century, the Ojibwa gradually moved into reservation life and have been losing their cultural identity. One persistent element is the drum, used to accompany the dance songs that constitute much of the musical repertoire. Vennum explores the history and symbolism of the drum, its construction, accessories, and its use in ceremonial contexts. He gathered inside information from William Bineshi Baker, Sr., an Ojibwa drummaker and singer, over a 15-year period. There are good photos of drum variants, of Baker at work, and of dances in progress. A glossary, extensive endnotes, and a bibliography of about 50 items are the reference features; unfortunately, this useful work was left unindexed.

Review: AM 1991, 112.

ML1211 : Orchestra

S2-999 ML1211 .S95

Craven, Robert R. Symphony orchestras of the United States : selected profiles / Robert R. Craven. — Westport, Conn. : Greenwood, 1986. — xxiii, 521 p. ISBN 0-313-24072-8.

A valuable directory of 126 orchestras, arranged by state and then by city, giving for each ensemble a narrative history, list of music directors, and a bibliography. There is a chronology of orchestras by date of establishment, beginning with the Handel and Haydn Society (Boston),

1815, and coming up to the Philharmonic Orchestra of Florida, 1984. There is a useful section that describes the acoustics of halls in the various cities. With a bibliography of 120 items and an expansive index.

Listing and reviews: ARBA 1987, #1238; Balay BH150; *Choice* 10/86, 320; LJ 9/15/86, 89.

S2-1000   ML1211.8 .P672 P72

Avshalomov, Jacob. The concerts reviewed : 65 years of the Portland Youth Philharmonic / Jacob Avshalomov. — Portland, Ore. : Amadeus, 1991. — 387 p. : ill. ISBN 0-9313-4028-4.

A performance history of the first youth orchestra in the United States, established in 1924. All concert programs are reproduced, and local reviews are printed. Player indexes cover 1924–1979. The author has been conductor of the ensemble since 1954.

S2-1001   ML1211.8 .S32 S37

Schneider, David. The San Francisco Symphony Orchestra : music, maestros, and musicians / David Schneider; foreword by Edo deWaart; discography by Victor Ledin. — Rev. ed. — Novato, Calif. : Presidio Press, 1987. — xii, 328 p. : ill. ISBN 0-89141-296-4.

1st ed., 1983.

The author, a violinist with the SFS, presents interesting personal observations on the conductors, fellow musicians, and the daily life of the orchestra. Musical commentaries are valuable, and there are good descriptions of the various halls the orchestra has played in, and of several tours. A chapter on the acoustics of Louise M. Davies Symphony Hall is useful. Unfortunately, the narrative is woven from undocumented conversations (there are no source notes). With a list of conductors, beginning with Henry Hadley (1911–1915, the only American ever to have been principal conductor), and of concertmasters. There is a discography from 1925, with release labels and dates only, and an expansive index.

Review: LJ 10/15/83, 1962.

S2-1002   ML1211.8 .U6

Harrison, Conrad B. Five thousand concerts : a commemorative history of the Utah Symphony / Conrad B. Harrison. — Salt Lake City : Utah Symphony Society, 1986. — xiv, 423 p. : ill. ISBN 0-916095-15-0.

ML1311 : Brass Band; Military Band

S2-1003   ML1311 .H3

Hazen, Margaret Hindle. The music men : an illustrated history of brass bands in America, 1800–1920 / Margaret Hindle Hazen and Robert M. Hazen. — Washington : Smithsonian Institution Press, 1987. — xix, 225 p. : ill. ISBN 0-87474-546-2.

A scholarly but readable story of bands (woodwind as well as brass) in the United States, with about 170 photographs. The place of bands in the community, the repertoire, the instruments and the industry that provided them, promotions, and many individual ensembles are discussed. With chapter endnotes and an expansive index.

Reviews: AM 1989, 329; *Choice* 9/87, 140; LJ 6/15/87, 74.

S2-1004   ML1311 .H66

Holz, Ronald W. Heralds of victory : a history celebrating the 100th anniversary of the New York Staff Band & Male Chorus, 1887–1987 / Ronald W. Holz. — New York : Salvation Army Literary Department, 1986. — xvii, 347 p. : ill. ISBN 0-89216-065-9.

A well-documented history of the New York ensembles of the Salvation Army, focusing on the famous, greatly admired band. The band has made world tours, played a command performance for George VI, performed in Yankee Stadium and Lincoln Center, and on a long radio series. Anecdotes enliven the presentation, and various reference features (lists of all musicians and administrators; chronology; concert programs; photos) give it research value. With a nonexpansive index. The author is a bandmaster at Asbury College; his father was leader of the Staff Band and Chorus from 1955 to 1963.

Review: AM 1991, 230.

S2-1005   ML1311 .R3

Railsback, Thomas C. The drums would roll : a pictorial history of U.S. Army bands on the American frontier, 1866–1900 / Thomas C. Railsback and John P. Langellier. — Poole, Dorset, England : Arms & Armour Press; New York : Sterling Pub. Co., 1987. — 63 p. : ill. ISBN 0-85368-876-1 (U.S.).

The first bands were formed during the Revolution, financed by and for the entertainment of officers. Early official bands were the Corps of Artillery Band (1795), the Second Infantry Regiment Band (1796), and the Marine Band (1798). Railsback provides a documented history of the band movement, with many interesting photographs, repertoire lists, instrumentations, financial accounts, and other documentation. The book is scholarly in approach, with chapter endnotes and a 150-item bibliography of primary and secondary sources. Without index.

S2-1006   ML1311.7 .P4 K73

Kreitner, Kenneth. Discoursing sweet music : town bands and community life in turn-of-the-century Pennsylvania / Kenneth Kreitner. — Urbana : University of Illinois Press, 1990. — xvi, 205 p. : ill. ISBN 0-252-01661-0.

Wayne County in northeastern Pennsylvania is the site of this interesting historical account of a number of ensembles and individual musicians.

There are photos, programs, tour itineraries, and extracts from memoirs. At least one group, the Maple City band, is still active. With chapter end-notes, a bibliography of about 80 items, and an expansive index.
Reviews: ARBA 1990, p. 528; *Choice* 9/90, 128.

ML1400–3195 : VOCAL MUSIC

ML1406 : Composing for Voice

S2-1007   ML1406 .T5
Thomson, Virgil. Music with words : a composer's view / Virgil Thomson. — New Haven, Conn. : Yale University Press, 1989. — x, 178 p. ISBN 0-300-04505-0.
A brief (76 pages) text that gives Thomson's ideas about various elements of songwriting and singing. He touches on the union of poetry and music, melody writing, accompaniment writing, and operatic writing; and he considers the coaching of singers. Examples of his own songs, with comments, take up the rest of the book. With an expansive index.
Reviews: AM 1993, 243; *Choice* 12/89, 642; LJ 10/1/89, 98.

ML1699–1950 : Music for the Stage : Opera and the Musical

S2-1008   ML1699 .O6
Opera annual, U.S. 1984–85 / ed. Jerome S. Ozer. — Englewood, N.J. : Author, 1988. — 642 p. : ill. ISBN 0-89198-132-2. ISSN 0899-3645.
A survey of productions by the four major opera companies (in New York, Chicago, and San Francisco) and a selection of regional companies. Arrangement is by opera, so that various productions can be readily compared. For each there is a photocopy of the program, onstage photographs, and reprints of local reviews. With a nonexpansive name index. As of October 1993, no further volumes in this projected series had appeared.
Reviews: ARBA 1990, #1270; *Choice* 2/89, 924; LJ 3/15/89, 68.

S2-1009   ML1711 .B66
Bordman, Gerald. American musical comedy : from Adonis to Dreamgirls / Gerald Bordman. — New York : Oxford University Press, 1981. — 224 p. : ill. ISBN 01950-3104-0.
A useful narrative of shows, covering 1884–1981; the productions are described and reviewer reactions are given. The entire libretto of *Adonis* (1884) is included. Without documentation; but with good indexing of shows, songs, and performers.

S2-1010   ML1711 .B67
Bordman, Gerald. American musical theatre : a chronicle / Gerald

Bordman. — 2nd ed. — New York : Oxford, 1992. — 832 p. ISBN 0-19-507242-1.

1st ed., 1978.

A narrative history from 1866 through the 1989/90 season, with long discussions of individual shows and extracts from contemporary reviews. There is a nonexpansive index of song titles, show titles, and persons.

Review: LJ 2/1/92, 90.

S2-1011   ML1711 .G735

Green, Stanley. Broadway musicals, show by show / Stanley Green. — 3rd ed. — Milwaukee, Wisc. : H. Leonard Books, 1990. — xix, 372 p. : ill. ISBN 0-88188-836-2.

1st ed., 1985; 2nd ed., 1987.

A narrative account of each production from 1866 to 1989, including song lists. There are useful indexes by composer, lyricist, director, choreographer, actor, and theater.

Listing: Balay BH107.

S2-1012   ML1711 .M2

Mast, Gerald. Can't help singin' : the American musical on stage and screen / Gerald Mast. — Woodstock, N.Y. : Overlook, 1987. — x, 389 p. : ill. ISBN 0-87951-283-0.

A straightforward history, with chapter endnotes; there are musical examples and scattered musical comments on the songs. The main interest of the book is in the critical discussions of the film adaptations. With a bibliography of 150 items and a nonexpansive index.

S2-1013   ML1711 .P67

Porter, Susan L. With an air debonair : musical theatre in America, 1785–1815 / Susan L. Porter. — Washington : Smithsonian Institution Press, 1992. — xiv, 631 p. : ill. ISBN 1-56098-063-X.

A scholarly consideration of genres and styles in stage performance, theaters, companies, orchestras, acting, and singing techniques; well placed in their historical context. In the musical theater category, Porter identifies many varieties, including ballad opera, pastiche, comic opera, ballet, and melodrama. This kind of research goes far beneath the usual surface of theatrical chronicles. The book is illustrated with contemporary playbills, pictures, and musical examples. A useful appendix lists by title about 1,100 musicals performed in the United States (1785–1815); another appendix gives performance details on shows given in New York, Philadelphia, Boston, Charleston, and Baltimore (1801–1815). With endnotes, a bibliography of 300 primary and secondary sources, and a partly expansive index.

Reviews: AM 1993, 112; *Choice* 6/92, 1556; LJ 12/91, 148.

S2-1014 ML1711 .R54

Riis, Thomas Laurence. More than just minstrel shows : the rise of black musical theatre at the turn of the century / Thomas Laurence Riis. — Brooklyn : Institute for Studies in American Music, 1992. — vii, 63 p. : ill. ISBN 0-9146-7836-1.

"An extended footnote" to *Just before Jazz* (S2-1020) that gives some further details on the period 1895–1905. Illustrated with sheet music covers and programs, graced with extensive comments; endnotes, but no index.

S2-1015 ML1711 .S95

Swain, Joseph P. The Broadway musical : a critical and musical survey / Joseph P. Swain. — New York : Oxford, 1990. — x, 384 p. : ill. ISBN 0-19-505434-2.

"The heart and soul of this study—indeed the reason for writing it when many other books on Broadway are available—are the musical examples contained in it." It is useful to have a strongly musical approach to this familiar repertoire, as a departure from the usual focus on the lyrics and plots. Greatest attention goes to *Showboat, Porgy and Bess, Oklahoma!, Carousel, Jesus Christ Superstar, Camelot, Evita, Kiss Me Kate, Most Happy Fella, My Fair Lady, West Side Story, Fiddler on the Roof, Godspell, A Chorus Line,* and *Sweeney Todd.* Swain's musical observations tend toward the program-note description type, but he occasionally considers difficult regions such as tonal structure. With chapter endnotes and a partly expansive index.

Review: LJ 6/1/90, 132.

S2-1016 ML1711 .W64

Woll, Allen. Black musical theatre : from *Coontown* to *Dreamgirls* / Allen Woll. — Baton Rouge : Louisiana State University Press, 1989. — xvii, 301 p. : ill. ISBN 0-8071-1469-3.

A well-documented narrative history, beginning with the nineteenth-century minstrel shows. Woll believes that black musicals have not been adequately covered in the literature; white writers may have avoided them because of racism, and black writers have wished to forget the indignities of blackface and "coon songs." Black composers remained trapped in the formulas of "darky entertainment" through the 1920s, and shows that offered a wider scope, such as *Shuffle Along* (Noble Sissle and Eubie Blake, 1921), were criticized for offering "white folks material." *Cabin in the Sky* (1940) offered a departure from the old format, but although it had a black cast the composer was white. When *Carmen Jones* (the adaptation by Oscar Hammerstein II of Bizet's opera) ran 502 performances on Broadway and toured successfully in the mid-1940s, black performers gained greater mainstream acceptance, but of course there

was no black composer involved. Langston Hughes wrote the book for *Simply Heavenly* (1957), a musical of interest and merit, but without Broadway success. Finally in the 1960s there emerged a genre of musicals written and performed by blacks, culminating in *Dreamgirls* (1981). With a bibliography of about 150 items and a nonexpansive index.
Reviews: *Choice* 9/89, 143; LJ 4/15/89, 78.

S2-1017   ML1711.8 .N3 M13
Mandelbaum, Ken. Not since Carrie : forty years of Broadway musical flops / Ken Mandelbaum. — New York : St. Martin's, 1991. — 372 p. ISBN 0-312-06428-2.
A behind-the-scenes perspective on 200 unsuccessful shows that appeared between 1950 and 1990. Reasons for the failures are presented, with extensive critiques of all aspects of the productions. Alan Jay Lerner and Rodgers and Hammerstein were among the composers who could flop as well as soar. With indexes of names and titles.

S2-1018   ML1711.8 .N3 M38
Annals of the Metropolitan Opera : the complete chronicle of performances and artists : chronology, 1883–1985 / ed. Gerald Fitzgerald. — New York : Metropolitan Opera Guild; Boston : G. K. Hall, 1989. — 2 vols. : ill. ISBN 0-8161-8903-X (set).
Volume 1 consists of a chronology of performances, with casts; volume 2 presents lists of performers, composers and librettists, production personnel, locations, broadcasts, administrators, chorus and ballet masters, and premieres (world and U.S.). Name index, referring to sections of the book only, not to exact pages. This thorough compilation supersedes the pioneering *Metropolitan Opera Annals* by William H. Seltsam (1947; three supplements; LOAM 155).
Listing and reviews: ARBA 1991, #1295; Balay BH95; *Choice* 12/90, 603; LJ 11/15/90, 64.

S2-1019   ML1711.8 .N3 M434
Jackson, Paul. Saturday afternoons at the old Met : the Metropolitan Opera broadcasts, 1931–1950 / Paul Jackson. — Portland, Ore. : Amadeus, 1992. — xvi, 569 p. : ill. ISBN 0-931340-48-9.
An elegant presentation of the Met's radio history, with casts of the broadcasts, fine photographs, stories about the artists, and perceptive technical critiques. Over 200 broadcasts have been preserved in whole or part; strange to say the Met itself has complete recordings only from 1950. Jackson singles out historic broadcast recordings for special discussion. With source notes, a selective bibliography, and an excellent expansive index.
Review: *Choice* 5/93, 1476.

S2-1020   ML1711.8 .N3 R51

Riis, Thomas Laurence. Just before jazz : black musical theater in New York, 1890–1915 / Thomas Laurence Riis. — Washington : Smithsonian Institution Press, 1989. — xxiv, 309 p. : ill. ISBN 0-8747-4788-0.

A scholarly account that begins earlier than the title indicates, with coverage of nineteenth-century black singers and dancers. As formal stage shows emerged, they followed certain dramatic formulae: "The humor and aspirations of black folk were central themes of the plots. The comic stars typically were tricksters or goodhearted ne'er-do-wells. . . . Often comments were made about social class, wealth, and the value of education." The music—tuneful and syncopated—included soloists with chorus backgrounds and male quartets. For a grand finale there was "the entire company singing and dancing, usually the cakewalk." Bert Williams and George Walker were the dominant vaudeville team during the boom of that genre after 1900; they starred in popular shows such as *In Dahomey* (1903), *Abyssinia* (1906), and *Bandanna Land* (1908). Later successful shows featured the Black Patti Troubadours, the Southern Smart Set, and the Negro Players. Riis has carefully documented his interesting history and provided useful reference lists: white shows with songs by black composers, New York shows by black composers, and songs in each black composed show. There is a bibliography of about 150 books and articles. Nineteen songs are printed in photocopy of the original sheet music. With a nonexpansive index. See also S2-1014.

Reviews: *Choice* 3/90, 1155; LJ 11/1/89, 91.

S2-1021   ML1711.8 .N3 S69

Suskin, Steven. Opening night on Broadway : a critical quotebook of the golden era of the musical theatre : *Oklahoma!* (1943) to *Fiddler on the roof* (1964) / Steven Suskin; foreword by Carol Channing. — New York : Schirmer, 1990. — xxii, 810 p. : ill. ISBN 0-02-872625-1.

About 300 shows are briefly described, then long extracts from reviews are given for each. In a useful feature not found elsewhere, biographical sketches for 19 critics are provided. With a nonexpansive index of shows, critics, and cast members.

S2-1022   ML1950 .L383

Lerner, Alan Jay. The musical theatre : a celebration / Alan Jay Lerner. — New York : McGraw-Hill, 1986. — 240 p. : ill. ISBN 0-07-037232-2.

A casual, lively history of musicals and operettas, featuring fine photos of stage productions. With a nonexpansive index. The author is a lyricist, best known for *Brigadoon* and *My Fair Lady*.

S2-1023   ML1950 .L8

Lynch, Richard Chigley. Broadway on record : a directory of New

York cast recordings of musical shows, 1931–1986 / Richard Chigley Lynch. — Westport, Conn. : Greenwood, 1987. — x, 347 p. (Discographies, 28) ISBN 0-313-25523-7.

An alphabetical list of shows, giving the opening date and theater for each, with songs, singers, and recordings (release labels only, without dates). Off-Broadway productions are included. There are 459 recordings and about 6,000 songs. Indexes provide access by composer, lyricist, performer, and musical director. With a chronological index of productions. Since Hummel (LOAM Suppl. S-902) covers all this material—plus earlier shows—and also gives noncast recordings, it is difficult to see why Lynch and Greenwood troubled to publish this.

ML2075 : Film Music

S2-1024　ML2075 .A5

Anderson, Gillian B. Music for silent films, 1894–1929 : a guide / Gillian B. Anderson; foreword by Eileen Bowser. — Washington : Library of Congress, 1988. — xlix, 182 p. ISBN 0-8444-0580-9.

A list of 1,047 film scores or cue sheets that were used to provide musical accompaniment to silent films. Material is drawn from research collections at the Museum of Modern Art, the Library of Congress, University of Minnesota, New York Public Library, Fédération Internationale des Archives du Film (Brussels), and the International Museum of Photography (Rochester, N.Y.). Anderson's scholarly assemblage, and useful introduction, will be of inestimable value in the study of this neglected genre.

Review: AM 1993, 254.

S2-1025　ML2075 .D33

Darby, William. American film music : major composers, techniques, trends, 1915–1990 / William Darby and Jack Du Bois. — Jefferson, N.C. : McFarland, 1990. — xvii, 605 p. : ill. ISBN 0-89950-468-X.

Discussions of 13 Hollywood composers: Max Steiner, Alfred Newman, Franz Waxman, Erich Korngold, Dimitri Tiomkin, Victor Young, Miklos Rozsa, Bernard Herrmann, Alex North, Elmer Bernstein, Henry Mancini, Jerry Goldsmith, and John Williams. Biographical sketches are followed by scene-by-scene descriptions of the movies that each man scored, showing how the music was crafted to fit the action. Thematic measures are included, but many are too brief to define the melodic statements. The descriptions are uniformly adulatory. Endnotes are given. There is a bibliographic essay, an appendix of Academy awards, and a nonexpansive index of names and titles.

Reviews: *Choice* 2/91, 944; LJ 11/15/90, 64.

S2-1026　ML2075 .F448

Film music, I / ed. Clifford McCarty. — New York : Garland, 1989. —

xv, 285 p. (Garland reference library of the humanities, 966) ISBN 0-8240-1939-3.

A useful collection of 12 essays—"the first anthology of new writings on film music to be published in English"—by various authors. Many interesting perspectives are included: experiences of the theater organist; extended analysis of two film scores; the composers who moved between Hollywood writing and standard concert writing; the Flash Gordon films. Memoirs and views of David Raskin and Bernard Herrmann are frank and sometimes surprising (Herrmann observes, "The people who make pictures are . . . vacuous stupid people"; and of electronic music, "It's all the same rubbish. It's not music. And the audience is smarter than all of them. It's bored"). With a nonexpansive index.

Review: AM 1993, 121.

S2-1027   ML2075 .F55

Flinn, Caryl. Strains of utopia : gender, nostalgia, and Hollywood film music / Caryl Flinn. — Princeton, N.J. : Princeton University Press, 1992. — 195 p. ISBN 0-691-04801-0.

An examination of "how a group of industrial, practical, aesthetic, psychoanalytic, and Marxist discourse alike uphold music's ability to conjure remote, impossibly lost Utopias." The term "utopian" is applied to film music "because it extends an impression of perfection and integrity of an otherwise imperfect, unintelligible world." The author, a literary scholar, is obviously transferring some of the approaches of criticism from her field into music; the results are problematic, often provocative, frequently obscure. It may be that Hollywood music is not strong enough to carry the load of so much "critical discourse." Flinn seems unaware of Palmer's study (S2-1030).

S2-1028   ML2075 .K2

Kalinak, Kathryn Marie. Settling the score : music and the classical Hollywood film / Kathryn Marie Kalinak. — Madison : University of Wisconsin Press, 1992. — 256 p. : ill. ISBN 0-299-133650-5.

A history of film music writing, plus discourses on a number of individual scores, explicating how they function in their visual contexts. Among the works studied in detail are *The Magnificent Ambersons* (Bernard Herrmann, 1942) and *Laura* (David Raskin, 1944). With a bibliography and an index.

Review: LJ 11/15/92, 77.

S2-1029   ML2075 .L35

Larson, Randall D. Musique fantastique : a survey of film music in the fantastic cinema / Randall D. Larson. — Metuchen, N.J. : Scarecrow, 1985. — vii, 592 p. : ill. ISBN 0-8108-1728-4.

A thorough, well-documented account of musical scoring for science fiction films, fantasy films, and horror films, largely drawn from interviews with many of the principal composers. Emphasis is on Hollywood material, but there is also coverage of "fantastic music" in Japan, Great Britain, and on the Continent. Max Steiner, Franz Waxman, Arthur Bliss, Miklos Rozsa, Bernard Herrmann, Jerry Goldsmith, and John Williams are among those whose works are examined. A checklist of compositions, arranged by composer, presents 1,300 titles. The discography, of 78s and LPs, is arranged by title. With an index of titles and composers (nonexpansive). Larson is editor of *CinemaScore;* he has written for *Cinefantastique* and *Soundtrack!;* and he is himself the author of short stories in the fantasy and horror genres.
Review: *Choice* 7/85, 1640.

S2-1030   ML2075 .P28
Palmer, Christopher. The composer in Hollywood / Christopher Palmer. — London : Marion Boyars, 1989. — 346 p. : ill. ISBN 0-7145-2885-4.

A description of major film composers at work, in roughly chronological sequence from about 1930 to about 1950. Individuals with the most coverage are Max Steiner, Erich Wolfgang Korngold, Alfred Newman, Franz Waxman, Dimitri Tiomkin, Roy Webb, Miklos Rosza, Bernard Herrmann, Alex North, Elmer Bernstein, and Leonard Rosenman. The author was an orchestrator who worked with several of the composers; he is able to give detailed descriptions of their films, scene by scene in some cases, and the challenges they encountered in setting music to them. Palmer is invariably impressed with the results: "There are times when the very endlessness of melody, the ceaseless surge and influx of wonderful ideas, almost overwhelms: I think of *Turandot,* the first act of *Madam Butterfly.*" Unfortunately, there is no actual music in the book, other than some illegible manuscript pages. With endnotes, a bibliography of about 60 items, and a nonexpansive index.
Reviews: *Choice* 1/91, 789; LJ 4/15/90, 95.

ML2811 : Art Song

S2-1031   ML2811 .F75
Freidberg, Ruth C. American art song and American poetry : Vol. III : The century advances / Ruth C. Friedberg. — Metuchen, N.J. : Scarecrow, 1987. — 351 p. : ill. ISBN 0-8108-1920-1.
Vols. 1 and 2, LOAM Suppl. SA-21.

In this volume Friedberg considers songs of Samuel Barber, Paul Bowles, Hugo Weisgall, Norman Dello Joio, David Diamond, Vincent Persichetti, Jack Beeson, Richard Owen, Jean Eichelberger, William

Flanagan, Ruth Schonthal, Richard Cumming, Ned Rorem, Richard Hundley, Robert Baksa, and John Corigliano. The studies are in program-note style, with some musical examples. There is a title index and a composer index.
Review: *Choice* 9/87, 140.

ML3111–3195 : Church Music

S2-1032   ML3111.5 .D4
Dean, Talmage W. A survey of twentieth century Protestant church music in America / Talmage W. Dean. — Nashville : Broadman, 1988. — 284 p. ISBN 0-8054-6813-7.
A well-researched and documented account of the church music scene: publishers, composers, hymnody in religious education, music on radio and television. With a bibliography of about 200 books and articles, and a nonexpansive index.

S2-1033   ML3161 .H56
Hinks, Donald R. Brethren hymn books and hymnals, 1720–1884 / Donald R. Hinks. — Gettysburg, Pa. : Heritage, 1986. — 205 p. : ill. ISBN not given.
The Brethren came from Germany to Pennsylvania in the early eighteenth century, using old German hymnbooks. In 1720 they published a book of 295 hymns and continued issuing hymn collections in English or German. Hinks considers the numerous publications in detail through 1884 and summarizes later editions. His concern is for the texts of hymns (rather than the music, which is largely ignored) and for the publications themselves. With a bibliography, but without index.
Review: AM 1988, 320.

S2-1034   ML3166 .R37
Rasmussen, Jane. Musical taste as a religious question in nineteenth-century America / Jane Rasmussen. — Lewiston, N.Y. ; Queenston, Ontario : Edwin Mellen, 1986. — xxvi, 603 p. (Studies in American religion, 20) ISBN 0-88946-664-5.
"One of the greatest concerns of nineteenth-century churchmen . . . was congregational singing," the author asserts; and she tells what they did about it: develop a more attractive hymnbook (1827), improve church music education, and create effective church choirs. Emphasis is on the music of the Episcopal Church. The special contributions of W. A. Muhlenberg receive attention. A scholarly, documented work, with a 300-item bibliography and an expansive index.

S2-1035   ML3172 .H37
Hartzell, Lawrence W. Ohio Moravian music / Lawrence W. Hartzell. —

Winston-Salem, N.C. : Moravian Music Foundation Press, 1988. — 201 p. ISBN 0-941642-02-X.

A scholarly study of the Moravian (United Brethren) music situation from 1722, in the Ohio Indian missions, to the music festivals that began in 1961. The emphasis is on individuals, whose lives were carefully researched in primary sources. Not much is said about the music itself. Endnotes by chapter; strong bibliography of primary and secondary sources; expansive index. Appendix features include concert programs and lists of church ministers from 1800, organists, instrumental music directors, and choir directors. Hartzell is a professor and organist at Baldwin-Wallace College, Berea, Ohio.

Reviews: AM 1989, 333; *Choice* 2/89, 951.

S2-1036   ML3174 .H5

Hicks, Michael. Mormonism and music : a history / Michael Hicks. — Urbana : University of Illinois Press, 1989. — xii, 243 p. ISBN 0-252-01618-1.

A scholarly, readable account of the rich and varied musical life in the Church of Jesus Christ of Latter-Day Saints, beginning in the early years of the institution. The first hymnal dates from 1836, and in the same year a singing school was established, leading to the first choir. Secular styles were embraced also, as early as 1841, with band music—to "elevate the people's tastes, stir their hearts with hymns and martial airs"—in the Nauvoo (Illinois) Music Hall, Brigham Young being among the musicians. Young also legitimized couple dancing as a means of worship, although without "clasping close." By the 1870s there were 85 voices in the Tabernacle Choir of Salt Lake City, a number that swelled to more than 300 for special occasions; the choir took second prize at the World's Columbian Exposition in Chicago, 1893. Hicks moves gracefully through these events and the subsequent impact of jazz and pop on Mormon youth. With footnotes and an expansive index.

Reviews: AM 1993, 119–121; *Choice* 4/90, 1332.

S2-1037   ML3187 .A44

Allen, Ray. Singing in the spirit : African-American sacred quartets in New York City / Ray Allen. — Philadelphia : University of Pennsylvania Press, 1991. — xx, 268 p. : ill. ISBN 0-8122-3050-7.

A well-documented study of ensembles active in the city, primarily in Brooklyn, in the context of the national movement of church quartet singing. Individuals and repertoires are given careful attention. Guidance for collectors of recordings is provided. With a useful bibliography and index.

Review: *Choice* 7-8/92, 1689.

S2-1038   ML3187 .B5

Big Mama. Them gospel songs : lore of the black church experience /

Big Mama. — Aurora, Colo. : National Writers Press, 1990. — xii, 74 p. : ill. ISBN not given.

S2-1039   ML3187 .C88
Cusic, Don. The sound of light : a history of gospel music / Don Cusic. — Bowling Green, Ohio : Bowling Green State University Popular Press, 1990. — iv, 267 p. ISBN 0-879720-497-8.
A very broad definition of gospel music (more or less equating it with religious music) underpins this volume, leading Cusic into a vast arena he could have avoided. He requires 10 chapters to escape the web of biblical, early Christian, Reformation, and early American hymn music— where he has nothing useful to say—and get to real gospel, the religious popular song that succeeded the spiritual. Once home, he presents good material on individuals prominent in the gospel movement: Mahalia Jackson, Sam Cooke, Bill Gaither, James Cleveland, Sandi Patti, Jimmy Swaggart, etc. There are interesting survey chapters on country and gospel, major labels, and "marketing the movement." Oddly enough, there are no musical examples in the book, and in fact the discussion avoids musical matters. Although there are source notes, they do not give a complete documentation; the author admits that his "countless interviews" and other gleanings have been "assimilated, digested and in many cases recycled until original sources have been lost." With a good bibliography of about 350 books and articles, and a nonexpansive index.
Review: *Choice* 4/91, 1319.

S2-1040   ML3187 .H37
Harris, Michael W. The rise of gospel blues : the music of Thomas Andrew Dorsey in the urban church / Michael W. Harris. — New York : Oxford, 1992. — xxiii, 324 p. : ill. ISBN 0-19-506376.
A useful history of sacred music that sets the text to blues tunes and often features improvisation in performance. The story is traced to turn-of-the-century Georgia, notably Atlanta, and religious musical styles that metamorphosed into gospel blues in the early 1930s, merging with old-line religious traditions in 1932–1937. Dorsey (1899–1993) was the first to publish a gospel song (1928); he produced about 400 others (best known is "Take My Hand, Precious Lord"), founding and directing the first gospel chorus. With extensive source notes, a bibliography of about 180 primary and secondary works, and an expansive index.
Review: *Choice* 11/92, 476.

S2-1041   ML3187 .L67
Lornell, Kip. "Happy in the service of the Lord" : Afro-American gospel quartets in Memphis / Kip Lornell. — Urbana : University of Illinois Press, 1988. — x, 171 p. : ill. ISBN 0-252-01523-1.

A well-researched account of gospel singing from the late 1920s to the early 1980s, based on the author's field recordings and interviews. The gospel quartet tradition in Tennessee is traced from 1871 with the Fisk Jubilee Singers to recent groups such as the Golden Gate Quartet, Spirit of Memphis, and Flying Clouds of Joy. Lornell deals with the American background for gospel singing, then with the ecology, migration, networks, social relations, training, and performances of many quartets, as well as the impact of mass media on them. He includes a 1952 travel diary for the Spirit of Memphis. Interviews, radio documentation, and other sources are listed. With an expansive index.
Review: AM 1991, 110.

S2-1042   ML3187 .M66
Montell, William Lynwood. Singing the glory down : amateur gospel music in south central Kentucky, 1900–1990 / William Lynwood Montell. — Lexington : University Press of Kentucky, 1991. — xi, 248 p. ISBN 0-8131-1757-7.
The subtitle is misleading, for this book is about singers, rather than about music, which is neither exemplified nor discussed. Montell traces the history of church singers from the shape-note period, the singing convention movement, early gospel quartets, the decline of popular participation, and contemporary groups and soloists. Oral history interviews were the basis for much of the study, which is well documented and illustrated. Individual performers and events are surrounded with imposing detail. With endnotes, a bibliography of about 75 primary and secondary sources, an appendix list of groups by county, and a partly expansive index of names and topics. The author is a professor of folk studies at Western Kentucky University.
Review: *Choice* 5/92, 1405.

S2-1043   ML3187 .T47
Terrell, Bob. The music men : the story of professional gospel quartet singing / Bob Terrell. — Asheville, N.C. : Author, 1990. — viii, 332 p. : ill. ISBN 1-8788-9400-5.
A casual account of principal gospel singers, such as James D. Vaughan, Virgil O. Stamps, the Rangers, the Speer Family, the Blackwood Brothers, and the Statesmen. Most of the book consists of undocumented conversations. Nothing is said about the actual music of these music men. With a nonexpansive index of names.
Reviews: *Choice* 9/87, 140; LJ 6/15/87, 74.

S2-1044   ML3195 .L48
Levine, Joseph A. Synagogue song in America / Joseph A. Levine. — Crown Point, Ind. : White Cliffs Media, 1988. — xxii, 232 p. : music. (Performance in world music, 4) ISBN 0-9416-7714-1.

A useful historical and technical study that shows how Jewish liturgical music developed in the United States. Various stylistic techniques are explained well in separate chapters: psalmodic, biblical (slower and louder than psalmodic), modal (combining elements of psalmodic and biblical), and performance (balancing intellect and feeling). Americanization of synagogue song took place with the incorporation of folk and popular elements. There is a glossary of 150 terms and—somewhat out of place in a general discussion—a compilation of 248 neume motifs from Lithuanian practice. Misinai tunes are given also (Mt. Sinai melodies, of biblical technique). The ideal reader of the book would be hard to conjure up, as it presents a wide range of discussion from basic to musicological. With an expansive index.

Review: *Choice* 4/90, 1333.

S2-1045   ML3195 .S55
Slobin, Mark. Chosen voices : the story of the American cantorate / Mark Slobin. — Urbana : University of Illinois Press, 1989. — xxv, 318 p. : ill. : 18 p. plates : with 35-minute audiocassette. ISBN 0-252-01567-7 (book), 0-252-01566-5 (cassette).

The interpretation of sacred texts through song began with the Second Temple, after the Exile. That rich tradition was established in America in 1685, with the cantor Saul Brown at the Congregation Shearith Israel, New York City. Slobin's account of subsequent developments, largely in the form of a sourcebook, is an interesting, scholarly tale, clarifying the synagogue setting and the function of the cantor. He shows how the "American cantorate recreated itself" after World War II "as a native-born institution, centered on newly founded training programs and professional organizations." Life histories of three immigrant singers are absorbing. It is of interest that the first accredited female singer dates only from 1976. With 40 extended musical examples, but no substantive discussion of musical elements. Endnotes, a bibliography of about 200 items, and an expansive index.

Reviews: AM 1992, 95; *Choice* 11/89, 498.

ML3470–3541 : POPULAR MUSIC

ML3470–3479 : General Studies

S2-1046   ML3470 .D46
Denselow, Robin. When the music's over : the story of political pop / Robin Denselow. — London : Faber & Faber, 1989. — xviii, 292 p. : ill. ISBN 0-571-15380-1.

The story of pop music as a political tool in the United States and several other countries, concentrating on the problems of racism, Vietnam, the antinuclear movement, apartheid, famine, and human rights in all aspects. Among the people involved are Harry Belafonte, Billy Bragg, Bob Dylan, Peter Gabriel, Woody Guthrie, the Rolling Stones, Pete Seeger, and Stevie Wonder. From the musical variety implicated in those names, it is clear that Denselow's "pop" covers a multitude of genres. The impact of theme concerts and other musical efforts on actual events is not clear, so it seems that the political songs bring the most benefit to those who perform them, in events "that have transformed the image of many pop singers . . . some musicians . . . treated as if they are the new priesthood, as caring, moral beings who concern themselves with human rights, peace, and hunger." With no footnotes, but with a bibliography of about 50 titles and a nonexpansive index.

Review: *Choice* 11/89, 496.

S2-1047   ML3470 .M36

The Marshall Cavendish history of popular music. — Freeport, Long Island, N.Y. : Marshall Cavendish Corp., 1990. — 21 vols. ISBN 1-85436-016 (vol. 1).

A useful encyclopedic treatment of pop performers and topics. Of the many contributors, the best known are Simon Frith, Peter Guralnick, and Nick Tosches. The articles are well illustrated but not documented. Convenient lists of the articles in each volume are given, and there is a nonexpansive index.

S2-1048   ML3470 .O5

Frith, Simon. On record : rock, pop, and the written word / Simon Frith and Andrew Goodwin. — New York : Pantheon, 1990. — xi, 492 p. : ill. ISBN 0-394-56475-8.

The rock era is over, says Frith, because the music became too formulaic, and there was a "replacement of authenticity by artifice." No particular evidence for this perception is given in the book, which is a random speculation about Bruce Springsteen, "Coventry Sound," John Barry, rock and video, sex in song, and film composer Ennio Morricone. With endnotes and a nonexpansive name index.

Reviews: *Choice* 4/92, 1192; LJ 12/89, 126.

S2-1049   ML3470 .P9

Pratt, Ray. Rhythm and resistance : explorations in the political uses of popular music / Ray Pratt. — New York : Praeger, 1990. — xii, 241 p. ISBN 0-275-92624-9.

A scholarly study of pop music as a vehicle of expression by minorities and disadvantaged groups in the United States—groups for whom "popular culture . . . remains the primary means of resistance" against oppression. Emphasis falls on the work of black musicians and on political protest figures such as Woody Guthrie and Bob Dylan. The

discussion is focused on the texts of songs, with nothing substantial said about musical elements. With a bibliography and index.
Review: *Choice* 1/91, 790.

S2-1050 ML3470 .W48
Wenner, Jann S. Twenty years of *Rolling Stone* : what a long, strange trip it's been / ed. Jann S. Wenner. — New York : Friendly Press, 1987. — 460 p. : ill. ISBN 0-914919-10-5.
A collection of "carefully trimmed" articles and interviews that appeared in *Rolling Stone* magazine. There are good color pictures, but there is no index.

S2-1051 ML3475 .B63
Boggs, Vernon W. Salsiology : Afro-Cuban music and the evolution of salsa in New York City / Vernon W. Boggs. — New York : Greenwood, 1992. — vii, 387 p. : ill. ISBN 0-313-28468-7.
Consists of 26 essays by Boggs (a teacher of sociology at City University of New York) and several other writers on the Latino pop genre known as salsa, widespread in the late 1960s. The forerunners of salsa are analyzed, among them the Cuban rumba, and pioneer artists are discussed. There are interviews with current performers, presented verbatim including hellos and goodbyes, but without source notes. A salsa song by David Zinn is presented in score. With a bibliography of about 50 books and articles; no index.
Review: *Choice* 10/92, 310.

S2-1052 ML3475 .G47
Gerard, Charley. Salsa! : the rhythm of Latin music / Charley Gerard and Marty Sheller. — Crown Point, Ind. : White Cliffs Media Co., 1989. — xvii, 137 p. ISBN 0-941677-11-7.
Salsa is regarded here as "a creation of the New York music industry," more particularly of the Fania record label. Gerard regards the genre as essentially an old Latino mode, enhanced for U.S. consumption by studio technology. In this useful introduction to salsa, he gives good descriptions of the musical elements, such as the clave (basic rhythmic formula), the instruments (percussions are prominent), and related styles like those of the Cuban Santería. There are clear musical examples, a glossary, a bibliography, and a discography (minimal data). With name and subject indexes.

S2-1053 ML3476 .C66
Cooper, B. Lee. Popular music perspectives : ideas, themes, and patterns in contemporary lyrics / B. Lee Cooper. — Bowling Green, Ohio :

Bowling Green State University Popular Press, 1991. — 213 p. ISBN 0-87972-505-2.

Following the idea of his 1986 book (S2-254), Cooper lists and discusses pop songs according to the topics of the lyrics: education, railroads, rebels, automobiles, Christmas, death, food and drink, and telephones. He also takes up "patterns": answer songs, cover records, nursery rhymes and fairy tales, and "social trends and audio chronology." Recordings are cited for the songs, and there are chapter bibliographies. There is also a general bibliography and a nonexpansive index.

Review: *Choice* 10/91, 293.

S2-1054   ML3477 .A48

Bindas, Kenneth J. America's musical pulse : popular music in twentieth-century society / Kenneth J. Bindas. — New York : Greenwood, 1992. — xviii, 301 p. (Contributions to the study of popular culture, 33) ISBN 0-2759-4306-2.

A collection of 28 essays by various authors, dealing with music and politics, class, economics, race, gender, and social thought. The work is footnoted and scholarly in tone. With an expansive index.

S2-1055   ML3477 .D44

Denisoff, R. Serge. Sing a song of social significance / R. Serge Denisoff. — 2nd ed. — Bowling Green, Ohio : Bowling Green State University Popular Press, 1983. — x, 255 p. ISBN 0-87972-0360.

1st ed., 1972 (LOAM 582).

An account of protest songs from the 1930s to the 1970s, somewhat vague in focus (rock music is treated as a protest mode, because of the generational conflict it supposedly represents). The most useful coverage is of urban folk music, religious revival music, class consciousness shown in song, and the work of Bob Dylan. The extent of updating in this edition is not discussed in the prefatory matter, but it appears to be minimal—all the endnotes precede 1972—except for the bibliography of some 300 "pop/ rock music books" and the final chapter, a perceptive bibliographical essay on popular music research that carries into the late 1970s. Denisoff's approach to this material is sociological rather than musicological and is thus concentrated on song lyrics and the extramusical elements of performance. The first edition had an index, but this one does not.

S2-1056   ML3477 .D67 P6

Dorough, Prince. Popular music culture in America / Prince Dorough. — New York : Ardsley House, 1992. — xiv, 352 p. : ill. ISBN 1-8801-5704-7.

A plain history of popular music, written at introductory level, with light documentation. Topics of interest include the folk music revival, Elvis Presley, and Tin Pan Alley; rock is generously covered. With an expansive index.

S2-1056a   ML3477 .E4
Elrod, Bruce C. Your hit parade : April 20, 1935 to June 7, 1958 : American top 10 hits, 1958–1984 / Bruce C. Elrod. — 3rd ed. — White Rock, S.C. : Author, 1985. — xviii, 462 p. : ill. ISBN 0-9614-8052-1.

S2-1057   ML3477 .H36
Hampton, Wayne. Guerilla minstrels : John Lennon, Joe Hill, Woody Guthrie, and Bob Dylan / Wayne Hampton. — Knoxville : University of Tennessee Press, 1986. — xiv, 306 p. ISBN 0-8704-9489-9.
An account of four musicians regarded by Hampton as prototypes of the protest singer, one who uses art "to serve political ends, specifically the cause of social justice." He identifies song lyrics by these four men that fall into the protest category and endeavors to form them into a sort of philosophy; but the effort is short on definitions, and it tends to ignore all the love songs and less belligerent material. The author often stumbles over his main thoughts, for example with Dylan, said to have two main themes: "that of the outcast" and "that of the seer in quest of visions"—neither one a protest motif. There are endnotes and a bibliography of about 400 books and articles about the artists and their times. With a list of songs by each man and a partly expansive index.
Review: AM 1989, 90.

S2-1058   ML3477 .J34
Jasen, David A. Tin Pan Alley : the composers, the songs, the performers, and their times : the golden age of American popular music from 1886 to 1956 / David Jasen. — New York : Donald I. Fine, 1988. — xxiv, 312 p. : ill. : 32 p. plates. ISBN 1-5561-1099-5.
The section of New York City that ran along 28th Street from Broadway to 6th Avenue was the songwriter's district from around 1886 to around 1950, known as Tin Pan Alley for all the noise from pianos. This interesting story concentrates on the business aspects of songwriting and gives useful information (albeit without documentation) about such publishers as M. Witmark and T. B. Harms. With a nonexpansive index.

S2-1059   ML3477 .L43
Lees, Gene. Singers and the song / Gene Lees; foreword by Grover Sales. — New York : Oxford, 1987. — xii, 272 p. ISBN 0-19-504293-X.
Sketches of Edith Piaf, Johnny Mercer, Frank Sinatra, Peggy Lee, Dick Haymes, Hugo Friedhofer, Jo Stafford, and Sarah Vaughan, infor-

mal and with invented conversations. There is also a curious essay, perhaps tongue in cheek, on "how to write lyrics," which offers such statements as, "English has drawbacks as a language in which to write lyrics. For one thing it is poor in rhyme." Another odd piece, "Pavilion in the Rain," seems serious in its theory that big bands faded away primarily because of the decline in public transportation. Without index.

Reviews: *Choice* 4/88, 1255; LJ 10/15/87, 83.

S2-1060   ML3477 .S33

Scheurer, Timothy E. Born in the U.S.A. : the myth of America in popular music from colonial times to the present / Timothy E. Scheurer. — Jackson : University Press of Mississippi, 1991. — xi, 280 p. ISBN 0-87805-496-0.

An interpretation of song lyrics that endeavors to connect them to American "mythemes," such as land, destiny, God's work, and the Founders. "The community accepts certain songs in which it finds . . . in lyrics or air, something that answers a need or states a feeling." "Myth fulfills a number of functions in our lives. As a result, so do our songs." Well, even granting this tenuous approach to cause and effect, and to the nature of myth, it was not much trouble to find song lyrics in the nineteenth century that dealt with these topics. But more recently, as Scheurer acknowledges, there emerged a problem with the concept: "Virtually no songs from the early and middle 1920s deal with the myth and only a very few from the 1930s." Indeed one could well say that hardly any modern song is concerned with land, destiny, God, or the Founders. The main topics (myths?) of popular song for a hundred years have been love and social protest. The author observes that in the 1970s there was "a culture that has abandoned the certainty of its mythology." With a bibliography of about 250 entries and nonexpansive index.

Review: *Choice* 12/91, 605.

S2-1061   ML3477 .S354

Scheurer, Timothy E. The nineteenth century and Tin Pan Alley / Timothy E. Scheurer. — Bowling Green, Ohio : Bowling Green State University Popular Press, 1989. — 181 p. : ill. ISBN 0-8797-2465-X.

S2-1062   ML3477 .S44

Shannon, Bob. Behind the hits / Bob Shannon and John Javna. — New York : Warner Books, 1986. — 254 p. : ill. ISBN 0-446-38171-3.

"Amusing, surprising, and factual pop music profiles" relating to the backgrounds of many recent hit songs and albums, with corrections of popular misconceptions (e.g., Madonna's "Like a Virgin" is revealed to be about spiritual rather than sexual innocence; Devo's "Whip It" refers to "moving quickly" rather than S & M). Various interesting speculations by the authors and contributed revelations by the performers provide good reading. With a title index.

S2-1063 ML3477 .S475
Shaw, Arnold. The jazz age : popular music in the 1920s / Arnold Shaw. — New York : Oxford, 1987. — x, 350 p. ISBN 0-19-503891-6.

A lively summary of the sea changes in popular music that occurred in the roaring twenties: jazz, blues, dance music, the musicals, the Harlem Renaissance, the pop ballads, the first big bands. With chapter endnotes, a representative list of LP records, a list of hit songs of the 1920s, and a nonexpansive index.
Reviews: *Choice* 3/88, 1109; LJ 9/15/87, 83.

S2-1064 ML3477 .S5
Smith, Joe. Off the record : an oral history of popular music / Joe Smith; ed. Mitchell Fink. — New York : Warner Books, 1988. — xiv, 429 p. : ill. : 64 p. plates. ISBN 0-446-51232-4.

A collection of first-person anecdotes and ruminations by several hundred jazz players, vocalists, and rock performers. Without documentation or index.

S2-1065 ML3477 .T24
Tawa, Nicholas E. The way to Tin Pan Alley : American popular song, 1866–1910 / Nicholas E. Tawa. — New York : Schirmer, 1990. — xii, 296 p. ISBN 0-02-872541-7.

An engaging history of popular songs, mostly "about those men and women who enjoyed, wrote, and published these compositions; . . . the singers . . . and also about subjects, textural structures, and musical styles." A sampling of song output is closely examined in terms of musical and textual content, revealing "craftsmanship of a high order" and an ability to "express an extraordinary American society that once existed in all its singularity." The discussion covers composers, publishers, modes and venues of performance, lyrics and themes, and songs by type. There is a useful section in which the music of 11 typical songs is given in full. With chapter endnotes, a bibliography of about 200 items, an alphabetical list of 230 principal songs, and a nonexpansive index of titles, names, and subjects.
Reviews: AM 1993, 114; *Choice* 11/90, 499.

S2-1066 ML3477 .W46
Wenzel, Lynn. I hear America singing : a nostalgic tour of popular sheet music / Lynn Wenzel and Carol J. Binkowski. — New York : Crown, 1989. — x, 150 p. : ill. ISBN 0-517-56967-1.

Fine color illustrations—mostly reproductions of sheet music covers—are the essence of this volume. A running commentary, casual and undocumented, accompanies the pictures. With an index of names and titles.

S2-1067   ML3477 .W8
Woliver, Robbie. Bringing it all back home : 25 years of American music at Folk City / Robbie Woliver. — New York : Pantheon, 1986. — xiii, 258 p. ISBN 0-394-74068-8.
Folk City, a New York City nightclub, is given tribute here through the reminiscences of owner Mike Porce and anecdotes by about 100 stars who performed there. Among those involved are Joan Baez, Oscar Brand, Judy Collins, Arlo Guthrie, and Carly Simon. Without documentation or reference features, except for a partly expansive index.
Review: LJ 5/15/86, 69.

S2-1068   ML3477 .Z64
Zollo, Paul. Songwriters on songwriting / Paul Zollo. — Cincinnati : Writer's Digest Books, 1991. — 194 p. : ill. ISBN 0-8987-9451-4.
A collection of "31 interviews featuring advice and inspiration" that were originally found in *SongTalk* magazine. Such writers as Pete Seeger, Paul Simon, Joan Baez, and Madonna were asked rather interesting questions, but the answers tended toward the mundane cliché. Without index.

S2-1069   ML3479 .C66
Cooper, Ralph. Amateur night at the Apollo : Ralph Cooper presents five decades of great entertainment / Ralph Cooper; with Steve Dougherty. — New York : HarperCollins, 1990. — x, 260 p. ISBN 0-06-016037-3.
Amateur shows at Harlem's Apollo theater began in 1934, bringing debut opportunities to such stars as Ella Fitzgerald, Luther Vandross, Sarah Vaughan, Dionne Warwick, and Michael Jackson. Cooper, impresario from the early days, offers his casual recollections, an assemblage of anecdotes and conversations, of interest for the cast of characters and many good photographs of them. It would have been useful to have a list of the celebrities who succeeded on the Apollo's stage; the expansive index leads to some of the names, but they are interfiled with other persons mentioned in the text.
Review: LJ 11/15/90, 73.

S2-1070   ML3479 .G4
George, Nelson. Buppies, B-boys, baps & bohos : notes on post-soul black culture / Nelson George. — New York : HarperCollins, 1992. — xii, 329 p. ISBN 0-0601-6724-6.

A book of essays on black music and entertainment after 1971, all but two of them from the *Village Voice*. The material is breezy and often vulgar in language, replete with invented conversations. Persons covered are rap performers, media personalities, Motown singers, sports figures, and others who represent—for George—the essence of contemporary black culture. There is a useful chronology of events concerning black people from 1971 to 1991. Without index.

S2-1071 ML3479 .M67
Morgan, Thomas L. From cakewalks to concert halls : an illustrated history of African American popular music from 1895 to 1930 / Thomas L. Morgan and William Barlow. — Washington : Elliott & Clark, 1992. — 132 p. : ill. ISBN 1-880216-06-X.

An informal tale of slave songs, coon songs, minstrel and early stage shows, blues, and jazz, noteworthy for its color reproductions of sheet music covers and good portraits. Individuals who get extended attention include Bob Cole and the Johnson Brothers, Will Marion Cook, Bert Williams, George Walker, James Reese Europe, Shelton Brooks, Joe Jordan, Noble Sissle, Eubie Blake, Cecil Mack, W. C. Handy, and Clarence Williams. Without documentation; with a song title index and name index.

Review: *Choice* 2/93, 973.

S2-1072 ML3479 .T21
Tate, Greg. Flyboy in the buttermilk : essays on contemporary America / Greg Tate. — New York : Simon & Schuster, 1992. — 285 p. ISBN 0-671-72965-9.

A collection of pieces by a writer for the *Village Voice,* reducing all art to political terms. The style is vulgar or hip, depending on the beholder, and totally unstructured. A hatred for "good old red-neck racist America" is pervasive. Performers treated to this approach include George Clinton, Cecil Taylor, Prince, Wynton Marsalis, Miles Davis, Ornette Coleman, Public Enemy, Ice-T, and Steve Erickson. Without index or reference features.

Review: LJ 6/1/92, 130.

ML3505–3508 : Jazz

S2-1073 ML3505.9 .N48
New perspectives on jazz : report on a national conference held at Wingspread, Racine, Wisconsin, September 8–10, 1986 / ed. David N. Baker. — Washington : Smithsonian Institution Press, 1990. — xvii, 133 p. ISBN 0-87474-332-X.

Consists of essays by Gunther Schuller (influence of jazz on concert

music), Gary Giddins (evolution of jazz), Amiri Baraka (i.e., LeRoi
Jones, on jazz criticism), and Billy Taylor (jazz in the marketplace), with
extended responses by Harold Horowitz, Dan Morgenstern, Stanley
Crouch, Jimmy Lyons, George Butler, and Martin Williams. The contributions are from major scholars, but the whole amounts to less than its
parts: the book lacks focus and presents nothing new. To claim that it is
"the most comprehensive exploration of jazz in this nation" (p. viii) is a
statement of intent, but hardly of outcome. Furthermore, the volume is
marred by Baraka's essay, a foolish diatribe against "racist America"
that is so irritating—and racist—that respondent Stanley Crouch accused
Baraka of reducing "the artistry of jazz to no more than political pulp."
Without index, source notes, or bibliography.
Review: *Choice* 9/90, 128.

S2-1074   ML3506 .A4
Annual review of jazz studies / ed. Edward Berger, David Cayer, Dan
Morgenstern, and Lewis Porter. — Metuchen, N.J. : Scarecrow, 1982– .
ISSN 0731-0641.
> Vol. 1, 1982. ISBN 0-87855-896-9. 178 p.
> Vol. 2, 1983. ISBN 0-87855-906-X. 224 p.
> Vol. 3, 1985. ISBN 0-87855-965-5. 224 p.
> Vol. 4, 1988. ISBN 0-88739-733-0. 224 p.
> Vol. 5, 1991. ISBN 0-8108-2478-7. 250 p.
The first four volumes were published by Transaction Books (New
Brunswick, N.J., and Oxford, U.K.). Edward Berger joined the other
three editors with the fifth volume. The *Annual Review* succeeds the
Journal of Jazz Studies, published from 1973 to 1979 (also distributed
by Scarecrow Press). All volumes carry important research articles on
jazz performers and jazz topics. It is not an annual review in the sense of
summarizing state of the art or developments of the previous year.
Review: AM 1987, 213.

S2-1075   ML3506 .B4513
Berendt, Joachim Ernst. The jazz book : from ragtime to fusion and
beyond / Joachim Ernst Berendt; revised by Gunther Huesmann; trans.
H. and B. Bredigkeit; new sections [in 1992 ed.] trans. Tim Nevill. —
6th ed. — Brooklyn, N.Y. : Lawrence Hill Books, 1992. — xvi, 541 p.
ISBN 1-5565-2099-9.
1st ed., 1953; 1st English ed., 1975 (LOAM 960).
A useful introduction to various aspects of jazz, including a summary
history, biographies of 14 major artists, elements of performance, the instruments, vocalists, big bands, and jazz ensembles. Without source
notes; with a selective bibliography and an expansive index.
Review: LJ 5/1/92, 103.

S2-1076   ML3506 .B8
Budds, Michael J. Jazz in the sixties : the expansion of musical resources and techniques / Michael J. Budds. — 2nd ed. — Iowa City : University of Iowa Press, 1990. — xiii, 185 p. ISBN 0-87745-281-4. 1st ed., 1978 (LOAM Suppl. S-716).
A scholarly study of recent jazz from several technical viewpoints: melody, harmony, meter, rhythm, dynamics, and tone color; and the role of electronics and tape. The meeting of jazz and rock, and the place of religious and racial themes are discussed. Contrasts with pre-1960 jazz are cited, and illustrative recordings are identified. This is a refreshing departure from the typical performer-based historical review. With chapter endnotes, a topical bibliography of about 350 items (books, articles, liner notes), and a nonexpansive index.

S2-1077   ML3506 .C75
Crow, Bill. From Birdland to Broadway : scenes from a jazz life / Bill Crow. — New York : Oxford, 1992. — viii, 273 p. ISBN 0-19-506988-9.
Consists of material gathered from personal interviews, recollections, published writings by musicians, and the oral history collection of the Institute of Jazz Studies; a by-product of research done for *Jazz Anecdotes* (S2-1078). The book's title is taken from Birdland, a club that opened in 1949 on Broadway, between 52nd and 53rd Streets in Manhattan (caged birds were a feature), and became the "jazz corner of the world." Includes essays (some of them previously published) on Stan Getz, Pee Wee Marquette, Papa Jo, Claude Thornhill, Gene Quill, Terry Gibbs, Marian McPartland, Gerry Mulligan, Charlie Parker, Duke Ellington, Erroll Garner, Thelonious Monk, Pee Wee Russell, Benny Goodman, and Peter Duchin. Crow, a bass player, tells about these artists in a casual first-person story, replete with conversations and anecdotes, saying nothing substantive about their music. Without source notes; with a nonexpansive index.
Reviews: *Choice* 4/93, 1322; LJ 9/15/92, 65.

S2-1078   ML3506 .C76
Crow, Bill. Jazz anecdotes / Bill Crow. — New York : Oxford, 1992. — xiv, 350 p. ISBN 0-19-506988-9.
Crow compiled these tales from personal interviews and conversations, published writings, and the oral history collection of the Institute of Jazz Studies (Rutgers University). They are grouped loosely under themes, such as traveling and style of dress, or by artists: Louis Armstrong, Bessie Smith, Bix Beiderbecke, Fats Waller, Eddie Condon, Pee Wee Russell, Duke Ellington, Benny Goodman, Coleman Hawkins and Lester Young, Art Tatum, Joe Venuti, Tommy Dorsey, Lionel Hampton, Charlie Parker, Dizzy Gillespie, Charles Mingus, Zoot Sims and Al Cohn, and Miles Davis and John Coltrane. The content is anecdotal, with

no examination of the music played by these artists. No sources are cited for the quotations. With a nonexpansive index.

Bill Crow is a bass player and has contributed articles and reviews to *Down Beat,* the *Jazz Review,* and *Jazzletter.* He writes a monthly column for *Allegro* [—D. P.].

Review: LJ 3/15/90, 92.

S2-1079   ML3506 .D3

Dean, Roger T. New structures in jazz and improvised music since 1960 / Roger T. Dean. — Philadelphia : Open University, 1991. — xxvi, 230 p. : ill. ISBN 0-335-09897-5.

A fine technical "analysis of changes in improvised music from 1960–1985," expressed in musical language, refreshingly free of "socio-political explanations." Developments in jazz idioms are the "result of autonomous change within music." Rhythm, melodic improvisation, and harmonic innovations are described and illustrated. With a bibliography of 157 entries, a selective discography of 139 records, and a nonexpansive index.

Review: *Choice* 9/92, 126.

S2-1080   ML3506 .D43

Deffaa, Chip. Swing legacy / Chip Deffaa; foreword by George T. Simon. — Metuchen, N.J. : Scarecrow Press and the Institute of Jazz Studies, 1989. — xi, 379 p. : ill. (Studies in jazz, 9) ISBN 0-8108-2282-2.

These biographical sketches of bandleaders and sidemen are based on interviews (conducted during 1982–1988) with the subjects and expanded from previously published articles. The interviewees include original swing musicians and recent champions of the style: Artie Shaw, Chris Griffin, Buck Clayton, Johnny Blowers, Maxine Sullivan, John Williams, Jr., Maurice Purtill, Lee Castle, Panama Francis, Stéphane Grappelli, Mel Tormé, Harold Ashby, Thad Jones, Frank Foster, Mercer Ellington, Warren Vaché, Jr., Scott Hamilton, and Woody Herman. In two additional chapters, Deffaa reflects on Count Basie and describes the condition of the Basie band in the year after his death.

The sketches, which vary in length from 10 to 45 pages, focus on the musicians' professional careers, including their recent activities; some background information is included. Well-chosen photographs of the musicians and their bands appear throughout; they have not been reproduced with great care. Sources of information beyond the interviews are very poorly cited. With a brief bibliography and a nonexpansive index of personal names and song titles (bands and clubs are inconsistently indexed).

Chip Deffaa is a jazz critic for the *New York Post.* He has also contributed to *Down Beat, Jazz Times,* and the *New Grove Dictionary of Jazz* [—D. P.].

Review: *Choice* 12/90, 639.

S2-1081   ML3506 .G56

Gioia, Ted. The imperfect art : reflections on jazz and modern culture / Ted Gioia. — New York : Oxford, 1988. — vi, 152 p. : ill. ISBN 0-19-505343-5.

An unfocused, rambling account of various jazz topics and personalities, by a jazz pianist and Stanford University teacher. He regards jazz as "imperfect" because improvisation is often unsuccessful. There is some interest in a chapter on Louis Armstrong and in another on jazz aesthetics. Gioia takes issue — unconvincingly — with the critique by composer/critic Virgil Thomson (misspelled Thompson) of Charlie Parker. Endnotes; nonexpansive index; without bibliography.

S2-1082   ML3506 .G736

Gridley, Mark C. Concise guide to jazz / Mark C. Gridley. — Englewood Cliffs, N.J. : Prentice-Hall, 1992. — x, 228 p. : with an audiocassette. ISBN 0-13-174467-4.

An excellent introduction to jazz, evidently drawn from the author's longer text (S2-1083), containing technical descriptions of performances that will serve the experienced listener as well as the initiate. Gridley starts out with helpful basics about jazz structure and history. He takes up the various styles and gives examples for them, in many cases going through a recording from beginning to end, noting the events of each timed segment. Individual styles are carefully explicated, and jazz instruments are discussed and illustrated. There is also a glossary, followed by a nonexpansive index.

S2-1083   ML3506 .G74

Gridley, Mark C. Jazz styles : history & analysis / Mark C. Gridley. — 3rd ed. — Englewood Cliffs, N.J. : Prentice-Hall, 1991. — xxi, 442 p. : ill. : with two audiocassettes. ISBN 0-13-50-7963-2.

1st ed., 1978; 2nd ed., 1985 (LOAM Suppl. S-664).

What are 10 technical differences between jazz and rock? Who were the principal trumpet players in the history of Duke Ellington's band, and what were their distinctive styles? What are the African and European elements in jazz? How did Dexter Gordon influence John Coltrane? This is a book of clear answers to such questions, and thousands of others. It is in textbook style, with a progression from basic theoretical concepts and historical roots through instrumentation and the great performers. There is no adulation and little appraisal; the essence is definite information. There is no better pathfinder to the inner life of jazz. With a nonexpansive index of persons, titles, and topics. S2-1082 is a briefer volume of similar content.

S2-1084   ML3506 .H38

Hartman, Charles O. Jazz text : voice and improvisation in poetry, jazz, and song / Charles O. Hartman. — Princeton, N.J. : Princeton University Press, 1991. — 192 p. ISBN 0-6910-6817-8.

The "text" here is the melodic material, not the words; Hartman uses the term in the manner of the literary critic. What exactly he is trying to establish does not become very clear, but in the process he offers some interesting musical analyses at a high technical level. Transcriptions of jazz performances (by Lee Konitz, Ornette Coleman, Joni Mitchell, etc.) are carefully studied for their chord progressions, phrasings, and melodic inventiveness. With chapter endnotes, a bibliography of about 150 items, and a nonexpansive index of notably obtuse character, giving such dubious entries as "performance" (30 citations) and "print" (26 citations).

S2-1085   ML3506 .J43
Abe, Katsuji. Jazz giants : a visual retrospective / Katsuji Abe. — New York : Billboard Publications, 1988. — 280 p. : ill. ISBN 0-8230-7536-2.

A book of fine photographs, with commentaries. Many of the pictures are large-size, color views of the performers in action. With a name index.

S2-1086   ML3506 .L44
Leonard, Neil. Jazz : myth and religion / Neil Leonard. — New York : Oxford, 1987. — x, 221 p. ISBN 0-19-505670-1.

Leonard examines religious responses to jazz from a sociological viewpoint, by applying such concepts as sect, gnosis, rituals, and myths to people's attitudes and behaviors in relation to jazz. Max Weber's studies of religious behavior are used to develop comparisons between religious behavior and behavior associated with jazz. Carefully annotated, but without separate bibliography. Includes expansive index.

Neil Leonard is chairman of the Department of American Civilization at the University of Pennsylvania [—D. P.].

Reviews: *Choice* 7-8/87, 1704; LJ 3/1/87, 78.

S2-1087   ML3506 .M43
Megill, Donald D. Introduction to jazz history / Donald D. Megill and Richard S. Demory. — 3rd ed. — Englewood Cliffs, N.J. : Prentice-Hall, 1993. — xii, 337 p. ISBN 0-1348-1854-7.

1st ed., 1984; 2nd ed., 1988 (LOAM Suppl. SA-417).

A useful textbook, with basic guidance about principal jazz styles (including rock and other recent idioms) and the work of many classic performers. Individual recordings are described in time lines, showing what happens at specific time intervals ("melodic extensions are used over a pedal point on the lowest string," "duet texture returns," etc.). The whole is arranged chronologically and concentrates on the music; there are brief career accounts of the persons whose playing is discussed. Jazz terms and elements are treated clearly in an appendix, and there is a glossary of about 150 terms. A selective discography provides titles and labels only. With a nonexpansive index.

S2-1088   ML3506 .P74
Priestley, Brian. Jazz on record : a history / Brian Priestley. — New York : Billboard Books, 1991. — xiii, 226 p. : ill. : 16 p. plates. ISBN 0-8230-7562-1.
"First published in Great Britain in 1988 by Elm Tree Books."
A narrative of jazz history and the recording industry attached to it, citing individual recordings as it goes—but without specifics about them. The historical approach is fuzzy, with actual dates avoided in favor of approximations (e.g., "in the 1960s MCA took over US Decca"; "by the mid-1930s there was even the first of the specialty retailers, in the shape of the Commodore Music Shop in New York"—MCA took over Decca in 1962; Commodore opened in 1924). A "record guide" by chapter cites mostly reissues and gives no comments or details. No source notes; partly expansive index.

S2-1089   ML3506 .R68
Rose, Al. I remember jazz : six decades among the great jazzmen / Al Rose. — Baton Rouge : Louisiana State University Press, 1987. — xii, 257 p. : ill. ISBN 0-8071-1315-8.
Rose reminisces about Jelly Roll Morton, John Casimir, Frankie Newton, Jack "Papa" Laine, Bill Russell, Mezz Mezzrow, Bobby Hackett, Alphonse Picou, Irving Fazola, Oran "Hot Lips" Page, Tony Parenti, Dan Burley, Allan Jaffe, Louis Prima, Adrian Rollini, Stéphane Grappelli, George Cvetkovich, Sidney Bechet, Tom Brown, George Girard, James P. Johnson, Chris Burke, Eddie Condon, Bunny Berigan, Alvin Alcorn, Muggsy Spanier, Wild Bill Davison, Joe Mares, Harry Truman, Jack Teagarden, Eubie Blake, the Original Dixieland Jazz Band, Armand J. Piron, the Jacobs Candy Man, Bunk Johnson, Edmond Souchon, Pee Wee Spitlera, Morten Gunnar Larsen, Danny Barker, George Baquet, Louis Armstrong, Knocky Parker, Johnny Wiggs, Jean Christophe Averty, Eddie Miller, Raymond Burke, Spencer Williams, Pierre Atlan, Claude Luter, W. C. Handy, David Thomas Roberts, Chink Martin, Walter Bowe, "Buglin' Sam" Dekemel, Harry Shields, Johnny St. Cyr, Sharkey Bonano, Armand Hug, Earl "Fatha" Hines, Gene Krupa, Pete Fountain and Al Hirt, Dizzy Gillespie, Miff Mole, Clarence Williams, the Dixieland Rhythm Kings, the Brunies (family), and Paul Barbarin.
The nonexpansive index includes names and titles; without bibliographical references.
Al Rose is a record producer, author, and radio host [—D. P.].
Review: *Choice* 7-8/87, 1705.

S2-1090   ML3506 .S36
Schuller, Gunther. The swing era : the development of jazz, 1930–1945 / Gunther Schuller. — New York : Oxford, 1989, — xviii, 919 p. : ill. (The history of jazz, volume 2) ISBN 0-19-504312-X.
Vol. 1, *Early Jazz,* 1968 (LOAM 1038).
The definitive history of the period, told from a musical point of view, with transcriptions, excellent analyses, and valuable interpretations throughout. Individuals receiving most attention are Benny Goodman, Duke Ellington, Louis Armstrong, Jimmy Lunceford, and Count Basie. There are also thorough discussions of the "great black bands," "great soloists," "white bands," "territory bands" [those from outside New York, mostly black], and "small groups." With a chronological table, glossary, and a nonexpansive index of titles and names.
Reviews: AM 1990, 111; *Choice* 9/89, 141.

S2-1091   ML3506 .S87
Stokes, W. Royal. The jazz scene : an informal history from New Orleans to 1990 / W. Royal Stokes. — New York : Oxford, 1991. — viii, 261 p. : ill. : 16 p. plates. ISBN 0-19-505409-1.
An anecdotal survey based primarily on hundreds of interviews Stokes conducted with musicians (and a few scholars) between 1970 and 1990. Some chapters are organized by locale (e.g., New Orleans, Kansas City and the Southwest, Chicago), others by type of performer (e.g., singers, big bands), and still others by era (e.g., post-bebop developments, the contemporary scene).
The 26 photographs are nicely reproduced; subjects and places are identified, and dates are given. Unfortunately, the text makes no references to the 16 plates, diminishing their value. There is a nonexpansive index of personal names and ensembles. Without bibliographic references.
W. Royal Stokes has been a jazz critic for the *Washington Post* and editor of *Jazz Times* [—D. P.].
Review: *Choice* 11/91, 460.

S2-1092   ML3506 .S89
Stroff, Stephen M. Discovering great jazz : a new listener's guide to the sounds and styles of the top musicians and their recordings on CDs, LPs, and cassettes / Stephen M. Stroff. — New York : Newmarket, 1991. — xii, 179 p. : ill. : 16 p. plates. ISBN 1-55704-104-2.
A useful discographical essay, discussing about 140 albums in the frame of jazz history. With a glossary of terms, a basic library of 60 albums, a view of jazz on compact discs, and a nonexpansive index of names.
Review: LJ 10/1/91, 103.

S2-1093   ML3506. T36
Tanner, Paul O. W. Jazz / Paul O. W. Tanner, David W. Megill, and Maurice Gerow. — 7th ed. — Dubuque, Iowa : W. C. Brown, 1992. — xii, 228 p. : ill. : with a CD or cassette. ISBN 0-697-14698-0.
1st ed., 1964; 2nd–4th eds. in LOAM Suppl. S-666.
A useful textbook, giving clear presentations of jazz idioms in historical sequence from African roots to fusion. Technology is discussed as well, and there are chapters on jazz in television and motion pictures, and jazz criticism. Musical examples and explanations are geared to the accompanying recording, using time lines that account for what is happening during every second of the performance. Terms are defined as they occur in the text. With a glossary of about 150 terms, a basic bibliography of about 300 books, and a nonexpansive index.

S2-1094   ML3506 .W44
Weinstein, Norman C. A night in Tunisia : imaginings of Africa in jazz / Norman C. Weinstein. — Metuchen, N.J. : Scarecrow, 1992. — xii, 244 p. : ill. ISBN 0-8108-2525-2.
An attempt to "raise questions about the relationship of Africa to jazz," with the so-called Afrocentric viewpoint seen to be "a major perspective crafted by jazz practitioners." Weinstein lists six characteristics of African music (which he treats as a homogeneous unity, although many distinct musical styles are found in Africa): 1) multileveled rhythmic activity, 2) improvisation, 3) collective participation, 4) speechlike vocalization styles, 5) societal and spiritual connotations, and 6) ancestral connections. These attributes, which—as the author recognizes—"are found in non-African musical traditions" also "provide an infrastructure for much of jazz." The book's title comes from Dizzy Gillespie's 1942 tune, suggesting that Weinstein's brush may be too broad for his topic, since Tunisia is not part of the black Africa he is thinking about (Africa north of the Sahara is basically Islamic and Middle Eastern in culture)—nor was Gillespie thinking about it. On the other hand, John Coltrane certainly did have black African inspirations (drawn from recordings) for some of his music. The rest of the narrative is dependent for its Africana on lesser-known jazzmen who actually traveled there or used African names in their compositions. With chapter endnotes, discography of music related to the theme of Africa in jazz, and a partly expansive index.
Reviews: *Choice* 11/92, 478; LJ 6/1/92, 130.

S2-1095   ML3507 .E55
Enstice, Wayne. Jazz spoken here : conversations with twenty-two musicians / Wayne Enstice and Paul Rubin. — Baton Rouge : Louisiana State University Press, 1992. — xi, 316 p. : ill. ISBN 0-8071-1760-9.

Interviews conducted between 1975 and 1981 with Mose Allison, Art Blakey, Ruby Braff, Anthony Braxton, Bob Brookmeyer, Dave Brubeck, Ray Bryant, Larry Coryell, Mercer Ellington, Bill Evans, Gil Evans, Tommy Flanagan, Dizzy Gillespie, Chico Hamilton, Lee Konitz, Charles Mingus, Joe Pass, Sonny Stitt, Gabor Szabo, Clark Terry, Henry Threadgill, and Bill Watrous. Despite the title, jazz is not spoken here: the conversations are entirely about personal matters, mostly trivial. Nothing is said about music. Indexed.

Reviews: *Choice* 3/93, 1161; LJ 8/92, 103.

S2-1096   ML3507 .G52

Giddins, Gary. Riding on a blue note : jazz and American pop / Gary Giddins. — New York : Oxford, 1981. — xv, 313 p. ISBN 0-19-502835-X.

Most of the material in this book appeared in somewhat different form in the *Village Voice* between 1973 and 1980. The mixture of profiles, interviews, and critiques, all of which are dated, includes the following subjects: Ethel Waters, Bing Crosby, the Dominoes, Otis Blackwell, Bobby Blue Bland, Sarah Vaughan, Betty Carter, Frank Sinatra, Jack Teagarden, Joe Venuti, Count Basie, Donald Lambert, Professor Longhair (Henry Roeland Byrd), Charlie Parker, Sonny Rollins, Arthur Blythe, Scott Joplin's *Treemonisha,* Irving Berlin, Duke Ellington, Charles Mingus, Ornette Coleman, Association for the Advancement of Creative Music, Willem Breuker, Dizzy Gillespie, Red Rodney (Robert Roland Chudnick), Dexter Gordon, Art Pepper, Wes Montgomery, George Benson, and Cecil Taylor. Includes a nonexpansive index of persons and groups. Without bibliographical references.

Gary Giddins is a jazz critic and historian. He founded the American Jazz Orchestra in 1985 [—D. P.].

Reviews: *Choice* 9/81, 94; LJ 2/15/81, 455.

S2-1097   ML3507 .J38 B9

Buckner, Reginald T. Jazz in mind : essays on the history and meanings of jazz / ed. Reginald T. Buckner and Steven Weiland. — Detroit : Wayne State University Press, 1992. — 185 p. : ill. ISBN 0-8143-2168-2.

A collection of documented essays, most of them presented at a 1987 conference at the University of Minnesota, some by musicians and some by specialists in other fields, such as communications, education, and African-American studies. Topics include James Reese Europe, a leading dance band and jazz leader who died in 1919; the autobiographies of Louis Armstrong; local jazz history in South Carolina; and an apologia for jazz autobiographies (by Kathy Ogren—perhaps the leading item in the book). There is a discography of James Europe and a nonexpansive index.

Review: *Choice* 9/92, 127.

S2-1098   ML3507 .K43

Keepnews, Orrin. The view from within : jazz writings, 1948–1987 / Orrin Keepnews. — New York : Oxford, 1988. — x, 238 p. ISBN 0-19-505284-6.

A gathering of essays by a major record producer and critic, including material on Pee Wee Erwin, Billie Holiday, Jelly Roll Morton, Art Tatum, Charlie Parker, Louis Armstrong, Lenny Bruce, Bill Evans, and Cannonball Adderly. The style is chatty, and there are undocumented quoted conversations. Without source notes, bibliography, or index.

Review: LJ 11/1/88, 96.

S2-1099   ML3507 .L47

Lees, Gene. Waiting for Dizzy / Gene Lees; foreword by Terry Teachout. — New York : Oxford, 1991. — vii, 251 p. ISBN 0-19-505670-1.

A collection of rambling tales that appeared originally in the *Gene Lees Jazzletter* (1981–), dealing with a number of musicians. Most of the content consists of loving appreciations, remembered episodes, and imaginary conversations on nonmusical matters. Persons in the cast include Benny Carter, Bix Beiderbecke, Al Grey, Joe Venuti, and Dizzy Gillespie of the book's title. Without notes or index.

Reviews: *Choice* 10/91, 293; LJ 4/15/91, 94.

S2-1100   ML3507 .M38

McPartland, Marian. All in good time / Marian McPartland. — New York : Oxford, 1987. — xvii, 174 p. ISBN 0-19-504871-7.

These articles, which originally appeared in *Down Beat* and other magazines between 1960 and 1983, combine McPartland's personal impressions of the subjects with historical, background information and quotes from other musicians, sometimes quoting the subjects themselves. Most of the portraits consider the professional and personal lives of the subjects, which include drummer Joe Morello, alto saxophonist Paul Desmond, pianist Mary Lou Williams, drummer Jake Hanna, Benny Goodman, pianist Bill Evans, bassists Ron McClure and Eddie Gomez, Dudley Moore, and composer Alec Wilder. There is also an article on the International Sweethearts of Rhythm band and another on women musicians in jazz.

Photographs of most of the subjects are included. Unfortunately, no sources are provided for the many well-chosen quotations. Without bibliographical references or index.

Marian McPartland is a pianist, educator, writer, and host of the radio program *Piano Jazz* [—D. P.].

Review: *Choice* 1/88, 778.

S2-1101   ML3507 .R29

Ramsey, Doug. Jazz matters : reflections on the music and some of its makers / Doug Ramsey. — Fayetteville : University of Arkansas Press, 1989. — xxi, 314 p. ISBN 1-55728-060-6.

A collection of essays previously published over a 30-year period, many from the *Texas Monthly.* Most of the pieces are too short (a page or so) to say much, but some of the longer studies—of Woody Herman, Dave Brubeck, Charles Mingus, the Modern Jazz Quartet, and Duke Ellington—reveal the author's ability to penetrate the music. Such insights are typically drowned, however, in a format of chat, anecdotes, and quotations, all undocumented. With a nonexpansive index.

Review: *Choice* 12/89, 643.

S2-1102   ML3507 .W525

Williams, Martin. Jazz changes / Martin Williams. — New York : Oxford, 1992. — xi, 317 p. ISBN 0-19-505847-X.

A collection of brief appreciations, previously published in *Down Beat, Saturday Review,* and other periodicals; some material was drawn from interviews. The author's comments are of most interest in longer essays, on Coleman Hawkins, John Coltrane, Jelly Roll Morton, Charlie Parker, and Lester Young. The approach is basically adulatory. Conversations and quotations are undocumented. With a nonexpansive index.

S2-1103   ML3507 .W53

Williams, Martin. Jazz heritage / Martin Williams. — New York : Oxford, 1985. — xiv, 253 p. ISBN 0-19-503611-5.

A collection of reviews, liner notes, and "appreciations" originally published in *Down Beat, Saturday Review, Annual Review of Jazz Studies,* and a few other periodicals. The most interesting material stemmed from direct observations at performances of Ornette Coleman, Gerry Mulligan, Duke Ellington, and Thelonious Monk. Other artists discussed include Louis Armstrong, Count Basie, Miles Davis, Dizzy Gillespie, Fletcher Henderson, Charles Mingus, Jelly Roll Morton, and Jack Teagarden. The discussions are often cast in musical terms, but there are also plenty of undocumented anecdotes and quotations. Without notes; with a nonexpansive index.

Reviews: *Choice* 1/86, 749; LJ 8/85, 99.

S2-1104   ML3507 .W535

Williams, Martin. Jazz in its time / Martin Williams. — New York : Oxford, 1989. — xii, 272 p. ISBN 0-19-505459-8.

A collection of reviews and short columns, previously published in *Down Beat, Saturday Review,* and *International Musician.* There is little of substance in these extracts, the longest of which offer adulatory impressions of John Coltrane, Duke Ellington, Miles Davis, Thelonious Monk, Dizzy Gillespie, Charlie Parker, and Lester Young. Stan Kenton does not fare so well, being the object of a mean-spirited essay. A

foolish attack on the *New Grove Dictionary of American Music* exemplifies critical imbalance. Without documentation; with an expansive index.
Review: *Choice* 9/89, 142.

S2-1105 ML3507 .W536
Williams, Martin. Jazz tradition / Martin Williams; foreword by Richard Crawford. — 2nd rev. ed. [i.e., 3rd ed.] — New York : Oxford, 1993. — xviii, 301 p. ISBN 0-1950-7815-2.
1st ed., 1970 (LOAM 1080); 2nd ed., 1983.
"An original blend of history and criticism, this book explores the work of nearly two dozen leading musicians and ensembles that have shaped the course of jazz." Williams offers insights into the music of King Oliver, Jelly Roll Morton, Sidney Bechet, Louis Armstrong, Bix Beiderbecke, Coleman Hawkins, Billie Holiday, Art Tatum, Duke Ellington, Count Basie, Lester Young, Charlie Parker, Thelonious Monk, John Lewis and the Modern Jazz Quartet, Sonny Rollins, Horace Silver, Miles Davis, Sarah Vaughan, Bill Evans, Charlie Mingus, John Coltrane, Ornette Coleman, Eric Dolphy, and the World Saxophone Quartet. His tone is faithfully adulatory, but he does have some musical language for it. With discographical notes and a nonexpansive index of names and titles.

S2-1106 ML3507 .W6
Wilmer, Valerie. Mama said there'd be days like this : my life in the jazz world / Valerie Wilmer. — London : Women's Press, 1989. — viii, 337 p. : ill. : 16 p. plates. ISBN 0-7043-5040-8.
A miscellany of scenes and conversations with various jazz performers, none of it documented. With a nonexpansive index.

S2-1107 ML3507 .Y6
Young, Al. Kinds of blue : musical memoirs / Al Young. — San Francisco : D. S. Ellis; distributed by Creative Arts, 1984. — 167 p. : ill. ISBN 0-916870-82-0.
A "prose album of musical memoirs, vignettes and reveries" by a poet, novelist, and writer on jazz. Young demonstrates or simulates a remarkable recall of his feelings while listening to various musicians, beginning with a detailed scenario of his three-year-old self being blessed and astonished by the Ink Spots doing "Java Jive," and carrying forward into similar joyous events produced by Thelonious Monk, Duke Ellington, Miles Davis, Janis Joplin, and others. These impressions are complete with conversations and details cast in what appears to be a poetic idiom. Without index or reference features. The following item is similar.
Review: *Choice* 4/85, 1149.

S2-1108   ML3507 .Y686
Young, Al. Things ain't what they used to be : a musical memoir / Al
Young. — Berkeley, Calif. : Creative Arts, 1988. — xvii, 233 p. : ill.
ISBN 0-8873-9024-2.
Further impressionistic memoirs (see S2-1107), inscribed in essays
(some previously published). Fictionalized conversations appear, along
with reflections. "Sometimes remembering takes the form of story or
personal myth." Personal myth? No index.

S2-1109   ML3508 .B52
Bird, Christiane. Jazz and blues lover's guide to the United States :
with more than 900 hot clubs, cool joints, landmarks and legends, from
boogie-woogie to bop and beyond / Christiane Bird. — New York : Ad-
dison Wesley, 1991. — viii, 385 p. ISBN 0-201-52332-9.
The title tells it all. A useful descriptive directory, arranged by region,
with a nonexpansive index of names.

S2-1110   ML3508 .C65
Collier, James Lincoln. The reception of jazz in America : a new view /
James Lincoln Collier. — Brooklyn, N.Y. : Institute for Studies in American
Music, 1988. — 95 p. (I.S.A.M. monographs, 27) ISBN 0-914678-30-2.
Collier takes issue with two ideas that have permeated histories of
jazz: that jazz was ignored or despised in the United States during its
early years, and that it was first taken seriously by European critics. He
offers strong evidence for the position that jazz was well liked in America, and after the sensational recordings (from 1917) of the Original Dixieland Jass Band jazz attracted an enormous following—primarily
among mainstream white audiences. Except for a few ill-informed affi-
cionados, Europeans came to understand jazz much later, and imper-
fectly at that. With endnotes; but without index.
Reviews: AM 1989, 345; *Choice* 3/89, 1172.

S2-1111   ML3508 .C7
Collection jazz (series).
A useful group of volumes issued by Oreos (Waakirchen, Germany)
from 1983; all are in German. Each book consists of a straightforward,
undocumented biography and a detailed discography with extensive
comments. There are illustrations of album covers and worklists for
composers. Indexes to song titles and album titles are included.
These are the 21 titles listed in Illinet (the database shared by Illinois li-
braries) in August 1993. The sequence is in reverse chronological order.
Jazzplakate = Jazz posters / Niklaus Troxler. 1991.
Sonny Rollins: sein Leben, seine Musik, seine Schallplatten / Peter
Niklas Wilson. 1991.

Count Basie : sein Leben, seine Musik, seine Schallplatten / Rainer Nolden. 1990.

Art Blakey : sein Leben, seine Musik, seine Schallplatten / Hannes Giese. 1990.

Pat Metheny : Biographie, Style, Instruments / Luigi Viva. 1990.

Sidney Bechet / Fabrice Zammarchi. 1989.

Bill Evans : sein Leben, seine Musik, seine Schallplatten / Hanns E. Petrick. 1989.

Ornette Coleman : sein Leben, seine Musik, seine Schallplatten / Peter Niklas Wilson. 1989.

John Coltrane : sein Leben, seine Musik, seine Schallplatten / Gerd Filtgen. 1989.

Charlie Parker : sein Leben, seine Musik, seine Schallplatten / Peter Niklas Wilson. 1989.

Miles Davis : sein Leben, seine Musik, seine Schallplatten / Peter Wiessmuller. 1988.

Dizzy Gillespie : sein Leben, seine Musik, seine Schallplatten / Jürgen Wölfer. 1987.

Thelonious Monk : sein Leben, seine Musik, seine Schallplatten / Thomas Fitterling. 1987.

Ella Fitzgerald : ihr Leben, ihre Musik, ihre Schallplatten / Rainer Nolden. 1986.

Keith Jarrett : sein Leben, seine Musik, seine Schallplatten / Uwe Andresen. 1985.

Django Reinhardt : sein Leben, seine Musik, seine Schallplatten / Alexander Schmitz. 1985.

Reminiscenses : piano solos and songs / Fats Waller. 1985.

Miles Davis : sien Leben, seine Musik, seine Schallplatten / Peter Wiessmuller. 1984.

Charles Mingus : sein Leben, seine Musik, seine Schallplatten / Horst Weber. 1984.

John Coltrane : sein Leben, seine Musik, seine Schallplatten / Gerd Filtgen. 1983.

Duke Ellington : sein Leben, seine Musik, seine Schallplatten / Hans Ruland. 1983.

S2-1112   ML3508 .D38

Davis, Francis. In the moment : jazz in the 1980s / Francis Davis. — New York : Oxford, 1986. — xiv, 258 p. ISBN 0-19-504090-2.

Davis brings together 26 profiles of artists and critical evaluations that he had originally written for the *Philadelphia Inquirer* and other periodicals between 1981 and 1986. Subjects include Anthony Davis, Wynton and Branford Marsalis, David Murray, Bobby McFerrin, Craig Harris, John Blake and Billy Bang, Mathias Rüegg, Scott Hamilton and Warren Vaché, Sumi Tonoka, Stanley Jordan, Keshavan Maslak, Sonny

Rollins, Ornette Coleman, Don Cherry, Warne Marsh, George Russell, Roscoe Mitchell, Arthur Blythe, Abbey Lincoln, Giovanni Bonandrini, Henry Threadgill, Sheila Jordan, Jay Clayton, Kim Parker, Susannah McCorkle, John Lewis, Ran Blake, the World Saxophone Quartet and the 29th Street Saxophone Quartet, and Miles Davis. Each article is dated. Comments by the performers are often insightful, and Davis offers many useful perceptions of the musical idioms. The nonexpansive index includes persons and groups. Without bibliographical references.

Francis Davis is a jazz critic who writes regularly for the *Atlantic,* the *Philadelphia Inquirer,* and *7 Days* [—D. P.].

Review: AM 1990, 238.

S2-1113   ML3508 .F74

Friedwald, Will. Jazz singing : America's great voices from Bessie Smith to bebop and beyond / Will Friedwald. — New York : Scribner's, 1990. — xvi, 477 p. : ill. : 16 p. plates. ISBN 0-684-18522-9.

Friedwald traces the changing styles of jazz singing from its beginnings in the blues to the present. While much of the text is about individual artists and groups, it is always incorporated into a description of a particular style or trend. The writing is loose and opinionated, with no sources given for factual information. Friedwald has tried to include everyone who could be considered a jazz singer and even those who have been slightly influenced by jazz. About 30 photographs of Friedwald's favorite singers appear on 16 pages of plates. A carefully annotated discography of 26 pages is organized by artist; recommended recordings include title, label, and the number of a recent release, typically a CD. The nonexpansive index consists almost exclusively of personal names. Without bibliographical referenes.

Will Friedwald is a frequent contributor to the *Village Voice* and the author of *Looney Tunes and Merrie Melodies: An Illustrated Guide to the Warner Bros. Cartoons;* he is also a record producer [—D. P.].

Reviews: *Choice* 11/90, 497.

S2-1114   ML3508 .G3

Giants of jazz (series).

Volumes issued by Time-Life Records, Alexandria, Va., offering brief (48–52 pages) life stories and discographies for jazz figures. The series ran from 1978 to 1982. In general these books are of slight value, but may be useful as introductions to their subjects. These are the titles listed in the OCLC-EPIC database in February 1994. The sequence is in reverse chronological order.

Bunny Berigan / John Chilton. 1982.
Johnny Hodges / Stanley Dance. 1981.
James P. Johnson / Frank Kappler. 1981.
Pee Wee Russell / John McDonough. 1981.

Teddy Wilson / George Gelles. 1981.
Sidney Bechet / Frank Kappler. 1980.
Benny Carter / Morroe Berger. 1980.
Earl Hines / Stanley Dance. 1980.
Red Norvo / Don DeMichael. 1980.
The guitarists / Marty Grosz. 1980.
Fats Waller / David Thomson. 1980.
Bix Beiderbecke / Curtis Prendergast. 1979.
Duke Ellington / Stanley Dance. 1978.
Benny Goodman / Frank Kappler. 1979.
Coleman Hawkins / John McDonough. 1979.
Billie Holiday / Melvin Maddocks. 1979.
Jelly Roll Morton / Chris Albertson. 1979.
Jack Teagarden / Leonard F. Guttridge. 1979.
Louis Armstrong / Chris Albertson. 1978.

S2-1115   ML3508 .G57
Gitler, Ira. Swing to bop : an oral history of the transition in jazz in the 1940s / Ira Gitler. — New York : Oxford, 1985. — 352 p. : ill. : 12 p. plates. ISBN 0-19-503644-6.

During the 1970s and early 1980s, Gitler interviewed 66 musicians who were active in the 1930s and 1940s. Rather than present the results as separate interviews, he reworked the information into several chapters that focus on various elements of the transition from big band to bebop. Gitler also wrote connecting narrative to create a context for the quoted information. Persons quoted most extensively include David Allyn, Johnny Carisi, Benny Carter, Kenny Clarke, Al Cohn, Earl Coleman, Billy Eckstine, Biddy Fleet, Terry Gibbs, Dexter Gordon, Jimmy Gourley, Al Grey, Neal Hefti, Milt Hinton, Henry Jerome, Budd Johnson, Barney Kessel, Lou Levy, Shelly Manne, Howard McGhee, Jay McShann, Billy Mitchell, Gerry Mulligan, Joe Newman, Chico O'Farrill, Red Rodney, Jimmy Rowles, Zoot Sims, Frankie Socolow, Billy Taylor, Allen Tinney, and Trummy Young. The 20 photographs are a mixture of individual publicity stills and ensembles in performance. Though well reproduced, most of the pictures are not very evocative. The nonexpansive index includes persons and titles. Without bibliographical references.

Ira Gitler is a New York–based writer, concert producer, and jazz radio host. He is the author of *Jazz Masters of the '40s* and has contributed to various other books and journals [—D. P.].

Reviews: AM 1987, 203; *Choice* 2/86, 877.

S2-1116   ML3508 .G674
Gordon, Robert. Jazz West Coast : the Los Angeles jazz scene of the

1950s / Robert Gordon. — London and New York : Quartet, 1986. — 242 p. : ill. : 8 p. plates. ISBN 0-7043-2603-5.

Gordon surveys the Los Angeles jazz scene from the mid-1940s through the early 1960s. There is a strong emphasis on the recordings of the period—both background information and critiques—but the other activities of groups and individuals are also discussed. The critiques seem very reasonable, and Gordon does well relating the local scene to national trends. While sources of direct quotations are carefully cited, no sources are provided for other information; since Gordon was an observer of the period, much of it is presumably first-hand. The annotated discography lists the most recent issues of over 100 recordings discussed in the text, by title and label number. The expansive index includes persons, companies, and titles. Without bibliographical references.

Robert Gordon is a musician who has taught jazz history courses at San Bernardino Valley College [—D. P.].

S2-1117   ML3508 .J12
Jazz life & times (series).

Volumes issued by Universe Books (New York) and Spellmount (Tunbridge Wells, England) from 1987. Each volume gives a biography of a jazz figure and a thorough list of recording sessions, bibliography, and index. These are the titles listed in the OCLC-EPIC database in February 1994. The sequence is in reverse chronological order.

Dizzy Gillespie : his life and times / Barry McRae. 1989.
Bunk Johnson : his life and times / Christopher Hillman. 1989.
Louis Armstrong : his life and times / Mike Pinfold. 1988.
Dizzy Gillespie : his life and times / Barry McRae. 1988.
Fats Waller : his life and times / Alyn Shipton. 1988.
Billie Holiday : her life and times / John White. 1987.
Gene Krupa : his life and times / Bruce Crowther. 1987.

S2-1118   ML3508 .J15
Jazz masters (series).

Volumes issued by Apollo (London) from 1981. Each gives biographical information and a selective record list (in print items) with full discographical data: date, matrix, personnel, label, and comments. Books are not indexed.

These are the titles listed in the OCLC-EPIC database in February 1994. The sequence in is reverse chronological order.

Ornette Coleman / Barry McRae. 1988.
Miles Davis / Barry McRae. 1988.
Stan Getz / Richard Palmer. 1988.
Benny Goodman / Bruce Crowther. 1988.

Sonny Rollins / Sonny Rollins. 1988.
John Coltrane / Brian Priestley. 1987.
Duke Ellington / Peter Gammond. 1987.
Thelonious Monk / Thelonious Monk. 1987.
Gerry Mulligan's ark / Raymond Horricks. 1986.
Woody Herman / Steve Voce. 1986.
Count Basie / Alun Morgan. 1984.
Coleman Hawkins / Burnett James. 1984.
Billie Holiday / Burnett James. 1984.
Charlie Parker / Brian Priestley. 1984.
Oscar Peterson / Richard Palmer. 1984.
Svengali : or the orchestra called Gill [*sic*] Evans / Raymond Horricks. 1984.
Lester Young / Dave Gelly. 1984.

S2-1119   ML3508 .J3 L9
Lyttelton, Humphrey. Basin Street to Harlem : jazz masters and masterpieces, 1917–1930 / Humphrey Lyttelton. — New York : Taplinger, 1982. — 214 p. : ill. : 4 p. plates. (The best of jazz, 1) ISBN 0-8008-0727-8.
A perceptive discussion of classic jazz, mostly through the examples of specific recordings made up to 1930. Among the items analyzed are "Tiger Rag" by the Original Dixieland Jazz Band, "Carolina Shout" by James P. Johnson, "Dippermouth Blues" by Louis Armstrong, "Wild Cat Blues" by Clarence Williams, and "St. Louis Blues" by Bessie Smith. Lyttelton describes jazz of the 1920s as tied to a basic rhythmic straitjacket of two beats. The great innovation of the period, credited to such artists as Bessie Smith, Sidney Bechet, and Louis Armstrong, was the change to a 12/8 meter on a four-beat foundation. See also the following item.
Review: *Choice* 3/90, 85.

S2-1120   ML3508 .L98
Lyttelton, Humphrey. Enter the giants, 1931–1944 / Humphrey Lyttelton. — New York : Taplinger, 1982. — 239 p. : ill. : 8 p. plates (The best of jazz, 2) ISBN 0-8008-0728-6.
A continuation of the interesting format of the first volume (S2-1119), dealing with the principal discs of Louis Armstrong, Fats Waller, Coleman Hawkins, Jack Teagarden, Art Tatum, Johnny Hodges, Dickie Wells, Lester Young, Billie Holiday, and Roy Eldridge. With an expansive index.
Review: LJ 4/15/82, 814.

S2-1121   ML3508 .O37
Ogren, Kathy J. The jazz revolution : twenties America and the mean-

ing of jazz / Kathy J. Ogren. — New York : Oxford, 1989. — vii, 221 p. : ill. ISBN 0-19-505153-X.

A reworking of the author's doctoral dissertation, this book presents a scholarly perspective on several topics, including "performance practice of bluesmen, minstrels, and jazzmen"; "location and setting for jazz performance"; "jazz performance and the black community"; and "white Americans debate jazz." A palpable image of the times is projected: the cities and streets, the clubs, and the record studios. Music itself is not often taken up. Whether or not this fascinating background forms "the meaning of jazz" or simply its accompaniment remains an open question, but Ogren's ideas and interpretations are always interesting and thoughtful. With endnotes and an expansive index.

Reviews: *Choice* 7/89, 1850; LJ 4/1/89, 91.

S2-1122   ML3508 .P45
Peretti, Burton W. The creation of jazz : music, race, and culture in urban America / Burton W. Peretti. — Urbana : University of Illinois Press, 1992. — xii, 277 p. : ill. ISBN 0-252-01708-0.

A well-documented sociological history of jazz, based largely on the oral history archives of Tulane University and the Institute of Jazz Studies. Commercial forces and race relations are much in evidence. Peretti takes the novel position that there was "considerable influence of European-American traditions on early jazz musicians," refusing to accept the view that jazz emerged from exclusively black roots. With an expansive index.

Reviews: *Choice* 3/93, 1162; LJ 9/1/92, 178.

S2-1123   ML3508 .R68
Rosenthal, David H. Hard bop : jazz and black music, 1955–1965 / David H. Rosenthal. — New York : Oxford, 1992. — 208 p. ISBN 0-19-505869-0.

A wide-ranging discussion said to have been based on interviews with performers. The style is casual, and the content is mostly on the level of personal activities; there are some comments bearing on the music, but they do not have much to tell ("upbeat, slow, two-beat feel," "lusher melodies," etc.). With endnotes and a nonexpansive index of names and titles.

Reviews: *Choice* 11/92, 477; LJ 1/92, 32.

S2-1124   ML3508 .W47
Werner, Otto. The origin and development of jazz / Otto Werner; foreword by Dick Gibson. — 2nd ed. —Dubuque, Iowa : Kendall/Hunt, 1989. — ix, 196 p. : ill. ISBN 0-8403-5511-4.

A useful introductory textbook on jazz, offering concise accounts of slave songs, minstrelsy, blues, ragtime, Dixieland, Tin Pan Alley, big bands, bebop, and cool. Full-length musical examples, in fakebook style, illuminate the narrative. There are "topics for discussion" after each chapter. With a jazz glossary, a general bibliography of about 50 books, and a nonexpansive index of names and topics.

ML3508.7–3508.8 : Jazz by State or City

California

S2-1125   ML3508.7 .C28 G5
Gioia, Ted. West Coast jazz : modern jazz in California, 1945–1960 / Ted Gioia. — New York : Oxford, 1992. — xii, 404 p. ISBN 0-19-506310-4.
Essays that offer "a critical re-evaluation" of the jazz scene in California during the 1950s and 1960s, the period of cool jazz—the crisp, soft, lyrical outgrowth of bebop. Major practitioners discussed include Dave Brubeck, Chet Baker, Shelly Manne, Art Pepper, Charles Mingus, Gerry Mulligan, Miles Davis, Jimmy Giuffre, and Dexter Gordon. These are well-documented accounts, with considerable musical discussion in addition to biographical and anecdotal elements. With endnotes and a nonexpansive index.
Reviews: *Choice* 10/92, 311; LJ 4/15/92, 92.

Kansas City

S2-1126   ML3508.8 .K37 D9
Durrett, Warren. Warren Durrett : his piano and his orchestra / Warren Durrett. — Shawnee Mission, Kans. : Author, 1987. — 314 p. : ill. ISBN not given.
"A chronology of the Warren Durrett big band in Kansas City, 1945–1986."

S2-1127   ML3508.8 .K37 P4
Pearson, Nathan W., Jr. Goin' to Kansas City / Nathan W. Pearson, Jr. — Urbana : University of Illinois Press, 1987. — xviii, 276 p. : ill. : 44 p. plates. ISBN 0-252-01336-0.
The book shares its title with a traveling exhibit that opened in May 1980, and toured for about three years, illustrating the jazz heritage of Kansas City. Presented in book format, the material obviously loses much of its impact and seems to have little new to offer on the topic except for good accounts of city life and nightlife in the 1920s and 1930s. Interviews with Count Basie, Buck Clayton, John Hammond, Jay McShann, Sam Price, Mary Lou Williams, and others, are recounted; they are anecdotal,

saying nothing about music. The whole is documented with chapter endnotes and benefits from good photographs and an expansive index. Review: LJ 2/1/88, 67.

New Orleans

S2-1128   ML3508.8 .N48 S61
Smith, Michael P. A joyful noise : a celebration of New Orleans music / Michael P. Smith; introduction and interviews by Alan Govenar. — Dallas : Taylor, 1990. — xiii, 210 p. : ill. ISBN 0-8783-3664-8.
A picture book that displays the great variety of musical life in the city: in the street, at funerals, in church, in parades, and at social occasions. Jazz is one element, but it is not allowed to dominate the book. Interviews with ordinary people who are also amateur music makers are of interest. Without index.

S2-1129   ML3508.8 .N48 S62
Smith, Michael P. New Orleans jazz fest : a pictorial history / Michael P. Smith. — Gretna, La. : Pelican, 1991. — 207 p. ISBN 0-88289-810-0.
A picture story of the New Orleans Jazz and Heritage Festival, held annually since 1970, attracting as many as a quarter of a million persons. There are some 400 photos, of crowds, star performers such as Miles Davis and B. B. King, brass bands, and church choirs. A running commentary connects the images. Without index.

New York City

S2-1130   ML3508.8 .N5 B34
Balliett, Whitney. Goodbyes and other messages : a journal of jazz, 1981–1990 / Whitney Balliett. — New York : Oxford, 1991. — 295 p. ISBN 0-19-503757-X.
Balliett has collected 53 short pieces he wrote during the 1980s; most appeared in the *New Yorker*. Subjects include the Red Norvo Trio, the Kool Jazz Festival, Charlie Parker, Duke Ellington, the Modern Jazz Quartet, Thelonious Monk, Sonny Greer, Dizzy Gillespie, Bill Coleman, Old and New Dreams (group), Teddy Wilson, Frank Sinatra, Bunny Berigan, Otis Ferguson, Warren Vaché, Earl Hines, Peck Kelley, Wynton Marsalis, "The Sound of Jazz" (television program), Ben Webster, Louis Armstrong, Michel Petrucciani, Paul Whiteman, Count Basie, Jelly Roll Morton, Blue Note recordings, Vic Dickenson, the Classic Jazz Quartet, Dave Murray's Octet, Zoot Sims, Al Cohn, the Mulligan Sextet, Paul Gonsalves, Cootie Williams, Jo Jones, Bill Evans, Charles Mingus, the American Jazz Orchestra, the Leaders (group), big bands,

Benny Goodman, Sidney Catlett, Jazz in July (festival), Keynote record-ings, Buddy Rich, John Hammond, Dick Wellstood, jazz on the S.S. Norway, Jimmy Knepper, Peggy Lee, Stéphane Grappelli, Warne Marsh, Gunther Schuller's book *The Swing Era,* Max Gordon, the *New Grove Dictionary of Jazz,* Roy Eldridge, Michael Moore, Gene Bertoncini, and Miles Davis.

Arranged chronologically; without bibliographical references or index [—D. P.].

Review: LJ 6/1/91, 140.

S2-1131   ML3508.8 .N5 G2

Gavin, James. Intimate nights : the golden age of New York cabaret / James Gavin. — New York : Grove Weidenfeld, 1991. — viii, 406 p. ISBN 0-8021-1080-0. (Alternative classification: PN1969.)

The story of small nightclubs in New York—for some reason identi-fied by Gavin as cabarets—from the 1940s to the early 1960s. Such clubs were frequented by a sophisticated clientele, who were rewarded with performances by outstanding jazz pianists, sultry vocalists, and comedi-ans. The clubs are described, and there are anecdotal biographical sketches of the owners, as well as about the performers (useful informa-tion is given on lesser-known artists). Extracts from routines exemplify the golden age of stand-up comedy. No bibliography or footnotes; but there is a selective discography (minimal data) and a nonexpansive in-dex.

Newark

S2-1132   ML3508.8 .N53 K8

Kukla, Barbara J. Swing city : Newark nightlife, 1925–50 / Barbara J. Kukla. — Philadelphia : Temple University Press, 1991. — xii, 269 p. : ill. ISBN 0-87722-874-4.

A "broad social history of nightlife in Newark, New Jersey," focused "on black life during the days of vaudeville and the swing era," "as much about the vicissitudes of life in urban black America." The local artists of renown included singer Viola Wells, trumpeter Leon Eason, pianist Clem Moorman, and pianist Bobby Tucker. Contemporary newspaper stories and interviews by the author were the basis for much of the book; sources are listed but not connected to the text by direct citations. There is a valuable "who's who" of about 500 persons, with concise accounts of their careers. With a nonexpansive index.

Sacramento

S2-1133   ML3508.8 .S2 W5

Wilson, Burt. A history of Sacramento jazz, 1948–1966 : a personal memoir / Burt Wilson. — Canoga Park, Calif. : Author, 1986. — ix, 101 p. : ill. ISBN not given.

ML3518 : Big Bands

S2-1134   ML3518 .B5 B2
Barron, Lee. Odyssey of the mid-nite flyer : a history of Midwest bands / Lee Barron. — Omaha, Nebr. : Author, 1987. — 288 p. : ill. ISBN not given.

Plain accounts of many "territory bands," the swing groups that traveled by bus from town to town; they did not reach the national stage but provided suitable music for proms and other local events. Although the book is made up primarily of routine anecdotes, there is reference value to the photographs and the personnel lists for many obscure ensembles. Without index or documentation.

S2-1135   ML3518 .B5 C8
Crowther, Bruce. The big band years / Bruce Crowther and Mike Pinfold; Franklin S. Driggs, picture editor. — New York : Facts on File, 1988. — 208 p. : ill. ISBN 0-8160-2013-2.

A chronological narrative of the big bands, well illustrated, without documentation. There are numerous unusual photos (many in color) that show theater interiors and exteriors. The nonexpansive index includes all personnel of the bands, a valuable resource. With a brief, selective discography (minimal data).

S2-1136   ML3518 .H28
Hall, Fred. Dialogues in swing : intimate conversations with the stars of the big band era / Fred Hall; foreword by Artie Shaw. — Ventura, Calif. : Pathfinder, 1989. — 223 p. : ill. ISBN 0-9347-9319-0.

Interviews with Bob Crosby, Dick Haymes, Jo Stafford and Paul Weston, Woody Herman, Mel Tormé, George Shearing, Wild Bill Davison, Peggy Lee, Artie Shaw, Jimmy Van Heusen, and Maxene Andrews; and comments by various persons about Glenn Miller. Hall—host of the radio program *Swing Thing*—did not make much of his grand opportunities, holding the material to career summaries and anecdotes. ("How was Sinatra to work with?" [to Stafford]: "Great, great.") George Shearing contributes the most memorable line to the query, "What got you into music at all?": "I'm a firm believer in reincarnation, and in a previous life I was Johann Sebastian Bach's guide dog." Undocumented; with a nonexpansive index of names. See also S2-1137.

S2-1137   ML3518 .H29
Hall, Fred. More dialogues in swing : intimate conversations with the stars of the big band era / Fred Hall; foreword by Jo Stafford and Paul

Weston. — Ventura, Calif. : Pathfinder, 1991. — 231 p. : ill. ISBN 0-9347-9331-X.

A sequel to S2-1136, presenting interviews with Kay Starr, Steve Allen, Teddy Wilson, Alvino Rey and the King Sisters, Herb Jeffries, Johnny Green, Les Brown, Helen Forrest and Helen O'Connell, Harry James, and Tony Bennett; with several people talking about Count Basie. The questions are not contrived to elicit musical information, nor indeed anything significant about the lives of the artists (Q: "What's your life style these days, Teddy [Wilson]? You work just as hard as you want to?" A: "I live on the road. I work from one job to another and in between the bookings I'm either in New Jersey or Boston." Q: "You have a son who is in music, don't you?" A: "Yeah, I have three boys . . ."; the interviewees say "yeah" quite often.) Undocumented; with a nonexpansive index of names.

S3-1138   ML3518 .L4
Leckrone, Michael. Popular music in the U.S. (1920–1950) : class outline : the big bands / Michael Leckrone. — Rev. ed. — Dubuque, Iowa : Eddie Bowers, 1986. — iv, 102 p. ISBN 0-9128-5516-9.

"Includes historical data of instrumental groups and individual artists of the big band era; glossary; lists and bibliography" (OCLC record).

No earlier ed. in LOAM or LOAM Suppl.

S2-1139   ML3518 .P64
Polic, Edward F. The Glenn Miller Army Air Force Band / Edward F. Polic; foreword by George T. Simon. — Metuchen, N.J. : Scarecrow, 1989. — 2 vols. : ill. (Studies in jazz, 8) ISBN 0-8108-2269-5.

A monumental tribute to the greatest of military swing bands, the Army Air Force Band organized and directed by Glenn Miller (1904–1944), which existed for only 1,032 days: 20 March 1943 to 15 January 1946. The ensemble performed normal military duties and also made radio broadcasts and recordings. One radio series was named *I Sustain the Wings,* from the AAF Technical Training Command insignia, "Sustineo alas." Various subunits of the band were developed under separate names. This discography provides complete information for all sessions, down to the Army serial number of each performer. There are extensive comments as well, some of a sort not usually found in discographies ("in a very cold hangar . . . the band wore woolen gloves while playing . . ."; "propaganda recordings for broadcast to German soldiers . . . dialogue in German by Ilse Weinberger . . ."). Biographical sketches for personnel are given. Volume 2 includes complete scripts of radio shows and a list of commercial record sessions in which Air Force Band musicians participated.

Review: ARBA 1990, #1289.

S2-1140 ML3518 .R38
Raymond, Al. Swinging big bands . . . into the 90's / Al Raymond. —
Broomall, Pa. : Harmony, 1992. — 245 p. ISBN not given.

An advocate of contemporary big bands, Raymond sets out to "encourage young dedicated musicians, and band leaders throughout the
country who are constantly battling the ravages of rock and 101 other
'goodies' in today's music world." He identifies over 100 bands that
have been active since the golden age of the 1940s. Although the commentary is breezy and unfocused, there are hundreds of photographs
not to be found elsewhere. Among the bandleaders emphasized are
Ashley Alexander, Lew Anderson, Lin Biviano, Gordon Brisker,
Matt Catingub, Sonny Costanzo, Bob Florence, Rob McConnell,
Paolo Nonnis, Rob Stoneback, and Zim Zemarel. With a nonexpansive index.

S2-1141 ML3518 .R64 A3
Rollini, Arthur. Thirty years with the big bands / Arthur Rollini. —
London : Macmillan; Urbana : University of Illinois Press, 1987. —
134 p. : ill. : 16 p. plates. ISBN 0-3334-3927-9 (U.K.); 0-2520-1454-5
(U.S.).

Versatile Rollini (1912–) played flute with the ABC Symphony and
tenor sax with Benny Goodman and other big bands. His life story is recounted here in casual style, built mostly of anecdotes and conversations,
and with no musical content. Without documentation; with a partly expansive index.

S2-1142 ML3518 .S551
Simon, George Thomas. The big bands / George Thomas Simon. —
4th ed. — New York : Schirmer, 1981. — xvii, 614 p. : ill. ISBN 0-
0287-24208.

1st ed., 1967; 2nd ed., 1971 (LOAM 1045).

A useful, insider account of the great swing and jazz bands of the
1930s and 1940s, offering history and commentary, with photographs
for each of about 300 ensembles. In some cases the band personnel are
identified. With a name index.

S2-1143 ML3518 .S555
Simon, George Thomas. The big bands trivia quiz book / George
Thomas Simon. — New York : Barnes & Noble, 1985. — 120 p. : ill.
ISBN 0-06-464096-5.

An amusing collection of questions about musicians of the swing era: readers may identify portraits, recall who played what solos, think of the song with the second line "She is all they claim," and wonder who sang "Got a Date with an Angel" on the Hal Kemp recording. Answers are given, fortunately; the general level of difficulty is high.

S2-1144   ML3518 .W39
Way, Chris. The big bands go to war / Chris Way. — Edinburgh, Scotland : Mainstream, 1991. — 288 p. : ill. ISBN 1-85158-475-7.
A valuable inventory of the American and British military bands formed during World War II by well-known musicians, including those of Tex Beneke, Larry Clinton, Sam Donahue, Wayne King, Glenn Miller, Artie Shaw, Claude Thornhill, Rudy Vallee, and Meredith Willson. Except for the Miller group, these ensembles have been largely forgotten. Way gives historical information, details of concerts and broadcasts, and interesting comments for each band. Discographies are included. With a nonexpansive index.

ML3519 : Bluegrass

S2-1145   ML3519 .B58
Deakins, Betty. Bluegrass directory : 1985–86 / Betty Deakins. — Murphys, Calif. : BD Products, 1986. — 216 p. ISBN not given.
"Who and where to write for bluegrass, old-time and folk music products, services, advice, catalogs" (OCLC record).

ML3521 : Blues

S2-1146   ML3521 .B36
Barlow, William. "Looking up at down" : the emergence of blues culture / William Barlow. — Philadelphia : Temple University Press, 1989. — xii, 404 p. ISBN 0-87722-583-4.
Although the introduction to this book is not promising—it attempts to document "the historical trajectory of African-American cultural resistance to white domination"—the volume turns out to be one of those rare approaches to blues (or jazz) that discusses musical matters in musical language. Song lyrics are also dealt with, and the author's social theme remains prominent, leading to a pleasing denouement, to the effect that we have achieved a "novel interracial melting pot," with whites and blacks bound "by their common love and respect for the music." With chapter endnotes, a good expansive index of names, and a song title index.
Reviews: *Choice* 4/90, 1331; LJ 12/89, 125.

S2-1147   ML3521 .B39

Bastin, Bruce. Red River blues : the blues tradition in the southeast /
Bruce Bastin. — Urbana : University of Illinois Press, 1986. — xiii, 379
p. : ill. ISBN 0-252-01213-5.

A close look at the emergence of blues in various communities of
Georgia, Virginia, North Carolina, and South Carolina, fully docu-
mented with chapter endnotes. There are strong chapters on noncom-
mercial recordings of the 1930s and 1940s (e.g., by John Lomax, and of
the festivals at Fort Valley State College, Georgia). The traditions and
perfomers of key cities are analyzed, such as Greenville, North Carolina
(Josh White, Gary Davis, etc.), and Spartanburg, North Carolina (Pink
Anderson). Among other blues artists studied closely are Brownie
McGhee and Sonny Terry in North Carolina, and Blind Boy Fuller in
South Carolina. With a tune index and partly expansive general index.

Bastin is a British folklorist and record company manager.

Reviews: *Choice* 2/88, 916; LJ 10/15/86, 97.

S2-1148   ML3521 .B47

Berry, Jason. Up from the cradle of jazz : New Orleans music since
World War II / Jason Berry, Jonathan Foose, and Tad Jones. — Athens :
University of Georgia Press, 1986. — xiv, 285 p. : ill. ISBN 0-8203-
0853-6.

A well-documented narrative of individuals and genres, covering musical families, club life, deejays, Mardi Gras music, and the "Caribbean
connection." Considerable attention goes to seminal figures such as Professor Longhair (Harry Roeland Byrd), Fats Domino, Allen Toussaint,
and Dr. John (Malcolm John Rebennack, Jr.). The contribution of American Indians is engagingly explored. With numerous photos, endnotes, a
bibliography of about 200 books and articles (giving minimal information), and an expansive index.

Reviews: *Choice* 4/87, 1229; LJ 9/15/86, 89.

S2-1149   ML3521 .B67

Booth, Stanley. Rythm [*sic*] oil : a journey through the music of the
American South / Stanley Booth. — New York : Pantheon, 1991. —
254 p. : ill. ISBN 0-679-40944-0.

"Originally published in Great Britain by Jonathan Cape, London, in
1991."

"The story of a journey . . . from slavery in 1940s south Georgia to
murder in 1960s Memphis and back again to savagery in 1990s Georgia, with many laughs along the way." There are more anecdotes than
laughs, about Elvis Presley, B. B. King, Janis Joplin, Aretha Franklin,
Phineas Newborn, Sam Phillips, and Muddy Waters, among others. The

material was previously published in a number of magazines. There is no documentation and no explanation of the misspelling in the book's title. With a nonexpansive index.

S2-1150   ML3521 .E42
Ellison, Mary. Extensions of the blues / Mary Ellison. — London : Calder, 1989. — 307 p. : ill. : 16 p. plates. ISBN 0-7145-3717-9.
A history of the blues with some musical considerations and some interesting sidelights: blues in poetry, blues in fiction, blues on stage, and so forth. The author, a British university lecturer, seems to outrun her material in the search for blues themes in T. S. Eliot and García Lorca. For some reason she spells Thelonious Monk's first name without the second *o*. With chapter endnotes, a bibliography of about 300 items, and a nonexpansive index of names and titles.

S2-1151   ML3521 .F56
Finn, Julio. The bluesman : the musical heritage of black men and women in the Americas / Julio Finn; illustrations by Willa Woolston. — London; New York : Quartet, 1987. — 256 p. : ill. ISBN 0-70043-2523-3.
A thorough account of the genesis of blues, which the author traces to Haiti (voodoo), Jamaica, Cuba (santeria), Brazil (candomoblé), African dance, gospel churches, and spirituals. The seminal songs of "neurotic genius" Robert Johnson are carefully discussed. Documented with chapter endnotes and readily accessible through an expansive index.
Review: LJ 3/1/92, 93.

S2-1152   ML3521 .G68
Govenar, Alan B. Meeting the blues / Alan Govenar. — Dallas : Taylor, 1988. — 239 p. : ill. ISBN 0-87833-623-0.
An endeavor "to examine the development and diversity of Texas blues," considering the different styles found in Dallas, Fort Worth, Houston, Beaumont, Austin, and other Texas cities. Govenar conducted 100 interviews with performers, but did not extract much musical information from them; the book is mostly comprised of gossip and casual chat. There is a short discography and a nonexpansive name index.

S2-1153   ML3521 .G73
Hyman, Laurence J. Going to Chicago : a year on the Chicago blues scene / ed. Laurence J. Hyman; photographs by Stephen Green. — San Francisco : Woodford, 1990. — 128 p. : ill. ISBN 0-942627-09-1.
A book of 230 photographs with brief comments, showing musicians in performance. There is no exact dating: "The year could be any year";

and indeed the city could be any city, since there are hardly any images that depict local settings. No index.

S2-1154   ML3521 .G9
Guralnick, Peter. Sweet soul music : rhythm and blues and the southern dream of freedom / Peter Guralnick. — New York : Harper & Row, 1986. — ix, 438 p. : ill. ISBN 0-06-096049-3.

A plain, undocumented history of non-Motown soul music, the "far less controlled gospel-based, emotion-baring kind of music" of the 1960s. Guralnick finds it significant that the popularity of the genre "accompanied the Civil Rights movement almost step by step" and does what he can to find political roots in the music. Among individuals getting much attention are Solomon Burke, Otis Redding, Aretha Franklin, and James Brown. The Stax Record Company is well discussed. Conversations and quotations are ubiquitous. There is a useful bibliography of articles on some individuals. With a selective discography (minimal data) and a nonexpansive index.

Reviews: *Choice* 10/86, 318; LJ 6/1/86, 125.

S2-1155   ML3521 .H38
Harrison, Daphne Duvall. Black pearls : blues queens of the 1920s / Daphne Duvall Harrison. — New Brunswick, N.J. : Rutgers University Press, 1988. — xv, 295 p. : ill. ISBN 0-8135-1279-4.

Documented life-and-career studies of Ida Cox, Bertha Hill, Alberta Hunter, Sara Martin, Ma Rainey, Bessie Smith, Mamie Smith, Victoria Spivey, Sippie Wallace, and Edita Wilson. Song lyrics are given, and record labels are discussed. With endnotes, a bibliography of about 80 entries, a subject index, and a song title index.

Reviews: AM 1989, 205; *Choice* 11/88, 501; LJ 4/1/88, 86.

S2-1156   ML3521 .M47
Merrill, Hugh. The blues route / Hugh Merrill. — New York : Morrow, 1990. — 236 p. ISBN 0-688-06611-9.

The story of Merrill's auto journey along the roads of "the greatest migration in America . . . from the Mississippi Delta to Chicago and from Louisiana and Texas to California"—the blues route, as he calls it—during which he talked to musicians and meditated on the various locales. It is all very casual, primarily comprised of undocumented conversations, and fundamentally uninformative. Without index.

Review: LJ 6/15/90, 114.

S2-1157   ML3521 .O42
Oliver, Paul. Blues fell this morning : meaning in the blues / Paul

Oliver; foreword by Richard Wright. — 2nd ed. — Cambridge : Cambridge University Press, 1990. — xxiv, 348 p. ISBN 0-521-37437-5. 1st ed., 1960 (LOAM 864).

Oliver considers blues to be the folk music of the American black. Topical chapters address the various themes of blues lyrics from the 1920s to the 1950s: love, crime, poverty, prison, war, etc. Each theme is discussed in a historical narrative, with song lyrics interspersed. About 350 songs are included in the discussions; they are also listed in a discography (78 rpm records only, no reissues; with matrix numbers, artists, recording locations, recording dates, and label information; no release dates). Expansive index. Without source notes, but with bibliographical references by chapter.

Reviews: ARBA 1991, p. 531; *Choice* 12/90, 640.

ML3524 : Country

S2-1158   ML3524 .C66

Country : the music and the musicians / foreword by Paul Kingsbury. — Nashville : Country Music Foundation Press; New York : Abbeville, 1988. — 595 p. : ill. ISBN 0-89659-868-3.

An adulatory narrative of country music from the 1920s to the late 1980s, in casual style. Needlessly large print and huge photographs turned this slim text into a giant volume. Without documentation or reference features, except for a selective bibliography of about 80 books.

S2-1159   ML3524 .D36

Daniel, Wayne W. Pickin' on Peachtree : a history of country music in Atlanta, Georgia / Wayne W. Daniel. — Urbana : University of Illinois Press, 1990. — xiv, 295 p. ISBN 0-252-01687-4.

Various approaches to Atlanta's country traditions: the Georgia Old-Time Fiddlers Conventions of 1913–1935; radio programming of the 1920s, 1930s, and 1940s; the WASB Barn Dance; television; and the local record industry. With chapter endnotes and a nonexpansive index.

Review: *Choice* 12/90, 639.

S2-1160   ML3524 .E5

Endres, Clifford. Austin city limits / Clifford Endres. — Austin : University of Texas Press, 1987. — 136 p. : ill. ISBN 0-292-70378-3.

A "photographic history of public television's favorite and most critically acclaimed music program," which included 140 shows over an 11-year period. There are 269 photos, 39 in color, of such stars as Kris Kristofferson, Willie Nelson, and Loretta Lynn. Some comments are appended, and some imaginary conversations. Without source notes;

with a "highly arbitrary" selective discography and nonexpansive index.

Reviews: AM 1990, 373; LJ 9/1/87, 184.

S2-1161   ML3524 .F36

Farragher, Scott. Music city Babylon / Scott Farragher. — New York : Birch Lane, 1992. — xv, 331 p. : ill. : 16 p. plates. ISBN 1-55972-134-0.

An insider view, by a talent agent, of the country music business: "a revelation of arrogance, greed and excess at all levels, from groupie to megastar." Nashville is "filled with hustlers of all shapes and sizes," providing Farragher with innumerable illustrative anecdotes. Among those in the cast are Jerry Lee Lewis, Fats Domino, Randy Travis, James Brown, Lou Rawls, Ronnie Milsap, and Mickey Gilley. Feelings and dialogues are created for the occasion. Without documentation; with an expansive index.

S2-1162   ML3524 .H22

Hagan, Chet. Grand Ole Opry / Chet Hagan. — New York : Holt, 1989. — 346 p. : ill. ISBN 0-8050-0543-9.

An anecdotal account of the Opry radio program, which began broadcasting in 1925—the longest running show in radio history. Prominent country singers are profiled, and there are about 100 photos, many in color. Index.

Review: LJ 6/15/89, 60.

S2-1163   ML3524 .M34

Malone, Bill C. Country music, U.S.A. / Bill Malone. — Rev. ed. — Austin : University of Texas Press, 1985. — xii, 562 p. : ill. ISBN 0-2927-1095-X.

1st ed., 1968 (LOAM 606).

An update of Malone's standard history, with a new chapter on developments from 1972–1984. A change in this edition is the removal of footnotes to a sort of summary bibliographical essay. Indexes for names and song titles, and a guide to recordings.

Listing and review: BCL; *Choice* 12/85, 614.

S2-1164   ML3524 .M36

McLaurin, Melton. You wrote my life : lyrical themes in country music / Melton McLaurin and Richard Peterson. — Philadelphia : Gordon & Breach, 1992. — x, 180 p. (Cultural perspectives on the American South, 6) ISBN 2-88124-548-X.

Seven interesting essays, including one on the changing image of the South in country music; others on the country music female, death in country music, and lyrical themes in Johnny Cash songs. With endnotes, a song title index (which cites recordings), and a name index.

S2-1165   ML3524 .R65
Rogers, Jimmie N. The country music message revisited / Jimmie N. Rogers. — 2nd ed. — Fayetteville : University of Arkansas Press, 1989. — xiv, 268 p. ISBN 1-5572-8051-7.
1st ed., 1983 (LOAM Suppl. SA-228).
An interesting collection of comments on about 1,400 country songs, all from the *Billboard* charts. Lyrics are discussed, and many of the performers are interviewed for their reactions. For a focus, Rogers considers how the various ideas of country music are processed through the industry and how audiences receive them. It is not surprising to learn that the "most commercially popular country songs speak of love between men and women," nor that the principal subthemes are "hurtin' love," "happy love," and "cheatin'." There are also many songs about "livin'." With chapter endnotes and a nonexpansive index.
Review: *Choice* 6/84, 1476 (for 1st ed.).

ML3527–3534 : Rock and Roll

S2-1166   ML3527 .G75
Gribin, Anthony J. Doo-wop : the forgotten third of rock 'n' roll / Anthony J. Gribin and Matthew M. Schiff. — Iola, Wisc. : Krause, 1992. — 612 p. ISBN 0-8734-1197-8.
"Doo-wop" is the name given to a style of vocal group singing that was popular from around 1954 to 1963; it featured nonsense syllables and (in the male groups) a falsetto tenor. Competing with rhythm and blues and with rock and roll, doo-wop recordings accounted for 15 percent of the number-one hits during their period. Among the major performers were the Cadillacs, Drifters, Harptones, Shirelles, Heartbeats, and Chantels. Gribin gives a useful historical account (without source notes), then a list of some 25,000 songs by artist, indexed by title, label, and album number. With a bibliography of about 150 entries.
Review: ARBA 1993, p. 545.

S2-1167   ML3531 .C67
Costello, Mark. Signifying rappers : rap and race in the urban present / Mark Costello and David Foster Wallace. — New York : Ecco Books, 1990. — 140 p. and unpaged music section. ISBN 0-88001-255-2.
The "first serious consideration of rap and its position as a vital force in our American culture" is a statement of the now-familiar perspective that portrays rap performers as social rather than musical phenomena. In an "edgy and perceptive discussion," the authors concentrate on "cul-

tural barricades that rappers alternately challenge, enforce, and decry."
Without index or documentation.

S2-1168   ML3534 .A68

Aquila, Richard. That old time rock & roll : a chronicle of an era,
1954–1963 / Richard Aquila. — New York : Schirmer, 1989. — xii, 370
p. : ill. : 32 p. plates. ISBN 0-02-870082-1.

"A historical investigation of the old hits and perfomers from rock's
first decade," consisting of biographies and studies of such topics as
youth culture, novelty records, and the relations of the music to society
and politics. There is a list of greatest hits, and there are various song lists
by performer. Without documentation or index.

Reviews: ARBA 1990, #1291; *Choice* 3/90, 1107.

S2-1169   ML3534 .B215

Bangs, Lester. Psychotic reactions and carburetor dung / Lester Bangs;
ed. with introduction by Greil Marcus. — New York : Knopf, 1987. —
xviii, 386 p. ISBN 0-394-53896-X.

Bangs, who died in 1982, was a rock performer who wrote for *Creem*;
this is a collection of essays from that periodical and a few other sources.
Although the *New York Times* (quoted on the cover) regarded Bangs as "one
of the best writers ever to appear on newsprint," these pieces are only casual
program notes, told in a vulgar idiom and featuring invented conversations.
Among the musicians discussed are James Taylor, John Coltrane, Chicago,
Jethro Tull, and David Bowie. With a nonexpansive index.

Reviews: *Choice* 4/88, 1254; LJ 9/1/87, 184.

S2-1170   ML3534 .B774

Brown, Rodger Lyle. Party out of bounds : the B-52's, REM, and the
kids who rock Athens, Georgia / Rodger Lyle Brown. — New York :
Penguin, 1991. — 221 p. : ill. : 8 p. plates. ISBN 0-452-26631-9.

The university town of Athens has become a center of rock performance; the emergence is narrated here in highly adulatory language,
framed in imaginary conversations and episodes. Without documentation or index.

S2-1171   ML3534 .C69

Cotten, Lee. Shake, rattle & roll : the golden age of American rock 'n'
roll. Volume 1, 1952–1955 / Lee Cotten. — Ann Arbor, Mich. : Pierian,
1989. — xxxii, 355 p. : ill. (Rock & roll reference series, 31) ISBN 0-
97650-246-X.

This chronology of the early years of rock music, announced as the
first of four volumes that will end with Woodstock, lists performances in
Baltimore, Chicago, Detroit, Los Angeles, New Orleans, New York

City, and Washington, D.C. New releases are also listed, as are other events in the industry. Cotten adds perspective by listing the top 10 rock and roll records for each month, by frequently adding comments in sidebars, and by writing a one-page biography of the "artist of the month." While rock is emphasized, there is also a significant amount of information on jazz and blues artists. Poorly reproduced publicity stills are sprinkled throughout. There are nonexpansive indexes of performers, song titles, record companies, industry personnel, and broadcast media. Since the entries refer to dates in the chronology, the monthly biographies are not indexed. The bibliography includes almost 100 books (author and title only), over 30 magazines, and a dozen newspapers.

Lee Cotten is the author of several works about the life and recordings of Elvis Presley [—D. P.].

Reviews: ARBA 1990, #1293; *Choice* 9/89, 76; LJ 9/15/89.

S2-1172   ML3534 .C87

Curtis, Jim. Rock eras : interpretations of music and society, 1954–1984 / Jim Curtis. — Bowling Green, Ohio : Bowling Green State University Popular Press, 1987. — 363 p. ISBN 0-87972-368-8.

A laborious effort at theorizing about rock, based on an incomplete understanding of Marshall McLuhan and much of modern culture. When did TV "operate as a force for innovation" is the "first question" of the book — one that is in fact not answered therein. What follows is a catchall monologue attempting to relate McLuhan's ideas to pop music. Rock history is divided into three decades and discussed in a fatuous manner. The chapter on electric guitars is of some interest. Numerous errors appear, including the egregious misspelling—for an entire chapter of discussion—"Sargeant Pepper." With endnotes (many mistaken entries) and a partly expansive index of names. All things considered, a book to be missed.

Reviews: AM 1991, 232; *Choice* 1/88, 776.

S2-1173   ML3534 .E44

Eliot, Marc. Rockonomics : the money behind the music / Marc Eliot. — New York : Watts, 1989. — xiv, 290 p. ISBN 0-531-15106-9.

A financial approach to rock music, offering dollar figures, sales, and market data in an undocumented narrative. With an awkward bibliography containing many errors and presenting some writers by their last names only. There is a partly expansive index.

Reviews: *Choice* 10/89, 325; LJ 5/1/89, 79.

S2-1174   ML3534 . F63

Flippo, Chet. Everybody was kung-fu dancing : chronicles of the lionized and the notorious / Chet Flippo. — New York : St. Martin's, 1991. — x, 294 p. : ill. ISBN 0-3120-6349-0.

A gathering of articles and interviews by Flippo, all of them published in various magazines over a 20-year period. They are made up primarily of remembered dialogues and stories, with no musical content. Among the persons considered are Waylon Jennings, Bobby Bare, Les Paul, and Jerry Lee Lewis. No index.

S2-1175   ML3534 .F75
Frith, Simon. Music for pleasure : essays in the sociology of pop / Simon Frith. — New York : Routledge, 1988. — viii, 232 p. ISBN 0-415-90052-2.

Essays previously published—mostly in the *Village Voice* and *Melody Maker*—on various popular musicians. The tone is casual and impressionistic, emphasizing personalities rather than musical matters. Bob Dylan, Madonna, and Elvis Presley are given considerable attention. With a nonexpansive name index.

Review: LJ 11/1/88, 96.

S2-1176   ML3534 .G2
Gart, Galen. First pressings : rock history as chronicled in Billboard magazine / Galen Gart. — Milford, N.H. : Big Nickel, 1986. — Vol. 1– . ISBN 0-936433-01-9 (vol. 1); 0-936433-00-0 (vol. 2).

Vol. 1: 1948–1950; vol. 2: 1951–1952; vol. 3: 1953; vol. 4: 1954.

Vols. 3 and 4 have subtitle: *The History of Rhythm & Blues*.

This interesting effort presents photocopies of *Billboard* articles, stories, pictures, and advertising from the years of coverage, reset into new page formats. Material is grouped by month of original publication, but exact dates are not given for individual items. An excellent source for timely and often obscure information, rendered accessible through nonexpansive indexes of names, record labels, and places.

S2-1177   ML3534 .G7
Greenwald, Ted. Rock & roll : the music, musicians, and the mania / Ted Greenwald. — New York : Mallard, 1992. — 120 p. : ill. ISBN 0-7924-5765-X.

A rock photo album, with many large color pictures, arranged more or less chronologically and accompanied by a casual commentary. There is some interest in the occasional table or graph, such as the family tree of rock styles, and a list of pseudonyms. A Grammy Award list in pop categories (winners only, minimal data) covers 1958–1991. With a one-page index.

S2-1178   ML3534 .H46
Henry, Tricia. Break all rules ! : punk rock and the making of a style / Tricia Henry. — Ann Arbor, Mich. : UMI Research Press, 1989. — xii, 152 p. (Studies in the fine arts. Avant-garde, 68) ISBN 0-8357-1980-4.

An interesting, scholarly treatment of a rock subgenre that offered the author few documents to work with, and problems with oral history as well, since the major figures refused interviews. Henry gathered what she could and put together this sensible account of the movement that she asserts began in England in 1976. Her definition of the phenomenon is cloudy: it carries "underlying implications of the amateur, the hoodlum, the useless element in society, together with the idea of volatility," and it stands "at the radical end of the rock-and-roll continuum." She concentrates on Lou Reed and the Velvet Underground, the New York Dolls, the Sex Pistols, the Manhattan rock club CBGB & OMFUG, and fanzines. As this is essentially a sociological study, the musical elements of punk are not discussed, but there are some tune/chord/word excerpts that reveal the poverty of the idiom. With endnotes, a bibliography of about 300 items, and an expansive index.

Review: *Choice* 3/90, 1159.

S2-1179   ML3534 .J68
Jones, Steve. Rock formation : music, technology, and mass communication / Steve Jones. — Newbury Park, Calif. : Sage, 1992. — xvi, 223 p. (Foundations of popular culture, 3) ISBN 0-8039-4442-X.

A study of the impact of recording technology on popular music, especially on rock—"a social history of music recording." There are chapters on "design and marketing of music technology," "technology, music, and copyright," "the process of sound recording," and "technology and the musician." Many performers are quoted along the way, discussing the relation between studio recording and live concerts and the like; their statements are documented, if not very illuminating. Indeed, the whole treatise deals with ground that has been made familiar by numerous predecessors. With a bibliography of about 300 items and a non-expansive index.

S2-1180   ML3534 .K44
Kelly, Michael Bryan. The Beatle myth : the British invasion of American popular music, 1956–1969 / Michael Bryan Kelly. — Jefferson, N.C. : McFarland, 1991. — xi, 221 p. : ill. ISBN 0-89950-579-1.

A study that intends to "set the record straight about the impact in America" of the Beatles and the so-called British invasion. Kelly offers an amalgam of facts and impressions (in casual style without documentation) to support his view that the Beatles did not wipe out current American styles and performers. Indeed, the Rolling Stones had a more lasting presence on the American scene. There is a long list of performers with hits in the United States during the 1950s and 1960s, only a few of whom were British. The author is also determined to show that the Beatles' hair and clothing styles did not produce the emulations that appeared to follow their American appearances: a position that few survivors of the period will accept. With a nonexpansive index.

Reviews: *Choice* 11/91, 459; LJ 4/1/91, 122.

S2-1181   ML3534 .K67

Kozak, Roman. This ain't no disco : the story of CBGB / Roman Kozak; photographs by Ebet Roberts. — Boston : Faber & Faber, 1988. — xv, 143 p. : ill. : 12 p. plates. — Discography, pp. 135–143. ISBN 0-571-12956-0.

The story of "CBGB-OMFUG, Hilly Kristal's notorious nightclub on New York's bowery," which flourished in the 1970s; it was identified with the emergence of punk and new wave. Kozak offers an undocumented account, told in a vulgar idiom, with anecdotes and quotations. There is a casual discography (minimal data). Without index.

Review: LJ 5/15/88, 84.

S2-1182   ML3534 .L4

Levitt, Ellen. Land of a thousand bands : the current American independent label rock 'n' roll band experience / Ellen Levitt. — Brooklyn : Midwood, 1987. — 143 p. : ill. ISBN not given.

S2-1183   ML3534 .L45

Lemlich, Jeffrey M. Savage lost : Florida garage bands : the 60s and beyond / Jeffrey M. Lemlich. — Florida Plantation, Fla. : Distinctive Publishing, 1991. — iv, 416 p. ISBN 0-942963-12-1.

The story of local groups in Florida, with their song lists and radio appearances. A major label for them, Marlin, is discussed in some detail. The discography gives minimal information. Without index or reference features.

S2-1184   ML3534 .M15

Marcus, Greil. Mystery train : images of America in rock 'n' roll music / Greil Marcus. — 3rd ed. — New York : Dutton, 1990. — xxi, 281 p. ISBN 0-525-48556-2.

1st ed., 1975 (LOAM 1369).

Generally interesting essays on a number of rock stars and "ancestors" Harmonica Frank and Robert Johnson. Attention is focused on the Band, Sly Stone, Randy Newman, and Elvis Presley. It is unfortunate that the Presley essay was not revised for this edition; it leaves him yet alive, his dissolute lifestyle unexposed, and still characterized as "a great nice person, and, yes, a great American." Extensive notes and discographies raise this book above the ordinary, and the critical comments on rock literature are candid. With an expansive index of names, titles, and topics.

S2-1185   ML3534 .M414
Martin, Linda. Anti-rock : the opposition to rock 'n' roll / Linda Martin and Kerry Segrave. — Hamden, Conn. : Archon Books, 1988. — vii, 374 p. ISBN 0-208-02153-1.

An unusual history of rock, presented through the words of its detractors, those who object to its sexuality, noise, musical vapidity, drug connections, and so forth. There is a variety of antirock spokespersons, not all of them old fogies, for example, Milt Hinton, Mel Tormé, John Lewis, Frank Sinatra, Mitch Miller, Jesse Jackson, Ronald Reagan, and Sammy Davis, Jr. Martin has been scholarly in her method, providing chapter endnotes and describing incidents that fueled the rock opposition, such as Jim Morrison's indecent exposure conviction in 1970. However, she holds to her own position—strongly prorock—and tends to brush off the criticisms. She promises that "rock will continue to fulfill cultural expectations by exciting an irrational response on the part of the establishment." With an expansive index.

Review: *Choice* 1/89, 816.

S2-1186   ML3534 .N59
Nite, Norm N. Rock on almanac / Norm N. Nite; foreword by Dick Clark. — 2nd ed. — New York : HarperCollins, 1992. — ix, 581 p. : ill. ISBN 0-06-271555-0.

1st ed., 1989.

A valuable compilation of data, presented in chronological order. For each year, 1945 to 1989, there are names of the hit songs of every month (6,400 of them), photos of new artists, personal facts on the stars, technological innovations, award winners, rock movies, and miscellaneous items. Discographical information in the record lists is limited to label names. With a glossary, a performer index, and a song title index.

Listing and reviews: Balay BH131; *Choice* 4/90, 1303; LJ 9/15/89, 106.

S2-1187   ML3534 .P37
Pattison, Robert. The triumph of vulgarity : rock music in the mirror of romanticism / Robert Pattison. — New York : Oxford, 1987. — xiv, 280 p. ISBN 0-19-503876-2.

Although its title may suggest an antirock stance, this book is in fact a defender of the genre; "vulgarity" is used to denote the voice of common people, as opposed to that of the elite. However, "the triumph of vulgarity does not mean the extermination of elite culture, but a reinterpretation of that culture in a popular mode." This vulgarity is none other than Walt Whitman's romantic pantheism, the driving force of American democracy. It seems that rock, rather than any earlier musical form that appeared to dominate the American scene (military band music, ragtime,

jazz, swing, Broadway), meets the vulgarity test, being "simple, inexpensive, and open to ordinary people." Pattison's arguments fail to distinguish rock from other genres on musical grounds; indeed, he says he is not talking about "rock as music, but about it as an idea"—clearly a challenge, in discussing any sort of music. He does not get very far with his thesis, one reason being that he gets mired in that ubiquitous slough of despond, racism. "Contemporary white civilization is effete, sterile, and impotent. The white man is overeducated and undersexed, unnatural and inauthentic. In a word, the civilized white man is boring." With endnotes, a bibliographic essay, and an expansive index.
Reviews: AM 1989, 93; *Choice* 6/87; LJ 3/1/87, 78.

S2-1188   ML3534 .P76
DeCurtis, Anthony. Present tense : rock & roll and culture / Anthony DeCurtis. — Durham, N.C. : Duke University Press, 1992. — xii, 317 p. : ill. ISBN 0-8223-1261-1.
Fifteen essays by various writers, presenting "a mix of theoretical, speculative, technical, and practical approaches to rock & roll," including one work of fiction. The editor finds that "rock & roll stands in a tense relationship with its own mythology, its own musicological history, and with the broader culture in which music plays a part. . . . The very nature of our subject is still up for grabs." Specific topics covered include the sonic guitar, "censorship" in rock, Laurie Anderson, Bruce Springsteen, rap, and life in a rock band. The essays are footnoted, and there is an expansive index.
Review: LJ 1/92, 139.

S2-1189   ML3534 .R3
Rees, Dafydd. Rock movers & shakers / Dafydd Rees and Luke Crampton. — Rev. ed. — New York : Billboard Books, 1991. — 585 p. : ill. ISBN 0-8230-7609-1. (Alternative classification : ML394 .)
British title: *Guinness Book of Rock Stars.*
A useful checklist of 700 British and American rock performers, giving for each a chronology of concerts and other events. Without index.

S2-1190   ML3534 .R4
Reynolds, Simon. Blissed out : the raptures of rock / Simon Reynolds. — London : Serpent's Tail, 1990. — 192 p. ISBN 1-85242-199-1.
Miscellaneous essays, most of them reprinted from *Melody Maker* magazine. No index.

S2-1191   ML3534 . R6335
Podell, Janet. Rock music in America / Janet Podell. — New York : H. W. Wilson, 1987. — 172 p. (Reference shelf, 58-6) ISBN 0-8242-0727-0.

Volumes in the venerable Reference Shelf series typically offer diverse viewpoints on issues of the day; this one takes a more historical approach to its topic. It presents 15 essays (reprinted from periodicals or books) by various writers, grouped into sections: "The Birth of Rock and Roll," "Rock Takes Root," and "The Rock Music Industry." Among the subjects treated with discernment are the Nashville sound, Elvis Presley, MTV, and punk. With a bibliography of about 200 books and articles (incomplete imprint data); without index.

S2-1192   ML3534 .S4
Schaffner, Nicholas. The British invasion : from the first wave to the new wave / Nicholas Schaffner. — New York : McGraw-Hill, 1982. — 316 p. : ill. ISBN 0-07-055089-1.
Although the title suggests that the book will examine the phenomenon of sudden British incursion into American pop culture (beginning with the arrival of the Beatles), Schaffner instead gives biographical material on British groups. He goes over familiar ground with the Beatles, the Rolling Stones, and the Who; but has some useful information to give about less fabulous invaders such as the Kinks and Pink Floyd. There are short sketches of about 100 other groups and lists of chart records (minimal data). A chronology takes note of day-to-day events beginning with January 1963, when the Beatles began their first tour, and covering to the end of 1980. With a partly expansive index of names, titles, and topics.
Reviews: AM 1988, 349; ARBA 1983, p. 448; LJ 8/82, 1465.

S2-1193   ML3534 .S42
Scheurer, Timothy E. The age of rock / ed. Timothy E. Scheurer. — Bowling Green, Ohio : Bowling Green State University Popular Press, 1989. — 267 p. : ill. ISBN 0-8797-2467-6. (Alternative classification: ML3477 .S32.)
Review: LJ 5/1/91, 78.

S2-1194   ML3534 .S83
Stuessy, Joe. Rock 'n' roll : its history and stylistic development / Joe Stuessy. — Englewood Cliffs, N.J. : Prentice-Hall, 1990. — xiii, 418 p. : ill. ISBN 0-13-782426.
A useful discussion of musical elements in rock of various decades, genres, and individual performers. There are musical examples and analyses dealing with the Beatles, other British invaders, folk rock, soul, and jazz rock. With a selective discography (minimal information), a bibliography of about 120 entries, and an expansive index.
Review: *Choice* 4/92, 1192.

S2-1195   ML3534 .S94
Szatmary, David P. Rockin' in time : a social history of rock and roll /

David P. Szatmary. — 2nd ed. — Englewood Cliffs, N.J. : Prentice-Hall, 1987. — xv, 239 p. : ill. ISBN 0-13-775339-X.
1st ed., 1987.
"A social history of rock and roll . . . from roughly 1950–1986," intended to illuminate the "many-faceted American experience." The author is concerned with a number of relationships: rock and black culture; technology and rock; business and rock; politics and rock. These themes are all touched upon, and many statistics and quotations are provided (without source notes) to support Szatmary's basic view that rock was essentially shaped by nonmusical forces. Indeed, not much is said in the book about the music itself. Major attention is paid to Dick Clark, surf music, Bob Dylan, the British invasion, Motown, acid rock, soul, MTV, heavy metal, disco, and punk. A chapter on Elvis and rockabilly is perhaps the strongest section. The story is told in a chatty style, with praise and admiration for all participants. With a bibliography for each chapter (about 300 entries in all) and a nonexpansive name index.
Reviews: AM 1989, 467; *Choice* 4/92, 1192; LJ 6/15/91, 80.

S2-1196   ML3534 .W33
Ward, Ed. Rock of ages : the Rolling Stone history of rock and roll / Ed Ward, Geoffrey Stokes, and Ken Tucker; introduction by Jann S. Wenner. — New York : Rolling Stone/Summit Books, 1986. — 649 p. : ill. : 38 p. plates. ISBN 0-671-54438-1.
An undocumented history of rock that locates its roots in the nineteenth century, including Stephen Foster among its pioneers. The principal value of the book is in its photographs. With a nonexpansive index.
Reviews: *Choice* 6/87, 1563; LJ 2/1/87, 80.

S2-1197   ML3534 .W45
Weinstein, Deena. Heavy metal : a cultural sociology / Deena Weinstein. — New York : Lexington Books, 1991. — 331 p. : ill. ISBN 0-669-21837-5.
Heavy metal has been severely denounced by nearly all observers for lyrics and performances that emphasize violence, promiscuity, substance abuse, satanism, and various perversions. Nevertheless, it is an idiom (the hardest hard rock) that has achieved enormous popularity. Sociologist Weinstein's study stands back from emotional involvement and analyzes the social context of the metal movement. Her purpose is "to show how sociology can inform public discussion," and she does this by focusing on the social dimension of the genre rather than on the performers. She is able to pinpoint the unique character of metal, finding that its "essential sonic element" is "power, expressed as sheer volume"—produced by an enhanced drum kit, including bass drum, electronic bass guitar (the bass emphasis results in the "heavy" effect), and

special vocal sounds such as screams. Aside from this general paradigm, she ignores the musical content of the genre. She is not much concerned with the lyrics either, noting that metal fans are not aware of them anyway. Those fans are "male, white, midteens," primarily blue-collar. They have no political stance; in school they are usually troublemakers and dropouts. So the phenomenon is reduced to a social event. There is interesting information about backstage work, the economics of concerts, bonding among the players and audience, and the negative critics. A listener's guide presents a selective discography. With endnotes, a bibliography of about 350 items, and an expansive index.

The author teaches sociology at DePaul University, Chicago.

Review: *Choice* 4/92, 1192.

S2-1198   ML3534 .W555
Whiteley, Sheila. The space between the notes : rock and the counterculture / Sheila Whiteley. — London and New York : Routledge, 1992. — x, 139 p. ISBN 0-415-06815-0.

A speculation about the "relationships central to the sixties counterculture: psychedelic coding and rock music." The idea is that rock performers of the 1960s utilized specific musical formulas to convey the sensations of drug trips. The study turns up nothing in the music examined that cannot be readily accounted for with a less bizarre scenario. Along the way there are some elementary musical analyses of work by Cream, Jimi Hendrix, Pink Floyd, the Beatles, and the Rolling Stones, with musical examples; the author finds sermons in stones and secret tales in every chord progression. With endnotes and an expansive index.

Review: *Choice* 2/93, 974.

S2-1199   ML3534 .W4
Wicke, Peter. Rock music : culture, aesthetics, and sociology / Peter Wicke. — New York : Cambridge University Press, 1990. — 256 p. ISBN 0-521-39914-9.

A commentary, translated from the original German, on British and American rock music from the mid-1950s to the mid-1980s. Wicke shows how the idiom was received in the societies of the United Kingdom and the United States, and how the place of rock has changed. With endnotes, bibliography, and indexes.

ML3534.8 : Rock by City

S2-1200   ML3534.8 .C4 P9
Pudlo, Van. Chicago's local rock / Van Pudlo and Joe Ziemba. —

Merrillville, Ind. : Toris Productions, 1982. — 94 p. : ill. ISBN not given.

An undocumented account of musicians in the Chicago area, most of them not widely known. Various authors contributed short essays, each of which contains biographical basics and some discographical information, with photos. The material is not organized at all, and there is no index.

S2-1201   ML3534.8 .L67 F4

Fein, Art. The L.A. musical history tour : a guide to the rock and roll landmarks of Los Angeles / Art Fein. — Boston : Faber & Faber, 1990. — 136 p. : ill. ISBN 0-571-12832-3.

A collection of about 200 photographs, offering interesting glimpses of locales that had some part in rock lives. Included are such shrines as residences of the Beatles in the mid-1960s, the Hollywood Boulevard "Walk of Fame," Janis Joplin's death site, and Foster's Freeze—where Brian Wilson was inspired to write "Fun, Fun, Fun." Each picture is well described; but access is difficult since there is no index.

ML3535 : Rockabilly

S2-1202   ML3535 .M35

McNutt, Randy. We wanna boogie : an illustrated history of the American rockabilly movement / Randy McNutt. — 2nd ed. — Hamilton, Ohio : HHP Books, 1988. — 285 p. ISBN 0-9401-5205-3.

This "history" is a collection of undocumented anecdotes and recollections by such individuals as Gene Perkins, Conway Twitty, Jerry Lee Lewis, Wanda Jackson, and Bonnie Lou. The connection between "boogie" and rockabilly is not clarified. With nonexpansive indexes of names and song titles.

ML3537 : Soul

S2-1203   ML3537 .G46

George, Nelson. Where did our love go? : The rise and fall of the Motown sound / Nelson George; foreword by Quincy Jones; introduction by Robert Christgau. — New York : St. Martin's, 1985. — xviii, 250 p. : ill. : 8 p. plates. ISBN 0-312-86698-4.

An informal story of Motown and the soul singers, relying mostly on anecdotes. There is a selective discography covering 1962–1971 (minimal data). Without documentation; with an expansive index.

Reviews: AM 1987, 339; LJ 1/86, 88.

S2-1204   ML3537 .P78

Pruter, Robert. Chicago soul : making black music Chicago style /
Robert Pruter. — Urbana : University of Illinois Press, 1991. — xx, 408
p. : ill. : 32 p. plates. ISBN 0-252-01676-9.

A strong history of rhythm & blues and soul in their Chicago manifestations: the record industry, radio, and live performance. The city was
a major center for R & B in the 1940s and 1950s, and as the changeover
to soul took place in the 1960s it had an important concentration of activities, notably "record row" along South Michigan Avenue. Capitol, Chess,
Constellation, King, and Vee-Jay were among the top labels to be found
there. Radio station WVON, established by Leonard and Phil Chess in
1963, had a major market share in the black community, guided by deejay
Herb Kent. After peaking in the 1960s, the record business—dependent on
indies, which were in decline nationally—faded; and "the Chicago soul
music recording industry was no more" after 1983. Pruter's account of all
this, which includes careful attention to hundreds of musicians as well as
to the movers and shakers, is documented with chapter endnotes and a bibliography of about 450 items, including a list of interviews held. There is
an expansive index of persons, labels, titles, and topics.

Review: *Choice* 5/91, 1497.

ML3541 : Western

S2-1205   ML3541 .D85

Dunbar, Tom. From Bob Will to Ray Benson : a history of Western
swing music, vol. 1 / Tom Dunbar. — Austin, Tex. : Term Publications,
1988. — 98 p. : ill. ISBN not given.

Discussion, photos, and discographies (minimal data) of Bob Wills,
the Tune Wranglers, the Hi Flyers, Bill Boyd, Shelly Lee Alley, Cliff
Bruner, Adolf Hofner, Johnnie Lee Wills, Floyd Tillman, Ted Daffan,
Jerry Irby, Apade Cooley, the Western Caravan, Jimmy Heap, the Texas
Tophands, Dave Stogner, Red Steagall, and Asleep at the Wheel. With-
out index.

**ML3550–3551 : NATIONAL MUSIC (FOLK,
ETHNIC, PATRIOTIC, POLITICAL)**

S2-1206   ML3550 .A5

Ancelet, Barry J. Makers of Cajun music / Barry J. Ancelet. — Austin :
University of Texas Press, 1984. — 159 p. : ill. ISBN 0-940984-48-2.

Biographies of 20 Cajun and Creole performers; they tell most of the
stories themselves, evoking the exotic background of their music al-

though saying little about the music itself. There is a useful historical introduction by Ancelet. With a selective discography (minimal information), but without documentation or index.
Reviews: *Choice* 2/85, 821; LJ 12/84, 2282.

S2-1207   ML3550 .A83 A832
Jairazbhoy, Nazir. Asian music in North America / Nazir Jairazbhoy and Sue Carole De Vale. — Los Angeles : Department of Music, University of California at Los Angeles, 1985. — 199 p. (Selected reports in ethnomusicology, 6) ISBN 0-8828-7020-3.

S2-1208   ML3551 .A6 E2
Eaklor, Vicki Lynn. American antislavery songs : a collection and analysis / Vicki Lynn Eaklor. — Westport, Conn. : Greenwood, 1988. liv, 564 p. (Documentary reference series) ISBN 0-313-25413-3.
The texts (not music) of 492 songs are given here, with sources; they are drawn from antislavery songsters and periodicals, excluding sheet music editions. Within each of six subject divisions, the songs are arranged chronologically and are briefly discussed. The total lack of attention to musical elements is a limitation on the value of this compilation. There are indexes by author, title, first line, and subject.
Review: AM 1989, 470.

S2-1209   ML3551 .B75
Bowman, Kent A. Voices of combat : a century of liberty and war songs, 1765–1865 / Kent A. Bowman. — New York : Greenwood, 1987. — xii, 172 p. (Contributions to the study of music and dance, 10) ISBN 0-313-254-08-7.
Bowman examines the lyrics of patriotic songs from the American Revolution through the Civil War, tracing the evolution of styles, concepts, and ideologies. Primary and secondary sources are carefully cited in this scholarly effort. Complete lyrics of a dozen songs are given in an appendix. The bibliography lists 25 anthologies, memoirs, more than 20 contemporary periodicals, and nearly 100 secondary sources. The expansive index includes persons, titles, events, and topics.
Kent A. Bowman teaches American history and English in Denton, Texas [—D. P.].
Review: *Choice* 12/87, 632.

S2-1210   ML3551 .G696
Greene, Victor. A passion for polka : old-time ethnic music in America / Victor Greene. — Berkeley : University of California Press, 1992. — xi, 355 p. : ill. ISBN 0-5200-7584-6.

Far exceeding the scope of its unfortunate title, this book is an excellent history of immigrant music in many genres and from many groups. It covers nineteenth-century and twentieth-century band music, the ethnic music and recording industry of the early twentieth century, the establishment of ethnic music in the mainstream (1940–1960), and the polka craze begun by Franki Yankovic. The treatment is scholarly, with copious endnotes including relatively obscure material in several languages, but lively. A useful bibliographic essay on ethnic music is included. With an expansive index of names, titles, and subjects.

Greene is a professor of history at the University of Wisconsin-Milwaukee; he has written two other books on the American immigrant experience.

Reviews: *Choice* 2/93, 972; LJ 8/92, 103.

S2-1211   ML3551 .H2

Halker, Clark D. For democracy, workers, and God : labor song-poems and labor protest, 1865–95 / Clark D. Halker. — Urbana : University of Illinois Press, 1991. — xiii, 243 p. ISBN 0-252-01747-1.

A study of themes in the lyrics of worker songs, concentrating on sociological background. The songs studied were parodies—new words adapted to familiar tunes—so Halker does not discuss the musical element (there are no musical examples). Grassroots republicanism and evangelicalism emerge as principal ideas in the songs. There is attention to the lives of individual songwriters. Footnoted; with bibliography and index.

S2-1212   ML3551 .L44

Lieberman, Robbie. "My song is my weapon" : people's songs, American communism, and the politics of culture, 1930–50 / Robbie Lieberman. — Urbana : University of Illinois Press, 1989. — xxiii, 201 p. ISBN 0-252-01559-2. (Alternative classification: ML3795.)

An account of "the political uses of art," in particular of music's role in the American communist movement of the 1930s and 1940s. That role was to energize the masses; it could do so because the songs "expressed the concerns of the common people." Names associated with these protest songs include Pete Seeger and Lee Hays (their Almanac Singers, and later People's Songs, were groups that promoted left-wing songs). But when the folk music revival, also credited in large measure to Seeger and Hays, arrived in the 1950s, the leftist element was scarcely noticeable in its repertoire. With endnotes and an expansive index.

Reviews: AM 1991, 225; *Choice* 12/89, 642.

S2-1213   ML3551 .S43

Seeger, Pete. Everybody says freedom / Pete Seeger and Bob Reiser. — New York : Norton, 1989. — xiv, 266 p. : ill. : music. ISBN 0-393-02646-9.

A collection of civil rights songs, written out with melody lines and chord symbols, with extensive comments that relate the songs to events in the movement. It is a good story, told mostly through eyewitness accounts; documentation is limited to a list of sources used. With a partly expansive index of names, titles, and topics.

S2-1214   ML3551 .S68
Carney, George O. The sounds of people and places : readings in the geography of American folk and popular music / ed. George O. Carney. — Rev. ed. — Lanham, Md. : University Press of America, 1987. — xii, 339 p. : ill. ISBN 0-8191-6416-X.
1st ed., 1977 (LOAM Suppl. S-833); 3rd ed. — Lanham, Md. : Rowman & Littlefield, 1994.
This is not a revision of the similarly titled book described in LOAM Suppl. S-833; it consists of a completely different set of essays, by different authors. Like its predecessor volume, it endeavors to show the connection between location and musical developments. Topics dealt with include country music, bluegrass, gospel, jazz, rock, Woody Guthrie, Miami sound, and "the image of place in American popular music." The geographical context is well displayed by numerous maps that show the diffusion of a style or instrument across the country. Articles are documented, but there is no index to the book.
Review: AM 1988, 327.

ML3556 : BLACK MUSIC

S2-1215   ML3556 .B17
Baraka, Imamu Amiri. The music : reflections on jazz and blues / Imamu Amiri Baraka and Amina Baraka. — New York : Morrow, 1987. — 332 p. : ill. ISBN 0-6880-4388-7.
A collection of essays and reviews by Imamu Baraka (LeRoi Jones), previously published elsewhere. Black performers discussed include Woody Shaw, Cecil McBee, Craig Harris, Jay Huggard, Bob Neloms, Chico Freeman, and Ricky Ford. Program notes on the music are given, along with personal anecdotes. Baraka's main concern is with the impact of "white chauvinism" on black music. He finds that rap "carries elements of the black democratic struggle" against the racism that pervades the music business. He and Amina Baraka provide some poetry, in a kind of beat idiom, and there is also a play. Without index.
Review: *Choice* 11/87, 486.

S2-1216   ML3556 .C37
Carruth, Hayden. Sitting in : selected writings on jazz, blues, and related topics / Hayden Carruth. — Iowa City : University of Iowa Press, 1986. — xii, 192 p. ISBN 0-87745-153-2.

This collection of prose and poetry brings together writings that date from as early as 1948; many of them have been previously published. Carruth expresses many opinions about jazz and jazz musicians; he examines the relations of jazz and blues to literature, blues to existentialist feeling, and the African-American sensibility to American aesthetic experience. Since there is no index, and since most chapter titles are not very descriptive, the work has little reference value. Without bibliographical references.

Hayden Carruth is a professor of English at Syracuse University [—D. P.].

Review: *Choice* 3/87, 1079.

S2-1217   ML3556 .E44

Ellison, Mary. Lyrical protest : black music's struggle against discrimination / Mary Ellison. — New York : Praeger, 1989. — 168 p. ISBN 0-275-92757-1.

A reflection on the theme expressed in the book title, traced through a number of topics: black power, revolution, socialism, black feminism, and world peace. Ellison, a teacher of American studies at the University of Keele in England, takes her starting point from Malcolm X, "You can't have politics without racism," and extends the idea to indicate that there is no music without politics. The limitations of her approach are considerable. She concentrates on song lyrics, and finding that often they do concern her chosen themes, is content with her proof. She has trouble dealing with the ubiquitous subject of love (basis of the blues and much black contemporary song) and says "it is unusual to find undue attention" paid to it. Of the actual music she has nothing to say. With chapter endnotes and a nonexpansive index.

Review: *Choice* 4/90, 1332.

S2-1218   ML3556 .F43

Keck, George R. Feel the spirit : studies in nineteenth-century Afro-American music / ed. George R. Keck and Sherrill V. Martin. — New York : Greenwood, 1988. — xii, 186 p. (Contributions in Afro-American and African studies, 119) ISBN 0-313-26234-9.

Eleven interesting papers from two Harvard University seminars (1982 and 1986), on such topics as the black female concert singers of the nineteenth century, black male concert singers, piano repertoire, the bands, the spiritual, concert management, and the Fisk Jubilee Singers. Each essay is footnoted, and there is a bibliographic guide to sources for the volume. With an expansive index.

Review: *Choice* 5/89, 1527.

S2-1219   ML3556 .G46

George, Nelson. The death of rhythm and blues / Nelson George. —

New York : Pantheon, 1988. — xvi, 222 p. : ill. : 8 p. plates. ISBN 0-394-55238-5.

"Drawing on hundreds of interviews and stories" since George began writing in the *Amsterdam News* in 1978, this collection of meditations approaches black music from the point of view that "something died" after World War II, but that "it may come back in some form." R & B was the voice of black opportunity and freedom in the 1950s, but the success of integration and social change "spelled the end of the R & B world." It was "called rock & roll to camouflage its black roots, and subsequently soul, funk, disco, rap and other offspring would arise from these roots." The assimilation of black music and black personality into white culture is decried, but also carefully described, by Nelson, whose account ranges over the record companies, black radio, deejays, and political movements. He apparently speaks for much of the black community in expressing unease over the two current black superstars, Prince and Michael Jackson, who "ran fast and far both from their blackness and conventional images of male sexuality"; it is alarming that Jackson, "an unblack, unmasculine figure" is the "most popular black man in America." Today's challenge is for black artists, producers, and radio programmers "to recapture their racial identity." A thoughtful, disturbing book. With an expansive index.

S2-1220   ML3556 .H224 A258
Hamm, Charles. Afro-American music, South Africa, and apartheid / Charles Hamm. — Brooklyn : Institute for Studies in American Music, 1988. — 42 p. (I.S.A.M. monographs, 28) ISBN 0-914678-31-0.

An intriguing, well-documented study of the reception of American pop music in South Africa, beginning with minstrel shows, going through vocal swing, and coming to twist (especially important there), soul, disco, and rock. The social forces of the era are treated perceptively. With endnotes, but no index.
Review: AM 1990, 120; *Choice* 3/89, 1174.

S2-1221   ML3556 .O456
Oliver, Paul. The New Grove gospel, blues, and jazz, with spirituals and ragtime / Paul Oliver, Max Harrison, and William Bolcom. — New York : Norton, 1988. — 395 p. : ill. ISBN 0-393-30100-1.

One of the numerous spin-off volumes drawn from the *New Grove Dictionary of Music and Musicians* (1980), with "additional information on individual artists." A good narrative approach, although without source notes. It benefits from an index (nonexpansive, covering names, topics, and titles), a feature conspicuously absent in the original *New Grove*. The bibliography of about 250 items is useful, despite its abbreviated imprint data.

S2-1222   ML3556 .R34
Southern, Eileen. Readings in black American music / Eileen Southern. — 2nd ed. — New York : Norton, 1983. — 350 p. ISBN 0-393-95280-0.
1st ed., 1971 (LOAM 698).
A useful collection of 41 (four more than in the first edition) essays or extracts, arranged under such topics as religious music of the nineteenth century, plantation music, nineteenth-century urban music, and music of a free people. Among the authors are James M. Trotter, W. E. B. DuBois, W. C. Handy, Ethel Waters, Dizzy Gillespie, Hall Johnson (a fine piece on the spiritual), Hale Smith, John W. Work, and Olly Wilson. With source notes, commentaries, and an expansive index.

S2-1223   ML3556 .S25
Spencer, Jon Michael. Protest and praise : sacred music of black religion / Jon Michael Spencer. — Minneapolis : Fortress Press, 1990. — x, 262 p. ISBN 0-8006-2404-1.
A "holistic perspective" on the history of spirituals, ring shouts, blues, freedom songs, and gospel singing. Music is found to be inseparable from the black struggle to overcome racist domination. There are footnotes, and nonexpansive indexes to names, topics, and song titles.

S2-1224   ML3556 .S27
Spencer, Jon Michael. Sacred music of the secular city : from blues to rap / Jon Michael Spencer. — Durham, N.C. : Duke University Press, 1992. — vii, 309 p. ISBN not given.
"A special issue of *Black Sacred Music: A Journal of Theomusicology.*"
Essays on such topics as "the blues as a secular religion" and "the mythology of the blues."

S2-1225   ML3556 .S5
Shaw, Arnold. Black popular music in America : from the spirituals, minstrels, and ragtime to soul, disco, and hip-hop / Arnold Shaw. — New York : Schirmer, 1986. — xi, 386 p. : ill. : 8 p. plates. ISBN 0-02-872310-4.
Like Nelson George (S2-1219), Shaw is concerned with how "white commercialization of the black original has affected the black style . . . and the overall result of that interrelationship." American popular music has become a fusion of white and black influences, so this study is "in a sense a history of the development of American popular music save that the view is from the other side of the tracks." Documented with chapter endnotes, the result is a valuable historical picture of all the pop forms, emphasizing black contributors. Discographies are cited for individuals

and movements, but information given is minimal. With a nonexpansive index.

Reviews: *Choice* 10/86, 319; LJ 3/15/86, 70.

S2-1226   ML3556 .S65

Small, Christopher. Music of the common tongue : survival and celebration in Afro-American music / Christopher Small. — London : Calder, 1987. — 495 p. ISBN 0-7145-4095-1.

A study of African music and culture and the impact on them of the encounter with white culture. When not adulterated, black music engages "fundamental qualities of identity and community"—which is the basis for its appeal outside of the black populations. Indeed, Small believes that Western classical music "can no longer serve us in this task, for its values have been completely identified with those of the state." The benefits of black music are not fully reaped because it has been "downgraded by the representatives of the official musical culture." With chapter notes and a nonexpansive index.

S2-1227   ML3556 .S74

Southern, Eileen. The music of black Americans : a history / Eileen Southern. — 2nd ed. — New York : Norton, 1983. — xx, 602 p. : ill. ISBN 0-3939-52797.

1st ed., 1971 (LOAM 697).

An update of Southern's indispensable standard work, showing "the long span of black music, from its African origins to the present, and to attest its wide range, from the humble slave songs to operas and symphonic music." This edition adds material to extend the story into the 1980s and makes some deletions to make room for the expansions. The bibliography is updated also, presenting about 600 items, some with brief annotations. There is an expansive index.

Review and listing: AM 1988, 108; BCL.

S2-1228   ML3556 .W8

Wright, Josephine. New perspectives on music : essays in honor of Eileen Southern / ed. Josephine Wright and Samuel A. Floyd, Jr. — Warren, Mich. : Harmonie Park, 1992. — xxiv, 561 p. (Detroit monographs in musicology/Studies in music, 11) ISBN 0-8999-0042-6.

A tribute book for Southern, the leading historian of black music (see S2-1227), containing essays on various topics, not all of them black-centered. Those that are include coverage of black religious music, jazz, and black women in classical music. Among the major authors are Dena J. Epstein, H. Wiley Hitchcock, Richard Crawford, Frank Tirro, Olly Wilson, and Adrienne Fried Block. Wright's bibliography of research studies on African-American music is selective, without stated criteria for inclusion. A thorough inventory of Southern's own writings is a major element of the book.

S2-1229   ML3556.8 .N5
Floyd, Samuel A. Black music in the Harlem renaissance : a collection of essays / ed. Samuel A. Floyd. — Westport, Conn. : Greenwood, 1990. — x, 228 p. (Contributions in Afro-American and African studies, 128) ISBN 0-313-26546-1.

An important collection of 10 essays, by Floyd and others, on the black cultural movement of the 1920s. Topics include vocal concert music, black music theater, writers and music, the Negro renaissance in England, and studies of individuals: Alain Locke, Robert Nathaniel Dett, William Grant Still, Florence Price, William Dawson, and Duke Ellington. There is a valuable bibliography of 725 concert pieces, compiled by Dominique-René DeLerma. References follow each essay, and there is an expansive index.

Reviews: AM 1993, 502; *Choice* 12/90, 638.

ML3557 : MUSIC OF NORTH AMERICAN INDIANS

S2-1230   ML3557 .D4
DeAngulo, Jaime. The music of the Indians of northern California / Jaime DeAngulo; ed. Peter Garland; introduction by Lou Harrison. — Santa Fe, N.M. : Soundings, 1988. — 41 p. and unpaged section of music and sketches. ISBN not given.

DeAngulo transcribed Indian melodies and sang them on tapes; he also wrote descriptions of instruments and ceremonies and drew pictures of events. His work was originally published in Paris, 1931. Interesting accounts of songs by region appear, and 28 songs are given in notation. Without index.

S2-1231   ML3557 .H66
Howard, James H. Choctaw music and dance / James H. Howard and Victoria Lindsay Levine. — Norman : University of Oklahoma Press, 1990. — xxvi, 143 p. : ill. ISBN 0-8061-2225-0. (Alternative classification: E99 .C8.)

One of the largest tribes in the southeastern United States, the Choctaw have undergone almost complete acculturation. The old dances are preserved only in isolated populations, the ones described here, in Mississippi and Oklahoma. In this fine volume, which serves to update the pioneer study by Frances Densmore (LOAM 403), there is a detailed, illustrated account of the choreography and an analysis of the songs. The repertoire is presented in classified arrangement, and 30 songs are given in score. Instruments and costumes are described. With a partly expansive index.

Review: *Choice* 11/90, 498.

S2-1232   ML3557 .K4
Keeling, Richard. Cry for luck : sacred song and speech among the Yurok, Hupa, and Karok Indians of northwestern California / Richard Keeling. — Berkeley : University of California Press, 1992. — xii, 325 p. : ill. ISBN 0-5200-7560-9.

An intriguing account of "the spiritual potency of crying"—sobbing sounds employed in the singing of certain California tribes. Ceremonials and dances are described, with this feature emphasized. The tale is well documented with endnotes and extensive references to earlier literature. Musical examples; index.

S2-1233   ML3557 .N38
Nettl, Bruno. Blackfoot musical thought : comparative perspectives / Bruno Nettl. — Kent, Ohio : Kent State University Press, 1989. — xii, 198 p. ISBN 0-87338-370-2.

A scholarly description by a prominent ethnomusicologist of musical life among the Blackfoot, a tribe in Montana numbering about 25,000 persons. Interviews and field recordings were conducted by Nettl, adding to the considerable quantity of earlier records (as early as 1897) and studies of the tribe. Songs are discussed and classified by type, and citations to recordings are given. Interesting speculations about basic musical concepts among the Blackfoot, and about the varied roles of music in different societies, are well supported by the data. Unfortunately, only three songs are given in musical notation. With a chronological discography, 1897–1986; a bibliography of about 200 entries; and an expansive index.
Reviews: AM 1991, 418; *Choice* 7/89, 1850.

S2-1234   ML3557 .V36
Vander, Judith. Songprints : the musical experience of five Shoshone women / Judith Vander. — Urbana : University of Illinois Press, 1988. — xxv, 317 p. : ill. : music : with a 60-minute cassette. ISBN 0-252-01492-8.

A fine study of the songs and music of five women living on the Wind River reservation in Wyoming. The songs are given in musical notation (taken from field recordings by the author) and fully placed in their tribal contexts. The material includes ghost dances, sun dances, war songs, and ceremonials of all kinds. Style and scholarship are well blended in this intriguing exploration. With endnotes and an expansive index.
Review: *Choice* 5/89, 1529.

S2-1235   ML3557 .W65
Keeling, Richard. Women in North American Indian music : six essays / ed. Richard Keeling. — Bloomington, Ind. : Society for Ethnomusicology, Inc., 1989. — 91 p. (Special series, 6) ISSN 0270-1766. (Alternative classification : ML3550.)

Essays by Judith Vander (drawn from S2-1234), Thomas Vennum, Jr., Charlotte J. Frisbie, Orin T. Hatton, Beverley Diamond Cavanagh, and

Richard Keeling, dealing with the female role in songs and ceremonies of a number of tribes: Shoshone (Wyoming), Ojibwa (Lake Superior), Navajo (southwest U.S.), Gros Ventre (Montana), Algonkian (northern Canada), and Yurok (California). All the contributions are interesting and well documented. With musical examples and a nonexpansive index of names and topics.

Review: AM 1991, 418.

ML3790 : MUSIC INDUSTRY

S2-1236   ML3790 .C3

Cimino, Al. Great record labels / Al Cimino. — Secaucus, N.J. : Chartwell Books, 1992. — 112 p. : ill. ISBN 1-55521-787-7.

A picture book of rock performers associated with 21 labels. Undocumented and frequently erroneous historical facts are presented about the record companies discussed: Sun, Chess, Atlantic, RCA, Stax, Motown, Decca, EMI, Capitol, Apple, A & M, CBS, Warner Brothers, Elektra/Asylum, Island, Stiff, Polygram, MCA, Virgin, ZTT, and Def Jam. With a partly expansive index.

S2-1237   ML3790 .C4

Corenthal, Michael G. Iconography of recorded sound, 1886–1986 : a hundred years of commercial entertainment and collecting opportunity / Michael G. Corenthal. — Milwaukee, Wisc. : Yesterday's Memories, 1986. — 243 p. : ill. ISBN not given.

An eclectic assemblage of historical sketches and comments on cylinder records, children's records, technology, religious records, and other topics; with interviews of five individuals. Pictures of labels and jackets are the heart of the book. Dates and facts are undocumented and not always reliable. A bibliography of about 125 items includes erroneous titles and gives incomplete citation data. With a nonexpansive index of names.

S2-1238   ML3790 .D15

Dannen, Fredric. Hit men : power brokers and fat money inside the music business / Fredric Dannen. — New York : Times Books, 1990. — 387 p. ISBN 0-8129-1658-1.

A blend of pop-sensational writing with scholarly documentation, reporting on the evolution of U.S. hit labels in the rock era and their executives. Labels prominent in the account are BMG, Warner, Capitol-EMI, PolyGram, MCA, Asylum, Casablanca, and CBS. Among the men discussed in detail are Godard Lieberson, Clive Davis, and Walter Yetnikoff. Much of the book is concerned with organized crime and payola. With endnotes and an expansive index of names and topics.

Review: *Choice* 11/90, 497.

S2-1239   ML3790 .D35

Davis, Sharon. Motown : the history / Sharon Davis. — Enfield, England : Guinness, 1988. — 368 p. : ill. ISBN 0-85112-894-7.

A casual history, undocumented, sprinkled with quotes, vague on facts; it deals mostly with the personalities associated with the Motown Corporation. An adulatory tone prevails; for example, appearing under a photo of the Motown founder is "Thank you Berry Gordy for the music." A good discography of Motown releases, by Gordon Frewin, gives records by label, with matrix numbers and release dates. With a nonexpansive name index that does not include the discography.

S2-1240   ML3790 .F56

Fink, Michael. Inside the music business : music in contemporary life / Michael Fink. — New York : Schirmer, 1989. — xiii, 401 p. ISBN 0-02-873110-7.

A presentation of the U.S. record industry in a textbook style, with chapters on recording history, managers, contracts, promotions, radio music, retailing, critics, musical theater, art management, and so on. Fink offers the most basic information for musicians entering or considering a career. Without source notes. With a glossary and a nonexpansive index.

S2-1241   ML3790 .F8

Fox, Ted. In the groove : the men behind the music / Ted Fox; foreword by Doc Pomus. — New York : St. Martin's, 1986. — xiv, 361 p. : ill. : 24 p. plates. ISBN 0-312-41166-9.

A valuable book of interviews with record industry figures, casual in approach but often informative on the names and backstage moves of the music business. Individuals who are queried are John Hammond (A & R man with Columbia and Mercury), Mitch Miller (A & R with Columbia), Milt Gabler (Commodore label), Alfred Lion (Blue Note label), Jerry Wexler (Atlantic label), Jerry Leiber and Mike Stoller (composers of "Hound Dog" and other Elvis songs), Clive Davis (Columbia executive), Phil Ramone (producer for Billy Joel, Paul Simon, etc.), Chris Strachowitz (Arhoolie label), Chris Blackwell (Island Records), and Nile Rodgers (producer for David Bowie, Diana Ross, etc.). With a partly expansive index.

Review: LJ 11/15/86, 99.

S2-1242   ML3790 .G74

Gray, Herman. Producing jazz : the experience of an independent record company / Herman Gray. — Philadelphia : Temple University Press, 1988. — xv, 171 p. ISBN 0-87722-574-5.

This profile of Theresa Records (based in San Francisco) traces the development of the company from its beginning in 1976. Gray considers the ideology and administration of the company, its relations with other independent record companies, and its function in the music industry. He also examines the significance of such small, independent organizations in the general culture.

The work is based on observational and interview data collected over 15 months. Primary and secondary sources are well cited. Because of Gray's background as a sociologist, the emphasis is on the company as an economic and cultural institution rather than on musical aspects of its recordings.

The bibliography of about 150 items documents many interviews and includes numerous monographs and articles. A discography of Theresa Records through 1986, organized by label number, includes album title and personnel, year of release, and titles of cuts for 21 albums. An expansive index includes companies, record labels, individuals, associations, titles, and topics. Without illustrations.

Herman Gray is an assistant professor of sociology at Northeastern University [—D. P.].

Reviews: AM 1989, 475; *Choice* 7/89, 1849.

S2-1243   ML3790 .H2

Halloran, Mark. The musician's business and legal guide / Mark Halloran; introduction by Gregory T. Victoroff. — 4th ed. — Englewood Cliffs, N.J. : Prentice-Hall, 1991. — 454 p. : ill. ISBN 0-13-605585-0.

A collection of topical sections, each by a specialist member of the California bar. There are good explanations of legal points in such areas as copyright, contracts, performing rights, and personal management. With a bibliography and index.

Review: *Choice* 10/92, 277.

S2-1244   ML3790 .K9

Koenigsberg, Allen. The patent history of the phonograph, 1877–1912 / Allen Koenigsberg. — Brooklyn : APM Press, 1990. — 72, 87 p. ISBN 0-937612-10-3.

"Printed in a signed, limited edition of 500."

A remarkable gathering of esoteric information pertaining to the history of recorded sound in the United States, focused on 2,118 patents and 1,013 inventors; 101 patent drawings are reproduced and illuminated by scholarly discussion. Patents are listed by patent number and under the inventors' names. Thomas A. Edison received 134 patents in this field, to lead all inventors. An essay by Raymond Wile discusses the U.S. patent system. There is so much scarce material in this volume that an index would seem indispensable; how unfortunate that there is none.

S2-1245   ML3790 .L2
Lambert, Dennis. Producing hit records / Dennis Lambert; with Ronald Zalkind; foreword by Al Coury. — New York : Schirmer, 1980. — xii, 196 p. ISBN 0-02-871950-8.

A description of record studio work, negotiations between artists and record companies, how to build a home studio, how to make a demo record, and handling contracts. With a glossary, but without index.

S2-1246   ML3790 .N3
Newsom, Iris. Wonderful inventions : motion pictures, broadcasting, and recorded sound at the Library of Congress / ed. Iris Newsom; introduction by Erik Barnouw. — Washington : Library of Congress, 1985. — 384 p. : with two 12-inch LP records. ISBN 0-8444-0445-4. (Alternative classification: PN1994 .L4824.)

A collection of useful articles by various specialists. Among the most interesting contributions are Jon Newsom's essay on music for animated films, James Smart's account of Emil Berliner and early disc recording, and Samuel Brylawski's "Cartoons for the Record: The Jack Kapp Collection." Indexed.

S2-1247   ML3790 .P25
Passman, Donald S. All you need to know about the music business / Donald S. Passman. — New York : Simon & Schuster, 1991. — xvi, 351 p. : ill. ISBN 0-6717-6139-0.

A chatty approach to managers, lawyers, agents, contracts, copyright, merchandising, and (above all) "deals." With an expansive index.

S2-1248   ML3790 .S5
Shemel, Sidney. This business of music / Sidney Shemel and M. William Krasilovksy. — 6th ed. — New York : Billboard Books, 1990. — xxxi, 688 p. : ill. ISBN 0-8230-7706-3.
1st ed., 1964.

A knowledgeable career guide, with ample detail on practical matters such as contracts, copyright, agents, managers, and taxes. All aspects of the music marketplace are well covered. Useful for business forms that cover numerous types of transactions. With an expansive index.

Listing and review: Balay BH71; *Choice* 5/78, 411 (for earlier edition).

S2-1249   ML3790 .S66
Bond, Sherry. The songwriter's and musician's guide to Nashville / Sherry Bond. — Cincinnati, Ohio : Writer's Digest Books, 1991. — 176 p. : ill. ISBN 0-8987-94579.

The approach here is very practical. There are interviews with local people in the business, maps of important parts of the city, descriptions of what to do before leaving for Nashville, and planning guidelines for itineraries and showcases. The second half of the book consists of lists of people and services grouped by headings such as arrangers, business managers, legal services, photographers, radio stations, and videotape duplications. The value of such a guide is in its currency; it will need to be updated frequently to remain useful. There is an expansive index of persons, groups, and topics, and a separate index to the lists. A dozen books are suggested for further reading.

Sherry Bond is active in copyright and royalty administration; she helped found the monthly *Country Chart Analyst* [—D. P.].

S2-1250   ML3790 .S9

Escott, Colin. Good rockin' tonight : Sun Records and the birth of rock 'n' roll / Colin Escott; with Martin Hawkins. — New York : St. Martin's, 1991. — x, 276 p. ISBN 0-312-05439-4.

The Sun Records label launched the careers of Elvis Presley, Jerry Lee Lewis, Carl Perkins, B. B. King, Roy Orbison, Johnny Cash, Charlie Pride, and other stars of the 1960s. Sam Phillips was the man behind the success of the label, and it is his story that unfolds in the books, through anecdotal accounts of the acclaimed artists. Sources for each chapter are cited, but there are no direct footnotes. With a selective discography (minimal data) and index. See also LOAM 1343.

S2-1251   ML3790 .T1

Taraborrelli, J. Randy. Motown : hot wax, city cool & solid gold / J. Randy Taraborrelli. — Garden City, N.Y. : Doubleday, 1986. — 213 p. : ill. ISBN 0-385-19799-3.

An informal account of Berry Gordy's record firm and its artists, highlighted by many good photos. A chronological section is useful for pinpointing key events. Quotes from the performers are offered without documentation. Without index, discography, or reference features.

S2-1252   ML3790 .V5 B1

Baumbach, Robert W. Look for the dog : an illustrated guide to Victor Talking Machines, 1901–1929 / Robert W. Baumbach. — Woodland Hills, Calif. : Stationery X-Press, 1981. — 326 p. : ill. ISBN 0-9606466-0-4. (Alternative classification: TS2301 .P3 B35.)

A valuable guide to all models of Victor record players, with photos reproduced from Victor catalogs and literature, specifications, and service notes for repair work. The models are discussed in relation to others and with regard to their market success. Appendix materials deal with accessories, Victor patents, and Victor repair manuals. Yearly sales figures are tabulated also, documenting the rise and fall of various models. Indexed.

S2-1253 ML3790 .W2
Wacholtz, Larry E. Inside country music / Larry E. Wacholtz. — Rev. ed. — New York : Billboard Publications, 1986. — 254 p. ISBN 0-8230-7532-4.
1st ed., 1984.
Bright, chatty contributions by various authors, dealing with aspects of the musical career. Topics include songwriting, copyright, publishing, record companies, management, producers, demos, promotion, MTV, and trade publications. With an expansive index.

S2-1254 ML3790 .W33
Wadhams, Wayne. Sound advice / Wayne Wadhams. — New York : Schirmer, 1990. — 2 vols. and 2 cds. : vol. 1, The musician's guide to the record industry, xiii, 545 p. : ill.; vol. 2, The musician's guide to the recording studio, xxii, 357 p. : ill. ISBN 0-02-872692-8; 0-02-872694-4. (Alternative classification: TK7881.4.)
Useful, sensible descriptions of all aspects of the American sound-recording industry, without idle chat. Among the topics covered: publishers, royalties, fees, rights, organizations, ASCAP and BMI, lawyers, managers, agreements and contracts, demo tapes, accounts, contracts (good detail and forms). The second volume shows the musician "how to work productively with engineers to make professional quality demo and master tapes on their own." The accompanying CDs present 200 examples of specific studio techniques; they take the listener through the complete recording process and mixdown session. With an expansive index.
Listing and review: Balay BH72; *Choice* 2/91, 945.

ML3795 : MUSICAL CAREER GUIDES

S2-1255 ML3795 .B33
Baskerville, David. Music business handbook and career guide / David Baskerville; foreword by Stan Cornyn. — 5th ed. — Los Angeles : Sherwood, 1990. — xx, 541 p. : ill. ISBN not given.
1st ed., 1979.
A practical introduction to songwriting, publishing, copyright, licensing, unions and guilds, agents, managers, attorneys, concert promotion and management, merchandising, record markets, artist contracts, studios, radio, television, music in advertising, film scoring, and career planning. Various forms and contracts are illustrated. With a glossary and bibliography.
Listing: Sheehy BH174 (for 3rd ed.).

S2-1256 ML3795 .D4
Dearing, James W. Making money making music (no matter where you live) / James W. Dearing. — 2nd ed. — Cincinnati, Ohio : Writer's Digest Books, 1990. — xi, 179 p. ISBN 0-8987-9414-5.
1st ed., 1982.
A rudimentary career guide, patronizing in approach, chatty in style. Topics treated include such lucrative activities as giving music lessons and selling music to publishers. With an expansive subject index.
Review: LJ 11/15/82, 2179 (for 1st ed.).

S2-1257 ML3795 .F497
Field, Shelly. Career opportunities in the music industry / Shelly Field. — 2nd ed. — New York : Facts on File, 1990. — 279 p. ISBN 0-8160-2401-4.
1st ed., 1986.
Descriptions of various jobs connected with music, with customary salaries, educational requirements, market prospects, and "tips." There are lists of universities that offer majors in the music industry, unions, associations, record companies, booking agencies, music publishers, rights societies, personal managers, and public relations firms. With a glossary and index of the jobs.
Review: *Choice* 10/86, 318 (for 1st ed.).

S2-1258 ML3795 .U4
Uscher, Nancy. Your own way in music / Nancy Uscher. — New York : St. Martin's, 1992. — xiv, 304 p. ISBN 0-312-05186-7.
An unusual approach to career guidance, presenting interviews with professionals in various areas. The value of the book is diminished by an amateurish index and curious bibliographical references.
Review: LJ 11/1/90, 86.

ML3838 : MUSIC AND PSYCHOLOGY

S2-1259 ML3838 .B696
Boyd, Jenny. Musicians in tune / Jenny Boyd; with Holly George-Warren. — New York : Fireside, 1992. — 288 p. ISBN 0-671-73440-7.
Interviews with musicians, carried out by a psychologist in search of the roots of creativity. Such artists as Eric Clapton, David Crosby, Mick Fleetwood, George Harrison, Paul Horn, Steve Jordan, B. B. King, Branford Marsalis, and Nancy Wilson were asked about their beliefs, reflections, and how they experience musical performance. Among the questions put to them: "Did you have any unexplained or psychic experiences or significant dreams as a child?"; "Do you believe in

a greater power?"; "What gives you the drive to create?"; "Are you in touch with the child within you?"; "Do you think the music today represents the unconscious feelings of the masses?" If Boyd is unable to make much sense of all the responses, it is not only because many of her questions are unanswerable, but because she has not discovered that the language of musicians is music, not prose. As one of them said to her, "Basic truths in life are so simple we can't talk about them." Musicians sing or play the truths instead. With an expansive index.

ML3849 : MUSIC AND THE OTHER ARTS

S2-1260   ML3849 .G83
Sumner, Melody. The guests go in to supper / ed. Melody Sumner, Kathleen Burch, and Michael Sumner. — Oakland, Calif. : Burning Books, 1986. — 383 p. : ill. ISBN 0-936050-05-5.

Set in a dinner-table atmosphere, this is a collection of thoughts about the arts by John Cage, Robert Ashley, Yoko Ono, Laurie Anderson, Charles Amirkhanian, Michael Peppe, and Kenneth Atchley. A prevailing theme is that art has become an open system, capable of interacting and drawing feedback from its environment.

Review: AM 1988, 342.

MT3–820 : MUSIC EDUCATION

S2-1261   MT3 .U5 E36
Egan, Robert F. Music and the arts in the community : the community music school in America / Robert F. Egan. — Metuchen, N.J. : Scarecrow, 1989. — xii, 461 p. : ill. : 16 p. plates. ISBN 0-8108-2117-6.

The community music school originated in the United States as "an institution which offers musical instruction at a nominal cost, and which is non-profit, non-sectarian." Such a school is typically located in a neighborhood community center or "settlement house." The Hull House Music School in Chicago was the first, dating from 1893. There were 160 members in the National Guild of Community Schools of the Arts in 1986. Among the distinguished alumni of community schools are Larry Adler, Lucine Amara, Clamma Dale, Benny Goodman, Martha Graham, Mario Lanza, Jaime Laredo, Jacob Lateiner, Johnny Mathis, Mitch Miller, Judith Raskin, Michael Tilson Thomas, Tatiana Troyanos, and Dionne Warwick. Egan's history is straightforward, documented, and thorough. With a bibliography of about 300 items and a nonexpansive index.

Review: *Choice* 2/90, 959.

S2-1262   MT3 .U5 M324
Mark, Michael L. A history of American music education / Michael L.
Mark and Charles Gary. — New York : Schirmer, 1992. — vii, 404 p.
ISBN 0-02-871365-6.
A straightforward account of music teaching in the United States, prefaced by some historical chapters on music education in Europe. Among
the topics covered are music in religious schools, class piano instruction,
competitions, the Music Teachers National Association, the recent aesthetic education movement, and multicultural developments. With a
name and topic index.

S2-1263   MT3 .U5 M76
Music education the United States : contemporary issues : based on
proceedings of symposia sponsored by the Alabama Project : Music,
Society and Education in America / ed. J. Terry Gates. — Tuscaloosa :
University of Alabama Press, 1988. — xi, 328 p. ISBN 0-8173-
0369-3.
Consists of 18 essays by various authors, covering such topics as aesthetics education, teaching methods, music in higher education, and programs for the gifted. With a bibliography of works cited and an expansive index.

S2-1264   MT4 .L2 U542
Clark, J. Bunker. Music at KU : a history of the University of Kansas
Music Department / J. Bunker Clark. — Lawrence : University of Kansas,
Department of Music and Dance, 1986. — 170 p. : ill. ISBN not given.
A topically arranged history (the choirs, bands, library, opera, strings,
theory, etc.) of the music activities at the university. Many great artists
have appeared in the concert series that began in 1903; the programs are
listed. Members of the music faculty from 1867 to 1985 are named. With
a bibliography of sources, but no index.

S2-1265   MT4 .N5 J844
Kogan, Judith. Nothing but the best : the struggle for perfection at the
Juilliard School / Judith Kogan. — New York : Random House, 1987. —
239 p. ISBN 0-87910-122-9.
The promise of the table of contents (auditions, teachers, competi-
tions, orchestra, student life) is unfulfilled in this foolish volume, which
makes each topic into a fictionalized capsule. It all ends with a love story.
No notes or index.
Reviews: *Choice* 2/88, 917; LJ 5/87, 70.

S2-1266   MT728 .B6
Blum, David. The art of quartet playing : the Guarneri Quartet in con-

versation with David Blum / David Blum. — New York : Knopf, 1986. — xiii, 247 p. ISBN 0-3945-3985-0.

A book by musicians for musicians, based on interviews with the Guarneri members: Arnold Steinhardt, John Dalley, Michael Tree, and David Soyer. Perceptive questions bring out intriguing information about how the distinguished ensemble works. Topics include tuning, vibrato, bowing, tempos, and passages from the repertoire that present special challenges. A long study of Beethoven's opus 131 is of great interest. With musical examples, a Guarneri discography (LPs, cassettes, and CDs—dates and labels only), and an expansive index. This is a unique and fascinating approach to musical artistry.

Reviews: *Choice* 11/86, 488; LJ 6/1/86, 124.

S2-1267   MT20 .C17
Ardoin, John. Callas at Juilliard : the master classes / John Ardoin; foreword by Nicola Resigno. — New York : Knopf, 1987. — xvii, 300 p. ISBN 0-394-563-67-0.

A collection of musical examples taken from arias in the repertoire of Maria Callas, with her helpful hints to students on interpretation of them. No index.

S2-1268   MT20 .L693
Lightner, Helen. Class voice and the American art song : a source book and anthology / Helen Lightner. — Metuchen, N.J. : Scarecrow, 1991. — x, 181 p. : ill. ISBN 0-8108-2381-0.

A teacher's guide to voice instruction in general (posture, breathing, etc.), with 32 illustrative songs in piano-vocal score by American composers. Stylistic features and performance problems are discussed for each song. With a name and title index.

Review: *Choice* 11/91, 459.

MT955 : ANALYTIC GUIDES

S2-1269   MT955 .K82
Kornick, Rebecca Hodell. Recent American opera : a production guide / Rebecca Hodell Kornick. — New York : Columbia University Press, 1991. — xvii, 352 p. ISBN 0-231-06920-0.

A list of 213 stage works (including certain operettas and musicals) in composer order; most were written since 1972. Information provided about each composition includes a plot summary, roles and their vocal ranges, orchestral and choral requirements, other production considerations, sources, and reviews of performances. There are indexes of titles, publishers, and durations (time needed for performance). There is no duplication with the similar book by Quaintance Eaton, *Opera Production* (University of Minnesota Press, 1961, 1974).

Listing and reviews: ARBA 1992, #1291; Balay BH98; *Choice* 7-8/91, 1791.

NB–NX : ARTS AND CULTURE

S2-1270   NB237 .H8 E34

Eden, Myrna G. Energy and individuality in the art of Anna Huntington, sculptor, and Amy Beach, composer / Myrna G. Eden. — Metuchen, N.J. : Scarecrow, 1987. — ix, 300 p. : ill. (Composers of North America, 2) ISBN 0-8108-1916-3.

Sculptor Huntington (1876–1973) and composer Beach (1867–1944) are brought together as two contributors of "remarkable individuality and unique energy to the cultivated tradition." Documented biographical sketches of the women are of interest, since neither has been the subject of detailed publication. There are also worklists for them. Eden encounters the so-called intentional fallacy, however, in attributing qualities to the art products that (she supposes) corresponded to ideas and beliefs in the minds of the artists. Of Beach's *Browning Songs,* for example, to which "she imparted her deep understanding of ethical values," it is said that "each song reflects a moral philosophy indicated in the text." Musical examples that accompany program notes of Beach's works are curiously printed in several different sizes and fonts. Huntington's fine sculptures are well photographed. With a partly expansive index.

S2-1271   NC1883 .U6 B58

Marsh, Graham. Blue note : the album cover art / Graham Marsh, Glyn Callingham, and Felix Cromey. — San Francisco : Chronicle Books, 1991. — 127 p. : ill. ISBN 0-8118-0036-9.

British edition: *The Cover Art of Blue Note Records* (London: Collins and Brown, 1991; ISBN 1-85585-096-6).

Reid Miles designed about 1,000 stylish covers for Blue Note, a premier jazz label of the 1950s and 1960s. His work is sampled in this good collection of photos. There is an index of performers.

S2-1272   NC1883 .U6 C2

Marsh, Graham. California cool : west coast jazz of the 50s & 60s : the album cover art / Graham Marsh and Glyn Callingham; foreword by William Claxton. — San Francisco : Chronicle Books, 1992. — 110 p. : ill. ISBN 0-8118-0275-2. (Alternative classification: ML3508.7 .C28.)

A picture book of about 300 album covers, most of them representing the Pacific Jazz Records label or the Contemporary label. Claxton was responsible for much of the distinguished artwork on the albums. Without index.

Review: LJ 10/15/92, 68.

S2-1273 NX456 .C37

Carr, Roy. The hip : hipsters, jazz, and the beat generation / Roy Carr, Brian Case, and Fred Dellar. — Boston : Faber & Faber, 1986. — 143 p. : ill. ISBN 0-571-13809-8.

The authors have tried to describe and depict "hip" through the juxtaposition of text and image. There are extended sections on jive, crooners, California jazz, Chet Baker, jazz in the movies, and record jacket art. The narrative is at times interesting, but it is the illustrations that make this work valuable, mixing photographic portraits, album covers, drawings, and advertisements to create a sense of what "hip" is. Unfortunately, there is no bibliography or index [—D. P.].

S2-1273a NX504 .G5

Giddins, Gary. Faces in the crowd : players and writers / Gary Giddins. — New York : Oxford, 1992. — x, 278 p. : ill. ISBN 0-1950-5488-1.

A collection of writings previously published since 1977, dealing with 37 actors, authors, and musicians. Good stories are included about Irving Berlin, Billie Holiday, Ella Fitzgerald, Dinah Washington, Sarah Vaughan, Louis Armstrong, Chick Webb, Larry Adler, Miles Davis, Sonny Rollins, and Dizzy Gillespie. Giddins is a knowledgeable and interesting writer, who does not depend too much on imaginary quotations from his subjects; but the essays are undocumented. With a nonexpansive index.

S2-1274 NX511 .C56 V58

Vitz, Robert C. The queen and the arts : cultural life in nineteenth-century Cincinnati / Robert C. Vitz. — Kent, Ohio : Kent State University Press, 1989. — xi, 322 p. : ill. ISBN 0-87338-376-1.

"Queen of the West," as Longfellow named it, Cincinnati began to make an artistic mark in the second half of the nineteenth century. In the 1870s, there were many glories: an outstanding new concert hall, a nationally known choral festival, and Theodore Thomas as director of the college of music. If later developments were not so spectacular, the city did maintain a wide range of activity in music and in the other arts. Vitz is not the most reliable guide, at least not in the musical sphere where he appears to have a shallow information base. But he does present a wide view of sculpture, painting, theater, and literature. Possibly the most useful feature in the book is its bibliography of primary and secondary sources.

Review: AM 1991, 314.

S2-1275   NX512.2 .A35 S6

Southern, Eileen. African-American traditions in song, sermon, tale, and dance, 1600s–1920 : an annotated bibliography of literature, collections, and artworks / Eileen Southern and Josephine Wright. — Westport, Conn. : Greenwood, 1990. — xlv, 365 p. : ill. : 6 p. plates. (Greenwood encyclopedia of black music) ISBN 0-313-24918-0.

A model bibliography, presenting 2,328 annotated references on African-American (Canada and U.S.) song, sermon, tale, and dance. All known items from the seventeenth century to 1920 are included. The chapters are arranged chronologically, then by subject. Full imprint data is provided. With excellent indexing by author, composer, artist, subject, and first lines of songs. A descriptive list of iconographic materials makes a useful appendix feature.

Reviews: AM 1992, 217; ARBA 1992, p. 354; *Choice* 3/91, 1108.

PC4813 : BALLAD TEXTS

S2-1276   PC4813.7 .J8

Armistead, Samuel G. Judeo-Spanish ballads from New York collected by Maír José Benardete / ed. Samuel G. Armistead and Joseph H. Silverman. — Berkeley : University of California Press, 1981. — viii, 149 p. ISBN 0-5200-4348-0.

A careful discussion of 37 ballads (words only) of the Sephardic community in New York City, with extensive notes and documentation. The index gives access by subject, first lines, and geographical places of origin for the ballads.

PN1590–1997 : TELEVISION AND MOTION PICTURES

S2-1277   PN1590 .B53 M3

Mapp, Edward C. Directory of blacks in the performing arts / Edward C. Mapp; foreword by Earle Hyman. — 2nd ed. — Metuchen, N.J. : Scarecrow, 1990. — xvii, 594 p. ISBN 0-8108-2222-9.

1st ed., 1978 (LOAM Suppl. S-503).

Personal and career facts for about 1,100 blacks in film, television, radio, theater, dance, and music. The information is conveniently displayed in clearly separated sections: education, special interests, career data, clubs, films, honors, relationships, and so forth (as appropriate for each person). While criteria are not stated, the inclusions represent living and dead persons from the nineteenth and twentieth centuries. With an occupation index and a bibliography of about 60 items. No general index.

Reviews: ARBA 1991, p. 543; *Choice* 11/90, 462; LJ 7/90, 88.

S2-1278   PN1992.8 .M87 K36
Kaplan, E. Ann. Rocking around the clock : music television, post modernism, and consumer culture / E. Ann Kaplan. — New York : Methuen, 1987. — ix, 196 p. : ill. ISBN 0-416-33390-7.

A contemplation about rock videos on MTV, the 24-hour cable channel that began broadcasting in 1981 and had viewers in 26 million households five years later. Kaplan finds five types of programming in the genre: romantic, socially conscious, nihilist, classical (voyeuristic; females as objects), and postmodern. Rock generally expresses the postmodern sensibility, as it "uses pastiche in place of the modernist parody" and is ambiguous about authority. The spectator is "decentered and fragmented"—in other words, posited in terms of deconstruction theory. MTV advertising and production are discussed along with these speculations, and there is a videography of examples. The whole is well documented with endnotes and accessible through an expansive index.

Review: *Choice* 12/87, 613.

S2-1279   PN1995.9 .M86 A5
Altman, Rick. Genre : the musical : a reader / ed. Rick Altman. — London : Routledge & Kegan Paul, 1987. — 386 p. : ill. (British Film Institute readers in film studies) ISBN 0-2533-0413-X.

A collection of 14 documented essays on diverse persons and topics, e.g., Vincente Minnelli, the Warner musicals. A useful bibliography by Jane Feuer includes books and articles, and has brief annotations. The index to the book gives access to studios, directors, actors, films, critics, journals, and subjects; it is a valuable stand-alone reference source.

S2-1280   PN1995.9 .M86 D45
Denisoff, R. Serge. Risky business : rock in film / R. Serge Denisoff and William D. Romanowski. — New Brunswick, N.J. : Transaction, 1991. — xi, 768 p. : ill. ISBN 0-88738-843-4.

Gossip and anecdotes about Hollywood movies with rock music scores or about rock musicians, beginning with *Flashdance* (1983). For each film there is a lengthy plot synopsis, description of the rock elements, an account of how the movie was made, costs, awards (in 1984 alone ten soundtracks became platinum records), and miscellaneous sidelights. With a partly expansive index.

Review: *Choice* 5/92, 1403.

S2-1281   PN1995.9 .M86 G74
Green, Stanley. Hollywood musicals year by year / Stanley Green. — Milwaukee, Wisc. : H. Leonard, 1990. — xiii, 351 p. : ill. ISBN 0-88188-610-6.

A chronological list of film musicals from 1927 to 1989, giving credits, short plots, song titles, and comments. There are useful indexes of titles, composers, lyricists, directors, choreographers, producers, photographic directors, cast members, and studios.

S2-1282   PN1995.9 .M86 H2
Harris, Thomas J. Children's live-action musical films : a critical survey and filmography / Thomas J. Harris. — Jefferson, N.C. : McFarland, 1990. — xiii, 193 p. : ill. ISBN 0-8995-0375-6.
Descriptions of 15 films that were intended for children, including *The Wizard of Oz, Babes in Toyland, Mary Poppins,* and *Willy Wonka.* For each film there is an account of its genesis, plot, production, and reception. With a nonexpansive index.

S2-1283   PN1995.9 .M86 H4
Hemming, Roy. The melody lingers on : the great songwriters and their movie musicals / Roy Hemming. — New York : Newmarket, 1986. — xi, 388 p. ISBN 0-937858-57-9.
Biographies and comments on the films and songs of Harold Arlen, Irving Berlin, George Gershwin, Jerome Kern, Jimmy McHugh, Cole Porter, Ralph Rainger, Richard Rodgers, Harry Warren, Richard Whiting, and six others. The sketches are "warmly affectionate," without novelty or much reference value (e.g., casts are not given for the movies). Index.
Reviews: AM 1988, 331; LJ 11/15/86, 109.

S2-1283a   PN1995.9 .M86 M4
McGee, Mark Thomas. The rock & roll movie encyclopedia of the 1950s / Mark Thomas McGee. — Jefferson, N.C. : McFarland, 1990. — x, 214 p. ISBN 0-89950-500-7.
Details on 35 important films from the early rock era, giving credits, cast, plot, songs, and excerpts from critical reviews. With indexes by personal name and song title.

S2-1284   PN1995.9 .M86 P37
Parish, James Robert. The great Hollywood musical pictures / James Robert Parish and Michael R. Pitts. — Metuchen, N.J. : Scarecrow, 1992. — vii, 806 p. : ill. ISBN 0-8108-2529-5.
An alphabetical list of musical films from 1927 to 1988, giving long descriptions, plot summaries, song titles, all credits, and critical receptions. With a chronology of titles, but without index.

S2-1285   PN1995.9 .M86 S26
Sandahl, Linda J. Rock films : a viewer's guide to three decades of musicals, concerts, documentaries, and soundtracks, 1955–1986 / Linda

J. Sandahl. — New York : Facts on File, 1987. — 239 p. : ill. ISBN 0-8160-1576-7.

"First published in the United Kingdom by Blandford Press, 1986, as *Encyclopedia of Rock Music on Film.*"

A useful compilation, in title order, of data on musicals, films of concerts, documentaries, and soundtracks. Each entry presents release data, cast, plot summary, songs, singers, and critical comments. There are many illustrations as well (stills and posters). Indexing by name, film title, and song title. Movies not included are those in which a rock star appears in a nonsinging role and those with only one rock song.

Review: ARBA 1988, #1321.

S2-1286   PN1995.9 .M86 T4

Terenzio, Maurice. The Soundies Distributing Corporation of America : a history and filmography of their "jukebox" musical films of the 1940s / Maurice Terenzio, Scott MacGillivray, and Ted Okuda. — Jefferson, N.C. : McFarland, 1991. — viii, 224 p. : ill. ISBN 0-8995-0578-3.

A corporate history of the Soundies firm, which made short subjects to be played on coin-operated machines by the name of Panoram. Between 1940 and 1946, they produced some 3,000 movies. With a title index.

S2-1287   PN1997 .J5583 M33

McClelland, Doug. Blackface to blacklist : Al Jolson, Larry Parks, and "The Jolson Story" / Doug McClelland. — Metuchen, N.J. : Scarecrow, 1987. — x, 283 p. : ill. ISBN 0-8108-1965-1.

A casual account of the genesis of the 1946 film *The Jolson Story;* with chapter endnotes but with many undocumented quotes and conversations. No index.

PN2270–2287 : BROADWAY AND THE THEATER

S2-1288   PN2270 .A93 V37

Kaplan, Mike. Variety's directory of major show business awards / Mike Kaplan. — 3rd ed. — New York : Bowker, 1989. — 750 p. ISBN 0-8352-2666-2.

1st ed., 1982, as *Variety U.S. Major Show Business Awards.*

A very convenient list of winners of and nominees for Oscars, Emmys, Tonys, Grammys, and Pulitzers for plays, through 1988. All categories are included for each award. With a name index.

S2-1289   PN2277 .N5 C515

Chevigny, Paul. Gigs : jazz and the cabaret laws in New York City /

Paul Chevigny. — New York : Routledge, 1991. — x, 215 p. ISBN 0-4159-0400-5.

City regulations, known as cabaret laws, of 1926–1990 inhibited the development of jazz clubs in New York. In addition to zoning restrictions, there were numerous obstacles before performers who sought the right to appear in the clubs. For instance, Billie Holiday was prohibited from singing after her narcotics conviction. Eventually, a campaign led by Chevigny (a lawyer) was successful in overturning the regulations. The story is told in plain style, with an index.

Reviews: *Choice* 5/92, 1402; LJ 11/1/91, 100.

S2-1290   PN2277 .N5 G8

Guernsey, Otis L., Jr. Broadway song and story : playwrights/lyricists/composers discuss their hits / Otis L. Guernsey, Jr.; introduction by Terence McNally. — New York : Dodd, Mead, 1985. — xiii, 447 p. ISBN 0-3960-8753-1.

Interviews with Leonard Bernstein, Elia Kazan, Arthur Laurents, Neil Simon, Edward Albee, Jules Feiffer, Harold Prince, and others. With name and titles indexes.

S2-1291   PN2277 .N5 L4

Leon, Ruth. Applause : New York's guide to the performing arts / Ruth Leon. — New York : Applause Books, 1991. — xii, 506 p. : ill. ISBN 1-55783-096-7.

A descriptive list of New York theaters, music halls, and venues for opera, symphony, jazz, chorale, chamber music, and dance. Information given for each of the 1,000 locales includes seating plans, ticket price ranges, directions for public transport, and suggested parking lots. With maps of the theater districts and Greenwich Village, and an expansive index.

Review: *Choice* 10/92, 277.

S2-1292   PN2287 .B69 G76

Grossman, Barbara. Funnywoman : the life and times of Fanny Brice / Barbara Grossman. — Bloomington : Indiana University Press, 1991. — xiv, 287 p. : ill. ISBN 0-253-326-532.

A straightforward, documented story of the singer/comedienne, who came to national prominence in the Ziegfeld Follies of 1934 and 1936; destined to be forever identified with her fictional creation, Baby Snooks. With chapter endnotes, a bibliography of 300 primary and secondary sources, and an expansive index.

S2-1293   PN2287 .P715

Latham, Caroline. Priscilla and Elvis : the Priscilla Presley story /

Caroline Latham. — New York : New American Library, 1985. — 189
p. : ill. : 8 p. plates. ISBN 0-4511-4419-8.
The story of Elvis Presley's wife, their baby, their divorce, and her
subsequent recovery and career in television. Latham's account is
straightforward and unsentimental, without fictionalized components.
There is no documentation and no index.

S2-1294   PN2287 .P73 I47
Ilson, Carol. Harold Prince : from *Pajama Game* to *Phantom of the
Opera* / Carol Ilson; foreword by Sheldon Harnick. — Ann Arbor, Mich.
: UMI Research Press, 1989. — xii, 461 p. : ill. ISBN 0-8357-1935-9.
A well-documented biography of Prince (1928–), producer of successful Broadway shows (*West Side Story, Fiddler on the Roof, Phantom of the Opera,* etc.). This is a fine perspective on the business and
daily operation aspects of the theater, including the problems of revisions, cast changes, and dealing with failures. With endnotes; a bibliography of reviews, articles, dissertations, letters, and other useful items;
and an expansive index.

S2-1295   PN2287 .R756 N4
Nelson, Stephen. "Only a paper moon" : the theatre of Billy Rose /
Stephen Nelson. — Ann Arbor, Mich. : UMI Research Press, 1987. —
xiv, 169 p. ISBN 0-8357-1796-8.
A revision of the author's 1985 doctoral dissertation, offering a scholarly account of notable productions by Rose from 1924 to 1962: *Jumbo,*
the aquacades, nightclub extravaganzas, and world's fair events. The
book's title is from the hit song in one of Rose's unsuccessful Broadway
efforts, *Great Magoo* (1932). With endnotes, a bibliography of primary
and secondary sources, and an expansive index.
Review: AM 1989, 99.

S2-1296   PN2287 .W46 S55
Smith, Eric Ledell. Bert Williams : a biography of the pioneer black
comedian / Eric Ledell Smith. — Jefferson, N.C. : McFarland, 1992. —
xiii, 301 p. : ill. ISBN 0-89950-695-X.
Williams, born in the Bahamas in 1874 or 1875, grew up in California, then joined a traveling minstrel troupe. Then he did vaudeville and
musicals in New York and broke the color barrier of the Ziegfeld
Follies in 1910. He and George William Walker formed a highly popular duo. Smith presents a straightforward, documented life story of
Williams (and shorter ones of Walker and Walker's wife, who sang
with them). With a list of 100 Williams songs, endnotes, and a partly
expansive index.
Reviews: *Choice* 10/92, 313; LJ 5/1/92, 84.

PS309–3523 : LYRICISTS

S2-1297   PS309 .L8 F8
Furia, Philip. The poets of Tin Pan Alley : a history of America's great
lyricists / Philip Furia. — New York : Oxford, 1990. — ix, 322 p. ISBN
0-19-506408-9.
A useful inventory of major lyric writers, with the names of their songs
and with comments about rhyming practice and idioms. Those discussed
are Dorothy Fields, Leo Robin, Johnny Mercer, Irving Berlin, Lorenz
Hart, Ira Gershwin, Cole Porter, Oscar Hammerstein II, Howard Dietz,
and Yip Harburg. With chapter notes and a nonexpansive index of names
and song titles.
Reviews: AM 1992, 219; *Choice* 2/91, 942; LJ 8/90, 112.

S2-1298   PS309 .L8 H3
Hischak, Thomas S. Word crazy : Broadway lyricists from Cohan to
Sondheim / Thomas S. Hischak. — New York : Praeger, 1991. — xvii,
241 p. ISBN 0-2759-3849-2.
A general narrative, presenting casual observations about lyric writers
and their songs. With a bibliography and a nonexpansive index of names
and song titles.

S2-1299   PS3523 .E76 H96
Lerner, Alan Jay. A hymn to him : the lyrics of Alan Jay Lerner. —
New York : Limelight, 1987. — 320 p. ISBN 0-87910-109-1.
This collection of Lerner's lyrics was edited by Benny Green (who is not
mentioned on the title page), who also supplied an introduction and notes
on individual shows—sometimes individual lyrics as well. The lyrics are
grouped by show, and the shows are arranged in chronological order.
While generally complete, only three lyrics are included from the earliest
show (*The Day before Spring,* 1945) and only seven from the next. There
is no indication of the sources used for the lyrics, and no variants are given.
In general the layout is satisfactory, but in numerous places lyrics run
in double columns for part of a page; it is never clarified when simul-
taneity is intended or when a second column was inserted to save space
(both were done). The characters who sing the lyrics are identified only
in ensemble numbers. There is no alphabetical index of song titles, so the
entire contents list must be scanned to locate a particular song. Without
bibliographical references.
Benny Green is the author of over a dozen books on very diverse subjects. He has his own radio program and has scripted over 2,000 radio
programs [—D. P.].

PS3552–3562 : WRITERS

S2-1300   PS3552 .O874

Sawyer-Laucanno, Christopher. An invisible spectator : a biography of Paul Bowles / Christopher Sawyer-Laucanno. — London : Blooms-bury, 1989. — xv, 501 p. : ill. : 16 p. plates. ISBN 1-55584-116-3.

An interesting story of the composer who became a best-selling nov-elist and went into voluntary exile in Morocco during the 1960s. He as-sociated with poets and avant-garde authors, gaining the designation "spiritual father of the beat movement." In this straightforward biogra-phy, music is passed over with little attention, although a checklist of compositions is included. With a bibliography of Bowles's literary works, chapter endnotes, and an expansive index.

Reviews: AM 1993, 383; *Choice* 10/89, 317; LJ 4/15/89, 76.

S2-1301   PS3554 .Y56 Z634

Day, Aidan. Jokerman : reading the lyrics of Bob Dylan / Aidan Day. — Oxford, England : Blackwell, 1988. — 189 p. ISBN 0-631-15873-1.

A study of Dylan's verses, offering "unprecedented insights" into their presentations of identity problems. Various disruptions and ambiguities are also disclosed, suggesting that the simple lines carry many deep meanings. With endnotes and a partly expansive index.

S2-1302   PS3558 .E575 H464

Hentoff, Nat. Boston boy / Nat Hentoff. — New York : Knopf, 1986. — 175 p. ISBN 0-394-40744-X.

In this memoir of his adolescence and young adulthood, Hentoff de-scribes his experiences of the 1940s Boston jazz scene, particularly at the Savoy Cafe. He recounts meetings and dealings with numerous musi-cians, including Jonathan "Jo" Jones, Lester Young, and Billie Holiday, and describes, in some detail, his relation with the jazz critic George Fra-zier. Without bibliographical references or index.

Nat Hentoff writes extensively on jazz and on civil liberties; he also writes fiction for adults and children [—D. P.].

Review: LJ 3/15/86, 64.

TITLE INDEX

Citations are to entry numbers. Initial articles have been deleted unless they are integral to the sense of the titles.

60 years of recorded jazz, 1917–1977 / Walter Bruyninckx. 230

1987/88 music business directory / August G. Blume. 37

1987/88 music radio directory / August G. Blume. 38

A & M records discography : including associated labels and alphanumeric index / R. M. Kosht. 196

A call to assembly : the autobiography of a musical storyteller / Willie Ruff. 666

A celebration of American music : words and music in honor of H. Wiley Hitchcock / ed. Richard Crawford, R. Allen Lott, and Carol J. Oja. 366

A heart at fire's center : the life and music of Bernard Herrmann / Steven C. Smith. 485

A hymn to him : the lyrics of Alan Jay Lerner. 1299

A joyful noise : a celebration of New Orleans music / Michael P. Smith. 1128

A left hand like God : a history of boogie-woogie piano / Peter J. Silvester; with a special contribution from Denis Harbinson. 992a

A life in jazz / Danny Barker; ed. Alyn Shipton. 577

A most wondrous babble : American art composers, their music, and the American scene, 1950–1985 / Nicholas E. Tawa. 378

A new song / Pat Boone. 685

A night in Tunisia : imaginings of Africa in jazz / Norman C. Weinstein. 1094

A passion for polka : old-time ethnic music in America / Victor Greene. 1210

A place of her own : the story of Elizabeth Garrett / Ruth K. Hall. — Rev. ed. 474

A satisfied mind : the country music life of Porter Wagoner / Steve Eng. 882

A star is torn / Robyn Archer and Diana Simmonds. 435

A time to sing / Dorothy Kirsten; discography by Stanley A. Bowker. 756

Abravanel! / Lowell Durham. 949

Absolutely Dylan : illustrated with more than 200 photographs / Patrick Humphries and John Bauldie. 713

Acquired of the angels : the lives and works of master guitar makers John D'Angelico and James L. D'Aquisto / Paul William Schmidt. 972

Adirondack voices : woodsmen and wood lore / Robert D. Bethke. 8

African-American traditions in song, sermon, tale, and dance, 1600s–1920 : an annotated bibliography of literature, collections, and artworks / Eileen Southern and Josephine Wright. 1275

Capitol record listing, 101 thru 3031 / Bill Bennett. 200

Career opportunities in the music industry / Shelly Field. 1257

Carnegie Hall : the first one hundred years / Richard Schickel and Michael Walsh. 396

Cash Box album charts, 1955–1974 / Frank Hoffmann and George Albert; with the assistance of Lee Ann Hoffmann. 260

Cash Box album charts, 1975–1985 / Frank Hoffmann and George Albert; with Lee Ann Hoffmann. 261

Cash Box black contemporary album charts, 1975–1987 / Frank Hoffmann and George Albert. 262

Cash Box black contemporary singles charts, 1960–1984 / Frank Hoffmann and George Albert; with the assistance of Lee Ann Hoffman. 249

Cash Box country album charts, 1964–1988 / Frank Hoffmann and George Albert. 226

Catalog : compositions of concert music. 106

Catalog of music by Pennsylvania composers / Kile Smith. 107

Catalog of the American musical : musicals of Irving Berlin, George and Ira Gershwin, Cole Porter, Richard Rodgers, and Lorenz Hart / Tommy Krasker and Robert Kimball. 132

Catalog of the musical works of William Billings / Karl Kroeger. 159

Catalog of the William Ransom Hogan Jazz Archive : the collection of seventy-eight RPM phonograph recordings / Howard-Tilton Memorial Library, Tulane University. 193

Catalogue of pre-revival Appalachian dulcimers / L. Allen Smith. 986

Caught in a trap / Rick Stanley; with Paul Harold. 841

Celebrating Bird : the triumph of Charlie Parker / Gary Giddins. 657

Chadwick, Yankee composer / Victor Fell Yellin. 461

Charles Ives : a bio-bibliography / Geoffrey H. Block; foreword by J. Peter Burkholder. 169

Charles Ives "My father's song" : a psychoanlytic biography / Stuart Feder. 490

Charles Seeger : a life in American music / Ann M. Pescatello. 970

Charles T. Griffes : the life of an American composer / Edward Maisel. — Rev. ed. 481

Charlie Barnet and his orchestra / Charles Garrod and Bill Korst. 286

Charlie Parker : sein Leben, seine Musik, seine Schallplatten / Peter Niklas Wilson and Ulfert Goeman. 658

Charlie Spivak and his orchestra / Charles Garrod. 360

Chartmasters' rock 100 : an authoritative ranking of the 100 most popular songs for each year, 1956 through 1986 / Jim Quirin and Barry Cohen. — 4th ed. 266

Cher! / Mark Bego. 700

Chicago soul : making black music Chicago style / Robert Pruter. 1204

Chicago's local rock / Van Pudlo and Joe Ziemba. 1200

Children's live-action musical films : a critical survey and filmography / Thomas J. Harris. 1282

Choctaw music and dance / James H. Howard and Victoria Lindsay Levine. 1231

Chosen voices : the story of the American cantorate / Mark Slobin. 1045

Chuck Berry : the autobiography / Chuck Berry; foreword by Bruce Springsteen. 683

Dick Haymes / Charles Garrod and Denis Brown, with special help from Roger Dooner and the Dick Haymes Society. 317

Dick Jurgens and his orchestra / Charles Garrod. 332

Dick Todd : king of the jukebox / Sheldon J. O'Connell. 872

Dictionary of Afro-American performers : 78 RPM and cylinder recordings of opera, choral music, and song, c.1900–1949 / Patricia Turner. 87

Dictionary of American hymnology : first line index / Leonard Ellinwood. 126

Did they mention the music? / Henry Mancini; with Gene Lees. 498

Dino : beyond the glitz and glamour : an autobiography / Dino Kartsonakis; with Cecil Murphey. 556

Dino : living high in the dirty business of dreams / Nick Tosches. 780

Directory of blacks in the performing arts / Edward C. Mapp; foreword by Earle Hyman. — 2nd ed. 1277

Directory of contemporary American musical instrument makers / Susan Caust Farrell. 34

Directory of music collections in the midwestern United States / comp. Publications Committee, Music Library Association, Midwest Chapter. 93

Directory of music faculties in colleges and universities, U.S. and Canada / comp. and ed. Craig R. Short. 27

Directory of music libraries and collections in New England, 1985 / comp. Publications Committee, Music Library Association, New England Chapter. 94

Directory of music research libraries / Rita Benton, general editor. 92

Directory of record and CD retailers / Keith Whelan. 31

Discography : traditional jazz, 1897–1985 / Walter Bruyninckx. 228

Discoursing sweet music : town bands and community life in turn-of-the-century Pennsylvania / Kenneth Kreitner. 1006

Discovering great jazz : a new listener's guide to the sounds and styles of the top musicians and their recordings on CDs, LPs, and cassettes / Stephen M. Stroff. 1092

Discovering great singers of classic pop : a new listener's guide to the sounds and lives of the top performers and their recordings, movies, and videos / Roy Hemming and David Hajdu. 440

Dizzy Gillespie, his life and times / Barry McRae. 637

Dizzy Gillespie : sein Leben, seine Musik, seine Schallplatten / Jürgen Wölfer. 638

Dolly : here I come again / Leonore Fleischer. 810

Don't explain : a song of Billie Holiday / Alexis DeVeaux. 730

Doo-wop : the forgotten third of rock 'n' roll / Anthony J. Gribin and Matthew M. Schiff. 1166

Doobie Brothers / Mark Bego. 903

Down Home guide to the blues / Frank Scott and the staff of Down Home Music. 223

Down thunder road : the making of Bruce Springsteen / Marc Eliot; with Mike Appel. 864

Dreamgirl : my life as a supreme / Mary Wilson; with Patricia Romanowski and Ahrgus Juilliard. 890

Drummin' men : the heartbeat of jazz : the swing years / Burt Korall ; foreword by Mel Tormé. 433

Jimi Hendrix : inside the Experience / Mitch Mitchell; with John Platt. 581

Jimmy Dorsey and his orchestra / Charles Garrod. — Rev. ed. 302

Joe Maddy of Interlochen : profile of a legend / Norma Lee Browning. 969

Joel Whitburn presents the *Billboard* hot 100 charts : the eighties / Joel Whitburn. 276

John Cage at seventy-five / ed. Richard Fleming and William Duckworth. 459

John Coltrane / Brian Priestley. 623

John Coltrane : sein Leben, seine Musik, seine Schallplatten / Gerd Filtgen and Michael Ausserbauer. 622

John Cougar Mellencamp / Tim Holmes. 783

John Kirby and His Orchestra : Andy Kirk and His Orchestra / Charles Garrod. 337

John Lewis / Thierry Lalo and Jacques Lubin. 558

John McCormack : a comprehensive discography / Paul W. Worth and Jim Cartwright. 342

John Philip Sousa, American phenomenon / Paul E. Bierley; foreword by Arthur Fiedler. 521

Johnny Hodges / Stanley Dance; notes on the music by Gary Giddens. 646

Johnny Mercer Chesterfield music shop, A.F.R.S. additions featuring Johnny Mercer, Jo Stafford, Pied Pipers, Paul Weston and his orchestra / Harry Mackenzie. 265

Jokerman : reading the lyrics of Bob Dylan / Aidan Day. 1301

Jolson : the legend comes to life / Herbert G. Goldman. 751

Judeo-Spanish ballads from New York collected by Mair Jose Benardete / ed. Samuel G. Armistead and Joseph H. Silverman. 1276

Just a gigolo : the life and times of Louis Prima / Garry Boulard. 660

Just before jazz : black musical theater in New York, 1890–1915 / Thomas Laurence Riis. 1020

Kansas City jazz and blues nightlife survival kit / Todd R. Wilkinson. 32

Kate Smith : a bio-bibliography / Michael R. Pitts. 190

Kay Kyser and his orchestra / Charles Garrod and Bill Korst. 340

Keeping score : film and television music, 1980–1988 : with additional coverage of 1921–1979 / James L. Limbacher and H. Stephen Wright, Jr. 130

Keith Jarrett : seine Leben, seine Musik, seine Schallplatten / Uwe Andresen. 551

Keith Jarrett : the man and his music / Ian Carr. 552

Kenny Rogers : gambler, dreamer, lover / Martha Hume. 851

Keyboard music of black composers : a bibliography / Aaron Horne. 114

Killer / Colin Escott; discography by Richard Weize. 765

Kinds of blue : musical memoirs / Al Young. 1107

King of the Delta blues : the life and music of Charlie Patton / Stephen Calt and Gayle Wardlow. 812

Kingston Trio on record / Benjamin Blake, Jake Rubeck, and Allan Shaw. 921a

Kitty : an autobiography / Kitty Carlisle Hart. 697

Klook : the Kenny Clarke story / Mike Hennessey. 616

Kurt Weill : a composer in a divided world / Ronald Taylor. 534

Kurt Weill : an illustrated biography / Douglas Jarman. 533

L.A. musical history tour : a guide to the rock and roll landmarks of Los Angeles / Art Fein. 1201

Prince : a pop life / Dave Hill. 848

Prince : his story in words and pictures : an unauthorized biography / Mark Rowland and Margy Rochlin. 849

Priscilla and Elvis : the Priscilla Presley story / Caroline Latham. 1293

Producing hit records / Dennis Lambert; with Ronald Zalkind: foreword by Al Coury. 1245

Producing jazz : the experience of an independent record company / Herman Gray. 1242

Profile of a lifetime : a musical autobiography / Ross Lee Finney. 473

Profiles in jazz : from Sidney Bechet to John Coltrane / Raymond Horricks. 420

Progressive jazz : free—third stream fusion / Walter Bruyninckx. 233

Protest and praise : sacred music of black religion / Jon Michael Spencer. 1223

Psychotic reactions and carburetor dung / Lester Bangs; ed. with introduction by Greil Marcus. 1169

Puerto Rican music following the Spanish-American war / Catherine Dower. 399

Purchaser's guide to the music industries. 40

Pure at heart / Stuff Smith; ed. Anthony Barnett and Eva Logager. 591

Queen of the blues: a biography of Dinah Washington / James Haskins. 884

Quincy Jones / Raymond Horricks; discography by Tony Middleton. 494

R.E.M. : behind the mask / Jim Greer; photographs by Laura Levine. 934

Ralph Flanagan and his orchestra / Charles Garrod. — Rev. ed. 311

Randy Travis : king of the new country traditionalists / Don Cusic. 876

Rap music in the 1980s : a reference guide / Judy McCoy. 144

Rap : the lyrics / Lawrence A. Stanley; introduction by Jefferson Morley. 51

Rare rock : a collector's guide / Tony Rees. 282

Ratt / Dominique DesCordobes. 935

Ravinia : the festival at its half century. 47

Ray Anthony and his orchestra / Charles Garrod and Bill Korst. 285

Ray Noble and his orchestra / Charles Garrod. 347

Readings in black American music / Eileen Southern. — 2nd ed. 1222

Real Frank Zappa / Frank Zappa; with Peter Occhiorosso. 894

Reba : country music's queen / Don Cusic. 781

Reba McEntire : the queen of country / Carol Leggett. 782

Recent American opera : a production guide / Rebecca Hodell Kornick. 1269

Reception of jazz in America : a new view / James Lincoln Collier. 110

Recollections : essays, drawings, miscellanea / Marion Brown. 613

Recording industry sourcebook 1993. 36

Recycling the blues : ZZ Top / Scott Nance. 948

Red, hot and rich : an oral history of Cole Porter / David Grafton. 506

Red Norvo / Don DeMicheal. 656

Red River blues : the blues tradition in the southeast / Bruce Bastin. 1147

Remarks : the story of R.E.M. / Tony Fletcher. 933

Remembering Buddy : the definitive biography of Buddy Holly / John Goldrosen and John Beecher. — 2nd ed. 735

Reminiscing in tempo : the life and times of a jazz hustler / Teddy Reig; with Edward M. Berger. 982

Resource guide to themes in contemporary American song lyrics, 1950–1985 / B. Lee Cooper; foreword by Wayne A. Wiegand. 254

Secular music in colonial Annapolis : the Tuesday Club, 1745–56 / John B. Talley. 386

Sennets & tuckets : a Bernstein celebration / ed. Steven Ledbetter. 454

Sequins & shades : the Michael Jackson reference guide / Carol D. Terry. 748

Sergei Vasil'evich Rachmaninoff : a guide to research / Robert Palmieri. 177

Settling the score : music and the classical Hollywood film / Kathryn Marie Kalinak. 1028

Sex / Madonna; ed. Glenn O'Brien. 767

Shake, rattle & roll : the golden age of American rock 'n' roll. Volume 1, 1952–1955 / Lee Cotten. 1171

She's a rebel : the history of women in rock 'n' roll / Gillian G. Gaar. 419

Shep Fields and his orchestra / Charles Garrod. 310

Shorty Rogers : a discography / Coen Hofmann and Erik M. Bakker. 352

Show music on record : the first 100 years / Jack Raymond. — Rev. ed. 248

Show tunes, 1905–1985 : the songs, shows, and careers of Broadway's major composers / Steven Suskin. — Rev. ed. 415

Sideman : the long gig of W. O. Smith : a memoir / W. O. Smith. 592

Sidney Bechet / Frank K. Kappler. 603

Sidney Bechet / Fabrice Zammarchi. 604

Sidney Bechet : the wizard of jazz / John Chilton. 602

Signature Record Company master listing / Bob Porter. 217

Signifying rappers / Mark Costello and David Foster Wallace. 1167

Silvio Scionti : remembering a master pianist and teacher / Jack Guerry. 570

Simon and Garfunkel : old friends / Joe Morella and Patricia Barey. 856

Sinatra scrapbook / Gary L. Doctor. 859

Sinatra, the man and his music : the recording artistry of Francis Albert Sinatra / Scott P. Sayers and Ed O'Brien. 359

Sing a pretty song / Edie Adams. 679

Sing a sad song : the life of Hank Williams / Roger M. Williams. — 2nd ed. 887

Sing a song of social significance / R. Serge Denisoff. 1055

Singers and the song / Gene Lees; foreword by Grover Sales. 1059

Singing about it : folk song in southern Indiana / transcribed by George List. 24

Singing in the spirit : African-American sacred quartets in New York City / Ray Allen. 1037

Singing the glory down : amateur gospel music in south central Kentucky, 1900–1990 / William Lynwood Montell. 1042

Sisters : a revealing portrait of the world's most famous diva / Jackie Callas. 691

Sitting in : selected writings on jazz, blues, and related topics / Hayden Carruth. 1216

Smokey : inside my life. / Smokey Robinson. 850

Soldier boy Elvis / Ira Jones; as told to Bill E. Burk. 831

Sondheim & Co. / Craig Zadan. — 2nd ed. 520

Song of the hawk : the life and recordings of Coleman Hawkins / John Chilton. 641

Songprints : the musical experience of five Shoshone women / Judith Vander. 1234

Songs, odes, glees and ballads : a bibliography of American presidential campaign songsters / William Miles. 120

Unforgettable : the life and mystique of Nat King Cole / Leslie Gourse. 703

Union of diversities : style in the music of Charles Ives / Larry Starr. 491

Unsung heroes of rock 'n' roll : the birth of rock in the wild years before Elvis / Nick Tosches. — Rev. ed. 425

Up from the cradle of jazz : New Orleans music since World War II / Jason Berry, Jonathan Foose, and Tad Jones. 1148

Van Halen! / J. D. Considine. 944

VanHalen / Philip Kamin and Peter Goddard. 945

Variety's directory of major show business awards / Mike Kaplan. 1288

View from within : jazz writings, 1948–1987 / Orrin Keepnews. 1098

Vincent Persichetti : a bio-bibliography / Donald L. Patterson and Janet L. Patterson. 175

Violin makers of the United States / Thomas James Wenberg. 446

Virgil Thomson: a bio-bibliography / Michael Meckna. 182

Virgil Thomson's musical portraits / Anthony Tommasini. 183

Virginia Piedmont blues : the lives and art of two Virginia bluesmen / Barry Lee Pearson. 406

Virginia's blues : country & gospel records, 1902–1943 : an annotated discography / Kip Lornell. 222

Viva! Zappa / Dominique Chevalier. 893

Voice of new music : New York City 1972–1982 : a collection of articles originally published in *The Village Voice* / Tom Johnson. 394

Voices of combat : a century of liberty and war songs, 1765–1865 / Kent A. Bowman. 1209

Voices of the jazz age : profiles of eight vintage jazzmen / Chip Deffaa. 427

Waiting for Dizzy / Gene Lees. 1099

Wanderer : Dion's story / Dion DiMucci; with Davin Seay. 710

Wanted man : in search of Bob Dylan / ed. John Bauldie. 717

Warren Durrett : his piano and his orchestra / Warren Durrett. 1126

Waylon : a biography / R. Serge Denisoff; discography by John L. Smith. 749

We danced all night : my life behind the scenes with Alan Jay Lerner / Doris Shapiro. 968

We wanna boogie : an illustrated history of the American rockabilly movement / Randy McNutt. — 2nd ed. 1202

We'll understand it better by and by : pioneering African American gospel composers / Bernice Johnson Reagon. 416

West coast jazz : modern jazz in California, 1945–1960 / Ted Gioia. 1125

What do they want? a jazz autobiography / Sammy Price; ed. Caroline Richmond. 567

What they heard : music in America, 1852–1881, from the pages of *Dwight's journal of music* / Irving Sablosky. 373

When the music's over : the story of political pop / Robin Denselow. 1046

Where are you now, Bo Diddley? : the stars who made us rock and where they are now / Edward Kiersh. 421

Where did our love go? The rise and fall of the Motown sound / Nelson George; foreword by Quincy Jones; introduction by Robert Christgau. 1203

Where's that tune? An index to songs in fakebooks / William D. Goodfellow. 150

SUBJECT INDEX

Entries in the index follow the style of Library of Congress subject headings, the access points found in most American library card catalogs and online catalogs. Appropriate modifications in the LC style were made in the interest of simplification; for example, the repeated qualifier "United States" did not appear to be necessary in most entries, since the entire book is about the United States. Also note that definite articles are indexed, i.e. The Doors, The Band instead of Doors, The and Band, The.

Citations are to entry numbers, not to page numbers. Where multiple citations appear under the name of a musician, italics have been used to identify items with the fullest treatment. The lack of any italicized items in such citation strings indicates that there is no useful distinction to be made among the citations.

JOINT-AUTHOR INDEX*

---

*This index contains listings for joint authors, editors, and other persons named in the entries in addition to the principal authors.

445

ABOUT THE AUTHOR

Guy A. Marco has been a Senior Fellow at the Graduate School of Library and Information Science, Rosary College (River Forest, Illinois) since 1989. He has a master's degree in library science and a Ph.D in musicology from the University of Chicago. His positions have included: Dean, School of Library Science, Kent State University; Chief, General Reference and Bibliography Division, Library of Congress; and Chief of Library Activities, U.S. Army, Fort Dix. Marco is the author of *The Art of Counterpoint* (1968), *Information on Music* (3 vols.; 1975–1984), *Opera: A Research and Information Guide* (1984), and *Encyclopedia of Recorded Sound in the United States* (1993). He edited the second edition of E. T. Bryant's *Music Librarianship* (1985) and is editor of the Composer Resource Manuals series for Garland Publishing.